UNTRODDEN FIELDS

OF

ANTHROPOLOGY

Nature understands no jesting; she is always true, always serious, always severe; she is always right, and the errors and faults are always those of man.   Him, who is incapable of appreciating her, she despises, and only to the apt, the pure and the true, does she resign herself and reveal her secrets.

GOETHE.

The web of our life is of a mingled yarn, good and ill together; our virtues would be proud if our faults whipped them not, and our crimes would despair if they were not cherished by our virtues.

SHAKESPEARE, (*All's Well*, IV, 3.)

Documents on Medical Anthropology

UNTRODDEN FIELDS

OF

ANTHROPOLOGY

OBSERVATIONS ON THE ESOTERIC

Manners and Customs of Semi-Civilized Peoples;

BEING A

RECORD OF THIRTY YEARS' EXPERIENCE IN

ASIA, AFRICA, AMERICA and OCEANIA.

By

Dr. Jacobus X.

(*IN TWO VOLUMES*)

Vol. I

Fredonia Books
Amsterdam, The Netherlands

Untrodden Fields of Anthropology:
Esoteric Manners and Customs of Semi-Civilized
Peoples

by
Dr. Jacobus X

ISBN: 1-4101-0582-2

Copyright © 2004 by Fredonia Books

Fredonia Books
Amsterdam, The Netherlands
http://www.fredoniabooks.com

THE EDITOR'S FOREWORD

πάντα καθαρὰ τοῖς καθαροῖς.

Periculosum est credere et non credere;
Ergo exploranda est veritas multum prius
Quam stulta prave judicet sententia.

PHAED. 3, 10.

THE EDITOR'S FOREWORD.

When the first edition of this little book appeared we
had no idea that it would excite so many different com-
ments and various conflicting criticisms. From all parts
of the world, men whose opinion is worth caring for,
wrote and thanked us for the step we had taken, saying
that such a work supplied a distinct want. The " little
cloud out of the sea no bigger than a man's hand " grew
to a size beyond our hopes, and our edition strictly limited
to 500 copies, rapidly ran out. The "note" however
most generally harped upon by our kind correspondents
was that concerning the absence of references to the
authorities cited here and there in the two volumes. It
was pointed out that while there could be no doubt as
to the authenticity of the names quoted, yet many students
and scholars preferred, when possible, to turn up and consult the original works and documents for themselves. We
have therefore supplied this deficiency; our only fear now,
is that we may perchance have overstepped the mark, and
gone to the other extreme. Our aim has been to be useful and experts alone can judge whether we have
succeeded. It is not for us to sound our own praises.

In announcing the first edition of this work we
issued a little leaflet which later gave rise to more than
one misunderstanding, many people supposing it to be a

different work entirely apart from "Untrodden Fields of
Anthropology."

The leaflet in question was headed as under, the difference of the title no doubt being the cause of the mischief :

"REMARKABLE STUDY

OF THE

'SIXTH SENSE' (1)

*And its Strange and Curious Manifestations and Aberrations
among Barbarous Races.   New and original work in
English, issued to Private Subscribers only."*

We then followed with an English translation of the
Author's Preface to the French Edition and we think
it will not be out of place to reproduce textually here
the weighty words of the French Traveller.   Some incon-
siderate persons, on the principle of "giving a dog a bad
name and hanging him at once," have, on the mere fact
that the book issued from Paris, imagined, without examination, that our work was of an improper character.   We
appeal to the judgment of sensible men whether the following words are those of a writer of indecent literature ;
and we have no fear of their verdict.— He says : —

---

(1) We are far from being the first to use this phrase.   Jacolliot
says "The most ancient traditions of India, the cradle of Humanity
and of Religions, mention and admit a sixth sense.   To man,
Brahma gave five organs,—Touch, Sight, Smell, Taste, Hearing and
a sixth, admitted by all Indian philosophers and called "Mamas",
which is the agent of the union of the sexes.—The Sankhyan philosophy defines it as follows:—"An organ by affinity, participating
in the qualities of the others, and which serves at once for sensation
and action."   L. Jacolliot, "La Bible dans l'Inde, Vie de Jezeus
Christna " (Paris, 1876).

* I have passed twenty-eight years of my life amongst diverse races, in all the five great divisions of the World. By giving my professional services to the natives of each place I visited, and by studying their language, I was able to gain their confidence, and learn much about their customs, manner of living, habits, etc. Having made diseases of the genito-urinary organ my speciality, I was often consulted in these cases, and therefore collected much valuable information:

I was not merely satisfied with observing the effect of the human passions, but it appeared to me indispensable to trace these passions back to their moral causes, and make a psychological study of those causes.

Whilst following in foreign countries the path of science which has been already traced by that eminent authority, Tardieu, I have avoided trenching on the ground covered by his remarkable Medico-Legal Study of Offences against Morals. I have chosen a wider field for my enquiries. Like Moreau (of Tours), I believe in a sixth sense, the *Genital Sense*, the existence of which he has psychologic-ally proved, by showing that its special functions were distinct from those of the other senses. It is the philosophical and medical study of this sixth sense that I had in view in compiling this work; and also an examination of those changes and irregularities which this sense undergoes, not only under the influence of temperament and constitution in the various races, but from manners, customs, and religious superstitions.

This is not an obscene work, but a psychological sketch of the history of the sexual passions of the human race; —a stone towards the building of a vast edifice which, as yet, is hardly commenced. And besides the medico-legal view of the question, I have made a thorough research into, and philosophical examination of, the original causes.

I have seen nearly all that I here relate, and have never hesitated to tell what I believed to be the truth. That which I have not seen I have derived from eye-witnesses who were worthy of credit. I have probed the depths of the human hearts of my patients, and too often found them cankered, and—conscious of my honest inten-tions—I have illuminated them with the torch of Philosophy. What I say may be believed.

I have written for a small number of studious, thinking people, seekers after the immutable truth, which is here presented to them unveiled,—stripped of the rags of conventionality. I have thus been able to boldly reveal that which it would have been impossible to write in an ordinary book of travels, which might. and ought to be, put into the hands of anyone.

Moreover, I have sought, and I believe I have succeeded (by a careful use of medical terms), in making my meaning clear without overstepping the bounds of decency."

Our work as far as we are aware, is absolutely unique in its kind. Of course, many little pamphlets have been written, with imposing titles but which were undocumented, and lacking entirely in scientific value. To judge for example, from the following array of words one would be led to think that an important treatise was forthcoming. We give the full title of this worthless production only as representative of many others of its class, equally misleading:

MŒURS ORIENTALES.

LES HUIS-CLOS DE L'ETHNOGRAPHIE.

DE LA CIRCONCISION DES FILLES — VIRGINITÉ — INFIBULATION — GÉNÉRATION — EUNUQUES — SKOPZIS — CADENAS — CEINTURES,

PAR

E. ILEX

LONDRES

Imprimerie particulière de la Société d'Anthropologie et d'Ethnologie comparées.

MDCCCLXXVIII

It is needless to say this *fumisterie* was no more printed in London for any "Anthropological Society" than it was printed in the Moon for a Society of Escaped Lunatics. Apart from a few stupid illustrations, wretchedly done, and all very much alike, there was no reason to conceal its place of origin, unless it was supposed that in surrounding the farce with an air of mystery, the gudgeons would be better attracted.

Our aim in "Untrodden Fields" has been precisely the same as that had in view by Sir Richard F. Burton, who was not afraid to illustrate his books on Travels and Voyages, with facts and observations of *real* anthropological value. We cannot do better than allow Sir Richard to speak in his own words; the extract is from his interesting "Foreword" to the original Benares edition of "The Thousand Nights and a Night":

"These volumes afford me a long-sought opportunity of noticing practices and customs which interest all mankind and which "Society" will not hear mentioned.

"Grote, the historian, and Thackeray, the novelist, both lamented that the *bégueulerie* of their countrymen condemned them to keep silence where publicity was required; and that they could not even claim the partial licence of a Fielding and a Smollet. Hence a score of years ago I lent my best help to the late Dr. James Hunt in founding the Anthropological Society, whose presidential chair I first occupied (pp. 2-4 *Anthropologia*. London, *Bailliere* vol. I., No. I, 1873).

"My motive was to supply travellers with an organ which would rescue their observations from the outer darkness of manuscript, and *print their curious information on social and sexual matters* out of place in the popular book intended for the Nipptisch, and indeed better kept from public view.

"But hardly had we begun when 'Respectability', that whited sepulchre full of all uncleanness, rose up against us. 'Propriety' cried us down with her brazen blatant voice, and the weak-kneed brethren fell away. *Yet the organ was much wanted, and is wanted still.*" BENARES (original) Edition pp. xviii to xix.

We printed these lines in a small leaflet and sent it to most of the subscribers to the book with the following remarks:

"Mr. Charles Carrington's object is precisely the same in 'Untrodden Fields of Anthropology', and all observations his Correspondents care, in the interests of Anthropology, to send him, will either be incorporated in a new and enlarged edition of the above-named work, or if of sufficient bulk and length, will be published separately under the title of "Anthropologia".

To these lines we added the undermentioned notice:

"CRITICISMS AND OBSERVATIONS INVITED"

"Medical, scientific, and literary men, and Travellers, especially those who reside Abroad and in the Colonies, who have read ' Untrodden Fields of Anthropology', are respectfully and earnestly invited to contribute their Criticisms, whether favourable or other-wise to Mr. Charles Carrington, 18, Faubourg Montmartre, Paris, with a view to an enlarged and revised Edition of this work.

Of course, it is unnecessary to add that while the Editor will be pleased to publish such criticisms over the name of the contributor, he is also prepared to reproduce them, if of sufficient weight and importance, without disclosure of name, and the anonymity would where requested, be strictly and steadfastly guarded."

We are pleased to say that many Doctors and scientific men responded to this appeal for co-operation in our intellectual enterprise, and generously sent in and left entirely at our disposal a collection of valuable and curious notes and observations which we hope one day to embody in a new work, to form a sequel to the present one, but we shall first have to arrange them in systematic order.

Some of these notes however, have been incorporated in the present edition.

The late Dr. Ploss the learned Author of Das Weib in der Natur und Völkerkunde was fully alive to the importance of the study of the organs of generation of both sexes as comparative points of radical differences, and agrees with us that this entrancing subject so vital in its results, is not sufficiently studied in its details, by the professional Anthropologist. We prefer to give his own words :—

"Die Anthropologen haben fich mit großem Eifer mit den Kraniologifchen und den Phyfiognomifchen Eigenthümlichkeiten der Menfchenraffen befchäftigt. Allein der Kopf und das Geficht bieten vielleicht nicht bedeutendere Ethnographifche Vergleichungspunkte dar, als wir fie bei den weiblichen Gefchlechtstheilen mit allem was dazu gehört zu finden vermögen. Man hat über die Befonderheiten im Bau der äußeren Sexualorgane nur bei einzelnen Völkerfchaften genauere Nachforfchungen angeftellt; denn es ift eben fchwer, eine genügende Zahl von Objekten zu bekommen und einer Betrachtung, oder gar einer genauen Meßung zu unterwerfen. Die Anthropo= logifche Bedeutung der Sache verdient es aber, daß wir das Material, fo weit es fchon vorhanden ift, an diefer Stelle zufammen bringen." (1)

("DAS WEIB", Vol I, page 133.)

What is Anthropology? What are its aims and objects? Has it any practical and beneficial bearing on daily life? These are undoubtedly the questions that will occur to a thinking man whose attention is directed to this matter. The field of Anthropology is very wide—one may say without exaggeration—as wide as the world of man is wide—for it concerns and embraces man in all the various branches and ramifications of his life. Its subject and object is at once Humanity. The reader will pardon us

(1) We subjoin a translation of this passage:--

"Anthropologists have very busily occupied themselves with the craniological and physiognomical peculiarities of the human races. But the head and the face do not perhaps present more important ethnographic points of comparison than we can find in the female sexual organs, with all pertaining thereto. It is only among a few races that exact studies have been undertaken of the peculiarities in the structure of the exterior sexual organs, for it is indeed difficult to obtain a sufficient number of subjects willing to submit to be examined, and still less so, to be measured. Nevertheless the anthropological importance of the matter deserves that we should here bring together as much of the material as already exists."

for quoting a few lines here from the short "Preface" to the first edition:—

"Hackneyed as the quotation is, that "THERE ARE MORE THINGS IN HEAVEN AND EARTH THAN ARE DREAMT OF IN OUR PHILOSOPHY", the appearance of this book will but give it fresh point and force.

Anthropology is a name for all that relates to Man in general; his Vices and Virtues, Loves and Longings, Hates and Failings, Passions and Peculiarities. The subject, as yet, is only in its Infancy. Able and brilliant writers have, however, dealt with phases of it in a style that defies competition. EDWARD TYLOR in "PRIMITIVE CULTURE" has analysed Man's Dream-life and traced the Evolution of the Gods from their birth in the agonies of Fear and Hope down to the present stage of what Cotter Morrison has cleverly termed the "deanthropomorphisation of the god-idea"; DARWIN in his famous "DESCENT" has traced his Evolution from the proto-plasmic, formless mass of pre-historic periods; while LUBBOCK, CLODD, and a host of others have envisaged him from various inter-esting standpoints, but NO WRITER save, perhaps the German, Ploss, has yet handled the ESOTERIC phases of barbarous life as the Author of these fascinating pages. That "TRUTH IS STRANGER THAN FICTION" is borne home upon the reader's mind with repeated impressiveness. The Crimes and Loves, Vices, Virtues and Indecencies of Savage and Barbarous Life, are painted by a master's hand on a strong canvas of facts drawn from personal observation and native chron-icles—those naïve accounts which, without embarrassment, "CALL A SPADE A SPADE".

Auguste Comte was not blind to the proper province of our study, he says:—

"Perhaps Sociology may be easily looked on as absorbing into itself Biology as its introduction, Morals as its con-clusion. When the word Anthropology shall be in more common and sounder use, it will be a better name for the three sciences which collectively have man as their object, as its literal meaning is 'THE STUDY OF MAN!'"

The pursuit of this science in the past has been too much dwarfed and confined. The President of the Anthropological Department of the British Association at Brighton, (1872), used these words:—

" *As to the myths, religions, superstitions and languages with which they (the material relics of our prehistoric ancestors) were associated, we may content ourselves by devoutly thanking Providence that they have not been preserved.*" (1)

Needless to add that this is not the position taken by our author. It would be an insult to the intelligence of our readers to ask which of the two should most be valued—the moral and social ideas, palpitating with the life-blood of the past—or the flint weapons and skeleton outlines of the prehistoric man. Let there be no misunderstanding here. We recognise well enough the value of flint implements and other discoveries as proving man's age upon the earth, (2) but we contend that fuller justice should be shown to the *social* side of Anthropology. Mr. Luke O. Pike in his valuable paper on the "Methods of Anthropological Research", sets his face resolutely against all balderdash of this sort. His words are worth quoting :—

"It is impossible to lay too much stress on the fundamental doctrine, that all Anthropology has for its end the good of the human beings of the present and the human beings of the future.

"Anthropology means the collection of facts, *not for the sake of the facts themselves*, but for the value of the laws to be discovered in them for the sake of future generations to be benefited by them. It means, if not peace on earth, at least goodwill towards men;

---

(1) We should be loth to believe that these foolish words were authentic, were they not quoted on the faith of Joseph Kaines (Vide "Anthropologia," page 33, London, 1873—5).

(2) We bear particularly in mind the use this side of the subject has been in combating the pernicious doctrine of Man's theological Fall (Vide vol. I, page 284, of Andrew White's "*Warfare of Science with Theology*" LOND. MACMILLAN, 1896).

and it would mean peace on earth if its enemies would allow it to be at peace. *It means the only kind of philanthropy which can be of service to mankind philanthropy founded upon science.*" (1)

We claim no finality for the work now issued. Even in its present enlarged forms it is offered to scientific students with much "fear and trembling." We know it is incomplete, while conscious of our inability to fill up the *lacunae.* Let it be regarded as a pioneer effort rather than as a finished treatise, bearing in mind that all knowledge is relative. Some day a greater man, with broader forehead and braver mind than his fellows will take up the work where our Author has left it and systematize his facts with useful results to mankind. In the meantime, we are guilty of no blear-eyed egotism in declaring that our book is unique in its kind, and occupies a place not filled by any other. We claim that it fully bears out its curious French title, (2) while in its English dress

---

(1) Quoted in (page 35) "*Anthropologia,*" (already cited).

(2)　　　　　　　　L'AMOUR
　　　　　AUX COLONIES

SINGULARITES

PHYSIOLOGIQUES ET PASSIONNELLES

observées durant trente années de séjour dans les Colonies françaises

Cochin-Chine, Tonkin et Cambodge—Guyane et Martinique—
Sénégal et Rivières du Sud—Nouvelle Calédonie,
Nouvelles-Hébrides et Tahiti.

PAR LE DOCTEUR JACOBUS X...

ISIDORE LISEUX
PARIS, 1893.

[This French edition beautifully printed by Unsinger, was issued at the price of 60 francs in one vol. of 396 pages on hand-made paper; only 330 copies were printed, and we believe it is now somewhat rare.]

it is supplemented by a choice variety of notes and facts
which considerably enhance its value. Isidore Liseux, the
Editor of the French edition, would not consent to add
any notes, an omission the reason of which we have never
been able to understand. A work of the present kind is
valuable only in proportion to the documents and authorities
cited as guarantee for its statements. We have given
therefore not only a complete and unexpurgated version
of the original text, but have added a number of notes
and useful appendices that, we are sure, will not fail to
be of the greatest use to searchers and students. We
believe in fact, that our work will have to be counted
with whenever a writer treats of these subjects in the
future. At the end of the second volume we deal briefly
with a couple of foul attacks—it would be a misuse of
words to call them criticisms—evidently inspired by the
lowest malice that penny-a-liners are capable of. Save
these two beautiful Billingsgate effusions, penned without
doubt, by what St. Paul would have termed " lewd (minded)
fellows of the baser sort," our little work has been well
and cordially received. The welcome accorded to it was
due above all to the stamp of truth and genuineness to
be found on every page. Those of our subscribers who
may not have seen the prospectus first issued will be
interested to read the following points, which we take
leave to repeat as most clearly explanatory of our position.

The Author's weight.

" The Author was a French army surgeon, and in that
capacity was sent by his Government to the different
Colonies about whose people he treats. The book is
consequently not based on hearsay, nor on learned researches
by beslippered Dryasdusts in long-forgotten archives.
As a French officer he had everywhere access to the best

society, while his medical duties brought him into contact with the lower orders. He was thus enabled to study every class in each community that he visited, and his observations have therefore a triple value, being the work of an acute physician, an experienced traveller, and a broad-minded man-of-the-world.

Depravity of Effete Civilizations.

Greater interest still is attached to the book, from the fact that the places under consideration lie in out-of-the-way corners of the earth, which the ordinary " *globe-trotter* " would never dream of visiting. His experiences cover THIRTY LONG YEARS IN ASIA, AFRICA, AMERICA, and OCEANIA; and, with the frankness of a medical student, he carefully and without fear, examines the effete civilizations of ANNAM, TONQUIN and CAMBODIA; laying open as with a scalpel, and exposing, the vices of people who have brought depravity almost up to the level of a fine art.

Questions and Difficulties.

Apart from curious details concerning the manners and customs of almost unknown peoples and tribes, questions are raised and difficulties solved, which must have occurred to the mind of every *thinking* man and woman, but, which hitherto no writer, except in some purely medical work, has dared to treat as they should be treated, and the result is a book which is a distinctly valuable addition to the history of mankind.

Esoteric Physical Peculiarities.

In GUIANA and MARTINIQUE his position as a French Medical Officer gave him an introduction to the best CREOLE SOCIETY, and his duties as a surgeon brought him into contact with the negroes and half-breeds. Esoteric physical peculiarities, that would escape the notice of an

ordinary traveller, who had not received a medical education, or which he would hardly dare to describe, find
a record in the author's voluminous note-books, whilst
the *viveur* side of his character displays itself in the
account of the amorous nature of the warm-blooded
Quadroon and Octoroon women.

Refined Sensuality of Society Islanders.

The differences between the Negro in the WEST INDIES
and in his native land, are exhibited in the author's
description of SENEGAL; and in the last portion of the
book, the reader follows with ever-increasing interest, the
history of the degraded savages of NEW-CALEDONIA and
the NEW HEBRIDES; or is entranced by the glowing
picture—painted as only French writers seem to know
how—of the voluptuous beauties of the SOCIETY ISLANDS—
the last remaining spot on the earth in which refined
sensuality, akin to that of the old Greeks, still lingers.
Of the esoteric portions of the book it would be impossible to speak in a prospectus which might fall into the
hands of women and children.

Weapons against Social Evils.

The work is divided into Two Volumes, each of some
300 pages, and we undertake to say that the most
indifferent novel-reader will find enough to sustain his
attention from the first page to the last, for the rest,
suffice it to say that the title of "UNTRODDEN FIELDS OF
ANTHROPOLOGY" seems the best that could be selected.
The anthropology, as we have hinted, is never dull, for
the author has had the happy inspiration to deal—not
with dry bones or cranial conformations—but with those
principles which ensure the continuity of the races he
describes, and which are physically matters of moment

to us who dwell in more civilized climes. Moreover, by showing us the causes of some of the vices which prevail amongst savage and semi-civilized peoples, he furnishes us with valuable weapons wherewith to combat those social evils, the existence of which amongst us is so deplored by every right-minded man and woman."

Our "foreword" would extend considerably beyond reasonable limits were we to attempt any delineation of the Rise and Progress of Anthropological Methods. An account of these must be sought for in the fascinating pages of Tylor, (1) Hunt, (2) Lubbock, (3) and other equally remarkable, if less known, writers whose contributions have rendered imperishable service to the multifarious History of Man. But we should be wanting in fairness to ourselves if we omitted to say a word in conclusion on what may be termed the less happy side of " Untrodden Fields of Anthropology"; we refer of course to the sketches we have been obliged to give of subjects generally "tabooed" except in medical circles. We may be allowed here to quote a few lines written by us with reference to a previous book (4) and which equally apply to the present work:—

In reply to those of our detractors who have raised an outcry against the contents of this book, we say once and for all that it is not meant for the "general public" but for a select few of private students, amateurs, and medical men who are interested in the strange and fanciful vagaries of wayward Human Nature.

A clever modern writer well says: (5) "We cannot be good by pretending not to know evil. When women go mad, the most innocent, the youngest, the most purely educated often utter the

---

(1) In "Primitive Culture".
(2) "Memoirs of the Anthropological Society of London, (vol. I).
(3) The Origin of Civilization, London, 1889.
(4) The Secret Cabinet of History (Paris, 1897).
(5) Hain Friswell in his "Essays on English Writers".

most horrid and obscene language; a proof that to them such evil
has been known; how acquired, how taught, it is in vain to ask.
What the teacher ought to seek, is, not to blot out and veil iniquity,
since that will always be visible, but to make the heart strong
enough to cast out the evil."

For the rest, we call to mind the larger freedom of discussion
now allowed in England and America, when conducted from the
right standpoint; and we have no fear as to the result. The smug-
faced, hypocrite and canting hirelings of (impure?) "Purity Societies"
may take to heart the wise and witty words of a modern French
literator: (1)—"La pudibonderie, si amusante et si gracieuse chez
la femme, n'est jamais que ridicule chez un mâle; elle prend même
un autre nom quand elle atteint les érudits. J'en appelle aux casuistes."

The sober-minded student will scarcely credit that so
serious a writer as Lombroso has himself had to complain
of this Mock-Modesty in the learned world. In the French
edit. of his book on the "Female Criminal and the Prostitute" (Paris, Alcan, 1896), the Italian scientist passes
the following strictures on the expurgating mania.

"We shall perhaps be reproached for having dealt in
too great detail with certain sexual phenomena which
conventional hypocrisy pretends entirely to conceal from
peoples' eyes; but far better not to publish this work at all
than to suppress these facts relating to the sexual life,
the female criminal would, in such case, no longer exist,
and less still, the prostitute. But, in the English versions
these facts *have* been omitted and suppressed, with the
result that in its castrated form, the book is undoubtedly
much less conclusive."

Our book, as we have fully evidenced, is written in a
temperate and scientific spirit. It is moreover, *not* intended

---

(1) Octave Uzanne, Le Livre, Mars 1884, p. 138:— "Bashfulness, so
entertaining and graceful in a woman, is never anything but ridiculous when found in a man; it calls even for another name when it
lays hold of the learned. I call the casuists to witness to the
truth of this."

for general circulation. An obscene work is one that is designed to stir up voluptuous passions where such passions would not otherwise exist. But the present work couched as far as possible in technicis terminis can have no such effect, being the mere recital of certain customs of barbarous and savage peoples, not dealt with except in widely scattered works, very difficult of access even to the leisured and wealthy scholar. That the present treatise is far removed from a pornographic basis is proved by the fact that many persons who wrote us for the first edition, expressed afterwards their disappointment, as they found the terminology employed too recondite for their hydrocephalic intelligence, and had evidently expected to receive something of a very different stamp. Dr. Schrenck-Notzing (of München) points out:—" that the injury done by implanting knowledge of sexual pathology in unqualified persons is not to be compared with the good accomplished. For the physician himself, sexual anomalies, treated as they are in a distinct manner in text books on psychiatry, are in greater part a terra incognita." (1)

Many eminent men in the past, famous alike for their sturdy thinking and philosophical acumen, have not considered such subjects as those discussed in this book, beneath their notice; among such we may mention curious old Dr. Schurigius, Etmuller, Flemming, Paullini, Beckherius, Rosinus, Lentilius; and lastly brave Levinus Lemnius. (2)   Of course, " there are people " as Adèle Esquiros cleverly says : (3) —

" Who if it were given them to dissect a corpse, would

---

(1) Die Suggestions-Therapie, etc., F. Enke, Stuttgart, 1892.

(2) All of these are mentioned in *Scatalogic Rites* by Capt. John G. Bourke, (Washington, 1891), in itself a wonderful piece of contempt of public opinion.

(3) " *Les Marchandes d'Amour* ", (pag. 189).

only see one thing, that it was naked. Minds like these are so unclean that they thereby become stupid, or are they stupid because they are so unclean? From a book, however bad it may be (someone has said) there is always something good to be gained. Take any impure thing, say a body already in the stage of putrefaction, and give it to the anatomist, he will not start back in horror, for science becomes beautiful in proportion as she is useful.

"I take this mass of impurity and subject it to observation in the crucible of analysis, separating its different principles and using the knowledge won from the lifeless clay for the benefit of living man.

"Cannot we create also an intellectual chemistry, seek how the originally pure elements have become corrupted, and thus find a way by which they may be transformed again to their first state? The elements that we analyse are filled for weak brains with corrosive venom—let us then seek to neutralise these bad influences.

"The decomposition of dead bodies we can well prevent, can we not also stay the decomposition of the human heart? If the weak know, if we know, that a given vice has a bad taste and 'turns but to dead ashes in the mouth', with what happiness should we fly from it. It is only necessary to see certain phases of degradation such as they really are, to hold them afterward in hatred."

Anthropology, as considered in this book, really enters more into the psychopathology of sexual life than probably any other work yet written on the same subject.

Such studies should be undertaken only by men—(i.e. Physicians and Magistrates)—whose duties compel them to make these matters the object of scientific investigation. Dr. R. von Krafft-Ebing has offered some weighty remarks on this head which are so very pertinent to our point that we tender no apology for repeating them:

"It is the sad province of Medicine," he says, "and especially of Psychiatry, to constantly regard the reverse side of life—human weakness and misery. (1)

Perhaps, in this difficult calling, some consolation may be gained and extended to the moralist, if it be possible to refer to morbid conditions much that offends ethical and æsthetic feeling. Thus Medicine undertakes to save the *honor of mankind* before the Court of Morality, and individuals from judges and their fellow-men. The duty and right of medical science in these studies belong to it by reason of the high aim of all human inquiry after truth.

The author would take to himself the words of Tardieu, who had the courage to deal in his day, with an equally repulsive subject: "No physical or moral misery, no sore however corrupt it may be, should frighten him who has devoted himself to a knowledge of man and the sacred ministry of medicine; in that he is obliged to see all things, let him be permitted to say all things." (2)

Burton, it will be remembered, was attacked in the Press for having printed his *magnum opus*, the *Thousand Nights and a Night*, which in our humble judgment is the most wonderful translation ever made from one tongue into another, and moreover in the truest sense, a deep "well of English undefiled". But he held, and justly, that "A Controversy *in* the Press *with* the Press is the controversy of a fly with a spider". He therefore replied

---

(1) Psychopathia Sexualis, with especial reference to Contrary Sexual Instinct: a Medico-legal study. Seventh edition (Philadelphia, 1895).

(2) Aucune misère physique ou morale, aucune plaie, quelque corrompue qu'elle soit, ne doit effrayer celui qui s'est voué à la science de l'homme; et le ministère sacré du médecin, en l'obligeant à tout voir, lui permet aussi de tout dire. (*Des attentats aux mœurs*).

to the critics in his caustic "Reviewers Reviewed". The crushing reply is typical of the man. The "Battle of the Books" says he, "has often been fought, the crude text *versus* the bowdlerised and the expurgated; and our critic can contribute to the great fray only the merest platitudes. There is an old and trusty saying that 'evil communications corrupt good manners,' and it is a well-known fact that the discussion (?) and reading of depraved literature leads (sic) infallibly to the depravation of the reader's mind. (Page 179 *Edinburgh Review*, No. 335 of July 1886). I should say that the childish indecencies and the unnatural vice of the original cannot deprave any mind save that which is perfectly prepared to be depraved; the former would provoke only curiosity and amusement to see bearded men such mere babes, and the latter would breed infinitely more disgust than desire. The man must be prurient and lecherous as a dog-faced baboon in rut to have aught of passion excited by either.

"I resolved that, in case of the spiteful philanthropy and the rabid pornophobic suggestion of certain ornaments of the Home-Press being acted upon, to appear in Court with my version of the Nights in one hand and bearing in the other the Bible (especially the Old Testament, a free translation from an ancient Oriental work) and Shakespeare, with Petronius Arbiter and Rabelais by way of support and reserve. The two former are printed by millions; they find their way into the hands of children, and they are the twin columns which support the scanty edifice of our universal home-reading. The Arbiter is sotadical as Abû Nowás, and the Curé of Meudon is surpassing in what appears uncleanness to the eye of outsight, not of insight. Yet both have been translated, textually and literally, by eminent Englishmen and gentlemen, and have been printed and published as an "extra series" by

Mr. Bohn's most respectable firm and sold by Messrs.
Bell and Daldy. And if the Nights are to be bowdlerised
for students, why not, I again ask, mutilate Plato and
Juvenal, the Romances of the Middle Ages, Boccaccio and
Petrarch, and the Elizabethan dramatists one and all?
What hyprocrisy to blaterate about the Nights in presence
of such triumphs of the Natural! How absurd to swallow
such camels and to strain at my midge!

" Having failed to free the Anthropological Society from
the fetters of *mauvaise honte*, and the mock-modesty
which compels travellers and ethnological students to keep
silence concerning one side of human nature (and that
side the most interesting to mankind), I proposed to
supply the want in these pages. The England of our day
would fain bring up both sexes, and keep all ages, in
profound ignorance of sexual and intersexual relations ; and
the consequences of that imbecility are peculiarly cruel and
afflicting. How often do we hear women in Society lamenting
that they have absolutely no knowledge of their own physiology ; and at what heavy price must this fruit of the know-
ledge-tree be bought by the young first entering life.
Shall we ever understand that ignorance is not innocence?
What an absurdum is a veteran officer who has spent
a quarter-century in the East without learning that all
Moslem women are circumcised, and without a notion of
how female circumcision is effected; without an idea of
the difference between the Jewish and the Moslem rite as
regards males ; without an inkling of the Armenian process
whereby the cutting is concealed, and without the slightest theoretical knowledge concerning the mental and spiritual effect of the operation. Where then is the shame
of teaching what it is shameful not to have learnt? But
the ultra-delicacy, the squeamishness of an age which is
by no means purer or more virtuous than its ruder pre-

decessors, has ended in trenching upon the ridiculous. Let us see what the Modern English Woman and her Anglo-American sister have become under the working of a mock-modesty which too often acts as a cloak to real *dévergondage;* and how Respectability unmakes what Nature made. She has feet but no "toes"; ankles but no "calves"; knees but no "thighs"; a stomach but no "belly" nor "bowels"; a heart but no "bladder" nor "groin"; a liver and no "kidneys"; hips and no "haunches"; a bust and no "backside" nor "buttocks": in fact, she is a monstrum, a figure fit only to frighten the crows.

"I have no apology to make for the details offered to the Students of Moslem usages and customs, who will find in them much to learn and more to suggest the necessity of learning. In no wise ashamed am I of lecturing upon these esoteric matters, the most important to humanity, at a time when their absence from the novel of modern society veils with a double gloom the nightside of human nature. Nay, I take pride to myself for so doing in the face of silly prejudice and miserable hypocrisy, and I venture to hold myself in the light of a public benefactor. In fact, I consider my labours as a legacy bequeathed to my countrymen at a most critical time, when England the puissantest of Moslem powers is called upon, without adequate knowledge of the Moslem's inner life, to administer Egypt as well as to rule India. And while Pharisee and Philister may be or may pretend to be "shocked" and "horrified" by my pages, the sound common-sense of a public, which is slowly but surely emancipating itself from the prudish and prurient reticences, and the immodest and immoral modesties of the early sixth century, will in good time do me, I am convinced, full and ample justice."

Burton's words in defence of his "Nights" so well-express our own opinions on these matter that anything we had written would have been but a far-off and feeble echo of the same sentiments. This must be our only apology for so lengthy an extract.

The modern Bayard's lines more than justify the existence of our book. Were more required, we would add that should the work even fall into the hands of young men, no more powerful deterrent to vice could be given than that which under the heading of prostitution in China, shows the terrible consequences of promiscuous intercourse. "God help" the man, young or old, who catches a dose of syphilis, or confirmed gonorrhœa with all their nameless and far-reaching results—sometimes involving the loss of the virile member, the nose, and eyesight. This is no place to sermonize, but we imagine that were sexual education less shirked in England, there would be vastly fewer men who, too late, learn the bitter truth of the Hebrew seer's words, about the "strange woman, which flattereth with her words, whose feet go down to death, whose steps take hold on hell, going down to the chambers of death." Let men learn about these things in an open and lawful way, and they will be less likely to search them out clandestinely.. Proscribe anything—a book or other object—and you at once put a premium on it. Men, as Napoleon shrewdly observed, are but "grown-up children", and after the manner of children we notice that they howl (in their way) for anything forbidden them until they get it.

If the false male prudes who fight, with a fanaticism worthy of Sudanese negroes, against the regulation of vice in India and at Home, knew what it is to suffer from the hideous diseases which are bred and spread by their system, we feel sure they would use their efforts in a more intelligent direction. In our judgment *they* are

responsible for the great multitude who go " as an ox
goeth to the slaughter, or as a fool to the correction of
the stocks till a dart strike through his liver; as a bird
hasteth to the snare, and knoweth not that it is for his
life."

Parent-Duchatelet in his monumental work on Prostitution has the following sentence :

" What good, in fact, could be effected without the
knowledge of these habits and customs? It will later on
avoid groping about, and may perhaps suggest to those
who shall come after me, some salutary measures that
our generation had not thought of."

These words seem singularly applicable to our work,
and we appropriate them because expressive, above all, of
our own aim.

CHARLES CARRINGTON.

CONTENTS

SECOND EDITION

ANALYTICAL

TABLE OF CONTENTS

PART THE FIRST

ASIA

Cochin-China—Tonquin—Cambodia

CHAPTER I.

Cochin-China thirty years ago.—A few words about Saigon as it was.—Other Asiatic races, besides the Annamites, inhabiting Cochin-China.—The Hindoos, otherwise known as Malabars.—Cambodians.—Malays.—Moys.—Anthropological characteristics of the Moys.—Chams.—The Tagals of Manilla.—The Chinese town of Cho-lon. —The Chinese race.—Trades and professions — Diversity of anthropological types amongst the Chinese.—The Minhuongs.—A few words on the manners and customs of the Chinese and Cochin-Chinese.—The Chinese theatre.   [Page 1

CHAPTER II.

The origin of the Annamites, otherwise called *Giao-Chi.*—Anthropological characteristics of the race.—Genital organs of the Annamites.—Their small size.—The child taken as a basis of comparison for the medical part of this subject.—The little Annamite girl, and her early loss of virginity.—Woman at the age of puberty.—The genital organs of the adult.—Franco-Annamite mongrels.   [Page 16

Chapter VII.

Study of the buccal, vulvar, and anal deformities caused by male and female prostitution in the Annamite race.—The vulva of the young girl before puberty, and of the Annamite woman; signs of the loss of virginity.—Sodomy and pederasty.—Anal Blennorrhœa.—Signs of inveterate passive sodomy.—The Anal Infundibulum.—Relaxation of the Sphincter.—Effacement of the Radiating Folds.—Signs of active pederasty in the Annamite and the Chinese.—Signs of active and passive pederasty in the European in Cochin-China.—Signs of Passive Sodomy.

[Page 115

Chapter VIII.

The European Colony thirty years ago.—The two first European prostitutes.—Rarity of the European woman.—Moral causes of the relative frequency of sodomy and pederasty in those days.—Saigon in the present day.—Increase of the feminine element.—Nocturnal amusements.—The European prostitute.—Great Improvement in the Morality of the Europeans in Cochin-China.—The Diminution in the Male and Female Prostitution of the Natives more apparent than Real.—How the Business is now managed.—The *boy* and the native collegian.

[Page 133

Chapter IX.

My visit to Tonquin.—Anthropological characteristics of the Tonquinese.—The Muongs, and the Xas or Quans.—The Chinaman, and the Tonquin-Chinese half-breed.—Chinese Piracy.—Manners, habits, customs, and religion.—Moral characteristics, forms and perversions of sexual passion.—The European Colony in Tonquin.

[Page 148

Chapter X.

My sojourn in Cambodia.—Anthropological characteristics of the Cambodians.—Organs of generation.—Foreign races inhabiting Cambodia.—The Malays and Chams.—The Chinese.—

CHAPTER XI.

PART THE SECOND

AMERICA

Guiana—Martinique

CHAPTER I.

XL CONTENTS

Chapter VI.

The convict under military law.—Capt. B*** President of the Council of War—Curious Cases tried before the Council.—Hindoo.—Pederasty amongst Arabs.—Arab Criminal Assaults and Rape.   [Page 286

Chapter VII.

My Stay at Martinique.—The whites, called pure Creoles.—Prejudice against Colour.—The Black race.—Moral characteristics of the Negress.—The Coloured Race.—The Mulatto.—The Quadroon girl and her passionate nature.—"Fricatrices" and Lesbians.—Depilation.   [Page 300

Untrodden Fields of Anthropology.

PART THE FIRST.—ASIA.

COCHIN-CHINA—TONQUIN—CAMBODIA.

CHAPTER I.

Cochin-China thirty years ago.—A few words about Saigon as it was.— Other Asiatic Races, besides the Annamites, inhabiting Cochin-China.—The Hindoos, otherwise known as Malabars.— Cambodians.—Malays. --Moys.—Anthropological characteristics of the Moys.— Chams.--The Tagals of Manilla.—The Chinese town of Cho-lon.—The Chinese race.—Trades and professions. —Diversity of anthropological types amongst the Chinese.— The Minhuongs.—A few words on the manners and customs of the Chinese and Cochin-Chinese.—The Chinese theatre.

Cochin-China thirty Years ago. Cochin-China was the first colony I visited, and the impressions I retain of it are like those of a beardless youth for his first mistress.

I had hardly left the class-rooms of the College of Medicine, in 186—, than I obtained a post as assistant-surgeon in the Navy, and was sent to Cochin-China. I will pass over the varied incidents of a voyage of

more than two months (the Suez Canal was not then
made), and enter at once upon the study of the manners
and customs of the various races inhabiting Cochin-
China at the period of which I speak. An uninter-
rupted residence of five years in the colony, and a
second visit twenty-five years later, are guarantees
of the correctness of my observations.

**A Few Words about Saigon as it Originally
was.** The impression produced by Saigon at this
time has been very well described by Pallu de la
Barrière, [1] only two years after the conquest in 1861,
for, until the capture of the intrenched camp at Ki-
hoa, the occupation of Saigon could only be regarded
as temporary:

"The traveller who arrives at Saigon perceives, on
the right bank of the river, a kind of street, the sides
of which are broken here and there by large empty
spaces. The houses—which for the most part are of
wood—are covered with leaves of the dwarf palm; a
few of the houses are of stone. Their roofs, of red
tiles, brighten and improve the scene. Then comes
the curved roof of a pagoda; then a shed, out of the
perpendicular, which serves as a market, and the roof
of which seems slipping down on the right side. In
the middle distance are some arrack palms, which
harmonize well with the soil of India; the other vegetation lacks character. Thousands of boats are huddled
together along the bank of the river, and form a little
floating town. Besides this there is not much to see
at Saigon, unless it is the Chinese *arroyo*, with its fairly
clean houses built of stone, some of them old, and

---

[1] Pallu de la Barrière. *Histoire de l'Expédition de Cochinchine.*
Paris 1888. in 8vo.

standing amidst copses of cabbage palms. Further off, on the heights, are the house of the French Commandant, that of the Spanish Colonel, the students' camp, and that is about all."

I have given this description of Saigon such as it was at the time when the colony of Cochin-China was in its infancy. We shall find it much changed a quarter of a century later.

Before studying the Annamite race, let us cast a rapid glance at the other Asiatic races inhabiting this country.

The Asiatic Races, besides the Annamites inhabiting Cochin-China. These various races are all represented, more or less, at Saigon. Moreover, five years spent in continual journeys in the interior of the country, have given me opportunities of studying them all pretty closely. The Chinese race, which has the pre-eminence over all the other foreign races, both in number and importance, deserves a special mention.

The Hindoos, known as Malabars. There is to be found at Saigon, a certain number of natives of India, known under the generic title of Malabars, as they usually come from the Malabar Coast, Madras, Pondicherry, Bombay, etc. Some of them are Catholics, other Brahmins, but the greater part are Mahometans. They breed cattle, drive carts, transport goods, and keep little retail shops, or they change piasters and other money.

The Mahometans have constructed a handsome mosque; after the Ramadan they celebrate their Bairam, [1]

[1] The ninth month of the Muhammadan year, which is observed as a strict fast from dawn to sunset of each day in the month. The word

and have a grand procession by night, when, by the
light of thousands of torches, they drag about an immense car.

The anthropological remarks that I shall have to
make further on about the Indian coolies of Guiana,
will apply to their congeners of Saigon, and I must
refer the reader to that part of the book. But the
Malabars of Cochin-China are taller and more robust,
and of a much handsomer type. Some have brought

Ramazân is derived from *ramz*, "to burn" The month is said to have
been so called either because it used (before the change of the calendar)
to occur in the hot season, or because the month's fast is supposed to
burn away the 'sins of men (*Ghiyâsu'l-Lughah, in loco*).

The observance of this month is one of the five pillars of practice in
the Muslim religion, and its excellence is much extolled by Muhammad,
who said that during Ramazân "the gates of Paradise are open, and the
gates of hell are shut, and the devils are chained by the leg, and only
those who observe it will be permitted to enter at the gate of heaven
called Raiyân." Those who keep the fast "will be pardoned all their
past venial sins" (*Mishkât*, book VII, ch. I. part I).

See Hughes' "*Dict. of Islam*" p. 533; London, 1885, for more
extensive details; also the realistic account given by Burton in his
Pilgrimage to Al-Madinah and Meccah (Lond. 1873). Sir Richard
thinks that "like, the Italian, the Anglo-Catholic, and the Greek fasts,
the chief effect of the "blessed month" upon True Believers is to darken
their tempers into positive gloom. Their voices, never of the softest,
acquire, especially after noon, a terribly harsh and creaking tone. The
men curse one another and beat the women. The women slap and
abuse the children, and these in their turn cruelly entreat, and use bad
language to the dogs and cats. You can scarcely spend ten minutes in
any populous part of the city without hearing some violent dispute. It
is only fair to Islam to add that of course all quarrelling, abuse, and
evil words are strictly forbidden to the Moslem during Ramazan. If
one believer insults another, the latter should repeat I am fasting,"three
times before venturing himself to reply. Such is the wise law. But
human nature in Egypt, as elsewhere, is always ready to sacrifice the
spirit to the letter, rigidly to obey the physical part of an ordinance, and
to cast away the moral, as if it were the husk and not the kernel."

their wives from India; others have married Annamite women, by whom they have mongrel children of a villainously low type of humanity.

Cambodians. The Cambodian race, being the subject of a special study later on, I will not speak of it here.

Malays. The Malays descended from Cambodia, whither they had emigrated from the isthmus of Malacca. They are, in general, sober, patient, and avaricious: they carry on the business of pawnbrokers, and charge a very high rate of interest. They inhabit separate villages, and rarely intermarry with the Annamite race. The Malays are Mahometans, and faithful to their religion. Many of them carry on trade by exchanging the products of Cambodia against those of Cochin-China, and they form amongst themselves associations analagous to those of the Chinese. As far as industries are concerned, they manufacture hardly anything but jewellery.

Their costume consists of cotton drawers, a tight-fitting waistcoat, a linen jacket, and a turban. The men are close shaved; the women who wear a *langouti*, and a long robe, have their hair dressed in the Annamite fashion.

In form, colour, and conformation, the genital organs of both sexes of the Malays greatly resemble those of the Annamite, though they are unquestionably more virile.

Moys. I have examined the Moys of the district of Baria, where they possess many villages. Their habitations may be found in groups of three or four,

each house holding perhaps a score of persons. These
houses stand on posts, and are raised four or five
yards above the ground. They look like large rectangular cages made of bamboo, with a thatched
roof. The primitive furniture consits mainly of a slab
of baked clay to make the fire on, and a few screens
of bamboo to contain the provisions.

The men wear a square of cloth over the genital
parts, and the young women cover their breasts with
a square of cloth hung round the neck. Both sexes
have their ears pierced, and wear ear-rings. Their
language completely differs from that of the Annamite.

In this race, so different from the Annamite, family
feelings, and extreme kindness to children are exhibited
in a marked degree. Young people marry, after they
have attained the age of puberty, without any ceremony, or written contract. The Moy respects customs,
however, and cannot repudiate his wife and take
another, without being obliged to provide for the first
wife and her children.

The manners of the people are very pure. Adultery is very rare, and the vices we shall find amongst
the Annamites almost unknown. The Moy copulates
with his wife according to the law of nature, and
without tricks of any sort. From this point of view
it is the Annamites, not the Moys, who ought to be
called savages, for they are one of the most corrupt
people in the civilized world.

The religion of the Moys is very elementary, and
is confined generally to a worship of the dead. [1]

[1] A very significant fact representing already no small state of culture.
Spencer (in chap. XX. on *Ancestor-Worship in general*", in his
masterful work dealing with the *Principles of Sociology*", Lond. 1885)
—points out that "in the Far East, another vast society which had

Anthropological Characteristics of the Moys.
This race may be classed as amongst the smallest in the world—smaller than the Lapps, according to Dr.

reached considerable heights of culture, while Europe was covered by barbarians, has practised, and still practices, ancestor-worship.... With the highly-developed religious systems of India, there co-exists a daily re-genesis of deities from dead men." (page 283). Further on he brings evidence to show that " *the word for a god means literally a dead man* ". The whole passage is so profoundly interesting that we may be pardoned for reproducing it:—" Ghost, spirit, demon—names at first applied to the other-self without distinctions of character—come to be differently applied as ascribed differences of character arise: the shade of an enemy becomes a devil, and a friendly shade becomes a divinity. Where the conceptions have not developed far, there are no differentiated titles, and the distinctions made by us cannot be expressed. The early Spanish missionaries in America were incovenienced by finding that the only native word they could use for God also meant devil. In Greek, δαιμων Θεός are interchangeable. By Æschylus, Agamemnon's children are represented as appealing to their father's ghost as to a god. So, too, with the Romans. Besides the unspecialized use of *dæmon*, which means an angel or genius, good or bad, we find the unspecialized use of *deus* for god and ghost. On tombs the *manes* were called gods; and a law directs that "the rights of the *manes*—gods, are to be kept sacred."

Similarly with the Hebrews.

Isaiah, representing himself as commanded to reject it, quotes a current belief implying such identification: "And when they say unto you, 'Consult the ghost-seers and the wizards, that chirp and that mutter! Should not people consult their gods, even the dead on behalf of the living?'" When Saul goes to question the ghost of Samuel, the expression of the enchantress is—"I saw gods [elohim] ascending out of the earth;" god and ghost being thus used as equivalents.

Even in our own day the kinship is traceable. The statement that God is a spirit, shows the application of a term which, otherwise applied, signifies a human soul. Only by its qualifying epithet is the meaning of Holy Ghost distinguished from the meaning of ghost in general. A divine being is still denoted by words that originally meant the breath which, deserting a man's body at death, was supposed to constitute the surviving part.

Néis. [1]   " The tint of their skin," says this author,
" is darker than that of the Annamites. They have
but little hair, though more than is usual with the
yellow races. It is always black and wavy, or in
some cases curly; the beard, which is sometimes thick
on the lips and chin, is wanting on the cheeks.

" The skull is dolicho-cephalous, slightly scaphocephal-
ous, the face is prognathic, the forehead narrow, the
cheek-bones slightly projecting; the eyelids which are
large and well-formed, are horizontal and not oblique
like those of the yellow races. The nose is very flat,
the mouth wide, the teeth are large, well-set, and
reddened with betel.

" The muscles are but little developed, and do not
project under the skin. The breasts of the woman,
which are of average size, are conical; they wither
soon, but without lengthening like the breasts of the
Negress. The ankles are small, the feet long, and
the toes wide apart, as is the case with all people
who walk bare-footed."

I have given this description *in extenso*, but that
of the genital organs is still wanting. I do not know
why the anthropologists have, until now, almost entirely
neglected to note in the various human races the
variations in form and colour of the genital organ,
for me the most important of all organs, since it in-
sures the continuance of the race. I shall have more
than once to refer to the results of these examinations,
which I made very carefully.

In the Moy, the colour of the skin of the genital
organs, and particularly the scrotum, is darker than
in the Annamite. It is the same with the colour of

[1] Néis (Paul) sur le Laos. *Bulletins de la Société d'Anthropologie
de Paris.* Vol. viii, 3rd Series. Paris, 1885.

the mucous membrane of the " great lips," the gland,
and the vagina, which are not so light, but of a tint
approaching more to dark red. The penis and testicles of the Moy are larger than those of the Annamite,
although their average height is less. The vulva and
vagina of the Moy woman are more developed than
those of the Annamite woman. The pubis is shaded,
in both sexes, by a fair quantity of curly hair, of a
very black colour.

None of the Moys I was able to examine showed
any traces of masturbation or unnatural habits. There
is a great difference in this respect between the Moy
and Annamite races.

There is no single point in common between the
two races. The Annamite, being more civilized, looks
down with contempt upon the savage Moy, and will
not ally himself with them. The number of Moys
was sensibly diminishing when I arrived in Cochin-
China, and the race will soon die out, as every inferior
race does in the presence of a more advanced people.

Chams. It is asserted that the Chams are of Malay
origin, and are descended from the remnant of the old
Kingdom of Ciampa, which was formerly conquered
by the Annamites. Some wandering tribes may still
be met on the confines of the colony, towards Tay-
Ninh and Chandoc. These people flee from civilization.
What I have said about the Malays will apply to the
Chams.

The Tagals of Manilla. At the time of my first
visit, there were still in Cochin-China some Tagals of
Manilla, forming part of the Spanish Expeditionary
Corps. They were generally hunters of wild beasts,

or sometimes *sais* and coachmen. It is a hardy and
sober race. They have adopted as their costume, white
trousers, with over them, a shirt with long tails. By
marriage with the Annamite woman, the Tagal has
founded a mongrel race which is not half numerous
enough.

The Town of Cho-lon. About three miles from
Saigon is the Chinese town of Cho-lon, built a century
ago by Chinese emigrants, and having the exact
appearance of a town of the South of China.

An old friend of mine, Luro, a Government inspector
of the natives, whom I knew intimately, has written
the following picturesque description of it: "In the
interior of Cho-lon are many retail shops; those which
do a large trade, kept by Chinese, and the smaller
shops kept by Annamite women. The goods are
neatly and cleverly displayed. The seeds-man, grocer,
restaurant-keeper, chemist, tailor, boot-maker, jeweller,
iron-monger, trunk-maker, confectioner, etc., all have
their name written in large Chinese characters over
the door, artistically painted in black, red, blue, or
gold, according to the taste of the proprietor. There
is a continual movement of customers entering and
leaving. The shops are open in the evening, the
streets are lighted by the Municipality (with gas at
present) and, besides that, are illuminated with Chinese
lanterns of the most varied and pleasing forms and
colours, on which are painted, in transparent characters,
the name of the tradesman."

The Chinese Race. There were, in 186—, in
Saigon and Cho-lon, more than 30,000 Chinese, and
as many more in the interior of the country. The

Chinaman is the Jew of the Extreme East, he has in his hands nearly all the wholesale and retail trade. He is sharp, and thirsty after gain, but he is satisfied with a small profit. The European merchant is obliged to use him as an intermediate agent. An Englishman who lived many years of his life in Hongkong has sketched the following picture of this peculiar race:

" Of the moral character of the people, who have multiplied until they are 'as the sand which is upon the sea-shore,' it is very difficult to speak justly. The moral character of the Chinese is a book written in strange letters, which are more complex and difficult for one of another race, religion and language to decipher than their own singularly compounded word-symbols. In the same individual, virtues and vices, apparently incompatible, are placed side by side. Meekness, gentleness, docility, industry, contentment, cheerfulness, obedience to superiors, dutifulness to parents, and reverence for the aged, are in one and the same person, the companions of insincerity, lying, flattery, treachery, cruelty, jealousy, ingratitude, avarice, and distrust of others. The Chinese are a weak and timid people, and in consequence, like all similarly constituted races, they seek a natural refuge in deceit and fraud." [1]

Various Trades and Professions of the Chinese. Compared with the Annamite, the Chinaman looks like a stronger and more robust cousin-german. The family resemblance is evident, in spite of the radical difference between the Annamite chignon and the Chinese pig-tail, This family likeness between the two

[1] J. H. Gray.—" *China.—The Laws, Manners, and Customs of the people.*" (London, 1878, page 15 of Vol 1.)

races is specially remarkable amongst the Chinese of
the lowest order (called *bambous*) who for a few *sapecks*
perform the duties of porters. He is scantily clad in
a pair of ragged breeches, coming only to his knees,
and his naked sun-burnt body has a tint as dark as
that of the Annamite field-labourer.

Above this lowest class come the peripatetic sellers
of food, and those who act as cooks to Europeans,
who enjoy what I must own to be a well-deserved
reputation. There are also, amongst the Chinese, *boys*,
who act as waiters in the European cafés and restaurants. They are generally very cleanly in their habits.

The Chinaman is also the proprietor of the gambling
houses and brothels. He is also a gardener, and
grows (using human excrements as manure) all sorts
of European vegetables in the gardens round Saigon.
It is not possible to take a walk in the outskirts of
the town, before sunset, without being stifled by an
abominable stench of night soil. On the other hand,
during eight months of the year, you can eat salads
and vegetables which are quite as cheap as in the
markets of London or Paris.

**Diversity in the Anthropological Characteristics
of the Chinese.** The skin of the Chinaman of Canton
(who is generally rich) is almost as white as the skin
of a native of the South of France. The tint resembles
that of weak tea. The mucous membranes are a
rather bright carmine, toned down with a dash of ochre.
This colour is more specially found in the mucous
tissues of the gland and the vulva. It is impossible
to confound it with that of coloured men, the result
of a cross between the Negro and the White, for in
them the brown tint of the mucous membranes of the

Negro asserts itself, and forms a marked anthropological characteristic.

At the opposite end of the scale of the Chinese race is the Chinaman of the South (from Fokien or Haïnam), whose skin is of the colour of dark yellow ginger-bread, and whose mucous membranes have a yellowish red tint, almost the colour of "raw Sienna," darkened with a little Sepia.

As to the size and conformation of the genital organs, it appeared to me that the Chinaman of the North closely resembled the European. The prepuce is but small, and imperfectly covers the gland when in a state of repose.

The Chinaman of the South appears to be less vigorous, as a male, than the Chinaman of the North, but he is still much superior in this respect to the average Annamite. He also presents the same characteristic of the imperfectly developed foreskin; and the gland, which is only half covered when the organ is flaccid, slips out very easily and completely when it is in erection. I have met very few cases of phimosis, [1] which, on the contrary, is so common in the European races.

The pubes projects, and is furnished with black hair slightly curly, and fairly thick in the case of the Cantonese. The testicles of the Chinese appeared to me to be a little smaller than those of the Europeans, but the difference is not very marked,

Wherever he may come from, and whatever may be his social position, the Chinaman shows one common

[1] Historical students will recollect that it was this infirmity which prevented Louis XVI from accomplishing his marital duties until eight years after his marriage, when he submitted to the necessary liberating operation. (For further interesting details on this subject, see "*The Secret Cabinet of History*", p. 77 and seq. Paris, 1896.)

characteristic—his lubricity, and his great fecundity with those Asiatic races to whom he allies himself. On that account he is a famous colonizer in times of peace. [1]

Minhuongs. This is the name given to children who are the offspring of a Chinaman and an Annamite woman; they are whiter and better formed than the indigenes. Amongst them, one may often meet very lovely children who have not attained puberty. The Minhuong is as active and intelligent as his father, and as stubborn as his mother. He inherits from his father the Chinese type, and *he preserves the manners, the religion, and the costume* of the Celestial. This is important to note. His skin is lighter, and his muscular strength much superior to that of the pure Annamite.

As a generator, the form, colour, and dimensions of his reproductive apparatus are almost like those of the Chinaman, with a slightly darker shade of the skin and the mucous membranes.

[1] To form an idea of the Chinaman abroad one must have seen him thirty years ago in California and particularly in the Chinese quarter in San Francisco. There he and his progeny swarmed; but without benefit to the country, for he does not breed citizens, but only Chinamen, who, as soon as they have amassed sufficient money, will sooner or later return to the land of their ancestors; even their dead bodies, are sent back; the transport of which is effected by Chinese insurance companies. The Chinaman is industrious, economical, persevering, avaricious, sober and indefatigable but devoid of moral sense, and his soul is profoundly debauched—there is no nobility or even dignity about him. Wherever he comes, it is as a devouring locust and a blood-sucker. He is either keeper of an opium-smoking den, of a gaming hell or of a brothel, combining with any occupation he may exercise, that of usurer. Jews, with all their astuteness, cannot compete with him, and where he settles, they retire.

The United States now actively oppose their immigration, and the Australian colonies have been obliged to do the same.

At Cho-lon, the Minhuongs have preserved all the habits, manners, and customs of their fathers, and you cannot get a better idea of a real Chinese town than by seeing Cho-lon.

The Chinese Theatre. The women's parts are played by young men, who are brought up to the profession from infancy. To such perfection do they imitate the manners, the walk, and the voice of a Chinese woman, that it is difficult to tell them from women. They even go further, and play the part of women in other ways. We shall mention this subject in discussing the perversions of manners in the Chinese race.

At the Chinese theatre they play tragi-comedies, and heroic melodramas, and you see heroines, kings, ministers, generals and their armies, buffoons, dragons, tigers, protecting genii, etc. Terrible combats often take place, amidst the explosion of crackers. There are also farces, which, in the matter of licence. are as far beyond the Palais Royal, as those vaudevilles are beyond the " moralities" of Berquin. Freedom of description and realism are carried to the extreme. I confess to having passed some pleasant evenings, when an obliging Chinaman was kind enough to translate the plot and action of the piece to me.

For their great family festivals, the rich Chinese (and the rich Annamites also) engage a theatrical *troupe* expressly, and build in front of their houses a bamboo shed, in which they give, during at least three days. a performance gratis to their friends. It is more especially at these representations that the most risky pieces are played,—if the taste of the host should happen to lie that way.

CHAPTER II.

The origin of the Annamites, otherwise called Giao-Chi.—Anthropological characteristics of the race.—Genital organs of the Annamites.—Their small size.—The child taken as a basis of comparison for the medical part of this subject.—The little Annamite girl and her early loss of virginity.—Woman at the age of puberty.—The genital organs of the adult.—Franco-Annamite mongrels.

The Origin of the Annamites, otherwise called Giao-Chi. [1]

According to the learned father Le Grand de la Liraye, the Annamites date nearly as far back as the Chinese [2] themselves. " Two thousand two hundred and eighty years before Christ, *that is to say less than a century after the deluge*, mention is found of the Giao-Chi, an aboriginal race inhabiting the

[1] *Giao-Chi*, literally " Big Toe " race—a still marked feature, for the toe is now used like a thumb. (See Forlong's *Short Studies in the Science of Comparative Religions.* London, 1897, page 74.) This work is a mine of information and deserves the attention of every searcher into the origins of the historic Faiths of Humanity.

[2] The *primordia* of all countries are enveloped in much that is obscure and fabulous, and it is extremely difficult for the historian to fix the period when civil history had its beginnings. China is no exception, but there can, I think, be no doubt of the antiquity of the Chinese Empire. It is not, I believe, rash to say that it has survived a period of four thousand years, without having undergone any great change either in the laws by which it is governed, or in the speech manners, and customs of its teeming population." (Gray's " China " vol I, London, 1878.)

southern confines of the Chinese Empire, and which became the parent stock of the Annamite race.   It originally formed part of the Chinese Empire, and only gained its independence in 1428, by the general massacre of the Chinese.   Annam has borrowed everything from China; language, education, literature, religion, law, medicine, and arts.   Thus it gives birthright and citizenship to all the Chinese who come to trade in Indo-China."

The Annamite, it will be seen, is not a savage, on the contrary his civilization dates further back than that of the European, but he also possesses a formidable number of vices, which he conceals from the eyes of an inattentive observer, but which you discover when you come to study the race closely.

Anthropological Attributes of the Race.   The Annamite is thus a separate branch of the yellow Chinese race.   He is under-sized, nervous, but of a weak appearance, often thin, and not muscular.   The lower limbs are often bent, on account of the mothers carrying their children astraddle on their hips.   Their walk is ungraceful, and the foot is often turned out; the great toe is far separated from the others and almost opposable.   Thus an Annamite can, like a monkey, pick up a piece of money from the ground, or hold the rudder of his boat with his toes.   The pelvis is not well developed, the bust long and thin, the chest thrown out, and well-formed.   The hands are long and narrow, and the points of the fingers knotted. There is but little strength in the muscles,—a white man could thrash ten Annamites with his fists,—but they endure fatigue very well, and can withstand the heat of one of the most unwholesome climates in the world.

The skull is round, and brachy-cephalous. The face is a very long oval, almost lozenge shaped. The forehead is low, the eye oblique, and raised at the external extremity, the eyelids long, and covering black pupils. The Annamite has excellent sight. The cheeks rise towards the temples; the nose is almost as flat as that of the Negro, very large at the root, but the lips, however, are not so thick. The mouth is of an average size, the chin short, and the ears large and projecting.

The teeth would be magnificent if the practice of lacquering them with black varnish, and the red froth caused by betel chewing, did not render the mouth, of even the most beautiful Annamite woman, frightful. However, you get used to it in time.

The facial angle, in both sexes, is 77°. The beard makes its appearance very late,—towards the thirtieth year,—is short, hard, and stiff like horsehair, and grows only on the lips and chin. The hair is black, long, and very thick, it closely resembles a horse's tail, and often falls below the hips. The men and women both wear it in a chignon, raised up behind the head. The skin is thick; the colour varies according to the caste, from the mahogany or dead-leaf tint of the peasant who is burned by the sun, to the pale yellow wax hue of the mandarin, who never goes out without an enormous umbrella, the mark of his position, extended over his head.

If the Annamite woman, or *Congai*, is displeasing on account of her flat face, and her black mouth with its red saliva, it must be confessed that her body is well-made and well-proportioned. When once you are used to the shape of the face, you may often find women with pretty features. The hands and feet are excessively small, and the ankles and wrists slender.

Annamites of both sexes develop slowly, and a young man of twenty does not appear to be more than fifteen; if it were not that the ears are not pierced, you would often take a youth, of from fifteen to twenty years, for a girl not yet formed, and the sweetness of the voice increases the illusion. After the age of twenty, the features of the man grow larger and harder.

In the pubescent girl, the breast is hemispherical, and very regularly formed; it hardly begins to develop before the seventeenth year; for a long time it remains small and hard, but during gestation and the period of suckling increases to a considerable size and becomes soft, though still retaining its horizontal position. The nipple is usually brown. The first birth ordinarily takes place at twenty or twenty-one years of age. The women are very prolific, and you often find families of from six to ten, or even twelve, children,[1] half a dozen being the average. There are, however, few twins. This fecundity is very remarkable considering the smallness of the genital organs of both sexes.

About the fortieth year the "periods" cease. The Annamite race ages very quickly; at fifty years a man's beard is quite white, and he is broken down by age; however, there are, as in Europe, octogenarians, and even—it is said—centenarians. I must confess that I never saw one.

The Genital Organs of the Annamites.—Their Small Size. A fact which struck me as soon as I

[1] Dr. Alexander Wilder was of opinion that: "Every woman has the capacity of producing twenty or more children. (The Countess of WINCHESTER and NOTTINGHAM, ANNE daughter of CHRISTOPHER, Viscount HATTON, had THIRTY! —See *the Saturday Magazine*, February 8th, 1834).

began to examine closely the genital organs of the Annamites, was their really remarkable smallness, which is quite in keeping, however, with the weakness of their bodies, and debility of their muscles. From this special point of view, the Annamites may be said to occupy the lowest place amongst all the races we shall study, and if we may call the Negroes of Africa *men stallions*, it would be just as logical to call the Annamites *men monkeys*.

They deserve this appellation in two ways, the monkey being of all animals the one that has the smallest genital organs in proportion to the size of its body. The monkey is also the only animal which masturbates intentionally; another point of resemblance to the human race. The Annamite, one of the oldest of civilized beings, is as lascivious as the monkey.

Annamite Children. Let us commence with the examination of the genital organs in infancy, which can be done without any offence to morals, girls and boys going completely naked until the age of twelve years. Before that age, the penis of the little boy is hardly the size of his little finger, and the finger of an Annamite child is not large. They do not arrive at puberty before fourteen or fifteen, which is as late as in Europe. At that age the penis is as large as the forefinger of a European. The complete development of the genital organs is hardly effected before the twentieth year, and sometimes even later. The foreskin of the young Annamite is of the average length, and does not form a cushion in front of the gland, as is characteristic in the Negro races of Africa. But the preputial ring is generally narrow. As nearly all the boys practise masturbation from the age of fourteen or fifteen years, this ring enlarges, and permits the free egress of the gland.

The little girl has the vulva placed very high, higher even than it is in the little French girl. When she is nubile, which is hardly before the fifteenth or sixteenth year (the average age is sixteen) there is no great change in the appearance of these parts.

The Little Annamite girl, and Her Early Loss of Virginity. In all the little girls of less than ten years of age I found the hymen present. After ten years the complete hymen is often wanting, but the genito-urinary organs then present certain traces of defloration, though much less characteristic than those noted by Tardieu in the case of little girls, victims of indecent assaults *without violence but repeated during a long period.* In that case the hymen was not usually destroyed, but simply rendered thinner, and drawn back, and having the appearance of a mere ring surrounding the entrance to the vagina, and which allowed the extremity of a greased forefinger to be inserted without causing pain.

I attribute this simply to the fact that the little Annamite girls are deflowered, after ten years of age, by the little boys with whom they play, and repeat together the lessons which their parents have unconsciously taught them, on account of the forced promiscuity of the family in a little thatched house, where all the family live in common, and where mere partitions in wicker-work, the height of a man, form the only divisions of the rooms.

Besides, there is an Annamite proverb of brutal cynicism, which I heard at Tonquin: "For a girl to be still a virgin at ten years old, she must have neither brothers nor father."

The Annamite Woman at the Age of Puberty.
At the age of puberty the organs assume their full
development, and a girl is nubile at sixteen years.
The pubes is covered with some hair, which is carefully
pulled out, and, taken on the whole, the genital organs
are less developed than in the French woman. The
vulva and the vagina are markedly narrower, and much
shallower.

In the woman, and the pubescent girl, the vulval
and vaginal mucous membranes are generally the seat
of that disagreeable affection known as the " whites "
or " the flowers," and which contributes, by the relaxation it causes in the tissues, to dilate the organ.
Thus, in spite of the disproportion, copulation between
a young Annamite and an adult European can generally be effected without too much pain for the first
named. It is to be noted that the Congai—already
a fully developed woman—always has the clitoris but
imperfectly formed, as well as the little lips, which
seldom project beyond the large.

The prostitutes of the public brothels, who have
frequent connection with Europeans, have the entrance
of the vulva and vagina greatly enlarged. Generally,
however, that is placed very high and the average
depth of the vaginal passage does not exceed $3\frac{1}{2}$ or
4 inches. It often happens that a penis of more than
average length will cause inflammation of the womb,
by the repeated shock of the gland against the nose
of the tench.

I have treated many women for this complaint, who
havé confessed that it was owing to this cause.

The Genital Organs of the Adult. It is but
natural that we should find in the adult Annamite a

slender penis, in proportion to the small dimensions of the feminine organs. The pubescent youth of from 15 to 20 years of age has some hair growing on the pubes round his member. The testicles are exceedingly small until the fifteenth year, and increase in size little by little; but at twenty the Annamite is hardly more formed than a European of 15 or 16, and his development is not complete until he is 25 years old.

At its full growth, the penis has an average length of from 4 to 4½ inches (in full erection) and a diameter of an inch and a quarter. They may be found 5 inches to 5½ inches long, with a diameter of 1¼ to 1⅜ inches, but few attain a length of 6 inches, and a diameter of 1¼ inches. I once met with a penis of 7¼ inches; but that was on a Franco-Annamite half-breed.

Usually the testicles of an Annamite of pure breed are the size of a pigeon's egg. The pubes bears some stiff and bushy hair, like that which grows on their chins after the thirtieth year.

Franco-Annamite Half-breeds. There are very few persons of half-breed, for there is not much copulation between the two races, and still less production. Moreover, it is a remarkable fact that the white race which is very prolific with the black woman, is much less so with the yellow woman. I cannot explain the cause, but content myself with noting the fact. It is a matter for regret, for the Franco-Annamite half-breed physically resembles the European. The skin is almost white, the shoulders squarer, the muscles more developed, and above all the genital organs larger. The face, however, preserves the indelible stamp of the yellow race, in the flat nose, and the oblique eyes.

From the moral point of view, the half-breed is a real Annamite, as much of a gambler, thief, and liar, as the native. The young man I have just mentioned as possessing the large penis, was, I was informed, the son of an officer of the Expeditionary Corps; he had received a certain amount of education, and on leaving the Colony, his father left him assured means of existence. Women, baquan, and opium, soon ruined him, and he ended his life miserably.

CHAPTER III.

**Woman in Annamite Society.—Marriage.—The
Legal Age.** Although the Annamite woman is not
nubile till about the sixteenth or seventeenth year, as
I have already said, she may, however, according to
the *Ly-Ky,* or "Book of Rites," marry after fourteen
years, and the man at sixteen. Any marriage prior
to those ages is null and void.

Marriages are arranged through the *mai-dongs,* or
matrimonial agents, who bring the two families together,
and arrange the question of the wedding portion. But
the woman does not bring her husband any marriage
portion, and it is he, on the contrary who pays for
the wedding presents, brings to the common lot his
fortune of rice fields and cattle, and often, indeed, has
to pay a sum of money to the wife's family.

In return he is generously presented with a tobacco
jar, a box for betel, and a cigarette case;—he has no
other compensation.

Weddings are distinguished by a pastoral simplicity;
the future husband and wife meet, mutually offer themselves to each other, and chew betel nut together.

Rights and Duties of the Annamite Woman.
Custom has given the Annamite woman—although her husband has paid for her—certain rights which the Frenchwoman does not possess. In fact, as she is more intelligent, and more industrious than the man, she looks after almost everything. She works constantly, keeps the shop, goes to market, decorticates the rice, picks the cotton, attends to the poultry, weaves the cloth, works in the sun like a man transplanting the rice, does the cooking, and, in sea-faring families, steers the boat.

Character of the Annamite Woman. She is the "grey mare" of the household, but she is as lying and deceitful as her husband, and a gambler and glutton. She is as lascivious as the man, and betrays her husband whenever she can, if she finds pleasure or amusement in it. I will presently show the picture of the Annamite woman married morganatically to a European;—he always plays the part of George Dandin.[1]

Adultery.— Its Repression. [2] The Annamite

[1] George Dandin, one of the characters of Molière, an easy-going, good-natured, rather dull-minded model of a husband.

Molière, *George Dandin*, I. 9,

[2] The eminent criminal anthropologist M. Guillaume Ferrero, says: "To-day the penalties enacted against adultery in the different modern codes are very mild; they do not exceed a few months imprisonment. But if the law is mild, customs are still brutal, at least partly so; for in reality the adulteress often meets with her death at the hands of her husband, who kills the guilty woman, and is acquitted by the jury. In Italy, particularly of late, the acquitals of such uxoricides have been very frequent: which shows that public opinion still considers death as a deserved punishment for adultery. Judges, jurists, and criminalists all protest against this barbarous custom; but jurors are none the less, in these absolutions, the interpreters of public feeling, which on this

woman does not live shut up, like the Chinese woman, and does not have her feet tortured into uselessness. She has thus every facility for making a cuckold of the man to whom, on her wedding day, she promised fidelity. At Saigon, and in the neighbouring villages, morals are very lax, and a man, who appreciates yellow women with black teeth, can have his pick. In the interior, I have not found much reserve in regard to the foreigner, especially if he is generous and discreet. The law, however, punishes adultery with severe penalties. Like the French Penal Code (before the Divorce Law) it excuses a husband who kills his wife and her paramour, if taken in the act of adultery. I never heard of an instance of this during my five years' residence, although, it may be added, such punishment has been witnessed by others. Archdeacon Gray reports a case of severe flagellation that he saw in China (the Annamites took their code of law from the Celestials); we give his graphic narrative in his own words:

"In 1870, I saw a young man, apparently not more than twenty-one years of age, and his paramour flogged through the streets of one of the suburbs of Can-

point is very conservative, as it is in all that concerns sexual customs.

The legislation on adultery has therefore, up to the present, been what may be called a *passional* legislation; that is to say one that was actuated by the sexual passion and jealousy of the male, which took neither into account the individual gravity of the fault, nor its social importance. It struck blindly. What basis therefore could be given to a *rational* legislation on adultery.

To solve this problem, it is first of all necessary to examine the different types of the adulteress. There are two, the characters of which are well defined and differentiated: adultery which may be called *vicious*, and adultery that might be styled *casual*. For these two types the penalty cannot be the same."

Le Crime d'Adultère, son passé, son avenir, par Guillaume Ferrero. Paris.

ton in a most unmerciful manner. His arms were
bound behind his back, and the upper part of his
body was naked. Immediately behind him came the
woman, apparently about thirty years of age. Her
arms were also bound behind her back, and she was
receiving quite as severe a castigation. They had
been seized by the woman's husband—a play-actor—
and two of his friends, and handed over to the elders
of the district. At a meeting of this body, which took
place at noon on the following day, some were of
opinion that the guilty pair ought to be bound hand
and foot and cast into the Canton river. But the
majority resolved that they should be flogged through
the principal streets of the suburb. When the flogging was over, the youth, whose name was Laong-à-
Ying, was permitted to return to the house of his
widowed mother. The adulteress was sold by her
husband for the sum of one hundred dollars to the
proprietor of a public brothel. I visited the youth on
the day following that on which he was flogged, and
I was shocked when I saw how fearfully lacerated
his back and shoulders were."

It may be remarked here that the punishment of
an adulterer by beating him severely with rods,
which has always been practised by the Chinese, was,
it would appear from Diod. Sic. I, 89, 90, also usual
with Egyptians; while, in Rome, under Justinian,
adulteresses, as in some instances in the present day
in China, were scourged.

Before passing from the subject of this chapter,
which I do with a sense of relief, I must not omit to
add that the crime of adultery is looked upon by the
Chinese as more heinous when it is committed between
persons bearing the same *surname !*

In passing it is interesting to note with Dr. Jean-nel [1] that under the Roman law adulterous women were at first condemned to pay only a fine (TIT. LIV. X 31), to exile (TIT. LIV. XXV, 2); later they were obliged to get themselves inscribed at the town-hall (édile) as prostitutes (JAC. *Ann.*, II, 85); or to follow the profession of procuress (SUET. *Tib.*, 35). Finally, if Paulus Diaconus is to be credited, they were obliged to abandon their persons to the first comer to the ringing of a bell in a house of ill-fame, and this custom was abolished by Theodorius (PAUL. DIAC., *Hist. miscell.* VIII, 2).

Moreover, the Annamite Code contains the following article: "*An adulteress shall receive ninety blows of the rattan upon her buttocks, and her husband may afterwards marry her to another, or sell her if he pleases, or keep her in his house.*" If our European women could look forward to receiving ninety blows of the rattan upon their white posterior rotundities, perhaps fewer husbands would be wronged. [2]

The Annamite Code also says: "*Shopmen who commit adultery with the wife of their master, shall be treated as servitors or slaves, and punished by strangulation.*" This excellent Code does not do things by halves. Another article appertains to shrews. "*Every legitimate wife who strikes or insults her hus-*

---

[1] *De la Prostitution* (Paris, 1868).

[2] M. Macé, the well-known *ex chef de la sûreté*, who lately published his highly-interesting memoirs, relates therein, that a lady belonging to a most honourable family, but hysterical, and married to a wealthy gentleman, used now and then to quit her home, and hire a room in a lodging-house, where she received friends of her husband and sometimes even men unknown to her, without accepting anything from them and, on the contrary, would treat them with money she had abstracted from her husband.

band, shall be punished with a hundred blows of the rattan, and may be repudiated." It will be noted that it is a little cheaper for the Annamite woman to cuckold her husband than to scratch him or tell him disagreeable truths.

Left-handed Marriages. Besides the legal union consecrated by the marriage ceremony, an Annamite is entitled to take as many concubines as he wishes, without any formalities; but the children born of these unions have the same rights as the children of the legitimate wife. There are no distinctions as to "natural" or "adulterine" children in Cochin-China.

While on this subject we take the opportunity of quoting from Gray's valuable book on China an account of a most extraordinary case of marriage and divorce that came under his notice:

"On the 3rd of December, 1871," he writes, "I was present at a similar wedding between a man named Pang Wing and a woman named He-asing, both in the humbler walks of life. The marriage was solemnized at the house of the bridegroom's mother, in the Ma-choo-pow street of the western suburb of the city of Canton. The mother of the bridegroom, who was a very aged woman, was *in articulo mortis*. She lay upon a bed in the *atrium* of the house, with her feet towards the door, in order that her soul upon leaving the body might have free exit on its way to Elysium. The ceremony was entered upon without delay, and duly and properly gone through. What a scene ensued! When the wedding garment, which with its wide folds enveloped the whole body and arms of the bride, was removed, it was discovered that she was a leper! When the fact was disclosed, a number of the female relatives of the bridegroom, gave vent to their feelings of indignation and anger in howls which made the welkin ring. They then turned, as if actuated by a common impulse, towards the bride, whose appearance was now ghastly, to pour upon the unfortunate woman a torrent of the keenest invectives and most sweeping vituperation. The poor woman at last looked towards me for pity; and evidently fearing that more serious evils might befall her, she earnestly begged that she might be extricated from the embarrassing situation. She was at once divorced, and returned to her mother, who positively refused, however, to refund to the bridegroom the dowry which had been paid by him for what he justly considered a very bad bargain. A part of the sum was eventually returned. During the scene, the bridegroom's aged mother, who " lay a-dying," never once moved. Indeed. so motionless was she, that it appeared as if she had passed away for ever. She lingered till the following morning, having witnessed on her death-bed, in one brief hour, the marriage of her only son, and its singular sequel, the immediate divorce of the bride whom he had unwittingly espoused." [1]

The Love of Children. The Annamite women are very fond of their children, and lavish on them every mark of tenderness. They embrace them, and press them against their breasts, and kiss them—the kissing is a drawing in of the breath through the nostrils, as we do when we inhale a pleasant odour.

Abortion is very rare. Children are not wrapped in swaddling clothes, and suckle until they are three or four years old,—if boys; and even longer if girls.

[1] China (Vol. I. pages 188—9) Lond. 1878.

When the Annamite child can walk alone, he is allowed to run free in the sun, almost or quite naked, or roll in the dust, or wallow in the mire. He has — until he is ten or twelve years old—a pot belly, which contrasts strangely with his weak limbs. After he is twelve he wears a ragged pair of trousers, and an old coat, the cast-off garments of his father, and then goes to work, minding the buffaloes, or helping his parents to cultivate the rice field, or steering the sampan or junk. Girls and boys mingle promiscuously,— with the result that might be expected. That is why it is rare to find an Annamite girl, of more than ten years of age, a virgin.

CHAPTER IV.

Other passions besides love in the Annamite.—Gambling.—The Congai and the European.—The Chinese gambling dens.—The baquan, and the gaming houses of Saigon.—The passion for opium.—The usual allowance of an opium smoker.—How opium is smoked.—The resistance of the human constitution to the continued effects of opium.—The moderate use of opium and its good effects.—The nature of the pleasure caused by opium.

Other passions besides love in the Annamite. I have already said that the Annamite has, in common with the Chinaman, a passion for gambling. The coolies, and the common people, will play for their daily wages, and their wretched rags of clothes. The Congai is even more addicted to the vice than the man is, when her social position does not compel her to spend all her time at work. In the brothels, the women, whilst they are waiting for "clients", smoke their cigarettes, and devote their energies to interminably long games.

The European who has a Congai for a mistress, will learn to his cost that she, like the others, has a passion for gambling. Often, on a holiday, the young lady, dressed in her finest silk robes (three or four one over the other) and wearing her ear-rings, necklaces, and bracelets of gold and amber, will start off to spend the afternoon with her lady friends and acquaintances.

She will return towards the middle of the night, looking haggard, and with her head bare, her hair dishevelled, and her face and hands scratched and torn.
Her fine robes have been replaced by wretched rags.
Her jewels have disappeared. She will recount, amidst
sobs, and a deluge of tears, how she was waylaid on
her return by a band of robbers, who have not only
outraged her, but entirely stripped her.

The European consoles the afflicted damsel, and lodges
a complaint with the police. He learns, a few days
later, that the supposed victim had been playing *baquan*
in some den where illicit gambling was carried on, and
had lost everything down to her shift. Then the unfortunate *Pholan-za* (the Annamite pronunciation of the
word *Français*) makes a mental calculation that he is
180 to 200 piasters out of pocket, and he looks forward, with no pleasurable feelings to having to buy
fresh dresses and new jewellery. He returns home
furious, and perhaps gives his mistress a good thrashing with a rattan, and turns her out of doors. More
often, he pays for the sake of peace, and the comedy
is played over again very soon.

Baquan, which is of Chinese origin, is in Cochin-
China what roulette is at Monaco. On a table, or even,
in the low gaming-houses, on the ground, is spread
a cloth; on this cloth is placed a small square wooden
table with the four figures 1, 2, 3, 4, written in Chinese
and French, in separate compartments down each side
of the table. The stakes are placed on the different
numbers, and certain special stipulations are made by
means of a small red or yellow card, marked with
Chinese characters, which is placed on the stake. When
the stakes are laid, the *croupier*, who has in front of

him a little heap of Chinese *sapecks* in yellow copper,
shovels a number of them into a tea-cup without a
handle, and then empties this cupful in the middle of
the table. Another *croupier*, or one of the principal
players (it is his privilege if he chooses to claim it) is
furnished with a long wand with which he counts the
coins into fours, pushing each four back to the heap
as he counts it out. This is the exciting moment, and
while this counting is going on, the third *croupier*, the
banker, keeps up a monotonous chant,—the song of
victory or defeat. At the end of the counting there
are one, two, three, or four sapecks over, and that
determines the winning number. The winners gain
three times their stakes, which gives the banker four
chances of winning to three of losing. This continues
for hours and hours; it is quite as much a passion as
roulette. The Chinese *croupier* is so skilful, that if a
large stake is put on a certain number before the coins
are put in the cup, you may be pretty sure that that
number will not turn up.[1]

I have known Europeans who spent entire evenings
in the *baquans* of Saigon and Cho-lon, and who often
lost hundreds of piasters. Sometimes a rich Annamite

---

[1] " The proprietors of these gaming-houses realize large sums of
money, and the gamblers are frequently ruined, and, driven into des-
perate courses, often end their days in prison. Sometimes they lose not
only all their money, but the clothes they are wearing. On one occasion,
passing the door of a gambling-house near the temple of the Five
Genii, at Canton, I heard a great noise. Entering the establishment
to ascertain the cause, I found the conductors of the games actually
engaged in stripping the clothes off a man who had staked and lost
them. The unfortunate man was then dressed in gunny-bags (*a*) and
turned into the street." (*b*)

(*a*) Gunny is a strong coarse kind of sacking. [ED.] (*b*) Gray's " China "
(vol. I. pp. 387—88).

or Chinese gambler will take the bank on his own account, but he must divide his profits with the real banker.

You are elbowed by all sorts of people in these establishments, and are sure to meet the boy who is risking the money he has stolen from his master, the cook who is spending the household money, and certain persons of disgusting morals, in search of their prey.

The Passion for Opium. But the most terrible vice, or passion, is opium smoking; from which even the European can hardly hope to escape, for I speak from personal experience. When the French came to Cochin-China, they found the use of opium had been already introduced by the Chinese. The first Governor of the Colony made the sale of opium a monopoly, and this monopoly remained for twenty years in the hands of the Chinese, who derived a considerable profit from it; since then it has been in the hands of the Excise.

It seems that the kilogramme of raw opium, which costs the Excise sixteen shillings when they buy it from the English Government, is resold to the consumer at about ten pounds. It is an expensive vice.

The Usual Allowance of an Opium Smoker. A *tael* ($1\frac{1}{8}$ oz. avoirdupois) costs two piasters, and in skilful hands gives an average of about 100 pipes. This makes the price come to a trifle under or a trifle over the penny, according to the rate of exchange of the piaster, which varies from 3s.7d. to 4s.5d. In order that the opium should produce the desired effect, the beginner should smoke ten pipes; with less than that number he would not feel much effect, but above that number there would be risk of intoxication.

I have, however, known an European (an inebriate it is true) who, after smoking five or six pipes, fell into a torpor which lasted forty-eight hours.

At the end of a few weeks, the tyro in opium smoking will already be able to take his twenty pipes a day—ten, an hour after each of his two principal meals—which he will find will aid digestion quite as well as a first-rate cigar would. If the smoker would stop at that, there would be no harm done. Unfortunately, he increases his allowance by one or two pipes almost every day, and soon takes his thirty pipes a day. This already means an expense of £40 a year; but confirmed smokers soon exceed that number, and smoke their fifty or sixty pipes a day.

Nature of the Pleasure induced by Opium. With the first pipe you feel a sensation of gentle warmth in the stomach, and this pleasant " velvety " feeling lasts all the time you are smoking. This sensation is renewed with each fresh pipe, and when you have smoked from ten to fifteen or twenty—according as you are habituated to the use of the drug—the heart feels happier and the spirits lighter. All mental cares and physical pains (especially neuralgia) vanish. The body feels buoyant. You might imagine that the air which surrounds you is purer, and you feel a pleasure in breathing it. This effect is, moreover, most marked when the lungs are oppressed by the heavy, moisture-sodden air of the rainy season, but which, after opium smoking feels like the soft warm air of a hot bath-room.

After that you sink into a sort of pleasant idleness, and your physical condition is exactly analogous to that of a weak invalid enjoying the beams of a radiant spring sun. The ideas of each person follow their natural course; the brain teems with thoughts which crowd upon it, and you can easily perform intellectual work which would otherwise be beyond your capabilities.

CHAPTER V.

Physical love amongst the Annamites.—Methods of copulation generally used.—Asiatic houses of prostitution.—The Annamite " Bamboo ".—The dangers of Annamite love affairs.—Gonorrhœa and syphilis.—The Chinese brothel.— Chinese prostitution.—The whore-houses of Cho-lon.—The habits of old Chinese debauchees. —The Japanese brothel.—Physical characteristics of the Japanese woman. —The Annamite mistress of the European.

Physical love amongst the Annamites. Physical love amongst the Annamite race is, before all and above all, a contact of—generally very dirty—mucous surfaces. Amongst no people in the world is there such danger of physical contamination.

Marriage is for the Annamite (and in that he resembles greatly our modern civilized peoples) a question of business and the procreation of descendants, rather than of sentimental love. On her side, the woman has not generally a very great affection for her husband, but concentrates all her love on her children. Her morals are also very lax, and the chief care of an Annamite woman is not to be caught, and as she is more intelligent than her husband, she may be relied on to effectually hoodwink her credulous spouse.

The most Usual Methods of Copulation. The bed of the Annamite is a mere hurdle of bamboos,

39

covered with a flimsy cloth. Such a bed is not very
well suited for the classical position of sexual relations,
—the man, on the top of the woman. The French
soldier, when he visits a woman in one of the brothels,
and rubs his knees against the knots and wattles of
the hurdle, calls this " going to the bamboo." [1] By
extension, the same term is applied to the Annamite
brothel.

China finds herself actually in the same situation.
For upwards of fifteen years she was being mutilated

---

[1] Anthropological students will be struck with the following strange
habit of Australian aborigines

THE POSITION OF THE COUPLE IN COITUS AND THE EXPULSION OF
THE SPERMA BY THE WOMAN.

In the " Anthropologie der Natur=Völker ", by Waitz-Gerland
(vol. VI p. 715) is to be found a curious description of the customs
of the natives of Vincent Gulf, in the neighbourhood of Adelaide, related
by von Koehler, which is to the following effect: " The women are
thin, with pendent breasts and the genitals very far backward, so that
the men usually accomplish the act of coition from behind." In answer
to the question whether the writer had been able to see the act of
copulation performed before him, he replied in the affirmative, supplying
at the same time two schematic sketches which we regret being absolutely unable to reproduce (Vide:—*Zeitschrift für Ethnologie*, vol. XII
[1880] p. 87).

With regard to the facility of obtaining the edifying spectacle of a
native couple giving a specimen of their copulative energy in broad daylight the bribe of a glass of gin to both parties is amply sufficient, and
is often done by European travellers in the interior " for fun ! "

An intelligent and very trustworthy observer, Mr. A Morton, confirms
the above, having been several times a witness of the same. He further
states that as soon as the act has been accomplished, the female, standing
erect with her legs stretched apart, by means of a sudden jerk, contrives to violently expel the semina she has received. It seems that
this custom is common among the women, in order to avoid the natural
consequences which might probably result.

by a fearful civil war, such as the world has seldom witnessed, whilst at the same time foreign enemies attacked the country and imposed upon this proud nation the most humiliating conditions, and it has only just now suffered the most signal and stinging defeat from a comparatively insignificant neighbouring power. The *Flowery Kingdom* continues to march with giant strides from downfall to downfall, and very powerful changes must take place before it can rise again out of the slough into which it is now plunged.

The cause of this situation is the illimitable moral corruption which infects every grade of Chinese society. Immorality and venality have cast their poisoned breath over the people and their rulers, from the humblest constable to the Emperor on his throne, and have destroyed all energy, all force, all nobility and all manliness in this sunken nation.

The task I have undertaken is to expose this situation in all its phases, in the hope of filling up a great void in the history of prostitution. The author of the work entitled: *Work and the Poor in London*, says at the beginning of a note on prostitution in this vast Empire (page 129): "China presents to us a rich and interesting field for research; if our information were complete, there would not be a single country in the world about which so interesting a study could be made regarding the system of prostitution. Unfortunately the negligence or the prudery of travellers has been such that we possess but very superficial knowledge on the subject."

The task is difficult, because the pen often refuses to trace the gross immoralities that the writer would like to expose, and modern languages are reluctant to describe practices which so deeply offend our notions of modesty; we shall therefore endeavour, as much as possible, in our expressions, to keep within the limits of morality and of propriety, and as for words which could with difficulty be accepted in our tongue, we shall have recourse to Latin expressions.

Pierre Dufour, in his *Histoire de la Prostitution*, divides it into three classes:

Hospitable prostitution.

Religious prostitution.

Political or legal prostitution.[1]

Neither of these three divisions can be applied to Chinese prostitution. Hospitable prostitution, with the exception of one solitary example, is unknown in China, and religious prostitution has never existed. Williams in his *Middle Kingdom* says:

"A remarkable thing in the Chinese idolatry is that it does not admit of the divinisation of sensualism, which, under the name of religion, has caused to be maintained for so long a time the existence of infamous ceremonies and disgusting orgies, and which in so many other idolatrous countries, weaken the intelligence and sully the heart of the devotees. There is neither a *Venus* nor a *Lakshmi* in the list of the Chinese divinities; no lamentations in honour of *Thamnus*, no

[1] In certain countries, when a traveller arrived, it was customary to give him the largest hospitality, including not only board and bed, but also a bed-fellow, the wife, sister or daughter of the host, and the host would have felt much hurt had his offer been rejected. The custom still exist in some parts of India. This is *hospitable* prostitution.

Religious prostitution exists to this day in India, in the shape of the *Nautch girls*, attached to the Hindoo temples, and was formerly known in ancient Egypt in the temples at Thebes and Memphis.

Political, or legal prostitution is simply that known in most European countries as a licensed legal institution, subject to strict government supervision and control.

parades in the temple of *Mylitta*, no indecent ceremonies in honor of *Durga Puja.* The Chinese priests
have never made such things matter of religion, and
even in their pagodas, they have never kept *nautch
girls* as in the Indian temples, nor courtesans as at
Corinth."

Their speculations on the dualism of the nature of
Yin and *Yang* have never degenerated into an abject
veneration of the *linga* or *yoni* of the Hindoos, or for
Amum-Kem, of which coloured representations are still
to be seen on the ruins of Thebes. Although in word
and action it is a debauched people, the Chinese have
however never attributed vices to their divinities, and
the *adorers of enjoyment* (by antiphrase) have never
been led, from depravation to depravation, to be placed
at last in the sacred paths beneath the protection of
a goddess.

Their mythology contains few accounts of the amorous
adventures of their divinities, such as swarm in the
histories of the Greek and Hindoo deities, and which
render them so obscene.

And yet legal prostitution exists in China where it
is regulated by severe rules.

The Book of Laws of the dynasty of *Tsing*, actually
reigning, with its latest modifications, is however silent
on this subject; nor do we any more find anything
in the other books specially devoted to this subject,
and the Chinese themselves assert that with them prostitution is not subjected to any legal disposition whatever.

Asiatic Houses of Prostitution. Here, as in
every civilized country, women are to be had at all
prices, and to suit every taste, from the Annamite

"bamboo" to the *horizontale* [1] who lives in her own
rooms, and is the kept woman or mistress of some
rich Asiatic, and who will condescend to bestow her
favours upon you,—but never without being paid.

Though the European courtesan was for a long time,
a rarity in the Colony, there has never, even during
the period of the conquest, been any scarcity of native
women. Here, as elsewhere, the wife and daughter
of the vanquished became the spoil of the victor.

We may divide the Asiatic houses of prostitution
into three very distinct categories.

The Annamite "Bamboo." We will use the
name "bamboo", which the soldiers have given it.
Here there is no luxury; a hut open to all comers,
the "hurdle," and upon it a cloth, some stools, and
a few lamps giving out a fetid odour of cocoa-nut oil.

In such a place, you would expect to meet with
only old prostitutes, but it is quite the contrary. You
often find girls hardly yet nubile, of only sixteen or
seventeen years, who have been sold by their parents,
or mistresses. The average age of the inmates is
scarcely more than twenty years. The costume of these
ladies is the Annamite costume of the lower classes;
a cotton robe. But they always have a silver necklace
and amber ear-rings, bought out of their first earnings.

When she first comes to the house, the "bamboo" does
not know a word of French, and is unversed in the

---

[1] "Horizontale" is one of the many names in French applied to
ladies of easy virtue. It refers, of course, to the position assumed by
them in the carnal act. As proof of the decadence of European morals
—French being the tongue still spoken in all European Courts—we give
a list of synonyms used to designate women who sell their love-favours,
and believe it will considerably interest the student and philologist.
(Vide page 87.)

rites of Venus, but you may rest assured she will quickly learn to prattle amiable speeches, and make ultra-erotic proposals in her own *sabir*, for she is in a good school to learn. She does not, however, earn much money as long as she is in the establishment, for the proprietor of the brothel takes nearly all she receives. The tariff at the " bamboos " is not high; it varies from tenpence to a half piastre. For a piaster you can have the right of sharing the bed of the young woman for the rest of the night.

It must be confessed that, to those who have just come to the Colony, the Congai is not attractive. In the first place there are the blood-red froth caused by betel-chewing, and the horrible appearance of the teeth covered with black lacquer. This last, however, is with her a mark of beauty, as is also the hairless pubes, which also tends to disgust the European. The Congai scorns the European woman, who, she says, has teeth like a dog, and hair like a beast. I have often heard the natives make this remark. Another cause of disgust is the smell of the Congai, which is *sui generis*, —an awful mixture of the stenches of rancid cocoa-nut oil, sweat, and the filth of a dress which is never washed for fear of wearing it out. This smell chokes you, and damps even the strongest venereal desires. You are a long time getting used to it, and some courage is needed, but at last you get habituated to it, especially if you have the luck to light upon a young girl with a well-formed body, and whose teeth are not yet lacquered.

The Dangers of Annamite Love.—Gonorrhœa and Syphilis. It would be enough if the Congai were content with being merely repugnant. But, in spite of the most careful medical examinations, it is far from safe to have anything to do with her. In the first place, she is almost certain to have the " flowers, " and she gives her adorers a gonorrhœa very difficult to cure, especially if they are at all weakened by the climate. Syphilis is also very common amongst this race. It is not within the province of this work to give the etiology of this disease. I simply remark that it has taken deep root in the country, and the want of rational treatment has caused its ravages to spread. The following remarks from Dr. Schlegel's small tract on " La Prostitution en Chine ", will give an idea of the seriousness of this subject:

" The curse attending debauchery, syphilitic disease with all its complications, prevails largely in China.

The flower-boat girls, as a preservative against disease, pour out, in honour of the gods, one half of the first glass of wine they drink with a guest. However, the effects of these diseases are less serious than with other nations, which may perhaps be attributed to the generally lymphatic temperament of this people.

Nevertheless, on the other hand they are far more injurious to the general health, by reason of the deplorable medical treatment employed by the Chinese doctors.

There are doctors in China who devote themselves specially to the treatment of these diseases. They are in the habit of placarding on the wall, near to their door, the remedies they have employed to cure their patients, the same as some dentists exhibit a quantity of the teeth they have drawn. They boast of their science and of their remedies in pompous and bombastic advertisements pasted on the walls.

The wording of these advertisements is embellished with expressions of the most inconceivable obscenity.

We have seen some, among others, in Canton, in which were depicted in tints the difference in colour between the blood of the eel, of the ox, of man and that of a maiden after being deflowered. Joined to this was the description, and clients were informed therein, of the artifices employed by prostitutes, bawds and brothel-keepers.

Another placard advertised pills to preserve from syphilis and gonorrhœa; a third gave a description of leprosy, together with the advice of doctor N. N.... who knew how to cure it perfectly.

Besides Syphilis, there are other diseases to be met with in China which have long since entirely disappeared from Northern Europe, for instance, leprosy, in all its forms, and elephantiasis; the former, during the first stage of the malady is called *ma foeng*, and in the final period goes under the name of *lai foeng* (in the Emoi dialect *thai ko*). The Chinese attribute the origin of this disease to a criminal assault contrary to nature, committed by a troop of soldiers on the dead body of a very beautiful woman who had been the partner of one of their emperors. The symptoms of this malady are horrible. A few days after the inoculation pricking begins to be felt on the face and hands, and the unfortunate sufferers are continually slapping their face and head, in the belief that they are covered with flies.

The evil soon gets worse, the breath becomes fetid; food is no longer digested, and the body is covered with pustules. The spaces between the pustules become wrinkled and like leather. The hair of the head and the beard fall off, and the hair that may still remain turns white; the face is covered with hard and pointed tubercles, sometimes white at the top and greenish at their base. Pustules break out all over the hands, the articulations, the chin and the knees; abscesses are formed on the cheeks and on the chest; the teeth turn black; the skin becomes thick and cracks, whilst pustules by hundreds grow bigger along the borders of the crevasses. It is during this culminating period of the malady that the patient is at last released from his torments by death.

This disease is supposed to be incurable, although it is asserted that certain Chinese physicians know how to limit the eruption it produces to certain parts, for instance, to the buttocks and the thighs.

As soon as any one is affected with it, he is of course driven out of society, so that all that is left him to do is to take refuge like an unfortunate pariah among those who are similarly afflicted, and to earn his livelihood by begging.

This malady is very frequent at Canton, because there it is aggravated by the dampness of the dwellings and the bad ventilation of the city; at every step these unhappy creatures are to be met covered with livid, brown, or blackish pustules, supporting themselves with difficulty by the aid of a stick, or else, to the disgust of the passer-by, squatting down in the midst of the markets and public squares.

However, as a general rule, these unfortunates, by reason of the misery in which they exist, descend soon enough into their grave.

The lazarettoes existing in Canton are unable to shelter or to feed these unhappy beings. There are two hospitals for lepers; one is in a village at a few hours distance from the city, on the banks of a river, and where lepers only are permitted to reside.

Notwithstanding their malady, they marry among themselves. The children, during the first eleven or twelve years of their existence are not attacked by the disease, which does not touch them until later. The attempts we made in isolating these children gave no satisfactory results; as a matter of course the malady can only increase instead of diminishing.

The leper hospital situated near to the town can contain three hundred patients, and this foundation has to subsist on an annual income of 300 *taels* (1500 florins), a sum naturally insufficient.

The Chinese pretend that, by means of the following trial, it is possible to recognize the presence of the leper virus in the blood, even when the infection dates from one or two days only; it is a known fact that on lighting a man's face by means of the flame of a bundle of tow steeped in alcohol, it assumes a cadaverous hue; the Chinese pretend that the leprous infection then makes it appear of a fiery red.

We have had no occasion to verify this fact, but it deserves in any case to be tried.

Elephantiasis is also very prevalent at Canton, and in the province of Chusan it is still more common. It appears that in China this affection does not always go under the same denomination, but that the name changes with the different symptoms which present themselves. For instance, at Emoi, the malady mostly affects the scrotum, hence it is there called *toa laan pha* (big scrotum); if it descends into the legs, it is called *Kha-ta* (dried-up legs). It appears that it is then more serious, for there is a proverb which says: *Khaam Kha-ta, boe Koa thsa* (hast thou Elephantiasis, go buy thee a coffin); in Canton they call it *tai scha thai* (big foot of sand).

Syphilis reigns particularly along the coasts, where it was imported by European sailors.

The Chinese who know it well, are careful to isolate, for the exclusive use of Europeans the women with whom they will no longer have intercourse. This goes indeed so far, that when the British troops besieged Canton in 1857, the Chinese mandarins drove all the prostitutes of the environs who were tainted with venereal disease, towards the city; in order to infect the barbarians as they called them, which plan succeeded only too well.

Some idea as to the dangers of this disease may be obtained, for statistics[1] show that, during the first

---

[1] The question of staying the progress of this disease in our Indian Army has from time to time considerably stirred public opinion. LORD DUNRAVEN deserves the credit of having recently braved the country with a clear statement of the position. In two powerful speeches in the House of Lords. See the " TIMES " of May 15th and 18th, 1897.

His lordship, in an able speech, quoted the following stubborn facts, from the official report drawn up by the military medical authorities for the Secretary of State:

In 1887 there were 362 soldiers per 1000 admitted to hospital infected with syphilis, in 1895 the proportion had increased to 537 per 1000; 5% of effective troops had been sent home invalided from this cause; 45 per 1000 were constantly in hospital, under treatment; 13% were rendered unfit for service; finally, out of a total effective British force of 70,000 men in Indian, 20,000 were known to be contaminated, at the same it is noted that the virulence of the disease has greatly increased. But the most appalling fact is that out of 13,000 expired service men returning every year to England nearly one half are more or less syphilitic, and liable, if they marry to transmit the taint to their children.

Compared with other European armies the British troops hold the worst place in this connection:

27 per 1000 are infected in Germany;
44 „ 1000 „   „   „ France;
43 „ 1000 „   „   „ Russia;
65 „ 1000 „   „   „ Austria;
71 „ 1000 „   „   „ Italy;

twenty years of the occupation of the country, it was the cause of half the cases in the hospitals, that is to say, as much as marsh-fever, cholera, dysentry, hepatitis, and the special diarrhœa of Cochin-China, put together.

But let us conclude the description of the Annamite, "bamboo." If she is pretty and intelligent, as soon as she has learned to make herself understood in her polyglot *sabir*, has acquired certain small talents of a special kind, and has put aside a few piasters, she leaves the brothel. She is pretty sure to find a husband, and the couple install themselves in one of the villages round Saigon, and the disreputable husband lives on the proceeds of her prostitution. They conceal their real character by pretending to do a small trade in fruit and various other productions.

In the morning the woman goes to the market of Saigon, but instead of returning home early, as a honest tradeswoman should, she visits the Europeans during the hour of their siesta. We shall shortly notice how she works.

The Chinese Brothel and "Flower Boats". The first Chinese harlots came from Singapore, about 1866 or 1867. The Chinese brothel is cleaner than the Annamite "bamboo".

The women attract their customers in this way. They sit before the door, under the shade of the veranda, and among the British home troops :

204 PER THOUSAND!

We would advise English Non-conformist Respectability, which strenuously opposes all preventive measures, prayerfully to study these figures fraught with the terror of gloomy portent.

Dr. Jeannel (*De la Prostitution*, page 158, Paris 1868) says that England dishonours Liberty and belies her common-sense through her misplaced tolerance of the scandals of prostitution.

and gathered round their *mama*, the proprietress of the brothel. Inside the house, near the door, is a kind of public saloon, where the "clients", seated on sofas of rattan or bamboo, select the girl they like best, and pay their court to her, in the presence of the coloured print of the female Chinese Buddha (the Goddess of Reproduction, represented as a huge female with enormous breasts) before which a lamp is always kept burning as an offering.

Having made your choice, you ascend to the first floor, by means of a staircase like the ladder of a mill, fixed on the back wall of the house. On this floor there are a lot of Chinese beds, almost as wide as they are long, and modestly covered with dark-coloured mosquito curtains, which conceal the temporary loves of the occupants.

The opium smoker will always find a pipe there, and someone to prepare it for him, many of the girls having been instructed in the art. Few of them smoke, however, though sometimes the *mama* does.

"No license is granted" says Schlegel "to the owners of *Flower-Boats* or of houses of ill-fame, but they are permitted freely to carry on their trade. The Flower-Boat girls are of modest appearance when in public. In their dress it would be impossible to distinguish them from honest women, and the non-initiated would hardly be able to discern between a respectable woman and one of these "gay" girls. They show themselves in a proper and decent manner. So that it is only after a lengthened stay in China that the foreigner is able to recognize a certain unrestraint in their manner and dress.

Their profession does not cast an indelible stain upon

them, for they may be taken as concubine by a man of the world, and then rise again to an honoured position. This rehabilitation is called *tsoeng-liang* (following the good path).

The houses of ill-fame are not relegated to any fixed place; they are to be found everywhere, in the gayest and finest quarters of the town, their blue venetian blinds displayed, and on the rivers are the floating houses of prostitution, the *Flower-Boats*, which mask the houses built here and there on the banks.

They have however to put up with the extortions of the Mandarins, and under the most trivial presumption of harbouring criminals their inhabitants may be mercilessly driven out. But these establishments are none the less a source of profit to the greedy functionaries who rule in China, for although they have to pay no regular taxes, the Mandarins take advantage of the first favourable occasion to extort large sums of money from their owners.

The actual condition of prostitution in China is abominable. Although the criminal laws forbid to their functionaries the frequentation of these houses under pain of sixty strokes of the bamboo, it is quite common to see them in the evening wending their steps towards the *Flower-Boats*.

The merchants and private individuals, in a word, all those who can afford to pay, follow this example. Decked out in their richest raiments, they may be seen going there, even in broad daylight. Immorality prevails to such an extent that fathers are not ashamed to hold the most obscene conversations in presence of their children. This has naturally the most detestable influence upon them. Young Chinese of from 7 to 8 years of age may be heard talking with consummate knowledge of things the most obscene, and the filthiest expressions are ever in their mouths. As they advance in years so grows their contempt for women, for as, according to Chinese custom, any intercourse between the sexes is almost impossible, the young Chinese lads hardly ever see any but the very lowest class of women. For them, woman is but a thing, a business article, a being necessary only for propagating the species and for the satisfaction of the passions.

Compared with the conduct of the men, that of the women in China is far more reserved; we may how-ever, have occasion, during the course of this study, to show some facts which may cast a shade upon this picture.

The houses of ill-fame in China are of two kinds: those that are on land, and those on the water. The first are to be met with everywhere, the others exist only along the banks of the rivers.

Those situated on land are called *Tsing-lao* (blue houses).

These establishments are sumptuous and in no way inferior in richness of decoration to the mansions of the most wealthy merchants and to the palaces of the gov-ernors. We find in a Chinese novel forming part of the " *Collection of tales of the present Time and of Former Days*" entitled: " *The Business in Oil that had been done by the Pretty Girl*," the description of the front of one of these houses:

" Before him was a house which he examined atten-tively; the door of this habitation was overlaid with a coating of gold-coloured lacker, and made of elegantly worked bamboo; within it there was an enclosure painted vermillion, flanked by a rampart of fine-leaved bamboos, so that it was impossible to see into the house."

This building which here served as a *Blue House*
does not seem however to have been erected for that
destination, for we read further on:

"While the attendant was pouring out wine, *Tsin-
tschoeng* asked him: 'who resides within this bamboo
door painted with golden lacker?' The servant replied:
'It is the country-house of the signior *Thsi*, but it is at
present occupied by Mrs. *Wang-Kioe.'* *Tsin-tschoeng*
continued: 'I have just seen a young lady enter a pal-
anquin. Who is she?' 'It is a celebrated courtesan
named *Wang-wei*, she previously dwelt outside the
Yoen-Kin gate, but as her lodging was cramped and
small, a son of the signior *Thsi*, who is her lover, has
let this house to her for six months.'"

This shows us that in China, people feel no shame
in letting out their country-houses to hire for purposes
of prostitution, for the continuation of the novel shows
us that several *Flower Maidens* lived in the house.
These establishments in *Canton* and in *Amoy* are
slightly different. Contrary to the other buildings, they
are generally two stories high; the interior arrangement
is purposely very irregular. The upper story is par-
titioned off into little rooms, each of which has its
female occupant, and nearly in the centre is the saloon
common to all, embellished with the richest furniture
and paintings. Another thing to be remarked is that
the ledges of the roofs of these houses, in Canton, are
not horizontal like those of the other buildings, but
are sloping. The reason of this particular architecture
has not been sufficiently explained, although it has been
attributed to the influence of local superstition (*foeng
schoei*); when the house stands alone, it is surrounded
by a gallery closed by Venetian blinds; if it is situated
between other houses, the gallery only exist in front.

These blinds are painted blue, whence the name of *tsing lao* or *blue houses* which has been given them. At about seven o'clock in the evening the blinds are lifted, and the whole place is brilliantly lighted up, while music and song resound through the building. In the novels these establishments still go by the name of the *Brilliant Field of Flowers*, and the *Club of the Mandarins' Ducks*. Other less choice names are given to them, too numerous to recapitulate. The streets in which these establishments are situated go by such flowery names as the following: *Flower Street*, the *Willow Avenue*; each house has also its name; for instance in Amoy we find the following: *the Saddle of Straw, the Eighteen Chairs*, the *Horse's Pillar*, the *Church of Rome*, so named because the house had formerly been used as a chapel for Roman Catholic missionaries. The second form of establishments of this kind is constituted by the *Flower-Boats*, or as they are called *hoa shing*. The biggest of these are called at Canton, *Wang loa*; there are besides the *sha Kwoe*, or *Gauze Tents*, and the *fa-thao-moen, Gate of the flowery Frontage*. They may be compared to gigantic Venetian gondolas. Their length ranges from 60 to 80 feet, with about 15 feet in width; the poop is tapering and carries a platform made in such a manner as to enable one to go from one boat to another, when, as is generally the case, they are anchored close together; in this case, each boat is solidly warped to a zinc cable by means of strong ropes which surround it entirely from stem to stern; the cabin in the elevated poop aft is a sort of ante-chamber, preceding the main saloon, which occupies about one half of the entire length of the boat: they are separated by panels of trellis work or by wainscoting. To the right and to the left, near the entry, are two couches for the use of opium smokers. Finally there is a third saloon, or bed-chamber, which is completely hidden from the view of the guests by wooden panels; the windows on either side may be closed by curtains and shutters. Above the entrance there is an ornamental three pointed front-age, artistically carved in wood and richly gilt all over; the rest of the wood-work is also cut out with art and ornamented with the most brilliant colours; the floor of the main saloon is covered with the richest carpets, and European lamps, with pendant crystal drops are suspended from the roof. The furniture consists of a large round table, some candelabras and chairs, the whole being of beautiful rosewood, or ebony inlaid with marble. These seductive boats produce at night a magical effect when they are brilliantly lighted up, and no one who has once visited Canton can forget the sight. The Flower girls do not usually live in the boats.

The Chinese never go there alone, but from ten to twenty acquaintances agree together to hire one of these boats for the evening. For the larger ones they pay as much as from four to six pounds a head sterling.

For this sum the owner of the boat supplies the lighting, the supper and as many girls as there are guests. He must also bring musicians and the girls have to entertain the guests with song and conversa-tion.

At about nine o'clock in the evening the supper is served up, and the guests all take their seats round the table, each one with a girl at his side. During the last service little games are played, among which the most frequently in usage, is that known to the Italians under the name of *Morra*. At the end of the entertainment, at about 11 o'clock each couple goes

away separately to little boats, built on the same model
as the big one, where they pass the night.

The Chinese Prostitute. She generally comes
from Southern China. She is short, and often plump,
and her skin is almost yellow, the colour of weak tea.
Her breasts are rounder, and the muscles of her thighs
and legs more developed than is the case with the
Congai. All the hair of the pubes is carefully pulled
out.[1] The vulva and vagina are rather larger than
those of the Congai.

[1] DEPILATION. This reminds us of what Martial says:—
Primum igitur pathicis studiose exstirpandi erant pili de toto cor-
pore. (a) *Depilabant labra, brachia, pectora, crura, virilia, ante omnia*
vero lævigabant aram voluptatis pathicæ, podicem.

MARTIALIS, II, 62:

    Quod pectus, quod crura tibi, quod bracchia vellis,
    Quod cincta est brevibus mensula tonsa pilis,
    Hoc præstas, Labiene, tuæ, quis nescit? amicæ.
    Cui præstas culum, quem Labiene, pilus.

IDEM IX, 28:

    Cum depilatos Chreste, coleos portes
    Et vulturino mentulam parem colle
    Et prostituis lævius capuc culis,
    Nec vivat ullus in tuo pilus crure.
    Purgentque crebræ cana labra volsellæ.

. . . .

(a) *Excepto quidem capillo.* Hor. Ode X.

(The translation of the above is given at page 91.)

Again, Quintillian tells us:

"*Igutur ut velli et comam in gradus frangere et in balneis per-*
potare, quamlibet hæc invaserint civitatem, non erit consuetudo,
quia nihil horum caret reprensione.

(QUINTILL. INSTIT. ORAT. I, 6.)

(Vide page 92 for the transl. of this passage.)

The student will find a most interesting chapter expressly devoted to Depilation in "*Marriage-love and Woman amongst the Arabs; otherwise en-*
titled in Arabic the Book of Exposition, etc." PARIS, *Carrington,* 1896.

Vide also the end of the present vol.

But the greatest difference between them is, that
the Chinese woman is very cleanly in her habits. She
washes herself all over every day, and her clothes,
which are white, or of a light hue, are clean and neat.
The Chinese woman does not stink like the Annamite.
When we add that she does not chew betel, and that
she has pretty, white teeth, which are carefully kept,
it will be seen that she is more like a European woman
than the Annamite is.

Unfortunately, for those who like voluptuous pleasures, she has one immense fault,—her frigidity. Copulation, with her, is accomplished mechanically; it is a
commercial transaction which brings her in a piaster,
and that is all.

The chief care of the Chinese woman is, above all
things, not to disarrange the elaborately constructed
edifice of her hair, which is arranged for her once a
month by the Chinese hair-dresser. Imagine an enormous *chignon*, of the form of a conch-shell, decorated
with bows and " corkscrews " of ribbon, and kept together
by cosmetics and pomades, in a most extraordinary
and absurd shape. It would not be considered an act
of gallantry to take down the hair of a Chinese woman.
When she lies down, she places her *chignon* on a little
table, hollowed out in the middle.

Never expect from a Chinese girl any refinement of
voluptuousness;—she is incapable of it. She only
knows how to lie down and take you passively. If
need be, she will consent to visit the European at his
own house, if, in addition to the regular price of three
piasters, he will pay for a carriage there and back,
for, to her little deformed feet, walking is painful.
Regarding this peculiarity, it has been asserted, and
I fancy I have read it in some book of travels, that

the object of the compression of the Chinese woman's feet was to develop the constrictor muscles of the vulva and the vagina. I must confess that I have rarely met with this vaginal peculiarity. In my opinion, it depends rather on the obesity of the woman, and there is no need to go to China to find this result. All European women who are rather stoutly built, and who have the pelvis and the thighs well developed—even old prostitutes—are generally tighter than small thin women. Brantôme remarked this, long ago.[1]

Life of the Flower-Boat girls. The education of the "Flower-Boat" girls is conducted on a systematic plan. In nearly all cases they are children that have been stolen, bought of poor parents, or furnished by houses of ill-fame; during the first six years they are brought up with great care; towards the age of seven or eight years, they are made to keep in order the rooms of the elder girls; they are richly dressed and taken to the Flower-Boats, where they hand the tea and narghilehs to the guests.

Towards the age of eleven years they begin to learn to sing and to play the lute or the guitar. If

[1] "*J'ay ouy compter à Madame de Fontaine-Chanlandry dicte la belle Torcy, que la reine Eleonor (a) sa maistresse, estant habillée et vestue paroissoit une très-belle princesse, comme il y en a encor plusieurs qui l'ont veue telle en nostre cour, et de belle et riche taille; mais, estant deshabillée, elle paroissoit du corps une géante, tant elle l'avoit long et grand: mais tirant en bas, elle paroissoit une naine, tant elle avoit les cuisses et les jambes courtes avec le reste.*"

Brantôme, *Vie des Dames galantes*, (page 207 of the Edit. Bibliothèque Gauloise, Paris, 1857).

(a). La reine Eléonore, sœur de Charles Quint, fut mariée à François I, devenu veuf depuis quelques années, lors de la signature du traité de Cambrai. (Translation of the above at the end of the chapter-page.)

one of these children shows natural dispositions, she is also taught to write, to count and to paint. This goes on until the age of 13 or 15; then they must endeavour, by their artifices and coquetries, to turn the head of some rich gentleman. If they are lucky, their keeper sells them for a large sum in money, from £70 to £125.

This happens at the earliest at the age of 13; this is called: *trying the flower;* if she is 14 years old they say: *regulate the flower*, and at 15, it is: *gathering the flower.* The same as with the Romans, that day is a festival with the Chinese.

The entire population of the other lupanars come in the morning to express to her their good wishes; these rejoicings last from a fortnight to three weeks. The novel previously quoted also gives a description of them. After an interval of a few days she is sold a second time; the individual who devotes her in this manner to the lupanar is called the *supercalculator*. If the girl is of more than ordinary beauty she is left at rest for another year, to have her honour sold again a second, and sometimes even a third time. She then bears the name of *Ki hang liao ti niu niang, a virgin twice over.*

After that lapse of time she belongs to the staff of the establishment and goes by the name of *tschang Ki*. The prices she demands are sometimes incredibly high, and particularly in the central provinces of China large sums of money are expended to buy them. The novel above quoted mentions 10 ounces of silver (about £4—5 as the price for one night). However in Canton seldom more than £2,10/- is ever paid for a beauty of the first order. The most profitable customers to the Canton girls, are travellers from the

provinces, or as they are called in the energetic dialect of the district: "*schau toek kwai*", *the wicked
devils of the mountain.* Like provincials coming to
Paris, they come here to lose fortune, health and
honour. Ignorant of all the tricks of the brothels,
they are robbed in all possible ways. In the Flower-
Boats, the stranger is attracted and seduced, sometimes
by two or three girls together, which never occurs
with the *Roués*, in whose presence in public these
girls observe the strictest *decorum.* A girl, already
sharp, is presented to him as a virgin; after a rich
supper, well qualified with strong wines, he is conducted to a small sleeping boat, where a little eel's
blood completes the illusion:

*Flavæ anguillæ sanguinis ejacularis ejusque brac-
carum hiatum obline*, says a procuress, in an erotic
story, to a timid Flower-Boat girl.

The next morning, the unfortunate and much astonished man has to pay an exorbitant sum. This goes
on as long as the money he brought with him lasts.
As soon as that is dissipated, should he venture to
show himself again, he is received coldly and with
contempt.

Lucky indeed for him if, instead of an amorous
girl, he has chanced upon a harpy greedy for money,
and that, though impoverished in purse, he wisely
returns to his home. But these men from the country
are often so giddy, to employ the Chinese expression,
that they get into debt, take to gambling or even
resort to theft in order to spend the money thus so
badly earned in the low pleasures of the lupanar.

All the girls attached to an establishment of this
kind are the absolute property of the owner, a *leno* or
lena (male or female bawd) who are known respectively

under the name of *Woekoei* and *Paorl* or *Roeipo*.

The girls call the lena, *mother*, and address each other by the name of *sister*. The matrons of other establishments are their *aunts*, and the latter call the them *nieces*. The most vulgar names given to the master and the matron are *Piao thao* and *Ba thao, chief of the house.*

These matrons exercise an almost uncontrolled authority over their girls. They can beat them, and maltreat them, and if they should by mischance kill one of them, the river is handy to receive her body. Or else she is buried in the sand without a coffin or funeral ceremony. There being no complainant, Justice knows nothing about it, and makes no enquiries, even if the body is seen floating down stream. The fate of these unfortunate creatures is truly miserable; they must give all they earn to the matron, who has only to supply them with food and dress. It sometimes happens that one of these girls retains something in secret, or that their gallants add something to the tariff price, which she puts by in order to be able later to purchase her emancipation. But should the matron suspect such a thing she may search the girl's room in her absence and take possession of all she can find. If the girls are refractory, the whip and the stick are at once brought into play, and they are flogged unmercifully. It several times happened that one of these matrons tied a cat inside the pantaloons of her victim and then beat the animal.

It is not only by their owners that these unfortunate creatures are maltreated; the guests also, when they chance to be in a bad humour, or fancy themselves offended by them, are not ashamed to raise their hands and strike them.

When the bloom of their youth has departed, their lot becomes worse and worse. The big firms sell them to inferior establishments, where they go by the name of *wall-flowers*.

Falling still lower, they are called *Piao* and other similar names; at Amoy, they are then called *little girls*, or *brown holland*, when they do not belong to a fixed establishment, *circulators* or *walkers*, *thit tho lang* and *loe lioe*. Finally they take the name of *thsan-hoæ* and *pai-lioe*, which corresponds to the Latin, word *Blitida*, contemptible women. [1] The contemptuous expressions used by the Romans: *scrantia*, disgusting; *scrapta*, vile, are to be met with in Amoy in the words *tsap dzi lo thao e dzio kung* (*trivii scrantia*). A very common nickname is also applied to them: *tschoen-tao-ma* (inoculatrix).

Schlegel says: " Cases of girls going astray are, in fact almost unknown, and when they do occur it is only upon the promise of a secret marriage; this, in the eyes of the Chinese, no longer constitutes a *faux pas*, a secret marriage being to them as valid as a public one.

The man who, without very good reason, abandons a girl to whom he has been united in secret marriage, is in most cases condemned to death by the magistrates; further the priests threaten him with terrible punishments in hell.

[1] Blitea et lutea est meretrix, nisi quœ sapit in vino ad rem suam. *Plaut. Truc.* 4, 4, 1.

At Canton, these women are generally called *Lo qneue* or *Man ugao*.

They more usually go by the name of *hoa niu* (the daughters of flowers), on account of the flowers with which they adorn themselves, and *fao thao* (painted faces), because they are addicted to that adornment.

However, adultery is more frequent in our days, although the opportunities are very difficult to be met with on account of the strict separation of the sexes.

Most women, under the pretext of pilgrimages to obtain posterity, seek for consolation from the priests.

In order to make good this assertion, we shall seek in the Chinese tales themselves a fact which will clearly show us the existence of this depravity.

In the ninth part of the *Treasure of Wisdom*, a collection of celebrated law-cases for the use of magistrates, is to be found the following account:

" In the canton of *Yoeng Schun*, district of *Nau-Ning*, province of *Koeang-Si*, there is a cloister called *The magnificent Water-lily*. It contains a hall, called *The Hall of the Children and Grandchildren*, at the sides of which are a row of cells. The tradition says that when women came there to pray for children their prayers were always granted.

" It was in every case necessary to bring rich offerings, and the women who came there to pray were required to be at their best time of life and in excellent health. They had previously to fast and to abstain from carnal connection ; then, if the oracles were favourable they had to pass one night in the cloister. Most of these women related having dreamed that Buddha had fecundated them ; others said that an Arhan, one of the eighteen disciples of Buddha, had made them pregnant; others on the contrary related absolutely nothing.

" Some of them never returned again to the cloister after having once passed a night there, whereas others returned there several times running.

" As the cells were carefully closed, and that the

husbands and the parents remained on guard at the door, all this was generally believed.

"An inhabitant of *Fo Kien*, named *Wang-ten*, was appointed governor of Canton. On hearing of these miraculous events, he had some suspicions which he wished to clear up. He ordered two loose women of the town to go to this cloister, dressed in their finest clothes. Their instructions were the following: 'Should any one approach you during the night, do not repel him, but stain his tonsure, without his perceiving it, with red or black ink.'

"The next morning, at day-break, he posted a detachment of soldiers around the temple, and went in himself to make his inspection. All the priests, about one hundred in number, hastened to come forward to greet him. They all uncovered their heads in his presence, and *Wang-ten* then perceived among them two who bore red and black marks on the bald part of their heads. He ordered them to be immediately seized, and put into chains, and asked the two prostitutes to relate the facts with all the circumstances. They said: 'After vespers had been rung, two priests approached us. They gave us a parcel of pills to regulate the menses, and to engender children.' *Wang* thereupon ordered all the women who had gone there to pray for children, to be taken to prison. They all denied, but further enquiry showed that, like the two gay women, they had also been given pills to engender children. He then set them at liberty, but ordered the soldiers to enter the temple. The frightened priests did not dare to resist and were bound together two and two. He had the place searched to discover the means resorted to by the priests to approach the women. It was discovered that underground secret passages gave access to the cells behind the beds. It was impossible ever to find out how many women they had thus dishonoured."

The conduct in the women's convents is far from being as it should be. They are inhabited by girls who, betrothed in their youth to a man whom they have later refused to marry, have taken refuge in these convents to escape the authority of their parents, and by girls that have been abandoned by their lovers.

They are seldom led there by religious convictions.

In the cloisters they enjoy greater liberty than at home, for they owe obedience to one person only, the abbess. There is very great debauchery in these convents, and that to such an extent that there is a Chinese proverb which says: *The nun is the wife of the monk, and the monk is the slave of the nun.*

Chinese novels often contain examples of the misconduct which reigns in these convents: for instance, among others, in the erotic novel *of the Tower of Jasper*, in which is related the history of the life of a nun, the details of which are to such a degree indecent and immoral, that Boccaccio has never written anything like it. Notwithstanding the severe penalties meted out to debauched priests or nuns, the authorities generally content themselves with from time to time closing the convents, and obliging the priests, the monks and the nuns to resume the life of the laity.

The severe laws against adultery, for both man and woman, are the cause of the rareness of cases of seduction and adultery. These impediments have even led women to the infamy of the vice against nature, a vice known to the Romans under the name of *fascinum.* The instrument used by them is made of soft leather, or of thin horn, and stuffed with cotton. In China it is called *la siang Koeng* (the great Lord); at Emoi and its neighbourhood, and in the entire province of *Fokien*, it bears the name of *Kak tshia* (the chariot of horn).

The Houses of Prostitution of Cho-lon. Though the Chinese houses of Saigon are used by Europeans, those of Cho-lon, on the other hand, are almost exclusively reserved for the Chinese. In some respects these latter resemble certain " society houses " in Europe. You must be ready to put your hand in your pocket, and you are not admitted unless accompanied by some Chinese *habitué*.

As in France, there are luxurious saloons, with divans, sofas, mirrors, and pictures painted on glass. The girls, richly dressed, are sent into the saloon to receive the visitors. Even the stereotyped phrase " *Toutes ces dames au salon*," is employed,—in Chinese, of course. [1] If you choose to order it, you can

---

[1] Travellers on the Continent will recollect that in the gay resorts of this kind a similar call is invariably used   From the German's : " *Die Damen mögen herunter kommen* " to the Spaniard's :—" *Niñas al salon que hay caballeros* (or " *senores que se esperan* ", there is not much to choose. In certain swell Madrid and Barcelona " houses " however, the " salon" is generally qualified by " *azul* " or " *verde* " according to the pre-dominant colour by which it is distinguished, several distinct parties being sometimes entertained in different rooms at the same time. In Spanish places of a lower class, politeness is thrown to the winds and the brutal call is then " *Putas al salon* (or *macarelle*) *que hay cabrones que se aguardan*."

Parisian establishments of a superior character appear to manage these things better,—the visitor's step on the staircase setting in motion an artfully contrived, concealed electric bell which warns the *demoiselles* (?) of his approach and before he has had time to reach the landing the *patronne* of the place is waiting to wish *Monsieur, bonsoir*, and usher

be served with a copious repast in the Chinese fashion,
and of which birds'nest soup, tripang, preserved ginger,
and ginseng form the base, helped out by other strongly
spiced dishes.   You hear the distant sounds of Chinese
music, for the performers are placed in another room,
in order that they should not disturb the loving couples.
They play melancholy, languishing airs, which, it would
appear, give the Chinese erotic thoughts.   The girls
are tender and cajoling; they assume poses likely to
stir up the senses of the old Chinese bankers, who
are not easily excited.   They are hardly more expert
in the art of Venus, however, than their rivals of
Saigon.

Fate of the Chinese Prostitute.   These women
end their lives most miserably.   When their bodies
have been ravaged by horrible diseases, so as to render
them improper for the continuance of their trade, they
seek to earn a livelihood as street needlewomen.
Everywhere in Canton, these hideous creatures may
be seen, often with an artificial nose made of paper
and big spectacles, sitting at the street-corners, with
a basket full of old clothes and rags at their side, ready
for a few cents to mend the old garments of passing
soldiers and coolies.

Very seldom do any of them have a happier fate.
Should a girl take the fancy of one of the *habitués*
and if she purchase her freedom, she may then become
his *second wife.*

In this case, her life is a most happy one, and if
it happens that the legitimate wife has no son, whereas
she has one, her position becomes an honoured one

him into a reception-room after a quick, businesslike glance that has
measured her man, before he has uttered a word.

for then the husband often promotes her to the rank of legitimate spouse, on the death of his first wife.

Others again, who, by means of large sums of money they have earned, and by their intelligence have raised themselves above their condition, purchase their freedom at a heavy price, varying from £250 to £1700, and choose for themselves a legitimate husband among their adorers.

Such cases are however very rare, for these girls seldom possess money enough to redeem themselves, and to provide against a rainy day and to economise is not among their virtues.

The only hope of most among them is to be able one day to keep a brothel themselves. One of these Flower-Boat girls, being asked what she most desired, replied that she would be the happiest of women if she were taken by somebody as wife or as concubine; but she added: " I shall never have such luck, and shall deem myself most fortunate if I can one day commence business on my own account."

Female Infanticide. The dread of such a miserable fate is the cause of another crime that prevails among the Chinese, and for which we have often blamed them: the drowning of new-born female infants. The misery which reigns in China in years of scarcity leaves no option to the Chinese but to sell their daughters or to drown them.

We have seen what is the lot of the girl that is sold. What wonder then that a father with a sensible heart should prefer to make the little innocent babe die before it has suffered or breathed, rather than to abandon it to crime or to an abominable fate. In his ignorance he conforms to the maxim: "*Better to kill the body than the soul.*" Better let this poor innocent perish than to allow it to gradually die slowly of cold and hunger, as it so often happens in Europe.

Nor must it be forgotten that in Europe there are numerous institutions which receive these children, whereas in China the instability of capital makes it impossible to establish such institutions on a large scale.

The debauchery contrary to nature so prevalent in the North of China is also an obstacle to the multiplication of the female population. At Canton, where this disgusting vice is more rare, so also are there fewer cases of infanticide.

During a stay of eleven months in this part of China, during which we visited daily even to the narrowest arms of the river, we never encountered but one infant corpse floating on the water, whereas during the same period we found the drowned bodies of six adults. The child might therefore have been drowned by accident.

Vicious Habits of Old Chinese Debauchees. I have not seen what I am about to describe, but I heard it from a Chinese friend, B***, who farmed the opium monopoly, and who had often assisted me in obtaining admission to these houses. I do not think he wished to impose on my credulity, and this is what he has many times told me.

When the senses of an old Chinaman are so worn out that all natural means of excitement cannot arouse his enervated genital organs, he has recourse to the following expedient.

The old Celadon [1] is accompanied by a servant or strong coolie, who copulates with a woman in his presence, and then retires. In France, the spectators of this kind of operation are generally invisible to the performers. At Cho-lon such delicacy is unknown, and the amateur [2] assists at the scene, all the phases of which he follows with interest.

[1] Céladon, a character in the romance of *Astrée* who, langourous and insipid, is always sighing after his shepherdess (*Littré*).

To the " Barber's Tale of his Second Brother" (" *Nights* " ORIG. EDIT. vol. I. page 327) Burton makes a short note on the " concealed spectator" trick resorted to in Paris, and adds that " it was put down when one of the lookers-on lost his life by a pen-knife thrust into the crevice."

This was written in 1885. But the *voyeur* or spier is still the dread of those who frequent the Parisian " *bordels*", and a French army-officer has assured me that special pecuniary inducements are held out to young and vigorous soldiers to visit these places of " amusement " for an object that may be easily devined. We could say many startling things under this head, but this work not being a History of Prostitution we reserve our information for some future book.

[2] In the French, men of this stamp are called *Gagas*, a most significant word. Littré derives it from *gâter* (to spoil), hence *gâteux*, " a spoiled, or ravager." The colloquial meaning, however, is one who has spoiled, or ruined, his health by excesses with woman-folk; such persons generally suffer from that pitiable malady—loco-motor ataxis, although of course, this complaint is not *always* the consequence of licentious, and uxorious practices.—Dubut de La Forest in his work, *La Pathologie Sociale* (Paris, 1886), has drawn a powerful picture of a man reduced to this state. He traces the " gaga " through the following stages:—([1])infantile manias and motor disorders of phonation—([2]) Illusions—([3]) Erotomania ; ([4]) Loss of the Moral sense—([5]) Period of Calm—([6]) Exposition of one's private parts under irresistible impulse—([7]) Grave troubles of speech—([8]) Idiocy ; Outrages against modesty—([9]) Hallucinations—([10]) Desire to commit incest—([11]) Fresh period of calm—([12]) Cure.

M. De La Forest prophesies " that an *apparatus* will one day be invented in the form of a thermometer adapted to the skull, fixed and graduated, " not to the circumvolution, for there are thousands of them ", but to the five regions corresponding to the senses. We could thus

When once the agent has retired, well and duly paid, the old debauchee is left alone with the woman, who is still resting upon the field of battle. Then the man approaches, and eagerly receives *in bucca sua*, the liquid which runs *e vulva fœminæ*. [1]

This habit, it is said, is widely spread. I have no intention to discuss here this strange freak of eroticism, I simply note the custom.

Chinese agents of prostitution. We have now to speak of three kinds of despicable agents of prostitution who, even in China are looked upon with much contempt. We mean the *proxenets*, the *indicators* and the *traders*. The first of these, called in the Amoy dialect *hum lang po*, are to be met with in the middle-class. In the Chinese novel: *Tsiang hing ko* (Finds his pearl-embroidered vestment), this profession is carried on by an old woman dealer in jewelry. In the novel: " The house of the singing phœnix ", there are two maid-servants who bring about a meeting between the

---

measure the degree of Touch, Taste, Smell, Hearing and Sight, and would perhaps, also discover the kingdom of the SIXTH SENSE (*le royaume du sixcème sens*), THE GENITAL—the only one which interests nature." (Introduction XVII).

[1] This revolting habit of the libertine has not escaped the intellectual activity of the age, as may be seen by the following bibliography:

Diderot, *La Religieuse, roman d'une dévote à l'amour lesbique;* Théophile Gautier, *Mademoiselle de Maupin;* Feydeau, *La Comtesse de Chalis;* Flaubert, *Salembo;* Krafft-Ebing (op. cit. p. 76) adds: Belot, *Mademoiselle Giraud, ma femme.* In German literature Krafft-Ebing also quotes: Wilbrand: *Fridolin's heimliche Ehe;* Emerich Count. Stadion, *Brick und Brack oder Licht in Schatten,* and Sacher Masoch, *Venus in Pelz.* Among other authors who allude to tribadism are: Zola, in *Nana* and in *La Curée,* and quite recently in Italy, Butti, in his novel " *L'automna*".

Lombroso, " *La femme criminelle;* (Paris, 1896, p. 401),

student *Ki* and dame *Sioeë-ngo*. The individuals
belonging to the second category, called in the Amoy
dialect *Kiah ang tıng*, or *Khaan Bee, Khaan Rao,
Khaan moei soh,* wait at the landing-stages and public
places, lantern in hand, to show young men the way
to the palaces of debauchery.

These are the *adductores, conductores, admissarii*
of the Romans. The expression *Khaan Bee* answers
precisely to what the Roman peasants understood by
the word *admissarius: he who leads the stallion to
the mare or the bull to the cow.*

To this last class belong also the traders, *Gee po*
or *Hoan sao po.* Notwithstanding the heavy penalties
attached to this traffic, they buy young children or
steal them in order to sell them underhand to houses
of prostitution. Entire bands of men and women are
to be met with united together for the purpose of
trading in children on a grand scale.

There are also attached to the staff of the *Blue
Houses* attendants, called at Amoy *Phang Phoen tsoei,*
who bring water for foot-washing, and *pang hoen ê,*
pipe-bearers; the last and lowest are the *toeng pha
tschioe,* or bullies, whose office is to appease quarrels
among the customers, and if necessary, to turn them
out, and the *hia hoen tsoei ê,* or preparers of alum,
who boil the alum-water which the Flower-Boat girls
use for their secret toilet.

The conventional signs employed by the Chinese
are as numerous as the *furtivæ notæ* used by the
Romans. The Chinese call them *Secret marks* and
most of the courtesans are very expert in their interpretation. The forefinger rubbed beneath the nose
signifies that a man finds a woman to his taste and
that he would like to make her more intimate acquain-

tance. The same finger gently rapping the tip of the ear means: *No!* The right hand slapping the back of the left is also a refusal.

Other signs consist again in closing the two fists, leaving the two forefingers free, which are rubbed one against the other, as if sharpening two knives; or else laying the two hands flat one upon the other, and shaking them like castagnettes.

The most infamous of these signs and one which is only employed by the very lowest of coolies, is to shove the right forefinger in and out of the closed palm of the left hand.

By means of signs also the price is settled and the hour of rendezvous indicated, or else the fan is employed, certain movements of which are made to convey the desired information.

Of course aphrodisiacs are not wanting in so depraved a country as China, and we shall give a detailed account of them later.

The composition of these mixtures is even still unknown to Europeans; we only know that musk, opium, *Ginseng* (the root of *Panax quinquefolia*) and dried shrimps reduced to powder form the principal ingredients. Phosphorus and cantharides seem to be unknown to them.

The Chinese "Flower-Boat" girls also believe that the addition of a small quantity of menstrual blood to the wine or tea presented by them to a client is a sure way of causing him to remain faithful. Whether this proves a greater attraction to European visitors we do not know; at any rate people who go to these places should be on their guard. We now pass on to a third class of Asiatic *maison de passe*, of which, however, there is not so much comparatively to be said.

The Japanese Brothel. The Japanese brothels are situated in the same street as the Chinese ones, often even side by side. But the Japanese girl does not sit at the door touting for custom. The house is quiet, and there is no one watching from the balcony, over the veranda. There is not even a reception-room on the ground floor; you must ascend to the first floor, were you find a room shaded by sun-blinds. [1]

[1] Something analogous exists, or did exist some years ago in Holland. In Rotterdam, there exists a certain street, the "Sandstraat", leading down to the Boompjes, or port, All the brothels are obliged to be located in this street, on either side of which are none other than these hospitable establishments, which are besides conducted with the strictest decorum: the entry, with folding-doors, gives directly upon the street, and as soon as night has fallen, and the lamps are lit, these doors are lifted off their hinges, and replaced by heavy curtains which, while keeping out the cold, enable the police outside to take note of what is going on within and to be able to immediately interfere efficaciously in case of any disturbance.

On entering, the visitor finds himself in a spacious hall, at the other end of which is stationed an orchestra. To the right and left are placed little round marble tables, with comfortable benches and chairs as in any café. The centre of the hall is kept free for dancing.

The new-comer is invited to take a seat and a small glass of *Schiedam* is presented to him by a young girl, in graceful Dutch national costume, who, first touching it with her lips, hands it to him, with the amiable salutation of, " *Welkom, Mynheer,*" welcome, Sir. He is not charged for this, it is a present from the house. He then sits down, and usually calls for something on his own account; and observes what is going on. If he did not know where he was, he would simply imagine to be in some decently conducted dancing-saloon. A number of handsome girls walk two and two round the hall in the intervals between this music; but they scrupulously refrain from addressing themselves to any of the numerous clients, until one of them is beckoned to come. Acquaintance is then made and, after perhaps a waltz or two or a polka and some refreshment, may be brought to a satisfactory conclusion in the upper part of the building, to which access is obtained through a door at the back of the orchestra.

From one end to the other of the Sandstraat the conditions are the

On prostitution in Japan Selenka [1] writes:

"The vile things that have become usual in some of the Tea-houses near the port, are in no way national to the Japanese, and have their origin only in the avarice of certain greedy exploiters. On the other hand, the crowd of professional *demi-mondaines* in the towns constitute an established caste, sanctioned by ancient habit and custom, for the reason that poor parents often sell their daughters to houses of ill-fame. The unfortunate girls submit without murmur to their fate, the deeply-rooted Confucian theory: "Pious respect towards parents", makes their daughters laws. In the more important Japanese towns there are generally special streets devoted to this trade in which are luxuriously mounted establishments, called *Yoshiware*. on the ground-floor of which are congregated the ladies of the place, who, richly clad, guitar in hand, are exposed behind a sort of wooden grating to the male visitors. As these girls have received a certain same, the different establishments varying only in richness of decoration and comfort, from those near the port where go sailors, stokers and trimmers and others frequented by boatswains, ship-carpenters' and pursers' mates, to more respectable saloons, the resort of captains, first and second mates and sometimes a well-to-do stevedore. Higher up are the aristocratie establishments visited by ship-owners, shipping and insurance agents, some passing tourists, but more particularly by certain wealthy, ponderous and lecherous old Dutch burghers, who go there regularly to absorb good Hollands, smoke long pipes and practise bad morals.

The writer of these lines remembers seeing, to his great astonishment. an entire marriage party; bride and bridegroom, parents and family, gravely enter one of these dens, and proceed to enjoy themselves; the bride seemed to be quite at home, and enquiry elicited the astounding fact that SHE HAD, AND PROBABLY, WITH THE CONSENT OF HER "FIANCÉ", PASSED A COUPLE OF YEARS IN THIS ESTABLISHMENT TO EARN HER DOWRY!

[1] "Emil und Leonore, *Sonnige Welten, Ostasiastische Reiseskizzen*, Wiesbaden, 1896.

amount of education, they as a rule, find a husband, even if he be of inferior rank, and after marriage are esteemed as honourable women. They are themselves rarely responsible for the life they lead.

One day in Kioto I saw a young girl in the midst of a great crowd. She had just been "dressed up"; she wore rich varied tinted silk dresses, had a perfect halo of golden pins in her head-dress, and was patrolled through the streets, in order to draw the attention of the men to her. This young lady novice in gallantry did not seem at all dissatisfied with her fate.

Physical Characteristics of the Japanese Woman. She is stronger and more massively made than the Chinese, or Annamite woman and her extremities are not so fine; the feet are never deformed; and she always wears sandals or babooches, like the Turkish woman. The skin is whiter, the general appearance of the body is like that of the Chinese woman, but the pubes is not always deprived of its hair. In that case it is scantily furnished with a little black curly hair. The mucous surfaces of the vulva and vagina are lighter than in the Chinese woman, and much lighter than in the Annamite woman. The general hue, a yellow red, is nearly like that of a Spanish woman. The genital parts are also much better developed than in the Annamite woman. The breast is also more rounded.

Ploss states that:—the exterior genitals of Japanese women present many particularities. WERNICH found the following in his gynæcological department in Yeddo:

"The larger lips show little stoutness of development and even among young people they lack firmness. The vulva stands out very prominently which may perhaps be attributed to the custom among the women of the lower classes of making water in a standing position. The vagina is short. Wernich never found it to exceed 2 $^8/_4$ inches in length. He was never able to perceive a hymen. The vagina did not in general appear to be particularly wide. Congestion and erection of the portia vaginalis took place during examination much more frequently than it does among European women."

It is said indeed that the genital parts of Japanese women are actually so narrow that medical men are appointed to choose out of the prostitutes those which permit the coitus with the more powerful virile member of the European. Whether this information is founded on fact deserves further consideration. DOENITZ, who was for many years an employé of the Japanese government, and introduced police supervision of prostitutes into Tokio declares the above assertion to be inappropriate. The vaginas also gave convenient admission to the medium size of the speculum usually employed in Europe. Besides, the Europeans residing in Japan usually choose their concubines themselves and do not receive them from the hands of the police.

In a collection of Japanese aquarelles in the *Royal Anthropological Museum* in Berlin, known under the name of *Physiognomical Studies*, which were painted by *Maruyama*, the most celebrated Japanese artist of the last century, there is one representing a naked woman squatting on the ground, with the motto — which Prof. Dr. Grube kindly translated for us. — " A woman who has sinned in lust." Her *Schamspalte* (shame-slit), is depicted wide agape; the clitoris, as well as the smaller lips, stand out prominently, the larger lips, on the contrary, appear small with but little stout development.

MORACHE says that among Chinese women the larger lips are more largely developed. [1]

The mode of dressing the hair is less complicated than that of the Chinese woman, and much resembles that of the Spanish ladies. The hair is always lifted off the forehead, and twisted at the back of the head into a chignon, through which is stuck a shell comb. But, as with her two Asiatic sisters, the hair is as stiff and hard as the hair of a horse's tail. The colour is a beautiful blueish black, which sets off admirably a red or white flower.

The Japanese woman is very fond of European perfumes, and drenches herself with *ylang-ylang*, *eau de Cologne*, etc.

She takes a bath every day, and washes herself before and after copulation, as the European prostitute does. The Annamite woman disdains this wholesome practice, for she is as much afraid of water as a cat.

In spite of her rather flat nose (though it is not so flat as that of the Annamite woman) the Japanese looks attractive by the side of the Congai, and even of the Chinese woman. It might be said of her, that she has a pleasant ugliness. She is more willing than the Chinese woman in performing the genital act, but is not so lascivious as the Congai who has been well trained by an experienced *Pha-lan-za*.

Of all the women of the Extreme East, the Japanese [2] approaches the nearest, in all her physical and moral

[1] *Das Weib*, vol. I, p. 160.

[2] To show the extreme difference between the ideas of sexual morality of the Japanese and those of Europeans, it may be noted that it is frequently the custom in Japan for a woman to get married only after having passed a year in a tea-house (which corresponds with European houses of prostitution) and to whom the nakedness of women (or of men) has nothing shocking and promiscuous bathing, without any veil

qualities, to the French woman; she is very gay, and loves to chatter and laugh with those who can understand her funny mixed jargon.

She has but one fault, and that is an abominable habit of thickly painting her face with white lead and Chinese vermilion, so that it is dangerous to kiss a Japanese girl on the cheeks in the European fashion.

But Japanese, Chinese, and Annamite women, all branches of the same stock, have one common characteristic; they do not kiss with the mouth, but sniff through the nose.

If the reader is anxious to know what these priestesses of Venus charge, we may inform him that they are the most expensive of all. They ask two piasters for an hour of private flirtation, and six piasters for an entire night, whereas, for this last price, you could have half a dozen of the poor girls of the Annamite "bamboo". These last, too, never dare to show themselves in public in the daytime, outside the brothel, whilst the Japanese girl, accompanied by one of her comrades, often takes a *zidore* (an open carriage) and goes for a drive.

She is often to be met in front of the tiger's cage, or the orang-utan's hut, at the Botanical Gardens.

The Annamite "Daylight Whore" is a real plague

whatever is freely indulged in. As a fact any Japanese woman may prostitute herself without at all lessening her value as future wife.

In Japan pornography is unknown, because the people consider certain things as simply natural, and call them by their names, without intending harm; indecency being more in the thought than in the intention. A clever Japanese once said to a European traveller: "how evil-minded you Europeans are, you come here and witness things *we* hold as quite natural, and then go and describe what you term our immorality.

to the European bachelor. She introduces herself into your house between noon and one o'clock. The officers, and functionaries, who are returning from the mess, or the restaurant, meet on their road, in the streets a little removed from the centre of the town, groups of women gathered round the table of some itinerant *restaurateur*, or seated in the shadow of a tree. It is not necessary to enter into conversation with one of them; a gesture, a sign, a glance will suffice, and even if you are passing rapidly in a carriage, you will soon be followed home.

The woman who prowls about the town has generally been in the " bamboo", and like the *marmite* of Belleville, she has her *souteneur*, who protects her from the police officers. These policemen are natives, for, in the hottest hours of the day, it would be dangerous for a Frenchman to be out in the streets; they can be easily bribed to shut their eyes.

When once she is in your house, the daylight whore begins to boast of her knowledge of erotic matters. " Me good *whore, me know much Phalan-za.*" She is not indignant if the European, disgusted by her horrible odour, proposes sodomy. She will even forestall him in making the proposal, and if that is not agreed to, will suggest the kneeling instead of the horizontal position; in fact there is no practice that she will not lend herself to.

It is a simple question of price. She will usually begin by mentioning in advance, the price she asks for such a kind of pleasure.

We sincerely pity the poor wretch, who, on the strength of the medical certificate she shows him (usually borrowed from some woman in the " bamboo") sacrifices to Venus in the natural manner. Syphilis, or gonorrhœa at the very least, will teach him that Annamite "flowers" have thorns.

When once she has been in your house, the daylight whore will try to come again, and, though you may refuse her admittance, she will manage to elude the "boys", or the orderlies. Some day, when, after a good lunch, you are sleeping soundly during the siesta, she will enter, and you will not hear the stealthy foot-falls of her light feet. She has noticed on which nail you hang your watch, in which drawer you keep your purse. Everything portable of value will disappear, and you will never again see your gold watch, which she has sold the same day for a mere trifle to the Chinese goldsmith and jeweller, who will perhaps give her in exchange a pair of cheap ear-rings.

The Annamite Mistress of the European. As may be imagined, the European, disgusted with the "bamboo", and the daylight whores, often prefers to have a woman for his special use. If he should prefer a virgin, he may purchase from her parents, for some twenty piasters, a young girl of fifteen or sixteen, selected from those whose fate it would ultimately be to be sent to the "bamboo."

He will be under the disagreeable necessity of having to break in a young savage, who knows nothing. It is true that he may nurse the delusion that he possesses a virgin, but, as we have seen, there are not many of those to be found. Her brothers and cousins have already tried her. There are also various annoyances, especially in the interior of the country. Besides the "portion" to be paid to the parents, there is—which is much more serious—an entire outfit to be bought for the "bride", for she is handed over to you scantily clad in a ragged, dirty, cotton chemise, that once was white.

If you are an officer, or official of any sort—an *òng-quan*—your mistress must wear a costume suited to your rank, and you must buy for her the complete outfit of a woman in a good position in life, which includes, white, blue, and black, silk chemises; blue, red, or green trousers; a huge, round hat with silk ribbons to keep it on, and Chinese varnished shoes. Total cost: thirty piasters. But that is not all. She must have two bracelets, one in gold, and one in silver; two gold buttons for ear-rings; a necklace in silver, and one in amber; a silver leg bangle, and a gold finger ring. Cost: 120 to 130 piasters. In short, at the lowest estimate, you wil have spent 150 piasters in purchases, and that with the marriage portion, and the "wedding" expenses, will quickly mount up to 200 piasters, that is to say £40. All this expense is incurred, and after all you only possess a *demi vierge*, who is a little fool, only fit to eat, drink, and sleep, until she learns the way to the *baquan*, and then she will let herself be robbed of everything.

Men who know what they are about, prefer to take the mistress of some friend or colleague, who is leaving the colony, and thus get a woman who has had some training, requires no outfit, and understands a little French. But, whether you take a novice, or one who is broken in, you have, even at the best, a spouse whose fidelity is on a level with her morality. She will sham virtue before your European friends and acquaintances. She will boast to you how she refused to listen to those who tried to seduce her. But she takes her fill of pleasure with Annamite rascals, who are ready and willing to deceive a *Pha-lan-za*. Some day or other, the officer or official, who believes he possesses a pearl of virtue, and who is not acquainted with the real conduct of his mistress, will cull the bitter fruit of the kindness she has shown to others.

The boy Body-guard. The only means for a European to prevent his Annamite mistress from going wrong with the first gallant she meets, is to set his own Annamite boy over her as a body-guard. He will play the part of the gardener's dog, and make an excellent sentinel; but, being more knowing than the dog, he will take his own share, and become the third member of the household.

I must confess that this method is wanting in morality, but it is the only one which affords any security from venereal diseases, for it is easy to look after the boy's health, and as, moreover, he will jealously drive away all other rivals, he will at the same time be working for his master's advantage. The method may be called a useful precaution.

EXCURSUS I TO CHAPTER V.

ADDITIONAL NOTE. ON THE PECULIAR AND EXPRESSIVE NAMES for PROSTITUTES.

ACCROCHEUSES (man-hookers)—ALICAIRES (Hebes, so-called because in ancient Rome they used to offer wine to their clients)—AMBUBAYES (courtesans, from the latin *ambubaia*, flute-girl)—BAGASSER (drabs)—BALANCES DE BOUCHER QUI PÈSENT TOUTES SORTES DE VIANDES (butchers' scales which weigh all sorts of meat)—BARATHRES (sinks of perdition)—BASSARAS (prostitutes, from the Greek)—BEZOCHES (street-women) —BLANCHISSEUSES DE TUYAUX DE PIPES (pipe-stem cleaners) — BONSOIRS (good-nights) — BOURBETEUSES (puddle-trotters)—BRAYDONES (ensnarers)—CAIGNAR-DIÉRES (good-for-nothings)—CAILLES (quails)—CAM-BROUSES (filthy sluts)—CANTONNIERES (street-corner-girls)—CHAMPISSES (strumpets)—CLOISTRIERES (cloister girls)—COQUATRIS (cockatrices)—COIGNEES (women on the town)—COURIEUSES (inquisitive dames)—DEMOISEL-LES DU MARAIS (young ladies from the swamp)—DROUI-NES (trollops)—DRUES (smart lasses)—ENSAIGNANTES (teachers)—ESQUOCERESSES (cooks for meat)—FEMMES DE COURT TALON (short-heeled women)—FEMMES FOLLES DE LEUR CORPS (women mad with wantonness) —FOLLES D'AMOUR (love-stricken women)—FILLES DE JOIE (glee maidens)—FILLES DE JUBILATION (joyful romps)—FILLETTES DE PIS (well-breasted lasses)— FOLLES FEMMES (wantons)—FOLIEUSES (frolicsome wenches)—GALLOISES (gallic or merry maidens)—JAN-NETONS (back-gammon girls)—GAST (belly lasses)— GAULTIERES (whores)—GAUPES (vicious sluts, derived from *guêpe*, a wasp)—GONDINES (loose women)— Godinettes (diminutive of the preceding)—GOUGES or GOUINES (prostitutes, derived from the old French verb *goyr*, to enjoy)—GOURGANDINES (low women, from *gourganne*, the commonest sort of bean, the food of convicts)—GRUES (cranes, a nickname for street-whores)—HARREBANES (prostitutes)—HOLLIÈRE (a loose woman, from the verb *holler*, to gad about)—HORES (whores)—HOURIEUSES (women to let by the hour)— HOURIÈRES (the same as the preceding)—LESBINES (Lesbians, or women addicted to vice)—LESCHERESSES (lecherous women)—LEVRIERS D'AMOUR (love-harriers, procuresses)—LINOTTES COIFFÉES (linnets with caps on their heads) - LOUDIÈRES (s trumpets)—LOUVES (wolve-bitches) - LYCES (bitches)—MANDROUNOS (procuresses)—MANEFLE (a Languedocian word signifying procuress)—MARANE (vile woman, the female of *maran*, a miscreant)—MARAUDE (a roguish hedge-whore)—MARTINGALE (a lewd woman)—MAXIMAS (bawds)—MOCHÉS (prostitutes, from the Latin *mœcha*, a fornicatrix)—MUSEQUINES (gay harlots, the name is in reality an allusion to the gadfly).—PANNANESSES (dirty drabs, from the Greek πανος, a rag)—PANTON-NIÈRES (harlots)—FEMMES DE PÉCHÉ (sinful women) —PÉLÉRINES DE VENUS (Pilgrims of Venus)—PEL-LICES (courtesans, from the Latin *pellex*, a concubine or mistress of a married man)—PERSONNIERES (female partners for enjoyment)—POSOERA (a woman who can put it *in situ*)—POSTIQUEUSES (vagrant whores)— PRÉSENTIÈRES (women who give themselves for *pre-sents*)—PRÉTRESSES DE VENUS (priestesses of Venus) —RAFAITIÈRE (a bawd and procuress)—FEMME DE MAL RÉCAPTE (women of bad repute, from the Spanish *recato*, proper conduct)—REDRESSEUSE (prostitute and thief)—REVELEUSE (a clandestine whore)—RIBAULDES (low harlots)—RICALDEX (a long-tongued and short-heeled whore [*Cotgrave*])—RIGOBETTE (a merry loose woman, from the verbe *rigober*, to enjoy life)—ROUS-SECAIGNES (strumpets, literally *red bitches*, from *rousse*, red, and *chienne*, a bitch)—SACS-DE-NUIT (night-bags) —SAFFRETTES (merry wantons, from *saffreté*, wanton dallying)—SOURDITES (prostitutes)—SCALDRINES (squa-lid drabs, from the Italian *squallida*.)—TENDRIÈRES DE BOUCHE ET DE REINS (women offering mouth and hips)—TIREUSES DE VINAIGRE (Vinegar drawers)— TOUPIES, (spinning tops, or loose wenches)—TOUSE (women on the town who fleece greenhorns, from the verb TOUSER, to pluck or shear, is also applied to woman in general)—TROTTIÈRE (one who trots about

the streets)—VIAGÈRES (women who roam about)—
FEMMES DE VIE (fast women)—VILLOTIÈRES (gadding
bawds)—VOYAGÈRES (travelling prostitutes)—WAUVES
(Drabs)—USAGÈRES (women for general use).

Besides the above expressions in use in the XVIth
century there are several others invented since that
period, such are the following:

GAURES or GORRES (literally means, sows)—FRI-
QUENELLES (base dirty trulls)—IMAGES (pretty faced
girls)—POUPINES (chubby-cheeked lasses)—POUPINET-
TES (diminutive of the preceding)—BRINGUE (a common
hussy)—BAGUES (rings; the allusion requires no explanation)—SUCRÉES PAILLASSES (sweet mattresses)—
PAILLARDES (lewd women)—BRIMBALLEUSES (women
who tumble topsy-turvy)—SÉRANES (prostitutes who
entice their customers from their windows; they do
not walk the street)—CHOUETTES (night-birds)—CAPRES
(capers)—CHÈVRES (she-goats)—ANCELLES (willing servants, from the Latin *Ancilla*, a hand-maiden)—
GUALLEFRETIÈRES (frisky whores)—PEAULTRE (a
woman of questionable character)—PEAU (the same as
above)—GALLIÈRE (for galley, synonymous with the
English "a tidy little craft")—CONSŒURS (coy
sisters)—BAS-CULZ (low-gaps).

The foregoing list, which will not fail to interest
philologists, has been drawn in large part, from the
important " *Glossaire pour les Oeuvres de Rabelais* "
(Paris, 1837); we have added an English translation
of these queer epithets, and where possible, explained
the derivation of the word. In its present form it will
we hope, be found useful to linguistic students for
whom alone it is intended.

For the meaning of a number of the above expressions

we consulted a book published under the following pompous title:—" *Vocabula Amatoria: a French-English glossary of words, phrases and allusions occuring in the works of Rabelais, Voltaire, Molière, Rousseau, Béranger, Zola, and others, with English equivalents and synonyms*" (London, 1896), and to our astonishment we found that words of vastly different import had been all baldly rendered—" prostituted " without any attempt at differentiation of the various and peculiar shades of meaning. " Vocabula Amatoria " appears to us suspiciously like a badly executed re-hash of Delvau's " *Dictionnaire Erotique* " carelessly rushed through the press.

For more modern epithets not given in the preceding list the reader is referred to the *Dictionnaire Erotique Latin et Français* par Nicolas Blondeau. (Liseux, Paris, 1885.)

EXCURSUS II TO CHAPTER V.

Translation of Note I on p. 60.

The patients took care in the first place, to entirely remove the hair from all parts of the body (*a*) from the lips, arms, chest, legs, the virile parts, and in parti-cular, from the altar of passive lust, the anus.

" Pluck out the hair from breast and legs and arms;
Thy rigid member must be free from fur.
We know you to do this, Labienus, for your lady=love
But why, Labienus, do this to your anus?"

MARTIAL, II, 62.

While you, Chrestus, appear thus with your parts all hairless,
With a mentula like to the neck of a vulture.
A head more shining than a prostitute's buttocks

(*a*) Always excepting the hair of the head of which great care was taken (HORACE, *Ode* X book IV.)

With not a hair appearing on your leg,
And with your pallid lips all shorn and bare....

MARTIAL. IX, 28.

TRANSLATION OF NOTE 1 P. 60.

" To pluck out the hair, get the hair on the head curled, to drink in the baths to excess; still they cannot be said to be customary; for nothing of all this is exempt from blame.

(QUINTILLIAN, ORATORICAL INST. I. 6.)

Vide FORBERG'S famous edition of " *Antonii Panormitae* HERMAPHRODITUS, *pornius in Germania edidit et* APOPHORETA *adjecit* Coburgi Sumtibus Meuseliorum 1824.

TRANSLATION OF NOTE 1 P. 62.

"I have heard it related by Madame de Fontaine-Chanlandry called the beautiful Torcy, that the queen Eleonora, (*a*) her mistress, being dressed and arrayed, appeared a very handsome princess, as there are still many who have seen her so at our Court; but being undressed, her body seemed that of a giant, so long and great was it: but lower down, she appeared a dwarf, so short had she thighs and legs and the rest.

(*a*) Queen Eleonora, sister of Charles V. became, at the signing of the peace of Cambrai, the wife of Francis I, who then had been for some years a widower. (See Brantome's *Vie des Dames galantes*, p. 207.)

CHAPTER VI.

*Perverted passions amongst the Annamites.—Male prostitution.
—The "nay" and the "boy".—Gamblers, thieves, and sodomites.—Usual methods of the Annamite pederasts.—The Chinese
pederast.—The shop of Ach., the Chinaman.—The male house
of prostitution at Cho-lon.—Horrible immorality of the Chinese
actors who play women's parts.*

Perverted passions amongst the Annamites.
At the head of this and the following chapter, I
might say with Tardieu, quoting Fodéré, "Why
cannot I avoid sullying my pen with an account of the
infamous wickedness of pederasts? Like Fodéré, I
hesitated as to whether I should insert in this work
the repulsive picture of sodomy, but I was bound to
confess that it was a necessary supplement, and also
the part of the subject least known.

What Tardieu and Martineau have done for Paris,
that pandemonium of all the vices, I ought to do for
foreign countries. It is necessary for me to include a
study of the "aberrations of love passions in the Colonies", or otherwise the work would be incomplete.

Male Prostitution. [1] The Extreme East enjoys the

[1] The prostitution of the male was not unknown amongst the
HEBREWS. (Cf. JOEL, III, 3; MACHAB., II, IV, 12.) Bat the laws
struck at the pederast with no gloved hand, and the punishment that
followed was terrible. (Cf. GEN., XIX, 24 et seq; LEV XVIII, 22, 29;
DEUT., XXVIII, 27; ROMANS I, 27.) In ROME this infamous usage

wretched privilege of being the chief nucleus of pederastic vice.

With the exception of shopmèn, and *employés* in
small businesses, the Annamites reside in the villages
round Saigon, and it is only the *nays* and the *boys*
who come in direct and permanent contact with the
Europeans. *Nay* signifies "basket". The *nays* are
children of from seven to fifteen years, who are provided with round baskets. They are found on the
quays, in the market, and in front of the shops, waiting for a customer to make a purchase of any kind.
The nay, or "basket", is thin and wretched; he wears
his hair long and hanging behind him. He abounds
at Saigon, and it is from these baskets that the class
of *boys* is recruited.

These latter are from fifteen to twenty-five years of
age; they are essentially liars, debauchees, gamblers,
and thieves. Woe betide the European who leaves,
for an hour, the key in the lock of the drawer, or
cupboard, in which he keeps his piasters; he is sure
to be robbed. The *boy* waits at table, or acts as
valet,—both in the most imperfect manner. [1] It is

was in full swing and moreover practised openly :—(See HOR., *Sat.*
I, 2, 116; MART., XI 46; MART., IX, 9; JUVENAL, VI, 34.) The
Vocabulary used to designate these *auvergnats* was very varied *i.e.*
Cinaedi; Pathici; Pædicator; Spado; Frater; Pusio; Concubinus;
Catamitus. Juvenal held, that the malady was fatal and could be
recognised both by the expression of the face and general bearing:—
"Hunc ego *fatis* Imputo, qui vultu *Morbum* incessuque fatetur." (Juv.,
II, 16.)—"I attribute to the fates his malady which he acknowledges, etc."

[1] From the writer's experience of some years' residence in India, the
native boy contrast very favourably with his Annamite confrère, with
whom he only shares the pilfering propensities. He however never
steals money, jewelry or portable objects, but will not hesitate to cheat
his master in his marketings. A gentleman in Bangalore, having perceived
this, upbraided his *cansammah* or butler for so doing, whereupon the

nearly impossible to obtain any regular work from him, for he is absent great part of the day, and all the night. For costume, he wears a little jacket, buttoning down the front, and white cotton, wide pantaloons, with a belt of red silk, the end of it hanging down in front. To this belt hangs a small silk purse, lined with hide, and ornamented with designs in gilt copper filagree work. The *boy's* hair is rolled up, and encircled by a silk handkerchief; the hair is often kept in place by a shell comb.

Annamite Gamblers, Thieves, and Sodomites.

In short, the *basket* and the *boy* are gamblers, thieves, and sodomites. Are they sodomites simply that they may earn money to satisfy their other vices? That is the theory of certain Annamitophiles, who pretend that this vice was introduced by the European conquest. It was nothing of the kind. The Annamite is a sodomite because he is lascivious. He belongs to an old civilized race that is now rotten. Vice was innate, and the Europeans found it flourishing, and some (very few, let us hope) have taken advantage of it.

The Frenchman who goes to the Antilles, Guiana, or Senegal, has not introduced sodomy and pederasty into those countries, because the natives of those countries abhor those vices. The same Frenchman, arrived in Cochin-China, has become a sodomite or a pederast, because he has found, without the trouble of seeking, women and children who have afforded him the opportunity, It is necessary to point out a mistake

latter replied: " *Yes sah! very true, me do little market robbery, but me no let anybody else rob master.*" When the gentleman related this to a lady friend of his, long a resident in India, she at once exclaimed: " *Never get rid of that boy, if you can help it, he is a jewel.*"

that has been thoughtlessly repeated by many travellers, that the soldiers of the Expeditionary Corps had acquired, in the Chinese campaign, certain depraved habits, which they afterwards carried into Cochin-China, where they have taken root. These travellers forget that the Chinese came to Cochin-China several centuries before we did, and have had plenty of time to vitiate the manners of the natives.

We must not even accuse the Chinaman, for the Annamite is naturally quite as depraved as he is, if not more so,—which is saying a good deal. *Nays* and *boys* are a kind of living merchandise which offers itself.

The *nay* is like the little girl not yet arrived at puberty, who offers you flowers on the boulevards of Paris, and whose parents speculate on the debauchery of *roués*, broken-down in health, and of perverted morals. Instead of a little girl, it is a little boy. He has no flowers, and gains his living by means of a basket. For a *tai-an* (a penny), he will put your purchases into his basket, and docilely follow you home.

When once he gets to your house, if he should suspect that you have depraved tastes, he will soon offer you his services: "Captain" (everybody was a captain in 186—) "me much know chewchew banana," and if the client appeared to hesitate, "me know ablic." That is *sabir (patois)*. *Chewchew* means to eat. The banana is the well-known fruit of the tropics, which resembles in shape a penis afflicted with phimosis; *ablic* is the corrupt form of an Annamite word signifying the act of sodomy, and the word is as cynically coarse and expressive as the vulgar French verb, which corresponds to it. It existed before our arrival, whilst the equivalent for the word "modesty" does not exist in the Annamite language. That is a double philological proof.

By way of reply, the *nay* generally receives a good kick on the backside, in which case he slinks away, and says nothing. In the case of acceptance, he knows that the most suitable time is the hour of the siesta, after the midday cannon has been fired.

About a quarter past twelve, a shadow will steal furtively into the chamber of the pederast. Like the daylight whore, the *nay* knows some means of penetrating, without being seen, into a house in which, perhaps, several Europeans live together.

If the *nay*, a child not arrived at puberty, and generally dirty and disgusting, displeases him, the depraved European has, in the evening, recourse to the *boy*. He is about 16 to 20 years old; he is a former *nay* raised to the dignity of a *boy*. The *boy* works in the evening, after nine o'clock and before midnight, after he has left his master's house. He is not averse to easily gaining a piaster, with which he can try his luck at baquan. We may here note that, owing to the difference in the value of money thirty years ago, a piaster in Cochin-China was worth a louis in France.

Though the *boy* often wears a handsome silk costume, a handkerchief round his head, and a red, or sky-blue, girdle round his waist, his body is quite as dirty as that of the *nay*. The most elementary notions of cleanliness are unknown to him. Unlike the Chinese, he never washes himself all over; not a bucket of water is ever emptied over his head; and this in a country where the lowest temperature, day or night, is 77°F. It is difficult, even to get him to wash his hands before waiting at table. The Annamite is as lewd as a monkey, and has the same dread of water.

Methods used by the Pederasts. The *nay* and the *boy* are generally—to use Tardieu's expression—" suckers of the dart. " It must not be supposed that this depraved Asiatic feels any repugnance, or has any objection, to this disgusting habit. He has even less than the daylight whore, who is also willing to perform the same operation. Whilst the European lies at full length on a long chair, or on his bed, the *boy*, —kneeling or stooping,—*inguina osculatur, sugit, emissumque semen in bucca recipit, usque ad ultimam guttam.*

Although by preference a " sucker of the dart ", the *nay*, or the *boy*, will not refuse sodomy, but he is not enthusiastic about it. It is not any moral reason which stops him, for he is above prejudices of that sort. It is simply the disproportion which exists between the anus of a lad of ten or twelve years, and the penis of an adult European, for two *nays* have no objection to committing the act with one another.

When the *nay* attains the age of sixteen, and has little by little become used to the business, he will not raise any objection, for the vice has by that time become a morbid habit with him. He seeks opportunities and occasions, with as much pleasure as a woman seeks copulation. This depraved taste becomes a pressing need with him. I can even say more: I have known Europeans in whom this " passive taste " was so developed, and who went so far as to give themselves up to the lewd caresses of their *boys*. I trust I shall be excused for not dilating on this subject, and merely mentioning it in passing.

The Chinese Pederast. [1] I have said that the

---

[1] Ellis in INTRODUCTION to his book on " *Sexual Inversion* " ([1])

([1]) LONDON, 1897 (pages 6—7). The reader interested in this curious aberration should attentively read this valuable work in its entirety.

Chinese are *boys* in the restaurants, and cook-shops. As a house-*boy*, the Chinese costs much more than the Annamite, but he has the appreciable advantage of being much cleaner. The Chinaman washes himself thoroughly morning and evening, emptying two or three buckets of water over his head. The clothes he wears are usually very clean, and instead of walking barefoot, he wears shoes with thick soles, He has not, either, the characteristic stink of the Annamite *boy*.

He comes to Saigon at the age of ten or twelve, and first acts as a *boy*, then as a cook, and finally calls attention to the fact that " homosexual " practices exist and have long existed in most parts of the world outside Europe, even when subserving no obvious end. How far they are associated with congenital inversion is usually very doubtful. In China, for instance, it seems that there are special houses devoted to male prostitution, though less numerous than the houses devoted to females. When a rich man gives a feast he sends for women to cheer the repast by music and song and for boys to serve at table and to entertain the guests by their lively conversation. The young people have been carefully brought up for this occupation, receiving an excellent education, and their mental qualities are more highly valued than their physical attractiveness. The women are less carefully brought up and less esteemed. After the meal the lads usually return home with a considerable fee. What further occurs the Chinese say little about. It seems that real and deep affection, is often born of these relations, at first platonic, but in the end becoming physical--not a matter for great concern in the eyes of the Chinese. In the Chinese novels, often of a very literary character, devoted to masculine love, it seems that all the preliminaries and transports of normal love are to be found, while physical union may terminate the scene. ([8]) In China, however, the law may be brought into action for attempts against nature even with mutual consent; the penalty is one hundred strokes with the bamboo and a month's imprisonment; if there is violence the penalty is decapitation; ([8]) I am not able to say how far the law is a dead letter.

([8]) Morache, Art. " Chine", *Dict. Ency. des Sci. Med.* In Annan, also, according to Mondière (*Mem. Soc. d'Anthrop.* T. i. p. 465), pederasty has always existed, especially among young people.

([8]) Pauthier, *Chine Moderne*, p. 251.

takes a wife. Before he arrives at that, he has taken
his part in the male prostitution of Saigon, but in a
most discreet and guarded manner. In the evening,
you may see Chinese *boys* leave their master's house,
and act as rivals to the Annamite *boys*. But, generally speaking, the mouth sucking disgusts him as much
as it pleases the other; he contents himself with anal
copulation, active or passive.

Not only the Chinese *boy*, but also the *employés* in
houses of business, tailors, boot-makers, etc., also give
themselves up to prostitution. It is rare for a Chinaman of that social position, when he finds himself
alone with a depraved European, to refuse to yield to
his wishes. He does it, not so much for the money
he may get by it, as for the pleasure; but if the
European has connection with an itinerant dealer in
curiosities, he will be forced to make some purchases,
and these purchases will often have to be renewed.

A European friend of mine used to receive, at ten
o'clock every morning, a number of young Chinese
merchants, who used to besiege the door of his lodging,
which was adjacent to mine. Two never entered together; the one who arrived last would discreetly
stand at the street door, or in the shadow of a tree,
waiting his turn. At last I learned the secret of this
comedy.

One of these young Chinese merchants, whom I had
occasion to attend medically, told me in return, and
out of gratitude, some strange revelations concerning
the unnatural customs of the great majority of his
compatriots, who belonged to the same social category.
Each patron disposes of his *employés* and apprentices,
according to his humour, and his taste. These youths
also form love liaisons between themselves, and Orestes

and Pylades are not uncommon amongst the people
with pig-tails. They usually change parts alternately,
each being in turn husband or wife. Later,—as the
perverted passions increase with age,—when the genital
powers decrease, and they become masters in their
turn, the passive part is the only one that suits them.
By "natural selection", the Chinaman seeks out the
European who is addicted to the same vice.

Dr. Schlegel, who resided as a medical practitioner
in Canton, had uncommon opportunities of noting the
Chinaman's proclivities and we quote the following
remarks from his interesting little study on the subject:

"In the neighbouring town of *Tschang tscheoe*. the
number of female prostitutes is relatively small, whereas
on the contrary the town swarms with individuals
addicted to passions contrary to nature, to such an
extent that it is said:

Tsiang tsioe kaan a thoen, Emoei tsa bo soe. (*In
urbe Tchang tcheou catamiti, in urbe Emoi meretrices.*)

Nearly all the people there practise this vice, not in
secret, but openly. At Canton there exists one word
only to designate *Amasii;* it is the word *Khai taai*
which is considered to be a grave and ignominious
insult, whereas the dialect of *Fokie* is very rich in
expressions to designate these children and their
trade.

Like the Romans who had their *Pathici*, their
Ephebi, Gemelli, Catamiti, Amasii, the Chinese have
their *sio kia a*, little boys, *sio kia tsia*, pretty little boys,
tshat sia kia, young brigands, *ka thang a*, little
basins for the feet, etc. For obscene manœuvres they
have numerous expressions, of which we may cite the
following: *Ke Kaam (ut gallus facere coitum), ka ka
tsiah (mordere dorsum), kia soa lo (in viam montis*

ire), *ho laam hong (puerorum voluptatis frui*), *to saai thang (volutare in sterculinio)*.

One only of their expressions would seem to indicate the shameful nature of the act: that is *Gik thien so hing* (to act contrary to the course of nature). Besides, the following proverb shows how small is the number: *it ta, dzie bong, sa i si pi (de omnibus vitüs masturbatio vilissimum, tum polutio nocturna, pæderąstia tandem necnon meretricium)*. Although they consider solitary pleasures to be the worst and the most immoral, yet children and grown up people are much addicted to them. It is to this unfortunate habit that may be attributed the laziness and cowardice of the greater part of the Chinese, particularly in the province of *Fokie*. They devote themselves only to tranquil occupations such as agriculture and commerce, and avoid all work at all violent, as also the profession of arms. The absence of this vice which weakens the body, kills moral energy, renders Canton Chinamen far more energetic. That is why all works requiring physical strength in the Dutch colonies are done by Chinese coolies from Canton. That is why also the Canton districts supply such a large contingent of labourers to the colonial mines, and that its inhabitants are far more enterprising and less effeminate than the Chinese of the other provinces. It is doubtless for the same reason that the Canton Chinese who accompanied the Anglo-French expedition to Pekin, and who were known by the name of the *Bamboo rifles*, behaved so valiantly. In the midst of showers of bullets, they carried off the wounded and brought ammunition to the troops, while with the greatest coolness they greeted each murderous volley with shouts of joy.

It is this shameful self-abuse that renders all Chinamen, excepting those of Canton, cowardly, effeminate, perfidious and false. We see the same effects produced upon Europeans who give themselves up to these shameful practices, and we notice that among the Chinese the same causes produce similar effects. It is not rare to meet in the province of *Fokïe* with young men of from 20 to 25 years old completely ruined in health and suffering from continual spermatorrhœa. Such is the condition of that province. Let us now glance at the northern provinces, as far as they are known to Europeans; let us hasten to quit as speedily as possible these details of debauchery, and finish our task. In these provinces the vice against nature prevails in the highest degree. The Anglo-French expedition found there a debauchery so immense and so abominable, that it is no wonder that a handful of Europeans could drive into flight the innumerable armies opposed to them by China.

In Canton we find that this vice prevails mostly among the governing officials, who, during their frequent journeys, find it more convenient to be followed by young boys than by women, but it is there held in abomination. In the province of *Fokïe* we find the *Amasii*, domestic slaves; but in Pekin the same individuals seem to form a regular and quite natural class; the English and French troops found there real establishments where young boys of from 11 to 12 years old are trained to the service of masculine prostitution. They are all dressed up as girls and they are taught all the coquetries of the opposite sex; these precocious debauchees are incompletely castrated at the age of from 14 to 15 years, unhappy creatures neither men nor women. If later on they are received into these establishments the castration is completed. When not attached to regular establishments, they are to be found, as in ancient Rome, at the Barbers (*tonsores*). There, the client, while being shaved, is surrounded by a crowd of young boys of whom it may be said with Donza, one of the commentators of Petronius: *Quorum frequenti opera non in tondenda barba, pilisque vellendis modo aut barba rasitanda, sed vero et pygiacis sacris sinedice, ne nefarie dicam, de nocte administrandis utebantur.*

The Chinamen of Pekin are not ashamed to be seen in public with their Gitons, and in the theatres one may see the richest Chinese with their *amasii* standing behind their chair.

The bestial orgies to which they abandon themselves can find no analogies but in the history of the ancient Romans. Concerning Chinese debauchery it is interesting to quote Barrow, who, in his *Travels* says:

" The practice of a vice so abominable and so contrary to nature seems there (in China) to be so little accompanied by shame or even restraint, that the principal officers of State make no difficulty in admitting their practice of it. One of these officers had always near to his person an individual called the pipe-bearer [1], who was generally a well-built youth of from 14 to 18 years of age, very richly dressed. These youths were pointed out to us by gestures and signs which it was not difficult to understand. The two Muhammadans I have previously mentioned, and who lived in the IXth century had also made this remark. I also find in the relation of the voyage of *Hüttner*, who was a member of the suite of the British embassy in Tartary, speaking of *Gehol*, he says: 'In one of the palaces I found, among other

[1] The Indian *Hookahbadar*.

works of art, two marble statues of young men, admirably executed. Their hands and feet were tied and their attitude left no doubt that the vice special to the Greeks was also in honour among the Chinese. It was an old eunuch who laughing showed them to us.'"

Immorality is still greater among the Tartar and Mongol races. Among these, as with all pastoral races, all kinds of debauchery against nature prevail, and their influence has spread all over China. That is why this vice is more prevalent in the Northern provinces and diminishes as one goes Southward. At Canton it disappears almost entirely, and is practised only by the Mandarins who are Mandchoos, or who, if they are Chinese, have been spoiled by a more or less prolonged stay in the North. But how long will this province resist the invasion of this abominable plague, and the example of the ruling officials will it not deprave the people, as it has already done in other provinces?

We have nearly reached the end of our enterprise. We have lifted the veil that obscured part of the Chinese character, and we have endeavoured in a few sketches to point the immorality reigning in China. If these sketches may appear too strong to some of our readers, let them bear in mind that an enterprise of this nature is extremely difficult, and that here and there energetic terms must quite necessarily be employed to show things as they are. No one can complain if we cut to the quick into an unhealthy wound, however repugnant the spectacle may be. We ask for the same indulgence towards our work.

May the above lines come beneath the eyes of the Tartar chiefs and show to the adversaries of the *Tai phing* rebellion how greatly reform is necessary in China.

It is only by an immense immigration of foreign elements, and by the opening out of China to other nations, that it will be possible to cure the horrible canker that is eating up that country.

Occidental civilization will come to the help of this nation, so remarkable in other points of view. But for that purpose, the work must not be confided to people, nearly as unpolished, ignorant, or fanatical as those whom they pretend to correct. It requires energetic and educated men, who know and can apply the remedy to the sore where it exists.

The Mandchoo dynasty must be thrown down unmercifully, and with it will disappear the seeds of immorality which it sows around it.

That is to what tends the revolt of the *Taï phing* however cruel or infamous the means they employ. Gentle means are of no avail. One must not apply palliatives to the sores of this great rotten body; the knife must cut down right to the quick, to remove the gangrened portions, in order that the rest may grow again and return to vigorous health. The Phœnix of the fable resuscitates only after having been consumed by fire; China also will never rise again until all that opposes her resurrection has been uprooted and destroyed

The Shop of Ach., the Chinaman. In 186—, one of the richest dealers in curiosities, Ach., the Chinaman, who afterwards became one of the leading Chinese residents of Saigon, had a peculiar and widespread reputation. Crowds of people went to his house to drink his excellent tea; but, of course, his customers never boasted of it, except privately and between themselves, for Ach. was too compromising. In spite of the tolerance of manners in those days, one had but to make a few purchases in his shop to be suspected of having enjoyed his lewd favours. Saigonese jokers defined this operation as "digging in the yellow clay". I give the expression for what it is worth. At Ach.'s shop could be found a complete assortment of Chinese and Japanese phalli, and the coloured albums of the Chinese Aretin.

Twenty-five years later, I found Ach. rich, and much esteemed by his compatriots, and looking stout, strong, and well. His little business had proved lucky, and he had succeeded in life.

Chinese Erotic Literature. It is agreeable to find that our observations are amply borne out by Dr. C. A. Schlegel who writes: [1]

In China, erotic books and engravings are largely employed as sexual excitants. Innumerable quantities of these are to be met with; nearly all of these light works, novels, anecdotes, etc., are full of expressions of so cynical a nature that it is almost impossible to choose among them.

The Roman poets in their *molles libri* still made use of metaphors and periphrases, whereas in the *Tschoen koeng tse* (erotic poems) history is brought forward for the sole purpose of describing the most scandalous affairs in the vilest language.

The governing authorities allow these books to circulate without any restriction. They have, as well as the priests, fulminated against these immoral books in the public papers, and their authors have even sometimes been severely punished; the priests do not fail

[1] "La Prostitution en Chine", (Rouen, 1880), an able booklet of some 40 pages, written originally in Dutch.

to preach that the authors of these obscene books will remain burning in hell as long as their works are still in existence on earth; and yet, notwithstanding, every day the most infamous plays are performed, at which women as well as men assist, and printers continue to publish novels daily more and more filthy.

It has happened that Governor-Generals of provinces have caused entire editions together with their plates of impression, after having purchased them, to be burned; but such cases are very rare, for the governors are generally themselves the very first to buy these impure works. The erotic plates and engravings surpass in richness, variety and in infamy, the most lubric imaginations, and meet with more sale than the books, for all the world can see, but it is not every one that can read. This trade must be very lucrative, for there exist in Canton studios where nothing but these *Tschoen koen hoa* are painted. In this city it is not only men who paint these pictures, but the Chinese themselves admit that in the town of *Soe-Tscheo*, in the province of Kiang-Han, young girls of from 11 to 14 years of age are employed at the same work, because they have a lighter hand, and know how to give these pictures a more agreeable colouring.

Lastly, in certain parts of China, they manufacture little articulated and movable puppets, in porcelain or in ivory, extremely obscene, known under the name of *Tschoen koeng siang*, and at Emoi under that of *Tschoen kiang ang a*.

In the face of such universal depravity, the moral tone of the women must necessarily be at a very low level. But nevertheless it is not nearly so bad as might be imagined, and the Chinese women are most of them far more modest than were the ancient Roman dames. [1]

The Male House of Prostitution at Cho-lon.

There remains to be mentioned an establishment at Cho-lon, which was known to very few Europeans, and of which the French police has always (most probably) ignored the existence. This was nothing else but a house of masculine prostitution.

It was clandestine, for the authorities would never have authorized such a den of infamy to be opened,

[1] Sir Rich. Burton, in the Vol. VI of his "*Supplementary Nights*" makes some sensible remarks on the subject of the circulation of English "erotics", which we here reproduce:

"It apppears to me that our measures, remedial and punitive, against 'pornographic publications' result mainly in creating 'vested interest' (that English abomination) and thus in fostering the work. The French printer, who now must give name and address, stamps upon the cover *Avis aux Librarres* under *Edition privée* and adds: *Ce volume ne doit pas être mis en vente ou exposé dans les lieux publics* (*Loi du* 29 *Juillet*, 1881). He also prints upon the back the number of copies for sale. We treat 'pornology' as we handle prostitution, unwisely ignore it, well knowing the while that it is a natural and universal demand of civilized humanity; and whereas continental people regulate it and limit its abuses, we pass it by, Pharisee-like, with *nez en l'air*. Our laws upon the subject are made only to be broken and the authorities are unwilling to prosecute, because by so doing they advertise what they condemn. Thus they offer a premium to the greedy and unscrupulous publisher and immensely enhance the value of productions ("*Fanny Hill*" by John Cleland for instance) which, if allowed free publication would fetch pence instead of pounds. With due diffidence, I suggest that the police be directed to remove from booksellers' windows and to confiscate all indecent pictures, prints and photographs; I would forbid them under penalty of heavy fines to expose immoral books for sale, and I would leave 'cheap and nasty' literature to the good taste of the publisher and the public. Thus we should also abate the scandal of providing the secretaries and officers of the various anti-vice societies with libraries of pornological works which supposed to be escheated or burned, find their way into the virtuous hands of those who are supposed to destroy them."

and, for that reason, this Chinese temple of love was
difficult of access.   Every precaution was taken to
throw the French police off the scent.   The house, in
fact, was situated in a suburb of Cho-lon.   Nothing
distinguished this illicit brothel from a honest house.
It was situated at the end of a court-yard, and no one
was admitted, unless introduced by one of the *habitués;*
without my friend B., the opium contractor, it would
have been impossible for me to enter.

At first sight, the house showed nothing abnormal,
and looked merely like a store of Chinese merchandise.
The sole occupant was an old Chinaman, the keeper
of the warehouse, and his worthy companion.   Ordinarily no one was to be found there.   But the clients
and *pensionnaires* knew the road and the right time,
for it was a house for nocturnal meetings, and only
filled towards midnight.   After the Chinese theatre
was over, the actors who played the women's parts,
used to come there to meet their protectors. [1]

---

[1] Customs of this nature are strangely alike in different countries.   Dr.
Jeannel notes that the principal characters in the plays of Plautus and
Terence are almost always procuresses and prostitutes.   That the actresses belonged to this class is proved by the following:—"Mox Hercle!
vero post, transacta fabula, argentum si quis dederit, ut vulgo sus-
picor, *Ultro ibit nuptum*, non manebit auspices." (PLAUT., Casin., 82.)
" . . . . . But by Hercules! after the play, if anyone gave her any money,
I believe that she would willingly get married, without waiting for the
nuptial ceremonies."

The theatres were known as places of debauch (see TIT. LIV. II, 18);
also ISODOR. (XVIII, 42), the latter we quote:—*Idem vero theatrum,
idem et postibulum*, eo quod post ludos exactos, *meretrices ibi proter-
nerentur.*"

("Theatre and brothel were synonyms; for after the plays were over,
the prostitutes there gave themselves up to the public.")   The famous
Folies Bergères at Paris in our own time has been wittily styled.
Les halles centrales de la Fornication.

On the far side of the house, at the end of a garden enclosed with high walls, was a fine pavilion richly decorated, and provided with handsome Chinese furniture. A good supply of apparatus for smoking opium was to be found there, for, with the Chinese, opium is the basis and motor of all voluptuous debauchery.

Instead of young girls, there were youths of from twelve to twenty years, richly dressed in silk costumes of tender hues, who waited on the guests, and acted as Ganymedes. Compartments similar to horse boxes, and containing a bed instead of a manger, permitted the amorous couples to isolate themselves. I say " couples ", but I may remark that the famous rule of the Jesuits, which forbade their pupils to ever be in pairs, was applied in a very singular manner. It would be impossible to give even a hint at the scenes of extraordinary lewdness which went on in these compartments, without entering into erotic details worthy of the Marquis de Sade, [1] therefore I forbear.

I cannot, however, pass over in silence, one eccentric form of the *lusus amoris*. The Chinese actors who play the women's parts, come in their costumes, and assume the character of a modest virgin, afraid of losing her virginity, a refinement of vice which is much appreciated. In the presence of a number of old men, not very particular, the scenes of the first night of wedded life are represented without any shame. But there is nothing new under the sun, as the proverb says. Petronius and Suetonius have re-

[1] No better idea can be given of the frightful state of Paris under the Empire in regard to the organised bands of pederasts which had for special object the corruption of the *Dragons de l'Impératrice* than the following systematic account given by a police official: —

counted the same thing long ago. The Chinese of
Cho-lon do but repeat the history of the Emperor
Nero, and his marriage with the eunuch Sporus.

EXCURSUS TO CHAPTER VI.

The undermentioned facts vouched for by Dr. Krafft-
Ebing will surprise many readers. The old proverb
concerning "people who live in glass houses" here
acquires fresh force. The vices, practised with such
revolting cynicism in Asia, are carried out with un-
speakable audacity in the great cities of Europe.

OF THE HOUSES OF MALE PROSTITUTION IN BERLIN:
" The following notice from a Berlin (national?) newspaper, of February, 1884, which fell into my hands
by accident, seems suited to show something of the
life and customs of Urnings:—

" *The Woman-Haters' Ball.* Almost every social
element,—the fat, the bald-headed, the young,—and
why not the woman-haters? This species of men, so
interesting psychologically, and none too edifying,
had a great ball to-day. The sale of tickets was very
rigorous; they wish to be very exclusive. Their
rendezvous was a well-known dance-hall. We enter
the hall about midnight. The graceful dancing is to
the strains of a fine orchestra. Thick tobacco-smoke,

"RAPPORT D'UN OFFICIER de la POLICE MUNICIPALE de PARIS.
Attribution des Mœurs. Le 16 Juillet, 1864."

It is signed by F. CARLIER. And the words " Approuvé les conclusions, et continuer les investigations vis-à-vis de toutes les personnes
sans distinction."

(signed) NAUNEY.

Follow Carlier's signature.

This report is very rare, very few copies having been struck off.

veiling the gas-lights, does not allow the details of
the moving mass to become obvious; only during the
pause between the dances can we obtain a closer
view. The masks are by far in the majority; black
dress-coats and ball-gowns are seen only now and
then.

"But what is that? The lady in rose-tarletan, that
just now passed us, has a lighted cigar in the corner
of her mouth, and puffs likes a trooper; and she also
wears a small, blonde beard, lightly pointed out. And
yet she is talking with a very *décolleté* 'angel' in
tricots, who stands there, with bare arms folded behind
her, likewise smoking. The two voices are masculine,
and the conversation is likewise very masculine; it is
about the 'd—tobacco, that permits no air.' Two
men in female attire. A conventional clown stands
there, against a pillar, in soft conversation with a
ballet-dancer, with his arm around her faultless waist.
She has a blonde 'Titus-head,' sharp cut profile, and
apparently a voluptuous form. The brilliant ear-rings,
the necklace with a medallion, the full, round shoulders do not permit a doubt of her 'genuineness,'
until, with a sudden movement, she disengages herself
from the embracing arm, and, yawning, moves away,
saying, in a deep bass, 'Emile, you are too tiresome
to-day!' The ballet-dancer is also a male!

"Suspicious now, we look about further. We almost
expect that here the world is topsy-turvy; for here
goes, or, rather, trips, a man—no, no man at all even
though he wears a carefully trimmed moustache. The
well-curled hair; the powdered and painted face with
the blackened eyebrows; the golden ear-rings; the
bouquet of flowers reaching from the left shoulder to
the breast, ornamenting the elegant black gown; the

golden bracelets on the wrists; the elegant fan—all
these things are anything but masculine. And how
he toys with the fan! How he dances and turns, and
trips, and lisps! And yet kindly nature made this doll
a man. He is a salesman in a great millinery store,
and the ballet-dancer mentioned is his 'colleague'.

"At a little corner-table there seems to be a great
social circle. Several elderly gentlemen press around
a group of *décolleté* ladies, who sit over a glass of
wine and—in the spirit of fun—make jokes that are
none too delicate. Who are these ladies? 'Ladies',
laughs my knowing friend. 'Well, the one on the
right, with the brown hair, and the short, fancy dress
is called 'Butterrieke' and he is a hair-dresser;
the second one—the blonde, in a singer's costume,
with the necklace of pearls—is known here by the
name of 'Miss Ella of the tight-rope', and he is a
ladies' tailor; and the third,— that is the celebrated
'Lottie'.

"But that person cannot possibly be a man? That
waist, that bust, those classic arms, the whole air and
person are marked feminine!

"I am told that 'Lottie' was once a book-keeper.
To-day she, or rather, he, is exclusively 'Lottie', and
takes pleasure in deceiving men about his sex as long
as possible. 'Lottie' is singing a song that would
hardly do for a drawing-room, in a high voice, acquired
by years of practice, which many a soprano might
envy. 'Lottie' has also 'worked' as a female comedian.
Now the quondam book-keeper has so entered into
the female *rôle* that he appears on the street in female
attire almost exclusively, and, as the people with whom
he lodges state, wears an embroidered night-dress.

"On closer examination of the assembly, to my astonishment, I discover acquaintances on all hands: my shoemaker, whom I should have taken for anything but a woman-hater—he is a 'troubadour', with sword and plume; and his 'Leonora', in the costume of a bride, is accustomed to place my favourite brand of cigars before me in a certain cigar-store. 'Leonora', who, during an intermission, removes her gloves, I recognize with certainty, by her large blue hands. Right! There is my haberdasher, also; he moves about in a questionable costume as Bacchus, and is the swain of a repugnantly bedecked Diana, who works as a waiter in a beer-restaurant. The real 'ladies' of the ball cannot be described here. They associate only with one another, and avoid the woman-hating men; and the latter are exclusive, and amuse themselves, absolutely ignoring the charms of women."

Dr. R. von Krafft-Ebing *Psycopathia Sexualis*, London, 1895, (pp. 417—418).

DUTCH EXPERIENCES:

In Amsterdam there exists perhaps the biggest and most luxurious brothel in the world. It is known as *De Fontein* (the Fountain). This establishment occupies an entire building and comprises: restaurant, ballroom, private saloons, café, and at the top of the house a billiard-room where the players are chosen from amongst the handsomest sisters of this very irreligious community, and are ABSOLUTELY NAKED! Around the room, seated at small tables, are a number of grave elderly gentlemen of serious and venerable aspect, smoking long clay-pipes or meerschaums, and drinking beer or grog. One of these worthies had a peculiar knack, whenever one of these nude beauties stooped to make a stroke at billiards and presented her buttocks in his direction, to gently touch them with the hot bowl of his pipe. This would make her start and the old fellow, his paunch shaking with laughter, would draw a florin from his pocket and hand it to the angry fair. It is probable that this honest old burgher used to distribute a goodly number of florins in this manner during the course of the evening.

CHAPTER VII.

Study of the buccal, vulvar, and anal deformities caused by male and female prostitution in the Annamite race.—The theories of Tardieu and Martineau confirmed.—The vulva before puberty, and in the adult woman; signs of the loss of virginity in the Annamite race.—Rarity of the vulvar infundibulum in girls who have been deflowered before puberty by young boys.—Peculiar signs of the habit of mouth suction.—Sodomy and pederasty.— Signs of recent passive sodomy.—Anal blennorrhœa.—Signs of inveterate passive sodomy.—Signs of active pederasty in the Annamite and the Chinese.—Signs of active and passive pederasty in the European in Cochin-China.

Study of the buccal, vulvar, and anal deformities. The notes from which I have written this chapter, date back to my first visit, at a time when Tardieu, and Martineau, who continued his work, had not thoroughly studied this subject of medico-legal science. I have the private satisfaction of here noting, that on nearly every point, my observations confirm the theories of those two learned physicians.

I am about to note in succession all the deformities —vulvar, buccal, and anal—caused in either sex, by deflowering, masturbation, Sapphism, or sodomy amongst the Annamites.

The Vulva before the age of Puberty, and in the Annamite Woman. I have already remarked,

115

in speaking of the little Annamite girl, that the hymen was frequently worn away after the age of ten, and I remarked that the appearance of the organs of generation, after that age, does not differ greatly from that of the pubescent women, of more than sixteen or seventeen years. I will now return to the discussion of this subject, and for the better comprehension of the reader, I will begin by quoting from Martineau, the essential differences which the organs of generation should show in the little girl, and the pubescent woman, of the French race:

In the little girl, the direction of the vulva is to be noted: it is vertical, and the opening is concealed by the big and little lips. The vulva is straight in front; it is half open at the upper portion. On putting aside the lips a little, you see immediately the clitoris, and the urinary meatus: the lower part of the vulva is closed.

In the pubescent girl, and especially in the woman who has often had copulation, the position is quite altered. The vulva then points downwards and backwards. The separation, of the lips is slight at the upper part, but more pronounced at the lower, so that, in the pubescent woman, the clitoris and the urinary meatus are covered, and concealed, by the great lips. It is important to remember these positions when we come to study vulvar deformities.

Marks of Defloration in the Annamite Girl, before and after Puberty. From the number of young girls who were submitted to me for medical examination, I am able to assert that the vulva in them is directly in front, and that it is also open at the lower end.

In the girl or pubescent woman who has been deflowered at an early age, the vulva continues to point forward: the lower separation is much more marked, but the greater and lesser lips are much less accentuated than in the European woman, and rarely conceal the clitoris and the urinary meatus. The downward and backward direction of the vulva is also less marked. The lesser inclination of the vulva and vagina of the Annamite woman decreases, in a marked degree; the total length of the apparatus, which is, no doubt, shorter than in any other branch of the human race (except perhaps the Lapps) and corresponds exactly to the small penis of the man.

According to Martineau, the clitoris of the Frenchwoman is ordinarily $1\frac{1}{4}$ inches long, and more in some cases. The clitoris in woman corresponds to the penis, and should be of a proportionate size, and therefore we shall not be surprised to find that in the Annamite woman its average length is barely three quarters of an inch.

I have also said that the Annamites prefer the pubes bare, and that they compare the European woman, whose pubes is generally more or less furnished with tufts of hair, to wild beasts. [1] The hair

---

[1] Our friend, Lombroso, has endeavoured to found a series of statistics concerning the amount of hair on the bodies of women who live by their shame. Of course his remarks apply only to Europeans, as depilation prevails almost exclusively in the East. It may interest some of our readers to see what Lombroso says :—

1.—The *Nævus piloris*, commonly called a "beauty mark" (*grain de beauté*), is a new characteristic hitherto but little studied, and which must be added to the other characteristics of female degeneration. It is a kind of indirect beard supplement, which assimilates the woman more to man. We found it in 14% of normal women, in 6% of female criminals, and in 41% of prostitutes. Gurrieri however noted it in only

is removed from the woman's pubes by rubbing it
with an ointment containing lime and orpiment (sul-
phuret of arsenic).

I have rarely (not to say hardly ever) remarked,
in the Annamite woman, the symptoms indicated by
Martineau as showing the signs of masturbation, or
buccal Sapphism. This, no doubt, results from the
ease with which the girl or woman can satisfy her
natural desires; moreover, the great frequency of the
" flowers" must help to limit this special form of vice.
I never met but two cases, and both these were the
mistresses of Europeans.

The vulvar infundibulum does not exist in those
young girls who have been touched by young boys.
It is only found when these girls have repeated copulation with a European. Although the rose he gathers
is already withered, the disproportion in the size of the
organs renders the first attacks difficult, and ultimately
creates an infundibulum which is sometimes deep.
The rule, as laid down by Martineau, is mathematically
verified, so to speak.

The production of vulvar deformities due to deflora-

8%. Zola speaks of the beauty marks of Nana and of those of the
lascivious Countess, her worthy rival.

2. *Hairs.*—Professor Riccardi found in 21% of prostitutes an exaggerated pilose development on the sexual parts, and Gurrieri also found
27%, at the same time that he noticed 18% where it was totally wanting; 8% had a genuine ombilico-pubic tuft. 16% showed a virile distribution of hair.

We have also found with Ardu a virile distribution of hair on 15%
out of 234 prostitutes, whereas it was observed on only from 5 to 6%
of normal women and on 5% of female criminals.

On the contrary peluria which amounts to 6% among the Russian
prostitutes and to 2% among homicides, is absent on honest women and
on thieves. In Italy it was noted in the proportion of 8% on honest
women, 36% on homicides and 13% on thieves and child-killers.

tion in copulation, is based on this principle; so long
as there exists a proper proportion in the size of the
sexual organs, the physiological act is easily accomplished, and vulvar deformities do not supervene.
But when the size or dimensions of the sexual organs
differ in either sex; when there is a disproportion in
the genital organs, copulation is accomplished with
more or less difficulty, and vulvar deformities are
caused. This disproportion may exist in either sex ;
either on the part of the man, the penis being too
huge, or on the part of the woman, the vulvo-vaginal
orifice being shrunken, owing to normal resistance, by
the physiological tonic condition of the constrictive
muscle of the vulva, or by the undue resistance of the
hymen.

Professor Tardieu gives a typical description of the
vulvar deformities produced by defloration. The description only applies to Annamites who have not
attained puberty, having habitual commerce with Europeans. I quote part of it. " In these circumstances
the greater lips are thickened, and separated at the
lower part, which is the exact contrary of what we
ought to find. The lesser lips are besides elongated
to such an extent that they pass the greater, as if
they had been repeatedly pulled out. The clitoris is
red, projecting, and half erect; it is partly uncovered.
That is not all; the narrowness of the parts, and the
resistance of the bony sub-pelvic arcade, hindering the
complete introduction of the virile member, and con-
sequent destruction of the membrane of the hymen,
fresh deformities are caused. The membrane of the
hymen is found to be driven backwards and slightly
upwards; at the same time all the parts which constitute
the vulva are also forced back. The result is the

formation—at the expense of the vulvar canal—of a kind of infundibulum, more or less large, and more or less deep, capable of receiving the extremity of the penis, and very similar to that which is formed in the anus in the case of anal copulation."

Of these characteristics, I have rarely remarked those relating to the lesser lips and the clitoris, but the infundibulum was never wanting.

Special Signs of the Habit of Suction. Tardieu notes a peculiar conformation shown in the mouth of certain persons addicted to the habit of sucking. "I have noticed in the most positive manner, in two amongst them," he says, "that the mouth was all awry, the teeth very short, the lips thick, turned back, deformed, and quite in keeping with the horrible vice they practised." I would add to this that in nearly all the women and *nays* who are addicted to such practices, the lips generally appeared to me thick and deformed, especially in the young *nays*. [1]

I have often found eruptions, ulcerations, and the scars of chancres, on the lips and tongue of the unhappy victims of this form of debauchery. When once they are affected, they in turn help to spread the

[1] This abominable and perfectly disgusting habit has come under our observation to a large extent in Paris, where it is practised by both sexes. Various names and expressions are used by its votaries to designate this vice:—*faire minette*, *gamahucher*, *faire soixante-neuf;* the latter term is used on acount of the peculiar position used in order to accomplish the filthy act.

Several anecdotes are current with regard to this practice, but we prefer not to sully our pages by repeating them. I have however not been struck with any special malformation in the subjects such as Tardieu describes. We may mention that Martial has some very powerful *Epigrams* on this aberration.

syphilitic virus, by a law of reciprocity which it would be very difficult to repress.

Sodomy and Pederasty. According to Martineau, sodomy is the term generally employed to designate unnatural acts, without distinction of sex as to the persons between whom these acts are effected.

Pederasty signifies unnatural acts between men, and may be divided into active and passive pederasty.

The anal deformities produced by unnatural copulation are the same in the woman as in the *boy* and the *nay*, except some trifling differences. I will confine myself here to studying them in the *nay* and the *boy*, where they are found more frequently than in the woman.

Signs of Recent Passive Sodomy. It has been already remarked, that the *nay* or *basket* is a youth of from eight to fifteen years. After that age, he is promoted to the rank of *boy*, but, whilst he is a *nay*, he has not usually reached the age of puberty. As may easily be imagined, these poor little wretches fall into the hands of " active" pederasts, who are not remarkable for gentleness and kindness, and who brutally assuage their lewd passions without caring what may be the result.

I have often found, in these unfortunate *nays*, marks of attempts that have been committed almost by violence, the fact being that a lad not yet arrived at puberty, and frail and weak, is incapable of making any serious resistance to brutal attempts at sodomy on the part of an adult European or Asiatic.

In order not to unduly extend this work, I will not give here the results of my medical observations, for

I should only be repeating what Tardieu and Martineau have already said. I will refer the reader to their works, and confine myself to discussing their opinions.

Let us, in the first place, take that of Tardieu. [1]

"A recent attempt leaves such well-marked signs that it is impossible to mistake them. The signs of recent attempt are more or less evident according to the degree of violence employed, the size of the parts, the youth of the victim, and the absence of previous vicious habits. They vary, according to circumstances, from redness, roughness, painful heat of the anus, and difficulty in walking, to the fissures, called *rhagades*, deep rents, extravasation of blood, and inflammation of the mucous membrane, and the underlying cellular tissue. This inflammation may be more or less extensive, and more or less prolonged; but if the examination does not take place till some days after the attempt, you will find usually, only itching, and a discoloration of the anus, due to the modifications, caused by the discharge of blood."

The symptoms mentioned by Martineau are more explicit. He remarks—which Tardieu does not—that there may result "abscesses or fistulas". Sometimes a bloody and purulent serum is spread over the anal region, which is very painful. The pain is either continuous, or merely passing; and comes on more especially during defecation; the woman (or man) then experiences a smarting pain, which is sometimes very violent. At other times, the pain comes on after defecation, and lasts several hours.

On examination of the region, the following marks

[1] *Etude Medico-Légale sur les Attentats aux Mœurs* par Ambroise TARDIEU, professeur de Médecine légale à la Faculté de Médecine de Paris. (Sept. edit., *Paris*, 1878.)

will be found. On touching the anus, it will be noticed that the orifice is slightly dilated. The anus is also driven upwards. The sphincter, not having yet lost its power, resists, but is also nevertheless driven upwards, with the result that a slight depression of the anal region is formed, the beginning of an infundibulum bearing towards the anus

Martineau's reasoning is complete. But I would remark that, in the majority of recent attempts, I have not found the infundibulum clearly defined;—not because there was not a great disproportion between the anus of the child and the penis of the adult, but because the anal sphincter (and the vulvar also) possesses less tonicity than in the European. Consequently, the sphincter is more easily dilated.

I have always found, in the medical examination, that the anus was dilated, and that the finger, when introduced, did not meet with that constriction which is found in the anus of a person who has not been sodomised.

In the woman, the anal infundibulum is more frequent and more pronounced than in the *nay*, and for a good reason. In the first place the muscles of the buttocks are more developed than in the *nay*, and the sphincter has also more tonicity. The *nay* is generally very young when he begins the practice, whereas the woman is old when she takes to sodomy, which she does rather from economic motives, on account of the money it brings, than from natural taste. The result in her case is that, the sphincter having greater tonicity, anal copulation is more difficult, which causes the production of an infundibulum.

In the *boy*, who has usually been a pederast for some years, only the signs of inveterate sodomy are found,

All the sodomites, both men and women, lubricate the anus, in order to make copulation easier, and use, for this purpose, some fatty substance, mixed with the thickened juice of a kind of mallow, which is boiled in a small quantity of water. This mallow possesses emollient properties.

Anal Blennorrhœa. Cases of anal blennorrhœa, which are very rare in Europe,—for Tardieu and Martineau only met with one case each,—are much less rare in Cochin-China. They occur when the *nay* is the victim of a *boy*, who has contracted the disease from a woman, which is the case with the majority of adults. I met with one case, however, in a young German, who was employed in a large house of business, and who had probably been infected by a *boy*, but he would never confess how he caught it, and related all sorts of improbable lies.

I cured him by employing cubebs internally, and injecting, by the rectum, his own urine collected in a glass, and used while tepid, with a syringe.

Signs of Inveterate Passive Sodomy. According to Tardieu these are the signs which it should present: " The characteristic signs of passive pederasty, which we will recapitulate in order, are, — excessive development of the buttocks, infundibular deformity of the anus, relaxation of the sphincter, the effacement of the folds or wrinkles, ridges and excrescences round the anus, extreme dilation of the anal orifice, inability to restrain the fæces, ulcerations, *rhagades*, piles, fistulas, rectal blennorrhœa, syphilis, and foreign bodies introduced into the anus. The mere enumeration of these different signs can give no idea of their importance: it is absolutely necessary to identify each separately, in all its essential peculiarities. "

Tardieu's summary having been thoroughly discussed by Martineau, it would be better to refer the reader to his book, and to note here the differences, which I think I have observed, as to the relative importance of these symptoms.

In the first place, I will put aside the sign of excessive development of the buttocks, which is without importance in the Annamite race, and come at once to that of the anal infundibulum.

The Anal Infundibulum. This deformity has always struck observers, but some of them have denied its importance, and others have exaggerated it. This difference of opinion is perhaps due to the fact that, in certain cases, this deformity exists, while in others it is absent. I have given the reasons for its existence, or its absence, by proving that the anal infundibulum resulted either from the resistance of the sphincter muscle, or from the disproportion in the size of the organs. I repeat, that in all cases in which these conditions exist, or have existed, you are certain to remark this deformity, both in the man, and in the woman.

The infundibular deformity of the anus is, I repeat, real, only you must know how to look for it, and how to understand its pathogeny. As regards this, I cannot do better than quote the very exact description given by Tardieu.

"The infundibular deformity of the anus," says that eminent professor, "results, on the one hand, from the gradual forcing back of the parts which are situated in front of the anus, and on the other hand, from the resistance shown by the higher end of the sphincter to the complete admission of the member into the rectum. The sphincter, in fact, forms above the anus a sort of contracted muscular canal, the depth of which is sometimes an inch and a quarter to an inch and a half, so that the lower part of the ring may give way, and allow itself to be pushed towards the upper, which resists still more, and remains at the bottom in a sort of funnel, the widest portion of which is circumscribed by the sides of the buttocks, and the narrow part of which extends through the anal orifice to the compressed sphincter, which is reduced to a mere ring, which closes, more or less completely, the entrance to the intestines.

If I have succeeded in making my meaning plain, it will be seen that the infundibulum will be more or less wide, and more or less deep, according to the state of fatness, or leanness, of the person, and the more or less pronounced projection of the buttocks."

In all the Annamite prostitutes addicted to practices of sodomy, I met with the infundibulum so well described by Tardieu, and of the shape mentioned above. I attribute this to the advanced age of these women when they begin anal copulation. But, on the contrary, I have not often met with it in the *boy* of from sixteen to twenty, or twenty-five years of age, who is a hardened pederast, and began the practice at an early age. The regular infundibulum had disappeared, to give place to another form quite as characteristic as the first, and which has not been noticed by Tardieu.

We owe the clear description of this form to Martineau, and I cannot do better than reproduce it. "When the anus is compressed upwards, if you do not find an infundibulum such as I have described, do not imagine that it does not exist. In many cases, in fact, by an attentive examination, and by feeling the anus, you will find an infundibulum formed, not at the expense of the buttocks, but of the anus and the softened sphincter, and flattened in such a manner, that the finger, directed from the back to the front, and from the bottom to the top, will meet with a small annular depression in the form of a cupola, in which the extremity of the exploring finger can lodge.

"I call your earnest attention to this infundibulum, formed at the expense of the anus, and partly of that of the sphincter, because other authors appear to me to have ignored its existence." [1]

It is generally in this special form that I have encountered the infundibulum in the *nay* of twelve or thirteen years of age, and especially in the *boy*.

Relaxation of the Sphincter.—Effacement of the Radiating Folds.
I again quote from Martineau. "Besides this infundibular deformity, the sphincter is relaxed, and the radiating folds are effaced. These two signs are very important. In fact, they are never wanting in the inveterate sodomite. Tardieu, very rightly, like Zachias Casper, attributes a great diagnostic value to the existence of these two signs, which, he says, are met with even when the infundibulum is missing. For my own part, I have always found this relaxation of the sphincter, and the effacement of the radiating folds or wrinkles. It may easily be understood, in fact, that these signs are invariable in the inveterate sodomite. It is not necessary that anal copulation should be accomplished easily, or with difficulty; to produce these signs it suffices if the act

[1] Martineau, *Leçons sur les Déformations vulvaires et anales* (Paris, 1883).

of sodomy is often repeated. The friction, the passage of the member, suffices to dilate the anus, and to produce the relaxation of the sphincter, and the effacement of the radiating folds. The tonicity of the constrictor muscle of the anus is lost little by little, the sphincter is insensibly relaxed, the folds and wrinkles are smoothed out, and anal copulation is then effected more easily.

" Along with these two morbid phenomena, if the anal orifice is dilated with the fingers, it will be found that the rectal mucous membrane forms creases, and sometimes a bright red, thick swelling. As to caruncula and excrescences, lesions which the Latin satirists called *cresta*, *mariscæ*, I have never met with them.

" Simultaneously with these deformities and anal lesions, will be noticed the weakening of the sphincter, the compression of the anus upwards, and the dilation of the anal orifice to such an extent that, with some patients, the fæces, and the intestinal gases, escape involuntarily.

" Owing to this dilation of the anus, you can easily introduce into the rectum, one, two, or even three, fingers. On separating the buttocks, you will find a hole, more or less gaping, in which you will be able to perceive certain lesions with which the mucous membrane is affected, such as ulcerations, piles, and fistula, etc., etc. These lesions, which are considered by Dr. Venot (of Bordeaux) as a consequence of habitual sodomy, are, in my opinion, nothing of the kind. They may occur without inveterate sodomy. They may exist with it, but they are not a consequence of it."

The marks of inveterate sodomy could not be described more faithfully than they have been by Martineau, but I have especially remarked in the elder *boys*, a considerable dilation of the anus, to such an extent indeed, that I introduced in some of them the thumb and the two first fingers, as far as the second joint, and that easily and without causing pain, by taking a little care. When relaxed to such an extent, the sphincter was incapable of keeping in the fæcal matter. Having once cured one of these unfortunate wretches, of excessive relaxation of the anus, by employing an astringent of myrrh and acetate of lead, mixed with simple ointment, I created for myself (without seeking it) an extensive practice, for the *boy*, when nearly cured, made me a reputation I was far from desiring, amongst comrades of the same kidney. They came from all parts, to my surgery, which allowed me, at the cost of a few pots of ointment, to closely study the deformities mentioned above, and to gather some information as to the methods used by these perverted wretches.

Signs of Active Pederasty in the Annamite and the Chinaman. Tardieu is the only author who has treated of this subject in detail, and he has done so in a remarkably complete manner. I will sum up the conclusions at which he has arrived.

" In the active pederast, the virile member is very slender, or very huge; slenderness is the very general rule, huge size the very rare exception, but, in either case, the dimensions are excessive. one way or the other. In the slim penis will be noticed a considerable reduction from the base to the extremity, which is very thin, like the finger of a glove, and resembles the *canum* more; this form is the most general.

" In the very large penis, it is not the whole organ

which undergoes a gradual thinning from the root to the extremity, but the gland, which being strangled at its base, is sometimes inordinately elongated, in such a manner as to give one the idea of the muzzle of certain animals. Moreover the member, throughout its whole length, is twisted in such a manner that the urinary meatus, instead of being straight up and down, is turned obliquely to the right or left. This twisting and change in the direction of the organ are sometimes carried to excess, and appear the more marked because the dimensions are so considerable, so that I once saw the dorsal side of the penis turned completely to the left, and the meatus transversal. "

I will content myself with making the following remarks. I have never noticed in an Annamite the signs of passive pederasty, without making an examination of the genital organs, and without at once asking if he practised active pederasty, or masturbation. The reply generally confirmed the medical diagnosis resulting from the examination.

I have often found, in the young *nays*, signs of masturbation, characterized by a gland very easily skinned, the mucous surface red, and the member becoming erect at the least touch. In the *boy* on the contrary masturbation was the exception, and, as a rule, signs of active pederasty--either by the *boys* amongst themselves. or perhaps with some European —were found.

But though the *boy*, for a sum of money and the promise of secrecy, would reveal to me the vicious habits he had practised with his master, it may be imagined that, even the most depraved European would not willingly confess his abject vices. Messrs. Y. and Z. would smile affably when spoken to concerning their taste for good looking *boys*, or the Chinese of Ach.'s shop, but the insinuation that they followed the Latin adage, *par pari refertur*, and that between them and the *boys* and Chinese, there existed an exchange of favours, would not have been well received.

From the Asiatics I examined, I deduced the following observations. The genital organ of the male Annamite, being, as we have seen, remarkable for its slenderness, I generally found in the *boy* who was an active pederast, the member conical, and similar to that of a dog, as has been remarked by Tardieu. In some only—those more especially addicted to masturbation—the gland was in the shape of a club.

The genital organ of the Chinaman, being more developed, and approaching nearer to the size of that of the European, did not so often assume this shape, but rather showed, on the contrary, the lateral twist of the penis, and the elongation of the gland from the crown.

Signs of Active and Passive Pederasty in the European. The signs of active sodomy in the Europeans, who consented to allow me to examine them, were usually those which Tardieu describes as exceptional. It is true, let me hasten to say, that the number of Europeans I examined was not considerable, and I cannot, therefore, deduce any general rule. In one of them, a M. B***, a man whose lasciviousness and misconduct were notorious, I found the member very much developed, and capable of satisfying the most exacting woman. It was not without some astonishment that I saw a man, provided with a genital apparatus of this size, in the habit of assuaging his lust upon unfortunate children not yet arrived at puberty. I remarked the same thing among the Arab sodomites of Guiana. I also remarked in the European active sodomite, the cork-screw form—often very pronounced—and the strangulation of the gland by the pressure of the anal sphincter.

Signs of Passive Sodomy. For reasons which will be well understood, I was only able to note these in two Europeans. The first, was the young German I have mentioned as affected with anal blennorrhœa, and whom I cured by injections of a special kind. He promised to show me the state of his rectum after he was cured, but he took care to never come back, in order not to have to confess the more than probable cause of the disease, which was evidently occasioned by anal copulation with some affected person.

The second was a young lad of seventeen, the son of a clerk in one of the Government offices. I made the voyage out in company with his father, and rumours were current on board the ship, about the morality of this young man. He came to me, one day, with a stinking chancre, which occupied the front part of the anus. This latter was much dilated, and admitted two fingers. On opening it, I found the anal mucous surface relaxed, red, and ulcerated. The radiating folds had partly disappeared, and the sphincter had sensibly lost its tonicity. This vicious youth pretended that he had acquired the disease from the mouth of a Congai, and I could not make him comfess the truth. I thought, on the contrary, after making a medical examination of his anus, that he acted (perhaps many times) as the "patient", and had caught his disease from some active sodomite infected with syphilis.

CHAPTER VIII.

The European Colony thirty years ago.—The European woman very rare.—Moral causes of the relative frequency of sodomy and pederasty in the early days of the occupation.—Saigon in the present day, thirty years after the conquest.—Increase of the feminine element in Cochin-China.—The life of the European in the present day.—Evening amusements.—The European prostitute.—Increased morality of the Europeans.—The diminution in the masculine and feminine prostitution of the natives is only in appearance.—Present manners.—The boy and the native collegian.

The European Colony.. Thirty years ago the European colony was not very numerous, and, except for some English and Germans, and a very few French merchants, was mainly composed of officers of the Navy and other corps connected with it, and a small minority of civil service officials.

There were not in all more than four of five hundred Europeans, besides the Expeditionary Corps. Daily existence was desperately monotonous, which, added to the unhealthiness of the climate made a sojourn in the place very unpleasant. In an atmosphere which is hot, damp, and frequently saturated with electricity, the climate very quickly enervates and weakens the physical strength, and this weakness of the body re-acts in its turn on the moral character.

Few amusements brightened the life of the European bachelor, for, at first, few people brought their families

to the Colony.   Consequently, there were none of those
social meetings which render civilized life nearly sup-
portable.   I cannot call to mind one agreeable réunion,
for though everyone was obliged to appear now and
then at the official soirées of the Governor, these were
nothing short of torture to the officer, or official, who
was forced to put on for the occasion, his regimentals,
and epaulettes, or the regulation black suit.   At the
first official ball at which I assisted, 186—, the female
element was represented by four ladies, who danced
a quadrille, with two hundred officers, and officials,
standing round them.   There were no evening amusements at Saigon, but for those who liked the Club,
and baccarat or écarté.   Lovers of music were reduced
to visiting the Chinese theatre, the only one in existence
at the time, for the French theatre did not open till
twenty years after the conquest, and it must be confessed that the Chinese theatre was not very amusing.
Confirmed gamblers had recourse to *baquan.*   The
admirers of the fair sex were the worst off, the female
element was conspicuous by its absence.   There were
two or three married ladies, who were not very cir-
cumspect, and were freely talked about, but as to ladies
of the demi-monde, or even of the " demi-demi-monde",
there were absolutely none.

The two first European Prostitutes.   If my
memory serves me faithfully, the two first European
prostitutes came to Saigon in 1866, or 1867.   They
were two Moldo-Wallachians, nearly forty years of
age, who had been in every brothel between Alexan-
dria and Saigon.   Installed as *dames de comptoir* in
a common beer-house, they caused almost a riot amongst
the male population; and the night of their arrival all

the bachelors of Saigon were collected in the establishment, though usually you did not find more than four
Europeans there. Some funny person had the absurd
idea of putting the ladies up in a raffle,—each at a
hundred tickets at one piaster. In an hour all the
tickets were sold, and the lottery drawn. I do not
know whether the happy winners were enchanted with
their good luck.

Except the café and the Club—or, indeed, baquan,
and the Chinese theatre—what amusements were there
in the evening, for Europeans who did not want to
drink, or gamble, or even listen to the senseless music
of the Chinese? None whatever, but opium smoking
and native prostitution. Unless a man possessed an
exceptionally strong will, it was difficult to avoid
gliding down the slippery paths of vice, in a country
where vice was to be found everywhere. In the daytime, the European was attacked in his house by the
" daylight whores ", and in the evening, if he had the
strength to take a stroll, in order that he might sleep
the better, quite a crowd of lewd boys came round
him, to impudently offer their unclean favours. [2]

It was not astonishing that persons of weak character, who did not know how to preserve their moral
dignity, fell into shameful vices. I cannot but repeat,
that the European did not import the vice of Sodom
into Cochin-China. The vice was a direct result of
Chinese civilization, and became part of the manners
of the Annamite people long before the conquest by the

[1] Vices such as these are not confined alone to Asiatic cities. We
recall an incident that occurred to ourselves in 1894 in Séville. While
traversing a short street in the centre of the city we were accosted by
a woman, who said "Si el señor no quiere mugeres hay niños muy pe-
queños y el señor puede tomarlos por el culo." The utter depravity of
other cities like Berlin, Marseilles and Naples is notorious.

French. It was the vanquished people who corrupted the European, and he was aided in that by the almost complete want of the European feminine element, at the beginning of the colonization.

Moral Causes of the Sodomy of the Europeans. [1] The real causes of the propagation of the vice of sodomy, in the European colony, are these. In the first place, the almost complete absence of the white woman. Obliged to take to the disgusting Congai, whose black mouth, with its red spittle, was enough to damp the warmest genital ardour, some preferred the mouth sucking used by these women; others, more depraved, took the road to Sodom. Others again, more depraved still (or perhaps from hereditary character) addressed themselves to the *nays* and *boys*, who offered themselves in shoals. This last category was much the smallest, I hasten to acknowledge.

All gave, as the reason for their vicious habits, the absolute want of security, and the great danger of catching syphilis from the Congai. A great change has taken place since then, and before describing the life which the European now leads in Cochin-China, let us cast a rapid glance at Saigon in the present day.

Saigon in the Present Day, more than thirty Years after the Conquest. Nearly a quarter of a century after my first stay in the Colony, I paid it a second visit, on my return from Tonquin. I can thus bear witness to the progress effected in thirty years.

Important changes in the appearance of Saigon had taken place, to such a degree, indeed, that of all the old houses and huts existing at my departure, I recognized one only, that of the great merchant, Wang-taï,

[1] See the Excursus at the end of this chapter.

transformed into the office of the " Contributions indi-
rectes." A magnificent Government House, a superb
Cathedral, a brand new Post and Telegraph Office,
Treasury, fine Law Courts, Government Offices, the residence of the Commandant, enormous barracks provided
with all necessary comforts, all had sprung out of the
ground as though by enchantment, with the help of
the Chinese labourer. The town had doubled in size,
and instead of small low narrow houses with tile roofs
and no ceilings, where the officers and officials formerly lodged, there are now fine houses of several
storeys, with verandas all round.

Instead of a few rare Malabar cabmen, never to be
found on the days when they were most needed, there
were hundreds and hundreds of carriages of all sorts,
from the regular old cab, formerly driven by a Malabar (whence its name) to the calash with two horses,
or the *zidore*, an open carriage with one horse. These
could be hired for fourpence a journey, or eightpence
an hour, with no *pourboire* for the driver,—an improvement worth noting. For half a piaster (1s. 8d.), you
could make a tour of inspection at five or six o'clock
in the evening, or at night after dinner, when the
temperature is heavy and oppressive. In the middle
of the Promenade is the Café Pré-Catalan, where you
can take your bitters before dinner, or your beer afterwards. If you feel so inclined, there is an excellent
restaurant, with private rooms on the first floor, where
you can enjoy a good supper in good company. And
the feminine element will not be wanting at the supper
as it was in the old days.

**Increase of the Feminine Element in Cochin-
China.** The number of European women has in-

creased enormously. Many of the officials who at the beginning of the occupation were bachelors, married during one of their visits to France, and brought out their wives and families. The officers of the various corps connected with the Navy, also obtained permission to bring out their wives.

Each family has its horses and carriages. The expense of purchasing these is from 300 to 400 piasters, with a cost of twelve to fifteen piasters a month for the keep of the horses, and the wages of the coachman.

On leaving, you can sell the whole turn-out (except the coachman), at a loss of about forty to fifty per cent, after you have used it for three or four years. It will be seen that the cost is a mere trifle.

The French shopkeeper, who used to keep a bazaar, has disappeared, and been replaced by a Chinaman, who sells the same articles much cheaper, for he imports them direct from France. But new shops of all sorts have arisen, florists, milliners, dressmakers, booksellers, jewellers, etc.; there are some of all sorts, not forgetting pork-butchers. Instead of the common eating-house, kept by a kind of cosmopolitan, whose cooking burned your palate, there are now many fine restaurants and hotels. It will be seen that the Colony is flourishing.

The Present Life of the European. After his daily work is over, if the European wishes to amuse himself in the evening the means are not wanting.

In the first place there are plenty of European families, who receive their friends, and offer them tea. When the Government ball takes place, there are some hundred of ladies in the immense ball-room, and dancing is carried on from ten at night till six in the morning in spite of the torrid heat.

A small and pretty French theatre, in which the heat is less felt than it is in some of the large theatres of Paris, has been built in the middle of the Rue Catenat. During the season, which lasts six months (from October to March), there are four performances a week, and the prices of admission are very moderate.

The Colony pays a subvention of £4000 a year to the theatre, which enables the manager to engage good artistes for every sort of entertainment, from farce to grand opera. We have heard *William Tell* given. The female members of the company are numerous, and well-trained, and include, besides the leading actresses, chorus ladies, and even a *corps de ballet.* All these ladies like to pass an evening at the Pré-Catalan, and a few glasses of iced champagne will not frighten them.

There are besides, numerous cafés and beer-houses, generally kept by women, or girls, who are not inclined to be too prudish. This is very different from the days when there was only one French Café,—la Rotonde, usually called the *Trois Tétons,*—kept by two women whose beauty was on the wane.

During the six months of the year when the theatre is closed, an orchestra of female musicians from Austria, plays in an immense hall constructed of bamboo, and filled with plants and flowers, and through which the air circulates freely. These concerts are frequented by all the European society.

The European Prostitute. In the daytime, you may see on the promenade of the Tour d'Inspection, many handsomely appointed victorias, with coachmen and *saïs* dressed in showy liveries. On the cushions of each carriage recline one or two ladies, bepowdered and berouged, and dressed in the latest fashion. They are the "old guard" of Saigon, taking a drive. In the evening, these *demi-mondaines* have their box at the theatre, or their seats at the music-hall, and are surrounded by a circle of admirers. We are no longer in 186—, when the two first European prostitutes were raffled for. A score or so of years has sufficed to radically alter the Colony, and, as we shall see, has caused an immense improvement in morals.

Great Improvement in the Morality of the Europeans in Cochin-China. This fact struck me as soon as I returned. In former days, the European sodomite had been far from a rarity; many persons, some of them of high rank, had this unfortunate reputation. They were not despised, or thought the worse of on that account. They were merely "chaffed". In the cafés, the most smutty stories were told, and laughed at.

Those who evinced a taste for male prostitution, used to meet together, and pass the evening with their associates; opium was smoked, and there were always boys hanging round the doors, waiting for customers.

Within less than a quarter of a century, a radical change has been effected, and this change is undeniably due to the introduction of the European woman, and a similar increase in the number of Chinese and Japanese prostitutes.

The number of Europeans addicted to the habit of opium smoking has also greatly diminished. They may now be counted. They have Annamite mistresses skilled in preparing the opium pipe; in the Army, the officer who was also an opium smoker—frequent enough thirty years ago—has completely disappeared.

As to the European sodomite, hardly more than the memory of him may be said to exist. Those who still preserve this reputation are old merchants, and officials dating back to the old régime. They are regarded as curiosities by the new-comers. That amongst these last, there may be some who have a weakness for " Greek love", is possible, for the vice exist even in Europe, but they form an infinitesimally small minority, and so far from boasting of their vice, sedulously conceal it. They require secrecy, and in order not to arouse suspicion, dare not even introduce the *nay* or the *boy* into their houses by night. "Other times" have produced "other manners".

The Diminution in the Male and Female Prostitution of the Natives more Apparent than Real. It must be owned, that the police of the Colony has made the most praiseworthy efforts to rid Saigon of the plague of sodomite *nays* and *boys*. Permission to reside in Saigon is only given to Annamites working for some European, and each person having such permission must possess a card, bearing his description and his photograph. Any native who is met with, who does not possess such a card, and who has no trade by which he gains his living, is arrested; if the medical examination shows that he is a sodomite, he is sent to the Penitentiary at Poulo Condore.

Unfortunately, the police regulation obliging the Chinaman or the Annamite to carry a lighted lantern after nightfall, and forbidding him to be found in the street after midnight, has been withdrawn. It was withdrawn at the request of the native members of the Municipal Council, who asserted it was an infringement of personal liberty. The *nay* also has no longer a

basket.   He sells flowers, which are now extensively
cultivated in the neighbourhood of Saigon.   The *nay*
is now found, in small bands, at the doors of cafés,
restaurants, etc.   He is no longer alone, as he used
to be, but is accompanied by a little girl, who passes
for his sister.   She generally carries a bundle of rose-
buds, which she offers to you with a most engaging
smile.   You have only to accept them, give her a few
halfpence, and at the same time show her one or two
piasters.   That is quite enough.

How the Business is now managed.   The following information I derived from one of my countrymen,
whom I had known in 186—, and whom I found on
returning again.   He had (for he is now dead) a great
liking for virgins,—a propensity which was well-known
throughout the town.   This is how soliciting is now
done, under the noses of the European policemen, the
only ones who can be trusted to look after morals.

"The boy slips away, and the little girl remains
within a few paces of you, without losing sight of you.
When you leave, she walks in front of you, and you
follow her, for she will conduct you into a quiet side-
street where you will find a closed cab, the driver of
which is *always an Annamite.*   The *nay* is near by,
and on the look-out for the police.   You enter the cab
with the little girl.   The little boy sits on the box, by
the side of the driver.   A drive of an hour will cost
you a piaster for the little wretches, and half a piaster
for the driver.   Of course, you are driven outside Saigon,
generally to the Botanical Gardens which are open night
and day, and the cab will take you back to your house,
if the drive has fatigued you.

If you want a whole night with the damsel, the

driver will conduct you, if you ask him, to a hut in
one of the suberban villages. These villages are not
"in the district" of the European police, and are only
looked after by the rural police of the commune, so
the proprietors of these hospitable hovels are never
disturbed. You will find a table laid, and provisions
at reasonable prices, and you can be served with
coffee, tea, or opium, with all the required apparatus
for smoking. But take care of your purse, for you
will be lucky if you find it in your pocket when you
wake up the next morning.

The Boy of the Present Day. The boy's morals
have not changed, but the fear of the police has led
him to take some extra precautions. He no longer
runs the risk of prowling about the streets of Saigon,
but has retired to the villages, and established the
centre of his operations in those hospitable cottages
of which I have just spoken, and also in the clandestine gambling dens, which, having been hunted down
by the European police, have now deserted Saigon.
It is in these places that the few remaining admirers
of depraved practices must seek him. They need only
take the trouble to drive out to these villages, and
they need be under no apprehensions that the villagers
will pay any attention to the comings and goings of
a few debauchees. The moment that you open your
purse-strings, the Annamite will be ready to display
unlimited indulgence to other people's vices. In this
respect his notions of liberty are wide.

The Native Collegian. I will conclude by noticing
one more category of young "amateurs", who were
almost unknown in old Cochin-China. These are the

pupils of the large French College of Saigon, and the French schools of the interior.

In the time of the mandarins, young men, who received an education above the average, might compete in the public examinations, and if they passed, obtain employment as " men of letters". Nowadays, when they have been taught the elements of primary instruction,—when they know how to speak French passably, and can write, somehow or other, French and Annamite in *coggnu* (phonetic characters)—when they are acquainted with the four rules of arithmetic, and a smattering of history and geography,—they are turned out at seventeen or eighteen years of age, but not even the most unimportant place is offered them. The most intelligent become interpreters in the law-courts. The others,—like Jérôme Paturot,—wander about the streets, looking for a place of some kind. They must live somehow. In the evening, like Diogenes, but without his lantern, they seek for a man. The absence of the lantern, and the change in costume, are the only differences between them and the *boy* of old days;—they are just as much wanting in moral sense, and capable of the same turpitude.

They wander about the quarters in which the native houses of prostitution are situated, ready to serve as guides, interpreters, assistants, and, if need be, associates. They extol the qualities of the merchandise, and, for a fair and moderate price, will acquaint the women with your habits and customs.

Woe betide the European green-horn who is caught in their snares! He will be bombarded with letters demanding employment, and if they gain admittance into your house in any capacity—as secretary, clerk, amanuensis, or what not—you will soon be inevitably robbed. In whatever hiding-place you conceal the key of your cash-box, they will be sure to find it. If you carry it about you, take care not to forget and leave it in your clothes. Your *boy*, too, will act as accomplice to the thief. When he has robbed you, he will not run away,—he is not such a fool. But if you threaten to give him in charge, he will reply that he also will prefer a complaint against you, for you "abused his virtue". The most simple method of avoiding a scandal,—which would not bring back the stolen money,—is to say nothing, and turn the thief out of your house, for if you act otherwise, he will not fail to bring a shameful charge against you; and when the case is heard, an Annamite lawyer (there are some who have taken their diploma in France) will be ready to abuse you in the heartiest manner. [1]

EXCURSUS TO CHAPTER VIII.

Homosexuality among Tramps in America.

There is much to be said on this subject. Every *hobo* (genuine tramp) in the United-States knows what "unnatural intercourse" means, and about every tenth man practises it, and defends his conduct. Boys are

[1] Strangers arriving in Tangiers are assailed, before they have had time to disembark, by the importunities of hotel touts, who at the same time proffer their services as interpreters and "guides" to anywhere and anything. If the unwary accept these offers, they will be led in the evening to some unwholesome den to see the *danse du ventre*, vilely executed, and woe betide the unhappy man who is enticed to ascend to the upper regions, where he is almost sure to get a splendid dose of syphilis besides being mulcted of dollars right and left by guide & Co., all combined for the same nefarious purpose.

The writer has seen the above-mentioned dance far better and more lasciviously performed for two sous in a booth on the Place de la République in Paris.

the victims of this passion. The tramps gain possession
of these boys in various ways. A common method
is to stop for awhile in some town, and gain acquaintance with the slum children. They tell these children
all sorts of stories of "life on the road", how they can
ride on the railways for nothing, shoot Indians, etc.,
and they choose some boy who specially pleases them.
By smiles and flattering caresses they let him know
that the stories are meant for him alone, and before
long, if the boy is a suitable subject, he smiles back
just as slily. In time he learns to think that he is
the favourite of the tramp, who will take him on his
travels, and he begins to plan secret meetings with
the man. The tramp, of course, continues to excite
his imagination with stories and caresses, and some
fine night there is a boy less in the town. On the
road the lad is called a "prushun", and his protector
a "jocker" The majority of "prushuns" are between
ten and fifteen years of age, but I have known some
under ten and a few over fifteen. Each is compelled by
hobo-law to let his jocker do with him as he will,
and many, I fear, learn to enjoy his treatment of them.
They are also expected to beg in every town they
come to, any laziness on their part receiving very
severe punishment.

How the act of unnatural intercourse takes place is
not clear. From what I have personally observed I
should say that it is usually what they call "leg
work" (intercrural), but sometimes *immissio penis in
anum*, the boy in either case lying on his stomach.
I have heard terrible stories of the physical results to
the boy of anal intercourse.

One evening, near Cumberland, Pennsylvania, I was
an unwilling witness of one of the worst scenes that

can be imagined. In company with eight hoboes, I was in a freight-car attached to a slowly moving train. A coloured boy succeeded in scrambling into the car, and when the train was well under way, he was tripped up and " seduced " (to use the hobo euphemism) by each of the tramps. He made almost no resistance, and joked and laughed about the business as if he had expected it. This indeed appears to be the general feeling among the boys when they have been thoroughly initiated. At first they do not submit, and are inclined to run away or fight. Even little fellows under ten have told me this and I have known them to wilfully tempt their jockers to intercourse.

CHAPTER IX.

My visit to Tonquin.—Anthropological characteristics of the Tonquinese race. — The Muongs, and the Xas, or Quans.— The Chinese, aud the Tonquinese-Chinese half-breeds.—A few words concerning the importance of the Chinese element in Tonquin.— Chinese piracy.—Manners, habits, customs, religion, etc., of the Tonquinese.—Moral characteristics, and forms and perversions of carnal lusts.— The European Colony, and its morality.

My Visit to Tonquin. I lived a little less than two years in Tonquin, a good long time after my return from Cochin-China. I was able, however, owing to the experience acquired in the last mentioned Colony, to turn my short visit to good account.

Anthropological Characteristics of the Tonquinese. The Tonquinese ascended from Central Annam towards the North, as the Cochin-Chinese descended from the same place to Cochin-China. They conquered, and drove back into the mountains, the native races of the Muongs, Xas, or Quans. At the time when we came to Tonquin, the Chinese had also come down from the North to conquer the land in their turn.

It would therefore be but natural that we should find almost the same anthropological characteristics in two peoples of the same race, who differ from one another as little as a Languedocean does from a native of Avignon, or a Provençal.

The observations I made in Tonquin did but confirm those I had previously made in Cochin-China, so that I shall note here only the differences, where they occurred. Moreover, I found at Tonquin, a number of old military Inspectors from Cochin-China, who declared that the Tonquinese showed the same moral qualities, and had the same customs, habits, etc., as the Cochin-Chinese. They are, besides, ruled by the same central Government of Hué, and use the same code of laws—the Gia-Long.

The Tonquinese is bigger, more robust, and better proportioned than the Cochin-Chinese; he is also much taller.

This is due to the influence of a climate in which the temperature descends below 68° F. in winter, and is only 75° F. in spring, whereas at Saigon the average temperature of those two seasons in 80½° F., or only 3½° below the average of the summer. The head of the Tonquinese is not so big, and the face less prognathous. The forehead is low, the limbs still slender, but the chest is more developed. The skin is a trifle whiter, but the mucous surfaces are absolutely of the same colour. The genital organs of both sexes are perhaps a little more developed, but their comformation is the same. In short it may be said that the Tonquinese is the elder brother of the Southern Annamite, but simply a little more robust, The Tonquinese woman is prettier than the woman of Lower Cochin-China, and you do not meet with pot-bellied children, as you do at Saigon. The race is incontestably finer.

The Muongs. The Muongs appear to represent the autochthonous race. Their anthropological characteristics are those of the Moys of Cochin-China, but they are stronger, and more intelligent, and although they have been driven back to the woods and the mountains, their number, which is nearly four hundred thousand, enables them to resist with more success the Giao-Chi. I have met some specimens of the race, in the neighbourhood of Ninh-binh; they are civilized, and divided into tribes under patriarchs, like the tribes of ancient Israel. On the upper waters of Red River, the Muong is more savage, and more resembles his degraded brother, the Moy of Cochin-China. The Muong lives by hunting, rearing cattle, and working in the forests.

He is brave, and uses, both in the chase and war, small poisoned arrows, shot out of a short cross-bow, which, however, has a good range; with this weapon they defended themselves against the matchlocks and flint guns of the Annamites. These last, finding they could not exterminate their enemies, brought them into subjection, and make them pay tribute. According to the traveller, Villeroi d'Auges, the Muongs have singular funeral customs; they enclose the body in a trunk of a tree, and place it in the hut of the nearest relative of the deceased, before confiding it to the earth.

The Moys and Muongs, being branches of the same race, and closely related, I refer the reader to what I have said regarding the characteristics, manners, etc., of the former.

The Xas, or Quans. These are savages, whose ancestors descended from the high lands of Laos, and who inhabit the mountainous district to the north of Tonquin. They talk a peculiar language, and they wear cotton drawers, a shawl of bright colours, and a kind of cap on the head. I possess very little information about this race, and I have never seen a specimen.

The Chinaman, and the Chinese Half-breed at Tonquin. The Chinese of Tonquin are identically the same as those who have emigrated to Cochin-China, but they are much more numerous, and in the regions of Cao-bang, Lang-son, and Lao-kay form the majority. The Chinaman often marries a native woman, and compels his companion to adopt his religion, his manners and customs, and even eat the same food, and wear the same clothes, as the children of the Celestial Empire. Half-breeds are met with in the coast-provinces, and I saw a good many at Hanoi. They are quite as intelligent as the Minhuongs of Cho-lon, but taller and more vigorous. The children of the Chinese follow their father's example and despise their compatriots, and even their mothers.

Before the arrival of the French, the Celestials had already invaded the land, and were slowly but surely transforming it into a conquered country. They had, undeniably, all the trade, and their language was driving out the native tongue. The French arrested this progress, and thus came into rivalry with a nation of three or four hundred millions of inhabitants. Time alone will show whether France has not been imprudent, in extending her conquests to the frontiers of China.

Chinese Piracy. The Chinese have always considered the Tonquinese as beings of an inferior race, only fit to be taxed and worked without mercy. The method of conquest of this old civilized nation — perhaps the oldst civilized nation in the world—has never changed, and still consists of the pillage, ruin, and devastation of the conquered country,—a method identical with that of the Romans, in regard to the peoples of Western Asia (Persia, Assyria, etc.) before the Christian era, and of the Europeans before the modern era.

Chinese pirates infest the Gulf of Tonquin, the coast of Hainam, the mouths of the Delta, and the islands of the coast. The bars, placed by the natives at the mouths of the rivers, have never been able to stop the Chinese junks. These pirates act much the same as the old Normans, who used to disembark, attack the villages and unprotected towns, massacre all those who resisted, and re-embark, carrying away with them all the marriageable girls and the young men. The French occupation has put some restraint upon these depredations, [1] but not stopped them altogether.

[1] Those people who may imagine that piracy on the high seas is a thing of the past, will read the following cutting from the "*Daily Telegraph*" of August 10th (1897) with some astonishment.

PIRACY IN THE EAST INDIES. ATTACK ON A BRITISH STEAMER.

LLOYD'S agents at Benang, under date of 14th ult., report as follows:

"The British steamer Pegu, owned in Penang, left this port on 7th, bound for Edie and the usual ports up to Olehleh. At Edie she took on board, as passengers, a party of some *ten Achinese, and one woman.* The men, as is customary on that coast, were searched for arms, but none were found, and it is supposed these were *all concealed on the woman's person.* At about seven p.m. on the 9th, when the master, Captain Henry Ross, and the chief engineer, Craigie, were at dinner in the saloon, they were set upon, without warning, by these men. The engineer, though wounded by stabs about the body and arms, managed to escape, and barricaded himself in the engine-room. Captain Ross also escaped from the saloon, but in trying to gain the bridge was overtaken, stabbed fatally, and *disembowelled.*

"The Achinese then turned their attention to the rest of the crew, killed the mate and steersman on the bridge, and five of the passengers, all natives, while five other passengers jumped overboard, and were drowned. In addition to these, *fourteen others of the crew and*

On land, the pirates infest the North and North West provinces, which they have rendered almost a desert. The Black Flags, under their old chief Luu-Vinh-Phuoc, have established themselves along the frontiers of China, and carry off the daughters of the luckless mountaineers, and sell them at Lao-Kay, to Chinese, who come specially from the North on purpose to buy them. The boys are either enrolled in the pirate bands, or held as hostages.

Manners, Customs, and Religion of the Tonquinese. There is very little difference between the Tonquinese, and the Annamites of Cochin-China. The Tonquinese are laborious, and you meet few poor wretches who spend their lives in begging. They are essentially labourers, though some exercise certain industrial professions, and are fishermen, brickmakers potters, etc. The women work a great deal, and, in the country, even cultivate the rice fields along with the men. In the towns they carry on business, and keep shops.

The costume is almost the same as in Cochin-China, except the shoes and sandals of plaited straw, worn in the winter. The women's dress is a little longer, and they tie a *kekouan* (a bright coloured scarf) round the waist, and round the neck.

The huts of the Tonquinese are analogous to those of the Annamites, and their food is the same, and quite as much salted and spiced. Chinese tea is only

---

passengers were more or less severely wounded. Having gained possession of the ship in this way, they proceeded to plunder the strong room, securing about $15,000 in coin, with which they *made good their escape in the ship's boats*, landing on the Achin coast near Simpang Olim.

drunk on feast days, on ordinary occasions a decoction of the native tea, called Hué tea, is used.

The religions are the same in Tonquin as in Annam and Lower Cochin-China; the religion of Confucius, for the educated classes; an altered form of Buddhism, superstitions, and belief in sorcery, for the people. The ceremonies of marriage and burial do not present any essential difference.

Moral Characteristics of the Tonquinese. The moral characteristics of this race greatly resemble those of the Southern Annamite, but this last enjoys some tranquillity under the French rule which has relieved him of the despotism of the Mandarins, whilst the unfortunate Tonquinese has to serve three masters, the old Mandarin, who, being still all powerful, continues his exactions; the French protectorate which defends him as well as it can from the Mandarin and Chinese pirate; and lastly the pirates, who rob him and hold him to ransom. France makes him pay a subsidy, the Mandarin keeps up the *Ka-doui*, which still flourishes in Tonquin, and the Chinese pirate puts the finishing touch, by burning down his house, and cutting off his head, if he shows the least resistance.

The Tonquinese peasant therefore, is gentle, timid, and fearful. He only asks to be left in peace to till his rice field, and earn his daily bread thereby. Being almost without defensive arms, it is impossible for him to defend himself against the incursions of the pirates, and the Chinese regular troops disguised as pirates, and armed with breech-loading rifles. His fate is worthy of interest and pity.

Forms and Perversions of Carnal Passions in

Tonquin. I can but repeat here what I have already said concerning the Southern Annamite, the race being the same, and Chinese civilization having produced the same effects in Tonquin as in Lower Cochin-China.

No appreciable difference is to be found in the forms, or perversions, of sexual intercourse. The *nay* and *boy* flourish at Hanoi and Hai-phong, as they do at Saigon, and are as impudent and depraved, and as great gamblers and thieves. The daylight whore, and the prostitute of the Tonquinese bamboo, practise the same methods, as in Cochin-China.

The Tonquinese are as passionately fond of gambling and opium as their congeners of the South, and are addicted to all the forms of debauchery connected with those habits.

Lasciviousness, gambling, pederasty, and sodomy, are innate in the race. Having definitely stated this fact, let us pass on to another subject.

The European Colony in Tonquin. The number of vicious Europeans addicted to the vice of sodomy, and the passion for opium, was sensibly less than when Cochin-China was first colonized. This is due to the more rapid progress in colonization in Tonquin, which, in less than ten years, had made as much progress as the elder colony did in twenty-five. Many have come here from the other colony, to say nothing of the English and Americans, who have been attracted by the mines of coal and various metals which do not exist in Cochin-China.

White women were implanted at Tonquin very quickly, the climate being decidedly superior to that of Cochin-China, the cool temperature of the winter correcting the anæmic effects of the intense heat of the summer.

Owing to all these causes, sodomy and pederasty have not had time to take very deep root in the European colony, and the number of worshippers of the anal Venus has been greatly reduced, and will be more so in the future.

What I wish chiefly to note here, is the radical difference between the pederasty of the Annamite of the North or the South, and also of the Chinese, and that of the European. It is a general characteristic of the Asiatics, who are lewd, and devoid of moral restraint, whilst on the contrary, in the European races it is of an esoteric character, peculiar to certain individuals, mere erotic idiots, whom the bulk of their fellows have always scorned and loathed as they deserve.

CHAPTER X.

My sojourn in Cambodia.—Anthropological characteristics of the Cambodian.—The organs of generation of the Cambodians.—Foreign races inhabiting Cambodia.—Malays and Chams.—Chinese.—Portuguese.—Annamites.—Social condition of Cambodia.—Decline of the country and of the Kmer race.—Royal prerogatives before the French Protectorate.—The Abbaioureach, and the Abbareach.—The five Ministers.—The Mandarin class.—The oath of the Mandarins.—The middle-classes.—Free men.—Slavery.—Habitations.—Costume.—Food.—Moral characteristics of the Cambodian.—Curious customs attending the castration of animals.—Bravery of the Cambodian.—Hunting the elephant and rhinoceros.—Religion.—The Bonze and the Kmer Pope.—The Somdach-Prea-Sam-Creach.—The idle life of the Bonzes.—The white elephant of Noro-dom.—Cambodian Creeds.—Religious festivals.—Family festivals.—Superstitions.—The Feast of the Dead.—The Festivals of Catsac and the Blessing of the Waters.—Human sacrifices.—Cambodian legislation and justice.—Causes of the decadence of the Kmer race.—The vulgar tongue and the sacred language.

My Sojourn in Cambodia. I lived several months in Cambodia in 1866, during the civil war caused by the struggle between Noro-dom, the reigning king, supported by the French, and his brother Pra-Keo-Pha, his rival for the throne. In order not to exceed the scope of this work, and swell the book immoderately, I shall deal very briefly with all those manners, customs, and habits, which do not directly concern sexual intercourse.

Ciampa, the ancient Kingdom of the Kmers, was formerly very powerful; it comprised the whole of Cochin-China, a part of the Empire of Annam, the present Kingdom of Cambodia, and the provinces of Baltambang and Angkor belonging to Siam. These countries formerly possessed a high degree of civilization, which is still shown by the magnificent monuments and buildings, especially by the fine city of Angkor. The present race of Cambodians, degenerate descendants of the old Kmers, cannot decipher the characters in the ancient language engraved on the monuments of their ancestors.

Anthropological Characteristics of the Cambodians. When one has daily been in the habit of seeing the Annamites, you are astonished to find the Cambodian so much bigger, for he is of the average height of the European of the South. He is better proportioned, and noticeably more robust than the Annamite. His body is square, his shoulders large, his muscular system is well developed, but, nevertheless, you never find the muscles at all salient. The skull is long and oval; the forehead flat or round, the eyelids are not oblique, but the upper eyelid is always pulled down at the corner of the eye; the nose is not so flat as that of the Annamite, and the nostrils less gaping. The mouth is of an average size, the teeth are lacquered, and spoiled by betel chewing. The chin is round, and slopes back, the ears low, and sticking out from the cheeks, but the cheek-bones are not so high, and less projecting than in the Chinese and Annamite races. The hair is generally a dark chestnut, instead of being black as in the Annamite, and is not so stiff, but on the contrary sometimes flat, sometimes slightly wavy. The hair of the Cambodian is not luxuriant. The shoulders are horizontal and large, the chest rounded, the pectoral muscles projecting, the arms strong. The hand and foot are very big, with strong ankles and wrists, and the fingers bony and long,—which is not the case with the Annamites and Chinese. The calves of the legs are well placed, and well developed, and in this respect the Cambodians are the best endowed of all the Indo-Chinese peoples.

The skin is of a very pronounced dark yellow; in those parts exposed to the sun, such as the face, back, hands, and legs, the skin is darker. The general colour of the skin very closely resembles that of the Mulatto, and to an inexperienced observer, there is a certain physical resemblance between a strong Cambodian, and the offspring of the black and white races, but an examination of the organs of generation would show an essential, and characteristic, difference.

The two physicians from whom I have borrowed the greater part of this description, have not examined the genital organs; my special studies have enabled me to supply this deficiency.

[1] The Organs of Generation of the Cambodian.
The organs of generation are much more developed

[1] MAUREL describes them as follows:

"Their buttocks are largely developed; the pubes but little prominent. The Labia majora, thin or medium, and not much garnished with hairs. The Labia minora are long or medium, and are recovered with a pigment layer, if not uniform, at all events pretty generally distributed. The Clitoris is of medium size, the vagina rosy, and the columns well marked. The distance from the anus to the fork varies from 0 in. 78 to

in the Cambodian than in the Annamite. In shape
generally, and dimensions, there is less difference between a Frenchman and a Cambodian, than between
the last mentioned and an Annamite. Though the
skin of the body, the scrotum, and the yard, are
nearly of the same tint as in the Mulatto, the colour
of the mucous surfaces of the gland, and of the vulva
in the woman, are nearly those of the European, but
of a darker red, with a light tint approaching to
yellow, but brighter than the colour of the same parts
in the Annamite, which is more yellowish, and never
of a dirty, reddish brown, as in the mulatto. In the
child, the prepuce is normal, and in the man, few
cases of phimosis occur. The pubes, in both sexes,
is rather scantily covered with hair of a dark chestnut,
and slightly curled. The Cambodian woman plucks
the hair out of the pubes. Her genital organs are
better developed than those of the Annamite woman.
In their general appearance, and in the oblique position
of the vagina, the Cambodian woman approaches nearer
to the Frenchwoman than the Annamite. The Cambodian woman does not suffer, like the last named,
from that distressing complaint, the flowers. The clitoris I found, in some cases, fairly well developed,
and also the lesser lips, but generally speaking the
dimensions of these two parts are normal.

Syphilis is tolerably rare in Cambodia, although
there are some skin diseases. Longevity is not rare

1 in. 18; and that of the neck of the vulva from 0 in. 98 to 1 in. 96;
that from the vaginal orifice to the anterior cul-de-sac from 1 in. 57 to
2 in. 35, and to the posterior cul-de-sac from 2 in. 35 to 3 in. 144."

Maurel. E. *Mémoire sur l'Anthropologie des divers peuples vivant
actuellement au Cambodge. Mémoires de la Société d'Anthropologie
de Paris. II série*, t. IV, *Fascicule* IV. Paris 1893, p. 528.

amongst the Cambodians; you meet many persons of from sixty to eighty years of age, and some even older.

In short, the Cambodian is physically superior to the Annamite, to whom the chignon gives a womanish appearance, whilst the closely cut brush of hair of the Cambodian gives him a more manly aspect.

Foreign Races inhabiting Cambodia.—The Annamites. The Annamite,[1] small and weak as he is, is the conqueror, and the Cambodian, though big and strong, the conquered. He has been slowly driven back from the South to the North by the Annamites, of whom there are nearly a hundred thousand in Cambodia, and who continue gradually to effect the peaceful conquest of the country.

The Malays and Chams. The Malays occupy, principally, the right bank of the Mékong. They much resemble their congeners of Cochin-China. The Chams inhabit the old Ciampa. They are scattered to the North and North West of our colony, towards Tayninh. They are an agricultural and commercial people. I have no particular information concerning them.

The Chinese. They come more especially from

[1] According to *Mondière* (a) the Annamite woman in Cambodia has her genital organs differently formed than the European woman. She has not the wide opening nor the large curving, which in our women results from the elongation of the perinæum; all the parts lying between the *Os Pubis*, the *Os Ischii* and the *Os Coccygis* take the form of a trapezoid. Neither the perinæum nor the exterior parts are arched; there exists a flattening of the large and small labia, and the mutterscheide (*vagina*) appears to be very short so that the orifice of the uterus is quite close to the entry of the vagina.

(a) Mondière—*Monographie de la femme de Cochinchina—Mém. de Soc. d'Anthrop. de Paris*, 1880, p. 250.

Hainam and Fo Kien. They carry on all the chief trade of Cambodia. The half-breeds, which result from their marriages with native women, preserve a good deal of the physical appearance of the Celestials, but —inversely to what happens in Cochin-China and Ton-quin, where they are real Chinese—they have adopted, in Cambodia, the manners and creeds of the Kmers. They are, however, more laborious than these latter, and devote themselves to tilling the land, which they prefer to trade.

The Portuguese. The Portuguese penetrated into Cambodia at about the same time as they did into Siam, where they established themselves in 1516. They have left some descendants, bearers of a string of high sounding names, but none of these descendants can speak the Portuguese language. Physically and morally, they are true Cambodians. The favourite counsellor and factotum of King Noro-dom is a certain "Da Sonza Inigos, etc.", a descendant of a Portuguese.

Social Condition of Cambodia. —Decadence of the Country and of the Kmers. When, in 1863, the French first took Cambodia under their protection, this unlucky country was being pressed by two power-ful neighbours, Annam and Siam, who for two hundred years had been disputing for portions of the land, and wresting in turn from it its most fertile provinces. The Cambodians of to-day are the last remnants of a great people,—the Kmers, with whom religion was all powerful, and whose government was an absolute monarchy.

The power of the Buddhist priests is equal to that of the King, and they are almost absolutely indepeudent. Next to them come the Mandarins, who do no work and ruin the country by their exactions and plundering. Under all these come the poor wretched people, robbed, taxed, and over-worked. There is no intermediate middle-class.

The Royal Prerogatives before the French Protectorate.

The King exercised the most absolute and unlimited power, he was sole governor and sole proprietor of the Kingdom. He appointed all officers, and his decrees were law; he fixed the amount of taxation, and had the power of life and death, the right to pardon, and to revise judgments.

According to Aymonier,[1] a former resident in Cambodia, from whom I have taken many of these details, any Cambodian who thought that he had been denied justice or fair play, could use the *rong deyka*, by going to the palace at the time of the King's audience, and having some blows struck on the tam-tam by an official who was paid four *ligatures* (two-thirds of a piaster) for each stroke. The King then sent to hear the complaint. The *sar tuhk* cost nothing. It sufficed for the complainant to prostrate himself before the King as he was passing, and hold above his head a written statement of his case, which the King then took.

The King is supposed to be of divine origin, and adds to his name such high-sounding qualifications as, " descendant of the Angels and of the God Vishnu; full of virtues as the Sun, precious as crystal, etc., etc." No one may speak to him unless prostrate on hands and knees. No one may dare to wake him when he is asleep, except one of his wives, who is permitted to

[1] AYMONIER—*Cochinchine-Excursions et reconnaissances*, (No. 16, *Globus*, 1885, vol. 48, No. 7).

lightly touch his foot.   It is high treason to put a
hand on his sacred person: Moura, one of the residents, relates concerning this, that in 1874 Noro-dom
was thrown violently out of his carriage, and lay
insensible on the ground.   None of his Mandarins, or
servants, who were present—for the accident happened
in the court-yard of the palace,—dared to help him,
and it was some European, who chanced to be there,
who carried the wounded King into the palace.   The
Queen of Spain, when the country was an absolute
monarchy, enjoyed the same privilege—if it be one.

The Abbaioureach and the Abbareach.   By
these names are designated the king who has abdicated, and the first "Prince of the Blood", or Second
King, who will inherit the crown on the death of the
King.   Next to him comes the *prea voreachini*, or
first "Princess of the Blood".   Each of these members
of the royal family bears rule, by virtue of peculiar
laws and customs, over certain provinces, as appanages
of his or her rank, and governs them absolutely.

The Five Ministers.   Five Ministers,—*the chaufea,*
or Prime Minister and President of the Council; the
ioumreach, or Minister of Justice; the *beang*, or Minister of the Palace and of Finance; the *chakrey*, or
Minister of War, and the *kralahom*, or Minister of the
Navy, rank next below the princes of the royal family.

The Mandarin Class.   Each minister has under
his orders a certain number of mandarins, who are
divided into separate corps.
The mandarins are much more numerous than is
needed for the administration of the country.   They

are insatiable, and ruin, or impoverish by their exactions, the people, who are unable to resist.

The Oath of the Mandarins. Twice a year, the mandarins come to Pnom Penh to drink the "water of the oath"; that is the form of the oath of fealty to the King. On these occasions they receive presents. Those who are absent get no gifts, and are, moreover, fined.

The Middle Class. The middle class is only represented by the Chinese and Malay merchants, who enjoy certain privileges.

Free Men. This caste of the people has liberty, and nothing else,—when they are not obliged to sell themselves to pay their debts. The people have hardly any property, and have to support all the expenses of the King. They are governed by the mandarins, against whom there is no redress. Men of the lower class are thus obliged to choose a patron amongst the mandarins of Pnom Penh. This custom, which is named the *Komlang*, calls to mind the clans of Germany and France in old times.

The more powerful the mandarin is, the more useful does the Komlang become, for nothing is to be feared from any mandarin less powerful than the one chosen for patron. It is true that the Komlang comes expensive, for a quarter of the taxes is claimed by the mandarin, who also requires from his clients a whole host of small services, and makes them escort him whenever he appears in public.

Slavery. Slavery exist in Cambodia. The supply is kept up by man-hunting, which is still carried on at Laos, and concerning which Dr. Harmand has given some curious details. The Cambodians buy their slaves from the Laotians.

Twins, children born deformed, hunchbacks, hermaphrodites, etc., are by law slaves of the King. The children of slaves are themselves slaves, as in old Greece and Rome. Creditors who are not paid become the masters of their insolvent debtors. These latter may be seized, along with their wives and children. They can, it is true, repurchase their liberty, by paying the debt and interest, or they may change their master, if they can find a new master who will pay the debt to the old one.

Also all criminals condemned for rebellion against the royal power, or against the authority of the mandarins, become slaves, as do also their families. The master has full power over his slave, even that of corporal punishment, and the law does not interfere, except in cases of serious injury or death, caused by excessive brutality. In the latter case the master may be condemned to death. There is a curious custom; if a master abuses his female slave, she recovers her liberty and receives compensation, if she can prove her case. In some respects this custom resembles the Mosaic law.

Habitations. The Cambodian huts, like those of the Annamites, are thatched, and built on piles by the banks of the rivers. On account of inundations, the basketwork floor is made movable, and raised whenever the river is in flood. The inhabitants of the same locality mutually assist each other in case of fire, or against thieves and pirates.

Costume. The Cambodian wears on the upper part of his body a short strait vest with buttons, and covers the middle part of his body with a *langouti*, which leaves the legs naked from the knee. The woman wears a *langouti* like the man, but covers it with a long robe, fastened in at the waist, and open at the breast. She covers her breasts with a scarf of silk or cotton, according to her means. The mandarins wear silk robes, and their wives cover their busts by wrapping round them a long silk scarf of some bright colour. Instead of ear-rings, the Cambodian woman wears in her ears small cylinders of ivory, or even wood. Whilst she is a young girl, she wears her black, or dark chestnut, hair long, but when once she is married, she wears her hair like the man, cut short and stubby. This custom, which is exactly the reverse of that of the Annamites, with whom the chignon is common to both sexes, gives the Cambodian woman, a harsh, unfeminine appearance.

Food. The food of the Cambodian is similar to that of the Annamite. Rice, in place of bread, pork— fresh, dry, or salted—vegetables and fruit, form his chief nutriment; his food is also strongly spiced. Water, clarified with a little alum, forms the chief beverage. Tea is not in such general use as amongst the people of the more southern country. A spirit made from rice, called *sra*, is drunk, but much more moderately in Cambodia than in Annam.

Opium is smoked by the rich. A mixture of Indian hemp and tobacco, called *Kanehka*, which produces an effect analogous to that of opium, is also used.

Moral Characteristics of the Cambodians. The people are mild-tempered, indolent, and very fond of amusement. They are passionately fond of boat races,

which are often made the subject of heavy bets, games
of ball, bowls, and kite-flying; they also make crickets
fight till they tear off each other's legs, or head; they
bet upon these insects like the English used to do on
game cocks.

Strange Custom used when Animals are gelded.
When a Cambodian has a buffalo, or domestic ox,
gelded, he makes the operation, says Pavie, the occasion of a certain solemnity. The master informs the
animal of his intention in phrases something like this.
" It is not from any whim, or private pleasure of my
own, that you have to suffer this disagreable operation.
It was the custom of my ancestors, and you ought
not therefore to bear me any ill-will, either in this
life, or in any future life."

Westmarck says:

" A like respect is testified for other dangerous
animals by the hunters who regularly trap and kill
them. When Kafir hunters are in the act of shower-
ing spears on an elephant, they call out, " Don't kill
us, great captain; don't strike or tread upon us, mighty
chief." [1] When he is dead they make their excuses
to him, pretending that his death was a pure accident.
As a mark of respect they bury his trunk with much
solemn ceremony; for they says that: " The elephant
is a great lord; his trunk is his hand." [2]

Amongst some tribes of Eastern Africa, when a
lion is killed, the carcass is brought before the king,

[1] Stephen Kay, *Travels and Researches in Caffraria* (London,
1833), p. 138.
[2] Alberti, *De Kaffers aan de Zuidkust van Afrika* (Amsterdam
1810, p. 95). Alberti's information is repeated by Lichtenstein (*Reisen
im südlichen Afrika*, i. 412), and by Rose (*Four years in Southern
Africa*, p. 155). The burial of the trunk is also mentioned by Kay, l. c.

who does homage to it by prostrating himself on the ground and rubbing his face on the muzzle of the beast.[1] In some parts of Western Africa, if a negro kills a leopard he is bound fast and brought before the chiefs for having killed one of their peers. The man defends himself on the plea that the leopard is chief of the forest, and therefore a stranger. He is then set at liberty and rewarded. But the dead leopard, adorned with a chief's bonnet, is set up in the village, where nightly dances are held in its honour.[2]

"Before leaving a temporary camp in the forest, where they have killed a tapir and dried the meat on a babracot, Indians (of Guiana) invariably destroy this babracot, saying that should a tapir passing that way find traces of the. slaughter of one of his kind, he would come by night on the next occasion when Indians slept at that place, and, taking a man, would babracot him in revenge."[3]

. . . .

Alaskan hunters preserve the bones of sables and beavers out of reach of the dogs for a year and then bury them carefully, "lest the spirits who look after the beavers and sables should consider that they are regarded with contempt, and hence no more should be killed or trapped."[4] The Canadian Indians were equally particular not to let their dogs gnaw the bones, or at least certain of the bones, of beavers. They took the greatest pains to collect and preserve these bones and, when the beaver had been caught in a net, they threw them into the river. To a Jesuit who

[1] Jerome Becker, *La Vie en Afrique*, (Paris and Brussels, 1887), ii. 298 *sq.* 305.

[2] Bastian, *Die deutsche Expedition an der Loango-Küste.* ii, 243.

[3] Im Thurn, *Among the Indians of Guiana*, p. 352.

[4] W. Dall, *Alaska and its Resources.* p. 89.

argued that the beavers could not possibly know what
became of their bones, the Indians replied, " You know
nothing about catching beavers and yet you will be
talking about it. Before the beaver is stone dead, his
soul takes a turn in the hut of the man, who is killing him and makes a careful note of what is done
with his bones. If the bones are given to the dogs,
the other beavers would get word of it and would not
let themselves be caught. Whereas, if their bones
are thrown into the fire or a river, they are quite
satisfied; and it is particularly gratifying to the net
which caught them." [1] Before hunting the beaver
they offered a solemn prayer to the Great Beaver, and
presented him with tobacco; and when the chase was
over, an orator pronounced a funeral oration over the
dead beavers. He praised their spirit and wisdom.
" You will hear no more," said he, " the voice of the
chieftains who commanded you and whom you chose
from among all the warrior beavers to give you laws.
Your language, which the medicine men understand
perfectly, will be heard no more at the bottom of the
lake. You will fight no more battles with the otters,
your cruel foes. No, beavers! But your skins shall
serve to buy arms; we will carry your smoked hams
to your children; we will keep the dogs from eating
your bones, which are so hard. [2]

[1] *Relations des Jésuites*, 1634, p. 24, ed. 1858. Nets are regarded
by the Indians as living creatures who not only think and feel but also
eat, speak, and marry wives. Lagard, Le Grand Voyage du Pays des
Hurons, p. 256. (p. 178 *sq.* of the Paris reprint, Librairie Tross, 1865).
S. Hearne, *Journey to the Northern Ocean*, p. 329 *sq.*; *Relation des
Jesuites.* 16, 36, p. 109; *ib;* 1639, p. 95.

Charlevoix, *Histoire de la Nouvelle France*, p. 225; Chateaubriand,
Voyage en Amérique, p. 140, *sq.*

[2] Chateaubriand, *Voyaye en Amérique*, pp. 175, 178. They will not

Food is prepared, also a bottle of *sra*, a gourd, a fine fat cock, and some pieces of the trunk of a banana tree, to which are attached areca nuts and betel. After an invocation to the *prah pisnoukar*, or Genius, of Industry and Commerce, the gelder performs the operation, and receives as his reward the *sra*, the cock, and the gourd.

Bravery of the Cambodians. The Cambodian is courageous, and uses with effect the few worthless guns, with no butts, which he possesses, and sticks of hard wood, of from eight to ten feet in length, which in his hands, become terrible weapons. He does not fear death. With nothing but these primitive arms he opposed, in 1866, our rifled guns, and in 1885-86, the Gras rifle of the French and Annamite sharpshooters. If he has been conquered by the Annamite it is because,—though more vigorous and quite as brave as the latter,—the military organization is not so perfect.

Hunting the Elephant and Rhinoceros. The Cambodian hunters, armed with wretched flintlock, or matchlock, guns, or even with nothing but sticks, hunt the elephants, rhinoceroses, wild boars, and wild bulls, which abound in the forests of Cambodia. Elephant hunting is very dangerous work: the animal is shot with a poisoned arrow fired out of a gun.

" To hunt the rhinoceros requires great courage," says M. Moura, a former resident in Cambodia. " Four or five skilful hunters meet together, armed with long

let the blood of beavers fall on the ground, or their luck in hunting them would be gone.

Relations des Jésuites, 1633 p. 21. Compare the rule about not allowing the blood of kings to fall on the ground, vol. i, p. 179 *sq*.

bamboos hardened in the fire. They discover the trail of the rhinoceros, and when they perceive the animal, advance towards it. When the rhinoceros sees the hunters close to its lair, it charges open-mouthed, and the men push the long bamboos, with which they are armed, deep down its throat. Having done this the hunters bolt, and climb up trees, and the wounded animal soon falls exhausted from loss of blood. Then the hunters come down, and finish it."

It must be acknowledged, that only men who are really brave would dare to attack a rhinoceros with no better weapons than bamboo sticks hardened in the fire.

Religion. The religion of the Cambodians is Buddhism, but disfigured by numerous superstitions foreign to the doctrine of the founder, Cakya Mouui, and more especially by the worship of ancestors a form common to all the people of China, and Indo-China.

Mr. Edward Tylor, in his fascinating work devotes many pages to this interesting subject. [1] The following illustrates, in a special manner, the remarks we have made, and although the passage is somewhat long, we take leave to quote it, on account of its importauce:

"It is quite usual for savage tribes to live in terror of the souls of the dead as harmful spirits. Thus Australians have been known to consider the ghosts of the unburied dead as becoming malignant demons. New Zealanders have supposed the souls of their dead to become so changed in nature as to be

[1] *Primitive Culture*: Researches into the Development of Mythology, Philosophy, Religion, Language, Art and Custom, by EDWARD TYLOR, D.C.L., etc.; *Reader in Anthropology in the University of Oxford* (2 vols—3rd edit. London, 1891).

malignant to their nearest and dearest friends in life; the Caribs said that, of man's various souls, some go to the seashore and capsize boats, others to the forests to be evil spirits: among the Sioux Indians the fear of the ghost's vengeance has been found to act as a check on murder; of some tribes in Central Africa it may be said that their main religious doctrine is the belief in ghosts, and that the main characteristic of these ghosts is to do harm to the living. The Patagonians lived in terror of the souls of their wizards, which become evil demons after death; Turanian tribes of North Asia fear their shamans even more when dead than when alive, for they become a special class of spirits who are the hurtfullest in all nature, and who among the Mongols plague the living on purpose to make them bring offerings. In China it is held that the multitudes of wretched destitute spirits in the world below, such as souls of lepers and beggars, can sorely annoy the living; therefore at certain times they are to be appeased with offerings of food, scant and beggarly; and a man who feels unwell, or fears a mishap in business, will prudently have some mock-clothing and mock-money burnt for these 'gentlemen of the lower regions'.

"Notions of this sort are widely prevalent in Indo-China and India; whole orders of demons there were formerly human souls, especially of people left unburied or slain by plague or violence, of bachelors or of women who died in childbirth, and who henceforth wreak their vengeance on the living. They may, however, be propitiated by temples and offerings, and thus have become in fact a regular class of local deities. Among them may be counted the diabolic soul of a certain wicked British officer, whom native worshippers in the Tinnevelly district still propitiate by offering at his grave the brandy and cheroots he loved in life.

" India even carries theory into practice by an actual manufacture of demons, as witness the two following accounts. A certain brahman, on whose lands a kshatriya raja had built a house, ripped himself up in revenge, and became a demon of the kind called brahmadasyu, who has been ever since the terror of the whole country, and is the most common village deity in Kharakpur. Toward the close of the last century there were two brahmans, out of whose house a man had wrongfully, as they thought, taken forty rupees; whereupon one of the brahmans proceeded to cut off his own mother's head, with the professed view, entertained by both mother and son, that her spirit, excited by the beating of a large drum during forty days, might haunt, torment, and pursue to death the taker of their money and those concerned with him. Declaring with her last words that she would blast the thief, the spiteful hag deliberately gave up her life to take ghostly vengeance for those forty rupees. By instances like these it appears that we may trace up from the psychology of the lower races, the familiar ancient and modern European tales of baleful ghost-demons. The old fear even now continues to vouch for the old belief.

" Happily for man's anticipation of death, and for the treatment of the sick and aged, thoughts of horror and hatred do not preponderate in ideas of deified ancestors, who are regarded on the whole as kindly patron spirits, at least to their own kinsfolk and worshippers."

Brahminism has also left many traces on the religion of Cambodia.

Sir John Bowring who was governor of Hong Kong and personally visited Siam and the adjacent countries, has some pertinent observations regarding the princi· ples underlying the Religious practices of these peo ples: [1]

"The Buddhist, whose contemplations lead their thoughts into calculations of infinite ages, as connected with the incarnations of the Divinity,· have sought to convey notions of eternity by images in which the fancy is made the handmaid to speculations the most adventurous. For example, they teach that, in order to estimate the ages needful for all the transmigrations which are preliminary to the creation of a Buddha, you are to fancy a granite rock of enormous extent, which is to be visited once in a hundred thousand years by a celestial spirit clad in light muslin robes, which should just touch the rock in flitting by; and that until by the touch of the garment, which must remove an infinitesimal and invisible fragment of the stone, the whole stone should be reduced in successive visitations to the size of a grain of sand, the period of transmigrations of a Buddha would not be completed. Again, the priests say, so many must have been those transmigrations, that there is no spot on earth or ocean which you can touch with the point of a needle where Buddha has not been buried in some form or other during the incalculable period of his transitions from one to another mode of existence. So, the descent into one of the lesser hells of Buddhism is said to occupy three thousand years, and the same period is required to

[1] See "*The Kingdom and People of Siam;* with a narrative of a mission to that country in 1855 (2 vols) London, 1857. Sir John was a clever linguist, and a man of wide and comprehensive study. It will be remembered that he occupied the post of plenipotentiary in China.

mount again from its abyss,—this being the penalty of a minor offence; the greater crimes demand a proportionate era for their purgation or punishment.

As regard the ultimate disposal of man after he has passed through his various transmigrations, and reaches a state of *Nirvani* (Pali) or *Nishvan,* there seems no small variety of opinion as to what is to be understood by that state of anticipated blessedness, which some call annihilation or extinction, others repose, others complacency, and some infinite felicity, be that felicity what it may.   But it is given to none to penetrate into the darkness beyond the grave; " it doth not yet appear what we shall be;" "eye hath not seen nor ear heard" the pleasures in store for the virtuous: and if we, to whom so much has been revealed, but from whom so much more has been concealed, are but wanderers in mists and clouds when we follow the dead into the regions unexplored, we ought not to wonder that others less enlightened, less instructed, should be more at a loss than ourselves.

To be entirely disconnected from the world is represented to be the most exalted stage of mortal virtue: so, one of the highest acts of merit, and which more than any advances the devotee towards final absorption (Nirvana), is the sale of all his property, and his own person, and the dedication of the proceeds to acts of charity.   Several instances of such self-sacrifice are recorded in the Pali writings.

In the teachings of ancient sages who have become the honoured among nations, there will be found much more of resemblance and affinity than would be anticipated, from the exercise of independent thought emanating from the minds of men placed in situations extremely remote from and unlike one another.   The

Book of Job contains much of Platonic wisdom, and the words of Confucius and Gaudama might well have fallen from many a Western philosopher.

"Attach not yourself," says Gaudama, "to the pleasures of this world; they will fly from you in spite of yourself. Nothing in the universe is really your own. You cannot preserve it unchanged, for even its form is perpetually varying." "Be not the slave of love or hatred, but learn insensibility to the vicissitudes of life; be indifferent to praise and blame, to rewards and persecutions. Endure hunger and thirst, privations, diseases, and even death, with the tranquillity of an imperturbable spirit."

The Bonze. [1] The bonze is called the lord priest (*luc sang*). Priesthood is rather a temporary function, than,—as in the Indian priest—an ineradicable qualification, for, in Cambodia, the bonze may quit the religious order at any time. A slave may even become a bonze, and in that case he regains his liberty. The vows taken by the bonze not being necessarily for life, young mandarins who aspire to public offices, and even the princes of the royal blood, pass a year in holy orders. The *somdach-Préa-sang-Creach,* or head of the religious orders, is a very high personage, and is equal to the King, as the Pope is to European monarchs. The bonzes are independent of the mandarins, and are

[1] It may interest readers to learn that "bonze" is given in the 1897 edit. of Ogilvie's "*Imperial Dictionary*" as a corruption of the Japanese word *busso*, u a pious man." It is European for a priest of the religion of Fo or Buddha in Eastern Asia, particularly in China, Burmah, Tonquin, Cochin-China and Japan. The state monastic of celibacy in which they live approximates them to the monks of the Roman Catholic Church. There are also female bonzes, whose position is analogous to that of nuns in Europe.

only amenable to a Council of Discipline, consisting of the King, the King who has abdicated, the " second King", and the Queen Mother. The composition of this Council will suffice to show what a high position the bonze holds in Cambodian society.

Notwithstanding all the precepts which are supposed to be protective of personal purity, the paintings seen in the Buddhist temples are often of a licentious and libidinous character.

The persons and property of the priesthood are removed from the general action of the law. There is a sort of ecclesiastical court, presided over by a bonze of high rank, in which the sacred code, written in the Pali language, constitutes the rule of judgment, in precisely the same way as the text of the Koran becomes the paramount law in the Superior courts of the Mussulmans. Within certain limits, a priest may both inherit and bequeath property; but its possession does not emancipate him from those privations to which he is condemned by his religious vows. In case of intestacy, the property falls to the convent of which the bonze was an inmate.

A priest is not allowed to take an oath. His affirmative answer to a question is received when he raises his fan; his negative is conveyed by letting the fan drop.

As the priesthood, as an institution, is more dovetailed into the social system than in any part of the world, no jealousy seems created by its laziness, no resistance is exhibited to its claims. It is supported by the spontaneous offerings of the whole people, in whose minds *merit* and its recompenses are constantly associated with reverence for the functions of the servitors of Buddha, the depositaries of his will and the expounders of his teachings. Among the priests will be found some subtle polemics, who are by no means unwilling to enter the fields of controversy. The Mohamedans aver that a few of the priesthood have recognized the authority of the Prophet, but the cases must be very rare.

The police to which the *Phra* are subjected is superintended by one of the princes, who has a number of commissaries, who are authorized to bring them up for judgment. On the proof of their delinquencies, they are unfrocked, flogged with the rattan, or condemned to prison, or other penalties, according to the gravity of their offences.

The Life of the Bonze. He perfoms no manual labour, and, beyond attending the classes in Buddhist theology, for the instruction of aspirants to religious orders, does not do anything but collect alms. With his head completely shaved, and clad in a costume of yellow cotton ornamented with embroidery, this pious do-nothing wanders through the villages and towns, from daybreak till noon, begging rice, fish, fruit, tobacco, and betel, all of which he jumbles together in a sanctified tin saucepan, which he carries under his arm. At eight o'clock, and at noon, he takes his meals in the convents, but, if he observe the rules, he ought to fast all the evening. They are but poorly instructed; they must mutually confess their sins to each other once a fortnight.

The principal commandments they have to keep, are, according to M. Moura: 1st, to kill nothing that has life, not even lice or fleas; 2nd, not to steal; 3rd, not to marry, or commit fornication; 4th, not to tell lies; 5th, to fast after noon; 6th, not to get drunk; 7th, not to sing or dance; 8th, to dress plainly; 9th, not to sit nor lie in any place that is high (*sic*); 10th, not to possess gold or silver.

Noro-dom's White Elephant. The Cambodian, like the Siamese, holds the white elephant in great veneration. Former kings were obliged, as a mark of their vassalage, to send to Siam all animals of this description captured in Cambodia, but the French protectorate put a stop to this custom. In 1867, I saw at Pnom-Penh, a white elephant which belonged to Noro-dom.

It will be remarked that the Kings of Cambodia, like the old Hebrew Kings, though the absolute heads of civil government, have no religious power, and are confronted by a powerful theocracy.

Creeds and Beliefs in Cambodia. The Cambodians attach great importance to the alms which they give to the bonzes, and they also often undertake the construction of a pagoda at their own expense. Acts like these, they believe, receive their reward in a future life, and hasten "the eternal annihilation", or Nirvana. They admit the immortality of the soul, and metempsychosis is a belief sanctioned by their moral law. There is a great difference between the Cambodian, who is a pious believer, and the Annamite, who is a doubter and a materialist. Like the Annamite, however, the Cambodian believes in genii, devils or demons, and ghosts. These last can be driven away by the *arac* (the spirit of some old dead friend), the protector of the family, who is worshipped as such, and to whose shade the flowers of the frangipanni are offered. He is invoked through the agency of old witches, who make incantations, and have prophetic inspirations like the sibyl of Cumea.

Religious Festivals are very numerous amongst the Kmers. The principal is the Col Chnam, the first day of the year, similar to the Annamite *Tet*, which is celebrated, as in Annam, by sacrifices and public rejoicings. The religious and believing Cambodian also gives offerings to the bonzes. In families, the children offer their parents the water of purification, as the Romans did, and slaves wash the bodies of their master. There is a holiday, called the *thngay-sel*, at each change of the moon; those of the new and full moon are the most solemn.

Fête days are celebrated by visits to the pagodas, and offerings to the bonzes. As may be imagined, these latter do not let themselves be forgotten.

The bonzes celebrate with great pomp, in their pagodas, the full moon in the month of May, the anniversary of the death of Buddha. Families give feasts on this occasion, and at these the bonzes occupy the seats of honour.

In February also, the bonzes walk in procession through the fields,—a ceremony samewhat akin to the Catholic "rogations",—and call down the blessings of heaven on the fruits of the earth. The farmers and labourers then provide copious repasts for the worthy bonzes.

The bonzes also keep, in the rainy season, a kind of Lent, called Prasa, in memory of the day of rest of Cakya Mouni, who devoted this season to giving religious instruction to his disciples. In each pagoda, a huge candle, called the *Tien-Prasa*, is kept constantly burning, like the Easter candles in the Catholic churches.

Family Festivals. At the beginning of the Prasa, every family offers a sacrifice to its ancestors, but in this ceremony the bonzes do not participate. Besides this worship of ancestors, the Kmers render homage to the *Neac-ta,* which, like the genii of the Annamites, are their household gods. These divinities are entrusted by the god *Indra* (Prea la) with the care of villages, houses, etc. Their aid is invoked in case of epidemic diseases, and great public calamities.

Superstitions. I have already said that the Kmer is very superstitious. Their doctors are crassly ignorant of medical science, and, from that very fact, each doctor is a sorcerer, and practises the counterpait of those magical spells so well-known to our ancestors in the Middle Ages. The doctor (*cru*) makes a clay figure, and buries it in some distant spot. Then he orders the demon, who is the cause of the disease, to leave the body of the patient, and pass into the clay figure. The screech-owl, and other night-birds, are reputed to bring ill-luck. The credulous Kmer has faith in talismans that are to render him invulnerable to bullets, make an enemy's gun miss fire, or drive away ghosts. There are even some charms which were to make wings grow, and waft the happy possessor up to heaven. I was gravely assured, however, that the art of weaving this particular spell had been unhappily lost. But, as there can be concocted from the tusks and whiskers of a tiger, a charm, which it is asserted,—for I have never tried it,—will act as a deadly poison, it seems a pity that such a beneficent invention as a talisman which would cause wings to sprout, should not have been also preserved.

The Kmers also believe in auguries and dreams, and even go to the cemeteries to sleep upon the graves of dead friends, in the belief that their dreams will be inspired by the spirits of the departed.

The Festival of the Dead takes place on the last day of the September moon, and is called the *pchum ben*. Crowds of people assemble together in the pagodas, and bring with them quantities of food of all sorts, for the dead, who, on this day, have Buddha's permission to leave hell.

It may be remarked, that this belief in hell is common to Buddhism, and to many other religions which have borrowed the same idea. According to M. Moura, from whom I have already quoted, the dead are, as may indeed be supposed, invisible, and the festival lasts three days. On the third day, the bonzes send away the spirits of the departed, with these words: "Depart to the land and to the fields where you reside; to the mountains, and beneath the stones which serve you for houses. Go! return! In this month, in all future years, your sons and grandsons will remember you, and you will return to them."

The Festivals of the Cat-sac, and the Blessing of the Waters. The Kmers also keep two other festivals, which are probably remnants of Brahminism: first, the *Cat-sac*, when the top-knot of children of from eleven to thirteen years of age is cut, when family feasts are held, and the bonze is called upon to give his blessing, and, second, the Blessing of the Waters, the occasion of a long religious ceremony on the part of the bonzes.

There is still in Cambodia a special caste, called Bakou, who pretend to be descendants of the old Brahmins, some of whose customs they still retain. They enjoy the prerogative of guarding the royal sword, wear their hair long, and are free from taxes, and compulsory labour.

Human Sacrifices. The terrible custom of offering to the divinity, as an expiatory sacrifice, human
beings, was continued almost until our own days.
Only criminals condemned to death are now sacrificed;
they are executed under the protecting tree of the
province, so that the punishment of a malefactor becomes
a sacrifice to the tutelary genii. This custom is similar
to that of the ancient Gauls and Britons, who used to
put to death condemned criminals, when the Druids
ordered human sacrifices to be made; but our ancestors
used to offer themselves voluntarily, if no criminals
were forthcoming.

Cambodian Legislation and Justice. The Cambodian code is very severe on unfortunate culprits,
who are divided into five classes, according to the
importance of their crimes; the first class comprises
treason against the State, or the King, or sacrilegious
offences concerning the bonzes, or the religion. This
calls to mind the edict of St. Louis, King of France,
ordaining that blasphemers should have their tongue
burned with a hot iron.

For punishing criminals, there are twenty-one methods
of execution, all of horrible cruelty. Amongst them,
I may mention, burning alive (as in the Middle Ages),
the wheel, being cast to wild beasts, flogging, etc.,
which are exclusively reserved for criminals of the
first category.

For the four remaining classes, there are chains,
imprisonment, fines, confiscation of property, and the
punishment of slavery for the guilty person and all
his family.

This atrocious code was applied without any sort of
impartiality, for it included an article by which in the

case of a fine being imposed, the King took one third of the sum, the judges who pronounced the sentence took another third, and the remaining third went to the complainant.

Causes of the Decay of the Kmer [1] Race. We must search for the secret of the decadence of the once famous Kingdom of Ciampa, in the absolute power of the King, the religious despotism of the bonzes, and in bad legislation: this will explain why the Annamite though less civilized than the Kmer, has yet been able to conquer him, and drive him from his native soil.

M. Jacolliot, in his remarkable essays on India, comes to the same conclusion; it is the influence of a bigotry which, from birth to death, enfolds man in its inextricable bonds, which has made the Hindoo a man without patriotism, and rendered his country, ever since the days of Alexander the Great, a prey to every conqueror.

The Kmer Vulgar Tongue. The Kmer is a language with a monosyllabic tendency, and is spoken *recto tono*,

---

[1] Otherwise known as *Çyam-bods* (no doubt Siām or Shan-bods). Forlong believes them to be the original Indian Colonisers who settled down at the head of the delta of the Mekong and around its great inland swampy sea, where flourished Indian arts and religions for some 2000 years. These people were known to other Indians as *Kmirs*, and were principally ophiolaters from Ceylon and the Tamil and Telagu coasts. Arabian sailors called them *Komirs* or *Kh'mars*, thought to mean " Cunning craftsmen " or " Artisans," which their elaborate sculptures and architecture showed they were. But *Kamirs* or *Chamirs* seems to be a corruption of *Tamils*. See similar Dravidian etymologies given by Prof. Oppert in his *Bhārata-Varsa*, here reading as usual *r* for *l*." (See Forlong's work on Comp. Religions, *London*, 1897).

and, consequently, differs completely from the Chinese
and the Annamite *vario tono.*

Francis Garnier, [1] the explorer, asserts that in the
savage tribes, which still exist upon the tops of the
highest mountains, he has discovered the sources of
the primitive language of the autochthones. They
were conquered, at some very remote epoch, by the
Aryans coming from India, who imposed on the conquered people Brahmanism, and themselves formed the
high caste of Brahmins.

The Sacred Language. This theory would seem
to be supported by the fact of the existence of a
sacred language, which is not understood by the common people, and is possessed by only a limited number
of priests and high personages. *Pali*, which is an
Aryan language, forms the basis of this sacred language,
sentences of which are inscribed upon the facades of
the temples of Angkor the Great, and the immense
sculptures, which cover the walls of these temples, are
reproductions of the legends of those sacred books,
the Hindoo Vedas.

The civilization of Cambodia came, therefore, from
India, and the conquest and ruin of the country are
due to Annam, which was pushed on by China. This
conquest of the ancient Kingdom of Ciampa by a less
civilized nation, reminds us of the fall of Roman
civilization, brought about by the Barbarians of the
North, and the invasion of the South by the tribes of
the North of France.

[1] Francis Garnier, was murdered in Cochin-China some ten or
twelve years ago, after rendering incalculable services, often in spite of
his own interests, to France. He reaped the usual harvest—neglect and
indifference till it was too late.

CHAPTER XI.

Sexual intercourse, its forms and perversions among the Cambodians. — The lover as a water-carrier. — Two Kmer proverbs. — Marriage. — Polygamy. — The rank of the first wife. — Adultery and its repression. — Divorce. — Various reasons for divorce. — Reconciliation of divorced couples. — Adoption. — Manners of the Kmer woman. — The life of a young girl. — King Noro-dom's harem. — The royal corps de ballet. — Singing and music. — Manner of copulating. — Perversions of the sexual passion amongst the Cambodians.

Betrothals. A marriage is always preceded by a betrothal. Recourse is first had to a sort of female go-between (of a serious kind), who adroitly sounds the family of the young girl as to their intentions. If these are favourable, three matrimonial agents are sent, and are accompanied by some of the relatives of the aspirant for the hand of the young girl, who bring with them presents. The girl's hand is then supposed to be granted, and the young *fiancé* must enter upon his love noviciate, which consists in carrying water and wood to the house.

According to M. Aymonier's account, on a certain day, previously fixed, the young man repairs to the house of his lady-love's parents, which he first salutes, before ascending the ladder which leads to his future wife's abode. He again salutes as he enters the house, where he is in future to reside, and perform the double duty of servant and sweetheart to the lady of his choice, to whom, by the way, he has never yet spoken a single word. The customs of the country forbid young people of different sexes to meet together, and render necessary a proceeding of the kind described, in order that a young man may pay his court to his future wife.

The amorous water-carrier is at the beck and call of the father and mother of the girl, and the girl herself, and they make him trot about on all sorts of errands, but, as a reward, his sweetheart prepares his food, and his "quids" of betel, and rolls his cigarettes for him. Whether she carries her condescension so far as to give him a light for them, M. Aymonier does not say. An intimacy is established, sooner or later, though, in the beginning, the modest young woman does not dare to leave the house, and sends her lover his quids and cigarettes by the hand of one of her little sisters; when she offers them herself that is considered as an avowal of reciprocated affection.

As a measure of precaution, the youth sleeps in the kitchen, and is thus separated from the chamber of the young woman by the bed-room of her parents.

There are, however, means of circumventing these safeguards of morality and prudence, for, when a courtship lasts a very long time, one or more babies may assist at the wedding of their procreators. This often happens amongst the poorer classes, when the marriage ceremony is long deferred, perhaps for several years.

It should be said, however, that the law recognizes the ceremony of betrothal as a half marriage, and gives the engaged couple certain privileges, though it imposes upon them sundry duties. When a girl is once seduced (that is to say has lost her virginity) the young man cannot draw back out of his engagement.

On the other hand the girl, when she has once accepted a young man, has no longer the right to flirt with, or be courted by, other young men, and, if her infidelity can be proved, she is punished exactly as though she were an adulterous wife. The children proceeding from a too warm courtship are regarded as legitimate.

Two Kmer Proverbs. There are two Kmer proverbs, which are rather amusing, concerning this ceremony of betrothal, and the results which generally spring therefrom. " To leave," says the first, " a young girl alone with a young man, is like entrusting an elephant with the care of a plantation of sugar-canes." [1]

[1] This quaint saying calls to mind a ball-room incident recorded by Burton:—

" To give a taste of 'Mother Damnable's' quality. I had been waltzing with a girl, who, after too much exertion, declared herself fainting. I led her into what would at home be called the cloak-room, fetched her a glass of water, and was putting it to her lips, when the old lady stood at the door. 'Oh dear! I never intended to interrupt you,' she said, made a low bow, and went out of the room, positively, delighted."

We cannot miss the opportunity of contrasting the customs of courtship in France and England. Our Gallic neighbours consider that a girl's reputation is lost if, before marriage, she allows herself *to be alone* with her *fiancé*. In England, on the contrary, sweethearts frequently pass hours, and sometimes a whole day together without the presence of a third person. Climate and character have undoubtedly much to do with this. Your Frenchman wisely thinks it better to keep the " cup from getting broken " than to try and mend it afterwards by an action for " *Breach of Promise.*" Frenchwomen are alive to this, and act on the principle of never trusting a man. Of course, in spite of all their precautions, some do fall into the seducer's trap, (or is it the contrary?) but as a rule, this is only because they wanted to.

It is well-known that the elephant is as fond of sugar-canes as a school-boy is of sugar-sticks. " Never trust hens' eggs to a crow," is the second;—the crow has a reputation of being extremely partial to eggs.

Marriage.—Polygamy. I shall not describe the marriage ceremonies, which are very long and complicated.

Polygamy is practised in Cambodia, but only amongst the rich class of mandarins, for the poor man of the lower classes has enough to do to support only one wife. The Cambodian law allows three legitimate wives, of whom the first (*thom*) is considered as the chief; she has been demanded in marriage, and espoused according to the traditional rites. The second, or " middle wife", is nothing but a legal mistress, for no demand is made to her parents for her hand, and the marriage ceremonies are not performed. Finally, the third wife is simply a concubine, and is generally a young slave, bought from her master by some rich man, who has been captivated by her beauty.

The Position of the First Wife. By a peculiar fiction, the first wife is considered the mother of all the children of her husband, even when they are the offspring of the other wives. Only the mandarins can (on account of the great expense) afford the luxury of several wives.

Adultery, and Its Repression. The penalty for

We may mention that the note re Burton is taken from the 1st vol. of the " Life and Achievements of Sir R. F. Burton by his wife Isabel Burton." This " Life," except in its main outlines, is about as much like the downright Agnostic and spicy story-teller (to his club-friends) as it is to the " man in the moon ".

adultery is not very heavy, and varies according to the rank of the guilty person. It costs much more to seduce the wife of a mandarin, than the wife of a common person. The paramour has only to pay a fine. As to the woman, a singular custom prevails, which recalls, in some respects, the ways of our jovial ancestors. Her face is covered with a basket, and on her ears and round her neck are placed red roses, as a derisive symbol of a modesty which can no longer blush, and then she is led through the streets and obliged to confess aloud the sin of which she has been guilty. With the exception of the rope and the chemise, this is much the same as the confession before the church-doors in the Middle Ages. What is more serious, however, is that the law of Cambodia punishes with the same fine, the gallant who makes a rendez-vous with a married woman, or kisses her, and the procurer who favours these illicit meetings. [1] But though the Cambodian law esteems a mere fine as sufficient penalty for the offence of taking another man's wife, it permits the outraged husband to kill the guilty parties if they are caught *in flagrante delicto*. [2] But, all the same, he is obliged to kill both, for if he should pardon his wife, and kill the paramour, or allow him to escape, and wreak his vengeance on his wife only, he is liable to have to pay a fine,

[1] Cambodian legislation, in punishing equally both the parties guilty of adultery, seems to us to be dictated by a stricter sense of justice than European law, according to which the burden of the penalty falls far more heavily on the woman than on the man.

[2] It has been particularly remarked that French juries, in the Department of the Seine, are generally inclined to extreme indulgence in cases of passional crime, and when death is inflicted on one or both the culprits surprised *in flagrante delicto*, an acquittal is almost certain to be dealt out to the death-doer.

in proportion to his social rank, to the Public Treasury.

If a wife, who has been more or less ill-treated by her husband, runs away, and takes refuge with her parents, they must bring her back to her husband within a month at the latest, or they are liable to be fined.

Divorce exists among the Kmers; a divorce can be obtained if both parties mutually agree to ask for it, —which seems to me a very sensible rule.

A woman who is plagued, ill-treated, or thrashed by her husband, can claim a divorce, especially, if during the time she is so treated, her husband should take a second wife. Such a case is forejudged. If the woman fails to prove her case, she must return to the conjugal domicile, and the husband has even the right to bring her back by force; but if she should stil resolutely refuse to live with him, a divorce is then pronounced.

Various Reasons for Divorce. Another cause for divorce is the prolonged absence of a husband, who does not return at the date fixed. The wife has then the right to demand a divorce, provided that she restore to his family, in the presence of the magistrate, the presents and goods that her husband has given her.

If the man absents himself without any reason, his wife may obtain a divorce after a delay of from nine to eleven months. The time will depend upon how far distant is the place where the fugitive husband is known to be living. But if he should return within the stipulated period, his wife is bound to receive him.

The husband who is absent on legitimate business connected with his trade or profession, and has gone to some distant place, and who neglects to send any tidings of himself for a year or more, is liable to have his wife divorce him.

A delay of three years is accorded if the husband has sent money to his wife, or if he has gone to China. The delay is extended to seven years if it is known that his boat has been taken by pirates, or been shipwrecked. We may compare this with the delay of five years granted by the French law, which in a similar case declares the husband to be dead after the expiration of that time.

Yet another cause for a divorce is a very odd one, and does not, I think, figure in any other code of laws. It is this. When a Cambodian, in a moment of anger, demolishes with a hatchet or cutlass, the conjugal domicile—which, as it is generally made of wicker-work is not a difficult task,—and removes all his property to his parents' house, and resides there himself, even for a period of only twenty-four hours, his marriage can be dissolved. In this case, the wife keeps the wedding presents. It is curious to contrast these various reasons with those regulating divorce in Annam, and it will be seen that there is a great difference in morals between the two nations.

The Reconciliation of Divorced Couples. If a divorced couple become reconciled, and sleep together, the decree of divorce is annulled.

We may mention in passing that the Kmer code recognizes community of property, and separation *a mensa et thoro.* The code also advocates the duty of gratitude on the part of children to their parents, and forbids a judge to receive any plaint from a son bringing an action against his father, for a bill which has been accepted and not paid.

Adoption is also permitted, and encouraged by law, and is not uncommon amongst people of dissimilar ages. It is celebrated by a ceremony at which offerings are made to the spirits. Adopted children are regarded as though they were the real offsprings of the persons adopting them, and are treated the same. When they leave the country, they take farewell of their adopted parents, who offer them betel and arrack at their departure. Generally, they do not forget their adoptive parents and write to them, and send presents. They are forbidden to marry with the daughters of their adopters, although they are not connected with them by blood. This is a very curious moral restriction.

The Manners of the Kmer Woman are much more pure than those of the Annamite woman. With some rare exceptions, Europeans never have anything to do with any of them, except prostitutes who are slaves, and exercise the calling for the benefit of their unscrupulous masters,

The Life of the Young Girl. It may be said that the young girl among the Kmers is watched as carefully as a saucepan of milk on the fire. She is entirely hidden from Asiatic foreigners, and *a fortiori* from Europeans. Sometimes you may see afar a young Cambodian girl going to the well, and wearing a small piece of cloth or cotton on her chignon (girls wear, as we have already said, their hair long), but, as soon as she catches sight of you, she rushes into the hut, where she remains shut up till the stranger is gone. They never appear in public, except at festivals, or to go to the pagoda. On account of these austere customs, prostitution of children, so common in Cochin-China, is unknown in Cambodia, and the Kmers have the right to regard with contempt, the depravity of youth which exists amongst their conquerors.

It may be said, that in Cambodia illegitimate children are almost unknown. The code, however, contains some stringent regulations concerning offences against morals, and a man is punished for seduction in proportion to the difficulty, or ease, he had in effecting his object. Rape is punished very severely, with chains and imprisonment. This Cambodian law resembles, in many points, the law of Moses.

Noro-dom's Harem. King Noro-dom has eleven legitimate wives. The one who is wanting to make up the dozen, is the queen who should occupy the chief rank, and who, in accordance with custom, must always be a princess of the royal blood; her title would be Ac-Kha-Mohé Sey.

He has also an unlimited number of concubines. In appearance, he is dried-up, and stunted, and looks as weak as his subjects look firm and vigorous. The best French brandy, opium, and women, have ruined his constitution. He evidently cannot satisfy all his wives, any more than Solomon could: as the song says

> "However ardent a man may be,
> Though he have the strength of a dozen men,
> If he has to sleep with six hundred wives,
> He will want a holiday now and then." [1]

[1] Our version is not exactly word for word. What translation in verse can be? We therefore think it proper to give the student the French text besides.

> ["Brûlât-on des plus vives flammes,
> S'il faut contenter six cents femmes,
> Quelque soit le tempérament,
> Ça doit gêner sur le moment."]

This verse comes back to my memory some years after I first heard it sung, which was at a music-hall in Saigon in 1889, during my second sojourn there, which was whilst Noro-dom, was on a visit to the Governor General. The European public applied these lines to Noro-dom, and encored them; it does not take much to amuse French people in the Colonies. The prospect of one day having the honour to be admitted to the royal bed must suffice for most of these ladies, for Noro-dom holds strong opinions concerning the privileges of a kingly husband.

The royal harem is contained in a special part of the palace, and the ladies are well and closely watched; no one can be admitted to their apartments without an order from His Majesty. In 1873, King Noro-dom had, it is said, two of his wives, whom he suspected of infidelity, publicly executed along with their supposed accomplices.

The Royal Corps de Ballet. Besides his concubines the King has his theatrical singers and dancers. They all receive a salary of food and money, and have a suite of attendants, and the regulations concerning etiquette, etc., are minutely observed. Noro-dom generally imports his dancing-girls and concubines from Siam; they come to Cambodia when they are about thirteen or fourteen years old. The dance of the royal bayadères is rather a representation than a dance properly so called. The subjects of the ballets are always borrowed from the Hindoo epics, and Buddhic tradition, and represent episodes in the life of Cakya-Mouni.

I assisted at one of these ballets, which was performed under a long rectangular shed, the sides of which being open, permitted the King's faithful subjects

to sit on the ground and witness the royal performance,
The throne is on a platform, in a small building at
the end of the shed. At the King's feet, sits the royal
band, and their music is not wanting in melody, even
to European ears: it does not torture you, like the
horrible Chinese music. One of the instruments is a
sort of harmonica, with bells of silver, and silvered
copper, which makes a very agreeable peal.

Singers and Music. There are also singers who
usually come from Siam, and whose rather tremulous
voices are accompanied by the music of string instruments, a kind of clarionet, or oboe, and the bell-har-
monica just mentioned. From time to time, the heavy
thuds of the tam-tam, and the click of wooden castanets,
punctuate the phrases of the music.

Forms of Copulation used in Cambodia. I
regret to have to confess to the reader that I can give
no precise information on this point, the almost universal
chastity of the women, and the modest reserve of the
Cambodian man, having prevented me from learning
any details of the secrets of the domestic life of this
people.

I may simply say that copulation is practised without
any sort of "tricks", in the classical manner, the
woman lying on her back, and the man on the top of
her. More I could not learn, for the Cambodian is as
silent in these matters as the Annamite is talkative.

**Perversions of Sexual Intercourse amongst
the Cambodians.** I ought also to say in praise of
this people, that, in spite of their decadence, their
manners have remained pure. Prostitutes are to be

found in Cambodia, as everywhere else, but they only practise natural methods, and are not like their southern neighbours, addicted to mouth suction, and they abhor sodomy.

Pederasty has not, in Cambodia, the place of honour that it holds in Cochin-China. There are, it is true, pederasts, or rather passive agents, amongst the poor homeless children who wander about the streets of Pnom-Penh, but they only constitute exceptions to the general rule. When they do consent to commit sodomy, it is with repugnance, and not like the Annamite, who is ready and willing to take either the active or passive part,—whichever is required.

The result of this is, that the Frenchman, who comes from Cochin-China to Cambodia, has to take a native mistress, for he finds neither the "daylight whore", the *nay*, or the *boy*. This is a fresh and evident proof that we did not import these disgusting practices into Cochin-China, since they do not exist in Cambodia, the boundary province of our Eastern colonies, and yet we meet with them again in Tonquin, which is also inhabited by the Cochin-Chinese race.

PART THE SECOND.—AMERICA.

GUIANA—MARTINIQUE.

CHAPTER I.

A short stay at Martinique.—Arrival at Guiana. — Yellow Fever and its preventive treatment. — The White Creole of Cayenne.— Prejudices against colour. — The fashionable world of Guiana.— Hospitality of the Creoles of Cayenne. — The Creole dialect and its uncouthness.—Liveliness of the Creole ladies.—" Lou Tafanari and her potato". — The misadventures of a singer of indecent songs. — Good manners and kindheartedness of the ladies of Cayenne.

A Short Stay at Martinique. After having taken part, as an ambulance surgeon, in the campaign of 1870-71, I was sent, a year or two after that terrible war, to Guiana.

On arriving at Martinique, I heard that yellow fever had broken out at Guiana, which place was then in quarantine. The military detachment, of which I formed part, received orders to disembark at Fort de France. I was thus able to spend three weeks at Martinique, and I also stopped there a fortnight three years later, on my return from Guiana.

To Martinique I shall devote a separate chapter.

Arrival at Guiana. The number of medical men at Guiana being barely sufficient, I was sent to reinforce the medical staff there.

Yellow-Fever and its Preventive treatment. This was the first time I had come face to face with this dangerous disease,—concerning which I intend some day to publish my observations. For the present, I will content myself with saying that, thanks to preventive treatment commenced a week before my departure from Fort de France, I was able to escape five deadly epidemics of yellow-fever,—some at Guiana, and some, later on, at Senegal.

The recipe is very simple, and I give it here for the benefit of any of my readers who may be obliged to stay in a country where yellow-fever prevails.

You take, when you sit down to lunch or dinner, at first two, and increase the dose to three, and finally to five, "pills of Dioscorides";—that is to say take four pills a day the first week, six a day the second week, and ten a day the fourth week.

At the end of the third week you take along with the arsenic, a gramme of iodide of potassium per day, which you drink either in your coffee, or your morning milk.

The action of these two powerful alteratives is as follows. Arsenic is a slow medicine but a powerful tonic, giving strength and muscle, and increasing lung power. It has but one fault, and that is that, in tropical countries, it settles in the liver. Then the iodide of potassium comes in, acts as a marvellously good purifier of the blood, and drives the arsenic out of the liver. Whether it was the effect of this preventive treatment, or some idiosyncrasy in my constitution, I cannot say, but I have attended many cases, and even made post-mortem examinations, without taking the disease.

At the termination of the epidemic, as my service at the hospital,—where I was entrusted with the charge of the dissecting-room—left me some leisure in the afternoon, I accepted with pleasure the offer of Dr. B***, an ex-naval surgeon, to make over his practice to me during his absence. Dr. B***, was suffering from liver disease, and wished to pass the summer at Vichy and Paris. He was the only civilian physician in the Colony, and, as he was a mulatto, his patients were almost exclusively negroes, and coloured people. The proposal was so tempting that I did not hesitate a moment, for it was a splendid opportunity for me, to study the manners and customs of the coloured races.

I was thus able to study the most minute details of their ways, for a doctor, when he knows what he is about, is like a confessor to his patients.

The White Creole of Cayenne deserves the place of honour in my description. He is the descendant of the old French colonists, who settled in Guiana under Louis XIV, and Louis XV. Their number has diminished so much that, it may be said, that nothing but a remembrance of them remains. The depressing and anæmic action of the climate of Guiana on the pure white race is so great, that after three or four generations the stock is completely exhausted, and marriages between white Creoles become nearly sterile. It is not the same, however, when the revififying action (in the physiological sense) of black blood is introduced. The Negro is, in fact, the branch of the

human race created expressly to inhabit the hot and
unhealthy countries situated under the equator. By
mixing with the white race, he gives the latter the
power to resist the climate. The offspring of the pure
White with a Quadroon is the *Misti*, who, consequently,
has but an eighth part of black blood in his veins.
This small proportion suffices, however, to preserve
him from most of the diseases which assail the Whites.
The White can never go out in the heat of the sun,
without a sun helmet and an umbrella, whilst the Misti
walks about, wearing nothing but a straw hat, without
any danger.

This immunity he derives from the Negro, who can
with impunity, expose his woolly head to the fierce
rays of the tropical sun.

Most of the Creole families of Guiana have more
or less black blood in their veins. In the entire
colony there were not more than five families in
187— quite free, both by direct descent and by indirect alliance, from all admixture with the Negro
race.

Prejudice against Colour. The real Whites being
so few in number, you do not find at Guiana that
prejudice against colour which is so strongly developed in the Antilles. The Whites with a black taint,
who form the great majority of the Creoles, or so-
called Whites, have Quadroon or even Mulatto parents,
and do not show the same contempt for the Blacks
which is exhibited by the Whites of the Antilles.
These latter are sufficiently numerous to stick together
and form a sort of " Belgravia ", and had, up to 187—
(the date of my visit) obstinately refused all intercourse
with the coloured people.

The Fashionable World of Guiana. In Guiana,
on the contrary, the Whites and the people of colour,
the officers and officials from France, live on the best
possible terms, and, according to their position frequent
fashionable society without paying the least attention
to the colour of the skin.

The salons of the Government House were open to
all, and at the balls there you might see dancing the
daughters of the millionaire W***, a white man from
France, married to a Negress, and the Mdlles. C***, the
representatives of one of the five real white families
of the country.

The common and dominant characteristic of all these
young women, whether pseudo-white or coloured, was
the desire to marry a man whiter than themselves. A
naval officer, or Government official, who was also a
man of fashion, was the *rara avis* they laid themselves
out to catch.

It should be remarked, that all the Creole families
of Guiana who are at all well to do, make the greatest
possible efforts to have their children instructed and
educated. Many girls and boys of twelve years of
age are sent to France, to be educated in the best
establishments till they are eighteen. The girls are
usually excellent musicians. Later they become excellent wives and mothers, and the European who
marries one has rarely cause to regret it.

Hospitality of the Creoles of Cayenne. The
Creole of Cayenne is thoroughly hospitable. Anyone
who is admitted into a household, and is not an un-
licked cub, becomes at once the friend of the family,
in the strictest sense of the word. If he possesses any
social accomplishment, and can sing a song, strum on

the piano, or is a good dancer, he is considered a valuable acquisition. Good dancers are especially appreciated. In spite of an average temperature of 85⁰ F., the Creole ladies are indefatigable, and will dance all night and until sunrise, and hardly rest for a moment. Some French ladies once tried to support the honour of the flag of Paris, but the next day they had to take to their beds, and were laid up for two or three days.

The Creole Patois and Its Uncouthness. The ladies of the Colony talk amongst themselves the soft sounding Creole *patois*, which is easy for a Frenchman to understand, for it is, like the dialect spoken in the Antilles, a corruption of the French language from which has been taken the *r* (so dear to the Marseillais) and certain nasal and guttural consonants, and to which are added some words from the Portuguese, and some from the language of the African Negroes.

It possesses no more syntax than a telegram, and in two months, or three months at the latest, you can talk it and understand it, especially if you choose a coloured woman for your professor. Latin is said to be a plain-spoken language, and the Creole *patois* has the same attribute. The Creole ladies have not the hypocritical modesty of the daughters of Albion who always say the " leg " of a fowl and never the thigh, and would never dare to pronounce the word " rump ". On the contrary, they like any word which has a good flavour about it. The coloured people of the lower class (like our ancestors in the time of Rabelais), see no harm in calling things by their real names. They call a spade a spade, and a τοολ a " fish ". They use rather a picturesque expression for this, for when a Negro

wants to urinate he says: " I am going to change the
water of my fish." It is not a little fish either which
these good Negroes possess, but a big eel with a black
head, which they inherit from their African ancestors.

The Sportiveness of the Creole Ladies. I will
allow myself here to tell one or two funny stories,
which will serve to show the playful humour of the
Creole ladies. I obtained a round of laughter, one
evening of the carnival, by relating, at a private party
given by a lady of the best society, a Provençal story
translated into the Creole patois.

"**Lou Nafanari**" and "**son Potato**". Here is the
story put into English:

Miss Rose, a rich town-lady went with her farmer
to visit her estate. She was mounted on a she-ass, and
the Spring, or something else, having made the animal
lively, it threw up its heels, with the result that Miss
Rose was thrown, and her petticoats flying up she
displayed all those graceful contours which she always
kept modestly covered. Having quickly regained her
feet, she sprang lightly on the donkey's back, and
gave it a well-deserved thrashing for throwing her.
The incident had passed so quickly that the farmer
did not appear to have noticed it at all. " Peasant,
did you see my agility? " asked the lady; to which
the farmer replied gravely: " *You may call that your
agility, but I call it your a—e.*" [1]

[1] Little need to say that this story is just a trifle "older than the
hills"; it has appeared, more or less modified in form, in most European
tongues and at least in one Oriental,—(*viz:* the Arabic, compare the
story in the *Thousand Nights and a Night*—Burton's trans. of course),
—of the "*Porter and the Three Ladies of Baghdad,*" where the jester
gets a severe slapping for referring in irreverent terms to the women's
" monosyllable "—It is moreover a " chestnut " of which most young,

The Misadventures of a Singer of Indecent Songs. At these pleasant evening parties, where you generally meet the same persons, I made the acquaintance of an officer named B***, a big man possessed of a stentorian voice which he used for singing comic songs. He had some specially adapted for ladies,—like the *Gros Chat gris, Le Soulier de Mélanie, Le Chapeau de la Marguerite,* etc., the best songs selected from the repertory of the provincial café concert.

By a singular arrangement, every Thursday night, instead of the usual mixed party, the ladies and gentlemen each had a separate gathering.

At that of the men, our musical *militaire* was accustomed to sing another repertoire, suited to his hearers, and comprising all the worst productions from the "ordure box" of Gouffé, enlarged, and embellished. The house where the men met on these occasions, stood almost alone, in the upper part of the town, and the neighbours did not complain,—far otherwise indeed. Owing to the heat they were obliged to keep their windows open, and thus were enabled to enjoy the concert, besides which, a dozen young rascals, of both sexes, used to congregate in the street, and listen to the deep bass of the singer, and so complete, quite gratis, their musical and moral education. The curiosity common to the daughters of Eve, also moved the ladies of the upper ten to wish to hear these songs, which they were not permitted to hear in their own drawing-rooms. To effect this, they used the following stratagem. They announced one evening, that they

innocent fledglings hasten to relieve their consciences in the after-dinner chat and smoke. Despite its questionableness, we were unwilling to exomit it from a translation, of which the chief claim to merit we think, consists, in its not being castrated. Those persons whom these things "please not" must skip the page.

intended, on the following Thursday, to pass the evening at the house of a lady who lived at the opposite
end of the town to the place where the men met.
But, on the night, they secretly repaired to a house
which was almost opposite the gentlemen's meeting-
place. They assembled together, and in a room without any light, which might have betrayed them, and
with the windows open, they were excellently placed
to hear the whole of the erotic repertory, without their
presence being suspected.

It chanced that on that evening the artiste felt
himself very much in the vein, and selected the hottest
songs in his collection, and all the smuttiest words were
trolled out, and fell on the listeners' ears like strokes
of the tam-tam. Not a syllable of this was lost. The
next day, at a soirée at which both sexes met, one
of the most amiable and most larky of the ladies, who
being an excellent musician, had remembered the airs
from once hearing them, [1] offered to accompany M. B***,
on the piano. " I hope you will give us something

[1] Let no one throw up their hands and exclaim against the shockingness
of these free-and-easy manners. They are equalled, if not out-distanced,
in certain religious circles, whose mysticism only makes them the more
specious and dangerous. Take the following:—"The 'Salvation Army'
is in itself a scandal, but let its disciples say and do as they please among
themselves, ourselves abstaining from listening to or following them. It
is impossible to push insanity to a greater extremity than do these people,
when it is remembered that the female *marshal* of this *army* dared to
assert, before an assembly of four thousand hallucinated fools: 'that one
night, being stark naked, she saw Christ *in person* and that she conceived
by his operation.' This is erotic love, or more surely pure mystical
onanism. Not satisfied with fornicating with the images of her *god*, the
marshal, like the Hebrews stigmatized by Ezekiel, invents a *virile* and
lewd god to satisfy the lascivious desires of an army of hysterical
maniacs ... The *Salvation Army* is a proof that there are to be found
everywhere *simples de cœur et d'esprit.*" (DR. BOUGLÉ, "*Les vices
du Peuple,*" Paris, 1888, in-8vo pp. 44—46.)

fresh," she said. "We have heard on good authority that you received by the last mail a lot of new songs which you intend to give us. These ladies are all looking forward to a great treat."

"Pardon me, Madame, you are mistaken, and I do not know who has——"

"Bah! Bah! do not be so modest. This, I know, is the air of one of your new songs," and Mme A*** began to play on the piano the tune of *La Clef d'Agnès*.

The gentleman, however, remained silent. "Perhaps you have forgotten the words, I will assist your memory," and the lady sang the first verse.

> "Agnès était une jeune innocente;
> On l'a mariée à grand Jeannot Nigaud;
> La premièr' nuit, la nuit la plus charmante,
> Jeannot ne put——"

"Well, go on; tell us the rest!"

M. B***, was stupefied, but maintained a prudent silence.

"If that song does not please you," continued the lady, "here is another," and she began to play the air of the 'Dispute entre le *Luc* et le *Noc*,' and sing:

> "Un jour un *luc* plein de fierté
> Tint au *noc* ce langage:
> Φουτρας-tu toujours à mon nez [1]
> Et dans mon voisinage?"

[1] The above curious French verses remind us that in Spanish and other languages, there are many similar in style and idea, among others the following, which we heard given *after dinner* in Madrid by an eminent contemporary politician

> "Si el coño tuviera dientes
> Como tiene fortaleza,
> Cuantos carajos valientes
> Quedarian sin cabeza."

We believe this to be a genuine "Andalusian native", if lacking in propriety, it can hardly be said to want either force or originality.

M. B***, looked at the lady with his eyes starting out of his head, and then fled precipitately from the drawing-room, pursued by a general burst of laughter.

Morality and Good-heartedness of the Ladies of Cayenne. Such freedom of manners does not lead (as might be supposed) to immorality. No doubt there are, here as elsewhere, husbands who wear horns, and ladies rather too ready to open their thighs, but they are the exception, and not the rule. Generally speaking, the Creole ladies do not betray their husbands. They are, moreover, excellent mothers, and extremely fond of their children. This love of progeny they even carry so far that if their husbands have bastards by coloured girls or negresses, instead of driving away the children as would be done in France, many of the ladies of Guiana support them, and provide for them. When they are of an age to take the first communion, they are sent to church, the girl with her white veil, handkerchief, and prayer-book, the boy with the orthodox wax candle, and white silk armlet. If the boy is intelligent, he is given some amount of education, and a place is procured for him as a clerk, or in some Government office. If the girl is pretty, she is often brought up in the house as a poor relation, or as a sort of lady's maid or companion.

One day I was on a visit to one of the best white families of the country, and I saw the lady of the house enter, carrying in her arms a fine child, almost white, but with some signs of black blood.

" Is that the child of one of your neighbours, Madame ? " I asked.

" No, *Mouché*, the child of *Mouché* S. R." (her husband.

I looked at her with astonishment. She smiled, and pointed to her maid, a handsome mulatress with a splendid bust.

" That is the mamma of the child, and Mouché S. R. is the father."

The legitimate wife was carrying in her arms the adulterine child of her husband. I confine myself to this one instance, but I could cite many others. [1]

[1] Primitive nations are not so squeamish about the husband getting children by other women than the legal wife. We can cite no better known illustration than that given in Genesis (chap. XXX verses 1—10); to which we recommend the reader to refer.

CHAPTER II.

The coloured races.—The influence of black blood on cross-breeds with the White man.—Mistis, Quadroons, Mulattoes, and Zambros.—The proportion of illegitimate children. — The easy morality of the coloured woman. — The thorough Negress.—From Saturday night to Sunday morning.—"Milady C***, the Queen of the Golden Wrists".—The musky smell of the Negress.— The genital organs of the Negro race.—Physiological peculiarity of the colour of the gland of the Negro's penis.—The genital organ of the Zambro.—The genital organ of the Mulatto.—Physical beauties of women of colonr.—Permanent influence of black blood on the genital organs of the male.

Influence of Black Blood on Crosses with the White Race. The cross between the White and the Negro produces, in the human race, a phenomenon analogous to that which is observed in horses. The pure blood stallion produces with mares of an inferior native race, foals which exhibit the qualities of its procreators. Though not so handsome as its father, the half-blood is much superior to its mother, from whom, however, it derives a certain "rusticity" and the power to resist the effects of the climate. This explains the almost complete dissappearance from Guiana of the pure white race, whilst on the contrary the coloured race has flourished. Guiana received, however, in the reigns of Louis XIV, and Louis XV., quite as many Frenchmen as the Antilles.

The climate soon got the better of them, as witness for instance the Kourou expedition, when fifteen thousand Alsatians were reduced to some hundreds only in a very few years.

Mistis, Quadroons, Mulattos, and Zambros. The Mulatto is the direct offspring (nine hundred and ninety-nine times out of a thousand) of the White man and the Negress. Those who are born of Europeans settled in the country, or who have a white Creole parent, who can bring them up, and furnish them with the means of living prosperously, quickly become people of fashion. There are already many families of this kind. But the offspring of the connections of the Negress with less fortunate Europeans, temporarily residing in the Colony, (called *Massogans*), or even with common soldiers, fall into the category of unfortunate beings.

It should be remarked, that the Mulatto is nearly always the offspring of the White man with the Negress, and only once in a thousand times, of the union of the White woman with the Negro. This is a clear instance of natural selection, in which the woman represents the inferior element, and the man the pure blood. We may note in passing, that, in the births, the girls are much more numerous than the boys. There are not—as is the case in Chili—four or five women to one man, but there are certainly more than two.

The Negress who gives birth to a child whiter than herself, will make the greatest sacrifices to bring it up properly; she will do any kind of work, and put up with any hardship, to ensure the existence of her

ANTHROPOLOGY. 213

progeny, [1] and gain *queque sous maqués* ("marked" halfpence, or copper money). But a living is easily earned in a country where you need neither wood nor coal for fuel, and where all you require for food is cooked banana (bacove), fruit, flat fish, cassava, and bread fruit.

To have a baby is no dishonour to a Negress or a Mulatta, especially if it is by a White man. She will select for its godfather, (who is considered as the putative father), whichever of her lovers has the best

[1] In the "*Princesse de Bagdad*" of Dumas, the woman who is about to abandon the conjugal hearth with her lover, is met by her child, who endeavours to retain her with kisses; the lover seeks brutally to thrust the child aside; that suffices to awaken the maternal feeling, and she refuses to go, saying: "*Ah! I was mad!.... I was mad!.... but when that man raised his hand on my child....!*"

In fact the predominance of the maternal feeling, is such that it suffices sometimes to weaken, to dissipate and even to suppress the phenomena of love, which are far more vigorous in the male.

That is why, in general, woman cares less for youth or beauty in her husband than for more solid qualities.

Unfortunately, among certain civilized nations marriage has become a business transaction, in which sexual intercourse is an almost extraneous matter.

On the other hand, and more particularly in France, marriage means for the woman, EMANCIPATION; she is at once freed from the social, or absolutely anti-social thraldom of the rules of SOCIETY.

According to Icard in his "*La femme pendant la Période menstruelle*, (Paris 1883), sexual desire diminishes and in fact expires as soon as gestation has commenced,

Nevertheless, the antagonism between the maternal feeling and the sexual instinct does not inhibit the sub-existence of a sensual basis; in fact women sometimes enjoy during the suckling period erotic feelings, and go so far as to seek to be again in a state of maternity, in order to be able to renew this enjoyment, greater to them perhaps than the act of copulation itself. This may perhaps be to some extent explained by the uterus and the great sympathetic nervous complexus.

Lombroso, *La femme Criminelle* (*loc. cit.* p. 115 *et seq.*).

social position. I will not go so far as to say that she is not capable of fidelity to her "protector" for the time being, but her fidelity is but relative. She will betray her lover with a man who is in a better position, but never with an inferior.

The Proportion of Illegitimate Births. Statistics showed that in 187—, there were born at Cayenne sixty illegitimate children to every forty legitimate. I do not know whether this has changed. The consequence of this tolerance in the matter of morals is that abortion is very rare. As to infanticides after delivery, they are almost unknown in Guiana; a woman who killed her child would be lynched by the other women. Within the last half century, there has never been but one case, and then the woman was nearly an idiot. The public indignation against her was so strong that the sentence of death was obliged to be carried out, or the women of the lower classes would have caused serious riots. The physician who is a philosopher must be gratified at such a result, and deplore the opposite condition in France, [1] where, in

[1] Christian England when a girl has tripped—due more often than not to the influence of a stronger will than her own—pitches her out-of-doors with the new-born offspring in her arms. Forsaken by her seducer as well as by her own kindred, without money or work she is driven to a life of shame, unredeemed by love, to support her child, while the man who has misled and betrayed her goes off scot-free to work his will elsewhere. When will the overchurched conscience of the British wake up to this terrible injustice! The lost woman's so-called "unfallen" sisters (because they were never tempted?) are the first to point the finger of scorn at her. Is it because they are jealous that she has eaten of the forbidden fruit which they have not been bold enough to taste?

The illiterate coloured people of French Guiana look upon illegitimate unions with indulgence, and the children resulting from them are as dearly cherished as those born in wedlock.

the large cities, (and notably at Paris), infanticide is far from being a rarity.

Easy Morals of the Coloured Women. The union of the Mulatta with the White man produces the Quadroon. It is amongst the Quadroon women (whose connection with the White man produces the Misti [1]) that are found the most beautiful prostitutes. But, like the Greek courtesans, they do not bestow their favours on the first comer. *Bonnes filles* as they are, they expect a little courting, and you must take some pains to please them. That not very honourable institution, the brothel, does not exist in Guiana,--or in the Antilles either for that matter. Love is quite free, but I hasten to say that, in spite of that, syphilitic diseases are rather rare.

The whoremonger has a varied choice of exotic flowers, ranging from the Negress to the Misti, who is almost white. We will say a few words about each.

The Full-blood Negress. We will begin with her, as she forms the great part of the feminine population, together with the Zambra, the offspring of the Negress with the Mulatto. To please her, and become her lover, does not necessitate any long or complicated proceedings. It suffices (or at least it did some twenty years ago) to walk on the Place des Palmistes after the evening meal. You met a girl, talked to her a bit, and after a few commonplace phrases, if her face, as seen by the light of a match, pleased you, you put the regular question, " *Ché doudou, ou qua oulé coqué avé moi?* " (Darling, where can you sleep with me?)

[1] Sometimes called the Octoroon.

The word *coqué* is a corruption of the old French *cocher*, that is to say expresses the idea of a cock treading a hen. You had but to follow the girl to a room in some neighbouring house. If need be, one of the benches of the Place des Palmistes would afford you free hospitality.

From Saturday Night to Sunday. The easy-going morals of the Negress and the Zambra were often the cause of a trick being played upon newcomers, who were unacquainted with the manners of the people. And here we enter upon the question of the influence of religion on morals. I should here state, that at Guiana the influence of the priests is very great. The coloured people possess sentiments of real piety, even amongst the men. The children, who are educated by the monks, are ardent believers, and quite the reverse of the young workmen of France. The Negress has simple and sincere faith, but her devotion is of a peculiar kind. She confesses, takes the communion nearly every Sunday, and, during the week, breaks in the most reckless manner, that part of the Decalogue which says,

> " Fleshly lust thou shalt desire
> In marriage only."

The priest contents himself with merely damming the current, for to forbid physical love to these warm-blooded creatures, would be lost labour.

On Saturday evening, absolution is given before attending the Sunday mass, and Saturday evening is therefore the time chosen to play a joke on any new-comer, who is sent to the Place des Palmistes to get a woman. To the regular question the first twenty women or so will be sure to reply, " *Mon ché, mo pas pouvé, mo gain asolution mon pé guyodo, mais dimain fini la messe mo qué vini ton case.*" (My dear, I can't, I am going to get absolution from the curé, but to-morrow after the mass I will come to your house). [1] Dear creatures! after having performed their duty to their Creator, they are ready to do their duty to their fellow-creatures. At last he will end by finding one who is ready to go with him, and he will naturally be inclined to ask her why she is not going to get absolution. " No," she will reply sorrowfully. " he won't give it me."

"The Queen of the Golden Wrists—Milady."

I have said that the fidelity of the coloured woman is only relative. If the person who wants her is in a position that flatters her vanity, or can serve her interests, she will not hesitate to break her previous engagement, if she believes that the secret will be well kept.

The surest means of getting her is not to run after

[1] This is of course *pigeon-French* but the same conditions still exist in the remote districts of Connaught (The wild West of Ireland):

" Two elderly Irish dames, residing in the highly respectable and intensely Catholic town of Ballinasloe, after having been for many years bosom-friends, were at daggers drawn. But, mindful of their Easter duties, they both went to confession, and the following morning, in due course, to communion. On leaving the church, after mass, the two old ladies unhappily chanced to knock against each other—whereat fierce passions seethed within their venerable bosoms, till at last the elder of the two matrons, shaking her fist at the other, exclaimed: " That's you, Mrs. O'Flaherty, is it? and bitter bad luck to you, by the same token! You may be thankful this blessed day that I am now in a state of grace, but plase God, that'll not last long, and then I'll sarve ye out, ye old hag!""

her too ostensibly, or appear too anxious; you will attain your end more easily by employing a go-between. The most intelligent of these women, and the one who had the largest number of clients in all Cayenne, was the celebrated Mulatta C***, called *Milady*, and who was connected, by the left hand, with one of the best families in the country. She was the "Queen of the Golden Wrists", as the coloured women were called, in distinction from the "Imperials". The struggles of these two factions reminded one, in a minor degree, of the party war that raged between the green and blue coachmen of old Byzantium, but this latter-day rivalry was more pacific, and had never caused blood to be shed.

It was in their dances that these young women tried to outdo each other in grace and abandon. These dances much resembled certain dances used in Senegal, and I will not therefore describe them here.

If you were one of the regular customers of *Milady*, and had not made any particular choice of a young woman, it was sufficient to ask her for a box of cigars,—light, dark, light-brown or dark-brown, as the case might be.

She would understand, and at the hour fixed, would send you the box of cigars by the hands of a Quadroon, Mulatta, Zambra. or Negress. Ah, there were some nice girls in Guiana, and, even now, I think of them with pleasure! But it is time to study them more closely.

The Musky Smell of the Negress. Let us begin with the Negress. In all the human races, there are, of course, individual differences in the desire for the carnal lusts. But it may safely be asserted that the

Negress of Guiana is certain to have warm blood, and a strong desire for intercourse with the male. She receives him with the most lively pleasure, and does all she can to satisfy him,—particularly if she has to do with a *Massogan*, or White man from Europe, — but she has no vicious or depraved habits. She performs a natural act naturally, and without any of the refinements of the prostitutes of our great cities, or of the Annamite *Congaï.* She shows a horror of sodomy. She is clean, one might say, morally and physically. If she does not take baths, she at least washes herself frequently, and the poor girl has a very good reason for these ablutions. That reason is that all the black race,—I may say once for all, not to have to repeat it,—has a very fine skin which perspires abundantly, and gives forth an indefinable odour *sui generis*, which reminds one slightly of the musky smell of the crocodile. [1] This influence is particularly noticeable when she is excited by sexual passions, and is annoying to beginners who are not accustomed to it, but you end by getting used to it. The Negress therefore anoints herself plentifully with all the strongest perfumes from Europe, in order to conceal her native smell, and she

[1] In the animal kingdom various odours and sounds are closely connected with the reproduction of the species. During the season of love a musky odour is emitted by the submaxillary glands of the crocodile, and pervades its haunts. At the same period the anal scent-glands of snakes are in active function, and so are the corresponding glands of the lizards. Many mammals are odoriferous. In some cases the odour appears to serve as a defence or a protection, but in other species the glands are confined to the males, and almost always become more active during the rutting season.

Westermarck "*The History of Human Marriage*,(p. 246, London, 1894).

See the Excursus at end of this Chapter for fuller information on this head.

always keeps herself very clean. But in any case her peculiar odour is not so repugnant as that of the Congai.

The Genital Organs of the Negro Race. Her odour, however, is but the least fault of the Negress. Her greatest disadvantage is the immense size of her vulva and vagina. In all the human races there is a close connection or proportion between the male and female genital organs. I have already remarked this in reference to the Cochin-Chinese. Now, in no branch of the human race are the male organs more developed than in the African Negro. I am speaking of the penis only, and not of the testicules, which are often smaller than those of the majority of Europeans. The result of this conformation is, that a Negress, though suitably provided to receive the Negro, is far too wide for the White man, especially if he is but moderately furnished, or "half cooked" as Rabelais might say. The Negress therefore,—being very desirous of the favours of the White man,—uses astringent preparations to strengthen the mucous surfaces and tighten the entrance of the vulva. The preparation which appeared to me to be the most used, was made of acajou nuts (an astringent) macerated in spirit, and mixed with tormentilla root, and vanilla beans (for perfume). A few spoonfuls of this liquid, mixed with water, form a lotion, which, when applied frequently, enables the desired result to be almost obtained.

Physiological Peculiarity of the Colour of the Gland in the Negro. The penis of the Negro affords a physiological peculiarity, as do also the mucous surfaces of the lips and the vulva in the Negress.

The colour is as black as that of the rest of the skin. It is not the same with the Negro of Oceania, as we shall see later. The peculiarity is absolutely special to the African Negro, and his descendants who have been brought as slaves to America. The mucous surface of the gland and the foreskin vary, in the European, from a pale pink to a bright red, and it is therefore not without a certain feeling of curiosity, that one examines for the first time the genital organ of the Negro, and remarks the uniform black colour of the skin and the mucous surfaces. The vulva of the Negress is black at the entrance, but becomes a bright red in the vagina. It is the same with the lips and the mouth in both sexes. The pubes is scantily furnished with hair, short and hard as the bristles of a brush. As to the head, everybody knows that that is covered with a woolly crop. The Negress of Cayenne always wears on her head a large handkerchief of striped silk, and the gallant who took it off, and passed his hand through her hair, would not find his caresses well received.

The Genital Organ of the Zambro. The Zambro is the offspring of the Negress and the Mulatto. Although one quarter of their blood is white, the Zambro and the Zambra differ very little from their black ancestors. The Zambro especially is almost a Negro, so far as his genital organ is concerned. The skin of the member, and of the scrotum, is a dark sepia colour, and the skin of the body is sepia colour. The mucous surface of the gland is of a reddish sepia. The hair of the pubes is like that of the Negro.

The Genital Organ of the Mulatto. The Mulatto commences to approach nearer to the White. The skin of the body varies from a light brownish yellow to a darker tint of the same hue. This tint is formed of sepia, gamboge, and vermilion. The skin of the scrotum and the member is darker than the rest of the body, but the mucous surface of the gland is of a dirty reddish-brown. The hair of the pubes is more plentiful, and more resembles the European, but is always stiff, and generally very black; there are some exceptions of which I will mention one. I attended medically a young Mulatto and his sister, who had been begotten by a father with carroty red hair. The girl had red and smooth hair, the skin fairly light, with here and there patches of red, and the hair of the pubes a dark russet, with the mucous tissues of the lips and the vulva, dark red. Her brother, on the contrary, had a skin not so light, the hair and the tufts of the pubes black, but the member, which was very much developed, had a gland of a deep brown colour, with the scrotum sepia colour.

In size, the genital organs of the Mulatto are less developed, as concerns the penis at least, than in the Negro. The testicles on the other hand are a little larger. As a logical consequence, the vulva and vagina of the Mulatta are not so wide and gaping as those of the Negress, though larger than those of the European woman.

Often in the same family there are great differences between the children of the same White father and the Negress. The girls generally have a fairer skin than the boys, the mucous tissues are redder, and their hair is not so woolly. The white blood predominates. It is just the opposite with the boy. There are many exceptions to the rule; sometimes, by a singular phenomenon of atavism, you may find Octoroons much darker than their mother, and almost Mulattos. But unite the Zambro with the White man, or the Mulatto with the Quadroon woman, and there will result from these admixtures, irregular crossings whose physical characteristics will approach to, or recede from, those of the white race. In the first case, there are five parts white against three black; in the second the proportion is the same, and nevertheless the two types are quite dissimilar.

EXCURSUS TO CHAPTER II.

MEDICAL NOTES ON THE SEXUAL VALUE of SMELL.

This subject alluded to in several places in the text merits perhaps some confirmation, and we therefore add the following extracts from well-known scientific writers. We think it preferable to give these notes here to putting them in smaller types at the foot of various pages, as in the present form they are much easier to read and consult.

Dislike of Urnings to the odor fœmina. The physical repugnance of true Urnings for women may be illustrated by passages from Krafft-Ebing's cases (pp. 117, 123, 163) which I will translate.

(1). "I had observed that a girl was madly in love with me, and longed intensely to give herself up to me. I gave her an assignation in my house, hoping that I should better succeed with a girl who sought me out of love, than I had with public women. After her first fiery caresses, I did indeed feel a little less frigid; but when it came to thinking about copulation, all was over—the same stark frost set in, and my part was played out. I sent her away, deeply excited, with some moral remarks; and I have never tried the experiments again. On all of these occasions *the specific odour of the female added to my horror.*

(2) " The proximity of wenches aroused in me qualms and nausea ; *in particular I could not bear the smell of them."*

(3) "It seems to me absurd to set up the female form as the prototype of human beauty, I regard a woman's person as displeasing, the formation of her hips as ugly and unæsthetic. Dancing is therefore an abomination to me. *I loathe the odour which the so-called fair sex exhales when heated by the dance.* The disgust inspired in these three Urnings by the smell of the female is highly significant; since we know that the sense of smell acts powerfully upon the sexual appetite of normal individuals. It may be remarked in all the instances of pronounced Urnings, sexual congress with women seems to have been followed by disgust, nervous exhaustion, and the sense of an unnatural act performed without pleasure. This is true even of those who have brought themselves to marriage. "

A PROBLEM IN MODERN ETHICS (pp. 54—55).
London, 1896.

(Since the death of John Addington Symonds, the talented author of the "*Renaissance in Italy*", this work has been formally attributed to him. (*Vide* HAVE-LOCK-ELLIS on "*Sexual Inversion*").

Odor Fœmina and Sexuality:—Zippe (*Wien. Med. Wochenschrift*, 1879, Nr. 24), in connection with a case of kleptomania in an onanist, likewise establishes such relations, and cites Hildebrand as authority, who in his popular physiology says: "It cannot be doubted that the olfactory sense stands in remote connection with the sexual apparatus. Odours of flowers often occasion pleasurable sensual feelings, and when one remembers the passage in the 'Song of Solomon', 'And my hands dropped with myrrh and my fingers with sweet-smelling myrrh upon the handles of the lock', one finds that it did not escape Solomon's observation. In the Orient, the pleasant perfumes are esteemed for their relation to the sexual organs, and the women's apartments of the Sultan are filled with the perfumes *of flowers.*"

Most, professor in Rostock (comp. Zippe), relates: " I learned from a sensual young peasant that he had excited many a chaste girl sexually, and easily gained his end, by carrying his handkerchief in his axilla for a time, while dancing, and then wiping his partner's perspiring face with it."

The case of Henry III shows that contact with a person's perspiration may be the exciting cause of passionate love. At the betrothal feast of the King of Navarre and Margaret of Valois, he accidentally dried his face with a garment of Maria of Cleves, which was moist with her perspiration. Although she was the bride of the Prince of Condé, Henry conceived immediately such a passionate love for her that he could not resist it, and made her, as history shows, very unhappy. An analogous instance is related of Henry IV, whose passion for the beautiful Gabrielle is said to have originated at the instant when, at a ball, he wiped his brow with her handkerchief.

Professor Jäger, the "discoverer of the soul", refers to the same thing in his well-known book (2nd ed.,

1880, chap. XV, p. 173); for he regards the sweat as important in the production of sexual effects and as being especially seductive.

One learns from reading the work of Ploss ("*Das Weib*"), that attempts to attract a person of the opposite sex by means of the perspiration may be discerned in many forms in popular psychology. In reference to this, a custom which holds among the natives of the Philippine Islands when they become engaged, as reported by Jäger, is remarkable. When it becomes necessary for the engaged pair to separate, they exchange articles of wearing apparel, by means of which each becomes assured of faithfulness. These objects are carefully preserved, covered with kisses, and smelled.

The love of certain libertines and sensual women for perfumes indicates a relation between the olfactory and sexual senses.

The following case, reported by Binet, seems to be in opposition to this idea. Unfortunately nothing is said concerning the mental characteristics of the person. In any event, it is certainly confirmatory of the relations existing between the olfactory and sexual senses:—D., a medical student, was seated on a bench in a public park, reading a book (on pathology). Suddenly a violent erection disturbed him. He looked up and noticed that a lady, redolent with perfume, had taken a seat upon the other end of the bench. D., could attribute the erection to nothing but the unconscious olfactory impression made upon him.

(*Vide*, Kraft Ebbing's (pages 26—28) " PSYCHOPATHIA SEXUALIS " *with especial reference to* Contrary Sexual Instinct: A MEDICO-LEGAL STUDY.

*Authorized translation of the seventh enlarged and
revised German edition,* by CHARLES GILBERT CHAD-
DOCK, M.D. (*Philadelphia and London,* 1895.)

The odour of nudity. Lombroso says :—" Civilization gave birth to false modesty when it suppressed
nudity, and habits of cleanliness attenuated that peculiar
smell of the body, which, exhaled by the female attracted the male. The attracting attributes depending
on sight and especially on tact, now developed themselves and transformed the feminine maternal organs
(lips and breasts) into erotic organs."
La Femme Criminelle (page 112), Paris, 1896.

["It is also remarkable that many animals (musk-
ox, civet-cat, beaver) possess glands near their sexual
organs, which produce secretions having a very strong
odour.]

The influence of age on the odor fœminœ. [1] It
is unnecessary for us to tell our readers, that it is
more agreable to sniff the odour of a rose or that of
a bunch of violets between two fresh Normandy
pippins, than when enclosed between two dried figs
of the desert of Sahara.
Thence comes the unhealthy lubricity of certain old
men who pay with gold, the freshest breasts in order
to soil them lecherously with their impure and disgusting slaver: here is a clear case of high-treason
against humanity, particularly if these pretty Magde-

[1] For this note and the following we are indebted to DR. AUG.
GALOPIN'S little book entitled: *Le Parfum de la Femme et le Sens
Olfactif dans l'Amour. Etude psycho-physiologique* (Paris, *Dentu*, 1889).

burg hemispheres resemble those the glory and love
of which were so aptly sung by Victor Hugo:

> "Jeanne est née à Fougère
> Vrai nid d'une bergère,
> J'adore son jupon
>   Fripon.
> Amour, tu vis en elle,
> Car c'est dans sa prunelle
> Que tu caches ton carquois,
>   Narquois.
> Moi, je chante et j'aime,
> Plus que Diane même,
> Jeanne et ses durs tétons
>   Bretons."

The odor fœminœ has like woman's life, three great
natural phases:

(1) the period of puberty;

(2) the period of marriage;

(3) the period of the menopausis.

Old age is seldom apparent, in women of the world
before the age of sixty.

After she has passed her fifteenth olympiad, woman
has no longer any age and still remains beautiful, if
she has the wit *to know how to grow old*.

The odour emitted by old women is sometimes very
pleasant, resembling that of dried rose-leaves, of iris
and of the faded flowers of the lime-tree.

As for young girls, they almost always smell agree-
ably, their odour is pleasing and awakens no carnal
desire.

However, the *Song of Songs* teaches us that all
meat was game to that old *polisson* Solomon. Listen
to what Cloquet says: "At the moment of puberty,
young virgins sometimes shed around them a perfume

that the poets of all ages have not failed to celebrate, and that the author of the *Song of Songs* has exalted with an enthusiasm, which may be still, though rarely, understood in our days."

The idea of the Odor Fœminœ could naturally not escape the observant mind of Zola who said: "Every thing exhaled an odour of woman..."

..."He smelt this woman's shoulders the fragrance of which intoxicated him."

It is incontestable that it is during youth that these olfactive impressions are most vivid. But it cannot be denied that they give a calm and legitimate pleasure at every age, even to octogenarians, of whose long and active life there remain only memories.

This reminds us of the words of an illustrious and estimable old man, Crémieux, who honoured us with his affection and who, on the day after the death of his dearly loved partner, said to us in his house at Passy:

"My dear boy, this atmosphere, so full of her, will soon choke me, now that she will return no more to renew the life of it..."

And a few days later, this noble old friend died of grief and of *hunger*, because he would not live any longer without *her*.

The awakening of erotic ideas. This is what one of the most eminent contemporary physiologists, Professor Longet, says on the subject:

"The olfactory sense intervenes with some people to awaken venereal desire. There are certain men who find, in the influence exercised by the odour of the vulva on the pituitary membrane, the principle of very erotic dispositions. The smell of man also, awakens

in some ardent women, the wish for pleasure. Here,
memory and imagination must largely contribute: is
it not the same with regard to the ardent impression
produced, particularly during youth, by the atmosphere
exhaled by certain women, whose garments even retain
the breath of voluptuousness after they have quitted
them?

"Among animals, the connection between the olfactory and the genital organs is as incontestable as it is
intimate. When they are in heat, individuals of the
same species are forced mutually to seek each other;
they therefore require a means of finding each other,
a means of excitation, and nature is careful to make
the sexual organs of most of them exhale, at this
moment, a strong and special odour. Nothing in fact
could more effectually serve this purpose than these emanations spread far around by the atmospheric currents."

Of course the odour of the vulva, alluded to by
Longet, is the smell peculiar to the special liquid
secreted by the glandular regions of that organ, and
the more or less unpleasant odours engendered by the
state of uncleanliness in which the said organ may
have been kept, have no connection with the animal
emanations with which we have to do.

Animals, bitches for instance, are careful to clean
themselves when they are in heat. Bitches that are
unclean find few or no gallants, with the exception of
some dogs whose olfactory sense has become vitiated,
examples of which depravation are frequently to be
met with in the human species.

Certain ardent women, gifted with a warm imagination, are usually highly perfumed. The temperature
of their body generally increases almost instantaneously,
to the extent of from $1^0.8$ to $3^0.6$ degrees Fahrenheit,

under the masculine attack. This increase of heat induces a considerable development of odorous vapours which envelop their lovers in a perfumed atmosphere which completes their intoxication, soldering their affections and their souls: such women are sure of being loved.

There are others, often more beautiful to the eye, who may be looked at, admired even and, who, not-withstanding, are not smelt... are not loved. They tire and repel to the tedium of monotony.

This explains those couplings, inexplicable to the ignorant vulgar public, between one of those whom it is agreed to call *handsome lads* (though nothing is uglier than a man who thinks himself handsome); and a woman whose face and whose body even have nothing of classical plasticity.

Such a woman, vanquished to-day in a first meeting, by one more beautiful than herself, will triumph to-morrow, over the prettiest of her sex, thanks to the magical power she exercises by her odour. She magnetizes the atmosphere. [1]

It often occurs, that the same *handsome fellow* who had neglected her in the morning will be madly in love with her in the evening. And all the other women, becoming jealous, exclaim:

" But what particular charm has she about her, with her head one way, and her shoulders another? "

[1] Wilkes, the last century agitator, and one of the ugliest men of his time was given to boast that he would, with an hour's start, compete with the handsomest man agoing for the favours of a beautiful woman—and win. His magnetism was attributed to his conversational powers. But may it not have been due to some such cause as above outlined?

The case of the Princess de Chimay (*Miss Clara Ward*) and the uneducated, gypsy musician, the violinist of a Paris café—Rigo, is too well known to need mention.

She has this ... that the odour she emanates is pleasant to the nostrils of men! That is what she has! And this quality, together with wit, suffices to the woman who likes the society of men and is herself fond of man. Talent, in a woman of good taste, does not alone consist in knowing how to choose the most delicate perfumes; it consists, mainly, in knowing how to choose that which amplifies, without in any way perverting, the natural odour peculiar to herself: in this there is a secret difficult to divulge openly; but it suffices to draw your attention to it to enable you to overcome all the difficulties connected therewith. If woman knows so many things, it is because she can guess at all that is hidden from her.

Céline Montaland (the celebrated actress), so beautiful and so dangerously perfumed, was she not always one of the most seriously and legitimately beloved of women?

Animals can never converse together, and, yet, they well know how to mark their preferences: do they not fight each other to the death, as we do, to preserve to themselves their favourite?

The nasal pituitary gland is the powerful laboratory in which are elaborated the living particles that detach themselves from the beloved being, and which, by the medium of the brain, are destined to be assimilated to the entire organism.

The purest marriage that can be contracted between man and woman is that which is engendered by olfaction and finds its sanction by common assimilation, in the encephalon, of the living molecules proceeding from the evaporation of two bodies in contact and which sympathise together.

The intoxication of confessors and of female penitents has no other cause.

In all ages of the Church, it is the perfume of virgins that has always intoxicated priests and given rise
to the immorality of the confessional, as well for
youth filled with desire as for musing and sighing
old age.

**Males thrown off the scent as to the odour of
their females during the act of copulation.** In
the stables of cattle-breeders, female animals are often
met with that cannot be fecundated; among cows particularly, to which the French then give the name of
" *Robinières* ". This results, among other causes, from
the greater or less degree of antipathy which exists
between the two individuals, and mostly on account
of the antipathy of the male for the female. The bull
commences a work that he is unable to finish: there
is fraud.

This antipathy can be overcome by dissimulating
the particular smell of the female, aromatizing certain
parts of her body, directly involved, in order to deceive
the male; or at least, to momentarily attenuate the
emanations from the female which were offensive to
him, and repelled him.

In the case of mares, very strong infusions of espar-
cet (French honey-suckle), wild thyme (Thymus ser-
pylum), sage and other aromatic herbs are employed.

Weak injections, penetrating but slightly, and directed
towards the sides of the canal of the female, are sometimes used to dissimulate or to attenuate the peculiar
scent proceeding from the secretions of the vaginal
glands.

For cows, infusions of all sorts of green herbs suffice;
for rabbits, infusions of white nettle or of wild thyme.

With certain females destined to the reproduction

of hybrids, it is sometimes necessary to blindfold the male and to impregnate the female he is expected to cover, with the natural scent of a preferred female of his own species.

The female stranger is made to inhabit for several days the same stable with the sultana, and next to her. Immediately before the moment of copulation the products of the female secretions destined to throw the male off the scent are removed to the field of action, he being blindfolded so that it is impossible for him to see the concubine that is substituted for his legitimate partner. Very often, in this case, the illusion is sufficiently complete to deceive the animal.

If however the male entertains a doubt of the fraud, the stranger must be removed and the preferred mare made to take her place; he is then led to smell her, and the first one promptly substituted as soon as the illusion seems to be sufficiently complete, and the moment at hand.

This is very difficult to accomplish and no detail must be neglected.

Another method was to make the stallions breathe certain odours in the stable, before leading them to the mares that are distasteful to them, but it did not succeed, except after impregnating the female with the odours of the stable, by making her live several days in that of the stallion, before the final bringing together.

When the sense of smell is perverted in a stallion, it makes him lose three fourths of his ardour. Some animals, indeed, then fall into a state of relative impotency, which becomes absolute if there is complete obliteration of the olfactory faculties, which to them are the most powerful excitants to sexual pleasure.

With man, a momentary or chronic coryza provokes similar accidents but not in so striking a manner.

Oliva recommends civet as useful to excite the sexual desire in some animals. The smell of it makes caged nightingales sing. "Fragrant odours," says he, "stimulate animals to sing, by increasing their amorous tendencies."

We have it on excellent authority [1] that there was a monk in Prague, who could not only recognize by their smell different persons, but also distinguish a chaste girl or woman from those that were not. What admirable precision, and in how vast a field of experiment must not the good monk have made his odorous and more or less savoury investigations!

Doctor Monin, in his curious and useful study of the odours of the human body (*Les odeurs du corps humain*), adds: "the thing is not very difficult, we know a certain ladies' physician who can admirably detect by smell, and without ever making a mistake, when any of his clients have their menstrual periods."

Baruel senior could perfectly distinguish by scent the blood of a man from that of a woman, attributing the difference in smell to certain volatile fatty acids.

According to the accounts of travellers, the North American Indians can follow by scent the track of their prey or of their enemies (*De la Hontan*, La Haye, 1715).

It would appear that the Mongol and the negro races, by reason of the amplitude of their nasal cavities, are endowed with a finer and more extended sense of smell than European peoples. Among Asia-

---

[1] *The Journal des Savants*, Paris, 1864, referring to the *Œuvres de Lecat*, Paris, 1767, (vol. II, p. 257).

tics, the Kalmucks are noted, for the extraordinary fineness of their olfactory powers.

Remarkable examples of the delicacy of this sense among negroes are also recorded: some of them are said to be able to distinguish the track of a white man from that of a negro, and can also follow the scent of those of their unfortunate comrades who, to escape slavery, have fled to the forest.

Lecat relates a very curious case: " A boy who got lost was brought up in the woods which he never quitted. His sense of smell was so finely developed that he knew of the approach of enemies, men or animals. Having later on returned to civilized life, all his olfactory power was retained intact by him. He married, and could always follow his wife by her scent.

This is a husband who . . . very luckily has not one like him in Paris.

Already, in 1789, Haller, in his *Elementa physiologiæ*, Lausanne, 4to, t. V, p. 162, had studied the sensations that are produced by odours. He divided them into *agreeable*, *disagreeable*, and *indifferent*, or mixed.

This classification being too arbitrary, does not deserve serious consideration.

What are in fact the odours that are agreeable and those which are not?

Those which please some people are displeasing to others; those which restore animation in some women, will provoke alarming syncopes, or intense nervous irritability, in others.

We need go no further: a perfume that pleases at noon, may at midnight be displeasing to the same individual.

Therefore Haller's classification is totally wanting in scientific character.

All our elegant lady readers know that the *inof-
fensive* cigarette which they smoke from taste or for
fashion, when they are well, is distasteful to them when
a slight attack of sick head-ache seizes them after
keeping too late hours, or on the occasion of a little
fatigue, nervousness, offended pride or lovers quarrel,
and so forth . . .

The olfactory sense is very capricious, very change-
able . . . particularly in those spoilt children, but our
charmers still, who have learned how to conquer the
right to command, while at the same time seeming to
be obeying our will.

CHAPTER III.

Eroticism of the Negress.—Methods of Copulation. The Negress is usually of a passionate nature and does not care to waste time in trifles. I shall speak later on of the *aubergine*, and the aphrodisiac drinks that she gives her lovers to excite their ardour, but she knows of no "refinements", and accomplishes the carnal act with brutal simplicity, and generally in regulation position. This is known at Cayenne by the name of "counting the shingle pegs", because, in this position, the woman has her eyes fixed on the ceiling, and can thus count the pegs in the shingles, or wooden tiles, which form the roof.

The Negress requires a "stallion-man" to make her feel the proper physiological sensation, and she seldom finds him except in the male of her own race. Added to this, her nervous system is not so delicately organized as in the White woman. Her mucous membranes are drier, especially as regards the genital organs. The "flowers" are as rare in Guiana as they are common in Cochin-China. I shall study this question more in detail in speaking of the Negroes of Senegal. The love of the Negress for the White man, though it is flattering to her pride, is rather an affection of the head than the physical senses.

Astringent Injections. The teeth are the chief beauty of the Negress, and the coloured woman. If the former takes little care of them, that is not the case with the latter. Morning and evening, you may see her chewing a tooth-pick made from a piece of lemon wood; half a green lemon, with the seeds picked out, makes the best possible tooth-brush for her. With the juice of this fruit also, mixed with a decoction of the husks of the mahogany nut, they also make a preparation used in the private toilet. Is it to this daily washing, which contracts and strengthens the mucous surfaces, that must be ascribed the rarity of vaginal discharges amongst the women? It seems very probable.

The Quadroon and Mulatta, of Guiana, have one special characteristic. Though not naturally jealous, the White man who gets into the clutches of one of these coloured women, may be pretty sure that she will never let him go. She will [1] use every species

---

[1] The Burmese women exercise an extraordinary and almost irresistible fascination on Europeans. A distinguished English officer, on the high road to promotion and dignity, who had been for some time stationed at Rangoon, being obliged to return with the detachment he commanded to the headquarters of his regiment at Madras, was so inconsolable at this forced absence from his pretty Burmese mistress, who refused to quit her country, that he threw up his commission, and sacrificed his

of pleasure to enchain him. Old Negresses will manufacture for her love philtres, called *piaies*, intended to
secure to her her lover's affections. These are generally aphrodisiac beverages, of which cantharides, *bois
bandé*, (and sometimes a little phosphorus) form the
active ingredients, and which are often dangerous to
use. As to the Misti or Octoroon, who has only an
eighth part of black blood in her veins, she is rare
at Guiana, except in the families of pseudo-whites.
The difference in the colour of the eyes, between her
and a White woman, is scarcely perceptible, and the
hair is soft and long. The shape of the face, the lips,
which are a little more prominent, and the breasts
which are slightly pear-shaped, are the only marks of
black blood.

The Aphrodisiacs used by the Coloured Women.
In the Mulattas and Zambras, the black blood is in
the ascendant, and they both preserve the special
odour of the Negro, and the large size of the genital
organ. If astringents do not produce the desired effect,
and the Massogan is willing to undergo the process,
they will propose to him a secret remedy, which will
cause his member to swell, and increase his voluptuous
delights.

The Decoction of "Tightening Wood". To make
him perform often, they will give him to drink, before
going to bed, a decoction of *bois bandé*, or "tightening
wood". The name well indicate its properties. It is
the bark of a kind of nux vomica tree, related to the

family ties, friends, and social position to return to the arms of his
beloved at Rangoon.

Such cases are far from rare, and are well known to those who have
served in the Madras Presidency.

" false Angostura", which contains brucine, and a little strychnine. According to Rabuteau, [1] it has a special action in exciting the erective muscles of the penis, and produces priapism.

This decoction taken in proper doses, will cause erections; but too strong a dose will produce symptoms of poisoning.

The Hot Aubergine. This last, however, is less dangerous than another method of enlarging the member (*li qua gain go posson*). For this an aubergine (the fruit of the egg plant), of an appropriate size, is taken, and split lengthways. In each half is hollowed out a deep groove capable of containing the member when erect. Then a paste is made with flour, and water, in which has been boiled some " tightening wood ". some phosphorus matches (six to twelve), two or three small pimentos (*zozos*), a dozen peppercorns, and as many cloves, with one or two vanilla beans to give it perfume. The foreskin is drawn back, and the penis and gland covered with this paste, and then enclosed in the aubergine. The plaster is left on for some minutes, and at once produces intense phlogosis. To allay this, the penis is bathed with a luke warm de-coction of mallow, and then is rubbed with soap suds, which are allowed to dry. If these various operations are performed in the morning, eight or ten hours before copulating, it will be found that the penis has really increased in size. It is hot and inflamed, springs into an almost permanent erection at the least touch, and copulation produces a sharp feeling, almost painful. If the aubergine is kept on too long, priapism, or cystitis, will ensue.

[1] Rabuteau, *De la Prostitution en Europe depuis l'Antiquité jusqu'à la fin du XVIe Siècle*, Paris 1851.

Depraved Lust of the White for the Negress.
The White man to whom the strong smell of the
Negress is rather attractive than repellent, is already
physiologically depraved. [1] I have known many such,
—officers and officials—who have returned to France
and married charming young women, but who long
for the black skin and the woolly hair of the daughter
of Ham. It must be confessed, that (to use a familiar
expression) the goods are always up to sample. The
custom of never wearing stays, and the high waisted
dress, fastened under the breasts, like the fashion of
the Directory, gives the body great suppleness, and
leaves the waist in its natural form, for woman was
not constructed on the same pattern as the wasp. If
her lips are black, her teeth are as white as those
of a puppy, and the mucous surfaces of her mouth are
of a coral red, which makes an agreeable contrast to
her black skin. Her breath is pure. If the breast of
the young Negress is pear-shaped, the nipples are nice
and firm. The Negress is, above all, remarkable for
her large pelvis, and has posteriors as ample as those
of the Venus Callipyge. You feel that Nature intended
her to be " a good bearer ". The thigh is of a fairly
good size, but the leg is thin, the calves are small.

---

[1] Pruner Bey defines:—

" The penetrating odour given out by the skin of the negro is ammo-
niacal and rancid; one might say the smell of the he-goat. There is
nothing in it of the aqueous perspiration, for that is not increased. It
is probably due to a volatile oil thrown out by the sebaceous follicles.
Measures of cleanliness greatly diminish it, without however causing it
entirely to disappear. We do not know if this characteristic of the race
can change by means of a uniform diet, as is the case with fishermen
and with opossum hunters in Australia." MEM. SUR LES NEGRES.—
Mém. de la Soc. d'Anthropologie (1860—63, p. 325).

For further details, see the Excursus to the last chapter.

and the foot flat and long. In conclusion, we may mention that the skin of the Negress is always fresh, —a charm that is not without its attractiveness in the heat of the day.

The Beauties of the Coloured Woman. The Zambra is almost a Negress, and her dark brown tint is not so agreeable—according to the opinion of many amateurs—as that of the full Negress. In the Mulatta both races have a partial predominance. Her hair is crisp and curly, though longer. The skin is often of a pretty golden brown colour. Sometimes her genital organs more resemble those of the white race, but the breast is always pear-shaped, and the nipple always black. In the Quadroon, on the contrary, the black type becomes much weaker; the eyes are sensual and languorous, the hair long and almost smooth, the skin often not darker than that of a brunette of the South of Europe; the lips, though, which are of a deep carmine red, remain rather thick. The breast is still markedly pear-shaped, and the nipples black; the pelvis, and buttocks well developed, as in her grandmother, the Negress. The hair of the pubes is almost like that of a European woman, brown, deep chestnut, or red, if the latter was the predominant colour in the males. The clitoris is of a normal size, the mucous surface of the vulva, carmine red, darkened with a dash of sepia. The leg and foot closely resemble those of the European women.

Permanent Marks of Black Blood in the Genital Organs of the Male. In the Quadroon woman the skin is often lighter than that of a dark European woman of the South of Europe; and the Quadroon man is of the same tint. I have known some quite fair, with blue eyes. But, it suffices to cast a glance at the genital organs, to find the indelible marks of black blood. The skin of the penis, and the scrotum, is always darker than that of the rest of the body. The mucous surface of the gland is of a deep red, darker than the clitoris and vulva of the Quadroon woman. By this colour, and by the blue circle at the root of the nails, the Quadroon can be always recognized, even when he is fair. This double mark still exists, though less strongly, in the Octoroon, who has but one eighth part of black blood in his veins.

Perversions of Sexual Passions in the Negro and Coloured Races. There only remains for me to give some details concerning the perversions of sexual passions. On this point, I shall be very brief, having very little to say. The Negresses, and Creole women of colour, are pure, as are also their brothers, in this sense, that pederasty and sodomy—those two vices so common in the Extreme East—are almost unknown to them.

Women are so easily obtained in this pleasant country, that this result is not astonishing. I have, however, attended medically a young Mulatto, who had contracted a gonorrhœa in unnatural copulation with an individual whose social position he refused to reveal.

Another case of unnatural offence, I found in a Negro boy of fifteen, who had accepted the immodest offers of a freed Arab. This latter kept a little liquor store, for the sale of tafia and other spirits. He first made the boy drunk, by offering him a lot of spirits, and, the money not being forthcoming, paid himself on the lad's body. As a natural consequence of the great disproportion in the size of the two parts, there was occasioned a rectal fissure, with acute inflammation of the anus. The mother of the boy, a washerwoman, came to me, and related the story which the young scoundrel had devised. He stated that a young goat had run after him, and had pushed its horn up his rectum! The young blackguard was, no doubt, accustomed to commit the act, for there was a well-marked infundibulum in his anus, and on my threatening not to cure him unless he told me the truth, he confessed everything. The case was cured by appropriate treatment, which cicatrised the rectal fissure, but the boy's anus remained sufficiently dilated to admit the finger easily.

These two cases are the only ones that I met with amongst the coloured races, during a stay of three years: but on the other hand, amongst the Hindoos engaged as coolies, and the Arabs released from the hulks, I found plenty of others.

The question of the deflowering of little Negresses, I shall treat of when I come to study the Negro race in Senegal.

EXCURSUS TO CHAPTER III.

The following astonishing, and hitherto unrecorded facts connected with this abominable propensity in Paris have been communicated by the erudite author of *Histoire de la Prostitution chez tous les Peuples du Monde.* I give them in his own words:

" Greece and ancient Rome, where sotadic habits enjoyed absolute liberty, had not thought of organising male prostitution, by consecrating to it special lupanars.

The Greek and Latin historians have not left us anything, which could indicate the existence of brothels
of youths and young men addicted to the exercise of
Socratic love. It would be necessary to go to Persia
in order to discover traces of such tolerated establishments devoted to the vice against nature, called by
euphemism in the eighteenth century, *the philosophical
sin* (see on that subject the *Voyage en Perse* of the
Chevalier Chardin, in the 17th century). It was never
suspected that an establishment of the kind could exist
in the very heart of Paris, in the middle of the nine-
teenth century. The fact is however incontestable, as
the rare survivors of the period of the Restoration
may testify. At that time the police was so closely
occupied watching political conspiracies, that it could
find no leisure to take much interest in moral disorders.
This only can explain the sort of impunity that, from
1820 to 1826, was accorded to an establishment, undoubtedly not authorised, but to whose existence the
authorities closed their eyes.

This establishment had been founded in the Rue
du Doyenné, which formed part of the ancient quarter
of Saint Thomas du Louvre, enclosed within the quadri-
lateral formed by the junction of the Louvre with
the Tuileries. This Rue du Doyenné was lower than
the level of the Place du Carrousel; it gave on one
side, on to the large avenue that the Revolution had
opened on the site of the houses which had been
demolished to enable the Place du Carrousel to com-
municate with the court of the old Louvre. On the
other side, the Rue du Doyenné had no issue, and
led only to blind alleys looking on to abandoned
gardens and waste grounds. This house of male prostitution was located in a mansion of the 17th century

appropriated to its new destination. The grand entrance
was suppressed, and in its place were two small
side-doors, which remained shut during the day and
were only opened at night. A lantern suspended to
a post opposite the building shed a dubious light upon
its approaches, and it might have been supposed to
be uninhabited, and indeed had probably during the
day for only inhabitants the master of the house and
his servants. We were however assured that the
employés resided there and that they were subjected
to a very severe discipline; when they went out they
were kept within sight and had nothing to do with
women outside of the house; for this establishment,
we were informed, served for two distinct purposes:
the door to the right was for men, that on the left
was for women. The latter, who were no doubt but
rare exceptions, came there in quest of men ready
for *any kind of work*, docile and indefatigable servitors, whom nothing should disgust or fatigue. The
men on the contrary (and in the outset the establishment was created solely for their use) on going to
spend the evening or the night in the male Gynæceum,
would have avoided it with horror, if they had been
exposed to meet with women there. I have also heard,
that the health of the active pensioners was closely
looked after by special doctors, whose mission was to
preserve them from an ugly malady called the *crystal-
line*. As soon as the shades of evening began to
fall, at 4 o'clock in winter, and at 8 o'clock in summer, the palace of male prostitution seemed to revive;
the blinds were seen to half open, the windows to be
illumined, and preparations made to receive visitors.
At each door of the establishment there could be seen
a young man, of effeminate appearance, his hair care-

fully curled, elegantly dressed, his neck bare, walking to and fro, in the street, beneath the glare of the lamp, awaiting *customers*. I remember having seen, more than once, such *goods*, and I was struck as much by their decent and candid features as by the provocation of their dress and appearance: they had exaggerated the strange fashions of the day: frock-coats with leg-of-mutton sleeves, very tight at the waist, showing off the hips and posterior development. It must also be borne in mind that they wore rose-coloured or blue neck-ties, and that they usually had on light coloured gay suits, hazel, grey, or greenish. These details might be called the *bagatelles* of the door-way.

This pretty institution suddenly disappeared in 1826, after the publication of a malicious article, in which the police was called over the coals by a theatrical journal, wherein the author expressed his astonishment that such a public or semi-public establishment could have so long have been able to peaceably exist next door to the office of the *Gazette de France!*[1] As the writer maliciously said: "Are we to presume neighbourly good fellowship between the two establish-ments", at the same time permitting himself an injur-ious allusion to the supposed tastes of Louis XVIII.

In the middle ages, the principal domain of prosti-tution in Paris was called the *Champ Flory*, perhaps by analogy with the *Field of Flowers* the privileged rendezvous of the courtesans in ancient Rome. In the 18th century and the first forty years of the 19th, it was in the Champs Elysées that sodomy held its nocturnal sessions. There are still living many wit-

---

[1] The oldest political newspaper in France (1660), the organ of legit-imate monarchy and of strictly orthodox catholicity.

nesses of the facts we are about to relate, enabling them to be recorded in a history of ways and habits. The entire planted square extending from the Place Louis XV (now Place de la Concorde) to the *Allée des Veuves*, between the main Avenue of the Champs Elysées and the Cours-la-Reine, was the reserved fief of *Ebugors:* these did not show themselves during the day, at all events ostensibly, but at even-tide they took possession of it, as masters absolute, until dawn. The *Allée des Veuves*, since become the superb *Avenue Montaigne*, bordered by handsome buildings and mansions, was at that time nearly uninhabited, and the low wine-shops, which invaded it at the time of the Directory, were all enfeoffed to the dominating sect of the Ebugors. LA TYNNA, in his *Dictionnaire topographique, historique et étymologique des Rues de Paris* (5ᵉ ed. 1812), did not know, or did not dare to divulge the truth, concerning the *Allée des Veuves:* "This alley" says he, "at the bottom of the Champs Elysées, but little frequented before the establishment of the drink-shops, is really most appropriate for *Veuves* (widows). *Veuve*, in the figured language of the sodomites, was synonymous of the passive actors or *patients*, in the sense of the latin word *patiens*. From all corners of Paris, those interested repaired every evening to the square of the *Allée des Veuves*, and as soon as these occupants had taken possession of it, they allowed no indifferent stroller to intrude within the friendly shade of the venerable trees beneath which the sodomites were wont to sport. It would indeed have been dangerous to venture in the dark beneath these trees, guarded by their usual frequenters, as the forests of antiquity were by sylvans, satyrs and fauns. But the people of the *Allée des Veuves* would not have tolerated the approach of any nymph of the woods. There was no doubt some pass-word, some sign of recognition, to enable late-comers to be admitted without opposition to the free exercise of their habitual pastimes. At any rate the police and night patrols never ventured into these quarters, where they would have found an offensive army to oppose their imprudent curiosity. There, during seven or eight hours of the night, at all seasons, was a prodigious concourse of sectaries, who abandoned themselves to their secret cult, without fear of being disturbed or troubled. It is asserted that at certain times the mysterious love-feasts of these neophytes degenerated into a sort of nocturnal *sabbat*, in which the horrible familiars of this infernal pell-mell seize hold of each other hap-hazard and indiscriminately. Then were heard cries, groans, complaints, confused sighs. In these sorts of occult and tenebrous solemnities, the entire sanctuary was enclosed by ropes stretched from tree to tree, and there were armed men charged to keep out all the profane, by threats or by force. Victor Hugo, who resided, in 1831, in the Rue Jean Goujon, in the then new and almost desert quarter of Francis I, when he had retained friends of his till a late hour at his home, would often accompany them, as walking in groups, they conversed on art and literature, as far as the Place de la Concorde, whence, after bidding his friends good-night, he would return home alone composing verses as he went. He had several times noticed certain men who, when he passed, arranged themselves in échelons along the border of the square of the *Allée des Veuves*, and who seemed to observe him from afar, but without attempting to approach him. He could not suppose these men to be robbers and he was curious to know what was the motive of their habitual presence in this solitary place; but poetry soon lifted him above the things of the earth, and he continued his walk, reciting his verses in a low voice, as if he had been in his study. On one occasion, he stopped, seeking for a rhyme, or staring at the moon, which was shining in all its brilliancy: a man detached himself suddenly from the shade of the trees, and advanced towards him, bowing: "Sir," said the stranger, with extreme politeness, "we must entreat you not remain here any longer. We know who you are, and we should be sorry that one of ours, not knowing you, should be disagreeable or hostile in addressing you."—"But what then are you doing here?" asked Victor Hugo, "Every evening I notice people glide along in the shade, and disappear beneath the trees." "Pray pay no attention to that, Sir," quickly answered the person, whom Victor Hugo had before him; "we do not disturb or get in the way of anybody, but we do not suffer anyone to disturb or interfere with us; we are here at home!" Victor Hugo understood, bowed and went his way. Another evening, that he had taken along with his friends the counter-alley which bordered the *Avenue des Veuves*, he found this counter-alley obstructed by a line of chairs bound together with cords. At the same time a menacing voice cried out, "no thoroughfare here." Another voice, less formidable and almost friendly, continued immediately: "Mr. Victor Hugo is requested, for this time only, to pass on the other side of the Avenue des Champs Elysées."

About this time, Guilbert de Pixerécourt, who was manager of the Theatre Royal of the Opera-Comique, had the annoyance of being informed by the com-

missary of police of his quarter, that the previous
evening, behind a heap of paving-stones in the Rue
Saint Fiacre, the Secretary-General of the Opera-Comique had been arrested, being discovered in intimate
liaison with a Limousin stone-mason. Guilbert de
Pixerécourt had the greatest difficulty in saving the
Secretary-General of his theatre from being prosecuted
in the Correctional Police Court; he sent for him
and overwhelmed him with his just indignation. " It
is true, *Monsieur le Directeur*," replied the guilty
man, shedding tears, "I was wrong not to know how
to contain myself until I should have arrived at the
Champs-Elysées, with the worthy fellow I met on the
Boulevard du Temple. I am grieved at a scandal
which would not have occurred, if we had gone
directly as usual to the *Allée des Veuves*."

When the municipal authorities at last decided to
morally cleanse the Champs-Elysées, and to hunt out
of it for ever the *Ebugors* of the *Allée des Veuves*
and neighbourhood, these gentry whom the police
forced to quit, used during some time to come back
again: it was necessary to drive them away at night,
and to make numerous arrests, which were often resisted with arms in hand and led to sanguinary reprisals.
Finally the law got the upper hand, and the sect of
the *Ebugors* was finally dispersed and subjected to the
police regulations."

One of the most abominable pederastic scandals of modern times, and which created an immense sensation
at the period, occurred during the reign of Napoleon III.
There are many persons now living, contemporaries
of the events, who perfectly remember the circumstances, the details of which oozed out notwithstanding

the strenuous efforts that were made to stifle the report of them.

The following are the facts as related by Pisanus Fraxi:—

The anonymous authors of *l'Histoire amoureuse des Gaules* have revealed to us one of the most singular episodes of the reign of Louis XIV, in writing the annals of *France become Italian.* It is known how indignant and humiliated the " *Grand Monarque* " felt to find his own son, the Count of Vermandois, was compromised in the ugly doings of the society of Franco-Italian *Ebugors.* The Emperor Napoleon III experienced a similar mortification when he learned that some of the most eminent men of his reign were compromised in a great Sodomy Company limited business. The originator, or at least the director of this affair, in which very important sums of money were invested on mutual account, was, it was said, Mr. C—n, the syndic (president) of the Parisian Association of Stockbrokers. This gentleman, one of the richest members of this association, was perhaps no more than the not over scrupulous and obliging friend of these personages of the Court, of the Senate and of Financial circles, with whom banking operations had brought him into intimate contact. However that might be, an association, or rather club, of sodomists had already been four or five years in existence without the fact being noted, when mere chance made it known.

The Colonel of the *Dragons de l'Impératrice* was advised that the soldiers of this crack regiment were making extravagant expenses of all kinds and that they had most of them gold in their pockets. It was not easy to explain how these men could possibly have so suddenly become rich, it being known that neither they nor their families possessed the least amount of income. They were chosen among the most handsome and pretty-faced men in the army, and their coquettish uniform appeared to be their sole appanage. Several of them were searched; they were found possessed of well-lined purses; one had 25 louis (£20) on him. They pretended that this money was gained at play, but they did not or would not say at what game they had made it. They were temporarily put for a few days under arrest. At the same time it transpired that the *Cent-Gardes* of the Emperor had made their fortune, at all events a great number of them, and particularly those who were specially remarkable for effeminate beauty of face, bodily beauty, or elegant appearance. These latter possessed, besides splendid jewels, watches, chains, rings, and a little stock of ready cash, which could not be the result of avowable economies. There were new questionings, new researches, but always with the same uncertainties. At last a witness declared that one of the dragoons, still under arrest, had told him, after a copious dinner largely moistened with wine, that he would one day become a millionnaire, because no one could do the Empress better than he. The question suggested itself what was the meaning of: *to do the Empress*. This was soon made clear, when the police, which had been put on the scent, discovered the headquarters of the *Ebugors*, in a mansion in the *Allée des Veuves*, the property of the Society and which served for the cult of Sodom. This mansion, purchased at the expense of the members, had been furnished and arranged specially for its purpose; there were to be seen there splendid apartments, that were never but transitorily

occupied, by unknown persons who were received only
on presentation of a medal or sort of *abraxas* showing
mysterious signs and monograms. The door-keeper
and the servants of this house were taken into custody,
after a visit to the premises had left no doubt of their
usual destination. In the interior two wardrobes were
discovered filled with all kinds of costumes, feminine
of course, and among them, the costumes worn by the
Empress Eugénie in ceremonies and official receptions.
This strange discovery led to another still more significant. A quantity of correspondence was seized, letters in all sorts of hand-writings, anonymous or pseu-
donymous, interchanged between the associates and
their adherents, who were none other than *Cent-gardes*
and *Dragons de l'Impératrice*. A judicial enquiry
was instituted, and the porter-manager of the establishment was forced to speak. The recognized head
of the affair, Mr. C....n, was summoned before the Procureur-Général who, after a simply confidential examination, thought it necessary to refer the matter to the
Emperor in person, communicating to him at the same
time the reports of the police, in which were mentioned the names of several eminent personages, who
were on the point of being involved in the most scandalous prosecution. The Emperor had no sooner listened to the Procureur-Général and perused the documents he had brought, than he judged it prudent to
suspend proceedings and to hush up the affair, keeping
at the same time in his possession all the documents
connected with it, and among them the famous corre-
spondences, in which the acts and doings of the interested
parties were exposed without any veil and in the most
figurative and burning language. As he said to the
Procureur-Général: "It is advisable to spare one's

people and one's country such shameful things; scandal
corrects nobody and does harm to every one. The
punishment of such turpitude must be altogether arbitrary and secret; I undertake to reach the guilty of
all ranks, without having recourse to the laws, which
I consider to be impotent against such acts of human
degradation." The subordinate culprits who were in
preventive arrest, were set at liberty. No one else
was troubled openly; but Mr. C....n resigned his
position as a stockbroker and retired to his country residence, where he continued to remain: two or
three senators no longer showed themselves at Court,
five or six other incriminated persons, more or less
compromised, exercised justice on themselves by disap-
pearing from Parisian society, where their unexplained
absence was remarked and much commented on. The
Cent-gardes and the *Dragons de l'Impératrice* were
not subjected to any disciplinary measures, but a great
number of them were passed into other regiments,
where they remained under the supervision of their
new chiefs. For ten or fifteen days low murmurs circulated about this affair and its consequences, but the
matter was stifled by superior order. No doubt the
correspondence and documents in the hands of the
Emperor, were completely destroyed, for not a single
one was ever found again, as the authors of the *Fourth
of September* hoped they would be when they made
a most minute examination of the private papers in
the Tuileries. Nevertheless the liberty was taken to
publish the love-letters of a senator to a dragoon who,
under different costumes, had played the part of the
Empress in the mysteries of the mansion in the *Allée
des Veuves.*

The house in the *Allée des Veuves*, although undoubt-

edly one of the most important, was by no means
the only establishment devoted to the practice of
sodomy, nor were its frequenters the only individuals
addicted to that vice. Paris was indeed at that time
infested with clubs of pederasts, and sodomy was very
generally practised by men of all classes. Although
the papers relating to the scandal in the *Allée des
Veuves* have no doubt disappeared, as my informant
surmises, yet other official documents, amply sufficient
to bear out my assertion, are still in existence. I
have had the opportunity of perusing one of these, a
police report, duly signed and approved, dated " 16
Juillet 1864", some time before the breaking up of
the band already mentioned. The chief of that society
was already known to the police, and is described in
the report before me as: " A very good-looking old
gentleman, and exceedingly rich, known at the Barrière
de l'Ecole (*sic*, intended probably for Étoile) under the
name of Father C—n, surnamed *l'homme à la Ringué*."
The report continues:

" He comes to the café Truffaut, notices some young
soldier who takes his fancy, makes the waiter convey
a message to him and leaves the café without waiting for an answer. If the soldier accepts, he goes to
the rendezvous, and as Father C—n is well known,
he never goes alone. Hardly has the meeting commenced, than immediately a lot of troopers appear,
fall upon Father C—n, beat him, and force him to
give them all the money he has about him, which he
does with good grace enough; then, when he has not
a sou left and that often he has even given up his
watch, he escapes with tears in his eyes, repeating as
he runs: ' What an unfortunate situation for such a
man as I.'"

The attention of the police was directed to these illicit practices by one of the sect, A. R .... m, from whom the Vicomte de M .. y had abducted his favourite youth and "maîtresse en titre", and who, in a fit of jealousy, gave information against the band. In the report in question the names and addresses of the persons implicated are given in full, together with numerous specimens of their love-letters to each other. On one occasion there were actually eye-witnesses of their practices; these are minutely described, and it appears that a bitch figured in these orgies. Again I transcribe from the report:

" When these assemblies were complete, they closed the curtains, and abandoned themselves to scenes of orgie and of scandal that disturbed the repose of the other dwellers in the house during a great part of the night. They were distinctly heard giving each other feminine names, and they could even be seen between the curtains masturbating and sucking each other. One of the specialities of these soirées was an act of beastliness which they called; *l'Omelette à la Grenouille*, [1] wherein there figured a bitch, which must have been put to great pain, to judge by the howls of the animal that these gentry tried to smother by songs with accompaniment on the piano. These facts were attested by most respectable persons, lodgers in the house."

I have elsewhere [2] mentioned, under reserve, balls of sodomites, and I am now able to confirm that assertion. In the report under consideration two balls are spoken of: the one given at no. 8, Place de la

[1] The frog omelette.
[2] INDEX LIBRORUM PROHIBITORUM.

Madeleine, January 2, 1864, by an "homme d'affaires",
E. D . . . . d; the other, a return entertainment by the
Vicomte de M . . y, at the Pavillon de Rohan, 172,
Rue de Rivoli, on the 16th of the same month. At
this assembly, there were at least 150 men, and some
of them so well disguised as women that the landlord
of the house was unable to detect their sex."

We consider it but justice to say that most of the
above extracts have been taken from that valuable
work by Pisanus Fraxi, the *Centuria Librorum Abs-
conditorum*. London (privately printed) 1879.

CHAPTER IV.

The Hindoo race in Guiana.—Laziness of the Black of Cayenne.
— The hired Hindoo.—Anthropological characteristics of the
Hindoo.—The genital organ of the race. Comparison of the
genital organ of the Negro with that of the Hindoo.—The four
kinds of temperament of the Hindoo woman.— Want of morality
in the Hindoo race.—Perversions of the sexual passion.

Laziness of the Black Man of Cayenne. The Black,
at Cayenne, generally dislikes the painful labour of
agriculture. If he is the possessor of a patch of ground,
he plants some bananas, a little manioc, and a few
roots of tobacco, and pimento. Mudfish form his chief
food; tafia costs sixpence a quart, retail. The Black
has few wants he cannot supply, and if he does work
at all, it is usually at the gold diggings, where he
can earn large wages, which are paid in nuggets, and,
perhaps, he manages to conceal a few other nuggets.
It is no rarity to see a Black arrive at Cayenne with
several thousand francs; the first thing he does is to
buy a complete suit of black, with a tall hat, and a
white tie, like a respectable lawyer. He spends all
his money on women, and when his cash is gone, he
returns to his work at the mines.

The Hired Hindoo. To cultivate the large estates
recourse is had to Hindoos, hired with the consent of

the English Government. For a small daily pay, his food, clothes, and lodging, the Hindoo must give five years' work. Practically, he is worse off than if he were a slave for life, for his master gets the greatest possible amount of work out of him, without caring if the poor wretch's strength is worn out at the end of the time. But we must pass over this subject. I will only state here, that this system of hiring Hindoos is a deplorably bad one. They are picked up from the dregs of the great cities of Calcutta, and Benares, which is as much as to say that they are totally unfit for the hard work of cultivating the fields. As I had found, in Cochin-China, the Malabar healthy, and robust, so did I find the hired coolie, puny, and unhealthy, for syphilitic diseases are soon communicated amongst these voluntary exiles.

I was able to study this race closely, having obtained from the Colonial Government, one of these hired coolies, to employ as my boy. I was lucky enough to meet with a lad of eighteen, almost a Caucasian in form and features, who was active, and intelligent; he spoke a little English, and quickly learned French, and served as an interpreter between me and my Hindoo patients. They were non-paying patients, and for a very good reason. I was thus able to gather some curious information about these unfortunate waifs, who generally belong to the class of pariahs, for they are almost the only persons who would consent to expatriate themselves, and quit the soil where their ancestors rest.

Anthropological Characteristics of the Hindoo.
Anatomically, the Hindoo appeared to me to resemble the European, but the more refined European of the

great cities.   His features are regular, the nose straight,
the eyes horizontal, and widely open, the lips thin, the
feet and hands small, and well-made.   The long and
smooth hair often falls to the hips.   The skin, however,
is almost as dark as that of the Negro, but has not
the same earthy tint, but often has the colour of old
bronze.   The breast of the woman is far from being
pear-shaped like that of the Negress, but is not hemispherical, like that of the White women: it is rather
arched, but, in the young girl, is small and firm.   In
the adult woman it is greatly enlarged, but does not
hang like the breast of the Negress.

The Genital Organ of the Race.   The *Kama
Sutra* [1] divides men into three classes, according to

[1] The *Kama Sutra* of Vatsayayana, a book of Hindoo Erotology
written in Sanscrit about the fifth century of the Christian era.

This book was done from the Sanscrit into English and privately
printed in London, in 1883, and is one of those important anthropological treatises for which India is famous. It appears that the collation
of original MSS. obtained from Calcutta, Benares and Jeypur was only
effected after immense trouble and with the help of several distinguished
scholars. The wealth of erotic Indian literature existing in Hindi and
Sanscrit may be gauged from the following:—

(1) Ratira has ya = *The Secrets of Love.*
(2) Pancha sayka = *The Five Arrows.*
(3) Smara Pradipa = *The Light of Love.*
(4) Ratimanjari = *The garland of Love.*
(5) Rasmanjari = *The Push of Love.*
(6) Kamaledhiplava = *The Boat on Love's Ocean.*

This last is also known as Ananga Ranga, or *the stage of the Bodiless one.*

Further information may be found in the learned introduction to the book
itself: in the *avant-propos* to the charming French edition translated
from the English version and published by Liseux (Paris, 1885)—not to
be confounded with a cheap, nasty and incorrect French text issued by
Carré and translated by Lamairesse—and in CATENA LIBRORUM TACEN-
DORUM (all about privately printed books) *by* PISANUS FRAXI, (London,
1885).

the length of their *lingam*,—the hares, the bulls, and the stallions. In comparison with the Negro—the type of the stallion in the human race—the Hindoo is a hare, but a little bigger, however, than the Annamite, who appears to me to occupy the lowest place in the scale of the comparative sizes of the genital organs. The penis of the Hindoo is generally covered by the foreskin, when in its normal condition, and when in erection, in the boy not yet arrived at puberty. It does not become bared in erection until the lad has arrived at puberty, and is of an average age of sixteen to eighteen, and then that is probably due to masturbation.

The skin of the penis, and the scrotum, is of a fine black, or deep chocolate, as in the Zambro, but, it should be remarked, the mucous surface of the gland of the Hindoo is never black. It is of a more or less darkened red; almost bright in the waifs of the higher castes, whose skin is lighter than that of the pariahs.

In its usual condition, the yard is extremely flaccid, but increases greatly when erect, being then almost treble the size, and as hard as that of the European. The average size appeared to me to be about 5 inches long, by $1\frac{1}{4}$ in diameter. Many are from $3\frac{1}{2}$ to 4 inches, by one inch. Few are from $5\frac{1}{2}$ to 6 inches, which is nearly the European average, and which here appears to be the maximum. The testicles are oval, and the size of a pigeon's egg.

Comparison of the Genital Organ of the Negro with that of the Hindoo. By the side of the Negro of Guiana, the Hindoo cuts but a sorry figure. The yard of the former, when limp, measures from five to six inches long by $1\frac{1}{4}$ to $1\frac{1}{2}$ inches in diameter.

When erect, it does not swell proportionally, but rises only to 6¼ to 8 inches by 2¼ or 2½ inches in diameter. But the erection is never hard like that of the European, the Chinese and the Hindoo. It is always rather soft, and feels to the hand like a strong elastic hollow tube of black india-rubber. The testicle of the Black is rounder than that of the Hindoo.

Another characteristic difference is that of the secretion of the mucous surfaces. Either from cleanliness, or from some other cause, a very small quantity of sebaceous smegma is found under the foreskin of the Negro. If the Negress very rarely suffers from discharges from the vulva, the Hindoo woman is, in this respect, almost a match for the Congai. This is evidently a difference of race, for the food of the hired coolies is the same as that of the low class Blacks, except that rice takes the place of manioc, or cassava.

The *Kama Sutra* does not give the dimensions of the *lingam*, but this omission is repaired by the *Ananga Ranga*, [1] written in the 16th century of our era, whilst the previous work dates from the 5th century. The *Ananga Ranga* gives, for the dimensions of the penis of the " hare-man ", a length of six fingers broad; for the " bull-man ", nine, and for the " man stallion ",

---

[1] *Ananga Ranga*, a Hindoo treatise on conjugal love, written in Sanscrit by the great poet, Kalyana Malla (16th Century).

This work, far from being obscene, is an intelligent study of the sexual functions of the married relations, and in the East is studied by people of high rank and low. Burton, with Arbuthnot's coadjutorship, made an English version (*Cosmopoli*, 1885), of it direct from the original Sanskrit texts, and it was privately issued in London in a limited number. In the Arabic it is known as *Lizzat al-Nisa* (Pleasures of Women), and the common folk of India style it *Koka Pandit*, the name of its *supposed* author. Isidore Liseux, the ex-Catholic priest, printed a translation of it in French (Paris, 1886).

twelve. It should be remarked that the finger of the Hindoo, being thin and delicate, is not more than 0.6 of an inch in breadth, and these measures would therefore correspond to 3.6 inches, 5.4 inches, and 7.2 inches. The result of my personal observations is, that the great bulk of the Hindoo coolies may be classed as " men-hares", only a small number are " men-bulls", and a smaller number still " men-stallions".

The dimensions of the depth of the *yoni* (vagina) correspond to those of the men of their class. Neither of the works mentioned gives the size; that depends, mainly, upon the more or less frequent usage that the woman makes of her *yoni*. [1] But, as a general principle, the vulva and the vagina of the Hindoo woman are much less widely open than those of the Negress, though they are in excess of those of the Congai.

The four Kinds of Temperament of the Hindoo Woman. [2] The *Ananga Ranga* classifies women in four orders, according to their temperament. It may be interesting to remark, that this excellent work (to which we refer the reader), was far in advance, at that time, of the medical science of Europe, which was then in its infancy. Not until the 17th century, did we get a classification analogous to that of the Hindoos,

[1] See the Excursus to this chapter.

[2] The Hindoo woman, according to Mantegazza (a) is pretty and has a gentle, passionate nature. She generally possesses certain beauties, eyes of raven black, glowing with the heat of the tropics, large, and shadowed beneath heavy eyebrows and lids; her shoulders, arms and breast are worthy of a Greek statue. Her pretty little feet, free from any tyrannical imprisonment of shoe or boot, are adorned with ankle bracelets and rings on the toes, which have retained intact their pristine beauty and freshness." PLOSS.—*Das Weib* (vol I. p. 68).

a Mantegazza—"*Indien*," (Jena, 1885).

for the four orders of women correspond almost exactly
to the four temperaments of the European doctors,—
the nervous, the sanguine, the bilious, and the lymphatic. I only met at Guiana with the two last orders,
the *Shankhini* (the woman conch) and the *Hastini*
(woman elephant). The anatomical details of the
Hindoo author are very exact. Whether the moral
details were equally correct, it is impossible for me
to say.

**The Want of Morality, and Sexual Perversions
amongst the Hindoos.** The coolie, it should be
remarked, is a pariah, and the pariah in India, as
Jacolliot has well pointed out, has no morality. Badly
fed and badly paid, the hired coolies try to make
money by any means they can,—the men that they
may procure tafia, and the women that they may buy
suitable clothes and jewels. Hence there is a complete
want of morality amongst these poor people.

The youth, of from fifteen to twenty years of age,
gives himself up to pederasty, and finds customers
amongst the Arabs and Europeans released from the
hulks. The woman also is ready to practise any
method, like the prostitute of Europe, and has not,
as the Negress has, a horror of sodomy. The admirers
of this sort of pleasure, moreover, claim in justification
(exactly as they did in Cochin-China at the beginning
of the occupation) the dangers of ordinary copulation.
Gonorrhœa and syphilis are the lot of those who
indulge in natural coition with the Hindoo woman;—
she shares this miserable distinction with the Congai.

A depraved man can therefore easily satisfy his
passions in Guiana. If natural copulation with the

Negress, or the coloured woman, have no attractions for him, he has the Hindoo woman or boy to fall back on. But I should remark here, that there is one remarkable difference between this last and the Annamite boy. The latter takes delight in unnatural acts, and will become an active agent if required; the Hindoo, on the contrary, is passive, and nothing but passive. In no case does he try to reverse the rôles. Besides which, the Arab (or the White man) who is an active pederast, would not permit this; he obliges the boy to suffer his attacks without giving him any compensation of the same nature.

As to the deformities of the vulva, or the anus, produced in the Hindoo race by coition, they much resemble those which I have described in the Annamite race. To enumerate them here would be a repetition, so I refer the reader to what I have already written.

I should also remark, that the Hindoo women are well acquainted with means for procuring abortion, analogous to those described in the *Ananga Ranga*, and that they do not hesitate to use them, if they find themselves pregnant by a foreigner.

EXCURSUS   TO CHAPTER IV.

Lombroso takes upon this matter a somewhat opposite position. We quote a most important series of statistics (given in his "*La Femme Criminelle*", pp. 320—21, Paris 1896):—

"With regard to the genital organs, I have been able to find among prostitutes, hypertrophy of the labia minora in 16 %, and monstruous in 2 cases; in 6 cases it was accompanied by hypertrophy of the clitoris and of the labia majora.

Gurrieri noticed an exaggerated development of the clitoris in 13 % and 13 % also in the development of the labia minora; there was excessive development of the labia majora in 6,5 % of the cases observed.

Riccardi noted on 30 prostitutes observed by him:

 5 with hypertrophy of the labia minora;
 2 „ „ „ „ clitoris;
 1 „ hypospadia „ „ „

Gurrieri found among 60 prostitutes:

8 cases of hypertrophy of the clitoris;
8 „ excessive development of the labia minora.

A woman who had gained celebrity as an adulteress as well as a murderess from lascivious motives, had an enormous development of the clitoris and of the labias minora: almost all the pseudo hermaphrodites noted by De Crecchio and Hoffmann had exaggerated sexual tendencies, either towards the one or towards the other sex.

However, I am of opinion that excepting the richer pilose development, the anomalous condition of the organ does not correspond with the extent of vice, at all events not in the proportion that has been asserted.

Among 3000 prostitutes, Parent-Duchatelet found only three with an exaggerated development of the clitoris, which in one case reached to the size of a child's penis (3,14 inches) but unaccompanied with any special tendencies nor with a masculine aspect, and notwithstanding the absence of uterus, of menstruation and of breasts: she declared that misery had driven her to this unhappy trade, which she would gladly renounce. The other two showed no trace of hermaphrodism and were quite indifferent. Among the numerous hairy ones (*barbues*) there was no anomaly of the clitoris, nor any special tendencies.

The profession does neither widen nor deform the vagina, as it is supposed; there are neo-prostitutes, with enlarged vagina and *vice versa*."

CHAPTER V.

The Penitentiary and its occupants.—Transported criminals, or old convicts.—Horrible customs of the convicts.—The innate liking of the Arab for pederasty.—A crew under the " Caudine forks."—Ferocious lust of the African Arabs.—The Arab as an active pederast.—Pederasty is primarily a question of race.—The organ of generation in the Arab.

Transported Criminals, or Old Convicts. Formerly there were sent to the hulks, under the name of convicts, those condemned to hard labour. In the present day, they are sent to the penal colonies, and are said to be " transported ". The hulks is called " a penitentiary ",—a mere change of name, for the institution is exactly the same.

When transportation first commenced, in 1854, it was intended to renew at Guiana, on a large scale, the attempts at forming an agricultural colony which began in the time of Louis XIV, and Louis XV, and reform the criminal by giving him the moral stimulus of labour. This attempt failed, on the whole. According to the medical statistics, the average life of the convict was hardly more than twenty months, in the Colony, and, ten years later, Guiana was abandoned for New Caledonia.

Foreign criminals continued to be sent there (from the Antilles, Reunion, India, and even some Annam-

ites) for crimes against civil law, and especially the
Arabs, who alone formed a great part of the population of the Penitentiary. The only convicts now
sent to Guiana are a few white criminals, art workmen, and clerks. At present, these form but a small
minority, but in reality they are the leaders of the
Penitentiary.

Fearful Immorality of the Convicts. [1] The convict, though disguised under the name of the transported prisoner, has retained all the horrible immorality
special to the hulks. These habits, in the opinion of
certain moralists, arise from the men being deprived
of the feminine element. I believe, however, that this
is but a secondary cause; and that the real source of
unnatural vice is hereditary depravity. It is a law of
atavism, and a real mental disease, as medical science
has now pointed out. In all assemblies of human
beings, "like will to like", and private associations
are formed between people having the same tastes,
and the same habits.

When transportation first began, a good many of
the convicts married, and set to work to cultivate the
land which was granted them by the Government.
Of all the establishments so founded, one only has

[1] The following note is by J. A Symonds: "Balzac in *Une dernière incarnation de Vautrin*, describes the morals of the French
bagnes. Dostoieffsky in "Prison life in Siberia", touches on the same
subject. See his portrait of Sirotkin, pp. 52 *et seq.*, p. 120 (Edition
J. & R. Maxwell, London). We may compare Carlier, *Les Deux
Prostitutions* (pp. 300—1), for an account of the violence of homosexual
passions in French prisons. The initiated are familiar with the fact in
English prisons. Bouchard, in his "*Confessions*" (Paris, Liseux, 1881),
describes the convict station at Marseilles in 1630.

H. Ellis, *Sexual Inversion*, p. 13. London, 1897, in 8vo.

survived, the Penitentiary of St. Lawrence at Maroni,
which still lingers on, thanks to a subsidy from the
mother country.

In order that the white race may prosper in a climate
so unhealthy, it must have the support of black blood.
The Negro, though shallow-witted, is honest at bottom,
and has a considerable contempt for the transported
prisoner; no Negress, however low she might be,
would consent to ally herself with a convict,—a Government slave as she calls him. The despatch of the
white criminals to New Caledonia consequently caused
the Arab element to predominate at Guiana, and increased the vice of sodomy, instead of diminishing it.
I shall devote a chapter specially to the white convicts
of New Caledonia, but, for the present, I shall only
occupy myself with the foreign convicts.

We know already the Negro of Guiana, and his
brother of the Antilles differs but little from him. As
to the Negro of Senegal, he is very rarely found in
the Penitentiary. We have studied also the Hindoo
and the Annamite. There remains to speak about the
Arab convict.

The Innate Liking of the Arab for Sodomy. The
Arab is an inveterate pederast, even in his own
country, where there is no lack of women. He willingly
puts into practice the parable which is attributed to
the *Koran:* [1] " A man finding one day that the
principal door of his house was blocked up with filth,
determined to enter by the back door."

[1] Our author is here undoubtedly in error. Islam, large and generous
in all that relates to normal sexual intercourse, stamps unnatural practices
with peculiar abhorrence. We quote from Charles HAMILTON's "*Hedaya
or Guide, a Commentary of Musulman Law,*"—" translated by order of

I do not know whether this parable is really to be found in the *Koran*, but the Arab acts as though it were. The fact has been observed by all travellers and moralists who have been in Arabia and Tunis.

A Crew under the " Caudine Forks". The Arab tribes of the coasts of Algeria and Morocco, it is well-known, take by force the unfortunate wretches who are wrecked on their shores. A little time before the Algerian expedition, a French ship of war, a brig called the *Silenus*, was thrown on the African coast, and all the crew had to pass under the " Caudine

the Governor General and Council of Bengal."—4 vols 4to. London, 1791.

In chap. IV (of vol. I, page 167) "of the Marriage of Slaves" the following remarkable paragraph is given.

If a man marry the female slave of another, and be desirous of committing the act of *Azil* with her (i.e. *emissio Seminis in Ano, vel inter Mamillas*), this shall depend upon her master's permission, according to *Hancefa*; and such also is the *Zâhir Rawâyet*.—According to the two disciples, the permission for this act rests with the slave, because [as being the man's wife] carnal connexion is her right, but by *Azil* that carnal connexion which is her right is frustrated; her consent, therefore, is a requisite condition to the legality of the act, the same as that of a free woman, contrary to the case of a female slave, who is the property of the person having such connexion with her, because carnal connexion is not her right (whence it is that she is not entitled to claim the carnal act of her master or owner), and consequently her consent is not a condition.—The principle upon which the *Zâhir Rawâyet* proceeds in this case is, that the act of *Azil* defeats the intention of marriage, which is the production of children, and this is a right of the master; whence it is thas *his* consent is a condition, and not that of the *slave*.—And herein appears a distinction between the state of a free woman and that of a slave [in marriage].

In vol. IV, of Hamilton's " *Guide* " further information is found under the significant heading of " ABOMINATIONS " and we have given an extract of same, bearing upon our subject, at the end of the present chapter.

forks ", whether they liked it or not. Amongst them was a young naval officer, [1] who suffered the same fate as the others. One day—some years after the taking of Algiers—in a drawing-room in Paris, a lady who was known to be rather "fast", and very free-spoken, asked him, with an air half serious half jesting, if he had really been——"forked".

" Madame," he replied coolly, "imagine yourself for the moment in my place. If there was before you a sabre ready to cut your head off, and behind you a big τοολ, what would you do?. I went backwards, and I think you would have done the same."

Ferocious Lust of the African Arabs. Less fortunate than these sailors, is the unfortunate wretch who falls into the hands of these infuriated beasts. They will commence by robbing him of all he has, not leaving him even a shirt. What follows need not be described, suffice it to say, that however numerous the Arabs may be, they will *all* satisfy their brutal and ignoble passions. Fortunate will it be for their victim if he has not fallen into the hands of fanatics, for horrible mutilations will follow his first torment, and after having thus tortured him, they will leave him naked, but still living, to the hot sun, which will end his sufferings eventually. [2]

[1] Burton relates a similar experience (in the 10th vol. of his "*Nights*", page 235). The original, *Benares* edition of course; in the reprints all the real, *anthropological* notes have been *carefully* omitted for fear of Mother Grundy's wrath and ... the *Purity Society's* man!

Those students unable to procure the original edition will find the famous essay of the 10th vol. containing the anecdote in question, reproduced *in extensó* in *Marriage-love and Women amongst the Arabs*." (Paris, 1896.)

[2] *Dix-huit mille lieues à travers le Monde*, par Jules Desfontaines.

It is unnecessary to quote other authorities;· this will suffice. That horrible instrument of torture, the *pal*, was invented by the Arabs,— it may be added.

Active Pederasty of the Arab. The Arab is, almost exclusively, an active pederast. The youths and boys, who, in Arabia and all Mussulman countries, prostitute themselves for money, are, in the beginning, passive agents. I do not know whether, when they have become men, they change their part and become active agents, but at Guiana, amongst the Arab convicts, who are all addicted to this vice, I never met any but active agents. For "patients" they take,—if they cannot find women who will lend themselves to these disgusting practices,—Hindoo coolies, or white criminals either undergoing their sentence, or released, but very rarely Negroes, except a few depraved lads. I have mentioned an instance of this a few pages earlier. Some Arabs have demanded, and legally married before the Mayor, a female prisoner from the Penitentiary, but they have never tried to get any children by her, and only use anal copulation with her. These Arabs also leave their wives free to gain their living as they think best, on condition that they bring the money to their Mussulman husbands. The Governors of the Penitentiaries at last discovered these goings on, and ended by refusing permission to these worthy followers of Mahomet to take a lawful wife, and so the Arab in Guiana, both by taste and necessity, remains a pederast.

Pederasty is principally a Question of Race.

[1] The reader will recollect, that the author is in direct conflict with the view held by Sir Richard Burton, regarding the origin and preva-

A strange fact is, that the Arab, an active pederast, is provided with a genital organ, which, for size and length, rivals that of the Negro. It is even larger than that of the Negro of Guiana, but is surpassed in turn by that of the Negro of Senegal. But, whilst this last is rarely addicted to unnatural acts, with the Semitic Arab it is almost a general rule. A physical cause might be understood, as for instance a very small penis, as in the Annamite, who is almost as great a pederast as the Arab. It is certain, that the friction of the penis against the sphincter, which possesses, as we know, great contractile power, is greater than it would be in a vagina, dilated and relaxed by the heat of the climate, especially if affected by the " flowers"

lence of homosexual passion. But on the other hand it is proper to point out that J. A. Symonds, in his *Problem in Modern Ethics*, contests Burton's position, and maintains that Burton's knowledge of the subject was incomplete. We quote from page 77 : " Though he (Burton) possesses a copious store of anthropological details, he is not at the proper point of view for discussing the topic philosophically. For example, he takes for granted that 'Pederasty' as he calls it, is everywhere and always what the vulgar think it. He seems to have no notion of the complicated psychology of Urnings, revealed to us by their recently published confessions in French and German medical and legal works."

In a foot-note, Symonds further adds : " Burton's acquaintance with what he called ' Le Vice' was principally confined to Oriental nations. He started on his enquiries imbued with vulgar errors ; and he never weighed the psychical theories examined by me in the foregoing section of this essay. Nevertheless, he was led to surmise a crasis of the two sexes in persons subject to sexual inversion. Thus he came to speak of the 'third sex'. During a conversation I had with him less than three months before his death. he told me that he had begun a general history of "Le Vice"; and at my suggestion he studied Ulrichs and Krafft-Ebing, It is to be lamented that life failed before he could supply his virile and candid criticism to those theories, and compare them with the facts and conversation he had independently collected."

The Organ of Generation of the Arab. If the Annamite can plead such an excuse, the Arab cannot. We are, therefore, compelled to acknowledge, that it is a question of the peculiar moral sense of each race. The Arabs I examined, and who for the most part had been sentenced for rapes, or sodomy, committed upon children of either sex, in the proportions of their genital members considerably surpassed the fair average of the Negroes. In the bodies of many Arabs I dissected, the penis, instead of being drawn up and reduced to a small volume, like that of the European, still showed a considerable development.

In its usual condition, their yard, instead of being quite limp, still maintains a certain consistency, and feels to the hand like hollow india-rubber, or like the penis of the Negro, of which I have spoken. The gland is of a normal form, well-developed, and of a dirty red brown, lighter, however, than that of the Mulatto, but not so red as that of the Quadroon. It is, in proportion, smaller than the shaft of the penis, which is swollen a little underneath; the maximum diameter is found where the foreskin is cut in circumcising. This part of the penis sometimes swells out, like a sort of external pad. According to the measurements I made, the penis of the Arab has an average length, when in erection, of 7.2 to 7.6 inches by 1,6 or 2.0 inches in diameter; but I have found often a penis measuring 8 to 10 inches in length, by 2.0 or 2.4 in diameter. The organ then becomes a sort of pole which only a Negress could accommodate whilst a Hindoo woman of the class called " woman hare " would shrink from it in terror, and it would produce serious mischief in the rectum of any poor wretch who

consented to suffer its terrible attacks. [1] With such
a weapon does the Arab seek for anal copulation. He
is not particular in his choice, and age or sex makes
no difference to him. At the hulks, he finds amongst
the other convicts, Blacks or Hindoos, or even Whites,
the scum of the great cities, upon whom he can satisfy
his miserable lust. When once he is liberated, he
lives soberly, and tries to gain a few pence by keeping a store, or a small retail shop. He easily gets
also a place as foreman in the diggings, or where
Hindoos are employed. His abstinence from alcohol
makes him a capital man to keep a grog shop, and
his physical strength inspires a salutary dread. Those
who employ him are acquainted with his vice, and
this vice necessarily brings him before the tribunals,
when he has tried to use violence to some hired coolie,
who has objected to his advances, not from modesty,
but from a fear of being impaled.

EXCURSUS I TO CHAPTER V.

Small size of Penis. Over against the inordinate
dimensions of the member here described, we may
place the following:—taken from the "**Zeitschrift
für Ethnology**," (Berlin, 1871, 8vo pp. 113, 14, 15).

"It is a known [2] fact, which I can confirm that the
Taui islanders are in the habit of adopting for sole garment a mussel shell (*Bulla ovum*) within which they
hide their penis. Having purchased and examined a
great number of these "garments", I was convinced
that the opening of the shells had been but slightly
enlarged; I therefore thought it not unimportant to

[1] See Excursus IV.
[2] Waitz-Gerland, *Anthropologie der Naturvölker*, Part. VI, p. 556.

ascertain whether the prepuce only or also the gland had been enclosed in the opening of the mussel. The close examination of the penis of a native (obtained thanks to a rich present) [1] showed that the gland of the penis was really inserted into the mussel. But, as the artificially enlarged orifice of the mussel could barely accommodate the entrance of the little finger, this singular custom can only be explained by the extreme smallness of the virile member. To prove that this "costume" does not at all compress the penis, it may be added that without detaching the shell, the natives are able to make water, another opening being made at the other end to let it escape.

The small size of the penis is the same here (Agomes Islands) as among the Taui islanders. The littleness of the virile member among these people was so evident that it was a source of astonishment to the crew of our schooner, and gave rise to many remarks. My attention was drawn to it by my servant and I managed by chance to be able to take a rapid sketch from nature of an example. The penis of a strong, grown-up man looked exactly as if it was withdrawn into the skin, leaving the gland alone exposed, which was entirely free, the skin behind the prepuce being gathered up in circular folds. When the man was erect the position of his member was horizontal. This size of the penis seems to be general, although individual exceptions may occur. Notwithstanding all my efforts I could never succeed in inducing any of the natives

[1] During this examination the above native was extremely afraid of my withdrawing his mussel; this prudery, combined with the very primitive nature of the "costume" reminded me much of the "mogull" or disgrace of exposing the naked gland in Pelau and of the shame the Polynesians in general have at the sight of it.

Waitz-Gerland, *loc. cit.* Part VI, p. 28.

to allow me to examine them, and it was therefore impossible for me to take any exact measures or drawings. But a chance observation of three men showed me that the member of the youngest (about 20 years old) was longer than that of the two others. In youth the smallness of the penis is not observable.

The fact of the littleness of the virile member among these Melanesian peoples is the more remarkable that the negroes who, among all human races, after the Hottentots and the Kaffirs, come nearest to the Polynesians, are, on the contrary, distinguished by the large dimensions of their member.

EXCURSUS II TO CHAPTER V.

ILLUSTRATING note ON PAGE 284.

ISTIBRA [1] OR WAITING FOR THE PURIFICATION OF WOMEN.

"A man, when he purchases a female slave, is not permitted either to enjoy her, or to touch, or kiss her, or look at her *pudenda*, in lust, until after her *Istibra*, or purification from her next ensuing courses; for when the captives taken in the battle of *Autàss* were brought thence, the prophet ordained that no man should have carnal connexion with pregnant women

---

[1] A phraseology runs throughout this section which renders the translation of it into *English* particularly difficult, as the precise meaning of the term *Istibra* cannot be expressed by any single word in our language.—The best *Arabic* lexicons design *Istibra* to signify: "*the purification of the womb*". The term, however, must here be received in a more involved sense; for *Istibra* does not, in fact, mean simply *purification*, but *a desire* of, or (as rendered in the text) a *waiting for* purification; for which reason the translator renders it *purification*, or *abstinence*, as best suits the content.

until after their delivery or with others until after one menstruation; which evinces that the abstinence so enjoined is incumbent on a proprietor; and further, that the *occurrence* of right of property and of possession is the occasion of its being incumbent. The end proposed in this regulation is, that it may be ascertained whether conception has not already taken place in the womb, in order that the issue may not be doubtful.

Abstinence until after purification is incumbent on the *buyer*, but not on the seller; for the true reason of its necessity is the desire of copulation; and as the buyer is presumed to possess this desire, and not the seller, the observance of it is therefore enjoined him, and not the other. If, moreover, desire be an internal operation of the mind, the obligation of the law, in this particular, rests upon the *argument* of such desire. Now the mere power of committing the carnal act is an argument of the desire for such act; and as this power is established only by property and possession, it follows that property and possession are the occasions of this obligation of abstinence. This law, therefore, extends to a right of property, in all its different modes of being acquired, such as by purchase, donation, legacy, inheritance, covenants, etc., whence it is that this abstinence is enjoined upon a person, who buys a female slave, either from an infant, or a woman, or from a slave licenced to trade, [1] or from a person who is by law prohibited from having any carnal connexion

---

[1] The slave licenced to trade is, in this case, supposed to have been prohibited from cohabiting with the slave, as the goods he sells or purchases are presumed to be the property of another, namely, his master.

with her. In the same manner, also, this abstinence is incumbent where a person buys a female slave who is a virgin; for the law proceeds according to the proof of the cause which prompted it, and not according to the proof of the propriety or expediency, as these relate to what is internal and unknown.

If a person purchase a female slave during her menstruation no regard is paid to this menstruation with respect to determining the abstinence. [1] In the same manner, also, no regard is paid to a menstruation which occurs between the time of taking possession and the time of the right of property being established, by purchase, or the like;—and so likewise, regard is not paid to the delivery of a female slave between the establishment of a right of property in her, and the act of taking possession (contrary, how-ever, to the opinion of *Aboo Yoosaf*).—The reason of this is, that the occurrence of right of property and possession is the cause of purification being required; and the obligation of observing the purification is an *effect* of property and possession; and the *effect* can-not take place before the occurrence of the cause. The same rule holds with regard to such menstruous purgations as may happen previous to the procuring of sanction, in the case of an unauthorized sale of a female slave, notwithstanding the purchaser may be seized of her;—and so likewise, where the courses happen after the seizing in the case of an illegal contract of sale, and before the slave is purchased by a valid contract : for in none of all these cases do the present courses determine the abstinence.

[1] Arab. *Fee bàbal Iftibra;* (literally) " *in point of purification*", meaning that purification requisite to determine the abstinence imposed on the purchaser of a female slave.

Abstinence is requisite in the case of a *partnership* female slave, where one of two partners purchases the other's share; for here the cause is complete, and upon the completion of the *cause* the effect takes place.

If a person purchase a Magian female slave, or receive her in donation, and she, after his taking possession of her, have her courses, and then become a *Mustimá*,—or, if a person purchase a female slave, and make her a *Mokàtibá*, and she, after his taking possession of her, having voided her courses, prove unable to discharge her ransom,—such courses are sufficient to establish the requisite purification, in either of these cases, as having happened after the occurrence of the *cause* for waiting, namely, right of property and possession.

In cases where a female slave, having eloped, returns to her master,—or, having been taken away, or hired out, is restored,—or, having been pawned, is redeemed —abstinence is not requisite, for the cause of it (namely, the acquisition of property and possession) does not exist in either instance. In every case where abstinence is enjoined, and carnal connexion prohibited, all sorts of allurements and dalliance, such as kissing and hugging are likewise prohibited, as these lead to the commission of ·unlawful acts. Add to this, the possibility of their being committed on the property of another, as may happen if the slave prove with child and the seller lay claim to her. (It is reported from *Mohammed* that dalliance with a *captive* slave-girl is lawful.)

The purification of a pregnant female slave is established by her delivery, and that of a girl in whom

the menses have not yet appeared, by the lapse of a
month; that space being, with respect to such a one,
a substitute for the courses, in the same manner as
holds in the case of a woman under Edit. [1] If, however,
the menstrual blood, should discharge itself *before* the
expiration of the month, the purification by lapse of
time is annulled, because of the ability with respect
to the *original* circumstance, prior to accomplishing
the object of the substitute.

It is not lawful for a person who has given abusive
language to his wife, [2] either to look at her *pudenda*
in lust, or to cohabit with her, or to kiss or touch
her, until, such time as he have performed expiation,
because, as it is unlawful for him to copulate with her
until after expiation, it is consequently, unlawful that
he enter into dalliances with her, since the cause of
an illegal act is likewise illegal;—in the same manner
as holds in cases of *Ytticaf*[3] and *Ihram*; [4] or where a
person, by mistake, cohabits with the wife of another,
—in which case she must observe an *Edit;* during
which, as it is unlawful for the husband to have connexion with his wife, so it is likewise unlawful for

[1] See *Edit.*, Vol. I. p. 360.—There seems here to be a small
mistake in the text, as the *Edit.* of a female slave not subject to the
courses is determined by the lapse of a *month and a half.*

[2] Literally, "it is not lawful for a *Mozàhir*," meaning a person who
has pronounced a sentence of *zihár* upon his wife. (This whole passage
will be better understood by a reference to *zihár*, Vol. I. p. 326.)

[3] *Ytidàf* is a religious austerity practised by the most pious of the
Mussulmans in the last ten days of the month of *Ramzan;* they
remain during that period in a mosque, without ever departing from it
but when the calls of nature absolutely force them, abstracting themselves
at the same time from all enjoyments.

[4] *Ihrâm* is the period during which the pilgrims remain, at *Mecca.*—
They are then subject to a number of strict regulations, and are
particularly enjoined to refrain from all worldly pleasures.

him to use any of its incentives with her. It is otherwise during the courses or fasting, for, although copulation be at such time prohibited, yet dalliance is lawful, because the courses are frequent and of long continuance, engrossing a great part of life, as they happen once every month, and continue ten days every time;—and, in the same manner, the days of fasting are protracted to one month by the divine ordinances, and (among pious persons) voluntarily occupy a considerable part of life;—whence if dalliances were forbidden during those terms, it would tend to restrain men too much in their enjoyments.

CHAPTER VI.

The convict before the Court Martial.—Military law applied to the convicts.—Captain B***, President of the Council of War.—Amusing cases tried before the Council.

Military Law applied to the Convicts. The law which authorised transportation to Guiana, was followed by a second law, which made the convicts amenable to the military tribunals for all crimes and offences against the ordinary penal laws. Besides the Government Commissioners and Deputies, appointed in France by the Minister, there were two Councils of War, of which the President and Judges were chosen amongst the officers of the garrison of Cayenne. The Council of Revision was composed of the Colonel commanding, the Captain of the principal war vessel, and the Major of Marines. The two senior captains of the garrison of the Colony were, *ex officio*, Presidents of the two Councils of War. It might be imagined, that an officer who by chance found himself the senior on the station, and who was suddenly called upon to apply the Penal Code, without any previous study or experience, might feel embarrassed. But, bah! a transported ex-criminal was not worth much regard. A fresh sentence of a few years, more or less, was of no great consequence.

The unfortunate convicts had a terrible sword of Damocles, suspended over their heads. This was the Draconian article of the Code relating to old offenders, —which of course all the transported prisoners and ticket-of-leave men were. Offences punishable only by imprisonment, for criminals condemned by the common law, involved, for the convicts, a return to the Penitentiary for a minimum period of five years, or the maximum penalty of twenty years at the hulks, might be doubled. I saw a coiner condemned to death for having made a Papal coin of half a franc, or five pence, out of lead. It should be mentioned, that this convict had already been sentenced to hard labour for life for coining. Being an old offender, it was necessary to inflict a heavier sentence than hard labour for life, that is to say, the penalty of death. It is needless to say the convict was not executed; his sentence was commuted to five years in the chain gang, but, strictly speaking, and according to the letter of the law, he ought to have been executed.

Captain B***, President of the Council of War. My friend, Captain B***, the singer of smutty songs, was President of one of the two Councils. The post was not a sinecure for him, for the Council met twice a week, and had, at each sitting, three or four cases to decide. But with friend B***, the business did not drag; twenty to thirty minutes sufficed to hear, and settle, a case. The advocate of the accused, a subaltern officer of the garrison, specially designated for the post, knew perfectly well that no attempt at defence would be any good, so he confined himself to recommending his client to the mercy of the Court—this mercy generally consisted of a sentence for double the

maximum penalty, that is to say, forty years. That
is the regular tariff. For those already sentenced to
penal servitude for life, who reappear before the Council,
the sentence, which also is always the same, is five
years in the chain gang. The worthy Captain B***,
had always a broad grin on his face when he was
pronouncing sentence, and no doubt was thinking about
the smutty songs he was going to sing in the evening.
But it was especially in attempted rapes, or other
offences of the like kind, which were common enough
amongst the convicts, that the jovial obscenity of the
President showed to the best advantage. [1]   He evinced
the greatest interest in these cases, tried to bring out,

[1] The following sensible remarks on cant are of some interest. We
take them from Blondeau's *Dict. Erot. Latin—Français.* Paris, *Lisieux*,
1885.)

"Why do writers, and the people also, have recourse to so many
metaphors, periphrases, and circumlocutions, whenever the sexual organs
or sexual connection are in question? If we are not ashamed of being
men, why should we only dare to speak in covered words of that which
in us is the manifestation of our manhood? Nature has made the
union of the sexes the condition of our existence and of the propagation
of our species, and has attached to it, in view of this perpetuity, the
most powerful attraction, the most voluptuous pleasure: why should we
dissimulate it as if it were an offence or a crime? Why stigmatize as
shameful the sexual parts upon which Nature has expended all her
skill, and be ashamed to show that of which we ought to be proud.
Even to consider the naked fact, it is again the wish of Nature, since
she has made it a necessity, and the satisfying of a necessity can have
in it nothing shameful. Moralists have seen in this singular prudery,
an unjustifiable hypocrisy.

Listen to Montaigne. " What has the genital act done to men, an
act so natural, necessary and just, that they dare not speak of it openly,
and exclude serious and regular expressions? We bravely say KILL,
UNROBE, BETRAY, and THAT only between the teeth. Does that mean
that the less we say in words the more there is in our thoughts? For
it is good that the words which are the least used, the least written
and the best hidden, should be the best learnt and known."

in the course of the trial, the most indecent side of the affair, and uttered jokes that would have made a dead man grin. The public, the gendarme who kept order, and often the prisoner himself, would roar with laughter; but the verdict was always the forty years, or the five years, as the case might be.

Curious Cases tried before the Council. The worthy Captain B***, informed his friends and acquaintances, whenever any case of at all a "risky" nature was coming before the Court. Needless to say the public was never excluded on these occasions, in order that his lady friends the young Mulattas and Quadroons might enjoy the entertainment. The President was of average height, rather fat, with a red face framed in a thick, black beard, and lighted up by two small lascivious eyes, so that he had very much the appearance of a satyr. Anything might be said before him, and he was never so happy as when he had made a witness, or the prisoner, utter some gross obscenity.

Moinaux's *Comic Tribunal*[1] was surpassed by a long way. I confess that, for my part, I listened to the extraordinary proceedings before this tribunal with a great deal of interest, for they threw a strange light on the worst side of human nature.

[1] A small illustrated publication that used to chronicle all the queer and ludicrous cases appearing before the French law-courts.

In *Règles pour former un avocat* (Chap. 13) it is stated that "it was formerly the custom in 'most of the tribunals of the kingdom, to plead on Shrove-Tuesday any cause of a specially gay and spicy character.' These cases were called "warm cases", and celebrated advocates, it is said, did not disdain to take them up."

This extract is given on the authority of *Bibliotheca Scatalogica*, Scatapolis 5850 (read Paris 1849?); a singularly well informed little book on books of a scatalogical nature, mostly in French.

EXCURSUS TO CHAPTER VI.

ON CRIMINALITY WITH REGARD TO SEX IN THE ARAB RACE.

The references made to this subject in the preceding and other chapters are supported by the following evidence of medical specialists.

ON PEDERASTY, SODOMY, BESTIALITY and TRIBADISM AMONGST THE ARABS, by DR. A. KOCKER.[1]

Like all other Orientals the Arab is a *pederast*. It may be remarked that this vice is observed principally among nations where polygamy is permitted: in certain cases, a man cloyed with enjoyment, enervated by excess, seeks in sodomy a means of re-awakening his desire, in other cases we have to do with moral hermaphrodites.

Sodomy was denounced in *Leviticus* and by Hippocrates; on this point the Koran is also explicit, and the Mussulman jurisconsults have edicted the most severe penalties against it; we read in fact in Sidi-Khalil the following passages :

" Any Mussulman of either sex, free, of age and responsible for his or her acts who shall have committed the act of sodomy, being united to another by the bonds of a legitimate and valid marriage materially consummated, shall be stoned to death."

" The execution will take place with stones of medium size until death follows."

[1] " *De la Criminalité chez les Arabes au point de vue de la pratique médicale judiciaire en Algérie,*" par le Dr. A. Kocker, Paris Baillière et fils, 1884, (pages 169 et seq.

"Any individual Mussulman or non Mussulman, free or a slave, who shall be found guilty of sodomy shall be stoned to death together with his accomplice, even if both are slaves or non Mussulman subjects." [1]

For those who are unmarried or who have not yet consummated marriage the penalty was reduced to one hundred strokes of the bastinado.

Notwithstanding this severe legislation, there exists among the Arabs, as among ancient Greeks and Romans, and among the Chinese of the present day, a disgusting race, whom laziness and the love of lucre impel to exploit the perverted passions of those around them.

We have here to examine two actors, the *passive* and the *active* sodomite.

The Arab passive agent is generally young, but not effeminate like the one described by Tardieu. He is, on the contrary, robust and well set up. He wears no ornaments likely to lead to suppose that another sex was hidden beneath his burnous.

If this is the case, it is not that he despises jewelry, there is a deeper motive underlying his apparent disdain. If he wore ornaments he would come nearer in appearance to woman, who would then become his equal, he would therefore be outraging himself: a vestige of pride is still hidden beneath his ignominy. He might perhaps also lose his clients who would no longer find in him the acrid pleasures they seek for, for he would then in too many ways remind them of their wives.

The *placcs* where they are to be met with are generally the public squares and the Moorish *cafés*. There they pass all their time, smoking *Kif*, and drinking coffee; the last term of their existence is simply moral and physical degradation.

[1] Sidi Khelit. *Transl. by Seignette*, art. 1948 and following.

The *costume* of the passive pederast presents a peculiarity worthy of being noted and which was observed by Dr. Bertherand. Their Turkish pantaloons frequently have *an orifice* behind on a level with the anus and perfectly dissimulated by the folds of the garment. This enables them commodiously and without undressing, to abandon themselves to their shameful trade. This orifice must always be looked after, and it is easy to understand the importance that may have the examination of the stains which must almost fatally surround it.

The expert, who is charged to examine these individuals is often struck by the slight amount of anal deformation existing. He is far from finding among these Arabs the characteristic lesions described by Tardieu, but which more recent observers unanimously say are not at all general.

The folds of the anus are slightly obliterated, the infundibulum is usually wanting ; those triangular basic erosions situated around the anus, and given as characteristic of sodomy, are seldom met with. Hardly is there to be found sufficient laxness of the sphincters to be felt with the finger. It is evident that the examination is far from furnishing such precise indications as might reasonably be expected.

So far for the passive sodomite who gives himself up to this shameful trade, but when the act happens to be accomplished with violence by an Arab on young children, the lesions produced are absolutely characteristic and can leave no doubt whatever as to what has taken place, on condition however that the medico-legal examination be not too long deferred after the criminal act has been committed.

The *active* pederast is seldom an interesting subject

of study unless he is examined a few moments after the accomplishment of the act. There are then usually to be found all the signs of recent coition, sometimes there are on the member traces of blood, of sperm and of fecal matter.

But, the question arises, does not the penis assume any particular form among sodomites who have been for a long time addicted to this disgustiug practice?

This important point we now pass to consider. Among the Arabs the gland is often big and club-shaped, the penis slim. In short, their virile member presents all the signs mentioned by Tardieu as special to pederasts. The consequence of this generality of conformation is that these signs lose all their value.

The examination of the clothes of sodomites may also lead to interesting discoveries. Very often a hole is found in the trowsers at about the level of the genito-crural fold.

Pederasty amongst Arabs:—(παιδνος ερασατυς), the love of young people, consisting mostly in finger touches, is also observed among the Arabs, but less frequently than sodomy; their brutal passions being unable to find therein a sufficient aliment.

Lesbian love, or TRIBADISM, is rare among the Arab women. It would seem as if a certain degree of civilization were necessary to give birth to this vice. The cause which it appears most natural to invoke in explanation of this fact, is the absolute absence of erethism in the Arab woman. She is simply a female. If it were otherwise, and if passion came to animate these sometimes so beautiful statues, would not these Arab women seek to emancipate themselves from the servitude in which their husbands keep them?

One thing is worthy of remark : the *friend* of the Arab woman is generally an *Européenne.* When fulfilling the duties of assistant-surgeon at the Dispensary at Algiers, we frequently heard the female attendants complain of the scandalous scenes they had been obliged to witness in the evening in the courts, and in which the guilty parties were always of different race.

In Egypt, sapphism, it would appear, is almost the fashion, all the ladies of the harem have each of them an *amie.*

Bestiality is sometimes observed among the Arabs. They have connection with goats, sheep, and even with mares. [1]

This custom seems to have existed at all periods of their history. The following curious extract from the *Paris Médical,* of 1883, is a confirmation of the above:

" In the tenth century, Jahya-ben-Ishaq, physician to the Emir El-nâcer Lidinillâh, being consulted by a peasant who could no longer support the pain caused to him by swelling and inflammation of the penis, placed the member on a stone and compressed it so as to cause a mass of pus to flow out of it, in the midst of which there was a grain of barley. The Arab doctor at once guessed that the patient had taken liberties with his mare and had thus introduced the grain into the urethral canal which the culprit was obliged fully to admit was true.

Arab Criminal Assaults and Rape. During four years time we only noted 81 cases of rape committed by Arabs. This figure is evidently far inferior to the

---

[1] A curious and lengthy case is given of carnal connection with a *bear* in the " *Old Man young again* " (MS.) (now in preparation for the press).

real facts. We therefore must here insist upon the large number of cases the prosecution of which was abandoned for lack of proof, and the still greater number of those which remained unknown to justice.

The study of this crime is one of the most interesting that Arab criminality presents to us. This question,— far from being a simple one as in France, *i.e.* relating solely to criminal assaults committed on women or on children,— becomes more complex when we pass to the Arabs, and presents a point which it is important to put clearly in the light, we mean *violation in marriage*, fatal consequences of the Mussulman and French laws, of which the first authorise and the latter tolerate the most dissimilar unions. It is on account of this culpable toleration by our laws, no article of which comes to regulate marriage among Mussulmans, so that there are frequent cases of quite young children being married to grown-up men and dying from the effects of conjugal approach.

The author of the assault is, it is true, prosecuted, and generally condemned. Is that sufficient? Evidently not. We have even already, in commencing this study, made it clear that often in such cases, the Arab is to be held irresponsible; but then who bears that responsibility? We will not go further into the study of these questions, which pertain to the domain of humanitarian philosophy and of jurisprudence, leaving to the ruling powers the care of solving them.

We may note at once that simple *criminal assaults* are rare among the Arabs, and that consequently it is only his bestiality that impels the Arab, notwithstanding all impediments, to accomplish the act he has begun.

Criminal Assaults. The following by Dr. Rique, [1] confirms our observations anent the ferocity of the Arab's lustful attacks:—" This series of offences seldom come to the knowledge of the French authorities. For this there are two reasons: the rarity of these crimes and the difficulty of discovering them.

The rarity of such offences among the tribes should not lead us to conclude in favour of the continence of the Arabs. Nothing can give any idea of the immorality reigning in the douars. The Arab woman is sequestrated as among the Turks and the Moors She goes about with face uncovered, works in the fields tilling the soil, goes into the woods to pick up sticks, poor beast of burden that she is, looked upon by lord and master as something intermediate between his horse and his donkey, having received neither principles nor education, not esteeming herself more than she is esteemed, what scruple therefore could restrain her? Consequently it appears perfectly proved to us that there is not a single one who has not got at least one lover, whom she calls in her cynically naïve language her *Khouïah* or brother. This much established, and as pretty nearly every Arab has either a mistress or a legitimate spouse, and his genesic instinct, which to him is above everything else, being thereby satisfied, very few of them would care to expose themselves, for the sake of change, to a terrible and above all legitimate punishment. The innate modesty and jealous repugnance of the Arab in all questions having reference to women, have passed into the language. In order to express the idea of violation, they employ a euphemistic form of expression

[1] Etude sur Med. légale in the *Gazette Médicale de Paris*, vol. 63 (pages 156—161).

sufficiently distant from its real signification: *serrac en nça*, rob women.

It is particularly in cases of criminal assault that one must be on one's guard against every sort of evidence and trust only to one's eyes. I remember a case of this kind which seems to me to be interesting enough to be recorded.

A Caïd, considered to be one of the most loyal and honourable in the country, one day came to me at the Arab Bureau, bringing with him a young girl of from 7 to 8 years old, the daughter of one of his servants. I was told by the Caïd that she had been ravished by a shepherd whom he had caused to be arrested by his mounted guard. I examined the young girl, and could discover no trace whatever of violence, no œdema or ecchymosis. And yet the hymen membrane had been broken through, and defloration had taken place, but as it appeared to me, not very recently. I next proceeded to examine the accused. This man, El Ambli ben bel Kassem, although only fifteen years old, presented an excessive development of the genital organs, even for an Arab, and quite out of proportion with the size of the girl's pudenda. I was much perplexed, and I was about to draw up a report with negative conclusions, when, with a view to further information, I wished once more to carefully examine the girl. I then discovered at the fork, a little to the right, a syphilitic excoriation, very slight, it is true, but well characterised, which had escaped me at my first observation. On making this discovery a certain suspicion passed through my mind. I remembered that this Caïd had a son, a good-for-nothing fellow, a frequenter of low haunts, and even suspected of going about at night for nefarious purposes, and that a few days previously this son had come to consult me about a chancre he had at the basis of the bridle. I at once sent one of the horsemen of the Arab Bureau to fetch him, his whereabouts being known, and he was brought without being told what for. As soon as the Caïd's son had entered the ante-chamber, I suddenly pushed open the door of the consulting-room, and pointing to the young girl: "There," said I, "is she whom thou hast contaminated (fuss'd)!" Taken thus without warning and confounded by this sort of theatrical effect, he did not dare attempt a denial; I had guessed rightly. I sent him to the disposal of the chief of the Bureau, who had him arrested, and liberated El Ambi. As for the Caïd, he was shortly afterwards revoked.

But when the Arab thinks himself sure of a certain immunity, his brutal instincts, seconded by a hot temperament will lead to excesses of frenetic lechery.

Two Arabs of the Djendel tribe met, one evening at about eight o'clock on a by-path leading from Aïn-as-Solthan to Milianah, the unfortunate wife of a colonist, who was obstinate in not taking the high road. They seized hold of her, threatening to kill her if she resisted, laid her down under a tree, and while she was held down by one of the two, the other violated her. His companion then took his place, and so they continued alternately relieving each other during two hours. The unfortunate woman calculated that she had been outraged about fifteen times. Subjected the next day to medico-legal examination, a real echymosis of the vaginal tunic was perceptible, and the mucous surface was in some places lifted up and eroded.

With regard to criminal attempts on those of the same sex, they are far from being rare; but facts of this nature being seldom revealed, naturally escape verification. Generally there is mutual consent: the infamous vice is so deeply rooted amongst the Arabs, that it is almost hopeless to find any efficacious means of repression.

CHAPTER VII.

My stay at Martinique.—The white race, called pure Creoles.
—Prejudice against colour.—The Blacks of Martinique.—Moral
characteristics of the Negress of Martinique.—The coloured race.
—The Mulatta.—The Quadroon and her passionate nature.—
"Fricatrices" and Lesbians.

My Stay at Martinique. I have already explained
the reasons which detained me three weeks at Martinique, before going to Guiana, where I was able to
remain nearly three years. On the return journey to
France, I again stayed a fortnight at Martinique.

I have no intention of writing a long description,
analogous to that I have done for Guiana, of the white,
black, and coloured races of Martinique. I should
only have to repeat myself, and uselessly lengthen out
the book. I will content myself therefore, with briefly
noticing some of the differences between the people
of the two countries. I shall treat Martinique as I
have already treated Tonquin.

The White Race, called Pure Creoles. The
first fact which strikes one, is the very large number
of white Creoles, who can here form a stock part of
the population without the support of black blood.
This is due to the chains of high mountains at Martinique, where we find, at altitudes of from 2700 to

3300 feet above the sea, a really temperate climate, which is almost cold in the winter, and where the white Creoles have built sanatoria, for cases of fever, anæmia, hepatitis, etc. When the affairs of the island were very prosperous, all the rich Creoles had country houses on these heights, where they passed the hot season, and recovered their strength. The white race was thus able to contend against the climate,—which, by the way, is never so injurious as that of Guiana.

Prejudice against Colour. It is not astonishing that we should find here,—at least it was so in 187—a prejudice against colour which does not exist at Guiana. The real white Creoles constitute a kind of Faubourg St. Germain,[1] from which the coloured element is rigorously excluded. The latter has become, owing to the franchise, which gives every Black a vote, the dominant political power, but the old Creole society still looks upon him with disdain, and refuses to open its *salons* to him. The white Creole has as much contempt for the " mixed bloods ", as a nobleman of the old school had for his valet, but the latter could not brag, as the former can, that his ancestors bought and sold on the market, the grandparents of the coloured people.

The Black Race at Martinique. The Negro and Negress of Martinique are taller, more lithesome, and slenderer, than their congeners of Guiana. I remarked this during my first visit, and an old white Creole of Cayenne gave me the explanation of it. It appears that, when the slave trade existed, the slaving vessels

---

[1] The home of the old French nobility in Paris, exclusively closed to the *parvenu* and *rastaqouère* class, which generally goes West.

first brought their human merchandise to the Antilles, where, naturally, those with the best physical qualities were picked out, and the remainder then taken on to Guiana. If this is correct—and I see no reason to doubt it,—the explanation of the corporal inferiority of the Guiana Black, is very easy. It should be added, that the climate of Guiana is also more weakening. The Black of Martinique is more robust, and wider in the shoulders, but he has a restless, uneasy look in his face. And while the Guyanais is peaceable, submissive, quiet, and avoids quarrels, the Martiniquer, though quite as lazy when manual labour is concerned, is noisy, insolent, and overbearing. In the street he will never give up the pavement to you, unless he knows you, and has need of your services. Scuffles between the soldiers and the Blacks, which are very rare at Guiana, are, on the contrary, very common at Martinique, and blood is often shed. I do not believe that, within the memory of man, a Black of Cayenne has ever deliberately set fire to a house. The torch, on the contrary, is the favourite weapon of the Martinique Black; it is to him what the *marmite* of dynamite is to the anarchist. During the war of 1870-71, there were several insurrections, and incendiary fires, at Martinique, and the incendiary Blacks cried " Long live Prussia". The terrible fire, which quite recently destroyed Fort de France, is believed to have been the work of an incendiary.

Moral Characteristic of the Woman of Martinique. The character of the Negress of Martinique is similar to that of the male. She is more lively, and more laborious, than the woman of Guiana, who is a weak, stupid *gnan-gnan*, a good mother of a family,

but not very wide-awake. The Martinique woman has
a great aptitude for business, and makes money in
every way. She works like a man, which the woman
of Guiana will not do. The coal for the great Trans-
atlantic steamers is loaded by hundreds of women, who,
singing at the top of their voices to the sound of a
wild tam-tam, come and empty their baskets into the
hold of the vessel.

The woman of Martinique has not the strong and
simple religious faith of the Guyanaise. Martinique is
so much visited, that its black population has not been
able to withstand the contaminating influence of a not
very devout civilization. The woman of Martinique
is, moreover, a dangerous character, and you had better
look out for yourself if you happen to have offended
a Negress.

In fact, on the whole, she is not a very nice kind
of woman. She does not like the Whites; but the
Blacks detest all the White race, and would turn
them out of the island if they had the power.

So far as concerns physical passions, their forms
and their perversions amongst the black race, I have
nothing to add to what I have written about Guiana.
I may mention, however, that if the "Massogan" goes
after the Negress at Cayenne, at Martinique the *Becqué
blanc* can find plenty of coloured women, and can
afford to leave the Negress on one side.

The Coloured Race. This race has greatly increased,
during the last half century, and has become so strong
that it is able to contend against the old Creole race,
and has wrested from the latter the predominance in
political matters. It is the succession of fresh strata,
foretold by Gambetta. The rich coloured people bring

up their sons as notaries, doctors, lawyers, and jour-
nalists, who occupy all the highest political situations
in the country. But not all are rich. The poorer
members of the race. Quadroons or Mulattœs, become
clerks, or enter some Government department. Many
of them go and try their fortune elsewhere. It seems
that, for some years past, Guiana has been invaded
by Martiniquers, who are not looked on very favourably by the people of Guiana, who are aware that the
new-comers have long teeth, and an appetite not
easily appeased.

The Mulatta. As to the poor coloured girl, she
sells herself for money without any scruple. All proportions being duly considered, there are more Mulattas, and many more Quadroons, at Martinique, than
at Cayenne, and the amateur has a greater choice. I
did not discover any very remarkable differences between
the Mulattas of the two countries. Both are very fond
of the White man, but the Martinique girl is bolder,
and more intriguing, and more certain to assert her
sway over the *Becqué blanc* who may fall into her
hands. She is unscrupulous, and will procure elsewhere
the presents which her lover may refuse to give her.
She is also more lascivious than the girl of Guiana.

The Quadroon, and her Passionate Nature.
The Quadroon of Martinique can certainly give odds
to any of the courtesans of Europe, and it is only at
Tahiti that I have found her equal. It must be confessed, that the mixture of one fourth of black blood
produces an almost perfect woman. The general form
of the body is that of a woman of the South of Europe.
The skin is a dull brown, and the face is lighted up

by a pair of magnificent gazelle-like eyes. The legs are well-made, and the thighs and buttocks lasciviously well-rounded. The hair is perhaps still rather curly. but often of a dark chestnut, or red gold colour. The lips are large. The breast still remains a trifle pear-shaped. The hair of the pubes is curly, and rather soft, sometimes very plentiful, and often of a tint not so dark as that of the head. But the dimensions of the vulva and vagina are not at all like those of the Negress, and do not sensibly differ from those of the European woman.

The passions of the Quadroon girl are strong, like those of her white ancestors. She has not the same dislikes as the Negress, and is less particular than the Mulatta,—in fact she is ready for any sort of pleasure that comes in her way. She is a real Circe, and will lend herself willingly to all your amorous fancies, however lewd they may be. If a Quadroon girl of Martiniqne has a *bon Becqué* for a lover, and she likes him, she will never desert him, and will leave her country rather than lose him. The people of Martinique are naturally fond of travelling, whilst those of Guiana are of sedentary habits.

It is asserted that *Fricatrices* and Lesbians [1] are not

[1] In Bali, according to Jacobs ([1]), homosexuality is almost as common among women as among men, though it is more secretly exercised; the methods of gratification adopted are either digital or lingual, or else by bringing the parts together (tribadism).

Among Arab women, according to Kocher, homosexual practices are rare, though very common among Arab men. In Egypt, according to Godard, Kocher and others, it is almost fashionable, and every woman in the harem has a "friend". Among the negroes and mulattoes of French creole countries, says Corre, homosexuality is very common. "I know a lady of great beauty," he remarks, "a stranger in Guadalupe

([1]) As quoted by Ploss-Bartels, *Das Weib*, 1895, (vol. I, p. 390).

uncommon amongst the coloured women of Martinique, but, though I met with some women who were reported to possess this taste, I should be sorry to deduce therefrom that the general habit prevailed. "In case of doubt, abstain from an opinion," as the proverb says.

Depilation. The best known and most extensively distributed custom connected with the MONS VENERIS, is certainly depilation, by which is to be understood the artificial removal of a growth of hair. Among the Muhammadans this operation is prescribed by their ritual, but we meet with it in many other parts of the globe, in Africa, Asia and America.

The substance mostly employed for that purpose in Turkey is known to be Orpiment (yellow sulphide of Arsenic) and calcined chalk, equal quantities of which are worked up into a paste with rose-water: after this paste has been applied and left for a few minutes on the spot in question and then carefully washed off, the hair is found to be completely removed. This method is in quite general use throughout the East and is called in Turkey *Rusma* and according to Polak, [1] *Nurch* in Persia, for in Persia also the Muhammadan women are obliged to regularly depilate the private parts and the arm-pits in a warm bath. The Muham-

and the mother of a family, who is obliged to stay away from the markets and certain shops because of the excessive admiration of the mulatto women and negresses, and the impudent invitations they dared to address to her". [1] He refers to several cases of more or less violent sexual attempts by women on young girls of 12 or 14, and observes that such attempts by men on children of their own sex are much rarer.

[1] *Polak* — Persien, das Land und seine Bewohner. I, Leipzig, 1865.

[1] Corre, *Crime en Pays Créoles*, (Paris, 1889).

madan maidens and the Christian Armenian women in
Persia do not do this, as it was asserted in *Häntsche*. [1]
Polak says: "The private parts are depilated in
obedience to ritual law by means of a preparation of
orpiment and chalk; this is called *hadschebi keschidew*,
which means submitting to the law; but elegant ladies
themselves pluck out the hairs, until they no longer
grow any more."

Petrus Bellonius relates, that the quantity of orpiment used in the East is so enormous on account of
its use in depilation, that the farmers of the metal tax pay
to the Sultan of Turkey a yearly tribute of 1800 ducats.

On the Coast of Guinea according to *Monrad*, [2] the
young and unmarried negresses also depilate the private
parts, but after marriage they let the hair grow again.

In the Dutch East Indies, as *Epp* [3] asserts, the
women of Malay race depilate their *mons veneris*
until it appears quite bald. This is confirmed by one
of the photographs in the collection of the Berlin
Anthropological Society, but the others in the same
collection prove that this cannot be considered as a
general custom, and also that the Chinese women
living there have not adopted it. But among the
Battas of Sumatra, according to *Hagen* [4] the women
pluck out the hairs from the *mons veneris* and shave
it, as soon as the hair begins to grow.

Maurel [5] says, speaking of the Khmers in Cambodia,

[1] *Häntsche*, Physikalisch-Medicinische Skizze von Rescht in Persien;
in Virchow's Archiv. 1862, 5 u. 6. Heft S. 570.

[2] *Monrad*, H. C. Gemälde der Küste von Guinea. Weimar, 1824, p. 47.

[3] *Epp*, Schilderungen von Holländisch-Indien. Heidelberg, 1852, p. 392.

[4] *Hagen*, Die künstlichen verunstaltungen des Körpers bei den Balta.
Zeitsch. fur Ethnologie. Bd. XVI. 218, Berlin, 1884.

[5] *Maurel*, Mémoire sur l'Anthropologie du Cambodge; mémoires de
la Soc. d'Anthrop. de Paris. Paris, 1893, p. 529.

that the woman's *mons veneris* is generally shaved; but "the women who seek the company of Europeans easily abandon the practice."

In several parts of India this custom also prevails generally; only for that purpose they employ, as *Jagor* [1] informs us, very peculiar rings of which the Royal Ethnological Museum in Berlin possesses a few examples contributed by known travellers. They are used solely for that purpose and, when they are required to operate, they are carried on the tumb. At first sight they have the appearance of a very large signet-ring, as on the upper side they present to view a large round flat shield, which bears in the centre, surrounded by tastefully carved borders, a little mirror, destined in reality firstly in the manipulation to reflect the private parts and secondly to throw light by reflection on to these rather hidden regions. It is with the rather sharp edge of the ring that the hairs are removed. The Indian name of these rings is *ârsi*.

The well-known Nestor of the German savants in South America, *Rudolph A. Phillipi* in Santiago, made some enquiries concerning the Chilian women who, he discovered were given to depilation, but not at all generally, and only among certain very low classes of the population.

Karl von den Steinen [2] found in Brazil that among the Indian women in the district near the sources of the Schingu, of the Trumai and other tribes, it was a general custom to remove the hair entirely from the *mons veneris.*

---

[1] *Jagor*, See Verhandl. der Berliner Anthropologische Gesellschaft, 1882, and Zeitschrift fur Ethnologie, 1880.

[2] *Karl von den Steinen*, Die Philosophie der Tracht, und Enstehung des Schamgefühls. Ausland 1891, No. 16.

Hyades and *Deniker* [1] mention also a woman of Terra del Fuego who had submitted herself to depilation.

In the East, depilation is not an invention of the Muhammadans; their forefathers practised it, and in far ancient times this popular custom travelled from Asia into Egypt, and from there to Greece and Italy. According to *Aristophanes* the hetaires and gay women particularly of his time, alone practised it in Greece; but it would appear on the same authority that the honourable Greek women had also adopted the custom. Martial [2] relates that the Roman women resorted to depilation of the private parts as they grew older, in order to dissimulate their age. Many authors assert that the custom was still prevalent in Italy until modern times; and it would appear to be as much for sake of cleanliness as for protection against vermin (Rosenbaum). [3]

It would seem altogether that in general those peoples like to practise depilation whose pilose system is the least developed, as those also are most addicted to shaving who have the scantiest beards. The apparent exceptions are no doubt due to this depilation of female private parts being elevated to the rank of a religious rite, and forcedly therefore adopted by all the nations converted to Islamism.

[1] *Hyades & Deniker*, Mission scientifique du Cap Horn (1882, 1883) vol. VIII, Paris, 1891.

[2] *Martial*. Lib, XII, epigr. 32.

[3] *Rosenbaum*, Geschichte der Lustseuche, etc. Halle, 1882, p. 372.

(This latter work, we hope, shortly to offer to English readers in their own language. It is a mine of anthropological knowledge as regards the Ancients.)

THE END OF THE FIRST VOLUME.

Vol. II

UNTRODDEN FIELDS

OF

ANTHROPOLOGY

"No physical or moral misery, no sore however corrupt it may be, should frighten him who has devoted himself to the Knowledge of Man; and the sacred Ministry of the Medical Man by forcing him to witness everything, also permits him to say everything."

TARDIEU, *Des Attentats aux Mœurs.*

Τὸ γὰρ ἀποστῆναι χαλεπὸν
Φύσεος, ἣν ἔχει τις ἀεί.

ARISTOPHANES (Vesp. 1457):—

"The decomposition of dead bodies we can well prevent, can we not also stay the decomposition of the human heart? If the weak know, if we know, that a given vice has a bad taste, and 'turns but to dead ashes in the Mouth', with what happiness should we fly from it. It is only necessary to see certain phases of degradation such as they really are, to hold them afterwards in hatred "

ADÈLE ESQUIROS, *Les Marchandes d'Amour.*

Lass uns, geliebter Bruder, nicht vergessen,
Dass von sich selbst der Mensch nicht scheiden kann.

GOETHE (Torq. Tasso, I, 2, 85).

DOCUMENTS ON MEDICAL ANTHROPOLOGY

UNTRODDEN FIELDS

OF

ANTHROPOLOGY

OBSERVATIONS ON THE ESOTERIC

Manners and Customs of Semi-Civilized Peoples;

BEING A

RECORD OF THIRTY YEARS' EXPERIENCE IN

ASIA, AFRICA, AMERICA and OCEANIA.

BY A FRENCH ARMY-SURGEON.

(IN TWO VOLUMES)

VOL. II

Fredonia Books
Amsterdam, The Netherlands

PREFATORY NOTE
TO THE SECOND VOLUME

"Dont ne m'a retardé l'opinion de ceux qui disent que c'est une chose vergogneuse et sale de traicter de cette matière, et que la lecture d'un tel livre peut induire quelque libidineux désir en la pensée de ceux qui le liront. Mais nul ne le lise qui n'en aura a faire. Nous désirons empescher le mal; si, ce faisant, nous ne pouvons fuir le scandale volontairement pris, cela ne nous doit pas être imputé, ains à la pernicieuse volonté de ceux qui d'eux-mêmes cherchent à se scandaliser sans sujet."

Dr. JAQUES DUVAL.

Traité des Hermaphrodites.
(Rouen, 1612, p. 58.)

"Scire est nescire, nisi id me scire alius sciret."

PREFATORY NOTE
TO THE SECOND VOLUME.

The following letter, received from a valued correspondent, is so just, and defines our Author's effort with such precision, that we think it of sufficient interest to reproduce. Others were sent to us, many of them couched in very appreciative and laudatory terms. We hope to include them all in a third supplementary volume to appear later.

SIR,

In reply to your request to contribute any criticisms one wishes upon "UNTRODDEN FIELDS OF ANTHROPOLOGY" by "A French Army-Surgeon" (published 1896), although I have not resided abroad, nor can claim any special knowledge of the subject, as a medical man, and having read the work very carefully, I should like to make the following general remarks. The title at once arrests the scientific attention and the book leads one straight into fields "untrodden" as far as I am aware—at all events little more than a note here and there appears—in the standard anatomical, physiological, or anthropological works; in its purely psychological aspects I believe it is wholly untreated. The author's numerous observations on the various races and species of mankind, with which his position brought him into contact; the careful differentiations he details in the several species and races, and the rough classification he sketches therefrom, are very interesting; while his description of relevant and characteristic customs, of the different races, and the incidents of travel in passing from place to place are equally attractive. The scientific aspects of the work are very interesting, but the details of the examples, brief, and in general scientific terms. From the purely scientific side it would be probably too much to look for the scientific minutiæ of Darwin, or numerous and exact measurements, under the circumstances of the compilation of the work and the newness of the subject as a speciality. Lastly I think it is to be regretted that as a work treating of a scientific subject, and further as being a speciality, it is not announced to and procurable by the scientific world through the ordinary channels. Apologising for these brief criticisms and congratulating the author on what he has achieved.

Yours faithfully,

" MEDICUS."

ENGLAND.

Our friend's name is withheld, as desired.

CONTENTS

OF THE

SECOND VOLUME

ANALYTICAL

TABLE OF CONTENTS

PART THE THIRD

AFRICA

Senegal and the South Rivers

CHAPTER I.

CHAPTER II.

PART THE FOURTH

OCEANIA

New Caledonia—The New Hebrides—Tahiti

CHAPTER X.

CHAPTER XI.

CHAPTER XII.

Chapter XIII.

𝔘ntrodden 𝔉ields of 𝔄nthropology.

PART THE THIRD.—AFRICA.

SENEGAL AND THE SOUTH RIVERS.

CHAPTER I.

Sent to Senegal.—Arrival at Saint Louis.—General impression of the Senegal coast.—A few words about the town of Saint Louis.—The Black Town.—Anthropological characteristics of the Wolof race.—The beauty of the young Negress.—Operation performed on the breasts of women lying-in.—The genital organs of Negroes.—Rapes and other offences against modesty amongst Creoles and Negroes.

Sent to Senegal. A short time after my return from Guiana, I was sent to Senegal, where a terrible epidemic of yellow fever had disorganised the medical service, and necessitated the despatch of more doctors, hospital attendants, etc.

Arrival at Saint Louis. The Government transport, which I was on board, arrived at Saint Louis one Sunday, coasted along the shore, and anchored before the bar at the entrance to the river.

The General Impression produced by the Senegal

Coast. M. Loti, of the Academy, has admirably described the aspect of the coast of Senegal, and the impression it produces upon the traveller who has just come from France. " In descending the coast of Africa, when you have passed the southern border of Morocco, you coast along, for days and nights, an interminable, desolate shore. This is the Sahara, the great sea without water, which the Moors also call *Balad-ul-atish*, [1] or 'the land of thirst.' Solitude succeeds solitude, with mournful monotony of moving sand-hills and indefinite horizon ; and the heat increases in intensity day by day. And then appears above the sand, an old and white city, planted with a few yellow palms; this is Saint Louis of Senegal, the capital of Senegambia. A church, a mosque, a tower, and some Moorish looking houses. These all seem to doze in the hot sunlight, like those Portuguese towns which formerly flourished on the Congo coast, Saint Paul, and Saint Philippe de Benguela. You approach, and you are astonished to find that the town is not built on the coast, that it has not even a port, nor any communication with the exterior ; the coast, which is low and straight, is as inhospitable as that of the Sahara, and an unending line of breakers prevents the approach of ships. You then notice, what you had not perceived from a distance; immense human ant-hills, on the shores thousands and thousands of thatched cottages, liliputian huts with pointed roofs, beneath which huddles an odd Negro population."

[1] This word is shortened in the " dog-like," Arabic patois of the Moors to Bled-al-atish. Senegal is the oldest colony of France, and dates as far back roughly speaking as 1368, when the hardy sailors of Dieppe first came across, and disputed its possession with the adventurous Portuguese. The narrative of its gradual conquest is one of the most exciting in the history of European colonisation.

A Few Words about the Town of Saint Louis.
Saint Louis is about eighteen miles from the mouth of
the Senegal. The town is entirely built upon an island
of a very long lozenge shape, a mile and a quarter
long, and 500 yards broad. In the centre are massed
the Government House, the Church, and the huge
Rogniat Barracks; a little to the south is the Hospital,
and in the north, the Mosque. All around, in the
central part, are streets in the direction of the axes of
the lozenge, and bordered with houses in masonry of
a cubical form, and generally of only one storey, and
with flat roofs forming terraces, called, in the language
of the country, *argamasses*. These *argamasses* serve
to receive the rain water, Saint Louis having no
springs or wells of really drinkable water. There is
no verdure, unless it be a few palm trees in occasional
corners, and the rudiments of a garden round the
Government House, kept up at a great expense during
the dry season, when a barrel of water costs a dollar.

A sojourn at Saint Louis is not enchanting, for the
place is the very opposite of that verdant spot, Cayenne,
where the vegetation is extraordinarily exuberant.
Here there is nothing but yellow grey sand, and walls
painted white, the reflection from which blinds you.
According to my custom, I took up my residence at
the north point of the town, at the extreme limit of
the European quarter, in order to be as much as
possible in contact with the Black population, whose
huts and low houses (in brick for the rich people) are
relegated to the two extremities of the town.

The Black Town. In that part of the island which
forms the Black Town, are crowded together the huts
and hovels of the Negroes, which are in the form of

our bee-hives. On visiting them you will find some
gutted, overturned, or burnt. From the conical roofs
of those which appear to be inhabited, hang dirty rags,
and scraps of meat and fish. Negro boys, quite naked,
run about here and there on the sand of the river
banks,—banks that have fallen in, and are covered
with filth. Some old Negresses, hardly covered with
miserable rags of cotton drawers, and their hanging
breasts all bare, —crouch down before the doors of the
huts, smoking their pipes, and watching any stray
European who is passing. In front of the door, is the
mortar for grinding meal, hollowed out of an immense
tree trunk, and you may often see a woman, carrying
her child astride on her buttocks, and handling the
heavy pestle. Young Negroes, quite bare, girls and
boys, with just a string of glass beads round their
waists, surround you and pursue you with the monotonous refrain, "Toubab, give me ha'penny."

If you pass from the extremity of the island to the
narrow sand-bank which extends between the sea and
the right bank of the river, you will come across the
suburban village of Guet 'N' Dar, which is connected
with the town by a little bridge, built on beams. In
this suburb is held the native market, so picturesquely
described by Loti. [1] If you leave the town by the East,
to go to the large island of Sohr, you must pass over
a bridge of boats half a mile long.

**Anthropological Characteristics of the Wolof
Race.** The town of Saint Louis is almost entirely
populated by the Yolof, or Wolof, race, but you may
also find there examples of all the Negro races of
Senegal. It would take too long to describe all these

[1] *Le Roman d'un Spahi*, by Pierre Loti, Paris, 1896.

different races, and by choosing the Wolofs as a type, I shall be able to point out the principal differences between this race and the others.

The first few steps that a traveller takes in Saint Louis and its Negro suburbs, will reveal to him a striking difference between the inhabitants of the American colonies, and the African Negro. The Blacks of the Antilles, and Guiana, are descended from slaves, imported from all corners of Africa, since the time of Louis XIII., and whose descendants were set free in 1848. The admixture of all these different tribes has produced a race without any original characteristics, more or less bastardized, and corrupted, by contact with the White man, and the stain of the slavery of their ancestors. In Senegal it is not the same. Although slavery exists, the various races have preserved their peculiar characteristics, and there is a great difference, for example, between a Wolof and a Peulh.

The Wolofs originally came from Walo, and little by little have established themselves in the capital of Senegal. But they have preserved the manners and customs of their forefathers, though they have allowed themselves to be converted to Islam. It is for their use, that a fine mosque has been erected at North Point. Their huts line the streets of the town, and are divided into groups, separated by *tapades*, or screens of woven reeds, five or six feet high. There is always a court in front of these huts. Whilst the woman works in the house, the man fishes, hunts, or does a little work of some sort.

The Wolofs are a fine race; their average stature is greater than that of the European. The arms and legs are long, but though the thigh is tolerably

fleshy, the calf is very thin. The foot is large and
flat, and the head small. Loti, in the *Roman d'un
Spahi*, exactly depicts the Wolof in a few lines: " If
a vessel anchors before Saint Louis, you will soon see
it surrounded by long pirogues, pointed at the prow
like a fish's head, and manned by Blacks who stand
and paddle. The boatmen are tall, thin, and of hercu-
lean strength, well-made and muscular, with faces like
gorillas, and possessed of true Negro obstinacy, and
the agility and strength of acrobats; ten times have
they been driven back by the breakers, and ten
times have they recommenced their task; their black
skins, wet with sweat and sea water, gleam like polished
ebony."

The children go about quite naked, until they attain
the age of puberty, and have no hair but one woolly
lock left on their otherwise clean-shaved heads. When
the boys attain puberty, which is generally at about
twelve or thirteen years of age, they don a blue or
white *boubou*, a sort of long full shirt in cotton, with
no sleeves, and no seam down the sides, and which
falls almost to the feet. When the girls become nubile,
that is to say at ten or twelve years at the latest,
they wear cotton drawers, and have the bust naked,
but they often replace this garment, when they grow
to be women, by a *boubou*, rather shorter than that
of the men.

The Beauty of the Young Negress. In the
children, we can therefore watch the progressive development of the race. The Wolofs do not, like some
races of the interior of Africa, tattoo themselves. If
it were not that the breasts are disfigured when the
first child is born, and the head with its flat nose and

thick lips, the Negresses would be perfect specimens of humanity. This may easily be imagined, for they live in the open air, the full development of their body and limbs is not interfered with, and they may be said to grow like plants out of doors; the bust is never deformed by the use of the corset, that instrument of torture of civilised woman. [1]

The Negress (girl or woman) having to handle for several hours a day, a pestle that weighs eighteen or twenty pounds, acquires by means of that repeated gymnastic exercise, a fine development of the muscles of the arm and shoulder. They are strong and vigorous, and the *Toubab* (White) who tried to offer violence to one of these Negresses, would soon find out his mistake. The breast of the young girl, who is of nubile age and has not had any children, is pear-shaped, but compact, hard, and resisting, and the nipples are very hard, and point out horizontally under the *boubou*. The walk is light and graceful, and the *pagne* or

---

[1] The ancients were strangers to this modern horror, unless we class the belt or *ceinture* worn by the Roman girls and matrons in this category. Various names were given to them, according to whether they were placed across the breasts or the hips, next to the body or over the clothes. The Latins called them: *Cestus, Capitium, Fascia, Taenia, Mamillare;* while among the Greeks they were known as: *Strophion, Zone, Apodesmos.* From such simple beginnings gradually evolved the complicated bit of machinery that European dames and virgins love to imprison themselves in to-day. In 1727, the Chevalier de Nisard became so enthusiastic on the subject, that he broke out into the following rhapsody:—

> "Est-il rien de plus beau qu'un corset,
> Qui naturellement figure,
> Et qui montre comme on est fait,
> Dans le moule de la Nature."

Those who feel interested in the subject may refer to Ernest Leoty's charming little work "*Le Corset à travers les Ages*" (Paris, 1893).

drawers, which cover the lower part of the body, if draped gracefully, does not detract from the grace of her movements. After she has borne her first child, all is changed. [1] The beauty of the breasts, and of the body in general, quickly fades. The breast becomes elongated, and hangs down like the udder of a she-goat, to which indeed it bears a certain resemblance. The cause of this is very simple, though I believe it is but little known, for I have not found it mentioned in any book of travels in Senegal, or Africa, with which I am acquainted.

Operation on the Breasts of Women lying-in. The Negress must have both hands free, when she works the heavy meal-pestle. That is why she carries her child astride on her buttocks, and supported there by a large piece of linen, which passes under the child's arms, and is fastened under the woman's breasts. When the child wants to suck, the mother pulls it to either side, then pushes her breast under her arm, and goes on with her work whilst the child is suckling. The mere weight of the milk would be insufficient to pull down the breast of a young woman, and make it sufficiently long. This curious deformity is caused by a surgical operation, which the old matrons perform upon the young women, when they are lying-in. This operation consists in cutting the subcutaneous muscles which support the breasts, by an oblique incision, which

---

[1] This peculiarity of a rapid change and loss of form and firmness in the breasts of the Black woman, on her attainment of motherhood, has also been noted in the Viennese ladies. Burton, with his usual 'cuteness, has already noted the fact (see "Terminal Essay" of the tenth volume of the UNBOWDLERISED edition of his "*Nights;*" also page 248 of the "*Book of Exposition,*" Paris, 1896).

is done very skilfully, but is so painful that it makes
the patient cry out. The young woman does not,
however, utter a cry or groan during the act of
parturition, and gets up two hours afterwards in order
to bathe her infant. The large size of the womb
renders the delivery very easy,—much more so than
is the case with the Annamite Congai, who remains
in bed forty days, and has to take the greatest precautions to prevent a deadly attack of peritonitis. The
method of carrying the infant on the back is very
convenient for the child, for the Negress has generally
very well-developed buttocks, and on this rounded
double cushion the child is as comfortable as though
it were on a seat. But this plan has the disadvantage
of bowing the legs, and the child very often acquires
much the same sort of walk as a dismounted horseman.

The Genital Organs of Negroes. It is only among
a few of the Negro races that the exterior genitals of
women have been as carefully examined and described
as in DE ROCHEBRUNE'S work on the Wolof Negroes.

These genitals he describes as being slightly developed.
A slit of only a few millimeters long represented the
big labia, the *nymphæ* are so to say rudimentary,
measuring 0.004 m. across, and 0.021 m. in length; the
entire vulva is thus characterised by a depression, the
surface being exteriorly bounded by two ellipsoid
wrinkles, which from the lower part and the middle
of the *Mons Veneris* spread out until they reach the
neighbourhood of the front region of the perinæum;
at the same the inner borders of these wrinkles join
together, forming merely a light wavy line, to be
observed even on women of a certain age. These
parts differ also from the others in colour, which is

paler than the rest of the skin which is black, in adults the *nymphæ* are of a slaty-blue, whereas in young girls they are dark red.

THE CLITORIS CONTINUALLY STANDS OUT; in all the cases where it was measured, its dimensions were 0.013 m. in the middle of the exposed part.

This formation differs considerably from that of European women. On the other hand, however, the usual lengthening out of the *nymphæ*, which other observers have described as being a characteristic of Negro women, is not found among the Wolof Negroes; on the contrary, with them the *nymphæ* seem to be to a certain extent atrophied; one might, as DE ROCHE-BRUNE, speak of a genuine arrest of development. [1] In fact, the outspringing of the clitoris excepted, the further development of the outer surface of the vulva cannot be better compared with other parts than with those of an European maiden of from 8 to 10 years of age.

Very remarkable also is the position which this organ occupies. If a perpendicular line is supposed through the body of the woman from head to foot, and if a perpendicular surface is supposed through this line at the level of the anus, it will be found that the *fossa navicularis* [2] is situated in this plane, and therefore the base of the vulva is situated in a point relatively high as regards the vertical line. This is also further observable in the length of the perinæum, which is very remarkable. Whilst its average length in European woman is 0.012 m., in the Wolof Negress it

[1] Rochebrune (A. Fremeau de) in the "*Revue d'Anthropologie*," 1881, IV. 2.

[2] *i.e. pudendum.*

attains to 0.025 m.; this difference of 0.013 m. shows, that the vulva lies back by that quantity.

Rapes and other Offences against Modesty amongst Creoles and Negroes. [1] Among the races inhabiting warm climates, there are several conditions which awaken and over-excite the genetic sense at an early age. The climate in this plays only an indirect part; for if at first it determines a more or less active sexual stimulus, it soon tempers and enervates, and renders continence easy to those who do not seek to violate it. But a warm temperature engenders habits only too likely to provoke licentiousness. There is in this opposition between the cosmical influence and the social influences derived from it, a contrast, the effects of which have long been the object of observation. The East, which in the early ages of Christianity produced such a number of illustrious virgins and pious hermits, and which at the present day shows us the high honour in which chastity is held in Buddhist countries, has also given to the world traditions of the vilest debauchery. Sexuality, where it is not sufficiently restrained by conventual or religious obligation, but where, on the contrary, its instinct meets with innumerable solicitations, must have many slips in consequence, and such is the case in Creole countries. In the French colonies the dominant race is that of the Negro, the most salacious of all, and there the White Man shows a sort of taste for the coloured woman, the origin of which may perhaps be traced to a mysterious

---

[1] We give this extract from Dr. Corre's book, *Le Crime en Pays Créoles*, as supplementing our observations on the manners and customs, prevalent in the FRENCH GUIANA, dealt with in the first volume.

law of renovation by crossing of races; however, the prejudice of colour prevents legitimate unions, which would be so profitable to the regular development of the population and to the improvement of morals, instead of which it contributes to maintain them in a deplorable state of dissoluteness.   The state of nudity, or that thin light costume which partly reveals the form of the body and presents it more seductively to the imagination, provokes desire.   The facility of intercourse increases the danger of the contact between the sexes, the more so that the numerical disproportion that has been observed between them obliges all the women to vie with each other in coquetry, advances, so to say, in order to attract the gaze and the choice of men.   Further, in the inevitably idle life woman is obliged to lead in the tropics, her natural aspirations are subjected to a compression which often transforms them into a particular vice.   Among Muslims, the concentration of a greater or lesser number of women into the possession of one male develops, in the men, by reason of satiety of the opposite sex, erotic habits, which lead them to *boy* love; in the French colonies, countries of Christian civilisation, official monogamy thrusts outside of the pale of married life many young girls, who interiorly rebel against their situation, at the same time that concubinage, permitted to the husband, deprives the wife, to the profit of the mistress, of a considerable share of the marital property; the man remains faithful to the cult of woman; for the lively and graceful beings to whom he addresses it have nothing of the inertia and passiveness of the sad sequestered women of the harem; but the wife seeks the satisfaction of her unsatiated longings . . . without compromising herself, among her friends or companions, already initiated into the Lesbian mysteries. Pederastic habits are hardly ever heard of among the Creoles, but, on the contrary, the celebrated dialogue between Megilla and Liena is often repeated among them. [1] The necessity of residing in a torrid climate in very open houses, if it diminishes the chances of adultery, while leaving a sufficient liberty to the women in a sort of intercourse which seems beneath suspicion, has the grave objection of furnishing to the curiosity of children, much too soon, unwholesome occasions for its exercise: so that a youth enters very early on his first campaign in the amorous career, and it is frequently the same with the young girl, under one form or another, if she is not protected by sufficient education. In the upper classes, there is always a proper varnish of good morals, often indeed based upon a foundation of real virtue. But in the others, they too ordinarily express by blamable, if not criminal, acts the perversions or the brutality of the sexual sense.

In January 1866, at Pointe-à-Pitre, three coloured girls were accused of a criminal assault on a Negress of 14 years of age, who repulsed their proposals.

In February 1888, in consequence of a complaint lodged by the parents of the victims, Dr. Blane was commissioned to go and examine, at Capesterre, the state of two twin Negro sisters, aged 12 years, whom a Mulatto woman had deflowered with her finger.

In matters of this nature the case is almost always dismissed or else the accused acquitted, not because the presumptions of a culpable action are entirely set aside,

---

[1] Lucian, *Hetaer. dial. V.* In the East, for similar reasons, the same tastes are developed among the women of the harems; the insufficiency of genetic satisfaction on the one side, and the excess of the same on the other, bring about naturally a seeking for anti-natural love.

but because they disappear behind the established fact of flagrant habits of precocious lasciviousness in young girls suddenly become so rigidly virtuous.

Men, here, very seldom commit criminal assaults on children of their own sex. The only case I have met with in the registers examined by me at Guadeloupe [1] was that of a White Man, of excellent family, admitted at too young an age to direct pupils, who but the day before had been his comrades: this vicious young fellow continued to practise, with others equally vicious, habits they had contracted together when sitting on the same benches at school, without understanding that the change in his position gave additional gravity to his acts!

Characteristics of Creole Criminality. The criminal assaults committed by men are generally on children or adults of the female sex, and are committed by young and vigorous Negroes, but not always of violent or brutal instincts; in Creole countries violation in this respect presents some particular characteristics. It is exceptional for it to be committed with violence on children; it is sometimes done by surprise or by moral constraint, under circumstances analogous or similar to those which generally distinguish this crime with us; more often, it seemed to me, when the attempt is made, it is with the complicity more or less proved or at least with the consciousness of the little girl, already initiated in the sexual act, obeying willingly, or even herself provoking it; the child

---

[1] I restrict myself to the study of Creole criminality, and therefore shall not mention a criminal assault committed on young boys by a schoolmaster of European origin, belonging to the "Christian Brothers Congregation."

dissimulates, or else admits the fact only when it has been discovered and that it has brought upon her the threats of her parents. [1]

Blackmail a Ground of Accusation. It may be understood that, in a population which presents such looseness of manners, the magistrates and doctors are obliged to use the utmost circumspection. More than one accusation hides beneath it either revenge or an attempt to blackmail. Sometimes the criminal attempt has been got up, with infernal immodesty, between the *victim* and her parents, or else any initial scene at all is dispensed with, and father, mother and child agree marvellously together to concoct a calumny against the man they wish to ruin. It is now 25 years ago, at Martinique, I was in the consulting-room of a physician, when a couple of Negroes brought in a little girl of from 5 to 6 years old, with a very wide-awake look and decided gestures; they wanted her to be visited, asserting that she had been violated the previous day, or the day before that, by a bad man, their next-door neighbour! The child was laid upon a table; before there had been time to say a single word to her, she quickly lifted up her clothes and, without hesitation, placed herself in the posture of a woman, who is holding herself ready for... whatever may be desired: she presented no traces at all of lesions... and the accusation was a false one. One of my colleagues related to me that he was one day called in, to a respectable family, to examine a little girl of from 8 to 10 years old, who, her parents pretended, had been violated by a personage... of

[1] I may observe incidentally that in many of these little girls precocity manifests itself, by the abnormal development of the external genital organs and the premature appearance of the menses.

quasi-official rank; the matter was grave! The child
of her own accord lay down on her back, exposing
her person with the utmost effrontery, but presenting
nothing more than an abnormal development of the
external genital organs and of the clitoris; my colleague, guessing with what sort of creature he had to
do, asked her under his breath if she was not in the
habit of *doing z'amie* [1] and she replied by a smile
and a cynical glance, as if there could be the least
doubt of *so natural a thing!* The child had built up,
piece by piece, an accusation against a man who had
doubtless taken her fancy, but whose reputation was
far above suspicion, and the parents had believed in
this odious falsehood! [2]

The Psychology of Negro Brutality. In criminal
assaults on adults, the Negro will sometimes resort
to brutal means, for instance, if he is drunk. But
usually, when he uses violence, it is with the con-
viction that he is merely carrying to the extreme his
part as lover, to the unavowed satisfaction of the resisting woman. He does not attack women of notorious
virtue, but those whom he has seen to easily grant to
others the favours he envies; he had supposed, in perfect good faith, that he might dare to take what was
only pretended to be denied him ... for form's sake,
and he is astounded when he hears a sentence pronounced against him.

Narcotization not a Factor. The way in which

[1] This is the current expression used to designate those enjoyments
which girls and women procure to each other.

[2] As I am writing for those persons who are interested in questions
of criminality, for serious reasons or professionally, I do not feel called
upon to sacrifice the instructive realism. of my observations to a silly
mock-modesty.

these outrages are committed excludes all idea of
the previous preparing of the victim by narcotization.
I would not maintain that criminal outrages or
attempts may not at times have been perpetrated
without their knowledge on persons rendered unconscious by opium, thrown into their food or drink.
At all events, I know of no case of the kind. The
crime, in ordinary cases, has been thoroughly
premeditated, in the sense that the aggressor has for a
more or less long time coveted the woman, that he has
sought for a propitious moment to get possession of
her: nevertheless, as he has prepared nothing to bring
about the circumstances which have favoured his
design, the assault remains accidental, and, for that
reason, is to some degree attenuated in the eyes of
the judges and of the jury; it seems even as if there
was a tendency to nearly always exclude the idea of
violence, for the penalties applied rarely exceed from
1 to 2 years' imprisonment. [1] But the frequency of
criminal assault by surprise, the audacity and off-hand
manner with which it is often accomplished, point to
a certainty of impunity, among the accused, the cause
of which may perhaps be referred to a new Creole
superstition. They believe over there that there are
sorcerers who possess secrets for *making people*

[1] The Court of Bourges and the Criminal Chamber of the Court of
Cassation had, not long ago, to decide in a case of criminal assault, of
quite colonial character. The accused party rejected the crimination of
assault with violence: "He had introduced himself, favoured by the
night, into the bed of his victim, who had let him have his will,
mistaking him for her husband." The woman did not discover her
error until the act had been consummated. The High Court decided
that the circumstance of violence could not be set aside, the crime
having been committed without the reflected consent of her who had
been the sufferer.

invisible,[1] and when a theft is spoken of, the author
of which has not been discovered, they never fail to
repeat that he surely had the means *not to be seen.*
The man who dares to risk himself, panting with lust,
but not besides much troubled with any great danger of
immediate correction and of legal punishment, near to a
woman lying next to her husband, has more than once
drawn his bold confidence from his reliance in some *piaï*
or *quimbois* (amulet), capable of hiding him from view. [2]

[1] That is to be found again in the "*Grand Albert*" (a book of magic)
between a receipt to make a person dance *stark naked* and another to
enable one to travel ten leagues in an hour!

"To become invisible. You have a black cat and you must buy a
new pot, a looking-glass, a flint and tinder-box, an agate, some char-
coal and tinder, taking care to draw water from a fountain at the
stroke of midnight; after which you light your fire. Put the cat into
the pot and hold the lid down with the left hand without ever moving
or looking behind you, whatever noise you may hear; then let the
cat boil for 24 hours, and serve it on a new dish; take the meat and
throw it over your left shoulder, saying these words: "*Accipe quod
tibi do, et nihil amplius*" (Take what I give thee, and nothing more).
Take the bones, and put them one after another between the teeth of your
left jaw, looking at the same time at your reflection in the mirror; and if it
is not the good one, you must throw it away, repeating the same words,
until you have found it; and as soon as you no longer perceive your reflection
in the glass, withdraw backwards, saying: "*Pater, in manus tuas com-
mendo spiritum meum* (Father, into thy hands I commend my spirit).

[2] The intrigue of a very free Creole novel, printed in 1697 (*Le Zombi
du Grand Pérou ou la Comtesse de Cocagne*, by Blessebois, a naval
officer), is based upon this belief in talismans which render a person invisible. The Countess of Cocagne, a beauty more exalted by amorous
ardour than adorned by the qualities of decency and modesty, goes to
a M. de C...., an expert in the magical art, to ask him for a means
to bring back to her the Marquis du Grand Pérou. M. de C. per-
suades her that he has rendered her invisible, and, thus transformed
into a Zombi (spirit, ghost), she causes trouble in the house of the Marquis.
The magician contrives to obtain a substantial reward for his assistance...
on the occasion of a private supper with the Countess.

CHAPTER II.

Various Races besides the Wolofs.—Mussulmans and Fetishists. I cannot thoroughly describe in detail all the moral characteristics, manners, customs, etc., of all the tribes and races to be found in Senegal. I must confine myself to a few general remarks, and only treat *in extenso* such points as more specially refer to the sexual passions. I shall, however, note the anthropological characteristics which distinguish the principal races.

These may first be roughly classed into two great divisions, the Mussulmans and the fetish worshippers. The Wolofs, Sereres, Toucouleurs, Peulhs, and Soninkés or Sarrakholais, are Mussulmans; on the other hand the Bambaras, Malinkés, Mandingos, and Kassonkés are fetish worshippers. Other races of the South of Senegambia, as the Diobas for example, were originally fetish worshippers, and have gradually become Mussulmans. Before the French came to Senegal, the Mussulmans were conquering with the sword the fetish worshippers, and French civilisation has greatly interfered with the extension of Mahometanism, which is the great

reason why the French are so hated by those who
profess that religion.

The Toucouleur. Above Walo, on the left bank
of the Senegal, in Fouta-Toro and the neighbouring
districts, are found the Toucouleurs, a very warlike
and thievish race, and soldiers of Islam. They were
always in the front rank of the enemies of the French.
To their love of war, they add a considerable degree
of intelligence, and often enroll themselves in the
regiment of native sharpshooters. It was from amongst
this race that El Hadj 'Umar recruited his best soldiers,
and by their help was able to conquer a large Empire
in the Soudan, but the best provinces were wrested
from him by the French some ten years ago.

The anthropological characteristics of the Toucouleur
differ but little from those of the Wolof. The Toucouleur
is more slender and less robust, than the Wolof. He
comes to Saint Louis, with only a simple strip of rag
to cover his nakedness. He lives on the charity of
his co-religionists, and sleeps in any shelter he can
find, for he has neither hearth nor home. Every
halfpenny he can earn he puts away, until he has
amassed the twenty francs he needs for the purchase
of an old flint musket, a little barrel (about 11lbs) of
"treaty powder", and a dozen spare gun flints. Any
scraps of metal which fall in his way,—door knobs,
bits of wire fencing, saucepan handles, etc.--are
carefully stored away, and with these the Negro
blacksmith will manufacture projectiles, which will
not carry far, or with any precision, but which, when
fired at short range, will make terrible wounds. Many
French soldiers have felt their effects.

The Peulh forms a large race, scattered about over the country between the Senegal and the Upper Niger. In the opinion of General Faidherbe, [1] the Peulhs came originally from Lower Egypt, and are descended from the Hyksos, a pastoral people driven out by the Pharaohs. They are fanatical Mussulmans, and were of great service to El Hadj 'Umar. Like their ancestors, they are nomadic, and live on the produce of their flocks. The Peulh, in fact, is evidently of Semitic origin; if his hair is not smooth, at least it falls in cork-screw curls on his shoulders. The general tint of his body is of a reddish brown, and the external mucous surface of the gland, and the vulva in the woman, are almost as light as those of the Mulatto. The features are regular, and he has not the thick nose of the other Negroes. The Peulh rarely visits Saint Louis, and is hardly ever found in the ranks of the Native Sharpshooters, of whom I shall presently speak.

The Sarrakholais. This people is certainly of Semitic origin, and its name is synonymous with *White man.* We will borrow from Colonel Frey, who in 1885-86 commanded an expedition against the Sarrakholais, who had been stirred up to revolt by the Marabout [2] Mahmaduz-Zamine, a description of the anthropological characteristics of this race.

[1] From 1854 to 1865 Faidherbe was the Governor-general of Senegal, which he administrated with great energy and ability. He has left several important works on the races and countries he had to deal with.

[2] *Marabout*, derived through the Portuguese *Marabuto* from the Arabic muf'aribi, is a Mohammedan "Saint" supposed to work miraculous cures. These religious "medicine" men wield immense influence over credulous and fanatical peoples who regard them as supernatural beings; they correspond to the *Mollahs* of the Indian frontier tribes and the *fetish men* of "Rhodesia".

" The face is oval, the eyes large, and well-shaped,
the nose straight, and the lips thin. A Semitic descent
is also shown in the carriage of the head, which is
proudly held high, and in the harmonious proportion
of the limbs, which are well made, and of a proper
length. If a young girl of pure race is examined,
the observer is still more struck by the resemblance
of her features to those of the white race. Her nose
is small, and often aquiline, with quivering nostrils;
the eyes—almond-shaped, and surmounted by long
lashes—are large, and have a strange expression, like
those of a frightened gazelle; the mouth, nicely and
sometimes prettily shaped, discloses a set of small,
very even, and extremely white teeth; her throat and
bust are admirably formed; her limbs well-proportioned,
though perhaps a trifle frail; her legs finely shaped;—
in fact the young Sarrakholais girl is 'a pretty little
thing,' not devoid of a seductive charm. Owing, however, to numerous crossings with black races, in a
great many of the Sarrakholais these marks of race
have become degenerate and degraded, and have
acquired from these other races a coarser, heavier form.

But there still remains, as a characteristic trait of the
Sarrakholais people, an intelligence superior to that of
the tribes amongst whom they live, a more advanced
civilisation, a greediness of gain which is peculiar to
them, and a really extraordinary aptitude for trade,
which has caused the Sarrakholais to be called 'the
pedlars of Western Africa.'

" These Sarrakholais pedlars constitute the whole body
of the *Dioulas*, or caravan men. Their stock consists
of a little salt, a few pieces of cotton, some powder,
and a few trading muskets. They travel from one
country to another, and barter and exchange their

goods, and when they have acquired some capital, they become slave traders, —that is the dream of their life. To provide for this event, the Dioula takes care to furnish himself, before his departure, with some very neatly made handcuffs and irons, which he uses for securing those captives, who, having been taken in war, cannot resign themselves to their wretched fate, and become violent and difficult to guard. Captives of this sort are sometimes sold to the Dioula for a handful of salt. Other Sarrakholais, who have no taste for travel and adventure, attain the coveted position of householder by other means. They come to Saint Louis, or to the outposts, or landing stages, at the age of fifteen, and secure the most lucrative and best paid positions which can be obtained by native· employés, and choose, as much as possible, those places which require the least amount of hard work.

"Almost all the native sailors *(laptots)* who, at Senegal, compose the crews of the despatch boats and the trading lighters, are Sarrakholais. All the best posts as servants, waiters, and clerks, which can be held by natives, are, at Saint Louis, occupied by Sarrakholais. Of the sixteen 'river captains',—a kind of pilot, whose position is much envied by the natives, on account of the privileges of various sorts they possess,—fourteen are Sarrakholais. On the other hand, not a man of this race is to be found in the ranks of the Spahis, or the Senegalese Sharpshooters, for the very good reason that the work is very hard, and the pay very small."

According to Colonel Frey, the Sarrakholais people formed, some centuries ago, a vast empire in the centre of the Soudan,—an empire, the remains of which are still scattered over the African Continent, under the names of Soninkés, Markankés, and Sarrakholais. They

are found on both the right and left banks of the
Senegal. We have given this quotation *in extenso*,
as being the most complete refutation of the popular
error that the Black of Senegal owes what civilisation
he has to the White man.

**The Civilisation of the White Man has no
Effect upon the Character of the Black.** In 1885-86,
the most intelligent native race, the Sarrakholais, though
then enjoying a high degree of material prosperity, —a
prosperity which they owed in great part to contact
with European civilisation,—rose like one man, and
attacked the rear of the small French column which
was fighting in the Upper Soudan against Samory. [1]
Foremost, amongst those who thus revolted, were the
old *laptots*, and the clerks of the merchants of Saint
Louis. Perhaps one reason was, that this race knows
what an aversion the Toubab has for slavery, that
great curse of Africa; and the Sarrakholais, though

[1] This Negro has been styled "THE BLACK NAPOLEON OF THE
FRENCH SOUDAN." He is the bitter enemy of Colonial France. For
relentless energy and great ability he may be fitly compared to the
Algerian Arab, 'Abd-ul-Kader. Like most of the native chiefs who
have played an important rôle in Africa, Samory's beginnings were
very humble. Son of a caravan-leader, during his absence on a journey,
his mother was kidnapped and carried away into slavery. Samory on
hearing of this, did not hesitate to seek out the powerful chief who
had abducted her and demand her freedom. This chanced to be the
turning-point in his destiny, for the chief pleased with his handsome
aspect, engaged him for his service. The rest of his career nurtured
by ambition and fostered by blood and fire, forms one of the most
extraordinary pages in the history of the Soudan. His army is said to
number 60,000 men, of which 5,000 are mounted. Many times has
his death been reported, and as many times the report proved false by
his sudden resurrection. Like his famous Corsican prototype, the
treaties made with his adversaries have been ruthlessly broken in
subservience to a tireless ambition.

they had lived amongst the Whites, are great slave dealers. The fanaticism of the Mussulman had also a great deal to do with the hate they felt for the Christian White man.

The anatomical description of the Sarrakholais I shall give in the chapter relating to the organs of generation of the black races.

The Kassonkés are another race of Semitic origin, but greatly bastardised by crossing with the native Blacks. The Kassonkés, or Kassonkais, are tall fine men, as strong and robust as the Wolofs, but that is the only trait they have in common, for they are very lazy. They inhabit Natiogo, Kosso, and Soyo, on the left bank of the Upper Senegal. The costume of the men is rather original, and deserves a special mention. For head-dress, they have a sort of small cap with two pointed peaks, which they wear on the side of the head, like a French soldier's *képi*. They wear wide trousers, like a Zouave, but shorter and fuller. Their costume is completed by a small *boubou*, which comes half way down the leg. This dress is made of native stuff, dyed yellow or brown. The women are very pretty, whilst they are young, but they tattoo their lips and gums a violet colour, with tincture of indigo.

The Kassonké is far from being as brave as the Sarrakholais. He is generally a thief, an idler, and a drunkard. In this latter capacity he does not admire a religion of which one of the leading precepts enjoins abstention from fermented liquors. In this also he differs from the Sarrakholais, who is a strict observer of the law. Though he is not brave, he is very fond of war, or rather pillage, which is the natural attendant of war amongst all these people, but should he encounter any serious resistance he will fly without feeling any shame. He is especially fond of stealing women and children, who may be heedlessly wandering round the villages, and selling them as slaves. Even an adult native man, travelling alone and unarmed, is by no means safe, and runs a great risk of being set on by two or three scoundrels, bound, and carried to the next village to be sold as a slave. But the Kassonké has a great respect for the White man, of whom he has a most salutary dread. He has not, as the Wolof and Toucouleur have, the bitter and vindictive hate of the Mussulman for the Christian dog,—a feeling which caused the Sarrakholais to revolt during a time of peace and prosperity. Round Medina, in the heart of the Kassonké country, Islamism has made some few converts, but they are not very fervent, and the religion rather tends to decline than increase. The marabouts' school is hardly attended by any but the children of the Wolof traders, who are established in considerable numbers at this post, on account of the commerce with the upper part of the river.

The Young Kassonké Girl. A very pretty description of the young Kassonké girl is given in Loti's charming romance, which has already been quoted. [1]

"Fatou-Gaye had on her feet pretty little leather sandals, kept on by straps, which passed between the big and second toes, like the ancient rothurnæ. She wore the scanty and clinging drawers,—a fashion which the Egyptian women of the time of Pharaoh had bequeathed to the Nubian women. Over that was a *boubou*, a large square of muslin with a hole through which to pass the head, and which fell, like a peplum,

[1] *Roman d'un Spahi.*

a little lower than the knees. Her ornaments were composed of heavy rings of silver, rivetted round the wrists and ankles, and necklaces of the fragrant *soumaré*.

" She looked very pretty, did Fatou-Gaye, with her high barbaric head-dress, which gave her the aspect of a Hindoo goddess dressed up for a religious festival. She had not the flat nose and thick lips of some of the African tribes, and which, in France, we are in the habit of considering as the type of the black race. She was of the pure type of the Kassonké race; a small nose, fine and straight, with thin nostrils, slightly pinched in and quivering, a well-formed, pretty mouth with splendid teeth; and, above all, large wide eyes like blue enamel, which sparkled, according to her mood, sometimes with a strange gravity, sometimes with a mysterious mischief."

The Malinkés and Bambaras are Negroes who are fetish worshippers, descendants,—according to Dr. Colomb [1]—of the Mandingo race, which came originally from the banks of the Niger. It has not been mixed by crossings, and is characterised by thick lips, a very flat nose, woolly hair, and a narrow facial angle. The Malinkés are found on the banks of the Niger, and the higher branches of the Upper Senegal, where they form the major part of the population.

The Bambaras are principally established upon the right bank of the Niger. They have the same anthropological characteristics as the Malinkés, but are more thick-set and not so tall; the calves of their legs are

[1] *Notice sur les Oasis du Sahara et les grandes routes qui y conduisent.* (Nouvelles Annales des Voyages, Juillet, 1860) par Lieut.- Colonel de Colomb.

more muscular than those of the other Blacks. They
are intelligent, strong, and brave, and are hated, and
incessantly attacked, by the Mussulman people who
surround them.

The Malinké is thinner, less robust, and much less
brave than the Bambara. According to Colonel Frey,
the Malinké, either owing to superstitious terror or to
cowardice, will not travel at night, or, at least, unless
he is compelled to by force of circumstances; for
though in the daytime he can rely on his weapons,
and his agility, to bring him safely through perils, in
the dark he is exposed to a thousand dangers he
cannot always avoid. After sunset his sight becomes
considerably weaker; it might almost be said that he
is struck with blindness. This peculiarity of the Malinké
is attributed to the immoderate use of *allo*, the dried
leaf of the boabab tree, and to the very small quantity
of salt which he consumes.

The Senegalese Sharpshooter is a volunteer,
recruited, for a certain wage, from amongst all the
races of Senegal. The Government is not particular
as to how the men are obtained, provided that they
are strong and healthy. I was surgeon to a battalion
of Sharpshooters at Saint Louis, and the captain of
the battalion assured me that three-fourths of the
Negroes, who were engaged to serve for three years
at the various posts on the river, from whence they
had been sent to head-quarters, were slaves, bought
from their masters at a fixed rate of £12 a head. By
the very fact of his engagement, the Sharpshooter
becomes a free man, as soon as he is released from
military service.

By giving medical attendance to the families of the

Sharpshooters, I was able to learn many details concerning their manners and customs. Colonel Frey has
devoted several pages to a description of the modest
Senegalese Sharpshooter, without whose aid it would
have been impossible to conquer the Upper Senegal
and the Soudan.

" The corps is formed," he says, " of divers elements,
borrowed from all the different races of Senegambia,
and a practised eye can tell each at a glance. The
Toucouleur can be recognised by his warlike temper,
and his noisy, boastful character; the Bambara, who
most usually has been captured on the Niger, by his
robust limbs and his quiet temper; the Peulh by his
regular features, his thin, nervous legs, and his extreme
agility; the Wolof, who is more civilised than the other
Blacks, by his mild temper and more polished manners.

" In spite of the fact that they are recruited from
such diverse elements, the Sharpshooters show a
remarkable *esprit de corps*. They are most useful
auxiliaries, of great intrepidity, and most of them really
brave. The Sharpshooter is the right soldier for
conquest. No one is fitter than he to make a forced
march, and execute the sudden attacks that a young
and bold commander may conceive and execute.
When once he has put on his *grigris* (leather amulets),
in which, by the way, he has no great confidence,
from having seen fall under his bullets many of his
enemies who were covered with them, but which,
nevertheless, he likes to wear as ornaments; when once
he is furnished with his goat-skin, holding five or six
quarts of water, and his wallet, containing a handful
of *couscous*, and a hundred and twenty cartridges, his
officers may ask him to march twenty hours at a stretch,
and he will regard it as mere child's play."

The Sharpshooter is not always distinguished for discipline, especially if he is commanded by officers who have only just arrived in the country, and are ignorant of the language, and the manners of the natives, and do not know what to give, and what to refuse, to their men. Moreover, as he passes nine months out of each year in the bush, he needs a firm hand, tempered with parental authority, or he will, without any scruples, desert, and take his arms and baggage with him. Besides, he is a natural pillager. If the men are not carefully watched, they will despoil any caravan they come across. The Sharpshooter is viewed with scorn and loathing by the traders, the well-to-do people, and, generally speaking, by every Mussulman. For is he not a mercenary in the pay of the Whites,—a turncoat, and almost a renegade?

When it was proposed to introduce into Senegal a law which should make military service obligatory on the natives, numerous protests were raised amongst the Blacks of Saint Louis. "We would resist such a law," they cried, "even if we should have to revolt against the French authority."

CHAPTER III.

Social condition and moral characteristics of the Negro race in general.—The Chiefs and Marabouts.—Free men, griots, and blacksmiths.—The Griot village of Krina.—Slaves.—The slavery question.—Moral characteristics of the Black.—The Black's opinion of the civilised Toubab.—Karamoko's carbine.—Various customs and superstitions common to the people of Senegal.—Mussulman amulets and the fetish man's "grigris".

Social Condition. All the Negroes—except the chiefs and marabouts—may be divided into three well-marked castes; the *free men*, the *griots*, and the *slaves*. All these peoples have chiefs, little "Kinglets" of a village, who oppress their subjects like the tyrants of antique Greece. Amongst the Mussulman people, the head-chief possesses both the civil and religious power, and is a great marabout, like El Hadj Omar Mahmadou Lamine, who stirred up the Sarrakholais to rebel, Abdoul-Bou-Ba-Kur in the Fouta-Toro, and many others. Beneath them they have ordinary marabouts, priests of the Mussulman religion, who fight for their faith. Some of them give their soldiers grigris, and amulets against bullets, steel, fire, etc.

The Free Men may be divided into many categories. At the head of them comes the warrior, who is a cultivator of the soil in his leisure hours. Below these come the industrial classes, the various trades of which form corporations analogous to those which existed in France before 1789. By a singular custom, which reminds one of the castes of India, a man may only marry amongst families of the same trade, and this trade is hereditary; the son of a blacksmith is a blacksmith all his life, even though he may never touch a hammer. I should remark in passing, that one profession often includes a good number of others. Thus the blacksmith is also a locksmith, armourer, potter, and carpenter, in his spare moments. He is even a goldsmith and jeweller, and his trinkets are not wanting in a certain barbaric elegance. He even adds to these vocations that of surgeon-sorcerer, and he it is who circumcises the little boys. The trade of weaver is generally exercised by the captives.

The Griot. On the same social level as the black-smith-surgeon-sorcerer is the griot *(Dieli-Ké)*. He is the musician, the singer of praises of whoever will pay him, the minstrel of the Middle Ages. The instrument he usually plays on, bears a striking resemblance to the hurdy-gurdy of the Savoyard, and from it he extracts some excruciating sounds. The accordion is also in favour with him.

The free man has a great contempt for the griot, but is afraid of him. He is more intelligent than the common run of the natives, and " exploits " everybody, either by singing the praises of the generous, or by making insulting songs about those with whom he has a quarrel.

The griot goes to war without any musket,—like the blacksmith-armourer,—but with a sword, which, however, he does not use. He contents himself, during the battle, with singing, and exciting the warriors to kill each other. If his side should happen to be van-quished, he will, without the least sense of shame, change his opinion and servilely exalt the victor, whom, before the battle, he had been cursing. Some of the griots often become the counsellors of the most powerful chiefs.

I knew, both at Saint Louis and in the interior, some griots of the Mussulman tribes. None of them could resist the temptation of a glass of good absinthe, or *sangara* (trade brandy), if it was offered on the quiet.

If the griot sings during the battle, the blacksmith has to repair the arms, manufacture the heavy bullets of wrought iron, and after the battle, as an improvised surgeon, cut off limbs, slash the flesh of the wounded, and extract the bullets. No European would be able to survive the often terrible mutilations which result from this not very conservative style of surgery. I should mention in passing, that the wife of the black-smith circumcises the young girls, amongst the tribes who practise that operation, and amongst the Kas-sonkés, dresses the hair of the women, and even of the men. But to return to the griots. They only marry amongst themselves generally: and at their death, are not deemed worthy of a funeral ceremony. They are usually buried, with their instrument, in the trunk of a hollow tree, which is then closed up.

Slaves. There are three categories of captives or slaves. The first includes the *house slaves*, who have formed part, for many generations, of the slaves of the family, and are born in that position. They are rather servants for life than slaves properly so called. They are very rarely sold, and then only for very grave reasons. In fact, they are considered by custom, as an integral part of the family, like the freed-men of old Rome. The second category is composed of the *slaves of the lougan*, so named because they undertake the farming and other works. Usually he has been bought young, and has grown up in the house. He is almost as much esteemed as the house slave, and his lot is not very hard. Then comes the *trade slave*. He is mere human merchandise; hardly nourished, ill-treated, often beaten, and hawked about from one caravan to another. When he falls on the road, ill, or worn out, he is allowed to die on the ground like a dog, and his body becomes the prey of the jackals and hyænas.

Every effort has been made by the French Government to put an end to this horrible traffic, but has proved unavailing, owing to the conservative routine, and the ill will, of the Negroes themselves. I have mentioned that the Sarrakholais, the most intelligent race in all Senegal, furnish the greater part of the Dioulas, or conductors of caravans. The French outposts have orders to stop these caravans, but the caravans escape surveillance by making long detours. When the inhabitants of a village are captured, the captors begin by murdering all the males above fifteen years old, and the old women. The rest are led away into slavery, and often are sold at an absurdly low price.

The Slavery Question is the stumbling block which will always prevent European civilisation from extending. We shall never make the Black understand that he has not the right to buy or sell his fellow man in the market, like cattle. But between the fetish worshipper of the interior of Africa, or of the Dahomey coast, who cuts his captive's throat, and the Mohammedan who makes him work hard it is true but takes as much care of him as he would of a beast of burden, the distance is immense.

Our efforts to suppress slavery have only alienated from us the good will of the people, and though the public sale of slaves is forbidden, an almost open traffic in flesh is, all the same, carried on amongst the tribes of the interior. At Saint Louis even, where all the complicated machinery of French law exists, there are found, in spite of it, slaves who have been brought from the interior by the traders. They are disguised under the name of domestics, and are, in reality, *servants for life*. There are young girls of this category, who are made over, before they attain puberty, to "amateurs" who want virgins. Of course, the Black traders who bring back these slaves, do not openly boast of it, but the fact is nevertheless certain, and I have good proofs of it. For instance, in my house, I often used to see a Negro boy, the colour of old bronze, a half-breed between a Moor and a Negress, whom a rich Black merchant,—my landlord, if you please,—had brought with him from the station of Podor, when he went to attend the gum market. This lad, who was completely naked, despite his thirteen years, used to come and help my cook to wash up the dishes, and his wages consisted of a bit of sea biscuit, which he used to devour with teeth as white as those of a puppy, with sometimes a lump of sugar. Although his skin was lighter than that of a Zambo, but not so light as that of a Mulatto, the mucous surfaces of the lips and the gland were a very dark red-brown. Seeing that I appeared interested a little in the creature, my landlord asked me one day if I wanted to buy him. I appeared to entertain the proposal. He asked me twelve pounds, saying that that was the value of the cloth he had given for him, and that he would only sell him under the express condition that the lad was to be circumcised, and never made a Christian.

The motives which caused me to refuse this proposal will be easily understood. Thinking that I wanted to beat him down, he lowered the price, and finally my landlord's son, a big booby twenty years old, proposed to trade the Negro boy for my central fire gun with spare rifled barrels, my faithful companion during fifteen years. I kept my gun, and resolutely refused the nigger boy.

Moral Characteristics of the Black. I shall only say a very few words about those moral characteristics common to all the Black races of Senegal.

The Black certainly differs more from the White, morally, than he does in the colour of his skin. Superficial observers often reproach him with his idleness, his apathy, his carelessness, his want of forethought. The Negro is only a great child, who takes no care for the future. When the harvest is good, he eats and drinks, and never troubles to put any by for the morrow, or even to reserve the grain needed for sowing the *lougans* (cultivated lands). If the harvest should fail, he dies of hunger. But he is honest and upright; he is grateful, and remembers benefits received. He often forgets ill-treatment even. During an illness, which kept me in bed a fortnight, my young Sarrakholais boy helped himself, from a sack of dollars, to all the money needed for the household expenses. He was my factotum: cook, groom, and valet. He gave an account of all the money spent every day, and took whatever money he required.

I wrote down, when he was not present, all the items in a small account book, and when I was well again, verified the balance, which was perfectly correct. Only, the rascal had eaten nine pounds of sugar in a very few days. In Cochin-China, my sack would have been emptied by an Annamite boy, the first day of my illness, and, perhaps, if I had been alone, as I was in Senegal, and had a large sum of money in the house, the thief would have poisoned me, to prevent unpleasant disclosures.

Opinions of the Black concerning the Civilised Toubab. The Black,—and I mean by this not the ignorant Negro, but the trader, or the Sarrakholais, who has come into contact with civilisation at Saint Louis,—does not understand our system of government a little bit. For him, the French Government is the husband of the Republic, who is a very rich woman, who rules France, which is her property. As to the soldiers, they are the slaves of the Government. What is the use of explaining the parliamentary system to such fellows? The right side of compulsory military service they do not understand, but the wrong side of it they can comprehend when,—on the very problematical chance of civilising a Negro,—they see the son of a Normandy peasant, or a Burgundian vine-dresser, sent to die in an unhealthy country, or be killed by one of the subjects of Behanzin, in Dahomey. The Senegalese Sharpshooter, however, knows something about discipline in his own way, and can obey orders, if they are given by a capable officer.

The Black gazes open-eyed at all the wonders of civilisation. At first they are astonished, but that soon

wears off, and, strange to say, they never try to understand or explain anything they see. All that they
say—when they say anything at all—is, "That's
another invention of the Toubab." The railway at
Senegal, the telegraph, telephone, rifled cannon, the
dynamite with which the walls of their *tatas* (fortified
redoubts) are blown down, etc., do not cause a single
idea to penetrate their thick skulls. The son of my
landlord, the big booby I have mentioned, who read
and spoke French, said to me one day, when I wanted
to lend him a handbook on Elementary Physics, to
improve his mind, "The White men are rich, and they
know, and can do, a lot of things; but everyone has
his turn, and the day will come when the Black man
will know as much as the Toubab."

Whatever amount of education you may give a
Black, you can no more change his character than you
can the colour of his skin, and, as the proverb says,
"The barber wastes his soap, when he tries to wash
a blackamoor white." From a moral point of view,
we are committing a great error, when we try to
instil European ideas of civilisation into the brain of
the Negro.

Karamoko's Carbine. As we know, some of the
sons of the principal chiefs were brought up at Saint
Louis, at the "School for hostages", founded by
Faidherbe. As soon as they returned home again,
they invariably proved to be the bitterest enemies of
the Whites. The example of Karamoko, the son of
Samory, who came to Paris, where he was received
like the son of a king—a strange manner of showing
our superiority!— is an unanswerable proof of the
failure of this method.

It appears that, on his return, his father sent an escort, to welcome him on re-entering the Kingdom. Karamoko was laden with gifts from the French Government, and amongst these was a fine repeating rifle, richly ornamented. The chief who commanded the escort, having left the ranks, and presented himself alone before the King's son, Karamoko ordered him to return to his place at once. The chief did not obey quite quickly enough, so he had a bullet through his head from Karamoko's rifle. In the recent combats between Achinard's column and the natives of the Soudan, Karamoko always showed himself to be our most intractable enemy, and yet he had not, as the other chiefs had, the excuse of being ignorant of the French military power. He had heard hundreds of field guns fired, at the camp of Chalons, and had seen a division of cavalry reviewed. My opinion, respecting the character of the Blacks is entirely corroborated by that of Dr. Lota. [1]

Various Customs and Superstitions common to the Different Tribes of Senegal. I do not propose to describe here the various customs of the numerous tribes which inhabit Senegal. I shall content myself by noticing, in a few lines, those manners and superstitions which are common to all, as the circumcision of boys, the manner of burying the dead with the face turned towards the East, the form of salutation with the hand over the heart, and the Mussulman chaplet, which is as common as the fan is in Spain.

It is evident that Islamism, having been imposed by force, has taken no real root amongst the tribes of Semitic origin. As to the real fetish worshipper, be-

[1] Dr. Lota, *Deux ans entre le Sénégal et le Niger.*

longing to the Mandingo race, the religion of Mahomet
has hardly been able to penetrate his thick skull, and
even, when he is converted, he nevertheless retains
his old superstitions.

When a Negro is ill, prayers are offered up to his deities,
but that does not prevent his friends and relatives from
having faith in the prayers and amulets of the marabouts ;
and, at the same time, recourse is had to a fetish wizard,
who cuts open an unfortunate fowl, and examines its
liver, exactly as the augurs used to do in old Rome.

Mussulman Amulets and Fetish "Grigris".
When a Mussulman is ill, verses of the Koran are
written on specially prepared slips of wood, which are
then washed in water, and the water given to the
invalid to drink, or little bags containing scraps of
paper, on which are inscribed verses of the Koran, are
placed on the seat of the disease. That is a kind of
remedy that is within the reach of everybody. As to
the fetish worshippers, they have a blind faith in the
grigris, which are sold to them by sorcerers, to preserve them from illness, poverty, the terrible bullets
of the Toubab, the knives of their enemies, etc., or
charms to render the possessor happy in his, or her,
domestic life. A severe wound will hardly serve to
undeceive them, and if, by chance, they escape from
a battle with a few bruises or a slight wound, they
continue to believe in their charm with blind credulity.
The sorcerers who sell grigris are generally of the
blacksmith class, and in order to astonish and impress
the people, they dress themselves in a strange garb
made of strips of bark, wear a large calabash on the
head, and wander about the villages at night, uttering
horrible howls.

CHAPTER IV.

The Negro woman.—Her social condition.—Marriage.—The wife purchased by the husband.—Vanity of the women who fetch high prices.—Marriage ceremonies.—Constancy of the Negress.—The wives of the Sharpshooters.—Their inconstancy.—Their virtues.— Polygamy amongst the Blacks.—The chief mistress of the house. —Jealousy unknown to the Negress.—Divorce.

The Social Condition of Woman. Travellers who dash helter-skelter through the country, represent the Negro woman as a kind of domestic animal, obedient and hard-working, and the property of her husband, who has purchased her, and may purchase several other wives besides. To an impartial observer, however, who studies matters closely, this custom of the husband purchasing his wife, or wives, does not involve social inferiority to the latter. When we understand the manners and customs of the Blacks, we see that woman is not in such a miserable condition as is said, and that, relatively at all events, she enjoys some measure of liberty. Let us select as an example the household of the Negro of Saint Louis. The husband brings in the wood, cultivates a patch of land, fishes, or hunts. The native traders, who serve the European merchants, ascend the river to trade. These last form a rather high caste, and quickly obtain a good position. In the interior of Senegal, the man goes where he likes, but very often squats on the door sill and tells his beads, if he is a good Mussulman; sometimes he makes his own clothes,—a task which not being very fatiguing he reserves to himself. Meanwhile his wife slaves at all the heavy work; she cultivates the field, gets in the harvest, looks after the animals, grinds at the mill, and prepares the couscous. The operation of grinding is very hard work, and often the woman is obliged to rise in the middle of the night, for she has to pound for many hours at the coarse millet, which is as large and heavy as maize. In the afternoon, the work recommences. Vain attempts have been made to introduce waterpower mills to grind the millet, but the Negroes have always refused them, saying that their wives would have nothing to do if they did not grind at the mill.

In short, the social condition of the Negress is no worse than that of women in many civilised countries, even including France, where, in certain districts, the peasant women work in the fields like men. When the Negro returns from war, or from hunting, or from pillage, and does not find everything in order at home, he complains, scolds, or perhaps even thrashes his wife a little— but is not that also the case in many civilised countries? Read the *Assommoir*, or *La Terre*, [1] of Zola, and tell me if our boasted civilisation is so superior to that of the "poor Negro"! The Negroes, both men and women, are very fond of their children, seldom scold them, and hardly ever beat them. Of how many parents in civilised Europe can the same be said?

[1] These books were translated into English by Vizetelly, who got 18 months "hard" for it. He was 70 years of age! A book was published with the title "*Extracts principally from* ENGLISH CLASSICS : *showing that the Legal Suppression of M. Zola's novels would Logically involve the Bowdlerising of some of the Greatest Works in English Literature* (Lond., 1888). For more particulars about this crapulous business see *Curious Bypaths of History* (Paris, 1897).

Marriage amongst the Blacks.—Purchase of the Wife by the Husband. Amongst all the Blacks, Mussulman as well as fetish worshippers, the husband buys his wife; that is an incontestable fact—but are the Annamites, or many nations more civilised still, any better? [1] In any case the girl herself is not allowed to have a voice in the matter. It is simply a matter of business between her future husband and her parents. The marriage portion is haggled over; —it varies according to the position of the two parties, and at Saint Louis consists of rolls of cloth, cattle, and

[1] Westermarck, in his *History of Human Marriage* (p. 143), Lond. 1894, writes : " There are, however, even in savage life, circumstances which compel certain persons to live unmarried for a longer or shorter time. When a wife has to be bought, a man must of course have some fortune before he is able to marry. Thus, as regards the Zulus, Mr. Eyles writes to me that 'young men who are without cattle have often to wait many years before getting married' (*see* Weber, *Zwei Jahre in Africa*, vol. II, p. 216 [Kafirs]). When Major-General Campbell asked some of the Kandhs why they remained single, they replied that they did so because wives were too expensive (Campbell, *The Wild Tribes of Khondistan*). Among the Munda Kols and Hos, in consequence of the high prices of brides, are to be found 'what are probably not known to exist in other parts of India, respectable elderly maidens' (Watson and Kaye, vol. I, no. 18). In the New Britain Group, too, according to. Mr. Romilly, the purchase sum is never fixed at too low a price, hence 'it constantly happens that the intended husband is middle-aged before he can marry.' (Romilly, *Proceed. Royal Geog. Soc. N.S.*, vol. IX, p. 8). Similar statements are made in a good many books of travels. "

The `customs of these savage tribes are the opposite of those of modern France, where wives buy their husbands, and where beautiful women, often neglected by the dowry hunter, because their purse is not of sufficient bulk, fall to a workman or waiter. Benj. Disraeli was of opinion that the *mariage de convenance* more often turned out well than the marriage for Love, the latter article having the habit of "flying out", according to the old English proverb, " at the window, when Poverty comes in at the door ".

sometimes money; in the interior, it is one or two slaves. An instalment is all that is necessary; a promise to pay the balance after the marriage ceremony is generally accepted by the parents of the bride. In the interior, amongst the Kassonkés, a young girl may be even "booked in advance", and a "retaining fee" paid; this is faithfully returned, if, when she is of nubile age, her parents do not wish to complete the marriage, but if it is the young man who refuses, he loses the money he has paid. There is one really valid cause for breaking the contract, and that is immoral conduct on the part of the girl; otherwise, as soon as she is nubile, or at about the age of twelve years, she is sent to her future husband. This custom of marriage, or rather of betrothal by mutual consent of the interested parties, also exists in the Negro villages of the Wolofs round Saint Louis.

Conceit of those Negro Women for whom Large Prices are paid. The Negress does not consider it a dishonour, that she has been purchased from her father. On the contrary, she boasts of the high price that has been paid for her. I heard of a very neat reply made by one of them on this subject. A European family made the voyage out with me. The husband was a Government official, and, from motives of economy, lodged in a little brick house in the North part of the town near the Mosque. His wife, a good-natured inquisitive little Frenchwoman, became acquainted with many of the Blacks in the neighbourhood, and had for a servant a little Negro girl twelve years old. One day the sister of this Negress, a fine strapping girl of sixteen, came to inform her sister's mistress that she was about to be married. She was going to marry a trader in rather a good position, and she was recounting what handsome presents he had made to her father. The Frenchwoman said, in a tone of reproach, " What! are you not ashamed to boast that you have been bought and paid for, as though you were a beast of burden ? " The Negress was nettled at this remark, and replied, " If my lover gave all that for me, it proves that he loves me, and will pay a high price to possess me, whilst you, and the other wives of the Toubabs, seem so ugly to your men, that you are obliged to buy your husbands, and, unless you gave them a large sum of money, they would never have you." The allusion to the *dot* usually given with European women was decidedly neat, and the retort was well deserved. [1]

Marriage Ceremonies vary a little amongst the various tribes, but in general they have rather the character of a festival than of a religious ceremony, even amongst the Mussulmans. The husband first prepares the house, which is empty. On the wedding day, the modest bride, covered with a long thick veil, but without a single spray of orange blossom—very

[1] Max Nordau holds that money matters should not enter into the sexual relations at all :—

" When material considerations enter no longer into the contracting of a marriage, when woman is free to choose and is not compelled to sell herself, when man is obliged to compete for woman's favour with his personality and not with his social position and property, then the institution of matrimony will become a truth instead of the lie it is now, the sacred and sublime spirit of Nature will bless every embrace, every child will be born surrounded by the love of its parents as with a halo, and will receive, as its first birthday present, the STRENGTH and VITALITY with which every couple which has been united by the attraction of affinity endows its offspring." *Conventional Lies of our Civilisation,* Lond. 1895 (page 307).

different from the European bride—is taken by a matron
to the conjugul domicile. All the female friends of
the family make a procession, carrying on their heads
the wedding presents, which consist of household utensils, such as screens, baskets, a mortar and pestle,
calabashes for couscous, millet, earth-nuts, earthenware
jars, etc.

The bride enters the house, accompanied by the
matron, whose duty it is to initiate her into the sweet
delights of love, and meanwhile the tam-tams outside
beat with redoubled vigour. Men are strictly forbidden
to enter the house, but the women of the village come
in turn to visit the bride, give her advice, and felici-
tations. She stands, covered with her veil, and listens
to all her friends have to say. Outside the tam-tams
beat wildly, and the griots sing the future exploits of
the husband, and how great he is to be. At last the
husband enters the house, turns out the women, locks
the door, tears off the bride's veil, and then—— but
the reader must guess the rest.

As soon as he enters the house, the noise increases,
the tam-tams nearly split, the old flintlock muskets,
charged with whole handfuls of powder, go off like
field guns, the women clap their hands in frenzy, sing
wedding odes, and dance round the house like bac-
chantes. The cries and groans of the bride are
drowned in this infernal hubbub, but it does not, I
have been assured, prevent the husband from doing his
duty. [1]

Faithfulness of the Negress. The Negress is
usually faithful to her husband, especially in regard

[1] See Excursus to chapter XII for curious Marriage Ceremonies in
Europe.

to the Toubab, for she is afraid of having a Mulatto child, which would be a living proof of her fault. This is particularly the case at Saint Louis, where it is easier to obtain the favours of a young girl than of a married woman. I have often, for a joke, asked some of the women who lived near me, and with whom I was in the habit of talking freely, to sleep with me. "*Allah terré!*" (God would slay me) they always cried, and rushed precipitately into their houses.

The Europeans who will not, or cannot, get a woman or "maid of all work", have no resource but the low class prostitutes,—regular old "jacks", who are scorned and despised by all the rest of the population.

The Wives of the Sharpshooters. The first thing a Sharpshooter does, is to try to get together a few pence, and buy a wife, but he has some difficulty in effecting this at Saint Louis, where he is not in the odour of sanctity, and is looked down upon with disgust by the Wolof trader, who is a fanatical Mussulman. Sometimes he marries the widow of a deceased comrade, but generally procures a wife in the Roman method, in the course of one of his expeditions into the interior. Captives—the wives, or daughters, of the vanquished,—furnish the greater part of the Sharpshooters' wives. Colonel Frey's book,—to which I refer the reader,—gives some interesting information on this subject. At Saint Louis, I saw women who came from all parts of Senegambia and the Upper Soudan. They all lived comfortably together.

Their Unfaithfulness. The wives of the Sharpshooters seemed to me to be less faithful than the other

Negresses, but that was evidently due to their social surroundings. The Sharpshooters at Saint Louis receive a fixed pay, and are not fed. The bachelors board with the married men, for a consideration, and often even sleep in the house. This promiscuity favours easy morals, and the wife of a Sharpshooter is regarded with as much scorn by a Wolof Negress of Saint Louis, as a sutler woman would be by the wife of a banker, in Europe. [1]

[1] Free and easy as undoubtedly is the virtue of these native ladies, there is many a high-born dame in Europe who could give them points in what honest old Daniel Defoe would call, "Conjugal Lewdness, or Matrimonal Whoredom" (Lond. 1727), as the two following works more than sufficiently show :—

THE CASE OF IMPOTENCY as debated in England in that Remarkable trial, Anno 1613, between Robert, Earl of Essex, and Lady Frances Howard, who after eight years marriage commenced a suit against him for Impotency.—THE TRIAL OF MERVIN, LORD AUDLEY, Earl of Castlehaven, FOR SODOMY AND A RAPE. Anno 1631.--The Proceedings upon the Bill of Divorce between the Duke of Norfolk and Lady Mary Mordant. London, 1715, 2 vols.—THE CASE OF IMPOTENCY debated on the late· Famous Trial at Paris between the Marquis of Gesores and Mademoiselle de Mascranny. London, 1714, 2 vols, 12mo.

THE TRIAL OF THE HON. MRS. CATHARINE NEWTON, wife of John Newton, Esq., and daughter of the Rt. Hon. and Rev. Lord Francis Seymour, at the Consistory Court of Doctor's Commons, upon a Libel and Allegations charging her with the CRIME OF ADULTERY WITH MR. ISHAM BAGGS, A YOUNG OXONIAN ; Mr. Brett. a Player at Bath ; Thomas Cope, her Coachman ; Isaac Hatheway, her Footman ; John Ackland, of Fairfield, Somerset, and other persons, WITH ALL THE INTERESTING SCENES, FULL, MINUTELY, AND CIRCUMSTANTIALLY DISPLAYED concerning the whole of the evidence in that very remarkable Trial. London, 1782. *Frontispiece*, "*Mrs. Newton bathing in the River Trent, assisted by Mr. Baggs*," 8vo.

Bear in mind that these are *not* erotic books produced in Belgium, or Holland, but sober English, *home-made narratives* where if nothing be "extenuated", naught has been "put down in malice".

The Good Qualities of the Sharpshooter's Wife.

Nevertheless she possesses some remarkably good qualities, and, without her aid, the expeditions into the interior would be unable to operate. In fact, the Sharpshooter will never carry any baggage, and the military authorities have never been able to compel him to bear the "ace of diamonds", or knapsack, carried by the French footsoldier. When he is on an expedition, his load consists of a huckaback bag, containing food, and a strip of tent canvas, worn across the body from left to right, and in which are placed some packets of spare cartridges. He fills the two cartridge pouches he carries in front, and puts the rest of his ammunition into a cartridge bag behind him. At his side is a goat skin filled with water. His wife and children follow him in his expeditions. The linen, food, kitchen utensils, etc., are all packed in enormous round baskets, which the Negresses carry on their heads; they often carry more than a hundred weight, and with that burden the unlucky wretches follow the march. The children go on foot; the very little ones are carried astride their mothers' buttocks. When a halt is made, the women build huts of boughs, wash the linen, and cook couscous. When the husband is on guard, the gallants take advantage of their opportunities.

If the wife of the Sharpshooter is too apt to open her thighs, at all events she is good-hearted. Ask anything of a Negress, and she will give it if she has it, even if she has to deprive herself. But as soon as she has any claim on your gratitude, she will often ask for her "Sunday".[1] Happily she is satisfied with very little, and a very small piece of money will satisfy

[1] Soldiers' slang; to ask for a Sunday is to ask for a "tip."

her. The Negro has an innate weakness for presents, and, whether he is rich or poor, a small gift will always afford him pleasure.

Polygamy exists amongst all the Blacks, but the poorer classes generally content themselves with one wife. The rich traders of Saint Louis have as many as six, one for each day of the week, except the Sunday, when they rest. [1] Only the marabouts and the great chiefs may have an almost unlimited number of wives, but I am bound in duty to say that they never abuse the privilege.

Man's right to possess a number of women has often

[1] In David's time people held far freer ideas about women than we do to-day, *e.g.* it was thought right for them to possess numerous wives and to have carnal connections with other women besides. According to Samuel (book II, 3rd chap., 2—3) six sons were born in Hebron by six different mothers to the Israelite king. Again in chap. V, verse 13 it is said: "*And David took him more concubines and wives out of Jerusalem, after he was come from Hebron;*" and yet it is said (in 1 Kings XV, 5) that "*David did that which was right in the eyes of the Lord, and turned not aside from anything that he commanded him all the days of his life, save only in the matter of Uriah the Hittite.*" Probably it was this which caused DRYDEN to write:

> "When nature prompted, and no law deny'd
> Promiscuous use of concubine and bride;
> Then Israel's monarch, after Heaven's own heart,
> His vigorous warmth did variously impart
> To wives and slaves; and wide as his command,
> Scattered his Maker's image through the land."
> *Absolom and Achitophel.*

Few people will dissent from the shrewd observations of Max Nordau:—"Man lives in a state of polygamy in the civilised countries in spite of the monogamy enforced by the laws; out of 100,000 men there would barely be one who could affirm that he had never had fleshly commerce with but one single woman during his whole life; and if the principles of monogamy are more strictly observed by women, *it is not because they have never had any inclination* to dis-

been called in question; yet such right after all is merely a question of latitude and longitude, of age and country. Bigamy is severely punished in Europe, but Oriental countries regard sexual weaknesses with great leniency, providing, of course, it is not a case of adultery.

Westermarck in his *History of Human Marriage* has the following masterly summing up of this fascinating study:—" Polygyny was permitted by most of the ancient peoples within the historic period, and is at present permitted by several civilised nations and by the majority of savage tribes. Yet, among not a few savage and barbarous races it is almost unknown, or even prohibited; and almost everywhere it is confined to the smaller part of the people, the vast majority being monogamous. Moreover, where polygyny occurs, it is modified, as a rule, in two ways that tend towards monogamy: through the higher position granted to one of the wives, generally the first married, and through the favour constantly shown by the husband to the wife he likes best. Among certain peoples polyandry occurs, and, like polygyny, is modified in a monogamous direction, the first husband usually being the chief husband. Among the causes by which the forms of marriage are influenced, the numerical proportion between the sexes plays an important part.

regard them, but because Conventional Morality keeps a sharper look-out upon woman's conduct and punishes her lapses more severely than man's." *Conventional Lies, etc.*, page 30.

See much more on this subject in the *Book of Exposition* on the "SENSUALISM OF THE KORANIC PARADISE" (XXI to XLI).

For comparison with POLYANDRY see the Excursus (p. 84) at end of this chapter; and also refer to CH. LETOURNEAU's *L'Evolution du Mariage et de la Famille* (Paris, 1888).

In some countries there are more men than women, in others more women than men. This disproportion is due to various causes, such as female infanticide, war, and disparity in the number of the sexes at birth. There are facts which seem to show that in rough mountainous countries more boys are born than girls, and that consanguineous marriages produce a considerable excess of male births. If this be so, it can hardly be a mere coincidence that polyandry occurs chiefly among mountaineers and peoples who are endogamous in a very high degree. As for polygyny, there are several reasons why a man may desire to possess more than one wife. Among many peoples the husband has to live apart from his wife during her pregnancy, and as long as she suckles her child. Female youth and beauty have for men a powerful attraction, and among peoples at the lower stages of civilisation women generally become old much sooner than in more advanced communities. The liking of men for variety is also a potent factor; and to have many wives is to have many labourers. The barrenness of a wife is another very common reason for the choice of a new partner, as desire for offspring, for various reasons, is universal in mankind.

" In a savage and barbarous state a man's power and wealth are proportionate to the number of his offspring. Nevertheless, however desirable polygyny may be from the man's point of view, it is prohibited among many peoples, and among most of the others it is exceptional. Where the amount of female labour is limited, and no accumulated property exists, it may be very difficult for a man to keep a plurality of wives. Again, where female labour is of considerable value, the necessity of paying the purchase-sum for a wife is a hindrance to polygyny, which can be overcome only by the wealthier men. Polygyny implies a violation of the feelings of women; hence, where due respect is paid to these, monogamy is considered the only proper form of marriage. The refined passion of love, which depends not only on external attractions, but on sympathy arising from mental qualities, forms a tie between husband and wife which lasts for life; and the true monogamous instincts, the absorbing passion for one, is a powerful obstacle to polygynous habits. It is certain that polygyny has been less prevalent at the lowest stages of civilisation—where wars do not seriously disturb the proportion of the sexes; where life is chiefly supported by hunting, and female labour is consequently of slight value; where there is no accumulation of wealth and no distinction of class—than it is at somewhat higher states; and it seems probable that monogamy prevailed almost exclusively among our earliest human ancestors. But, though civilisation up to a certain point is favourable to polygyny, its higher forms invariably and necessarily lead to monogamy."

Burton comes to the following conclusions based on the reasoning that the relations of the sexes are all a question of climate.

"The world shows that while women have more philoprogenitiveness, men have more amativeness; otherwise the latter would not propose and would nurse the doll and baby. Fact, however, in low-lying lands, like Persian Mazanderan versus the Plateau; Indian Malabar compared with Marátha-land; California as opposed to Utah and especially Egypt contrasted with Arabia. In these hot-damp climates the venereal requirements and reproductive powers of the female greatly exceed those of the male; and hence the dissoluteness of morals would be phenomenal, were it not obviated by seclusion, the sabre and the revolver. In cold-dry or hot-dry mountainous lands the reverse is the case; hence polygamy there prevails, whilst the low countries require polyandry in either form, legal or illegal (*i.e.* prostitution). I have discussed this curious point of 'geographical morality' (for all morality is, like conscience, both geographical and chronological), a subject so interesting to the lawgiver, the student of ethics and the anthropologist, in ' The City of the Saints.' But strange and unpleasant truths progress slowly, especially in England." [1]

The Head Mistress of the House is always the first wife married; the others are considered as servants, which reminds one ot the history of Sarah and Hagar, the two wives of Abraham. But if there are any quarrels or discord in the house, amongst the women, the husband will restore harmony by thrashing them all round, with strict impartiality. Any man may take a captive to wife, and as long as she is sterile, he may sell, or get rid of her. If she has any children, she acquires legitimate rights, and becomes an integral part of the family.

Jealousy is unknown to the Negress. All Negresses, to whatever race they may belong, have one characteristic in common, and that is the almost entire absence of jealousy in regard to their lord and master. This is evidently the result of the right of the husband to possess several wives. The same Negress, who was boasting to Mme D ... of the high price her husband had paid to obtain her hand, came some months afterwards to pay a visit, and announce

[1] *Arabian Nights* (vol. III, page 241) (BENARES ?), 1885.

that she was in an interesting condition. She had also a favour to ask. Her husband was about to leave for the Upper River, and needed some money to purchase a second wife; she had therefore come to borrow two hundred francs for this purpose. The money was needed for a payment on account, and the marriage was to take place before the departure of the trader, who on his return would be sure to repay the loan, and complete the payment due to the parents of his second wife. On hearing this very naïve request, little Mme D... burst into a passion and cried, " What! unhappy woman, you want to borrow money for your husband to buy another wife? Are you not jealous?" "Jealous, what is that?" asked the Negress. " Why," replied the White woman, " to be the only wife, the only mistress in your own house, the only one to share your husband's bed."

"Oh, I don't care about that," answered the other " My husband is always on me now, and that is very fatiguing. [1] When there are two of us, we shall each have half of the work. When there are three, there will always be one resting, and when there are four, we shall have almost nothing to do except take care of the children, and we can talk, and amuse ourselves. Besides, if our husband beats us, we can defend ourselves all the better."

If a Negress is beaten undeservedly, by her husband, the other wives will take her part. He had better not go too far, if he is in the wrong, for, in her hands, the heavy pestle for grinding millet becomes

---

[1] A very curious story is that given in No. XXXVIII *Les Cent Nouvelles Nouvelles*, where the question of " marital fatigue " plays an important part. *Vide* also on " Flagellation in France " in " *The Curious Bypaths of History* " (Paris, 1898)

a formidable weapon. In this case, the husband has but one alternative; he must either knuckle under, or clear out of the house as quickly as he can.

Divorce. When a woman is ill-treated too much, she is free to leave her husband, and even take another, provided she returns the sum paid for her. This summary method of divorce, though it does not agree with the ethics of civilised nations, has the great advantage of rendering the relations between husband and wife more affectionate than might at first be believed. Children do not interfere with this amicable arrangement, for they follow the mother, and the new husband takes both hen and chickens.

As to the slave who is a temporary mistress, so long as she has no children by her master, she has no rights. To be kept as long as she is young and pretty, and sold as soon as she has ceased to please, is her usual fate.

CHAPTER V.

The hymen.—Large and small lips.—Clitoris.—The fork and the navel.—A study of the genital organs of the Negro races of Africa.—Marks of virginity in the young girl.—Circumcision of young girls.—The festival of same.—The nubile Negress.—The genital organ of the Negro.—The Perforated Kabyle woman.—Circumcision the probable cause of the size of the Negro's penis.—The effect of circumcision on the size of the penis of the pubescent boy.—Mantegazza on the genital organs of the Negroes.—His opinion on circumcision.—The incontestable advantages of this operation.—The suppression of masturbation in the circumcised.—The festival of circumcision amongst Fetish worshippers.—Excursus by Dr. Godard on the defloration of virgins in Egypt.—Sir R. F. Burton on Dahomeyan customs.—Female Infanticide.—Thibetan nuptial customs.—The Hottentot "Apron".—The perforation of the penis amongst Australian tribes.

I INSERT here some of the medical observations and notes I made at Guiana, concerning the young Negresses, as these observations agree perfectly, or with very slight differences, with those made at Senegal.

The Hymen exists in the Black race, as it does in the White. But it is much less developed, and constitutes a much less efficacious barrier against copulation, especially when it is effected with a penis like that of the White man, which is not so huge as that of the adult Black. I am speaking now of the pure Black race. Amongst races of Semitic origin, like the Sarrakholais, the hymen is more resisting.

According to Tardieu, in the French virgin, the hymen will not admit the end of the first finger. In the case of the young Negress, however, you can generally put in the first finger without destroying the hymen. With her the vulva is not so open at the upper part, but hardly closed, if at all, in the lower part. The opening rarely points forward, it is rather obliquely downwards.

Large and Small Lips. In the Negress, the small lips assume, at an early age, an immense development, and considerably exceed the great. Is this caused by repeated pulling, or is it a peculiarity of the race? I cannot say, but this lengthening coincides with nubility, and amongst the fetish worshippers, excision is the general rule.

Clitoris. The clitoris of the young Negress is very much developed. After the nubile age it increases greatly.

The Fork and the Navel. The projection of the fork is not so great as in the European woman.

Operations on Female Sexual Organs. Before proceeding to study the customs relating to the circumcision of girls, we think it will be of interest to quote a few remarks by our late, indefatigable friend, Dr. Ploss (of Leipzig), on the operative treatment of female sexual organs among different peoples.

"Certain savage tribes," he writes, "are accustomed to lengthen and widen the female *pudenda*. In the South-East of Africa, in the Wahia tribe, near the lake Nyassa, it is usual to artificially lengthen the clitoris until it attains the dimension of a finger. An artificial elongation of the labia has also been observed in Dahomey" (*Vide*, Adams, *Remarks on the country East from Cape Palmas to the Congo river*, 1823, p. 15—75). Prince Max of Neuwied noticed a similar artificial deformity among the women of the Mandan Indians in North America, and mentions also the same custom of elongation of the *labia pudendi* among the Menitary and Crow Indians, both externally and internally. Similarly the *Tribadie* or *Amor lesbicus*, among the Arabs, leads also to an artificial extension of the clitoris.

But what is far more important from the anthropological point of view is the study of more sanguinary operations: the circumcision and infibulation of maidens. Among some nations both operations are simultaneously performed, in others either of the two. We will now examine the *modus operandi*, the importance, the object and the results of the operation, and the countries where it is most practised.

The Excision of the Clitoris. This operation consists in a bloody extirpation and uprooting of the clitoris, together with the *præputium clitoridis* and a part of the small *labia*, and even sometimes a part of the entry to the vagina.

This strange and cruel custom prevails in a great number of countries, not only in Africa, but in many other lands. It is found among the Arabs, in Egypt, in Nubia, in Abyssinia, in Kordofan and the neighbouring districts and among numerous tribes on the East coast of Africa, as well as among those of the West coast. It has also been noticed in the Malay Archipelago, particularly in Java, and among the Chuncho and Campas Indians in Peru.

It is very difficult to trace the cause of this custom.

Some are of opinion that it is for the purpose of diminishing sexual lust in the female. There are others, however, who pretend that in those tropical climates the clitoris and labia often take such undue development as to become objects of repulsion to the male, and consequently an obstacle to marriage. According to Mungo Park, the Mandingo Negroes, in West Africa, do not attach any religious signification to the operation, but consider it useful and favourable to the fecundity of the woman. This is also the case in the Malay Archipelago, where the development of the pudenda is often excessive. The operation is generally performed as early as possible, but seldom later than the eighth or ninth year. The operators are women, who go about crying: "Any girls to be cut;" the instrument employed is simply a sharp knife.

It is usual in all parts of Africa, where this custom is practised for a number of girls to be circumcised together, and when they are healed, which requires about eight days, a festival is held in their honour. A girl uncircumcised would be repudiated by her husband, as he could also be by his wife if he had not undergone the operation.

Infibulation.—The Sewing up of Maids. This operation consisted principally in sewing up the labia, or in removing them by excision and causing the wounded surfaces to heal together by adherence, leaving only a small orifice free. It is common among the Gallas, Somalis and Bedschas above the Nile cataracts and from there extends among the inhabitants of Harrar to Massowa on the Red Sea. The custom seems to be of very great antiquity and is mentioned by the celebrated ancient Arab doctor Rhazes, in his

work of ten volumes dedicated to King Al Mansur,
Lib. V, c. 69.

The object of the operation is evidently to insure
the chastity of the maiden until her marriage, previous
to which she has to undergo the counter-operation.
When the husband starts upon a journey, he often
submits his wife to a new infibulation to make sure
that no one shall trespass on his premises during his
absence. Slave-dealers also employ that method to
insure the value of their merchandise. According to
Brehm (*Reiseskizzen in Nord-Ost Africa*, Jena, 1885,
Th. I, S. 169): the Mohammedan law requires circumcision only, but the inhabitants of the Sudan are not
satisfied with this, "*sed etiam labiis minoribus (Nymphis)
abscissis labia majora inde a Veneris monte usque ad
vaginam sanando ita copulant, ut fistula sola ad
urinam fundendam pateat*" (but also, the lesser lips
or nymphæ being cut away, the greater lips, right
from the *mons Veneris* to the vagina, unite in process
of healing, so that only a narrow pipe is left open for the
discharge of the urine). When marriage is decided
upon, the future bridegroom sends a wooden model of
his priapus to the parents of the young lady, and
according to its dimension a corresponding opening is
made. Cailliaud, in his *Travels on the White Nile to
Meroé and Senaar*, Paris, 1826, II, alluding to this
barbarous custom, expresses himself as follows: "Après
avoir élagué ces deux membranes, les plaies de l'une
et de l'autre sont rapprochées, et la patiente est tenue
dans un état d'immobilité presque entière jusqu'à ce
qu'elles se soient réunies ensemble par agglutination;
au moyen d'une canule très mince on ménage une
ouverture, à peine suffisante pour les écoulements
naturels. Quelque temps avant le mariage, il faut

détruire par incision cette adhérence contraire à la nature." It is usually not less than twenty days before marriage that the young girl is submitted to this cruel operation of opening out. When the wife is about to give birth to a child the opening has to be enlarged, and after her confinement is often sewn up again (Rüppel's *Travels in Nubia and Kordofan, etc.,* Frankfort, 1829, p. 42). [1]

Circumcision of Young Girls. This form of circumcision is peculiar to those tribes that are fetish worshippers, and consists of the excision of the lesser lips. It is not a religious ceremony at all, but simply a matter of hygiene. It should be remarked, that amongst these races, it is the blacksmith-surgeon who circumcises the boys, and it is his wife who circumcises the girls. The instrument employed in both cases is an iron knife, very badly sharpened, and more like a saw than a surgical instrument. But though the operation is not a religious ceremony, it is celebrated by a curious festival, which is a kind of holiday for the whole population of the village. On that day, everyone puts on his best clothes, and all the people meet on the public place, to the sound of the griots' tam-tam.

The Festival of the Circumcision of Girls. Accompanied by horrible music, consisting of tam-tams and other instruments, and the songs of the griots, the young girls who are to be operated upon, —superbly dressed, and wearing all the family jewels, —make the circuit of the village, and return to the public place, when a ball immediately commences, and

[1] *Zeitschrift für Ethnologie* for 1871.

See Dr. Godard's article, in connection with this subject, on the defloration of virgins, in the Excursus to present chapter.

lasts twenty-four hours. When they are worn out with fatigue, they are carried by the old matrons into the hut where the circumcision is to take place. The operation is performed at daybreak, when all the women of the village go alone to the hut of the blacksmith and his wife, who has to perform the operation. She sets to work in this manner. The patient is seated on a block of wood about eighteen inches high, placed at a little distance from the wall of the hut. When she sits she opens her thighs as widely as possible; the body is bent back, and the head, which is held nearly horizontal, touches the wall. The arms, which are thrown back, lean on a little bench, which runs along the side of the wall. In this position, the vulva is open, and the "little lips" project. The woman squats down in front of the girl, lays hold of the right lip with the left hand and cuts if off with a sharp stroke; then she performs the same operation on the left side. To stop the bleeding, she applies a plaster, the base of which is ferruginous mud from the smithy, mixed with water containing a little alum. This plaster is not only a styptic, but cicatrises the wound. The patient must remain in the house a week. During the three or four following weeks, a troop of girls may be seen every morning, limping, with sticks in their hands, to the river, to perform their ablutions. At last the bandage is taken off, and they can play about as much as they please. [1]

The Nubile Negress. The epithet vast may be applied even more fitly to the Negresses of Senegal, than to those of Guiana. On account of the size of

[1] Refer to notes by Sir Rich. F. Burton on certain Customs of the Dahomeyans in the Excursus to this chapter ; also to the Hottentot "Apron".

the vulva, and the vagina, and the want of nervous susceptibility in the Negress, delivery is effected almost without pain. In the adult Negress, the vulva is placed very low, and descends almost vertically, as does also the vagina, which is much longer than in the European woman. There is a very pronounced clitoris, which is often the size of the little finger of an adult. The pubes is prominent, and is covered with some stiff and hard hair. The Negresses shave themselves with the neck of a broken bottle.

The Genital Organ of the Negro. According to the usual law, to which this is no exception, the genital organ of the male is in proper proportion, as regards size, to the dimensions of the female organ. In fact, with the exception of the Arab, who runs him very close in this respect, the Negro of Senegal possesses the largest genital organ of all the races of mankind. It is even more developed than that of the Negro of Guiana. While dealing with this subject, we may be permitted to cite the following case, reported by a brother officer, of perforation of the vagina of a young Kabyle woman non-nubile, caused by the sexual approach of her husband.

The Perforated Kabyle Woman. [1] On the 25th of September, 1869, in the village of El-Mesloub, the young Aïni-Ntamrant, of the Beni-Raten tribe, aged twelve and married since about thirty days to El Haoussin or Ali, a youth of from 15 to 16 years old, died suddenly.

Public rumour, from the very next morning, accused

[1] This note was communicated by M. Prosp. Albert, *médecin aide-major de 1re classe*, at the military hospital of Tizi-Ozou (Algeria)

the husband of having killed his wife by premature
and forced conjugal approach. The Amyn or judge
of the tribe thought it his duty to have the body sent
to the *Bureau Arabe*, and we were charged to proceed to a *post mortem* examination of it. The following was the result.

The body is that of a quite young girl not yet
developed. She is thin, and the *mammæ* are not yet
elevated above the surface of the breast, nor is there
yet any hair on the pubis, which is merely covered
with down. The vulva is but imperfectly developed,
and the girl had never been nubile. Her conformation and her exterior genital organs were those of a
child. A close examination showed that the fork was
torn vertically downwards for a distance of three
tenths of an inch; the rent extends through the *navi-
cular fossa* into the vagina. There is no trace of the
hymen left, but in its place red excoriations. On
further examination the vagina was found to be extremely short, measuring not more than 1¼ inch in depth,
and at its inner extremity there was an opening
through which the finger could penetrate right into
the abdomen.

The uterus is that of a child and weighs only three
grammes. All these facts show positively that Aïni-
Ntamrant was quite unfit for marriage, and her husband must have used the utmost violence to have
caused the lesions we noticed. The examination of the
brain showed that death was owing to intense cerebral
congestion.

We caused the young husband of the victim to
appear before us. He is a lad of 15 or 16 years old:
of middle height, well constituted, but thin. He has
no beard, and but little hair on the pubis, which

besides is shaved. His genital organs are greatly developed for his age. His testicles are voluminous. From the tip of the gland to its insertion in the pubis the penis measures three inches and one sixth in length; its average circumference is 4¼ inches.

Is it necessary to draw attention to the enormous disproportion between the volume and length of the penis of this young man, when in a state of erection, and the opening of the vulva and length of the vagina of his wife.

From his own admissions we gleaned the following: the marriage took place a month ago, but the first conjugal approaches were so painful to her that the girl wanted to go back to her mother. But he refused to let her do so, promising however, to have patience Unfortunately he could not contain himself and the extreme violence he used, notwithstanding the supplications of his wife, ruptured the vagina, the walls of which we had besides noticed to be very thin.

This unfortunately is one of the examples of the disadvantages of the Koran, which omits to assign an inferior limit of age to marriage between young people. [1]

Circumcision the Probable Cause of the Size of the Negro's Penis. Without any hesitation I attribute the size of the penis to the operation of circumcision. It is certain that the removal of that portion of the skin, and the mucous surface of the foreskin, which compresses and caps the gland, and often prevents it coming out even when in erection, interferes with the free development of the young boy's organ. We know that at the time of puberty, in the European, consid-

[1] *Mémoires de médecine et de chirurgie militaires.* Paris, 8vo., p. 142—146.

erable changes in the genital organ are produced in a few months. The testicles grow very quickly and the member develops rapidly. But in many young people there is complete phimosis, owing to the smallness of the free extremity of the foreskin, more especially in those who at the age of puberty are not addicted to masturbation. It has often occurred to me, in the course of my medical visits to the barracks, to notice that many of the young French soldiers had the member of a completely conical form, diminishing gradually from the root of the gland. The foreskin covered it entirely, and the member was skinned with difficulty, when it was limp, and with more difficulty still when it was erect. In other cases, if an incomplete phimosis allowed the gland to partly come out, the shortness of the " bridle " of the foreskin curved the gland, and prevented it from assuming its normal form and position. This is phimosis, which is common enough in all the European races, and which can only be got rid of by a more or less complete circumcision, which, however, many persons refuse to have done, unless it is an absolute necessity. Now let us look at the young Negro of thirteen or fourteen, who is circumcised at the age of puberty. [1]

The Effect of Circumcision on the Size of the Penis of the Pubescent Boy. A fairly large cushion of flesh and skin is removed, and the retraction draws the skin of the penis behind the crown of the gland, to the extent of two-fifth to four-fifths of an inch at least; when the penis afterwards develops, the gland, having nothing to check it, will assume its

[1] See also *The Perforation of the Penis in Australia*, at end of chapter.

normal size. Cicatrisation, assisted by the healing growth which repairs the loss of the skin and mucous surface taken away, causes the largest part of the member to correspond with the circular scar caused by the operation. Although the gland may be much developed, its diameter still remains slightly inferior to this part of the penis, which on the whole greatly resembles a large fish, with a round head and a short tail. We can then understand why the Negroes of Guiana call their member, a fish.

The Negro is a real "man-stallion", and nothing can give a better idea (both as to colour and size) of the organ of the Negro, when erect, than the tool of a little African donkey. The absence of hair on the pubes—which the Negroes remove,—makes the resemblance more complete. Nor is it confined merely to colour and size, for the yard of the Negro, even when in complete erection, is still soft like that of the donkey, and when pressed by the hand feels (as I have already said) like a thick india-rubber tube full of liquid. Even when flabby, the Negro's yard still retains a size and consistence that are greater than that of the European, whose organ shrivels up and becomes soft and limp. The average size of the penis generally appeared to me to be about $7\frac{3}{4}$ to 8 inches in length, by two inches in diameter. Except with young lads, just arrived at the age of puberty, the penis is rarely less than $6\frac{1}{2}$ inches in length by $1\frac{3}{4}$ inches in diameter. I took these measurements from the Sharpshooters, amongst whom I met specimens of most of the races of Senegal and the Upper Niger. I often came across a penis of $9\frac{3}{4}$ to 10 inches. by $2\frac{1}{4}$ inches, and once, in a young Bambara, barely twenty years of age, found a monstrous organ $11\frac{3}{4}$

inches long by 2.6 inches in diameter at the circular
circumcision mark.

**Mantegazza's Opinion as to the Size of the
Genital Organs of the Negroes.** I find in Mantegazza [1] an exact confirmation of what I have just
said. " Observations as to the shape and dimensions
of the genital organs, in the various races, are not as
yet very numerous; it is proved, however, that the
Negroes generally have the virile member more voluminous than other people, and I myself verified this
statement, during the years in which I practised
medicine in South America. The size of the genital
parts in the male corresponds to the huge dimensions
of the vagina in the Negresses. Falkenstein remarked
that the Negroes of Loango had huge members, and
that their wives reproached our men with having such
small yards. He rejects the singular idea of Topinard,
who states that it is only when flabby that this
enormous size is noticed, and that, on the contrary,
the penis is reduced in size when erect. Falkenstein [2]
also observed amongst the Negresses of Loango, as
amongst us, a great difference as to the beginning of
menstruation in different individuals."

But I do not agree with Mantegazza when he
discusses the advantages, and disadvantages, of circumcision.

Mantegazza's Opinion of Circumcision. " The
historians of the Jews have exaggerated the hygienic

---

[1] *Gli Amori degli ·Uomini* di Paolo Mantegazza, Senatore del Regno
(Milan, 1892).

[2] *Die Loango-Küste in 72 Original-Photographien* (35 Blatt) *nebst
erläuterndem Text*, Berlin, 1876.

value of circumcision. It is true, that circumcised persons are rather less disposed to masturbation, and to venereal diseases, but circumcision is above all a distinctive mark, and a cruel mutilation of the protecting organ of the gland, and destroys the pleasure of copulation. It is a bloody protest against universal brotherhood, and though Christ was circumcised, he protested on the Cross against all those marks and symbols which divide and separate men. Dimerbroek says, that the foreskin increases a woman's pleasure in the act of copulation, and that is why, in the East, women prefer uncircumcised men. I should not like to affirm that this is so, because, when the member is in erection, the circumcised and uncircumcised yard are exactly alike. In any case it would need a woman to resolve this difficult problem, and no one has ever given her opinion on the subject. I only know that, amongst civilised people, circumcision is an absurdity, and though I am by no means an antisemite, and have a great esteem for the Israelites, I say, and shall always say, to the Jews: Do not mutilate yourselves, and imprint on your bodies this hateful mark, which distinguishes you from other men. As long as you do so, you can never pretend to be our equals. For, from the first days of your life, you yourselves proclaim, by means of the knife, that you belong to a distinct race, that will not and cannot mingle with ours."

For my part, my opinion is RADICALLY OPPOSED to that of Mantegazza, for reasons which I will explain in detail.

The Incontestable Advantages of Circumcision.
The fact is, that circumcision offers great advantages, without any serious inconveniences. The painful ope-

ration is the principal objection, but when the operation is once done, the gland remains always uncovered, and, by rubbing against the clothes, the mucous surface dries, hardens, and becomes tanned. The sebaceous glands of the crown dry up, and their disagreeable secretion disappears almost entirely. The general sensibility of the organ is also blunted, and copulation requires a long time before emission takes place. But if it is longer, the result is the same in the end for the man, and the woman gets the advantage. I do not think there are many women who will contradict this statement.

The immense advantage which I find in circumcision is the almost complete suppression of all the maladies which are brought on by completely developed phimosis, either directly or indirectly ; —balanitis, prostatitis, phlegmons of the penis, etc. A penis with a dry gland, the skin of which is slightly tanned, is infinitely less likely to contract syphilis than a gland that is capped by a phimosis, and has a fine and delicate skin, and a " bridle " that curbs it in. The least scratch or roughness, in the mucous covering of the vagina, will prove infectious to such a member.

I hope that the reader will be of my opinion, and conclude that Mantegazza is wrong.

The Suppression of Masturbation in the Circumcised. An indisputable, and not less valuable advantage of circumcision is, that it almost completely suppresses, in the pubescent youth, the vice of masturbation. In fact, I have remarked that the Negro boy, who practises masturbation before he is circumcised, does not practise it afterwards. He never experiences that continual tickling, which the European, provided

(unfortunately for him) with a perfect phimosis, feels
to such a degree, that, if he does not take daily precautions as to cleanliness, the gland, surrounded as it
is by a filthy layer of sebaceous smegma, remains,—
as does also the urinary meatus,—in a state of morbid
irritation.

The Arab and the Negro are guarded from all that.
Circumcision is of the greatest necessity to them, and
that is why the fetish worshipper, who hates the
Mussulman, is, like him, circumcised. In the Negro
boy before puberty, the yard, which is nearly as large
as that of the Hindoo ("man-hare") is provided with
a foreskin, which is very long and prominent. Moreover, the child learns at an early age the habit of
pulling his member by the foreskin, and this little
amusement being often repeated, the skin becomes still
longer. This habit is a kind of tradition with them,
and these young rascals glory in possessing an abnormally
long foreskin, when the day arrives for being circumcised. Well may it be said that the spirit of emula-
tion will take strange forms.

**The Festival of Circumcision amongst the Fetish
Worshippers.** With the Mussulman, circumcision is
almost a religious ceremony, whilst, as we have seen,
marriage is not. On the other hand, amongst the
fetish worshippers, it is a festival celebrated with great
rejoicings, but devoid of any religious character. I
quote from the author of a very interesting book [1]
a description of the festival of circumcision in a Malinké
village.

"We must assist to-day at a great festival. To-
morrow the young lads of the village of Makadiam-

[1] Bechet, *Cinq Années dans le Haut Soudan.*

bougou are to be circumcised, and the most renowned musicians have come to give their assistance at this solemnity. The orchestra is composed of eight bala-fours, five koras, a score of guitars, flutes, tambourines, and tam-tams, and, in short, all the musicians and instruments that can be got together; there are also choruses of women and young girls.

"Frequent libations of *dolo* (millet-beer) consumed during the day, have much to do with the musical and Terpsichorean excitement, which everyone evinces whilst awaiting the beginning of the festival. The price of *gouro* has doubled, and this valuable aphrodisiac is hardly to be found on the market, such stores of it have been laid in by the villagers. About three o'clock in the afternoon, we see a large crowd making for the Fort. These are the young heroes of the day, who, accompanied by the Griots, come in great pomp, to salute the Commandant, and try to obtain presents from him. The candidates for circumcision are about thirty in number, and from twelve to fourteen years of age. They wear their best boubous, and are covered with the jewels and amulets of their respective families. Their faces are radiant; and everyone crowds round them to excite them, and encourage them to support bravely the brutal operation.

"The chief Griot, in a hoarse, wild voice, sings: 'To-morrow you will be pure, to-morrow you will be men. You can go to war. The horsemen of Samory will fly before you.' The women and young girls repeat in chorus almost exactly the same words; then the Griots sing all together: 'A Malinké does not fear to shed his blood.' The young girls reply: 'The sons of the Malinké do not fear the knife.' The Griots: 'To-morrow all the women will be satisfied with you.'

And during all the festival, similar litanies are chanted in every variety of tone.

"I will be silent as to the details sung concerning the operation itself. The heroes of the day, each armed with a sabre, come one after the other, stamping, and performing a war dance, which consists in imitating cuts and thrusts, and making menacing gestures at an imaginary foe; whilst, with a yet unskilful hand, they try to turn the shining blade above their head; the movements of their legs give to their supple young bodies a motion from left to right, which is exceedingly graceful. Then, in their turn come the women and young girls, dancing and rolling their heads round on their shoulders with such vigour that the back of the head often touches the spine, which, to the spectators, has a most disagreeable effect.

"The songs and dances continue thus all the night, but being desirous of assisting at the ceremony, which takes place at daybreak, we only put in an appearance for about half an hour, at the evening festivities. The interpreter told us that the circumcision is performed publicly, and that, except the women, anyone can assist at it, that usually the Blacks did not like the Whites to be present, but an exception would be made in the case of the Commandant, and the officers from the Fort. Though I had been three years in the country, this was the first time that I had assisted at a ceremony which is very interesting in many respects. I will not speak here of the really astonishing courage shown by the children. The instrument used by the blacksmith-surgeon was a common iron knife of the country, sharpened with a file, and whetted on a flint stone: the patients sang, waved their arms, and smiled

at the excited spectators, who fired off their guns and
uttered wild cries.   When the operation was finished,
the boy was seated on the hot sand which was heaped
up round him to his waist.   He is then shut up for a
month, in a hut, which he must not leave until he is
completely cured."

I will complete this recital by giving some details
of the operation itself.

These particulars I had from one of my colleagues,
who witnessed the operation.   The blacksmith-surgeon
is provided with a small plate of yellow copper, about
the tenth of an inch thick, with a hole of about half
an inch in diameter in it.   He draws through this
hole the lad's foreskin, and with the left hand pulls it
forward, till he gets the right quantity (which varies
according to the length of the foreskin and the thick-
ness of the boy's yard), whilst, with his right hand, he
stops the point of the gland from coming through.
He takes care to pull, with the finger and thumb of
the right hand, the skin of the gland a little towards
the base of the penis, whilst the foreskin is held in
its place.   That being done, he takes his knife, which
he had held between his teeth, and with a single
stroke cuts clean off that portion of the foreskin which
is on the plate.   Having removed the plate, the
blacksmith-surgeon sucks with his lips the blood which
comes out of the wound, gently draws back the skin
of the penis to uncover the gland, and washes the
wound with water containing a resinous essence
(probably an extract from some kind of fir-tree), which
has the property of stopping the flow of blood.   The
foreskin which has been cut off is wrapped in a bit
of rag, and used as a wad for an old gun, which is
charged like a small cannon, and fired in the air,

amidst loud cries of joy. The operation ends, as I have already said in the case of the girls, by daily bandaging the wound with ferruginous mud, which is sedative and healing.

EXCURSUS TO CHAPTER IV. *

Polyandry. Polyandry is met with in many different countries. It should not, however, be confounded with the customs of certain warlike castes, devoted to celibacy, whose wives are in common. Such are the Naïr on the Malabar Coast, [2] in Southern India, and the same custom formerly prevailed among the Toporague Cossacks.

Genuine polyandry exists among the Esquimaux, the Aleutians, the Koriaks and the Kolouches. Sir John Lubbock notices the same custom among the Iroquois and among several tribes on the banks of the Orinoco. In the South Seas it exists among the Masris of New Zealand and in some other of the smaller islands. [5] In Southern India, in the Neilgherry Hills, polyandry is an institution among the Todas, where all the brothers of the same family become successively the husband of the wife of the elder brother, and, *vice versa*, the younger sisters of the wife becoming the wives of this matrimonial association. [6] A somewhat similar institution existed among the ancient Britons in the time of Cæsar, [7] as also, according to Mr. Lagneau, among the Agathyrses and the Liburnea. Mr. Rousselet relates, that on the Malabar Coast, among

* *Vide* note p. 59 *ante.*
[1] Oscar Peschel, *Voelkerkunde*, 1875. [2] Graul, *Ostindien*, vol. 3.
[3] G. v. Kessel, *Ausland*, 1872, No. 37. [4] Waitz, *Anthropologie*, vol. 3.
[5] Oscar Peschel, *ibidem.* [6] Baierlein, *Nach und Aus Indien.*
[7] *De Bello gallico*, lib. V, cap. XIV.

the Nair tribe, a young girl takes legally a husband, that is to say a protector, for he never becomes a husband *de facto:* this advantage is reserved to a number of younger men whom the lady later on attaches to her household.

In South Africa polyandry exists in the Herero tribe. [1] Samuel Turner, in his travels, in Thibet, [2] saw that it existed in certain parts of that country, and Vigne [3] also notices it as prevailing in the Himalaya Mountains, East of Simla, near Mossouri, and even in the Chitral district there are traces of this strange custom. [4]

In another locality of the Himalayas, Kooloo, polyandry exists, but sporadically only, so that in the same village polyandry and polygamy may exist together. Mr. Lyall, British political agent in the Himalayan districts of Kooloo, Lahool and Spiti, [5] relates that he saw in one Kooloo house four men with one wife; next door, three men with three wives and, a little further on, one husband with four wives. These arrangements always depend upon the relative wealth of the respective households. This opinion is indeed that of most of the travellers who have visited these regions. " I have myself," says Mr. Ujfalvy, " seen in the village of Manglaoor matrimonial associations in which four or six men, all brothers, lived with one wife. Colonel Jenkins, for many years chief of the Kooloo district, informed me that it was not indispensable that these men should be brothers."

[1] G. Fritsche, *Die Eingeborenen Südafrika's.*
[2] Samuel Turner, Embassy to Thibet.
[3] Vigne. Travels in Kashmir, Ladak and Iskardo, 1842.
[4] Biddulph, *The Tribes of the Hindoo-Kush,* Calcutta, 1880.
[5] Harcourt, *The Himalayan Districts of Kooloo, Lahool and Spiti,* 1871.

In the Kooloo district there is not much land fit for cultivation; property is therefore very limited and would finally tend to disappear by continuous portioning out: the proprietor would no longer be able to live on the produce of his land. In order to obviate this inconvenience, female infanticide is common in these valleys, and consequently the increase of the female population becomes impossible. It was this barbarous custom, according to Rousselet, which, prevailing in Rajputana, obliged the haughty Rajpoots to seek for wives outside of their own territory. The matrimonial associations in Kooloo live on the best terms one with the other; the children issued from these strange unions speak of an elder and of a younger father; and when one of the husbands perceives on the threshold of the marital chamber the shoes of one of his colleagues, he knows that he must not enter. This custom is called the *djoutika tabou.* [1]

Female Infanticide. With regard to the dilemma in which an otherwise friendly critic wished to enclose me, saying: " If really three fourths of the women become nuns, we do not see why female infanticide, which Mr. Ujfalvy thinks is so general, should be practised at all. Either this infanticide is without an object, and is but little practised, or the number of women is not sufficient to people the convents, *the existence of which is well established.*" My only answer is that *there is not even one woman's convent in the whole country.* All the travellers who have visited these districts will confirm me on this point.

In Ladak polyandry also exists, but not in quite the same manner as in Kooloo. Here the women

[1] The prohibition of the shoe.

enjoy a particular privilege, they have the faculty of choosing, outside of the association of brothers of whom they are the spouse, a fifth or sixth supplementary husband, according to their taste.

But in Ladak polygamy is also to be met with; and it even sometimes happens that a rich heiress will choose one husband only and remain satisfied with him.

I have not visited the Lahool district itself, but I have been able to obtain accurate information concerning the manners and customs of the country. The inhabitants are Buddhists, but their religion is far less pure than in Thibet. There are lamas and nuns; the latter, few in number, reside but two months of winter yearly in their convent. The rest of the time they live with their family, and as they have taken no vow of chastity, they can marry. They also often marry lamas. It would appear that the life they lead during their brief sojourn in the convent is very far from being edifying.

Polyandry undoubtedly exists in the Lahool country, and perhaps also in the Spiti districts, but documents are wanting on the subject: however, one of the Pandits, *Nain Singh*, sent by colonel Montgomery to explore the southern slopes of the Eastern Himalaya, noted its existence to the North of Spiti. Besides the manners and customs of Lahool and of Spiti are very similar to those of Thibet proper, where polyandry was already noted by Samuel Turner at the end of the last century. The reflections added by Turner to the relation of his travels are, besides, most instructive. We have ourselves been able to notice, particularly in Lahool, a great degeneracy of Buddhism, intermixed with Hindoo-

[1] Samuel Turner, *An Account of an Embassy to the Court of the Teshoo Lama in Thibet.* 1800.

ism; in proof of which the almost absolute liberty enjoyed by the nuns in this country.

In Ladak polyandry seems to have taken root for the same reasons as in the Kooloo district; in Ladak the amount of available arable land is still less than in Kooloo, and the conditions of the climate are such that it would be impossible to extend it. Schlagintweit [1] and Drew [2] seem to be right when they ascribe to economic reasons the prevalence of polyandry in Ladak; for in Ladak, more than elsewhere, the population would die of hunger if, by reason of regular succession, the landed property should become infinitely subdivided, and all the more so on account of the geographical isolation of the country. Drew, who was for a long time governor of Ladak, was never able to obtain any information concerning female infanticide in that country.

Drew seemed to think that the small number of female births in Ladak was one of the consequences of polyandry. It appears, however, that in this country, to prevent a too great diminution of the population polygamic and monogamic marriages are now and then contracted which re-establish the equilibrium. It is certain that polyandry has an injurious effect on the morals of the women; for neither in Kooloo nor in Ladak can the women pass for models of conjugal fidelity. In Kooloo particularly they have the reputation of being coquettish and fickle.

At Leh, the capital of Ladak, there is a whole quarter of the town inhabited by half-breeds resulting from the union of Ladak women with foreign fathers. As for Kooloo, travellers relate strange stories. In

[1] *Vide* Schlagintweit, *Indien*, vol. II.

[2] Drew. *ibidem*.

fact we were assured that the assistant commissioner of the country had taken the most stringent measures to protect the Kooloo husbands. When an English officer passing through the country succumbs to the charms of a Calypso of this country, the husbands are required to refuse him all means of subsistence, so as to force him to quit the country as soon as possible. I had myself occasion during my journey to meet with a young officer, the victim of an adventure of the kind, and to whom, for reasons of humanity, I ceded some boxes of tinned provisions.

However, at Kooloo, these strange families live together on the very best terms, without the least signs of jealousy. It must also be remembered that the numerous temples in this country are ministered by young girls devoted to the worship of Mahaderi, the wife of Siva, and these maidens are far from being averse to gallant adventure.

The men work in the fields or become coolies to carry travellers' baggage; the wife manages the household and looks after the children; she receives and takes care of the money earned by her husbands. She is therefore the real guardian of the property earned by the matrimonial association.

In the discussion which followed the communication of Mr. Ujfalvy, Mr. Rousselet made the following remarks: "It is evident that polyandry is a social form much spread about in ancient times among the wild peoples of Asia. But it is in India that the custom has been best preserved up to our days, and traces of it are to be met with throughout the whole of the peninsula, from the Himalaya to Cape Comorin.

"The Naïr or Nagar tribe on the Malabar Coast have best preserved the practice of polyandry, of which traces are also to be found among some other tribes of the Deccan, such us the Ramoosis, and the Metars, and also under form of a prostitution consecrated by usage, as among the Ouled Naïl in Algeria.

"The Naïr are evidently of Turanian origin; they settled in Southern India long before the Aryans and imposed their domination on the aborigines. Their name which signifies *master conqueror*, is sufficient to show that origin. After the introduction of the Aryan influence, they refused to accept the Brahmanic organisation, and were relegated among the Sudras, without however losing all their importance.

"Although adopting the worship of Vishnoo, they have preserved their veneration for the sanguinary Marima, to whom they sacrifice various animals, cocks, goats and even oxen, of which they afterwards eat the flesh, contrary to the Brahmanical precepts.

"Their organisation is based upon the principle of what may be called the *matriarcat*, that is to say that the woman holds the first rank.

"At the age of ten years, the young girl is legally joined to a man of her caste; but as soon as the union is consummated, the husband is dismissed with a slight present to remunerate him for his service, and henceforward he is forbidden all connection with the woman whom he has so to speak enfranchised. From this moment the Naïr woman may go with whomsoever she pleases, but in reality she does not contract any durable union, she can only have more or less passing lovers, and she may choose them where she likes, even among strangers. Nevertheless custom imposes upon her a sort of selection and, under pain of losing in consideration, she must choose her lovers among men of the highest castes or else of particularly vigorous constitution, so as to add to the credit and to the beauty of her tribe. But the lover possesses no rights whatever in the house; the authority always belongs to the woman. The head of the family is always the mother, and in her absence the eldest daughter; it is she who administers the property of her brothers or of her sons; inheritance goes by collateral line, that is to say the nephew inherits from his uncle; the supposed father can leave nothing to his children; in the family he has not even any recognised title and is considered merely as a friend and protector.

" The soil itself always belongs to the wife, head of the community; the mother leaves it to her eldest daughter and all the brothers cultivate it for the benefit of the entire community; men having no living sister or nephews, and therefore having no heirs, get themselves adopted as brothers by some woman outside of their family. This organisation was extended even to royalty, for during a long period the crown of Travancore was transmitted in female descent only, to the exclusion of the males.

" Among the tribes of Southern India who still practise polyandry it is necessary to note the *Tir* and the *Poliyar*, on the Malabar Coast, and in the Mysore country. Here, marriage exists; only the brothers or members of the same family combine to have one wife in common, and the estate passes undivided to the children of the community, who, on their side, continue this indivision by common unions.

" In the North-East of India, at the foot of the Himalaya, among the mountaineers of the Garros tribe, there still exist traces of this ancient custom, although polyandry has practically disappeared. Among the Garros the woman is still the head of the family; she administers the property and transmits it directly to her children. However, marriage mostly affects there the form of monogamy or of polygamy, but it is always the daughter who seeks and chooses for herself her husband, and it is she who, on the eve of her marriage, has her favoured one carried off by her friends and brought to her house.

" As in all other polyandric tribes, among the Garros the son never inherits the paternal property, which always goes to the son of his sister, but this nephew inherits at the same time from the widow and is obliged to take her to wife, even should she be the mother of his own wife.

" The polyandric system seems to be practised only according to the real wants of the population. So that, when the number of the population diminishes, a woman contents herself with one husband only.

"Another peculiar custom in Ladak is worthy of notice, that is the retirement from social life of the parents after they have attained a certain age. When the daughter is married and has children, the father and mother abandon their property to her benefit, reserving to themselves only what is strictly necessary for their keep. In most cases each community has a little house and field reserved for this purpose. When two or several fathers attain together the age of retirement, they continue to live together."

N.B. It is but fair to add that we are indebted for the preceding notes on Polyandry to an article on the subject in the *Bulletin de la Société d'Anthropologie* for the year 1883.

Dr. Godard on the Deflowering Virgins in Egypt.[1]

The Turks do not care to marry a woman still in possession of her virginity, but such is not the case with the Arabs, the schismatic Copts and the Catholics. To them, as I have already said, virginity is the first quality of woman.

In Nubia, girls are married at the age of from eight to ten years, but the husband does not lie with them. In order to verify that the girl is still a virgin, the Nubian makes her sit upon a chair, one woman holds the right arm, another holds the left, two other women hold the thighs stretched apart. The future husband then introduces the leading finger into the vagina to assure himself that the girl is a virgin. He then keeps her for one or two years in his house, until she is about ten years old. Then, instead of having her *incised*, as in the Soudan, he himself dilates the vagina in the following manner: he introduces first one finger, and then two, and repeats this manœuvre during several days.

The rich husband is carried into the nuptial chamber by his eunuchs. There he finds his bride enveloped in a great veil which hides her from his eyes. He says a prayer; that terminated, he says to her: "Thou art my love, I will give thee slaves, jewels, and what thou mayest desire." He then lifts her veil and must exclaim—"How beautiful she is?" Then the first handmaiden of the household enters and makes the bed, and then leaves the married couple alone. The next morning she re-enters the chamber to find beneath the pillow the usual present from the husband, which corresponds to the beauty he has found.

[1] Dr. Godard, *Observations médicales &c. en Palestine et en Egypte*, 8vo. Paris, 1867 (p. 85—88).

Customs of the Dahomeyans. I now proceed to notice certain peculiarities in the Dahomeyan race, which in the usual phrase, are "unfit for the drawing-room table."

The Dahomeyan is essentially a polygynist; and Dalziel's *History* is correct in asserting "The Dahomeyan women do not admit the embraces of their husbands during pregnancy, nor at the time of suckling, which continues two or three years, nor while under the *catamenia*, during which they retire to a part of the town allotted to their reception. The prostitutes, who in this country are licensed by royal autority, are also obliged to confine themselves to a particular district, and are subject to an annual tax." The latter class, called *ko'si* (twenty-wife), because the honorarium was twenty cowries, is supplied from the palace; and the peculiar male and female system which pervades the court rendering eunuchesses necessary as well as eunuchs, demands *Hetæræ* for the women as well as for the male fighters. I was hardly prepared for this amount of cynicism amongst mere barbarians; although in that wonderful book, the "Arabian Nights," which has been degraded by Europe into mere Fairy Tales, the lover is always jealous, not of his own, but of the opposite sex.

Another great peculiarity in Dahomey is as follows: —Almost all the world over, where man is circumcised, the woman is subjected either, as in Egypt, to mutilation of the clitoris, performed in early infancy, when that part is prominent, or as in the Somal and the upper Nilotic tribes, described by M. Werner *(Reise zur Entdeckung der Quellen des Weissen Nil)*, to mutilation combined with excision of the *nymphæ* and fibulation, the wounded surfaces being roughly stitched together. The reason of such mutilation is evident. Removal of the prepuce blunts the sensitiveness of the *glans penis*, and protracts the act of Venus, which Africans and Asiatics ever strive, even by charms and medicines, to lengthen. The clitoris, called by old authors *fons et scaturigo Veneris*, must be reduced to a similar condition, or the too frequent recurrence of the venereal orgasm would injure the health of the woman. This is the case in the old Calabar River of the Biafran Bight; in Dahomey it is reversed.

Adagbwiba, or circumcision, which in parts of West Africa,—the Gold Coast for instance,—appears sporadic, is universally practised in Dahomey. During the days of the *History* (Introd., p. XVIII) the time of submitting to the rite was left to the boys themselves, and their caresses were not admitted by the women as long as they remained in the natural state. At present, circumcision is undergone in Whydah and about the seaboard at the age of twelve to sixteen; in the interior it is often delayed till the youth is twenty years old, when it becomes cruel and sometimes dangerous. It is apparently not a religious ceremony: a lay practitioner, and not the fetishman, being the performer. The patient sits over a small hole dug in the ground. The operator draws out the prepuce, which, as amongst Africans generally, is long and fleshy, and removes the blood from it by manipulation. He then inserts under the prepuce the forefinger of the left hand, and wetting with saliva a splint or a bit of straw, marks the circle which is to be removed. Two cuts with a sharp razor, one above, the other below, conclude the operation. This would argue an origin unconnected with the Jewish and with the Moslem forms, which also vary; amongst circumcising peoples, however, the

rite is everywhere differently performed. The favourite
styptic is heated sand thrown on the wound, which is
washed every third day with simples boiled in water.
The drink is ginger and warm water; the food preferred
is ginger soup, but anything may be eaten except pork.
"A certain operation peculiar to this country," says
the *History* (*loc. cit.*), "is likewise performed upon the
women," and this the foot-note thus explains — *Pro-
longatio, videlicet, artificialis labiorum pudendi, capellæ
mamillis simillima* (That is to say the artificial lengthening of the lips of the pudendum, so as closely to resemble
a she-goat's dugs). The parts in question, locally
called "*Tu*," must, from the earliest years, be ma-
nipulated by professional old women, as is the bosom
amongst the embryo prostitutes of China. If this be
neglected, lady friends will deride and denigrate the
mother, declaring that she has neglected her child's
education, and the juniors will laugh at the daughter
as a coward, who would not prepare herself for marriage. The sole possible advantage to be derived from
the strange practice is the prevention of rape, but the
men are said to enjoy handling the long projections,
whose livid slaty hue suggests the idea of the turkey-
cock's carbuncle. It is popularly said, "There can
be no pleasurable Venus without 'Tu'." I find the
custom amongst the cognate tribes of Grand Popo, but
not in any other part of the West African Coast.

As a rule the Dahomeyan eunuch still marries, and I
have heard of cases similar to that quoted in Dalziel's
History, when relating the end of the rebel eunuch
"Tanga:"—"To his wives he appeared not the rigid
jailer, nor the tyrannic usurper of their affections, but
the generous arbiter of their liveliest pleasures. Hence
they could not but be charmed with a freedom which

no other seraglio enjoyed, and" (all devoted themselves
to death) "they would not survive that felicity and
protection which was to terminate with the existence
of their master and their lover, whose ruin seemed
inevitable." It is difficult to obtain information in
Dahomey concerning eunuchs, who are special slaves of
the king, and bear the dignified title of royal wives.
The operation is performed in the palaces, by evulsion
of the testicles, and is often fatal, especially when
deferred till the age of twenty. Throughout Yoruba
these neutrals are found at the different courts, and
the practice may have migrated from the East.

Amongst all barbarians whose primal want is progeny,
we observe a greater or a less development of the
Phallic worship. In Dahomey it is uncomfortably prominent; every street from Whydah to the capital is
adorned with the symbol, and the old ones are not
removed. The Dahomeyan Priapus is a clay figure of
any size between a giant and a pigmy, crouched
upon the ground as if contemplating its own Attributes.
The head is sometimes a wooden block rudely carved,
more often dried mud, and the eyes and teeth are
supplied by cowries. A huge penis, like the section
of a broom-stick, rudely carved, like the Japanese articles
which I have lately been permitted to inspect, projects
horizontally from the middle. I could have carried off
a donkey's load had I been aware of the rapidly
rising value of Phallic specimens amongst the collectors
of Europe. The Tree of Life is anointed with palm-
oil, which drips into a pot or a shard placed below it,
and the would-be mother of children prays that the
great god Legba will make her fertile. Female Legbas
are rare, about one to a dozen males. They are, if
possible, more hideous and gorilla-like than those of

the other sex; their breasts resemble the halves of German sausages, and the external labia, which are adored by being anointed with oil, are painfully developed. There is another Phallic god named " Bo ", the guardian of warriors and the protector of markets. [1]

The Apron of the Hottentot Women. [2] A peculiarity belonging to the Hottentot or Bosjesman women is the enormous elongation of the nymphæ. Their labia minora, of extravagant length, presenting a reddish blue livid coloration, remain joined together in their entire length, and descend vertically between the thighs. According to certain travellers these nymphæ, thus in juxta position, might at first sight be mistaken for a male member, for a narrow flabby penis.

This deformity has been called by all travellers the *Apron*; some, who had been unfortunately too discreet to examine the thing closely, took it for an article of dress placed in front of the genital organs, either from modesty, or else from simple coquetry; others have considered this appendage to be a special organ; very few, indeed, among those who have examined more closely, have been able to exactly understand the disposition of this anomaly. But the *apron* is not a distinctive characteristic of the Bosjesman race. Cuvier relates that in Abyssinia it was usual to perform excision of the deformed labia minora and that one of the first reforms sought to be introduced by the Catholic missionaries, in the sixteenth century, when they introduced their religion into the country, was the suppression of this operation. But the young girl

[1] From Sir R. F. Burton's article in *Memoirs of Anthropological Society of London* (Lond., 1863, pages 317—320).
[2] *Bulletin de la Société d'Anthropologie*, 1881 (pages 385—388).

converts, who had not been operated upon, being no longer able to find any husbands, the Pope, who was then not yet infallible, authorised the shortening of the labia.

This elongation of the labia minora is also observable among Negresses: Mr. L. Vincent saw some measuring from 2 to 3 inches. This deformation is also sometimes observable on White women, but in a far less exaggerated degree.

But if this anatomical peculiarity is not exclusively the privilege of the Bosjesman race, in no other does this deformation attain such prodigious proportions; in fact, some of these women have been found wearing *aprons* of from 6 to 7 inches in length.

Many opinions have been expressed concerning this apron: some have simply denied its existence; others have considered it to be the result of certain practices, as an artificial deformation; and lastly, among the authors who reasonably believed that this peculiarity was to be attributed to nature, not only have the most various ideas and hypotheses been expressed, but the most fantastical descriptions have been traced.

Perron, who seems to have adopted the opinion of General Jansens, thinks that the apron is a special organ placed in front of the genitals and not the development of one of their parts.

Levaillant's error is less serious, but he also has not looked close enough, and if he has seen that the apron is a part of the organs of generation considerably developed, he has not sufficiently noted the starting-point nor the cause of this deformation; he thinks that it is an artificially promoted elongation of the labia majora: "The apron," he says, "may attain to the length of 3½ inches, more or less, according to the age of the individual, or to the trouble she has taken to cultivate this strange ornament; I saw a young girl of fifteen whose nymphæ were already 4 inches long. Until then it is friction and traction which have begun to distend, suspended weights complete the work."

Barrow, with much reason, protests against this opinion. In fact, the apron is so little of an ornament, that a great many women, not only among the Hottentots, but also among the Bosjesmans, hide it. Some of the latter who go about naked, when before strangers, keep their nymphæ squeezed between their thighs so as to dissimulate them from view. This it was that caused certain travellers to imagine that the deformation did not exist. And this dissimulation may be complete, for this is what Cuvier says of the Hottentot Venus: "While she was being examined she kept her apron hidden between her thighs; it was only after her death that she was found to have possessed one."

Besides all the Bosjesmans questioned by Barrow affirmed to him that this deformation was natural and that the means employed to obtain it, mentioned by Levaillant, were never resorted to. Many Bosjesman women transported into Cape Colony in early age, never having revisited the country of their birth, and consequently ignorant of such practices, had deformed genitals like the Bosjesman women of the Bush.

Of all travellers, Barrow is he who has most carefully examined this anomaly. He relates as follows: "Everybody knows the history of the appendage which the Hottentot women possess at a place not usually exposed to view; a conformation not belonging to the fair sex in general. This fact is absolutely true. As for the Bosjesman women, all of them were the same

in the tribe we met, and we were able to satisfy our
curiosity on that point, without in the least offending
their modesty. After examining them carefully, it
seemed to me to be an elongation of the labia minora,
more or less extended according to the age of the
subject. The longest we measured were a little over
5 inches; the woman carrying them was of middle
age. Some are said to have them longer. These
elongated nymphæ, joined together and pendent, seem
at first sight as if belonging to the opposite sex. Their
colour is a livid blue with a reddish tint, very much
like the comb of a Turkey-cock, an excrescence which
can give a pretty good idea of it, with regard to
appearance, size and form. The interior parts of the
nymphæ, wrinkled and creased in the White woman,
lose this character among the Hottentots and become
perfectly smooth; but then they no longer possess that
stimulating nature for which certain anatomists pretended that they had been created; these appendages
have at least the advantage of protecting the women
from all violence on the part of the other sex; for it
seems almost impossible that a man should have connection with such a woman without her consent or
even without her aid."

The best description of the apron is that given by
Cuvier, after the Hottentot Venus, whose body he
had: " According to necroscopic examination," he says,
"it was apparent that the apron was not, as Perron
had supposed, a particular organ, but the development
of the nymphæ; the labia majora were not salient,
they intercepted an oval of about 4 inches in length.
From the superior angle between them there depended
a semi-cylindrical protuberance of about 18 lines in
length with 6 lines in width, the lower extremity of

which widens out, divides and prolongs in the shape
of two fleshy petals, creased, of about 2½ inches in
length, with 1 inch in width; each of these is rounded
at the end; their basis spreads out and falls down
along the interior border of the *labia majora* and
terminates in a fleshy crest at the lower angle of the
labia. If these two appendages are lifted up, they
form together the figure of a heart, the lobes of which
would be narrow and long, the middle being occupied
by the opening of the vulva. Each of these lobes
bears, on its outer surface, close to the inner margin,
a furrow deeper than the other creases, and which
continues deepening until the two bifurcations join
together; so that where they have thus united there
is a double border encircling a dimple in the form of
a wedge; in the middle of this dimple there is a slender
prominence terminating in a little point at the place
where the two borders join again together.

"Consequently the two fleshy lobes are formed above
by the prepuce and the summit of the *nymphæ,* the
rest of them consisting only in the extra-development
of these same *nymphæ.* The vulva and the matrix
show nothing particular."

The above can be verified by a visit to the Museum
of Natural History at the *Jardin des Plantes* (Paris),
where there is a life-size exact model of the Hottentot
Venus, *in naturalibus.*

Thibetan Nuptial Customs. In Thibet the young
girls about to marry are previously relieved of their
virginity by the priests, either Buddhist or Tao-See,
according to their religion. In either case, the priest
of one or the other faith has mission to prepare the
bride for the nuptial rite.

In the Chinese text this ceremony is called *t'chin-than*. [1] Each year, at the fourth moon, the officer of the Province announces the day fixed for the *t'chin-than*. On that day each priest has his female client and can have but one.

On the marriage day, the procession of friends, with music and drums, goes in grand parade to meet the priest and accompanies him to the residence of the bride.

There, two canopies have been prepared covered with brilliant coloured stuffs. The priest occupies one seat, the bride the other.

As soon as night has fallen, the principal persons of the escort disappear, but the gongs and trumpets continue more than ever to make as much noise as possible before the house of the bride.

During this night full license is granted to the priest, and this is, as modestly expressed as possible, what takes place:

"*Audivi illum cum virgine simul in proximum cubiculum ingredi, ibique eam, manu adhibita, con-stuprare. Manum deinde in vinum immisit, quo, si quibusdam credideris, pater, mater, proximi tandem atque vicini frontem signant; si aliis, vinum ore ipsi degustant. Sunt et qui sacerdotem puellæ pleno coïtu miscere asserunt, alii contra contendunt.*"

(I have heard tell that the priest going into a neighbouring chamber with the maid, there deflowers her, making use of his hand for the purpose. Then he plunged his hand in wine, with which, if you believe some authorities, the father, mother, relations generally and neighbours, put a mark on their forehead; if others

[1] In Latin: *strati dispositio*. (Abel Rémusat, *Mélanges Asiatiques*, t. I, p. 71 & seq.)

are to be credited, they actually swallow the wine. Some moreover declare the priest enjoys full coition with the girl, but others deny this).

The Perforatio Penis in Australia. [1]   " Before leaving Australia I made the acquaintance of a Mr. B. . . ., an experienced squatter, who gave me some interesting information concerning the Mica operation in Central Australia.

" This operation consists in a slitting up of the lower side of the urethra, in consequence of which the penis is no longer a tube but more exactly a gutter. The operation is performed by means of a sharp flint and a piece of bark is placed in the wound to prevent primary healing of the severed surfaces by agglutination. After the operation the young men may go about perfectly naked, which they are forbidden to do previously. They are now permitted to marry. In micturition they stand erect, the legs apart and urinate like women. In the moment of erection the penis is broad and flat and the sperm is ejaculated *extra vagina* (outside the vagina). This fact was also noticed by other European travellers who had paid natives to perform coition in their presence. It was also particularly remarked that among about 300 natives there were only three or four who had not been operated, and it appeared that upon these devolved the duty of insuring the propagation of the tribe. One of these, who had been no doubt specially selected for the purpose, was a splendid specimen of humanity, fully six feet two inches in stature. "

Edward J. Eyre, in *Journ. of Expedition of Discovery*

[1] *Extracts from Travellers' Note-Books.*

into Central Australia, etc., Lond. 1840—41, Vol. I,
p. 212, says: "In the Port Lincoln Peninsula and
along the adjacent coast the natives not only are circumcised, but have in addition another most extraordinary ceremonial: *Finditur usque ad urethram a
parte infera penis*, p. 213. (The penis is cleft right
to the urethra from underneath). Among the party at
the camp I examined many and all had been operated
upon. The ceremony with them seemed to have taken
place between the age of twelve and fourteen years,
for several of the boys of that age had recently undergone the operation, the wounds being still fresh and
inflamed. This custom must contribute to prevent a
too rapid increase of the population . . . "

In another work by several authors: *The Native
Tribes of South Australia*, Adelaide, 1879, the Rev. G.
Taplin, in a note at page 14, gives a description of
the operation: " *Operationem hoc modo perficiunt:
os Walabii attenuatum per urethram immittunt illud-
que ad scrotum protrudunt ita ut permeet carnem.
Scindunt dein lapide acuto usque ad glandem penis...*"
(They perform the operation in the following way:
they insert the slender bone of a Walaby down the
urethra, and push it home to the scrotum, so as to
pierce the flesh. Then with a sharp stone they slit
up the penis right to the glans). In the same work
(p. 231), the missionary C. W. Schürmann writes as
follows: "Another operation is also performed at
this period. It consists of a cut, with a chip of
quartz from the orifice of the penis, along its lower
side down to the scrotum, opening the passage out
in its whole length. I have not been able to
ascertain the motives of this strange mutilation."
—S. Gason says in *Manners and Customs of the*

Native Tribes of South Australia, p. 273: " So soon as the hair on the face of the young man is sufficiently grown to allow the end of the beard to be tied, the ceremony of the Koolpie is decided on . . . The operation is then commenced by first laying his penis on a piece of bark, when one of the party, provided with a sharp splinter of flint, makes an incision underneath the penis, into its passage, from the foreskin to its base; this done, a piece of bark is inserted in the wound so as to prevent its healing by first intention . . ."

CHAPTER VI.

Erotic dances of the Senegal Negroes.— The " Anamalis fobil"
and the " bamboula" of the Wolofs.— The " belly dance" of the
Landoumans of Rio Nunez.— Obscene dance of the massacre of
the wounded, and mutilation of the dead, on the field of battle.—
The Gourou or Kola nut, the aphrodisiac of the Negroes.

ALL the tribes of Senegal have dances which are
peculiar to them. Amongst the Bambaras of the Upper
Niger, it is a character dance, a sort of war dance
performed by armed men. But, amongst the greater
number of the other tribes, the dance has an erotic
character. The most striking of these is the famous
dance of the Wolofs of Walou, generally called by the
generic name of *bamboula.*

The Anamalis Fobil, or Bamboula of the Wolofs,
is frequently danced[1] in the streets of Saint Louis and
the Negro suburbs of the town, by the light of the
chaste Diana (which is then full moon), by the brilliant

[1] Compare the dances of the Greeks and Romans. SCALIGER (J. C.),
in his *Poetica* (book I, p. 64). "Among the infamous dances were
the ῥίκνωμα, ῥικνοῦσθαι, that is to say the shaking of the hips
and thighs, called by the Latins *crissare.* Among the Spaniards this
abominable dance is still in honour. The meaning of this dance is
very significant: waving their buttocks, these young dancing girls stooped
to the ground, and finally threw themselves down on their back, as
if to receive the amorous assault. The Lacedemonian βίβασις differed
from this dance, in that the girls jumped so as make their heels strike
their buttocks." ARISTOPHANES in *Lysistrata* (v. 82) says: "I dance
naked and with my heel smite my buttock." POLLUX (IV, ch. 14):—
"With regard to the βίβασις, it was a kind of Laconian dance.

light of which not a single detail is lost to the spectators. As soon as night falls, you hear the sound of the tam-tam, calling the Negro population to the Place. The beginning is quiet enough, the tam-tams beat without any *entrain*, the dancers, male and female, timidly essay a few steps, and then regain the ranks of the spectators. Little by little, they become warmer, the dance becomes bolder and more risky, the tam-tam marks the time faster and faster, the spectators clap their hands and utter obscene cries, particularly the famous *anamalis fobil*, and the paroxysm of lust reaches its apogee. Loti, in the *Roman d'un Spahi*, gives a

Prizes were offered for competition, not only between young men but also between young girls. It was required to jump and strike the buttocks with the heels; the jumps of each of the competitors were counted and marked; and the score of jumps went up to ONE THOUSAND!" Another and more difficult dance was known under the name of ἐκλάκτισμα, in which the foot was required to touch the shoulder. POLLUX (*ibid.*). "The ἐκλακτισματα were danced by women; it was required to kick higher than the shoulder." For an interesting choreographical theory see John O'Neill's erudite work, *The Night of the Gods, an Enquiry into Cosmic and Cosmogonic Mythology and Symbolism* (London, David Nutt, 1897), Vol. II. He traces the origin of certain forms of Dancing to a primitive religious practice; and connects the same with the circular perambulation of Eastern shrines and with the use of the Prayer-wheel, and then explains all three—round dancing, circular worship by perambulation, and the twirling of the prayer-wheel —from the extremely ancient worship of the (apparently) revolving Heavens. Schopenhauer's philosophy of dancing is curious. Irritability, he says, objectified in the muscular tissue, constitutes the chief characteristic of animals, and of the animal element in man. Where it predominates to excess, dexterity, strength, bravery—that is fitness for bodily exertion and for War—is usually to be found. Nearly all warm-blooded animals, and even insects, far surpass Man in irritability. It is by irritability that animals are most vividly conscious of their existence; wherefore they exult in manifesting jt. There is even still a trace of that exultation perceptible in Man, in dancing. *The Will in Nature*, Bell and Son, 1889, p. 250.

description of this dance, which I may be permitted
to borrow.

"*Anamalis fobil!* shrieked the Griots, striking on
their tam-tams, their eyes glaring, their muscles strung,
their bodies glistening with sweat. And everyone
repeated, clapping their hands in frenzy—*anamalis
fobil—anamalis fobil*—the translation of which would
burn this page. *Anamalis fobil!* the first words, the
dominant note, and the refrain of a maniac song, mad
with fervour and licence, the song of the bamboula of
Spring! *Anamalis fobil!* the cry of wild unrestrained
desire, of the vigour of the Negro overwarmed by the
sun into a terrible hysteria, the alleluia of Negro love,
the hymn of seduction.

"To the bamboulas of Spring come the young lads,
mingling with the girls who have just assumed, with
great pride, their costume of nubility, and to a wild
rhythm of unearthly melody, they all sing, dancing on
the sand, *Anamalis fobil!—Bamboula!* A Griot, who
is passing, strikes a few blows on his tam-tam. It is
the call to arms, and all gather round him. The women
run up, and range themselves in a closely packed ring,
chanting one of those obscene songs of which they
are so fond. One of them leaves the crowd, and rushes
into the middle, into the empty circle where the tam-
tam is beating: she dances to the sound of grigris and
glass beads; her steps, which are slow at first, are
accompanied by gestures which are terribly licentious.
Her movements become quicker until she is in a perfect
frenzy; they seem like the frisking of a mad monkey,
the contortions of a maniac.

"Her strength is at last exhausted, she retires, breath-
less, and worn out, with the sweat glistening on her
black skin; her companions welcome her with applause

or yells, then another takes her place, and so on until
all have taken part."

In a literary work, that everybody may read, the author
could not say everything, and was obliged to be very
particular, as to what he wrote. Not having, in this
book, the same reasons for reticence, I may explain
that *anamalis fobil* means, "the dance of the treading
drake". The dancer in his movements imitates the copulation of the great Indian duck. This drake has a member of a cork-screw shape, and a peculiar movement
The woman, for her part, tucks up her clothes, and
convulsively agitates the lower part of her body, by
an indescribable movement of the haunches; she alternately shows her partner her vulva, and hides it from
him, by a regular movement, backwards and forwards,
of all the body. The presence of a Toubab does not
interfere at all with the erotic passion of the dancer,
who, on the contrary frisks about more than ever, and
addresses him with obscene phrases, more especially
if she is an old woman. They are always the most
excited, as Loti has remarked. " The old women are
distinguished by the wildest and most cynical indecency.
The child, which she often carries fastened on her
back, and packed up in the most uncomfortable manner,
utters piercing shrieks, but in their excitement the
Negresses are deaf to everything, even the maternal
instinct, and nothing stops them."

I have already said that the *anamalis fobil* is danced
in Saint Louis, under the paternal eye of the authorities,
and without any interference from them. At least it
was so, barely more than ten years ago.

The "Belly Dance" of the Landoumans of Rio

Nunez. The Kassonkés and Sarrakholais have also a lascivious dance, but not of such a pronounced character as the Wolof dance. At Rio Nunez, the Landoumans have a dance, which resembles the *danse du ventre* of the Arabs. The dance is performed by a woman. She executes a series of steps, sometimes forward, sometimes backwards, sometimes sideways, accompanied by a wagging of the pelvis, meant to imitate the movements of a woman copulating in the regular classical method. The Arab dances at the Paris Exhibition of 1889, gave a tolerably exact, though not very forcible, idea of this dance. [1]

Obscene Dance of the Massacre of the Whites, and Mutilation of the Dead. Not one of the authors who has written about Senegal, has described the horrible doings of some of the races of the interior, especially the Toucouleurs and the Malinkés, after a battle in which the Europeans have been defeated or repulsed, and have left their dead and wounded on the field of battle. These last are most horribly mutilated by the old women, who come to despoil the dead. For the dead the inconvenience is not great, but the unfortunate wounded suffer horribly before they die. The subject has been touched upon very

---

[1] This dance is highly indecent. We shall not soon forget the first time we saw it executed by two Jewesses *absolument nues*, in some house to which our courier led us in a back street in Tangier. Most "greenhorns" freshly come from Europe are caught in this way. We were "bled" of about ten "pesetas" each, of which the "courier" mentioned no doubt received halves. The same dance, much more skilfully done, we have since witnessed at the *Casino de Paris* for one *franc* and in a travelling booth at *fête* time on the *Place de la République* for two *sous*. The *danseuse* was this time clothed in gauze and thus executed, the display is vastly more graceful and suggestive.

delicately in the "Roman d'un Spahi," the best book that we have about Senegal. Fatou-Gaye, the mistress of Jean, the Spahi,—who, with the advance guard of his squadron, has been killed by an ambuscade of the enemy,—comes to search for the corpse of her lover, which she at last finds. The description of the scene is very powerful. " Fatou-Gaye stopped, trembling and terrified. She had recognised him, lying there with his arms thrown out, and his mouth open to the sun, and she recited some unknown prayer to a pagan deity, touching meanwhile the grigris hung round her black neck. She remained a long time, muttering to herself, and gazing with haggard eyes, the whites of which were suffused with blood. Afar off, she saw approaching the old women of the enemy's tribe, wending their way towards the dead, and she suspected that something horrible was about to happen. Hideous old Negresses, their wrinkled skins shining under the torrid sun, approached the young man, their grigris and glass beads clinking as they moved; they touched the body with their feet, laughed, performed obscene rites, and uttered strange words which seemed like the cries of monkeys; they violated the dead with ghastly buffoonery."

We will complete this quotation by an exact recital of what takes place,—the details were furnished to me by persons in whom I have implicit confidence. The old Negresses cut off the organs of generation of the wretched Toubabs, with a common knife, [1] badly

---

[1] This terrible form of mutilation was practised by the Abyssinians in the late war with Italy. After the battle of *Adoua* (in 1896) a sergeant who had been temporarily stunned, came to himself and followed the line of retreat, when, near a pile of slain soldiers, overcome with fatigue, he again fainted. On recovering his senses he felt a sharp,

sharpened, whilst the young women dance round in a characteristic dance of the same nature as the *anamalis fobil*, and showing their vulva, and insulting in his distress the unhappy wretch, who is sometimes conscious, and saying to him, " Toubab, look at this κυντ : you shall never more enjoy it." The mutilation being effected, the old women stuff the poor man's yard into his mouth, and leave him to perish miserably. The dead are treated the same, but of course it makes no difference to *them*. It is usual, amongst the officers engaged on expeditions in Senegal, to always reserve for themselves the sixth shot of the revolver, so that they may not fall alive into the hands of these devilish hags. The young white soldiers are also recommended to fight to the last drop of their blood, and never under any circumstances leave the field of battle without orders. The removal of the wounded is rigorously insisted upon. The native Sharpshooters know well what fate to expect if they are defeated, and fight with the utmost energy, for they are not spared any more than the Whites. The Romans fought *pro aris et focis*, and if the subject were not so serious, one might say that in Senegal they fight *pro mentula et coleis*.

The "Gourou" or Kola Nut, the Aphrodisiac of the Negroes. The Blacks only know of one aphrodisiac, the *gourou* or Kola nut, which, strictly speaking, is not a nut at all, but a large chestnut, very much

burning pain at the junction of the thighs, and then, to his horror, found he had been deprived of the attributes of manhood. Endowed with uncommon strength and courage this man was able to crawl into the Italian camp, more dead than alive, and a record of his experiences appeared in *La Stampa*. (See *Eunuchs and Eunuchism ;* Paris, 1898, for similar cases).

like a horse chestnut. This fruit comes from the South rivers. The Negroes of Senegal and the Soudan chew the *gourou* with delight, although it has a sharp and astringent taste. It produces on the Black a sort of general nervous excitement, which sensibly increases all the physical faculties, including of course the generative powers. A Negro who chews a few *gourou* nuts, can go twenty-four hours without eating, and march or dance, almost without interruption, the whole time: at the great bamboulas and fêtes, the *gourou* is therefore much used. It is a most valuable fruit when exceptionally hard work (amorous or otherwise) has to be done, but its use should not be abused. Kola is now admitted into European therapeutics, and is used for restoring lost strength, and stimulating the forces of the body. It contains a greatar quantity of caffeine and theobromine than the best teas and coffees; and it has a direct, immediate, and certain effect upon the heart and the circulation, which it regulates and strengthens. Kola is a most useful medicine, active, and energetic, and a restorative of the best kind. I found it of great service when I accompanied the expedition to Fouta-Toro, and I chewed it from time to time, in order to restore my strength. [1]

[1] A most interesting account is given by Edouard Heckel under the title of " Des Kolas Africains " in the *Bull. de la Soct. de Géographie de Marseille*, Avril-juin, 1883.

For a detailed account of certain Aphrodisiacs see *The Old Man Young Again* (1898) and *Aphrodisiacs and Anti-Aphrodisiacs*, by John Davenport, Lond. 1869.

CHAPTER VII.

The unimportance of the signs of virginity in the Negress.—Negro girls deflowered by Toubabs.—Amorous subterfuges used in Europe.—Artifices used by Asiatic peoples.—Former American customs.—Report of Carletti, the Traveller.—Savage habits regarding perfumes.—Tumefaction of the gland.—Influence of chastity on health.—Elements of social science.—Dr. Verga on celibacy.

Forms of Sexual Intercourse amongst the Negro Races. I must, in the first place, do my best to destroy the common impression that prevails, that the Negress is " a hot woman," passionately fond of the pleasures of love. She is nothing of the kind, and only cares for the normal form of sexual passion. I have already remarked, concerning Guiana, that the pure Negress had only an " affection of the head " for the White, and that the woman of real lively passions was the Mulatta, and, more especially, the Quadroon. The observations I made at Senegal, coincided exactly with those made at Guiana.

Unimportance of the Signs of Virginity in the Negroes. The Negroes of Senegal do not attach, as the Arabs do, considerable importance to the presence of the real signs of virginity in the young girls. I have already mentioned that the husband purchases

his wife, and that marriage is a festival, and not a
religious ceremony.   The non-existence of the material
proofs of virginity seldom give rise to any complaint
on the part of the husband.   Cases in which a young
woman is sent back to her parents are not common,
for half the marriage portion would be retained by
the girl's father, as damages.   Moreover, the size of
the virile member of the Negro renders it difficult for
him to detect any trick.   The Black bride, on the
wedding night. shows herself expert in the art of
simulating the struggles of an expiring virginity, and
it is considered good taste for the girls to require to
be almost raped.   The least innocent young women
are often the most clever at this game.   Thus throughout nearly all Senegal, the European, who has a taste
for maidenheads, can easily be satisfied, provided he
is willing to pay the price. [1]   At Saint Louis certain
women of ill-fame procure young girls, who bear the
significant name of the " unpierced", and vary from
eight or nine years to the nubile age.   It is even
easier to obtain a young girl before she is nubile than
afterwards, on account of the certainty of her not
bearing any children.   The price is within the range
of all purses, according to quality, and you can have
a Negro girl, warranted " unpierced" (belonging to
the category of domestic slaves), for the modest sum
of from eight to sixteen shillings.   Of course, the
respectable matron pockets half this sum, for her
honorarium.

---

[1] A celebrated Parisian courtesan used to boast, according to MAN-
TEGAZZA, that she had " sold " her " virginity " on 82 different occasions !!   See " *Curious Bypaths of History* " (Paris, 1898, pages 275
to 300) for further uncommon details on this subject.

The Medico-Juridical Importance of Signs of Virginity. Taylor has treated this subject at great length in his valuable work on Medical Jurisprudence, and inasmuch as "Untrodden Fields" will be read by Doctors and Anthropologists living abroad and who may not have Taylor's book within reach, we trust to be excused for quoting so long a passage. We have fully detailed our own views and experience on this subject in another part of the present work.

"The question," says Taylor, "may become of importance not only as it affects the reputation of a female, but the credibility and character of the person who makes the imputation of a want of chastity. In 1845, a gentleman was brought to a court-martial on a charge of having deliberately and falsely asserted that on several occasions he had connection with a native woman. This was denied by the woman, and evidence was adduced to show that she had still what is commonly regarded as the main sign of virginity, namely, an unruptured hymen. In consequence of this, the gentleman was found guilty and cashiered. The woman was at the time about to be married, and this rendered the investigation all the more important to her. A surgeon, who examined the girl, deposed that he found the membrane of a semilunar form, and tensely drawn across the vagina; and his evidence was corroborated by that of a midwife. The inculpated person took up a double line of defence—1st, that the examination of the woman was incomplete; and 2nd, that the hymen, if present, would not justify the witness in saying that intercourse could not possibly have taken place. On the first point, it is unnecessary here to make a remark; but it appeared, from their own admissions, that the witnesses had never before examined women

with this particular object. Assuming that there was
no mistake, it became a question whether non-inter-
course could in such a case be inferred from the
presence of the membrane. Fruitful intercourse, it is
well known, may take place without rupture of the
hymen. Some instances of this kind were referred to
at the court-martial; but such cases are usually regarded
as of an exceptional nature. The real question is,
whether, unless the hymen be in an abnormal state,
intercourse can possibly occur between young and
active persons without a rupture of this membrane.
Intercourse is not likely to be confined, under these
circumstances, to a mere penetration of the vulva. The
membrane in this woman is stated to have been tensely
drawn across the canal, and it was not tough; it was
therefore in a condition to render it most easy for
rupture. In the case of an old man, or of one of
weak virile power, vulvar intercourse might be had
without destroying the membrane; but such a case
could only be decided by the special circumstances
which accompanied it. The presence of the unruptured
hymen affords a presumptive but not an absolute proof
that the woman is a virgin; and if the membrane is
of ordinary size and shape, and in the ordinary situation,
it shows clearly that, although attempts at intercourse
may have been made, there can have been no vaginal
penetration. Admitting the statements of the examiners
to be correct, it is improbable that this woman had
had sexual intercourse several times, or even on one
occasion.

"In the case of DELAFOSSE v. FORTESCUE, [1] which
involved an action for defamation of character, the
plaintiff, a married man, æt. 64, had been charged

[1] Exeter Lent Ass., 1893.

with committing adultery with a certain woman. Several witnesses for the defendant positively swore that they had seen these persons in carnal intercourse. This was denied by the plaintiff; and, as an answer to the case, medical evidence was tendered to the effect that the woman with whom the adulterous intercourse was alleged to have taken place had been examined, and the hymen was found intact. In cross-examination, however, this was admitted not to be a conclusive criterion of virginity, and a verdict was returned for the defendant. The form and situation of the hymen in this case were not described; but it is to be presumed that these were not such as to constitute a physical bar to intercourse, or this would have been stated by the medical witness. Hence the existence of the membrane was not considered to disprove the allegations of eye-witnesses. In Scotland this kind of medical evidence is not admissible. A wife sued the husband for divorce, on the ground, *inter alia*, that he had committed adultery with C. In defence the defendant denied the adultery, and adduced C. as a witness, who swore that such connection had never taken place. She also swore that she had submitted to an *inspectio corporis* by Simpson. The defendant then proposed to examine Simpson, that he might speak to the result of his examination. He argued that this was the best evidence that he could adduce in support of his innocence, as if the girl was still a virgin the adultery alleged could not have been committed. The court refused to admit the evidence, on the ground that the evidence proposed was merely that of an opinion from the professor; that other medical men might differ from him in opinion, even from the same observations, and that, as the court could not compel

C. to submit to another examination, the proposed evidence must be considered *exparte* and inadmissible. [1] In HUNT v. HUNT a verdict was obtained at common-law against the alleged paramour in a case of adultery. It was subsequently proved that the lady was *virgo intacta*. So long as there are facts which show that women have actually conceived with the hymen still in its normal state, it is inconsistent to apply the term 'virgo intacta' to women merely because this membrane is found entire. A woman may assuredly have an unruptured hymen, and yet not be a 'virgo intacta'. This can only be decided by the special circumstances proved in each case. Such *virgines intactæ* have frequently required the assistance of accoucheurs, and in due time have been delivered of children. [2]   A similar question arose in REG. v. HARMER. [3]   The prisoner was indicted for perjury. He was a waiter at a tavern, and being called as a witness in a divorce suit, swore that he had seen one of the parties in adulterous intercourse on more than one occasion. The lady with whom the adultery was alleged to have been committed, denied this on oath, and Lee and another medical expert gave evidence that they had examined this lady, and found her to be a *virgo intacta*. He was found guilty."

Negro Girls deflowered by Toubabs. The " unpierced" soon lose their right to the title, when they have to do with a Toubab, but, on account of the size of their genital parts, the loss of their maidenhead

[1] *Sessions Cases* (Edin., Feb. 11, 1860).
[2] "Amer. Journ. Med. Soc." Ap., 1873, p. 560.
[3] C.C.C., June, 1872.

is not such a serious affair for them as it would be for a little French girl who was not yet nubile. I have never remarked in a little Negress, who had been deflowered by a White, the vulvar inflammation, which, with us, is noticed as the result of premature copulation.

Amorous Subterfuges used in Europe. Mantegazza makes some very interesting remarks on this subject.

In opposition to those who exact the virginity of the bride, there are others who attach no importance whatever to it.

According to Hureau de Villeneuve, [2] the hymen is not described in the Chinese works on medicine and surgery, and he explained the fact by saying that the mothers and nurses succeeded in obliterating it by continual washings of the genital parts. It is said to be the same in India.

Epp enthusiastically applauds these customs. They contrast with the want of cleanliness among us Europeans who, out of modesty or through neglect, transform this nest of love into a putrid sink.

[1] Much fuss is made by men over this matter, but we think that if they were purer in their own lives they would be less likely to suspect their wives' chastity. Women have as much right *morally* to expect purity in the men they marry as the contrary; although, we know that of course, the old cry will be raised about the inequality of the sexes and the husband having to pay for children not his own, yet the fact remains that healthy offspring are given to those who have learnt "self-governance". Too often, the libertine, so jealous and exacting as regards his partner, brings a syphilitic body to the marriage bed, and in the scrofulous faces of his children reads for the first time the meaning about the "sins of the fathers descending upon the children until the third and fourth generations."

See "Excursus" to the present chapter on the *Influence of Chastity on the Health.*

[2] *De l'Accouchement dans la Race Jaune,* thèse de Paris, Ploss, *op. cit.,* t. I, p. 219.

The ancient Egyptians used to make an incision in the hymen previous to marriage, and Saint Athanasius relates that among the Phœnicians a slave of the bridegroom was charged by him to deflower the bride.

The Caraïb Indians attached no value to virginity, and only the daughters of the higher classes were shut up during two years previous to marriage.

It appears that among the Chibcha Indians in Central America virginity is not at all esteemed. It was considered to be a proof that the maiden had never been able to inspire love.

In ancient Peru the old maids were the object of high esteem. There were sacred virgins called *Wives of the Sun* [1] somewhat similar to the Roman vestals. They made a vow of perpetual chastity and passed their lives in weaving and in preparing *chicha* [2] and cakes of Indian corn for the King (*Inca*). [3]

It is also said that they were buried alive when they happened to break their vow of chastity, unless indeed they could prove having conceived, not from a man, but from the sun. The seducer was put to death and his race dispersed.

Several authors worthy of credence assure us that these vestals were guarded by eunuchs. The temple at Cuzco had one thousand virgins, that of Caranqua two hundred. It would appear, however, that the virginity of these vestals was not so very sacred after all, for the Inca Kings used to choose from among them concubines for themselves or for their principal vassals and favourite friends. According to Torquemada, these

---

[1] The nuns of the present day, do they not style themselves the " *Spouses of Christ?* "

[2] A fermented intoxicating beverage.

[3] Read the priests of the Temple. (Trnsl.).

vestals remained only three years in the temple, and were then replaced by others. The Inca used to choose three whom he consecrated priestesses of the sun, then three for himself and the others he married to his subjects or else gave them their liberty.

Marco Polo narrates how young girls were exposed by their mothers on the public highway in order that travellers might freely make use of them. A young girl was expected to have at least twenty presents earned by such prostitutions before she could hope to find a husband. This did not prevent them from being very virtuous after marriage, nor their virtue from being much appreciated.

Waitz assures us that in several countries of Africa a young girl is preferred for wife when she has made herself remarked by several amours and by much fecundity.

It was impossible ever to find the signs of virginity among the Machacura women in Brazil, and Feldner [1] explains the reason in latin: " *Nulla inter illas invenitur virgo, quia mater inde in tenera ætate filiæ maxima cum cura omnem vaginæ constrictionem ingredimentumque amovere studet, hoc quidem modo manui dextræ imponitur folium arboris in infudibuli formam redactum, et dum index in partes genitales immissus huc et illud movetur, per infundibulum aqua tepida immittitur.*" (Among them a virgin is never to be found, for this reason that the mother from her daughter's tenderest years endeavours with the utmost care to remove all tightness of the vagina and obstacle therein. With this end in view, the leaf of a tree folded into the shape of a funnel is held in the right hand, then while the index finger is introduced into the genital

---

[1] *Voyage à travers le Brésil*, Liegnitz, 1828, vol. II, p. 148.

parts and worked to and fro, warm water is admitted by means of the funnel).

Among the Sakalaves in Madagascar the young girls deflower themselves, when the parents have not previously seen to this necessary preparation for marriage.

Among the Balanti of Senegambia, one of the most degraded races in Africa, the girls cannot find a husband until they have been deflowered by their King, who often exacts costly presents from his female subjects for putting them in condition to be able to marry.

Barth (1856), in describing Adamad, says that the chief of the Bagoli used to lie the first night with the daughters of the Fulba, a people under his sway. Similar facts are related of the aborigines of Brazil and of the Kinipeto Esquimaux. In many of these cases it is not easy to determine if we have to do with the right of the strongest or with a strange taste on the part of voluntary victims.

Demosthenes informs us that there was a celebrated Greek hetæra, named Neæra, who had seven slaves whom she called her daughters, so that being supposed to be free a higher price was paid for their favours. She sold their virginity five or six times over and ended by selling the whole lot together.

The god Mutinus, Mutunus or Tutunus of ancient Rome, used to have the new brides come and sit upon his knees, as if to offer him their virginity. Saint Augustine says: " *In celebratione nuptiarum super Priapi scapum nova nupta sedere jubebatur.*" (In the celebration of nuptials the newly wed bride used to be bidden sit on the shaft of Priapus). Lactantius gives more precise details: " *et Mutunus in cujus sinu pudendo nubentes præsident, ut illarum pudicitiam prius deus delibasse videatur*" (and

Mutunus, in whose shameful lap brides sit, in order that the god may appear to have gathered the first-fruits of their virginity). It appears, however, that this offering was not merely symbolical, for when they had become wives, they used to return to the favourite deity to pray for fecundity.

Arnobius also relates: "*etiam ne Tutunus, cujus immanibus pudendis, horrentique fascino, vestras inequitare matronas et auspicabile ducitis et optatis ?*" (is it Tutunus, on whose huge organs and Βριστλινγ Τοολ you think it an auspicious and desirable thing that your matrons should be μουντεδ ?)

Pertunda was another hermaphrodite divinity that Saint Augustine maliciously proposed rather to name the *Deus Pretundus* (who strikes first); it was carried on to the nuptial bed to aid the bridegroom. "*Pertunda in cubiculis præsto est virginalem scrobem effodientibus maritis.*" (Pertunda stands there ready in the bed-chamber for the aid of husbands excavating the Φιργιν πιτ) (Arnobius).

The Kondadgis (Ceylon), the Cambodgians and other peoples charged their priests with the defloration of their brides.

Jäger communicated to the Berlin Anthropological Society a passage from Gemelli Cancri, which mentions a *stupratio officialis* practised at a certain period among the Bisayos of the Philippine Islands: "There is no known example of a custom so barbarous as that which had been there established, of having public officials, and even paid very dearly, to take the virginity of young girls, the same being considered to be an obstacle to the pleasures of the husband. As a fact there no longer exists any trace of this infamous practice since the establishment of the Spanish rule ...

but even to-day a Bisayo feels vexed to find his wife
safe from suspicion, because he concludes, that not
having excited the desire of anyone, she must have
some bad quality which will prevent him from being
happy with her."

Influence of Chastity on Health. [1] A man may
kill himself by excess of venereal pleasure; as he may
also impose upon himself an absolute continence. But
in this case it is not so complete as might be supposed,
the nocturnal pollutions amounting to positive copu-
lations with loss of semen and voluptuous spasm. A
virgin perfectly pure in herself may even experience
in dream the spasms of pleasure.

Nevertheless, voluntary chastity reduces to a minimum
the secretion of sperm and of venereal desire; it may
even cause the gradual dying out of these wants, which
constitute the greatest delights and also the greatest
tyranny of humanity.

It must be recognised to what a degree chastity
favours health, longevity, energy of intellect and of
sentiment, and the limits beyond which it ought not
to extend so as not to disturb the harmony of life
dependant on the regular action of all the organs.

It seems at first that by being sparing of so precious
a product as the sperm and economising the strength
expended in every sexual intercourse, the individual
should be able to accumulate an important reserve
force; but this is only partly true, and it is difficult
to precise the amount of chastity necessary for the
maintenance of health.

With regard to man, statistics supply us with no
elements for solving the problem; they prove on the
contrary that marriage is conducive to health and

[1] From Mantegazza, *Igiene dell' Amore* (Milan, 1892).

longevity, but here we have only a comparison between married life and celibacy, and celibacy is not always synonymous with chastity. Bachelors are, very often, the worst of libertines. But if we could meet around us a dozen of men really chaste, we should find them superior to others in vigour, in longevity and in intellectual energy. I think also that priests owe the old age to which they often attain to their chastity, admitting at the same time that their minor responsability and the ease and comfort of their lives are also advantageous to their health, conceding at the same time to malicious persons that the servants of God are not all of them chaste.

All men, particularly the young, may experience the immediate benefits of continence. Blumenbach has said that the reabsorption of sperm at the time of their loves renders animals ferocious; but, many centuries before him, Aretaeus said that the sperm made us lively, ardent and vigorous. Martin of Lyons relates the case of a man, in whom the spermatic secretion having become suppressed, he used to have sweatings having the smell of sperm, accompanied by the voluptuous sensation of ejaculation. We leave aside this latter question of the voluptuous sensation, but accept the idea of the sperm-smelling sweat, because we have ourselves recognised a strong odour of sperm among very chaste but very ardent young men. It is certain that a certain part of the semen is reabsorbed and strongly excites the muscles, the brain and the nerves, and in the second part of my book will be seen the importance I give to this reabsorption in the production of the secundary sexual characters. The semen accumulated for a long time in the spermatic vesicles constitutes a real reservoir of force, which may reveal itself under the most varied forms. Memory becomes prompt and tenacious, thought is rapid and fecund, the will is energetic and the whole character shows a vigour quite unknown to libertines.

Some sublime egotists had soon observed that their life was being exhausted in the pleasures of love, and by condemning themselves to absolute chastity were able to preserve unto the extremest old age their ardent enthusiasms, their juvenile energies and a life always enjoyable. No magnifying glass enables us to see the celestial blue so well as the prism of chastity.

It is perhaps fortunate for the future of humanity, that we cannot put into balance, on the one hand all the voluptuous spasms of a life spent in the cult of Venus, and on the other all the harmonies, all the joys and all the poesy of a chaste life. Everybody would then perhaps be chaste and the world would perish.

In all books of history and of morality, thousands of facts are met with which show that in all times and in all places, man has sought in chastity the means to double his forces in order to devote them to higher purposes. We see athletes condemn themselves to continence, warriors preparing for the fight by abstaining from sexual pleasure and many religions commanding their priests to observe celibacy and chastity. A fact less known, is that in the University of Paris, during nearly six centuries, no married men could be admitted to profess in any of the faculties. Before granting the licentiate of arts the chancellor of the University required the oath: *Jurate quod non estis matrimona-liter conjuncti* (Swear that ye are not conjoined matrimonially), and, on the 29th April, 1566, some married men having contrived to introduce themselves into the University thanks to the civil wars, the chancellor had them expelled and the rector concluded his sentence of exclusion in these terms: *Unanimi omnium consensu et ore communi vultis puniendos mulcta certè primarios, qui in eorum collegio admiserunt viros uxoratos.* (By the unanimous consent of all and the common voice ye hereby declare those governors should be punished at any rate with a fine, who have admitted married men in their college).

Considering the great economy of force resulting from chastity, many persons imagine that it must give an unusual energy to the genital organs. This is true only for short periods of chastity. When it is prolonged, the organs, on the contrary, are weakened.

Absolute chastity is a rare exception and is possible only to a chosen few; but a temporary chastity is to be recommended to those who, at certain periods of their life, have to spend a great amount of intellectual power.

Elements of Social Science. Chastity has also its evils; but they have been exaggerated by several writers and specially by the anonymous author of the *Elements of Social Science.* He who reads the terrible case of the curé Blanchet, who wrote such harrowing letters to Buffon, must turn pale with horror at the effects of absolute chastity: but this worthy priest is a rare exception. At the utmost there are a few weeks or some months of wrestling, but the victory then becomes easy and certain. First of all desire becomes excessive, there is extreme disquietude, sleepless nights, continuous and violent erections; then all calms down and beneficial nocturnal pollutions supply a safety valve. It is true that in some cases there is headache, vertigo, but this is almost always when chastity comes after venereal abuse. I have seen many individuals without force, stupified or paralysed after venereal excesses, I could count twenty diseases resulting from this cause: I never saw one produced solely by chastity.

Women support it much better than men, and many cases of hysteria said to have been produced by unsatisfied love must be ascribed to another cause.

I speak of virgins; young widows may prove an exception, particularly when they have other habits and are voluptuous by nature. They may have congestions of the brain, vertigos and divers forms of neuroses. Habit is the element which exercises the greatest influence on all the acts commanded by the cerebro-spinal axis, and this truth should be deeply meditated by those not over vigorous husbands, who during the honeymoon, from self-conceit or by the aid of momentary excitation, have accustomed their wives to a regimen they are unable to continue to provide them later. Putting aside " women of ice " and " women of fire ", who are exceptions, the others become lascivious, chaste or moderate, according to what their partners design them to be.

Dr. Verga on Celibacy. Doctor Verga, a remarkable author and philosopher, has well studied the influence of celibacy and of marriage on insanity. May I be permitted to briefly give the substance of his interesting researches : [1]

" It is generally accepted that for mental as well as for bodily maladies, the efficient and determinant

---

[1] Prof. Andrea Verga, *Si le Célibat prédispose a la folie.* Milan, 1869.—*Si le Mariage contribue à la Folie*, Milan, 1871.

causes obtain all their value from the hereditary or acquired individual predisposition.

"This predisposition, which manifests itself usually in infancy, may later on engender an aversion or exterior obstacles to marriage. Some young people, born of parents cerebrally affected, having themselves such a morbid sensitiveness that they feel irritated at the least contradiction, I might almost say at all opposition to their will, and who have a horror of any restriction to their liberty, understand that they are not made for marriage, and condemn themselves voluntarily to celibacy; the malady which threatens them finds them naturally inclined to a single life. For it must be remarked, marriage is a dignity that requires a vocation and special aptitudes; it is the crowning glory of the individual. Others again, even more inclined to insanity, but less persuaded of the danger, or having fewer scruples, either stimulated by instinct or constrained by special circumstances, seek to marry; but certain peculiarities, certain excentricities cause families and young girls to receive them very coldly. Time passes and at last insanity manifests itself.

"It is evident that in such cases the effect of celibacy is merely apparent. All those bachelors of either sex did not go mad because they were unmarried, but because they were already on the highroad to madness.

"You may tell me that young girls are in far different conditions from those of young men; that they do not choose, but are chosen; that their parents more easily dispose of their hand and willingly allow them to go away, knowing how capricious they are and how difficult to govern; all that is very true.

"But that is precisely what must render the proportion

of insanity less among young girls and also less pronounced among married women: two facts entirely corroborated by statistics.   We have also determined by our calculations that the adult female insane unmarried are in the proportion of 35.17 per cent, whereas the bachelor insane amounted to 64.83 per cent, and on the contrary the married women insane were in the proportion of 48.93 per cent, while the married men insane amounted to 51.07 per cent.

"It is with insanity as with epilepsy, with idiocy and crétinism: all these maladies might be styled *the maladies of celibacy*, so much do they preponderate among bachelors of both sexes.   But, if we except epilepsy, which sometimes manifests itself late in life, idiotism and crétinism are essentially peculiar to early youth.   Idiots and crétins remain children all their lives and never acquire the matrimonial capacity.

"From which it follows that with them celibacy is the consequence and not the cause of their infirmity."

CHAPTER VIII.

Perversions of the sexual passion amongst the Negroes.—The Negress is neither a Sodomite nor a Lesbian.—Parent-Duchâtelet on " Lesbian Love".—Tribads despised by other prostitutes.— How the vice is contracted.—The strange affection of Tribads. —Lawful love thought shocking.—Pregnancy frequent among them. —A White Messalina.—A White woman violated by a Negro.—Taylor on raping adult women.—Evidence of signs of violence.—Trick of a Negro to get a White women.—A little White girl deflowered by a Negro.

The Negress is neither a Sodomite nor a Lesbian. After the explanations just given, as to the want of genital sensitiveness in the Negress, it would not appear strange that we should discover few cases of erotic perversion, which are so common amongst Asiatic people. The Negress is not a Lesbian, although her clitoris is well-developed. Neither is she a sodomite, but, on the contrary, has a profound aversion for that depraved habit. [1] The reason perhaps is, that when practised with the Negro's yard, anal copulation would be a real torture,—a kind of impalement. The only traces of sodomy I found, were amongst the lowest class of Black women of Saint Louis,—cheap prostitutes of the worst sort. I may mention particularly one of these women, who was still young,

[1] See Krafft-Ebing on tribadic practices among European " fast women " —*Psychopathia Sexualis* (page 429).

and who presented a notable development of the buttocks, with a deep infundibulum, a sphincter completely relaxed, and an orifice so considerably dilated that it admitted three fingers without pain. This woman confessed that it was the Whites (Is this quite certain?) who practised sodomy upon her, and that before she allowed them to do it, she demanded in advance a bottle of sangara, which she drank till she was dead drunk, and in this way she felt nothing, or next to nothing.

Parent-Duchâtelet on "Lesbian Love."

While dealing with this subject we think it not inopportune to contrast the careful and conscientious study of this great man in regard to the prevalence of unnatural vice amongst Parisian prostitutes [1] and the *causes* that originate it. "I cannot refrain here," he says, "from treating of a very important item in the history of the habits of prostitutes, but I am forced to do it with the utmost reserve. I am about to speak of those loves which a depraved taste contrary to nature impels some prostitutes to seek to satisfy among members of their own sex.

"These disgusting and monstrous *marriages*, so common in houses of correction, that but very few female prisoners can escape from them, are they as frequent among prostitutes as some people seem to think? The following are the details on that subject that I have been able to collect from all those who by their situation were able to make observations.

"Regarding the number of prostitutes addicted to

[1] *La Prostitution dans la Ville de Paris* considérée sous le Rapport de l'Hygiène Publique, de la Morale et de l'Administration par A. J. B. Parent-Duchâtelet, 3ème édit. (Baillière et Fils, Paris, 1857).

this vice, I have found an extreme difference of opinion: there are some who pretend that all or nearly all of them abandon themselves passionately to it; others on the contrary have assured me that very few are given to it. This contradictory opinion was based with the former, not with the latter, solely upon a vague supposition, on some flying reports, gathered by chance here and there, and not upon a careful study of the question, destined to elucidate it, and having for basis a certain number of observations.

" This contradiction can be in great part explained by the fact that none of these women will ever admit of being addicted to this vice, for when they are questioned, they reply quickly and with impatience: *I am for men only, and I never was for women.* All the persons who have been enabled to study them at all moments of their life, and particularly in hospitals and prisons, have assured me that they are absolutely silent on that subject; that they are as ashamed of this vice for themselves as they are ashamed for their comrades who are given to it; those only in prison, who are really guilty, do not hesitate to shew themselves in their true light.

Tribads despised by other Prostitutes. Generally speaking, *tribads*, for that is the name given to these women addicted to unnatural practices, are despised and looked down upon by the other prostitutes; indeed to some of these they inspire a sort of horror which impels them to fly from and avoid them. During the moments of coming together and of conversation in prison they are not spared reproaches and jeers, but always in covered words; and even in their disputes, when they abuse each other in the coarsest language, they still preserve a certain restraint on that point. Jealousy alone or the wish for revenge can induce them sometimes to denounce each other, but that is rarely observed.

A woman who kept a house of prostitution, and who was addicted to this vice, had received into her establishment a very pretty girl whom she wished to attach to herself; but the girl quitted the place solely for that reason, regretting at the same time, she said, the well-being and comforts of all kinds with which her mistress surrounded her.

A girl of low degree, while in a state bordering upon intoxication, wishing to do violence to one of her comrades who refused to comply with her desires, caused such a disturbance in the house that the police had to interfere. All the women attached to the brothel denounced her to the commissary of police as guilty of *a criminal assault.*

How the Vice is contracted. Some persons who have given me information on the subject, are of opinion that it is mostly with women keeping brothels that prostitutes contract the vice here in question, which may be attributed to the abundant food supplied to them, the idle life they lead and the conversations they hold with each other; but a crowd of other details tend to convince me that, if such conditions are not without influence, they act only upon a very small number, and the origin of these depraved tastes must be sought for elsewhere.

An observation made and repeated in the interior of a prison, the only place where it is possible to properly study certain tastes and inclinations which dominate among prostitutes, has proved that nearly all

the tribads belonged to the class of independent prostitutes (not attached to licensed brothels), and also that
those who made themselves remarked by their tendency
to pervert the others, had invariably passed some years
inside of prisons. [1]

Who does not know, in fact, that it is in the
prisons, and more especially in the prisons for women,
that these shameful vices most generally prevail, and
there are but few female prisoners who can resist,
particularly if their detention extends over more than
eighteen months or two years. It is towards the age
of from twenty-five to thirty years that prostitutes
usually take to this sort of libertinism, and after having
already plied their trade during six, eight or ten years,
unless they have passed some time in prison. If at
times there are found young women novices in the
business of prostitution who show similar inclinations, it
is not that they were naturally impelled to it, but that
they are more properly to be considered as the victims
of others who have led them astray. There are but
few old prostitutes who may not be ranked among
the tribads; they at last come to have a horror of
men, and to become the associates of thieves and of
all that is most abject and most crapulous.

[1] It is in fact in prison, that women most often contract this shameful vice.
Nearly all young girls, who remain some time in prison, are contaminated with
it; this and other considerations, show the necessity of the cellular system.

The terms of the Regulations of 1824 mentioned by Parent-Duchâtelet
are strictly observed, and the licensed houses are visited at night by
the police to see that they are executed. But notwithstanding these
precautions, corruption has progressed, and there are now but few
prostitutes that are not tainted with it. How can it be otherwise, seeing
that these unfortunate creatures meet only with contumely, humiliation
and insult from men, who are often the very first to excite them to
practise a vice which ought rather be to them a subject of horror.

It is worthy of remark that there is often a considerable disproportion of age and of charm between two women who conjoin in this manner; and what is likely to surprise, is, that, once the intimacy established, it is usually the younger and prettier who shows the greater attachment and more passionate love to the other.

The Strange Affection of Tribads. Whence comes this attachment, and how are these *liaisons* formed? I was able to procure in a prison communication of the correspondence between these tribads; I invariably found it romantic, full of the usual expressions employed by lovers, and evidencing throughout a much exalted imagination. The most curious specimen of the kind that I saw, was a series of letters addressed by one prisoner to another; the first of these was a declaration of love, but the style of which was veiled, covered, and extremely reserved; the second was more expansive; the last ones expressed in burning terms the most violent and unbridled passion.

In most cases the want of education excludes the manner of communication peculiar to cultivated minds; it is by caresses, care, attentions, kindnesses of all sorts, that the superannuated and sometimes even old prostitutes manage to seduce quite young girls, and succeed in attaching them to themselves in a really most astonishing manner. These old dames are then seen to work with extreme ardour in order to augment their gains and be able to make presents to those whom they want to seduce; they offer to do work for shops, and use all the powers that the art of seduction can suggest to them, to compensate by peculiar and artificial qualities, what in them is deficient, and which might tend to inspire aversion.

When such *liaisons* are established they present certain curious peculiarities which we will now endeavour to unveil.

With prostitutes the loss of a lover of the same sex is far different from the abandonment by a lover of the opposite sex. In the latter case, consolation is quickly found, another is soon met with who will cause the unfaithful one to be forgotten. But what a difference with the others! In fact their attachment approaches more to frenzy than to love: they are tormented by jealousy, and the dread of being supplanted and of thereby losing the object of their affections, makes them never quit each other, but watch each other's footsteps; they get *run in* for the same offences, and manage to quit the house of correction at the same time.

When they are taken to prison, supposing they are purposely placed in separate dormitories, there is no end to their observations, child-like complaints, cries and howls; they play all sorts of tricks so as to rejoin those from whom they would not be separated; they simulate illness so as to be sent to the infirmary, some indeed have been known, in that intention, to inflict very serious wounds upon themselves. Some of them, more cunning than all the others, and consummate mistresses of all the tricks of their trade, have applied to certain parts of their genital organs little pieces of caustic potash, by means of which were produced slight ulcerations so closely resembling venereal chancres that the most experienced surgeon might be misled. They have most of them a wonderful talent to simulate the itch, which they accomplish by pricking the parts, where that eruption usually shows itself, with a needle made red hot.

The abandonment of a tribad by the object of her affection becomes in a prison a circumstance requiring the closest vigilance on the part of the warders; the woman who has been abandoned is decided to take a striking revenge on the unfaithful one, as also on the other who has supplanted her; hence real duels in which the combatants employ as weapons the basins in which the food is served, and sometimes even with knives; but the instrument most frequently made use of in these single combats is the hair-comb. This often causes very serious wounds, mortal results have even been several times observed. Formerly such duels were of frequeut occurrence in the prison of *La Force*, [1] and the governor, M. Chefdeville, whenever he became cognizant of any infidelities of that kind, used to write to the Prefect of Police, for the authorisation to put into a separate place the woman who had thus become an object of hatred to another.

This hatred and rage among such excitable beings as prostitutes cannot last very long; her vengeance once sated, the abandoned woman seeks to bring back to her the unfaithful one, in which she sometimes succeeds; or if her efforts are useless, she attempts new conquests, and plies again her pernicious talents.

Lawful Love thought Shocking. There is, however, one case, which in itself is absolutely unpardonable, and demands perpetual revenge; that is when a woman quits another to attach herself to a man whom she makes her lover. This crime, we repeat, is one that is never to be forgiven. Nothing can cause it to be

[1] This prison was demolished a great many years ago. All female delinquents are now sent to the prison of Saint-Lazare, specially destined for women. (Trans.).

forgotten. Woe to her who has thus sinned! for, if she is not the stronger of the two, she is sure to get a beating every time she meets the other who thinks she has the right to reproach against her the most outrageous affront that a prostitute can receive.

This vengeance of a tribad who has been abandoned, under the circumstances above alluded to, presents a remarkable particularity, which is, that in such a case the other prostitutes never interfere, by offering their friendly offices *to endeavour to separate the combatants*, which they never fail to do in cases of ordinary disputes. But in the cases in point, they look on with indifference, and allow the quarrel to be settled as it may. Does this manner of acting result from any agreement or rule among themselves? or is it motived by the contempt they entertain for creatures who, by the excess of their infamy, have plunged themselves even below their own level? We are inclined to adopt the latter explanation, but without maintaining that it is the more exact.

Pregnancy frequent among them. Several inspectors and some former warders of prisons, have informed us that pregnancy is more frequently met with in tribads than among other prostitutes who have not yet contracted this foul taste. This may be understood and to a certain extent explained. The same witnesses have also remarked that in these cases the pregnancy became the subject of jokes and of inuendoes throughout the prison, and that she who presented those symptoms was not the object of the particular care and attention which the imprisoned prostitutes are ready to show to their comrades who may happen to be in that situation.

It may therefore be taken for granted that tribads have come to the lowest stage of vice to which a human creature can descend, and that, for that very reason, they require to be more specially looked after by those who are charged with the supervision of prostitutes, but more particularly by those to whom is confided the direction of the prisons destined to receive these women.

The attention of the authorities has at various times been drawn to these unfortunates. For instance, in the police regulations of 1824, the keepers of brothels are expressly forbidden to allow any of their women to sleep two in the same bed, [1] and when on inspection at night any infraction of this regulation was noticed, the two delinquents were punished with several days imprisonment; the same severity is meted out to free prostitutes who are found in the same condition; lastly the license was withdrawn from a woman keeper of a brothel, because she was found in bed with one of her boarders.

In summing up these details, in considering the circumstances which, among prostitutes, contribute to develop these infamous proclivities, in studying at what age this vice generally begins to develop itself among them, taking also into consideration the limited number of prostitutes who continue their trade more than two or three years; finally, seeing how the tribads are treated, and despised by those who have not yet followed their example, it may be concluded that the number of those who have descended to the lowest stage of vice is far more limited than certain persons have asserted, and that it is impossible to say what is the exact proportion in which they stand to the

[1] These regulations are still in force.

others, but with some approximation to the truth it may be said that they do not constitute one fourth of the prostitutes actually plying their trade in the city of Paris.

The above details show how important it is that those who are charged to maintain order and good morals should know in their least particularities the customs and habits of prostitutes.

Masturbation and Pederasty very rare amongst the Blacks. The free Negro is neither a sodomite nor a pederast. He even masturbates very little. Besides, the rubbing of the hand on the slightly sensitive mucous surface of the circumcised gland would require a much longer time than in copulation before it produced emission. The uncircumcised Negro boy masturbates, by pulling the foreskin which he elongates considerably. But, when once he is circumcised, he considers it almost a disgrace to masturbate, for there are plenty of women with whom to satisfy his sexual needs. It is not the same with the slave, who, whether circumcised or not, has fewer facilities for copulation than the free Negro, and amongst the slaves we find, what we always find in collections of human beings when the female element is wanting. There is an exchange of reciprocal pederasty, and each is active and passive in turn. At least, that was the result of a medical examination I made, of two young Bambara Sharpshooters, who came from the station at Kita, where they had been set at liberty after the capture of a batch of slaves belonging to the Sarrakholais caravan men. They enlisted at an early age, before they were twenty years of age. They confessed to me that, amongst the captives and slaves, pederastic practices were carried on.

Dr. Paul Moreau (of Tours), cites a remarkable case which has some bearing on the lascivious woman alluded to, showing that these erotic proclivities are strictly speaking congenital. A little girl not yet three years old, lying down on the floor or leaning with force against a piece of furniture, used to agitate her body with singular violence. Her parents at first saw in this only play; but recognising with pain that it proceeded from a sort of libertinism, they endeavoured carefully to correct so unfortunate a habit, employing alternately caresses and prayers, or threats and shame, and lastly punishment: they seemed, however, in no wise to succeed.

The child grew up and the evil increased to such a degree that at table, in company, in church, at sight of an agreeable object, she gave herself up in all possible ways to these manœuvres, which were followed by copious ejaculation. On being questioned as to the moment when her paroxym was about to take place, she remained silent or else admitted she experienced great pleasure. At the moment of her crises she seemed to have almost entirely lost all sense of sight and of hearing. The threats and reprimands of her parents had the effect of making her abstain from giving way in their presence at least to her unhappy propensity; but, nevertheless, she sought for solitude in order to satisfy it: and often was she found exhausted and drowsy.

Nothing could stop this excess of lasciviousness; a physician was called in whose advice was without effect. Her parents then decided to marry her, and fixed their choice upon a very vigorous man. She became enceinte, and from that moment was exempt from her infirmity; but she always came out of the most frequently repeated amorous assaults, fatigued but not satiated.

At last, her accouchement having been very laborious, she died under it. Her clitoris was of the size of a penis. The period of her greatest salacity lasted from the beginning to the end of spring, and during the whole of that time the patient exhaled the smell of a male-goat.

This lubricity was it seems heriditary. [1]

A White Messalina. This unfortunate woman made her husband ill by excessive copulation. I was obliged to send him to the hospital, to give him a little rest.

Being left alone in a small lodging, not far from the Negro quarter, in the North part of the town, she soon began to misconduct herself in a most scandalous manner. In the middle of the day, in the hottest hours, when you are sure not to find either a White man or a Creole in the street, she would sit, half naked, at her window, and make signs to any Negro who was passing. They came, at first singly, then by twos, by threes, and finally in parties, and all in turn assuaged their brutal passions upon her. They had never had such a good time. The scandal became so great that it reached the ears of her husband, and he obtained from the authorities permission to shut up his wife in the hospital. Ill she really was, for her erotic excesses had produced a severe affection of the womb. [2]

Moreau, says Krafft-Ebing, considers these cases peculiar to themselves, but he is certainly in error.

[1] *Ephémèrides des curieux de la nature.*

[2] Refer, for the imaginative side, to Burton's "Nights" (Vol. I. Benares

The sexual complexus of symptoms is always but the partial manifestation of a general psychosis (mania, hallucinatory insanity?).

The essential element of the state of sexual excitement is a condition of psychical hyperæsthesia with involvement of the sexual sphere. The imagination calls up only sexual images, which may lead to hallucinations, illusions, and true hallucinatory delirium.

The most indifferent ideas excite sensual association, and the lustful colouring of the ideas and apperceptions is very much intensified.

The abnormal state of consciousness implicates the whole course of feeling and desire, and is accompanied by general physical excitement like that which accompanies coitus.

Giraud (*Annal. méd. psychol.*) has reported a case of rape of a little girl by a religious paranoiac, aged 43, who was temporarily erotic. Here, also, belongs a case of incest (Liman, *Vierteljahrsschr. f. ger. Med.*)

M. impregnated his daughter. His wife, mother of eighteen children, and herself pregnant by her husband, lodged the complaint. M. had had religious paranoia for two years. "It was revealed to me that I should beget the Eternal Son with my daughter. Then a man of flesh and blood would arise by my faith, who would be eighteen hundred years old. He would be a bridge between the Old and New Testaments." This command, which he deemed divine, was the cause of his insane act.

Sexual acts that have a pathological motive sometimes occur in persecutory paranoia.

A married woman of thirty had, by means of money and sweetmeats, enticed a boy of five, who played near her, handled his genitals, and then attempted coitus. She was a teacher, who had been betrayed and then cast off. Previously moral, for some time she had given herself to prostitution. The explanation of her immoral change was given, when it was found that she had various delusions of persecution, and thought she was under the secret influence of her seducer, who impelled her to sexual acts. She also believed that the boy had been put in her way by her seducer. Coarse sensuality as a motive for her crime came less into consideration, as it would have been easy for her to satisfy sexual desire in a natural way.

(Küssner, *Berl. Klin. Wochenschrift.*)

Cullere ("Perversions sexuelles chez les persécutés," in *Annal. médico-psychol.*, March, 1886) has reported similar cases, the case of a patient who, suffering with paranoia sexualis persecutoria, tried to violate his sister, giving as a reason that the impulse was given him by Bonapartists.

In hysteria the sexual life is very frequently abnormal; indeed, always in predisposed individuals. All the possible anomalies of the sexual function may occur here, with sudden changes and peculiar activity; and, on an hereditary degenerate basis and in moral imbecility, they may appear in the most perverse forms. The abnormal change and inversion of the sexual feeling are never without effect upon the patient's disposition.

The following case, reported by Giraud, is one of this nature worthy of repetition:—

Marian L., of Bordeaux. At night, while the household was asleep under the influence of narcotics she had administered, she had given the children of the house to her lover for sexual enjoyment, and had looked on at the immoral acts. It was found that L. was hysterical (hemianæsthesia and convulsive attacks), but before her illness she had been a moral, trustworthy person. Since her illness she had become a shameless prostitute, and lost all moral sense.

In the hysterical the sexual sphere is often abnormally excited. This excitement may be intermittent (menstrual?). Shameless prostitution, even in married

women, may result. In a milder form the sexual
impulse expresses itself in onanism, going about in a
room naked, smearing the person with urine and other
things, or wearing male attire, etc.

Schüle (*Klin. Psychiatrie*, 1886, p. 237) finds very
frequently an abnormally intense sexual impulse " which
disposes girls, and even women living in happy marriage, to become Messalinas."

The author cited knows cases in which, on the
wedding-journey, attempts at flight with men, who
had been accidentally met, were made; and respected
wives who entered into *liaisons*, and sacrificed everything to their insatiable impulse.

In hysterical insanity the abnormally intense sexual
impulse may express itself in delusions of jealousy,
unfounded accusations against men for immoral acts, [1]
hallucinations of coitus, [2] etc.

Occasionally frigidity may occur, with absence of
lustful feeling,—due, for the most part, to genital
anæsthesia.

A White Woman violated by a Negro. A
Frenchwoman, of whom I have previously spoken,
Mme D***, was the victim of a horrible outrage.
During the epidemic of yellow fever, she had lost
both her husband and her son. I attended them, but
I could not, in spite of all my efforts, persuade her,
when she fell ill in her turn, to enter the hospital,

---

[1] *Vide* Fall Merlac, in the author's *Lehrb. d. ger. Psychopathol.*, 2.
Aufl., p. 222.—Morel, *Traités des maladies mentales*, p. 687.—Legrand,
La folie, p. 337. Process La Roncière, in *Annal. d'hyg.*, 1e Série, IV;
3e Série, XXII.

[2] The incubus in the witch-trials of the Middle Ages depended on
them.

which was already crowded. Her house and mine were both in the Negro quarter. She had no one to assist her but Negresses, whose attentions are well meant but not very useful. I had no hope of saving her, and one day diagnosed that she would die in the course of the night. I told a Negress, her neighbour and servant, to attend to her as usual, but to leave her quiet if she did not ask for anything.

Being on duty, and obliged to pass the night at the hospital, I could not return until the following morning. Mme D*** was dead. The Negress thought she was dead at about three o'clock in the morning, and had then left the house, after having covered the body with a sheet; when she came again in the morning at seven o'clock, a little before I did, she had found the sheet on the ground, and the body of Mme D*** lying across the bed, with the chemise removed. The Negress declared that she had shut the door, to prevent any animals entering, but one of the windows was open; the house was of only one floor. I saw at the first glance, that the face of the dead woman presented a peculiar appearance of suffering and horror. The body bore on the breasts marks of bites, and large bruises. The nipple of the left breast was almost completely torn off. Serious injuries had been done to the genital organs. These were well formed, the clitoris of a normal size, but the vulva was widely open. The great lips were parted, showing the vagina gaping. You could not distinguish any trace of the myrtiform caroncula, the fork, the navel pit, or the vestibule. The entrance to the womb, distended to such an extent as to admit a child's hand, was in place, but the mucous surface of the passage was hanging down, as it is in the case of women who have had a great number of children, or who frequently indulge in copulation. The finger met with clots of blood, which obstructed the bottom of the wound, and I could feel that the "tench's nose" had lost its usual power of resistance, and could be pushed back. The whole genital apparatus had the appearance of having been pounded, with a hard wooden pestle. There was not the slightest doubt in my mind, but that Mme D*** had been violated before her death. The Negress servant had left early, in order not to be present at her death, and a Toucouleur burglar (perhaps even several—unless it was the neighbours) had entered the chamber of the unfortunate woman, and outraged her. It is very probable that the poor woman, so martyred, had recovered consciousness before dying; from the expression of the face this might be guessed at all events. Mme D***'s house was rather removed from the others, and near the bank of the river. The neighbours had heard nothing, and their dogs had not barked, or at least not more than usual. An enquiry discovered nothing, and in the midst of the general confusion, which the yellow fever had created throughout the entire colony of Saint Louis, the tragical end of Mme D*** passed unnoticed. [1]

Taylor on Raping Adult Women. In this case we have, of course, a woman in a weak or rather

[1] For a similar case that occurred to the *Cantinière* of a French regiment during the occupation under the Second Empire, see the realistic story of my friend M. Hector France, *La Vache enragée*, which appeared, together with other tales, some years ago in *Le Réveil*, under, the general title of *Musc, Haschish et Sang*. The present editor has in hand, we understand, an English edition of these stories. Sir Rich. F. Burton refers to this work in very high terms in one of his notes to the "*Nights.*"

helpless condition. Mention has often been made of
the possibility of committing rape on adult women in
a good state of health and possessing normal strength.
Napoleon, in an anecdote recounting the story of the
woman who came in tears to him with a complaint
of having been violated by one of his soldiers, is said
to have drawn his sword and wriggled the empty
scabbard before her face in demonstration of the
absurdity of her tale unless she had been a consenting
party. This incident is also related as having taken
place between Queen Elizabeth (of England) and one
of her waiting-women who complained of a courtier;
and we are more inclined to believe it emanated from
a woman's wit than from a man's. But it is not
advisable to give too much account to "old wives'
fables". It is a question which properly belongs to
Medical Jurisprudence, and it is to one of the great
English exponents of this science that we now turn.
Saith our author: [1]

"Some medical jurists have argued that a rape cannot
be perpetrated on an adult woman of good health and
vigour; and they have treated all accusations made
under these circumstances as false. Whether, on any
criminal charge, a rape has been committed or not,
is of course a question of fact for a jury and not for
a medical witness. The fact of the crime having been
actually perpetrated, can be determined only from the
evidence of the prosecutrix and of other witnesses;
still a medical man may be able to point out to the
court circumstances which might otherwise escape
notice. Setting aside the cases of infants, idiots,

[1] *Vide* Taylor's *Principles and Practice of Medical Jurisprudence*,
4th edit. by Thomas Stevenson, M.D., Lond. Vol. II, Lond. *Churchill*,
1894.

lunatics, and weak and delicate or aged women, it does not appear probable that intercourse could be accomplished against the consent of a healthy adult, except under the following conditions :—

1. When narcotics or intoxicating liquids have been administered to her, either by the prisoner or through his collusion. It matters not, in a case of this kind, whether the narcotics have been given merely for the purpose of exciting the female, or with the deliberate intention of having intercourse with her while she was intoxicated,—the prisoner is equally guilty. [1] The nature of the substance whereby insensibility is produced is of course unimportant. Thus the vapours of ether and chloroform have been criminally used in attempts at rape. In a case which occurred in France, a dentist was convicted of a rape upon a woman, to whom he had administered the vapour of ether. The prosecutrix was not perfectly unconscious, but she was rendered wholly unable to offer any resistance. [2] A dentist was convicted of rape under somewhat similar circumstances in the United States, but it was thought that the woman had made the charge under some delusion. In REG. v. SNAREY (Winchester Lent Ass., 1859), there was a clear attempt at fraud. The prosecutrix asserted that she was INSTANTLY rendered insensible by the prisoner forcibly applying a handkerchief to her face, and she accused him of having committed a rape upon her. The charge was disproved by a distinct alibi, as well as by the improbability of all the circumstances.

Casper met with a solitary case in which a girl, æt.

---

[1] See REG. v. CAMPLIN, *Law Times*, June 28th, 1845; also *Med. Gaz.*, vol. 36, p. 433.

[2] *Med. Gaz.*, vol. 40, p. 865.

16, accused a man of having had intercourse with her
while she was sleeping in her bed, of which she was
not conscious until he was in the act of withdrawing
from her. On her own statement she was VIRGO
INTACTA up to the date of this occurrence. Upon the
facts of the case, Casper came to the conclusion that,
if her statement was true, the man could not have
had intercourse with her without causing pain and
rousing her to a consciousness of her position. The
hymen was not destroyed, but presented lacerations
in two places. This and other facts showed that there
had been intercourse, but did not prove that this had
taken place without the consciousness of the woman. [1]
In WHITE v. HOWARTH, [2] it was alleged that the
defendant's daughter, having gone to consult the plaintiff, who was a dentist, he took an opportunity of
rendering her suddenly insensible by chloroform, and
then had intercourse with her. In cross-examination,
however, it transpired that the girl was not rendered
insensible at all, but was conscious of all that was
going on, and she might have given an alarm but did
not. Most of these stories, when properly examined,
will be found inconsistent and untrue. It is not the
property of chloroform or of any narcotic substance,
in a non-fatal dose, to render a person instantaneously
insensible and powerless. In BROMWICH v. WATERS [3]
it was alleged on the part of the plaintiff, that the
defendant had given to a woman some liquid, which
she had only tasted, and then suddenly became incon-
scious. It was suggested that while in this state the
defendant had had intercourse with her, which he

[1] Klin. Novellen, 1863, p. 31.
[2] Liverpool Wint. Ass., 1861.
[3] Chester Lent Ass., 1863, p. 253, *ante*.

denied; the woman herself alleged that she was not conscious of her pregnancy until some months after this visit. But such symptoms could not be reasonably ascribed to any of the known narcotic substances. If given in a non-fatal dose their effects are slowly and gradually produced; if they come on in a few minutes, the dose must have been large, and then it is probable the person would die. There is no doubt that many of the charges made against medical men and dentists by women who allege that they have been violated whilst under the influence of anæsthetics are false charges. Anæsthetics stimulate the sexual functions, and the anogenital region is the last to give up its sensitiveness. [1] These charges are sometimes made in all good faith by modest females. A woman under the partial influence of an anæsthetic may mistake the forcible attempts to restrain her movements, whilst she is passing through the preliminary stage of excitement induced by the anæsthetic, for an attempt upon her person. In one instance, a lady engaged to be married was accompanied to a dentist by her affianced husband. Chloroform was given, and a tooth extracted in the presence of this gentleman. She could hardly be convinced that the dentist had not made an attempt upon her chastity.

Evidence of Signs of Violence. We have seen from the preceding section that the English law is very severe in the punishment dealt out to those who dare to trifle with woman's honour. But sometimes the cleverest jurist alive is non-plussed by the absence of any external marks which would indicate that force had been used. The charges of prostitutes, for instance,

[1] Bull. of the Medico-Legal Soc. of New York, May and Dec., 1881.

are received with suspicion and closely scrutinised. Something more than medical evidence would be required to establish a charge under these circumstances. The question turns here, as all cases of rape upon adult women, on the fact of *consent* having been previously given or not. This is the point at which the greater number of these cases of alleged rape break down; and it need hardly be observed, that this question has no relation to the duties of a medical witness; all that he can do is to establish, occasionally, whether or not sexual intercourse has been had with or without some violence. It is obvious that there may be marks of violence about the pudendum or on the person, and yet the conduct of the woman may have been such as to imply consent on her part: we must not suppose that medical proof of intercourse is tantamount to legal proof of rape. When a woman has already been in habits of sexual intercourse, there is commonly much less injury done to the genital organs. The hymen will, in these cases, be found destroyed and the vulva dilated. Still, as the intercourse is presumed to be against the consent of the women, it is most likely that when there has been a proper resistance, some injury will be apparent on the pudendum; and there will be also, probably, extensive marks of violence on the body and limbs. These cases are generally determined without medical evidence by the deposition of the woman, corroborated, as it should always be, by circumstances. This statement regarding the presence of *marks of violence* on the pudendum of a married woman, on whom a rape is alleged to have been committed, requires some qualification. In two cases of rape on married women, in which the crime was completed in spite of the resistance of the women, there were no marks of violence on the genital organs in either case. In one, [1] it appears, that while an accomplice held the head of the woman with her face downwards between his thighs, the prisoner had forcible intercourse with her from behind,—her thighs having been first widely separated. In the second case an accomplice held the woman down on a bed by her neck, while the prisoner separated her thighs, and thus had intercourse with her. She was examined nine hours afterwards by an experienced surgeon, and he found no mark or trace of violence on or anywhere near her pudendum. There were bruises on her arms, neck, and legs, where she had been forcibly held down. In each of these cases, it will be seen that the woman had not to struggle with a single assailant; and there can be no doubt that, if a married woman is rendered powerless by many persons being combined against her, or if rendered insensible by intoxicating drinks or narcotic vapours, a rape may be perpetrated, without any injury whatever to the genital organs. A separation of the thighs in a married woman will cause such a dilatation of the parts, as to render it easy for the male organ to penetrate the vagina without leaving any traces of violence on the labia or the female organs generally.

On the other hand, the vagina may be the seat of violence, and no marks to indicate a struggle or the application of force be found on the body. A woman was knocked down, her clothes were pulled over her face, and a rape was perpetrated by the assailant. In the position in which she was held, with her arms and hands covered over, she was half suffocated, and unable to offer any effectual resistance. She was examined on the evening of the day of the

[1] REG. v. OWEN AND OTHERS (Oxford Circ., 1839).

assault. No marks of violence were found on her body, but the mucous membrane of the vagina at its commencement was contused, and in some portions lacerated; and blood was oozing from these parts. It was considered that, under these circumstances, the statement of the woman was consistent with the fact that there were no marks of violence on her body. There was no reason to suppose that the injury to the vagina had been caused in any other way than by a criminal assault.

Trick of a Negro to get a White Woman. I had, as boy, in my service, a young Sarrakholais named Demba, sixteen years old, and therefore, of course, past the age of puberty, and none the worse for being one of the finest specimens of his race. He was the son of a *laptot*, who had brought him to Saint Louis when quite young,—in his tenth year. At twelve years old, he had been servant to an officer of Spahis. This officer had resided a long time in Algiers, and was the intimate friend of an official, who had also come from Algiers, and had married an Algerian woman of Spanish descent.

The intimacy between the two friends was carried to such an extent, that the officer, who lived next door to the official (there was a terrace connecting the two houses), was constantly in the house of the latter. The wife of the official, a woman of ardent temperament and warm passions, was, as may be guessed, the mistress of the officer, and when her husband had gone to his bureau, used to go along the terrace to her lover's room. Demba, the Negro boy, served as the messenger of love, and during the absence of the husband, watched at the door in case of his sudden

and unexpected return. One day it happened that the
husband had already left, and the lady had just entered
her lover's room, when the officer was called away,
on some military duty requiring his immediate attendance. The Negro boy, who was a very handsome
lad, with eyes like a gazelle, and a form like an antique
aun, but already a man, so far as the size of his
genital apparatus was concerned, though he had not
yet arrived at the age of puberty, ventured to enter
the chamber where the lady was still fretting over the
absence of her lover. I cannot describe here, in full
and realistically, the scene in which Demba showed
the lady, proofs in hand, that he was in love with her,
and that he was of a size to satisfy her desires. I
will content myself with saying that the pleasure of
the lady was all the greater, since the Negro boy,
though capable of taking his master's place, in respect
to the dimensions of his penis, being still under the
age of puberty, did not secrete any seed, and the
copulation could go on for an indefinite time, without
any danger of producing fruit— a double advantage of
pleasure and security.

I had this story from the Negro boy himself. The
young rascal, who was as intelligent as he was unscrupulous, also related to me the following anecdote. [1]

A Little White Girl deflowered by a Negro.
He related to me, that when he was hardly more than

[1] This inordinate salaciousness in the Negro (man) is an established
fact, and has given rise to more lynchings in the Southern States of
America than anything else, cases of robbery and brigandage not excepted.
The *Scented Garden* of the Sheikh Nafzáwi records two or more
notable cases of Negro lust and brutality, and Burton's note (on page 6
BENARES edit. of Vol. I of his *Nights*) respecting the genital organs
of the Zanzibar Negroes, will recur to all students of Anthropology.

ten years old, and came to Saint Louis, his father, a *laptot* in the employ of a European merchant of Saint Louis, procured him a place in the merchant's house, as boy. This merchant had married a Signare (a coloured Creole) from Gorea, and had a little daughter almost of the same age as the young Negro, but who was nubile, for, according to the Negro boy, she made blood (*sic*). Anyhow, her parents did not distrust him, and did not look very well after their daughter, and she, with the lasciviousness natural to coloured girls, took the Negro boy for her lover. She used to rise in the night, and go into the warehouse where he slept. Their amorous delights were carried on, quietly and mysteriously, for a year, but were at last discovered by traces of menstrual blood, which were found one day on some flour sacks, which had served for their improvised bed of love. The Negro boy was turned out of doors with a good kicking, and the girl was sent to a boarding school at Bordeaux, to complete an education that had commenced so well. [1]

EXCURSUS TO CHAPTER VIII.

THE CHARACTER OF MESSALINA VALERIA. [2]

Although often referred to, the real character of this "lady of lust and death" is little known. She would probably be regarded by the medical profession to-day as a "case" of uterine fever:—

[1] See Burton's *Nights* (Vol. II, page 49 of the BENARES edition) for a note by the chevalier on the criminal connection of Negro boys with White girls. The confiding parents who entrust their children to the care of these enterprising Blacks too often suffer a rude awakening. We shall probably revert to this subject later.

[2] From DR. PAUL MOREAU, *Aberrations du Sens Génésique.*

There are vices, said Serviez (in 1728), as well as
virtues, which seem to be hereditary in families.   The
bad examples of fathers sometimes spread a sort of
contagion which contaminates their descendants, and a
witty lady once said in elegant language "that a
coquettish mother would rarely engender strict daughters."

Valeria Messalina is an unhappy example which
confirms this maxim.   Born of a mother not over
virtuous, she imitated and even surpassed her in her
debauches.   Her life was filled with crime, she stained
her reputation with the most shameful and crying
licentiousness.   Her prostitutions were altogether infamous, her lewdness was beyond measure, and her
dissolution public and unlimited.   The most brutal
pleasures were those which had the liveliest attraction
for her, and the most horrible licentiousness revealed
itself to her in seductive garb.   The only thing she
looked upon with eyes of horror was virtue, and what
gave her the least trouble wes her reputation.   She
forgot her dignity, her birth, the natural modesty of
her sex, the fidelity she owed to her husband and to
her emperor, to give herself up brutally to her passions, without any care for decency, and without fear
of the fate of those whom she resembled.   Never was
such dissolution seen before.

She was the daughter of Valerius Messala Barbatus
and of Lepida who was accused of prostitution and of
sorcery, and of having had incestuous intercourse with
her brother Domitius Ahenobarbus.   It was this impure
spring that gave birth to a stream still more impure.
She was married to her cousin, the emperor Claudius.

Messalina had been gifted by nature with so violent a
tendency for lechery, that it was very difficult for her

to contain herself within the legitimate bounds of marriage, too limited for a heart burning with a thousand desires.

She had beauty and credit enough to attract lovers and too little virtue to let them long languish. The corruption of her temperament awakened her lubricity; the love of riches and of great inheritances excited her cruelty against those who were rich, so that debauchery and avarice were the two baneful things which underlay all the desires and all the actions of this infamous princess.

Messalina thought only of satisfying her passions; she made those who were virtuous enough to resist her shameful advances suffer from her cruelty. She accused those who would not consent to be her accomplices of crimes against the State, and the penalty of their resistance was death. In this way she caused her brother-in-law Silanus, who had repelled with horror all her offers, to be put to death . . . . and how many others!

Such extravagant lubricity would allow no limit to the crimes of this princess. Always athirst for pleasure, she was not satisfied with plunging brutally into the grossest and most infamous debauchery, but gave herself up to the first-comer, and sacrificed everything to her burning desires, without being ever able to gratify them to satiety. She wanted still to have companions and imitators of her prostitutions; and authority having great influence, she thought to diminish the horror of her infamies in associating in her crimes ladies belonging to the highest families in Rome, whom she forced to live with her in shameful libertinism.

Further, in order to carry her brutality to the last

point, she forced them to prostitute themselves to people
abandoned to debauchery in presence of their husbands,
whom she made the witnesses of their infamies and
often the accomplices and approvers of their crimes.

Juvenal sketched a fearful but sublime picture of the
libertinism of Messalina.

We beg permission to quote:—

EXTRACT FROM JUVENAL'S
SIXTH SATIRE.

Respice rivales Divorum: Claudius audi
Quæ tulerit. Dormire virum quum senserat uxor,
Ausa Palatino tegetem præferre cubili,
Sumere nocturnos meretrix augusta cucullos,
Linquebat, comite ancilla non amplius una;
Et nigrum flavo crinem abscondente galero,
Intravit calidum veteri centone lupanar,
Et cellam vacuam atque suam: tunc nuda papillis,
Prostitit auratis, titulum mentita Lyciscæ,
Ostenditque tuum, generose Britannice, ventrem.
Excepit blanda intrantes, atque æra poposcit,
Et resupina jacens multorum absorbuit ictus.
Mox, lenone suas jam dimittente puellas,
Tristis abit: sed quod potuit, tamen ultima cellam
Clausit, adhuc ardens rigidæ tentigine vulvæ,
Et lassata viris, sed non satiata recessit.
Obscurisque genis turpis, fumoque lucernæ
Fœda, lupanaris tulit ad pulvinar odorem.

Juvenal, Sat. vi. 115—132.

It is no easy task to render into English the vigour
of the original; for those unacquainted with Latin we
offer the following translation.

" Look at the rivals of the Gods: hear the treatment Claudius had to bear. Soon as ever his consort saw her husband was asleep, recklessly preferring a pallet to the Palace bed and donning the hood of night-walkers, the Imperial harlot would leave his side, accompanied by a single maid: [1] and hiding her dark hair under a yellow wimple, entered the reeking brothel with its patchwork quilts, and made for the chamber that stood vacant, her own. Then naked and with gilded nipples she took her stand for hire, under the feigned name of Lycisca, [2] and exposed the Βελλι that bore you, noble Germanicus, to all. She welcomed her visitors with a fawning smile, and asked for the fee, and throwing herself on her Βαχ drank in the Βλωζ of many lovers. Presently, when the whore-master dismissed his girls, reluctantly she left; but doing all she could to delay, was the last to close her chamber, still raging with the lust of a turgid womb; and retired, wearied with men, but unsatisfied. Then, with soiled face and darkling cheeks, and rank with the lamp's smoke, she carried the stench of the brothel to the Emperor's couch."

We append also Gifford's well-known metrical translation of the passage.

Turn to the rivals of the Immortal Powers,
And mark how like their fortunes are to ours.
Claudius had scarce begun his eyes to close,

[1] This confidante, according to Pliny (lib. VII), was one of the most famous prostitutes known in Rome; he adds that she even at times surpassed her mistress: *eamque die ac nocte superavit quinto et vicessimo concubitu.*

[2] The haunts of vice in Rome were divided into little cells, on the doors of which could be read the names of each of the courtesans who occupied them.

Ere from his side his Messalina rose;
(Accustom'd long the bed of state to slight,
For the rank mattress, and the hood of night;)
And with one maid, and her dark hair conceal'd
Beneath a yellow tire, a strumpet veil'd!
She slipt into the stews, unseen, unknown,
And hir'd a cell, yet reeking, for her own.
There flinging off her dress, the imperial whore
Stood with bare breasts, and gilded, at the door,
And shew'd, Britannicus, to all that came,
The womb that bore thee, in Lycisca's name:
Allur'd the passers by with many a wile,
And ask'd her price, and took it, with a smile.
And when the hour of business was expir'd,
And all the girls dismiss'd, with sighs retir'd;
Yet what she could, she did; slowly she past,
And saw her man, and shut her cell the last.
Still raging with the fever of desire,
Her veins all turgid, and her blood all fire,
Exhausted, but unsatisfied, she sought
Her home, and to the Emperor's pillow brought,
Cheeks rank with sweat, limbs drench'd with poison-
                                        ous dews,
The steam of lamps, and odour of the stews!

It is useless to insist further upon this woman who
carried impudicity to such a point that it would be
impossible, without shame, to write the entire history
of her obscenities. The few extracts that we have
given amply suffice to demonstrate the really morbid
character of her debaucheries.

Des Aberrations du Sens Génésique, Dr. Paul Moreau, Paris, 1880, 8vo., p. 30—33.

CHAPTER IX.

Differences between the organs of generation of the various races of Senegal.

Races of Senegal, their Genital Organs. So far as I was able to judge from a certain number of observations, although all the races of Senegal present common characteristics as to their genital organs, nevertheless certain differences may be found between them.

Amongst those people who have a Semitic origin, the yard is less developed when in a flaccid condition, and the difference when in a state of erection is more considerable, than in the Black of pure race, as the Wolof for instance. I have already said that there is an infiltration of Semitic blood amongst the Peulhs and Sarrakholais.

In the Peulh, the penis is relatively smaller than in the pure Black, but the testicles are more developed. In its shape, the yard much resembles that of the Mulatto. Moreover, there are Peulhs who differ little, as to general colour, from certain Mulattos. However, the ordinary hue of the body is a reddish brown, whilst that of the Mulatto is rather a yellow brown. The mucous surfaces of the lips, the gland, and the vulva, in the Peulh, are a little darker than in the half-breed between the White and the Black.

With the Sarrakholais, who, according to Dr. Lota,

are a cross between the Peulhs and the pure Black race, the male organ of generation is not sensibly smaller than that of the Wolof, and presents the same characteristic of being very large when it is flaccid. But as the Sarrakholais have a general tint of skin a reddish brown, similar to that of cooked chocolate, we find in them the mucous surface of the lips, the gland, and the vulva, to be a little lighter than that of the skin of the penis, and of a hue much resembling that of the Zambo of Guiana.

The other races,—the Wolofs, Kassonkés, Malinkés, Toucouleurs, Bambaras, etc.—present the common characteristic which is a type of the race,—that is to say that the penis is almost as large when flabby as it is in a state of erection, and the external mucous surfaces are of the same black colour as the skin. It was amongst the Malinkés of Kita, that I found the most developed penis, and notably the one of the maximum dimensions, being nearly twelve inches in length, by a diameter exceeding 2$\frac{3}{4}$ inches. This was a terrific machine, and except for a slight difference in length, was more like the yard of a donkey than that of a man.

PART THE FOURTH.—OCEANIA.

New Caledonia.

The New Hebrides—Tahiti.

CHAPTER I.

My stay in New Caledonia.—Anthropological characteristics of the Kanaka of New Caledonia.—The Kanaka "Popinée".—Degraded condition of the Popinée.—The genital organs of the Kanaka race.—Circumcision at the age of puberty.—Seclusion of girls at puberty.—"Hunting the Snake".—Beating as a means of purification.—Division of the Kanaka race into independent and hostile tribes.—The man's "manou".—Strange modesty of the Kanaka.—The girdle of the Popinée.—A few words about manners and customs.—The position of the Chief in the social state.—Habitations.—Food.—The Kanaka stove.—Beliefs and superstitions.—The wizard-doctor (Takata).—Prof. Frazer on "Killing the God".

My Stay in New Caledonia. I arrived in New Caledonia at the moment when the fierce insurrection of the natives, which commenced in 1878, had just finished. It had cost the Colony two years of war. Everyone remembered incidents of the struggle, and I collected a good deal of information from eye-witnesses whose evidence could be trusted.

In order, however, not to unduly lengthen this book, I will say nothing about the Europeans in New Caledonia, except the transported convicts, who have special and peculiar manners and customs.

Anthropological Characteristics of the New Caledonian Kanaka. New Caledonia was colonised by the Melanesian Negro in the first place, and afterwards received the accession of a superior race,— the Maoris. According to the greater or less infusion of Maori blood, which is different in the various tribes, the tint varies considerably, from a smoky black to chocolate, and to a dark Florentine bronze with coppery gleams. On the east coast, you more especially find tribes of a lighter colour. The Kanaka, therefore, is rather a Negro half-breed than a real Negro, and even when the colour of his skin is darkest, it is impossible to confound him with the Negro of Africa. In fact, his head differs notably from that of the African. It is asymmetric, the facial angle is wider, the forehead is open, high, narrow, and convex. The skull is flattened across, especially in the temporal region. It is covered with woolly hair, stiffer and less curly than that of the Negro, and which is often stubbly, which is never the case with the hair of the Negro. The eyes are widely open, but the conjunctiva is often injected with streaks of blood, which gives them a fierce expression. The cheek-bones are slightly projecting, the jaw prognathous. The lips are fairly thick, and are turned back, the mouth wide, the teeth very fine, and regular. The Kanaka has nearly always a moustache, and often a good sized beard, which is rarely the case with the African. The colour of the hair and beard is a dark black, but you often find men who have the hair and beard a fine coppery red as clear and bright as that of the European.

But, more especially, it is in the exactness of his proportions, and the regularity of form of his body, that the New Caledonian excels. The race is generally thin and supple; the obesity of the European never vulgarises and disfigures his shape. The arms and legs are not of a disproportionate length, as in the Negro. The muscles, which are hidden in the flesh during youth, assume a vigorous projection in virility; those of the arms are often as well developed as in a robust European; those of the thighs and legs are less so, but they are firm and nervous. The Kanaka is indefatigable on the march, especially if animated by pleasure, or passion.

The Kanaka Popinée. This is the name given in New Caledonia, to the fairest half of the human race, which in this country is incontestably the ugliest. In fact, there exists such a striking difference between the two sexes in respect to beauty, that one is almost inclined to wonder whether the male Kanaka has not the right to consider such a companion as much below him, or whether, on the other hand, it is the state of degradation in with the woman lives that has made her so ugly. The hair of the woman is short and frizzled, and is worn in a ball-shaped knob like the helmet of a Bavarian soldier. Whilst she is a young girl, the Popinée is worth looking at. The breasts, which are arch-shaped, are firm, and though she is generally slender, her form is fairly well rounded, and her skin soft. But this fleeting beauty lasts but for a flash, and the Popinée soon withers under the hard existence that savage life compels her to lead. The skin dries, the scars, with which she covers herself as a sign of mourning, render her repulsive, and mater-

nity completes the work Suckling greatly develops
the breast, which lengthens and falls naturally, although
the practice of sub-cutaneous incision is unknown to
her. The nipple of the breast is large and black.
When she no longer gives suck, the breast remains
flabby and wrinkled, and falls down like a she-goat's
udder. The belly shows several parallel wrinkles, and
the skin hangs down over the pubes, like an old
kitchen apron. An old Kanaka Popinée is an object
of disgust, whereas the maid, even when aged, always
retains a certain carriage. A young Kanaka of twenty,
on the contrary, is a magnificent specimen of the race,
and resembles an antique bronze.

Degradation of the Popinée. Every day, the
unfortunate Popinée works like a beast of burden.
She does all the work for the squad (I use this word
purposely) both in cultivation and war. On the march
she carries the provisions, the culinary utensils, the
tools. She marches on and on indefinitely, weighed
down by her burden; if she gets weak, a good blow with
the handle of a war club will restore her strength.
At night the she-donkey with four legs can sleep on
its litter, but the Popinée cannot. She must satisfy the
passions of the squad, and, even when she is pregnant,
this double work is hardly interrupted by child-birth.

The average height of the women is much inferior
to that of the men, and in this respect there is nearly
the proportion between the two sexes as in our own
race. The women suckle their children for a very long
time—from three to five years. The oppression under
which they groan, the hard work put upon them, and
the privations which are too often their lot, rapidly
wear out the strength of their constitution.

The Genital Organs of the Kanaka Race. The genital organs of the man are well-proportioned, but much less developed than those of the Negro. They resemble rather those of the South European, both as to shape and dimensions, whether flaccid or erect, though a little superior in size. The penis, when in erection, is from 5¾ to 7¼ inches in length by 1½ to 2 inches in diameter—rarely more. Once only did I find a penis of 7¾ inches. This size, on the contrary, is very frequent amongst the African Negroes. The average appeared to be 6¼ inches by 1⅘ inches. The testicles are as well developed in length as those of the European, but appeared to me to be a little flatter. In the colour of the mucous surface of the lips, the gland, and the vulva, the Kanaka also resembles the European. With those natives who have the skin of a smoky black colour, the mucous surfaces are never black, as they are in the Negro. It is of a fairly bright red, darkened by a touch of sepia. With those who have the skin the colour of Florentine bronze (they are almost pure Maoris) the mucous surface is of a bright red, toned down by light sienna,—almost the colour of red brick.

The reader must bear in mind that we must go back to the Quadroon (three quarters white), and should still find the mucous surfaces not so light and bright as in the Kanaka. I shall revert to this subject, when I compare the organ of the African Negro with that of the Melanesian Black of Australia. It may be said, that in the coloured man, a cross-breed between the White and the Black, the mucous surface of the gland is darker than the skin of the penis. With the Kanaka it is absolutely quite the contrary, who in this anthropological peculiarity resembles the South Italian,

the Sicilian for instance, who often has the skin of
the penis and the scrotum very brown, and the gland
bright red. The pubes is covered with a black and
curly fleece,—red, in individuals of that colour—and
fairly abundant.

Circumcision at Puberty. Usually, in the boy
before the age of puberty the foreskin is fairly long.
At the age of puberty, in certain tribes,—generally
speaking, those who have the darkest skin and who
live on the western coast (such as the Koné tribe)—
they make those boys who have phimosis, and whose
gland does not skin easily, undergo a sort of demi-
circumcision. The surgeon-sorcerer of the tribe splits
the upper part of the foreskin, with a piece of quartz,
sharpened and polished, down to the crown of the
gland, a length of about an inch.

This operation, which is much less painful than the
complete circumcision of the Negro, produces almost
the same effect, and the gland, even when in a flaccid
state, is completely freed. The foreskin thus divided
is tied up with *bourao* leaves, steeped in the juice of
certain herbs which the surgeon-sorcerer chews, and
which make it quickly heal, and draw it back behind
the gland. But when in erection, the foreskin that
has been operated upon in this way, sticks up in the
form of a comb, very much like the cut ears of a
terrier, forming an unpleasant looking projection above
the penis. This would be rather uncomfortable in
copulation, if the Kanakas were particular in their
pleasures. This pseudo-circumcision is simply a hygienic
measure, and nowise a religious custom. [1]

[1] Watermarck (see his work on Marriage), it is only right of me to
point out, thinks differently and quotes authorities on the tribes he

Seclusion of Girls at Puberty. While dealing with the customs pertaining to males prevalent amongst savage peoples on the arrival of the age of puberty, it may not be uninteresting to quote the curious remarks of Frazer regarding girls in whom also the signs of womanhood begin to appear. "Amongst the Zulus," this author says, "and kindred tribes of South Africa, when the first signs of puberty show themselves, while a girl is walking, gathering wood, or working in the field, she runs to the river and hides herself among the reeds for the day so as not to be seen by men. She covers her head carefully with her blanket that the sun may not shine on it and shrivel her up into a withered skeleton, assured result from exposure to the sun's beams. After dark she returns to her home and is secluded in a hut for some time." [1]

In New Ireland girls are confined for four or five years in small cages, being kept in the dark and not allowed to set foot on the ground. The custom has been thus described by an eye-witness. "I heard from a teacher about some strange custom connected with some of the young girls here, so I asked the chief to take me to the house where they were. The house was about twenty-five feet in length, and stood in a reed and bamboo enclosure, across the entrance to which a bundle of dried grass was suspended to show that it was strictly '*tabu*'. Inside the house were three

names. Of course, I do not deny that in the cases he cites hygiene is not the object of the operation; but notwithstanding, my observations hold good with regard to the Kanakas, amongst whom I have personally moved and have known perhaps with too *dangerous* intimacy not to be sure of my facts about them.

[1] Rev. James Macdonald (Reay Free Manse, Caithness), *Manners, Customs, Superstitions, and Religions of South African Tribes* (in manuscript).

conical structures about seven or eight feet in height,
and about ten or twelve feet in circumference at the
bottom, and for about four feet from the ground, at
which point they tapered off to a point at the top. These
cages were made of the broad leaves of the pandanus-
tree, sewn quite close together so that no light, and
little or no air, could enter. On one side of each is
an opening which is closed by a double door of plaited
cocoa-nut tree and pandanus-tree leaves. About three
feet from the ground there is a stage of bamboos
which forms the floor. In each of these cages we
were told there was a young woman confined, each
of whom had to remain for at least four or five years,
without ever being allowed to go outside the house.
I could scarcely credit the story when I heard it; the
whole thing seemed too horrible to be true. I spoke
to the chief, and told him that I wished to see the
inside of the cages, and also to see the girls that I
might make them a present of a few beads. He told
me that it was 'tabu,' forbidden tor any men but
their own relations to look at them; but I suppose the
promised beads acted as an inducement, and so he
sent away for some old lady who had charge, and who
alone is allowed to open the doors .... She had to undo
the door when the chief told her to do so, and then the
girls peeped out at us, and, when told to do so, they
held out their hands for the beads. I, however, purposely
sat at some distance away and merely held out the
beads to them, as I wished to draw them quite outside,
that I might inspect the inside of the cages. This
desire of mine gave rise to another difficulty, as these
girls were not allowed to put their feet to the ground all
the time they were confined in these places. However
they wished to get the beads, and so the old lady had

to go outside and collect a lot of pieces of wood and bamboo, which she placed on the ground, and then going to one of the girls, she helped her down and held her hand as she stepped from one piece of wood to another until she came near enough to get the beads I held out to her. I then went to inspect the inside of the cage out of which she had come, but could scarcely put my head inside of it, the atmosphere was so hot and stifling. It was clean and contained but a few short lengths of bamboo for holding water. There was only room for the girl to sit or lie down in a crouched position on the bamboo platform, and when the doors are shut it must be nearly or quite dark inside. The girls are never allowed to come out except once a day to bathe in a dish or wooden bowl placed close to each cage. They say that they perspire profusely. They are placed in these stifling cages when quite young, and must remain there until they are young women, when they are taken out and have each a great marriage feast provided for them." [1]

[1] The Rev. G. Brown, quoted by the Rev. B. Danks, "Marriage Customs of the New Britain Group," *Journ. Anthrop. Institute*, XVIII, 284 *sq.;* cp. Rev. G. Brown, "Notes on the Duke of York Group, New Britain and New Ireland," *Journ. Royal Geogr. Soc.*, XLVII (1877), p. 142 *sq.* Powell's description of the New Ireland custom is similar (*Wanderings in a Wild Country*, p. 249). According to him the girls wear wreaths of scented herbs round the waist and neck; an old woman or a little child occupies the lower floor of the cage: and the confinement lasts only a month. Probably the long period mentioned by Mr. Brown is that prescribed for chiefs' daughters. Poor people could not afford to keep their children so long idle. This distinction is sometimes expressly stated; for example, among the Goajiras of Colombia rich people keep their daughters shut up in separate huts of puberty for periods varying from one to four years, but poor people cannot afford to do so for more than a fortnight or a month. F. A. Simons, "An exploration of the Goajira Peninsula," *Proceed Royal*

In some parts of New Guinea " daughters of chiefs, when they are about twelve or thirteen years of age, are kept indoors for two or three years, never being allowed, under any pretence, to descend from the house, and the house is so shaded that the sun cannot shine on them." [1] Among the Ot Danoms of Borneo girls at the age of eight or ten years are shut up in a little room or cell of the house and cut off from all intercourse with the world for a long time. The cell, like the rest of the house, is raised on piles above the ground, and is lit by a single small window opening on a lonely place, so that the girl is in almost total darkness. They may not leave the room on any pretext whatever, not even for the most necessary purposes. None of her family may see her all the time she is shut up, but a single slave woman is appointed to wait on her. During her lonely confinement, which often lasts seven years, the girl occupies herself in weaving mats, or with other handiwork. Her bodily growth is stunted by the long want of exercise, and when, on attaining womanhood, she is brought out, her complexion is pale and wax-like. She is now shown the sun, the earth, the water, the trees, and the flowers, as if she were newly born. Then a great feast is made, a slave is killed, and the girl is smeared with his blood. [2] In Ceram girls at

Geogr. Soc. N. S. VII (1885), p. 791. In Fiji, brides who were being tattooed were kept from the sun. Williams, *Fiji and the Fijians*, I, 170. This was perhaps a modification of the Melanesian custom of secluding girls at puberty. The reason mentioned by Mr. Williams, " to improve her complexion," can hardly have been the original one.

[1] Chalmers and Gill, *Work and Adventure in New Guinea*, p. 159.

[2] Schwaner, *Borneo, Beschrijving van het stroomgebied van den Barito*, etc., II, 77 *sq.*; Zimmerman, *Die Inseln des Indischen und Stillen Meeres*, II, 632 *sq.*; Otto Finsch, *Neu Guinea und seine Bewohner*, p. 116.

puberty were formerly shut up by themselves in a hut which was kept dark. [1] Amongst the Aht Indians of Vancouver Island, when girls reach puberty they are placed in a sort of gallery in the house " and are there surrounded completely with mats, so that neither the sun nor any fire can be seen. In this cage they remain for several days. Water is given them, but no food. The longer a girl remains in this retirement the greater honour is it to the parents; but she is disgraced for life if. it is known that she has seen fire or the sun during this initiatory ordeal." [2] Amongst the Thlinkeet or Kolosh Indians of Alaska, when a girl shows signs of womanhood she is shut up in a little hut or cage, which is completely blocked up with the exception of a small air-hole. In this dark and filthy abode she had formerly to remain a year, without fire, exercise, or associates. Her food was put in at the small window; she had to drink out of the wing-bone of a white-headed eagle. The time has now been reduced, at least in some places, to six months. The girl has to wear a sort of hat with long flaps, that her gaze may not pollute the sky; for she is thought unfit for the sun to shine upon. [3] Amongst the

[1] Riedel, *De sluik- en kroesharige rassen tusschen Selebes en Papua*, p. 138.

[2] Sproat, *Scenes and Studies of Savage Life*, p. 93 *sq.*

[3] Erman, "Etnographische Wahrnehmungen u. Erfahrungen an den Küsten des Behrings-Meeres," *Zeitschrift f. Ethnologie*, II, 318 *sq.;* Langsdorff, "Reise um die Welt," II, 114 *sq.;* Holmberg, "Ethnogr. Skizzen über die Völker d. russischen Amerika," *Acta Societatis Scientiarum Fennicae*, IV (1856), p. 320 *sq.;* Bancroft, *Native Races of the Pacific States*, I, 110 *sq.;* Krause, *Die Tlinkit-Indianer*, p. 217 *sq.;* Rev. Sheldon Jackson, "Alaska and its Inhabitants," *American Antiquarian*, II, 111 *sq.* W. M. Grant, in *Journal of American Folk-Lore*, I, 169. For caps, hoods, and veils, worn by girls at such seasons,

Koniags, an Esquimaux people of Alaska, girls at
puberty were placed in small huts in which they had
to remain on their hands and knees for six months;
then the hut was enlarged enough to let them kneel
upright, and they had to remain in this posture for six
months more.[1] When symptoms of puberty appeared on
a girl for the first time, the Indians of the Rio de la Plata
used to sew her up in her hammock as if she were
dead, leaving only a small hole for her mouth to allow
her to breathe. In this state she continued so long as
the symptoms lasted.[2]

Hunting the Snake. In similar circumstances the
Chiriguanos of Bolivia hoisted the girl in her hammock
to the roof, where she stayed for a month; the second
month the hammock was let half way down from the
roof; and in the third month old women, armed with
sticks, entered the hut and ran about striking everything
they met, saying they were hunting the snake that
had wounded the girl. This they did till one of the
women gave out that she had killed the snake.[3]
Amongst some of the Brazilian Indians, when a girl
attained to puberty, her hair was burned or shaved off
close to the head. Then she was placed on a flat stone
and cut with the tooth of an animal from the shoulders

compare G. H. Loskiel, *History of the Mission of the United Brethren
among the Indians*, I, 56; *Journal Anthrop. Institute*, VII, 206; G.
M. Dawson, *Report of the Queen Charlotte Islands*, 1878 (Geological
Survey of Canada), p. 130B; Petitot, *Monographie des Déné-Dindjié*,
pp. 72, 75; *id.*, *Traditions indiennes du Canada Nord-Ouest*, p. 258.

[1] Holmberg; Bancroft, I, 82; Petroff, *Report on the Population, etc.
of Alaska*, p. 143.

[2] Lafiteau, *Mœurs des Sauvages Américains*, I, 262 sq.

[3] *Lettres édifiantes et curieuses*, VIII, 333. On the Chiriguanos
see Von Martius, *Zur Ethnographie Amerika's zumal Brasiliens*, p.
212 sq.

all down the back, till she ran with blood. Then the ashes of a wild gourd were rubbed into the wounds; the girl was bound hand and foot, and hung in a hammock, being enveloped in it so closely that no one could see her. Here she had to stay for three days without eating or drinking. When the three days were over, she stepped out of the hammock upon the flat stone, for her feet might not touch the ground. If she had a call of nature, a female relation took the girl on her back and carried her out, taking with her a live coal to prevent evil influences from entering the girl's body. Being replaced in her hammock she was now allowed to get some flour, boiled roots, and water, but might not taste salt or flesh. Thus she continued to the end of the first monthly period, at the expiry of which she was gashed on the breast and belly as well as all down the back. During the second month she still stayed in her hammock, but her rule of abstinence was less rigid, and she was allowed to spin. The third month she was blackened with a certain pigment and began to go about as usual. [1] Amongst the Macusis of British Guiana, when a girl shows the first signs of puberty, she is hung in a hammock at the highest point of the hut. For the first few days she may not leave the hammock by day, but at night she must come down, light a fire, and spend the night beside it, else she would break out in sores on her neck, throat, etc. So long as the symptoms are at their height, she must fast rigorously. When they have abated, she may come down and take up her abode in a little compartment that is made for her in the darkest corner of the hut. In the morning she may cook her food, but it must be at a separate fire and in a vessel of her own. In

[1] Thevet, *Cosmographie universelle* (Paris, 1575), II, 946B *sq.*; Lafiteau.

about ten days the magician comes and undoes the spell by muttering charms and breathing on her and on the more valuable of the things with which she has come in contact. The pots and drinking vessels which she used are broken and the fragments buried. After her first bath, the girl must submit to be beaten by her mother with thin rods without uttering a cry. At the end of the second period she is again beaten, but not afterwards. She is now " clean," and can mix again with people. [1] Other Indians of Guiana, after keeping the girl in her hammock at the top of the hut for a month, expose her to certain large ants, whose bite is very painful. [2]

Beating as a Means of Purification. The custom of stinging the girl with ants or beating her with rods is intended, we may be sure, not as a punishment or a test of endurance, but as a purification, the object being to drive away the malignant influences with which a girl at such times is believed to be beset and enveloped. Examples of purification, both by beating and by stinging with ants, have already come before us. [3] Probably, beating or scourging as a religious or ceremonial rite always originated with a similar intention. It was meant to wipe off and drive away a dangerous contagion (whether personified as demoniacal or not) which was supposed to be adhering physically, though invisibly, to the body of the sufferer. [4]

[1] Schomburgk, *Reisen in British Guiana*, II, 315 *sq.*; Martius, *Zur Ethnographie Amerika's*, p. 644.

[2] Labat, *Voyage du Chevalier des Marchais en Guinée, Iles voisines et à Cayenne;* IV, 365 *sq.* (Paris ed.), p. 17 *sq.* (Amsterdam ed.)

[3] Above, p. 213 *sq.* vol. I, p. 153 *sq.*

[4] This interpretation of the custom is supported by the fact that beating or scourging is inflicted on inanimate objects expressly for the

The pain inflicted on the person beaten was no more
the object of the beating than it is of a surgical
purpose indicated in the text. Thus the Indians of Costa Rica hold
that there are two kinds of ceremonial uncleanness, *nya* and *bu-ku-rù*.
Anything that has been connected with a death is *nya*. But *bu-ku-rù*
is much more virulent. It can not only make one sick but kill. "The
worst *bu-ku-rù* of all is that of a young woman in her first pregnancy.
She infects the whole neighbourhood. Persons going from the house
where she lives carry the infection with them to a distance, and all
the deaths or other serious misfortunes in the vicinity are laid to her
charge. In the old times, when the savage laws and customs were in
full force, it was not an uncommon thing for the husband of such a
woman to pay damages for casualities thus caused by his unfortunate
wife. *Bu-ku-rù* emanates in a variety of ways; arms, utensils, even
houses become affected by it after long disuse, and before they can be
used again must be purified. In the case of portable objects left un-
disturbed for a long time, the custom is to beat them with a stick
before touching them. I have seen a woman take a long walking,
stick and beat a basket hanging from the roof of a house by a cord.
On asking what that was for, I was told that the basket contained
her treasures, that she would probably want to take something out the
next day, and that she was driving off the *bu-ku-rù*. A house long
unused must be swept, and then the person who is purifying it must
take a stick and beat not only the movable objects, but the beds, posts,
and in short every accessible part of the interior. The next day it is
fit for occupation. A place not visited for a long time, or reached for
the first time, is *bu-ku-rù*. On our return from the ascent of Pico
Blanco, nearly all the party suffered from little calenturas, the result of
extraordinary exposure to wet and cold and want of food. The Indians
said that the peak was especially *bu-ku-rù*, since nobody had ever been
on it before." One day Mr. Gabb took down some dusty blow-guns
amid cries of *bu-ku-rù* from the Indians. Some weeks afterwards a body
died, and the Indians firmly believed that the *bu-ku-rù* of the blow-
guns had killed him. "From all the foregoing, it would seem that
bu-ku-rù is a sort of evil spirit that takes possession of the object, and
resents being disturbed; but I have never been able to learn from the
Indians that they considered it so. They seem to think of it as a
property the objects acquire." W. M. Gabb, *Indian Tribes and
Languages of Costa Rica* (read before the American Philosophical
Society, 20th August, 1875), p. 504 *sq.*

operation with us; it was a necessary accident, that was all. In later times such customs were interpreted otherwise, and the pain, from being an accident, became the prime object of the ceremony, which was now regarded either as a test of endurance imposed upon persons at critical epochs of life, or as a mortification of the flesh well pleasing to the god. But asceticism, under any shape or form, is never primitive. Amongst the Haupes of Brazil a girl at puberty is secluded in the house for a month, and allowed only a small quantity of bread and water. Then she is taken out into the midst of her relations and friends, each of whom gives her four or five blows with pieces of *sipo* (an elastic climber), till she falls senseless or dead. If she recovers, the operation is repeated four times at intervals of six hours, and it is considered an offence to the parents not to strike hard. Meantime, pots of meats and fish have been made ready; the *sipos* are dipped into them and then given to the girl to lick, who is now considered a marriageable woman.[1]

When a Hindoo maiden reaches maturity she is kept in a dark room for four days, and is forbidden to see the sun. She is regarded as unclean; no one is allowed to touch her. Her diet is restricted to boiled rice, milk, sugar, curd, and tamarind without salt. [2] In

---

[1] A. R. Wallace, *Narrative of Travels on the Amazon and Rio Negro*, p. 496.

[2] Bose, *The Hindoos as they are*, p. 86. Similarly, after a Brahman boy has been invested with the sacred thread, he is for three days strictly forbidden to see the sun. He may not eat salt, and he is enjoined to sleep either on a carpet or a deer's skin, without a mattress, or mosquito curtain. *Ib.* p. 186. In Bali, boys who have had their teeth filed, as a preliminary to marriage, are kept up in a dark room for three days. Van Eck, "Schetsen van het eiland Bali," Tijdschrift voor Nederlandsch Indië, N. S. IX (1880), 428 *sq.*

Cambodia a girl at puberty is put to bed under a mosquito curtain, where she should stay a hundred days. Usually, however, four, five, ten, or twenty days are thought enough; and even this, in a hot climate and under the close meshes of the curtain, is sufficiently trying. [1] According to another account, a Cambodian maiden at puberty is said to "enter into the shade." During her retirement, which, according to the rank and position of her family, may last any time from a few days to several years, she has to observe a number of rules, such as not to be seen by a strange man, not to eat flesh or fish, and so on. She goes nowhere, not even to the pagoda. But this state of retirement is discontinued during eclipses; at such times she goes forth and pays her devotions to the monster who is supposed to cause eclipses by catching the heavenly bodies between his teeth. [2] The fact that her retirement is discontinued during an eclipse seems to show how literally the injunction is interpreted which forbids maidens entering on womanhood to look upon the sun.

Woman during the Menstrual Period. Mr. Frazer has gone deeply into this subject and quotes a mass of authorities to prove that the ground of this seclusion of girls at puberty lies in the deeply engrained dread which primitive man universally entertains of menstruous blood. Evidence of this has already been adduced, but a few more facts may here be added. Amongst the Australian blacks "the boys are told from their infancy that, if they see the blood, they

[1] Moura, *Royaume du Cambodge*, I, 377.

[2] Aymonier, "Notes sur les coutumes et croyances superstitieuses des Cambodgiens," *Cochinchine Française, Excursions et Reconnaissances*, No. 16 (Saïgon, 1883), p. 193 *sq.* Cp. *id. Notice sur le Cambodge*, p. 50.

will early become gray-headed, and their strength will fail prematurely." Hence a woman lives apart at these times; and if a young man or boy approaches her she calls out, and he immediately makes a circuit to avoid her. The men go out of their way to avoid even crossing the tracks made by women at such times. Similarly the woman may not walk on any path frequented by men, nor touch anything used by men; she may not eat fish, or go near water at all, much less cross it; for if she did, the fish would be frightened, and the fishers would have no luck; she may not even fetch water for the camp; it is sufficient for her to say *Thama* to ensure her husband fetching the water himself. A severe beating, or even death, is the punishment inflicted on an Australian woman who breaks these rules. [1]   The Bushmen think that, by a glance of a girl's eye at the time when she ought to be kept in strict retirement, men become fixed in whatever position they happen to occupy, with whatever they were holding in their hands, and are changed into trees which talk. [2]

" The Guayquiries of the Orinoco think that, when a woman has her courses, everything upon which she steps will die, and that if a man treads on the place where she has passed, his legs will immediately swell up. [3] The Creek and kindred Indians of the United States compelled women at menstruation to live in separate huts at some distance from the village.   There

[1] *Native Tribes of South Australia*, p. 186; E. J. Eyre, *Journals*, II, 295, 304; W. Ridley, *Kamilaroi*, p. 157; *Journ. Anthrop. Inst.* II, 268, IX, 459 *sq.;* Brough Smyth, *Aborigines of Victoria*, I, 65, 236. Cp. Sir George Grey, *Journals*, II, 344; J. Dawson, *Australian Aborigines*, 101 *sq.*

[2] Bleek, *Brief Account of Bushman Folk-lore*, p. 14; cp. *ib.* p. 10.

[3] Gumilla, *Histoire de l'Orénoque*, I, 249.

the women had to stay, at the risk of being surprised and cut off by enemies. It was thought 'a most horrid and dangerous pollution' to go near the women at such times; and the danger extended to enemies who, if they slew the women, had to cleanse themselves from the pollution by means of certain sacred herbs and roots. [1] Similarly, among the Chippeways and other Indians of the Hudson Bay Territory, women at such seasons are excluded from the camp, and take up their abode in huts of branches. They wear long hoods, which effectually conceal the head and breast. They may not touch the household furniture nor any objects used by men; for their touch 'is supposed to defile them, so that their subsequent use would be followed by certain mischief or misfortune,' such as disease or death. They may not walk on the common paths nor cross the tracks of animals. They 'are never permitted to walk on the ice of rivers or lakes, or near the part where the men are hunting beaver, or where a fishing-net is set, for fear of averting their success. They are also prohibited at those times from partaking of the head of any animal, and even from walking in or crossing the track where the head of a deer, moose, beaver, and many other animals have lately been carried, either on a sledge or on the back. To be guilty of a violation of this custom is considered as of the greatest importance; because they firmly believe that it would be a means of preventing the hunter from having an equal success in his future excursions.' [2] So the Lapps forbid women at men-

---

[1] James Adair, *History of the American Indians*, p. 123 *sq.*

[2] S. Hearne, *Journey to the Northern Ocean*, p. 314 *sq.;* Alex. Mackenzie, *Voyages through the Continent of North America*, CXXIII; Petitot, *Monographie des Déné-Dindjié*, p. 75 *sq.*

struation to walk on that part of the shore where the fishers are in the habit of setting out their fish. [1]

" Amongst the civilised nations of Europe the superstitions which have prevailed on this subject are not less extravagant. In the oldest existing cyclopædia — the *Natural History* of Pliny—the list of dangers apprehended from menstruation is longer than any furnished by savages. According to Pliny, the touch of a menstruous woman turned wine to vinegar, blighted crops, killed seedlings, blasted gardens, brought down the fruit from trees, dimmed mirrors, blunted razors, rusted iron and brass (especially at the waning of the moon), killed bees, or at least drove them from their hives, caused mares to miscarry, and so forth. [2] Similarly, in various parts of Europe, it is still believed that if a woman in her courses enters a brewery the beer will turn sour; if she touches beer, wine, vinegar, or milk, it will go bad; if she makes jam, it will not keep; if she mounts a mare, it will miscarry; if she touches buds, they will wither; if she climbs a cherry-tree, it will die. [3]

[1] C. Lemius, *De Lapponibus Finmarchiae eorumque lingua vita et religione pristina* (Copenhagen, 1767), p. 494.

[2] Pliny, *Nat. Hist.* VII, § 64 *sq.;* XXVIII, § 77 *sqq.* Cp. *Geoponica*, XII, C. 20, 5 and 25, 2; Columella, XI, 3, 50.

[3] A. Schleicher, *Volkstümliches aus Sonnenberg*, p. 134; B. Souché, *Croyances, Présages et Traditions diverses*, p. 11; V. Fossel, *Volkmedicin und medicinischer Aberglaube in Steiermark* (Graz, 1886), p. 124. The Greeks and Romans thought that a field was completely protected against insects if a menstruous woman walked round it with bare feet and streaming hair. Pliny, *Nat. Hist.* XVII, 266; XXVIII, 78; Columella, X, 358 *sq.;* XI, 3, 64; Palladius, *De re rustica*, i, 35 3; *Geoponica*, XII, 8, 5 *sq.;* Aelian, *Nat. Anim.* VI, 36. A similar remedy is employed for the same purpose by North American Indians and European peasants. Schoolcraft, *Indian Tribes*, v. 70; Wiedemann. *Aus dem inneren und äussern Leben der Ehoten*, p. 484. Cp. Hal-

Division of the Kanaka Race into Independent and Hostile Tribes. The peopling of the island by successive immigrations of the Black, coming from the West, and the Maori, from the East; the elongated shape of the island, which resembles a chain of mountains emerged from the sea, and separating completely the East and West coasts; the division of the basins of the rivers by numerous lesser chains of mountains, very difficult of access, all concur to separate the New Caledonian race into a number of tribes, which are often enemies to each other. Nevertheless, the root of the language is common, and so are the manners and customs. A tribe consists of villages, the chiefs of which depend on the chief of the tribe;—an organised feudalism, like the clans of old Scotland.

The Man's "Manou." The costume of the Kanakas is of primitive simplicity. The man wears on his head a handkerchief, tied into a turban by means of his sling, and often ornamented with feathers, or plants. He ornaments his body with necklaces of shark skin, and bracelets of shells on his arms and legs. The lobe of the ear is often pearced with a hole, in which is inserted a round piece of wood, as big as an ordinary cork. The belly is tied round with a girdle of leather and cord, and the acme of "high life" is to have the chest smeared with a mixture of lard and cocoa-nut oil. But the real costume of the Kanaka is the *manou*, an article of clothing of a bright colour, generally red. This is what the *manou* is. Some Parisian play-wright has made a naval officer, supposed to have returned from New Caledonia, say, that with a pair of gloves you can clothe ten Kanakas. The fingers of the gloves would have to be of extra size if so. Another witty "boulevardier" says, that a Kanaka much resembles a gentleman in evening dress, for both wear a *tail* coat. I ask the reader's pardon for inserting this joke.

This solitary article of dress is called the *manou* which the Frenchman has translated by the word *moineau*. To manufacture his *manou* the Kanaka takes a cotton handkerchief of some bright colour, rolls it, twists it round his yard, so that it makes a comic looking hood the point of which falls to the knee, then he passes the two opposite ends under his testicles and fastens them on the pubes, at the root of his penis. The singular effect that this strange costume gives, when it is seen for the first time, may be easily imagined. One soon gets used to it however, even European ladies. In the jumps and bounds, which the Kanaka makes in dancing the *pilou-pilou*, his national dance, the manou waggles about like the clapper of a bell, which has an irresistibly comic effect. When two chiefs meet, it is considered a mark of courtesy and good taste to exchange *manous* with each other. It would be a serious insult to a Kanaka to lay hold of the end of his *manou* and unroll it; you would stand a good chance of getting a rap on the head from his club. I found it very difficult to persuade a Kanaka to take off his *manou*, and show me his genital organs. He would never do so in public, but only in a hut, and when free from observation. He even carries his scruples to such an extent that he is shocked at seeing a European bathe stark naked. I experienced this myself. One fine morning, I wanted to take a bath in the Thio, and as I was alone, and there was no policeman to summon me for indecent exposure, I jumped into the water in the

costume of Father Adam When I came out, I found
that some Kanakas had assembled on the shore whilst
I was taking my bath. They were extremely shocked
at my nakedness, and pointed at me, and made fun
of me.

One of the Missionary Fathers told me the following,
which he declared to be true. Some sailors were
bathing, quite naked, near a village, without suspecting that they were scandalising the villagers. Suddenly they all began to cry out, for each man felt
himself caught hold of by the genital parts. Some
Kanaka divers were trying to put caps, made of leaves
rolled up, over the members of the men.

Strange Modesty of the Kanaka. The Kanaka
carries his prudery even further. The civilised European makes water against a wall, and often hardly
hides himself, when there is no urinal at hand, but I
have never seen a Kanaka make water in public. He
hides himself, and crouches down behind a bush or a
hut, before he takes off his *manou*, which of course
would interfere with the operation. In this respect
the Kanaka can give the Englishman points.

Our distinguished friend Letourneau, the professional
anthropologist, has made a careful study of the strangely
different ideas prevalent amongst various races on the
subject of modesty, and his remarks are so apposite
that we take leave to quote them: " Throughout
Polynesia, " he says, " nudity was formerly the fashion.
Tasmanians and Polynesians would, if necessary, cast
a mantle of Kanguru skins over their shoulders, but
it was solely on account of the cold, or as a protection against thorny briars. The women did not even
dream of modesty, and one must be affected with the

monomania of the human race to find any intention
of decency in the custom of the Tasmanian women,
when squatting down, to bring up one or both their
feet so as to cover their nudity. [1]

"It often happens that European travellers, particularly missionaries, who are prone to attribute to inferior
races all or a part of their own ideas on decency,
have seen an intention of modesty in mere rudiments
of clothing, used only for purposes of protection. The
strings and bit of bark of the Neo-Caledonians and
of the Mallicollo islanders, the shells worn by the latter
do not in any way reveal a moral intention; [2] the
part they play is that of a special armour destined to
protect delicate organs.

"In New Caledonia (the Isle of Pines), the missionaries
provoked violent protests, when they raised the preten-
sion to make the girls wear the girdles of married
women, and these latter energetically claimed their
rights. [3]

"The Polynesian women, always very lightly clad,
would undress, without thought of evil, on the slightest
motive and invariably when they went to bathe. In
the Sandwich Islands, the native ladies, already somewhat touched by European civilisation, used to swim
stark naked towards the ships, bearing on their heads
their silk dresses, their shoes and stockings and their
parasols, wherewith to deck themselves out when they
got on board. [4]

"The perfect absence of scruples, with which the

[1] Labillardière, quoted by Bonwick (*Daily Life*, etc., p. 58).

[2] Cook's *Voyage round the world.*—De Rochas, *Nouvelle Calédonie*,
p. 153.—D'Entrecasteaux, *Hist. Univ. des Voyages*, t. XV, p. 56.

[3] De Rochas, *loc. cit.* p. 153.

[4] Beechey, *Hist. Univ. des Voyages*, t. XIX, p. 374.

Polynesians considered what we call *par excellence* 'morals', gave rise to incidents most singular to Europeans. During a passage of one of Cook's boats between the islands, a Tahitian lady of high rank wanted to convince herself *de visu*, that Englishmen were, in every way, made like the men of her own country, and that, out of pure curiosity. [1] On another occasion, a missionary was forced to hurry back to the ship that had brought him: the islanders, being quite unable to understand his continence, had imagined that he had some sort of malformation and had endeavoured to assure themselves of the fact. With slight variations, similar customs may also be observed elsewhere than in the Pacific Ocean. In general, primitive men are strangers to any trouble about decency. For instance, the most savage of the American Indians, the Fuegians, [2] the Californians, [3] satisfied their necessities at the very place where they happened to be at the moment, and without taking heed of their neighbours.

"In 1498, at Trinity Island, Christopher Columbus found the women entirely naked, whereas the men wore a light girdle called *guayaco*. At the same epoch, on the Para Coast, the girls were distinguished from the married women by their absolute nudity. The same absence of costume was observed among the Chaymas, [4] and Du Chaillu noticed the same among the Achiras on the West coast of Africa. [5] It is besides well known how very primitive is the female

[1] Cook, *Second Voyage round the world.*
[2] L'Hermitte, *Hist. Univ. des Voyages*, t. VII, p. 435.
[3] La Perouse, *Hist. Univ. des Voyages*, t. XII, p. 194.
[4] Humboldt, *Hist. Univ. d. Voy.*, t. XXXVIII, p. 362.
[5] Du Chaillu, *Journey in equatorial Africa*, p. 466.

costume throughout Black Africa. That of the men
is often still more so. Sometimes it is entirely absent,
as Schweinfurth relates in the notes of his travels,
that the Dinkas glorified in their complete nudity, and
contemptuously called the traveller 'the Turkish lady'
on account of his attire. [1]

"I will here cease this enumeration, which might be
much longer. In making it my object was in no wise
to group strange facts shocking to our European ideas
of modesty. My object was only to shed a light upon
these primitive customs, which surely were those of
our former ancestors.

"But from these facts some general ideas may be
deduced, very important for the study of the origin
of morals.

"The animal kingdom altogether ignores modesty,
and yet love, considered as an exclusive sentiment,
does not seem to be foreign to all animals. The
delicacy with which the males of certain species of
birds court and love their females, is such as to bring
shame not only to savage humanity but to many
so-called civilised peoples. To the Illinois parrakeet
(*Psittacus pertinax*), widowhood and death are synonymous; but even, when these monogamists are constant,
these animals ignore modesty. Why therefore, and
how is it, that this sentiment plays so considerable a
part in the morality of the superior races? Montaigne
put the same question to himself when he wrote
as follows: 'What has the genital act, so natural, so
necessary and so just, done to men, that it may not
be mentioned without shame and is to be excluded from
serious and regulated language? We boldly say *kill*,

[1] Schweinfurth, *The Heart of Africa*, p. 152.

rob and *betray*, and dare speak of the other only between our teeth.' (Livre III, chap. V).

"This is one of those questions of psychological evolution, which comparative ethnography alone can clear up.

"First of all the primitive man makes no moral distinction between the different wants which solicit him, between hunger and love; he does not discuss either of them, and modesty is quite as unknown to him as it is to beasts. But, among these latter, even an exclusive choice does not engender the sentiment of modesty. It is that this sentiment is the result of two combined causes: selection and life in society. It is not delicacy of sentiment, it is the brutal egotism of the primitive man that has, quite involuntarily, determined the genesis of decency and of sexual morality. The first seeds of these high sentiments were sown when men, liberating themselves from the primitive promiscuity, began to consider women as private property. The chief began by reserving this property to himself, protecting it as well as he could from the enterprises of other men, and more particularly severely punishing the least slip of his wife or wives, of course without subjecting himself to any restriction whatever. Little by little, thanks to these brutal prohibitions, there began to germ in the female mind a certain sentiment of conjugal duty, of sexual reserve, a care to veil her person more or less, and this sentiment ended in being transmitted hereditarily.

"In this connection, Polynesia is still a precious field for observation. In the islands, where, as at Tahiti, the sexual liberty was pretty nearly unlimited, the married women even being themselves let out or lent by their husbands with the greatest facility, all modesty

was unknown.   In New Zealand, on the contrary, where
the owners of women were more jealous of their rights,
they almost invariably punished with death the woman
guilty of unauthorised adultery, which they authorised
but with difficulty, the women were relatively decent.
Even when swimming, or during their sleep, they used to
keep on them their girdles of *phormium tenax* which
encircled their waists. [1]

    " Before giving themselves to Europeans, they usually
required the consent of their family or of their husband
and, after having obtained this consent, in consideration
of a proper present, it was still necessary to negotiate
with them. [2]

    " Some of them also became attached to their European
lovers and remained faithful to them. [3]   The men did

[1] Duperrey, *Hist. Univ. des Voy.*, t. XVIII, p. 152.
[2] Cook's " First Voyage round the World."
[3] *Editor's note.*—One of our contributors, Mr. Costello, communicates
the following:—" In 1843 a cousin of mine was acting as surgeon on
board one of H.M. ships which anchored off New Zealand to overhaul
and repair.   The islands were then almost entirely possessed by the
Maoris, and one of the chiefs, who had met with an accident, sent on
board to ask for a surgeon.   My cousin, a handsome young Irishman,
was sent ashore, where he remained several weeks, saying that he had
many other patients, and only occasionally visited the ship.   The fact
was that our inflammable Hibernian had been captivated by the charms
of the chief's lovely daughter ; a sort of marriage ceremony was performed,
the enamoured doctor promising to remain with the Maoris and be their
' Medicine-man.'   The ship was, however, now ready to sail, and the
Captain sent an order to the surgeon to come on board at once.   Instead of obeying he ran away to the woods with his Maori wife.   This,
however, was of little avail ; an armed party of seamen discovered his
retreat and brought him forcibly to the ship, the girl following and
lamenting behind.   As the ship began to move, she could be seen
from the deck, as standing on the shore, with a sharp shell she cruelly
cut and lacerated her face, so that no other man should ever afterwards
take a fancy to her.—Later, a whaler which came to the same place,

not consider it at all immoral to lend or to let out their wives; it was the right of the proprietor of the thing possessed, but already a certain jealousy held them back. In order to test how far their scruples went with regard to conjugal faith, as we read in the relation of Dumont d'Urville, Mr. Gaimard made all sorts of offers to a chief in order to obtain the favours of his wife, but this *rangatira* was deaf to all these seductions, even to the offer of an ordinary gun, simply replying each time: *taboo* (sacred or forbidden). But when the doctor came to offer him in, in joke, a double-barrelled gun, the savage chief, incapable of resisting so seductive an offer, merely answered by pushing his wife into the arms of the stranger, at the same time extending his other hand for the gun." [1]

The Woman's Girdle. The costume of the women is as rudimentary as that of the men. It consists merely of a girdle, which encircles the hips, and hardly hides the buttocks.

A Few Words concerning Manners and Customs. I shall deal very briefly with all that does not concern sexual passion.

The Chief's Place in the Social State. The Chief of the tribe is an omnipotent ruler,—a monarch by divine right and by heredity. Salic law prevails throughout the entire island. The Chief is a kind of god,—a fetish. Men bow down at his approach. Women are even still more unworthy to gaze upon

ascertained that the poor thing did not long survive, but had died of a broken heart."

[1] *Voyage de* l'Astrolabe, p. 171.

his venerated face. To present themselves before him,
they commence, when they are quite a hundred yards
distant, to go on all fours, and to complete the resemblance to an animal, they fasten to their girdle a
bundle of tow, which hangs down behind like a horse's
tail.

The Chief has a kind of supreme council, composed
of the most renowned warriors, and the most prudent
and experienced old men. Peace and war are decided
by this council; cultivation and the harvests are in
common. The Great Chief by divine right has a sort
of Mayor of the Palace, who is called the War Chief;
he trains the warriors to military tactics, and leads
them to combat, whilst the Great Chief prudently
remains within his tent, far remote from blows. On
the death of the Great Chief, everyone in the tribe
assumes mourning, which, for the women, consists in
whitening the upper part of the body with chalk, and
painting the face black, with a white streak at the
corner of the nose, and the eyebrows painted white.
As may be imagined, this funeral masquerade makes
the young women ugly, and renders the old Popinées
horrible. Before the French occupation, the fattest
wives of the deceased Chief were knocked on the head
with a club, and eaten at a funereal *pilou-pilou* performed in his honour.

Habitations. The Kanaka hut is of the shape of
a bee-hive, with a low and narrow door for the only
opening. In the centre of this hive, a fire burns
incessantly, and on it is thrown the refuse of the cocoa-
nut tree, to drive out the mosquitoes, which are the
curse of the country. No European can remain in
one of these huts, on account of the vermin and the

stench. The Chief's hut is higher than the others, as is also the hut of the Council of the Old Men. On the top is placed a fetish, a man or a woman, roughly carved, and with the genital parts out of all proportion. The whole is crowned by an immense weathercock, with an arrow fifteen or twenty feet long, and a star, the symbol of the Chief's power.

Food. The food of the New Caledonian is almost exclusively vegetable (taro, yams, patatas, and fruits). The coast tribes also eat fish, which is an important addition to their diet. Before the arrival of the Europeans,—with the exception of some birds, a large bat, the rat, and the dog,—there were no animals. The introduction of pigs and poultry has been a great benefit to the Kanakas, for these animals require hardly any care.

The Kanaka Stove. To roast a fish or a pig, the Kanaka requires neither spit, meat screen, nor stove. The savage cook lights a large fire, and makes red hot therein some large stones; then digs an oval hole in the ground, the size of the joint, and puts in the bottom the hot stones. On these hot stones he places the fish or pig, well wrapped up, with spices inserted, in banana leaves. Above this he puts some leaves of the *miaouli*, previously damped; then covers the whole with earth, and lets the meat cook in this concentrated heat. The steam mingles with the acrid aroma of the *miaouli*,—which is much like the laurel tree,—and the joint has a delicious flavour. That is how the cannibal cooks his dinner.

Beliefs and Superstitions. The Kanaka has a

vague idea of the immortality of the soul, which will survive the body, and depart into another world,—a veritable Mohammedan paradise, where it will dance interminable *pilou-pilous*, stuff itself with yams, and everyone will have as many women as he wants.

He believes also in the ghosts or manes of his ancestors and others,— strange beings who interfere for good or evil in this world, and are the cause of favourable or unfavourable events. Amongst these spirits of the dead, those of the chiefs have the greatest power, and public prayers are addressed to them, to cause a good crop of yams, or a good haul of fish. As may be guessed, the authority of a Chief is therefore never questioned by his subjects.

The Wizard-doctor (Takata). The *Takata* is at once wizard, physician, and the buffoon of the Chief, whom he amuses. He is the interpreter of the spirits. to whom he is reputed to talk, is doctor to the whole tribe, and also casts spells and enchantments, like the sorcerer of the Middle Ages. To cause an enemy to die, the Kanaka applies to the Takata, who makes a statuette, carries it to the grave-yard, and buries it with various invocations to the spirits of the dead. Does he wish the canoe of an enemy to founder?—he buries a small canoe. Does he wish to " put a spoke in the wheel" of a favoured rival?—the Takata makes an enormous Priapus, upon which the person requiring the spell makes water, uttering, at the same time, some mysterious words which the sorcerer has taught him. The charm will work if he can slip the figure of the Priapus between the legs of his rival, whilst he is sleeping. To spoil the fishing of a neighbouring tribe, a young girl takes off her girdle on the beach. If only one of the crew has erotic desires, no fish will be caught. This superstition especially prevails upon the East coast.

Killing the God. This curious belief in regard to fishes is not confined to the Kanaka alone. Mr J. C. Frazer, with whom I have had the pleasure to converse on these matters at Cambridge University in years gone by, and who has frequently rendered me valuable help, has consecrated a few lines to this interesting subject of piscine folk-lore in his carefully documented work, " The Golden Bough, a study in Comparative Religion " (London, Macmillan, 1890). He says, in the chapter entitled " Killing the God " : " A tribe which depends for its subsistence, chiefly or in part, upon fishing is careful to treat the fish with every mark of honour and respect. The Indians of Peru adored the fish that they caught in greatest abundance; for they said that the first fish that was made in the world above (for so they named Heaven) gave birth to all other fish of that species, and took care to send them plenty of its children to sustain their tribe. For this reason they worshipped sardines in one region, where they killed more of them than of any other fish ; in others, the skate ; in others, the dogfish ; in others, the golden fish for its beauty ; in others, the crawfish ; in others, for want of larger gods, the crabs, where they had no other fish, or where they knew not how to catch and kill them. In short, they had whatever fish was most serviceable to them as their gods. [1] The Otawa Indians of Canada, believing that the souls of dead fish passed into other bodies of fish, never burned fish

[1] Garcilasso de la Vega, *Royal Commentaries of the Yncas*, First Part, bk. i. ch. 10, vol. I, p. 49 *sq.*, Hakluyt Society. Cp. *id.*, II, p. 148.

bones, for fear of displeasing the souls of the fish, who would come no more to the nets. [1] The Hurons also refrained from throwing fish bones into the fire, lest the souls of the fish should go and warn the other fish not to let themselves be caught, since the Hurons would burn their bones. Moreover, they had men who preached to the fish and persuaded them to come and be caught. A good preacher was much sought after, for they thought that the exhortations of a clever man had a great effect in drawing the fish to the nets. In the Huron fishing village, where the French missionary Sagard stayed, the preacher to the fish prided himself very much on his eloquence, which was of a florid order. Every evening after supper, having seen that all the people were in their places, and that a strict silence was observed, he preached to the fish. His text was that the Hurons did not burn fish bones. 'Then enlarging on his theme with extraordinary unction, he exhorted and conjured and invited and implored the fish to come and be caught, and to be of good courage, and to fear nothing, for it was all to serve their friends who honoured them and did not burn their bones.' [2] The disappearance of herring from the sea about Heligoland, in 1530, was attributed by the fishermen to the fact that two lads had whipped a freshly-caught herring and then flung it back into the sea. [3] The natives of the Duke of York Island annually decorate a canoe with flowers and ferns, lade it, or are supposed to lade it, with shell-money, and set it adrift to pay

---

[1] Relations des Jésuites, 1667, p. 12.

[2] Sagard, *Le Grand Voyage du Pays des Hurons*, p. 255 *sqq.* (p. 178 *sqq.* of the Paris reprint).

[3] Scheiden, *Das Salz*, p. 47. For this reference I am indebted to my friend Prof. W. Robertson Smith.

the fish for those they lose by being caught. [1] It is especially necessary to treat the first fish caught with consideration, in order to conciliate the rest of the fish, for their conduct may be supposed to be influenced by the reception given to the first of their kind which is taken. Accordingly, the Maoris always put back into the sea the first fish caught, 'with a prayer that it may tempt other fish to come and be caught.' [2]

"Still more stringent are the precautions taken when the fish are the first of the season. On salmon rivers, when the fish begin to run up the stream in spring, they are received with much deference by tribes who, like the Indians of the Pacific Coast of North America, subsist largely upon a fish diet. In British Columbia the Indians used to go out to meet the first fish as they came up the river. 'They paid court to them, and would address them thus: "You fish, you fish; you are all chiefs, you are; you are all chiefs. " ' [3] Amongst the Thlinket of Alaska the first halibut of the season is carefully handled, addressed as a chief, and a festival is given in his honour, after which the fishing goes on. [4] In spring, when the winds blow soft from the South, and the salmon begin to run up the Klamath river, the Karoks of California dance for salmon, to ensure a good catch. One of the Indians, called the Kareya or God-man, retires to the mountains and fasts for ten days. On his return the people flee, while he goes to the river, takes the first salmon of

[1] W. Powell, *Wanderings in a Wild Country*, p. 66 *sq.*

[2] R. Taylor, *Te Ika a Mauri; or, New Zealand and its Inhabitants*, p. 200; A. S. Thomson, *The Story of New Zealand*, I, 202; E. Treger, " The Maoris of New Zealand," *Journal Anthrop. Inst.* XIX, 109.

[3] Lubbock, *Origin of Civilisation*, p. 277, quoting Metlahkatlah, p. 96.

[4] W. Dall, *Alaska and its Resources*, p. 413.

the catch, eats some of it, and with the rest kindles
the sacred fire in the sweating-house. 'No Indian
may take a salmon before this dance is held, nor for
ten days after it, even if his family are starving.
The Karoks also believe that a fisherman will take no
salmon if the poles of which his spearing-booth is made
were gathered on the river-side, where the salmon
might have seen them. The poles must be brought
from the top of the highest mountain. The fisherman
will also labour in vain if he uses the same poles a
second year in booths or weir, 'because the old
salmon will have told the young ones about them.' [1]

"Among the Indians of the Columbia River, 'when
the salmon make their first appearance in the river,
they are never allowed to be cut crosswise, nor boiled,
but roasted; nor are they allowed to be sold without
the heart being first taken out, nor to be kept over
night, but must be all consumed or eaten the day
they are taken out of the water. All these rules are
observed for about ten days.' [2] They think that, if
the heart of a fish were eaten by a stranger at the
beginning of the season, they would catch no more
fish. Hence, they roast and eat the hearts themselves. [3]
There is a favourite fish of the Ainos which appears
in their rivers about May and June. They prepare
for the fishing by observing rules of ceremonial purity,
and when they have gone out to fish, the women at
home must keep strict silence, or the fish would hear

[1] Stephen Powers, *Tribes of California*, p. 31 *sq.*

[2] Alex. Ross, *Adventures of the First Settlers on the Oregon or
Columbia River*, p. 97.

[3] Ch. Wilkes, *Narratives of the U.S. Exploring Expedition*, IV,
324, v. 119, where it is said, "a dog must never be permitted to eat
the heart of a salmon; and in order to prevent this, they cut the heart
of the fish out before they sell it."

them and disappear. When the first fish is caught he
is brought home and passed through a small opening
at the end of the hut, but not through the door; for
if he were passed through the door, 'the other fish
would certainly see him and disappear.' [1] This explains
the custom observed by other savages of bringing
game into their huts, not by the door, but by the
window, the smoke-hole, or by a special opening at
the back of the hut." [2]

[1] H. C. St. John, "The Ainos" in *Journ. Anthrop. Inst.* II, 253;
id. Notes and Sketches from the Wild Coasts of Nipon, p. 27 *sq.*

[2] Scheffer, *Lapponia*, p. 242 *sq.; Journ. Anthrop. Instit.* VII, 207;
Revue d'Ethnographie, II, 308 *sq.*

CHAPTER II.

Moral characteristics of the Kanaka.—Causes of the insurrection of 1878.—The Kanaka's courage.—His weapons.—The attack on the post at Foa.—Heroic death of sixteen warriors.—Ferocity of the Kanaka.—The philosophy of man-eating.—Devourers of their own offspring.—Men eaten to win glory.—Anthropophagy a motive for war.—Dogs v. women at Terra del Fuego.—Flagrante delicto of animality.—Cannibalism.—Its causes.—The "pilou-pilou".—The erotic "pilou-pilou".—Scenes of cannibalism.—The massacres of the "Alcmena", and la Poya.—The Chief's part in the feast of human flesh.—The reward of the French Government.

Moral Characteristics of the Kanaka. The Kanaka is nothing but a big boy; he has all the worst instincts of the child,—he is ferocious, cruel, and pitiless, but he is a man endowed, as we are, with moral sense. He is distinguished by a blind obedience to his Chief. The Chief has but to command him, and he will obey. He does not think himself a whit inferior to civilised man, and does not fear him. Moreover, the colonist, with whom alone he has the opportunity of comparing himself, is not remarkable for morality. The Kanaka thinks our civilisation is too complicated, and he sincerely pities the White man who cannot exist without all the apparatus of Government. There are only two things he envies us,—alcohol, and weapons of precision. At bottom he is honest and in that respect differs radically from the Annamite, who is as thievish as a magpie. You may leave within his reach the things he most

196

likes, food, meat, wine, and spirits even, and he will
touch nothing. You may leave upon the wharf all
the provisions destined for some European post, and the
Kanaka will even help you to load them, but he will
steal nothing. He is generous. Give a Kanaka a
bottle of brandy, or something good to eat, and he will
share it with his companions. He is very proud, and
feels an insult deeply. In spite of the injury done by
the cattle of the colonists, which devoured his fields of
taro and yams, the Kanaka would never have revolted,
if the gendarmes of la Poya had not been so imprudent
as to arrest the chiefs of thirteen tribes, and handcuff
them. The next day the whole of the thirteen tribes
had revolted.

Causes of the Insurrection of 1878. The insurrection of the Kanakas commenced with the murder
of the gendarmes of la Poya, and the pillage and
burning of the colonists' houses followed. It became a
war of races. The attack on, and destruction of, the
gendarmerie was led by a young Kanaka, who had
been brought up amongst the gendarmes. A little
later, I shall have a few remarks to make on the part
played by certain other Kanakas, who had been educated
amongst Europeans.

The Courage of the Kanaka. — His Weapons.
The insurrection showed fully the courage of the
Kanaka, who with nothing but the primitive weapons
of barbarism, dared to attack civilised men, armed
with the most perfect engines of modern warfare.

The principal weapon of the Kanaka is the *tamio*,
a small axe with a long handle, or the club with a

head like a bird's beak. This is the weapon for close combat. For fighting at a distance, he has a sling, which throws polished oval stones, then three or four darts of thin flexible wood, which he hurls from a distance of fifteen or twenty paces, like the Roman legionary who threw his *pilum*, and, at close quarters, he uses the *tamio*, or the club. With these pre-historic weapons, he did not hesitate to attack brave soldiers armed with Chassepots, or colonists provided with Lefaucheux rifles, or English breech-loading Sniders. The Chassepots and Sniders which the Kanakas captured at the outbreak of the insurrection, became, in their hands, terrible weapons. If the tribes of the North and East, instead of declaring for us, had also revolted, all the Europeans in the interior would have been massacred, and Noumea blockaded. It would have required a formidable expedition, sent from France, to relieve the remaining Europeans.

In spite of the help given by those tribes which remained faithful, it took two years to put down the insurrection. A good description of the fighting can be found in Commandant Rivière's book.

The Attack on the Post of La Foa. I have stated that the very fact of these badly armed Kanakas revolting, was a proof of their courage. An instance of this courage is given by Commandant Rivière, who relates that an attack was made, by daylight, on the post of la Foa, which was protected by palisades, and a "blockhouse" furnished with quick-firing guns. These so-called savages must have had an astonishing courage to undertake such an enterprise. The attack, however, failed, though it was led with considerable skill. For two hours the Kanakas hurled stones from their slings at the palisade and blockhouse, in spite of a well-directed fire from the breech-loading guns.

Heroic Death of sixteen Warriors. I will quote here another instance, which I heard from an officer employed in one of the flying columns sent against the Kanakas. The insurrection had been put down, and the remnants of the tribes were being pursued, in order that they might be captured and transported to Pine Island. A tribe (that of the great Farinos) was surrounded by the column, aided by the warriors of the friendly tribe of the Kondis. The rebel Chief assembled all his warriors, and explained to them the impossibility of continuing the struggle, and that, to save the lives of the children and old men, it would be better to surrender, and give up their arms. Sixteen warriors replied that they preferred death to slavery. These sixteen fought to the last gasp, against more than a hundred Kanakas, who struck them down with darts, and stones from their slings. To my mind, their action was quite as noble as that of Leonidas at Thermopylæ.

Ferocity of the Kanaka. But it cannot be denied that, in spite of his bravery, the Kanaka is ferocious, and his ferocity is mingled with cunning. All the colonists who were killed, were murdered by Kanakas they believed to be friends, and struck from behind at the moment when they least expected it. A Kanaka entered the house of a colonist in a friendly way, and asked for a bit of biscuit, a leaf of tobacco, or a glass of tafia; when his victim turned or stooped, to get the article demanded, he was struck on the back of the head with a *tamio*. Many of the colonists, hearing of the massacre of their neighbours, assembled together, armed with their guns, but the Kanakas they deemed their friends, and who had been charged by their chief to murder them, told them to fear nothing, and they would be guarded and protected. The unhappy wretches, men, women, and children, fell under the clubs of their pretended defenders. The general massacre of the Whites was systematically arranged. If the insurrection had been universal amongst all the tribes, not a colonist would have remained alive.

Only two instances are known in which a Kanaka took pity on a White, and warned him that if he did not fly he would be murdered. But in extenuation of the conduct of the Kanaka, it should be said that he was crushed and ill-treated by the colonists, his plantations were ravaged by their cattle, he was mercilessly overworked, insulted, and often beaten. I am not excusing the Kanaka; I am simply stating facts. The greatest massacres took place in that part of the island where the Whites were most mixed with the natives, and they were struck down by these natives who used to come most frequently to their houses.

The Philosophy of Man-eating. Professor Letourneau [1] has made an extensive study of this subject based on reports of travellers. His observations are so pertinent that we may be excused for quoting them. "In a curious chapter of his 'Essays,' that incarnation of common sense, by name Montaigne, wrote as follows: 'I think that there is more barbarity in eating a live man than to eat him when he is dead; to tear to pieces by torments and by gehennas a body full of feeling, to roast it little by little, to

---

[1] In his profound work, *L'Evolution de la Morale*, Paris 1894, of which an edition bowdlerised—as usual, has appeared in English.

deliver it to be bitten and torn by dogs and swine
(as we have not only read of, but ourselves have seen
in recent times, not between old enemies. but between
neighbours and fellow-citizens, and what is worse,
under pretence of piety and of religion) tnan to roast
and eat him after he is dead.'

" From the strictly utilitarian point of view, Montaigne
seems to be in the right. It is evident that the real
crime consists in killing a man and, when the crime
is committed, as it happens in civil and religious
wars, with the approval of a perverted moral sense,
the crime is then still more lamentable. Nevertheless,
cannibalism is a moral aggravation of homicide. It
amounts to pushing to the utmost extremes the contempt of one's neighbour; it means rigorously to
assimilate man to game or to a domestic animal.

" Besides, ethnography throughout attests the reality
of this assimilation. Only the human races that have
remained at the lowest degree of savagery, practise
cannibalism in its primitive and absolutely bestial
form. As the moral sense begins to form and the
intelligence becomes more developed, man is more
and more ashamed of cannibalism. He limits its
practice, dissimulates it and finally succeeds in reducing
it to a pure symbol. In this embryonic stage, and as a
survival, anthropophagy persisted for a long time, even
into the very heart of the latest phases of morality.
It is only in its altogether primitive form, when it is
practised openly, and simply, that it is the characteristic
of bestial morals. This evolution of cannibalism is
curious. I will briefly review its principal stages. At
the outset man is to another man as one animal is to
another, not only is the enemy devoured, that is to
say a competitor on the other side of such and such

a brook or mountain, but often even, in case of
necessity, the women, the children and old men of
their own tribe. Afterwards, cannibalism becomes
restricted, except in case of famine, to enemies.

" Restriction now follows restriction; for conscience
becomes more sensitive, and on the other hand, with
the progress of civilisation, the food supplies become
less precarious. As a rule religion is also mixed up
with it, and it regulates and consecrates anthropophagy. Little by little, it finishes by limiting the
practice to rare and exceptional cases, and even brings
it down to be no longer anything but a religious ceremony, and to make it symbolical. Under this last
form, cannibalism may continue to exist even among
the most advanced civilisations. In 1874, at the Anthropological Congress at Bologna, Carl Vogt not a
little scandalised certain of his auditory when he said
that he could trace and note in the Catholic mass a
last vestige of the anthropophagy of our ancient ancestors; and yet Carl Vogt was right.

" But religious anthropophagy is not its only attenuated form derived from ancient cannibalism. Juristic
anthropophagy also competes with it, and can also
co-exist with a relatively advanced stage of civilisation.
We shall have to speak of the judicial anthropophagy
of the Battaks of Sumatra, who till quite recently condemned adulterers, night-robbers and others to be eaten.

" But it is with the lower forms of cannibalism that
we have to do at present. The lowest of all is bestial
anthropophagy, having for sole motive the desire and
the want to eat meat. Cannibalism out of greediness
follows very closely, and cannibalism out of vengeance,
or from warlike fury, is often but a hypocritical form
of the same "

Devourers of their Own Offspring. "After having laid down these preliminaries, we can now enter upon the exposition of the facts and will begin with Australia. 'In this country,' says Oldfield, [1] 'there exists a very decided taste for human flesh. The flesh of women is particularly esteemed; therefore they but rarely attain to old age. The men look upon them as beasts of burden, domestic animals, which may be not only beaten, wounded and killed at will, but also eaten without scruple. As Father Salvado [2] says, in times of dearth they are sacrificed without hesitation.'

"Oldfield goes even further: 'They are generally despatched, says he, 'without the least scruple, before they become old and thin, lest so much good food should be lost.... In fact, so little importance is attached to them, either before or after death, that it may reasonably be questioned whether the man does not put his dog, when it is alive, on absolutely the same level as his wife, and whether he thinks more frequently and more tenderly of the one than of the other, after having eaten them both.'

"Cunningham also relates that, in the bag of one of the Australians of his suite, he found a woman's neck put by as food reserve. The same traveller makes a general observation proving evidently that the brutal practice of cannibalism is the sign of an altogether inferior mental condition. According to him, anthropophagy exists in Australia particularly among the tribes living in a state of anarchy, without organisation, where the brutal force of the individual reigns uncontrolled, that is to say among the least intelligent of the tribes.

Oldfield, *Historical Memoirs on Australia.*
[2] Trans. Ethnol. Soc. (New Series, vol. III, p. 220).

"If the Australian woman is frequently devoured, by reason of her relative weakness, it is of course still more often so with regard to the child, who is still weaker.

"'It is a common practice in Australia,' says Oldfield, 'to eat children in times of famine. Then,' he adds, 'the mother must not lament too loudly, under penalty of being beaten. She is only permitted to utter some smothered moans. But, however great may be the grief of the mother, it is appeased when she is offered her legal share, the child's head, which she begins to eat, although she continues her sobbing.' [1] At first sight this assertion of Oldfield seems incredible. But it surprises less, when we consider the psychology of the Australian, who is a very curious type with regard to the origin and formation of his moral sense. The Australian is in fact, as we shall see, susceptive of retaining tenacious mental impressions, barely more reasoned than those of our domestic animals, and which, like them, he obeys instinctively.

"In any case it is certain that the Australian is quite willing to devour his own children. Sturt [2] also confirms the information furnished by Oldfield. He relates in fact, that an Australian smashed on a stone the head of his sick child, which he then roasted and devoured."

Men eaten to win Glory. "Similar customs, but stamped with greater brutality, used to reign or still reign in many parts of the Polynesian archipelagos. At Viti, murder and cannibalism were not only absolutely simple things, but even perfectly honourable.

[1] Journal of two Expeditions of Discovery in Australia, etc., p. 286.
[2] *Hist. Univ. des Voyages* (vol. XLIII, p. 362).

A man was more esteemed the more often he had been covered with blood and gorged himself with human flesh. A chief of Raki-Raki, the great Ra-Undre-Undre, used to glory in having eaten nine hundred persons, all to himself, and without having allowed anyone else to have a share.

" A Viti-islander, of the name of Loti, who, it appears, afterwards became an excellent Christian, roasted his wife on a fire that he had made her prepare and light herself; he then cut her up and devoured her: all that without animosity or anger, solely to acquire notoriety, to be some one out of the common. The love of glory, so habitually and so emphatically vaunted in Europe by the panegyrists of heroes is, says Pritchard, [1] much developed among the Viti islanders, and there, it is to great murderers and great cannibals that fame is attached. In no other part of the world is the deviation so striking from what we call the 'moral sense', or rather the complete absence of moral ideas, innate and necessary according to our metaphysicians.

" But it is necessary to point out at once that we have not here before us a stupid, sleepy race. The Viti islanders are in no wise inferior to the other Polynesians, with whom, besides, they are largely crossed by inter-marriage. But among them, extreme discredit attaches itself to whoever has never killed and eaten an enemy. In that case, indeed, the culprit was subjected to a degrading punishment; he was sentenced to turn up the mud with his dishonoured club, which he had not known how to wield. [2] But with that, all was not finished here below. After human justice came that of the gods. In the future life of the Vitians, the

[1] W. T. Pritchard, *Polynesian Reminiscences*, p. 371.
[2] Wake, *Evolution of Morality*, vol. I, p. 323.

jealous gods, great amateurs of human blood, lay in waiting for the shades of mortals and called them severely to give an account of the number of enemies they had massacred and eaten during their passage on the earth.

" But, at the Viti Islands as at New Zealand, which we shall soon have occasion to study, and where the Melanesians seem to have preceded the Polynesians, cannibalism was absolutely animal. It was on the field of battle itself that, in the manner of wild beasts, the enemy, wounded or prisoner, was torn to pieces and devoured.

" Those of the vanquished, who were not immediately sacrificed, were simply put by in reserve for future banquets. They were therefore fattened: they were then slaughtered and eaten, according to necessity. At Viti, human flesh was much prized. Certain *gourmets* allowed it to become 'gamey.' In the language of the country it was called 'long pork' meat, and it was the rule that a dish of human meat should be served at all gala banquets. It was the ideal food, and to vaunt the excellence of a dish, they would say: 'It is as tender as dead man.'"

Anthropophagy a Motive for War. " Similar customs, though less refined, for the race is not so intelligent, prevailed in New Caledonia. The desire to eat human flesh was the most usual motive for war between the tribes. 'It is now a long time, the chiefs would sometimes say, since we have had any meat to eat: let us go and fetch some.' Sometimes, as M. de Rochas [1] tells us, before starting on the war-path, a sort of anthropophagic poem, an alternate dialogue between

[1] De Rochas, *Bull. de la Soc. d'Anthrop.* v. I, p. 414.

the chief and the warriors was sung: 'Shall we attack
the enemies?—Yes.—Are they strong?—No.—Are they
brave?—No.—We will kill them?—Yes.—We will eat
them?—Yes.' The fight ceased as soon as a few men
had been killed. The cutting up of the dead bodies
was a joyful and glorious ceremony. It was preluded
by a dance, during which one of the dancers bore a
spear in one hand, and in the other a special instrument,
destined to cut up the bodies. [1] After the battle the
chiefs picked out for themselves the lion's share and
put apart also certain choice morsels, destined to be
sent as presents, to dubious allies. [2] But it was not
alone war cannibalism that existed in New Caledonia,
domestic cannibalism was also practised. For instance,
a provident chief would now and then slaughter and
salt one of his subjects, so as to be able to have
every day a dish of meat. [3] Another chief, whose
name is legendary, Bouarate the great, used often
with his family to enjoy a good meal off one of his
inferior subjects. Public opinion in New Caledonia
was far from condemning such princely modes of
action, and in fact Bouarate has left behind him a
brilliant reputation: 'Great chief, Bouarate! Handsome lord, Bouarate!' used to say with enthusiasm
those of his subjects whom he had not yet devoured. [4]
Paternal love itself was silent before so much glory.
A Neo-Caledonian father placidly related how his
child had been eaten by his prince, who, said he, was
a great chief. [5]

[1] D'Entrecasteaux, *Voyage au Pacifique.*
[2] De Rochas, *Nouvelle Calédonie*, p. 206.
[3] Bourgarel, *Race de l'Océanie*, in *Mém. de la Soc. d'Anthrop.*
vol. II.
[4] De Rochas, *Nouv. Calédonie*, p. 246.
[5] Ch. Braine. *Nouvelle Calédonie.*

" To sum up, at the Fiji Islands as at New Caledonia, the stranger, member of another tribe, was considered as game, while the women, the children and inferiors often served for butchers' meat."

Dogs v. Women at Terra del Fuego. " At this place, woman is, as in Australial and in many other places, an object of food provision. Fitzroy [1] saw an old woman sacrificed, at a moment of scarcity of food. She was suffocated by having her head kept for a certain time in the smoke of a fire made of green sticks. The answer given to the remonstrance of the English traveller on this occasion, is quite typical; it puts beyond doubt the perfect innocence, the absence of scruple with which these to us so horrible acts are committed in primitive countries. 'Why,' said Fitzroy, 'do you not rather sacrifice your dogs?—The dog catches the *iappo*' (otter), quietly answered the natives.

" These manners are not special to such and such a race, to such and such a country; they are to be met with, almost identically, wherever man has but little become disengaged from animality, wherever also his food is scant and precarious. Everywhere, in Melanesia, in Africa, in America, there are certain tribes who have less humanity than wolves.

" I will now briefly mention a few more of these instructive cases before speaking with detail of Polynesian cannibalism, more specially interesting for the study of the evolution of morals.

" 'The Guarayos' (South America), say the authors of the *Lettres édifiantes*, [2] 'pursue men just as they would pursue beasts: they take them alive if they can, and

---

[1] Fitzroy, Voyage of the Adventure and of the Beagle.
[2] *Lettres édifiantes*, t. X, p. 231.

carry them away to be slaughtered one after another according as the necessity of hunger becomes felt.' Not only were they preserved as food provision, but they were fattened, and they were even supplied with wives; then, at a given moment, they were slaughtered with great ceremony, care being taken to besmear the male children with their blood, in order that they should become courageous. The victims, quite as ferocious as their tormentors, died like the Red Indians, striking up their death-song, during which they defied their tormentors, reminding them of how many of their friends and relations they had themselves devoured." [1]

Flagrante Delicto of Animality. "As to bestial ferocity, certain Red Indian tribes of the extreme North are, even at the present day, quite equal to the Guaranos mentioned by the ancient missionaries. Let us give ear to what is told us by a Brittany missionary, Monsignor Faraud, Bishop of Mackensie, who lived for many years amongst tribes that had preserved their old custom : 'These savages (the Deuèl-deli-Ottiné, or inhabitants who eat men) carry their passion for anthropophagy to such an extreme that the mother is not in safety with her child, nor the children with their father. Relations eat their relations, and friends devour each other. The least dearth re-awakens in their heart this horrible passion and then the strongest devours the weakest.' [2] Other Red Skins, neighbours of the above, the Cris, practise only war anthropophagy but in an absolutely bestial manner. On the battle-field itself, the victor, having scalped his vanquished enemy, cuts open his breast, and extracts from it the

[1] Thevet, *Singularités de la France antarctique*, p. 187.
[2] *Dix-huit Ans chez les Sauvages*, p. 374.

still palpitating heart, into which he greedily bites. [1]

" These atrocious customs exhibit man to us *in flagrante delicto* of animality. They alone would suffice to set at naught the time honoured theory of innate, necessary moral ideas. I need not further insist; there are many other facts which will come to confirm these latter and constitute a superabundant demonstration." [2]

We will now return to our Kanakas, and I shall give my reasons in the next section for differing with my master, Letourneau, on the causes that give rise, at any rate amongst these people, to the lust after human flesh.

Cannibalism.—Its Causes. The food of the Kanaka, being almost entirely vegetable,—especially amongst the tribes of the interior who cannot add sea fish to their diet,—is not sufficient to give strength, and sustained resistance to fatigue. The Kanaka eats enormously. He consumes at a single meal quantities of food which would be extraordinary for a European, but they are sugary and starchy foods. rich in carbon, but poor in nitrogen. He lacks convertible, blood-making food. He is like a steam-engine which has the furnace loaded with coke, and no water in the boiler. In the expeditions, the auxiliaries, although less heavily laden than our soldiers, were worn-out by fatigue, whilst the Europeans could still keep on marching. They were obliged to be fed on biscuit and bacon.

With all due respect to the vegetarians, a vegetable diet is nonsense. No vegetarian could undergo the hard work and fatigue, which a meat-eater could.

" Nothing can come of nothing," as Shakespeare

---

[1] *Dix-huit Ans chez les Sauvages*, p. 374.
[2] Letourneau, *opus cit.*

says; [1] to have muscle you must have meat. The Kanaka having in New Caledonia neither poultry, nor pork, and nothing but *notous* (pigeons as large as a fowl), ate his vanquished enemy, and, by atavism, this depraved taste continued to exist amongst the race after the introduction of the pig and cattle. The most handsome gift you can make a Kanaka is,—next to a gun,—a quarter of salt beef. Toussenel [2] has well described cannibalism.

" Cannibalism is one of the diseases of the childhood of primitive man, that poverty explains, though it does not justify. Let us pity the cannibal, and not abuse him too much, we civilised beings, who slay millions of men. The evil is not so much in roasting your enemy, as in killing him before he wanted to die."

The Pilou-pilou is an important factor in the life of the Kanaka. Nothing can be done without a *pilou-pilou*, which is danced in war, after victory, in love, and as an enjoyment. Each tribe has its own *pilou-pilou*, differing somewhat from that of other tribes. It would take too long to describe them here, but I will give a general idea of the principal varieties of the dance.

The Pilou-pilou of War. Only the warriors take part in this. They are in war paint, that is, painted black, with white marks here and there on the body, which gives them a most diabolical appearance, and with their darts and *tamios* in their hands. A large

---

[1] Our author has slipped here, or is he purposely facetious? " *Ex nihilo, nihil fit*" can hardly be fathered on Shakespeare; it must be considerably older, we fancy, than William's time.

[2] In his *Zoologie passionnelle.*

fire is lighted, round which the warriors stand in a
circle. After repeated groans, and a sharp whistle,
which has a horrible effect, they brandish their arms,
leap, grind their teeth, and make awful grimaces.
Then the band of warriors separates into two circles,
which turn round, the men meanwhile uttering hoarse,
guttural cries like wild beasts. At last the two bands
rush at each other with savage cries, and imitate a
deadly combat. I was present at Koné at a *pilou-
pilou* of this kind, and I could not prevent giving a
shudder, though I was under the protection of the
chief, who was seated beside me.

The Pilou-pilou of Love. The women take part
in this *pilou-pilou*, which is intended to celebrate the
sports of love, but they do not mingle with the men.
They form a small circle within that of the men, and
dance without moving from their place, moving their
haunches backwards and forwards in very supple
movements, with now and then a lascivious kind of
leap. This is an imitation of the movements of a
woman in copulation. The men dance round and round
them, leaping, bounding, squatting, and, as they rise,
pushing their bellies forward to imitate the movement
of **copulation.**

The Pilou-pilou of the Cannibals. Although the
Kanaka has now poultry and pork, he has nevertheless
retained his hereditary taste for human flesh. I was
informed, during my stay in New Caledonia, that the
tribe of Kanala ate from time to time, at an enormous
pilou-pilou, captives of some of the insurgent tribes
captured in 1878. Not having seen it, I cannot say
how true this was, but I can give extracts from trust-

worthy writers to prove the existence of this horrible custom.

In the first place, there was the massacre of the boat's crew of the *Alcmena*. The ship's long boat was sent to land, to get water. As a matter of form, three rifles were put in the bottom of the boat. Fourteen Whites, of whom two were officers, landed, and a quarter-master and two sailors remained in the boat. These last heard the cries of their comrades, and guessing that they were being massacred, tried to escape by swimming to the vessel, but they were overtaken by the Kanakas, brought back to land, and bound. They saw their unfortunate comrades cut up, cooked, and eaten, at an enormous pilou-pilou.

The first insurrection, that of 1868, began by the massacre of a sergeant and eight men, who had been sent to a tribe to requisition by force a body of men to construct the road to Noumea. The soldiers were received in a friendly manner, so they stacked their arms, and separated. They were immediately struck down, and their bodies cut to pieces. Some of their limbs were sent to all the neighbouring tribes who were on good terms with the murderers. Those which accepted this new kind of *gigot*,— there were three other tribes,—declared against the French. It took eighteen months to subdue these four tribes.

An eye-witness of the insurrection of 1878, Paul Branda, [1] gives some very interesting and previously unpublished details concerning this insurrection, and relates several instances of cannibalism. " During the preparations for the massacre," he says, " the Kanakas surrounded a captain, the commander of the district, an enormously fat giant, named Chausson. They

[1] In his book, *Les Lettres d'un Marin*.

danced a *pilou-pilou*, singing in chorus 'We will eat
Chausson!' Then each warrior advanced in turn,
brandishing his arms. One said, 'Chausson, I will eat
your hands;' another, 'Chausson, I will eat your feet,'
and they all gazed longingly at the fine juicy captain.
The worthy man, who understood the language of the
country, laughed heartily, and said, 'What funny devils
these Kanakas are.' Twenty-four hours later, the
entire tribe was up in arms, crying, 'Let us go and
eat Chausson.' By a lucky chance, the over-confiding
commander of the district had that day been called to
Noumea, and so escaped the teeth of his admiring
subjects."

I will also quote, from the same author, an account
of the massacre of la Poya. " The insurgents captured
a vessel, laden with supplies and cartridges, and having
a crew of eleven men. The unaccountable delay in
the arrival of this ammunition caused great uneasiness
as to the fate of the vessel and its crew, and a steam
launch, fully armed, was ordered to go and look for
it. Our sailors soon disturbed the horrible feast at
which the Kanakas were celebrating their triumph.
Near the feasting place were the trunks of men, horribly decomposed, and hidden in the rushes by the
river. The heads had been cut off as spoils of triumph,
and the limbs had been eaten.

" In an open space overshadowed by tall trees, near
the limpid river of la Poya, were chairs and sofas, taken
from the houses of the colonists, which had been sacked,
and forming a circle. In the middle, as the centre
piece of the table, was a putrefying human head. Here
and there lay human bones, carefully cleaned, especially the shin bones. The captain of the boat said,
'They are to make flutes.' In baskets hung on the

branches, were slices of grilled flesh, neatly packed, and of an appetising odour; one of the crew, formerly a pork-butcher, said they were pork; a butcher declared they were beef; one of the friendly Kanakas in the crew, said, 'That? white tayo!' A silence of terror and horror fell upon all the men. The grilled flesh, and the few bones, were piously collected, and buried with funeral honours. Of course this was very proper, but it seemed odd, nevertheless, to accord military honours to kitchen scraps."

A little further on the same author adds, "Our allies did not put themselves out of the way on our account; they ate their enemies in sight of our soldiers. The absolute need of their services obliged us to shut our eyes. The chief of the Konés came, and presented to the colonel four left ears. 'Why,' said the colonel, 'you have had them cooked!'—'Yes,' replied the chief, 'so that they might keep good.' After having received his reward, *he went off munching the ears.*

"The Government paid ten francs each for the head of every rebel Kanaka. The Arab convicts, who were the best sharpshooters, used to bring in the ears of those they killed, in order to claim the reward. They were accused of sometimes bringing women's ears, and after that they used to bring the penis and testicles of the dead Kanakas, finding the head rather awkward to carry on horseback."

The Chief's Share in the Feast of Human Flesh.

I will terminate these few remarks relating to anthropophagy, by an account of the chief's part in the feast.

Formerly, long before the advent of the French—when the struggle for life between the tribes was at its height, the conquering chiefs used, by the aid of an instrument which I have never seen, and of the shape of which I am ignorant, to tear out the genital parts, the heart, and the eyes of the conquered chief. These ferocious warriors did not content themselves with cooking their enemies in the Kanaka stove, but preferred to devour on the field of battle the parts thus torn off, all raw and bleeding. They thought that they should thus acquire the piercing sight, the courage, and the virility, of their adversaries. This custom now is nothing more than a tradition. According to some travellers, it also used to exist among the Maoris of New Zealand.

The Reward of the French Government. Of course, these customs are horrible, but it must be remembered that the Kanaka is uncivilised. What shall we say though to the action of the French Government during the insurrection? I am not inventing statements, but again quoting from Branda.

"We found allies on the following conditions; all the spoil, the women, and ten francs for every head brought in.

"The Kanaka mutilates dead bodies, but he does not, as the Indian does, wish to inflict pain on his enemy. On the other hand, I have heard Europeans seriously complain of the incapacity of certain officers, who would not wring information from prisoners by means of torture." [1]

---

[1] The "soft-hearted party" who are fearful of shedding blood, and whose timorousness is too often the cause of its being shed, will not accept the Jesuitical doctrine that "the end justifies the means." Yet in primitive societies none but iron measures can prevail, and the man, or tribe, not prepared to strike hard blows runs a risk of being wiped out by the "other side". There are men in the United States who

maintain that the perpetuation of criminal families can be prevented only by THE AMPUTATION OF THEIR REPRODUCTIVE ORGANS, and we hope to deal with this subject in a future work on *Eunuchs and Eunuchism.*

We quote the following from THE MEDICAL WORLD:—

"The matter of the castration of those who persist in crime is receiving more and more attention. In the *Legislature* of *Michigan* a Bill was introduced which provides for ASEXUALISATION. Feeble-minded and epileptics who become inmates of the feeble-minded institution of the State, 'before he or she is discharged, shall be caused to submit to an operation that causes asexualisation, that such person shall cease to be able to reproduce their kind.' All persons convicted the third time for felony, and those convicted of having ravished a child or woman, after the first year's incarceration, must submit to the operation which causes asexualisation."

CHAPTER III.

Forms of sexual intercourse amongst the Kanakas.—The Popinée the property of the Chief.—The Kanaka marriage.—Polyandry.—The condition of the Popinée.—The Kanaka "break wood," the usual method of copulation.—Accouchement.—Vulvar deformities produced by the repeated coition of the Kanaka Popinées.—An original form of punishment for adultery.—Not confined to the Kanakas.—Mrs. Potiphar and Joseph.—Lust of the Kanaka for the White woman.—The head chief Atai and Mme F***

The Popinée the Property of the Chief. Every girl of the tribe is born the property of the Chief, and his rights over her do not cease until the time when he gives her to his warriors. Until then he can sell her, hire her, or even eat her, if that is his pleasure. The Chief of Koné would not sell his women to the Europeans, but he let them out on hire. Kaké, the Chief of the Kanalas, was not so particular, and is said to have sold women to some of the colonists. I was assured that, hardly more than ten years before my visit, many of the tribes of the interior ate the women captured from hostile tribes. I have already remarked, that the unfortunate Kanaka Popinée has not only to do all the cooking and household work, but to satisfy the sexual needs of her squad of husbands—a term which I will hasten to explain.

The Kanaka Marriage.—Polyandry. As a matter of fact, marriage does not exist in New Caledonia.

The Chief gives the women to those of his warriors
with whom he is most satisfied, and in that consists
all the ceremony of marriage. But, as the number
of women is much inferior to that of the men, the
result is that every woman is the property of several
husbands. It is this collection of husbands, having
one wife in common, that I have designated under
the name of the " squad." They live together in a hut,
with their common wife. [1]

The Condition of the Popinée. Every day the
Popinée has to work like a beast of burden, and at
night she has to satisfy the desires of all the males.
How does each of the husbands manage to get his
share of the conjugal cake? That is a subject on which
I could gather no precise information. Does each
gentleman have a proper day for visiting Madame,
like some of the Parisian fast men, who keep a woman
between four, or even eight, of them? Or do the
stronger and more vigorous husbands take the lion's
share, and only leave their associates the scraps of the
feast, after they themselves are completely satisfied?
I could gather no trustworthy information on the point.
It is probable, however, that love, that noble sentiment
that sways the human breast, finds no place in a
Kanaka household. The wretched Popinée has to
permit the embraces of the males whenever they are
"in rut." Pregnancy does not cause any remission in
their attacks, nor does the period of suckling either,—
which by the way extends over three or four years.

[1] HERB. SPENCER in *The Principles of Sociology*, Lond., Williams
and Norgate, 1885; and CH. LETOURNEAU, in *L'Evolution du Mariage
et de la Famille*, Paris, 1888, both treat the subject of POLYANDRY
in a very full and competent manner, although from standpoints, of
course, rather different.

The Kanaka "Break Wood." As might be expected, the Kanaka does not show much consideration, or affection, for his common wife,—the more so, perhaps, because she is ugly enough to frighten a man. Sexual connection is performed without any preliminary preparation. After a hard day's work it often happens to the unfortunate Popinée, that she is obliged to support the amorous assaults of her squad of husbands all night.

Accouchement takes place without any sort of ceremony. The female neighbours help the women in labour as they best can. After a day or two's rest, she goes to work again. As to the labour of love, the genital organs are hardly given time to recover from the disorders caused by the accouchement. There is always one husband, more impatient than the others, who cannot wait, and very often, though at the risk of crippling his wife, he recommences copulation with her. Owing to this little amusement, the woman is worn out, and rarely brings forth more than two children, and although married at twenty, or twenty-five at the latest, she is soon used up; at thirty, she is a wretched decrepit creature horrible to behold.

An Original Form of Punishment for Adultery. It might be imagined that with the incessant amount of prostitution—as it may be called —that the Popinée undergoes almost every night, that she had quite enough of copulation, and never committed the sin of adultery. That, however, would be to fail to take into account the fancies and failings of a woman's brain. Adultery exists, and is punished in an original manner, which is not, I believe, practised anywhere else in the world.

When a woman is convicted of adultery, the Chief condemns her to die in the manner in which she has committed her offence. I will explain what I mean. The woman is fastened down in a hut in such a manner that she cannot move. Her hands are tied behind her back, her legs are bent to the thighs and fastened to them by means of a rope which passes round the thigh and the shin, and is then fastened to that which secures the arms and the hands; the woman is thrown on her back with her thighs open, and the opening of the vulva widely gaping. The description may not be very clear; it would need a photograph to show the position plainly. But I do not know of any photographer who has ever been able to take such a picture, for what I am relating was told me in confidence by Kaké, the Chief of the Kanalas. When she is powerless to move, the woman is given over to the young warriors of the tribe, each of whom enters the hut in his turn. The men dance the *pilou-pilou* whilst awaiting their turn. The operation, or rather the execution, continues without cessation until the victim dies,—as may be imagined—in horrible sufferings. According to Kaké, it takes about a hundred of these assaults to kill the woman. [1]

Not Confined to the Kanakas. The ingenuity of man has found out " many curious inventions", but surely nothing more revolting than this barbarous practice. Unfortunately this custom is not confined to

---

[1] De Rochas, in his book, *Nouvelle Calédonie* (page 262), confirms my account. L. Moncelon, Réponse au *Questionnaire de Sociologie*, in *Bull. Soc. d'Anthrop.*, 1886, states that he has seen a man sentenced to death for having looked at the wife of a chief when she stooped down to pick up some shells; crime of *lèse-majesté*.

Melanesia alone.   It is to be found in all countries and
in all times.   The adulterous man, it should be noticed,
is never punished for having forsworn his conjugal
vows, but wholly and solely for having injured another
husband.   I have no space here to go into the laws
of adultery prevalent among various nations and tribes.
The philosophy relating to this has been clearly sketched
out by able teachers like Letourneau and other professional experts. Still I would call attention to the
fact that this savage doctrine of *lex talionis* is carried
out with the same brutal and lascivious ferocity amongst
the Omahas.   These people tie the wretched female
to a stake in the prairie, and abandon her to the obscene embraces of twenty or thirty men.   Bancroft [1]
affirms that the Modocs of California publicly slit open
the guilty woman's belly; while the Hoopsa, another
tribe of Red Skins, tore out one of the adulterer's eyes
or, were he married, took away his wife.   If, quitting
modern times and savage countries, we travel back to
classical antiquity, we find that hardly any better state
of things existed in the more polished lands of Greece
and Rome.   Here marriage was crudely considered as
nothing more than a civic duty and thought of only
from the standpoint of population.   Strange as it may
sound to us, Lycurgus and Solon encouraged the impotent husband to favour the adultery of his young
wife.   "It was not reproachable," says Plutarch, speaking of the laws of Lycurgus, "for a man already fairly
stricken in years and who owned a young spouse, to
allow a fine young man who had the talent to please
him and was of kindly nature to take his place in the
conjugal bed with his wife, '*pour la faire emplir de
bonne semence*,' and afterwards recognise the fruit which

[1] *Native Races*, I vol., p. 350.

was born of the relations, as though it had been engendered by himself. Therefore, was it allowable in
an honest man who loved the wife of another through
seeing that she was virtuous, modest and bore fine
offspring, to beg her husband to permit him to have
connection with her so as to sow there, as in rich and
fertile earth, beautiful and good children, which by this
means should come to have a community of blood and
relationship with people of wealth and honour." [1] This,
of course, is marriage considered without the least prejudice, and from the strict point of view of social utility,
and I doubt much that the world has yet attained to
so philosophical and, as it seems to me, elastic an
interpretation of the wedded state as to sanction this
practice to-day, except, perhaps, as a private arrangement.

" Solon," says Letourneau, " imitated Lycurgus on this
point with the following restriction, recalling the code
of Manou, that the wife of an impotent husband ought,
with the authorisation of course of her conjoint, to select
a lover from among the nearest relatives of the said
husband." [2] Manners went sometimes beyond the laws,
and Plutarch mentions that Cimon of Athens, example
of soul-greatness and of goodness, lent his wife to the
rich Callias. [3] But that did not at all prevent the laws
of Solon from authorising the husband to kill the
adulterer whom he might catch *in flagrante delicto.*
Further still, the law struck with civil degradation the
too indulgent husband and authorised family tribunals
to sentence to death the guilty woman, whom the
outraged husband himself executed, before witnesses. [4]
Finally, a law of Draco, which was never repealed,

[1] Plutarch, *Lycurgus*, XXIX. [2] Plutarch, *Solon*, XXXVI.
[3] Plutarch, *Life of Cimon.* [4] Legouvé, *Hist. morale des femmes* (p. 182).

handed over the adulterous lover to the tender mercies of the husband. [1] In sum, save for the care of the good of the State, before which all gave way, this Grecian legislation did no more than consecrate the old primitive right, which made the woman the husband's chattel.

Rome's Code of Adultery. Rome followed strangely hard on Greece in all that concerned the marriage bond. [2] For the wife, her manners and legislation were at first of savage atrocity. The term "adulterer" was at the outset applied only to the wife, and the law of the Twelve Tables conferred the right to drag up the guilty woman before a domestic tribunal; she was condemned, and executed by the relatives themselves: *Cognati necanto uti volent* (Let the kinsmen kill her as they shall please). These family tribunals lasted all through the Republican *régime*, and even later, concurrently with the *Lex Julia;* but manners became less harsh, and death as a penalty of adultery was replaced with banishment of at least 200 miles from Rome and the obligation to wear the courtesan's toga. Of course, if the husband surprised the adulterous wife in the very act he still possessed authority to kill her on the spot; [3] and the lover he could keep to torture or mutilate, as the warmth of his lost love, or the cold-blooded calculation of revenge, might dictate. The character of the mutilation was of the savagest kind. A picturesque word for it exists in French, *raffaniser*, and its meaning may be better imagined than explained. The outraged husband could also deliver the hapless lover to the

[1] Ménard, *Morale avant les philosophes*, p. 303.
[2] Lecky, *History of European Morals*, vol. II, p. 312.
[3] Wake, *Evolution of Morality*, vol. II, p. 85.

ferocious lubricity of his slaves. One would think in these days that it were enough to render the poor wretch an eunuch and expose him to unnatural *passive* treatment. But law and opinion further authorised the husband to demand a sum of money for the ransom of his wife's lover and this consequently opened the door for torture as a means of blackmailing.

It was reserved for the philosophical Emperor, Antoninus, more clement and equitable' than his forerunners, to amend this terrible state of things. He forbade by law the husband, himself *presumed* guilty of adultery, to kill or judicially prosecute his wife surprised in her lover's arms. In time, the reaction that was to be expected took place, and manners affecting the conjugal couch became daily more licentious. Tolerance gave birth to license, and Septimus Severus laid down new laws against breaches of the marriage vow. That such laws were needed and appreciated is proved by the fact that Dion Cassius found on the public registers at Rome three thousand cases of adultery. [1] Socrates, the ecclesiastical historian, informs us that Theodosius not only softened the penalties waiting upon adultery, but did very much more. He swept away the old Roman custom, born of cruelty and lubricity, which sanctioned the locking up of the guilty woman in a small lodgment where she was delivered to the sensuality of all-comers, the latter even being obliged to carry small bells to attract attention. [2] The same ignoble practice, I have pointed out already, was in vogue amongst certain red-skinned tribes of North America, and if the community of the custom does not prove that the Romans

[1] Friedländer, *Mœurs romaines*, etc., vol. I, p. 367.
[2] Socrates, *Hist. Eccles.* lib. V., cap. XVIII.

were less civilised than the Red Skins, it at any rate demonstrates, combined with other facts, "the original equality of the most diverse races in the state of primitive savagery."[1]   In the name of Religion many crimes have been wrought, and the pious Constantine, to whom the imperial purple next fell, once more showed that the newest converts are the worst fanatics.   This Christian neophyte, with a fury that knew no bounds, waged pitiless war against all infractions of the public peace.   On the assumption that cruelty was the only cure for viciousness, he launched forth a law making adultery in both sexes punishable with death.

"Justinian reacted against this and moderated the rigours of the law.   His code condemns the adulteress to be whipped, to have her hair shaved off and to be shut up in a convent for the rest of her days, unless her husband should take her back again before the expiration of two years.   Compared with the excessive zeal of Constantine, this appears almost merciful.—It is also too well-known how previously, under the much wiser pagan emperors, the Roman morals had become so relaxed; an almost free marriage procured to the young women of the aristocracy an almost unlimited independence, or, at all events and despite the laws, adultery had ceased to be an abominable crime, as it had begun to be considered among the ancestors."[1]

In the realistic stories of Algerian experience written by my old friend and brother officer, Hector France (ex-Captain of the "Chasseurs d'Afrique"), there is a powerful narrative of an old man's revenge on his young wife's lover, whom he had succeeded in trapping. I shall give no account of this here, although Hector

[1] Letourneau, *L'Evolution du Mariage et de la Famille* (Paris, 1888), page 279.

France assures me it is thoroughly true in fact, as I understand that the editor of the present work intends bringing out an English version of these extraordinary stories, which have already been done into the Anglo-Saxon tongue by a master-hand.

A Kanaka "Joseph and Potiphar's Wife." Branda relates, in a very graphic manner, the story of a Kanaka " Potiphar's wife ".

" The son of the terrible Bouarate came to complain to the commander of the district of the rape of one of his wives by six of his subjects. What a sign of the times! respect for sovereigns is on the wane, even in New Caledonia. Who had dared to molest the wife of the noble lord, Bouarate? In former times the noble lord, instead of coming whining to the French authorities, would have knocked the delinquent on the head with his war club, and afterwards eaten him;— perhaps also eaten his faithless spouse into the bargain. Philip, however, was more good-natured, and after having extorted as large a fine as he could from the guilty parties, had requested that they might also have a week's hard labour in the prison. But the result of the inquiry showed, that, if there had been any rape, it was that of the six striplings, who had been seduced by this Messalina of Hienghen. [1]   I was present

[1] "So far as we can ascertain rape by females on males is a crime unknown to the English law. Several cases of this kind have, however, come before the French criminal courts. In 1845, a female, aged eighteen, was charged with having been guilty of an act of indecency, with violence, on the person of a boy under the age of fifteen years. She was found guilty. In another case, which occurred in 1842, a girl, aged eighteen, was charged with rape on two children,—the one eleven and the other thirteen years of age. It appeared in evidence that the accused had enticed the two boys into a field, and had there had forcible

at the examination of one of the accused, a handsome young man of sixteen or seventeen years, with a soft skin, of a relatively light colour, a modest face, and mild, soft eyes. This youthful Apollo energetically denied that he had been guilty of showing such disrespect to his chief; the lady had been the real culprit, and he had only been the passive instrument. Whenever he met Mrs. Philip she shot terribly amorous glances at him, asked him for a light for her pipe, put her hand on his shoulder, caressed him, etc., etc. He refused to understand. Whereupon she explained herself more categorically, and invited the handsome lad to come with her into the brush, and 'break wood.'

"The Caledonian Joseph answered Mrs. Potiphar with a formal refusal. Unfortunately, one day, the lady (still under the pretext of wanting a light for her pipe) seized Joseph by the hem of his garment—I mean that

connection with them. This female was proved to have had an unnatural contraction of the vagina, which prevented intercourse with adult males. She was found to be labouring under syphilitic disease, and the proof of her offence was completed by the disease having been communicated to the two boys. She was convicted. * Casper describes cases of this description which have fallen under his observation. † By the Penal Code of France, it is a crime in either sex to attempt intercourse with the other, whether with or without violence, when the child is under eleven years of age. That this offence is perpetrated in England cannot be doubted. It is by no means unusual to find, in the wards of hospitals, mere boys affected with venereal disease. In some instances this may be due to precocious puberty; but in others it can only be ascribed to that unnatural connection of adult women with male children with is punished as a crime in the other sex. The only accessible medical proof would consist in the transmission of gonorrhœa or syphilis from the woman to the child." (Taylor's Medical Jurisp.).

* "Ann. d'Hyg." (1847, I, p. 463).

† "Gerichtl. Med." (vol. 2, p. 129), and "Klin. Novellen" (1863, p. 15).

Caledonian garment for which, on wet days, a rolled-up leaf, kept in its place by the stalk of some plant, can be advantageously substituted. This kind of garment is called in the country, *moineau*. It is the height of fashion to wear it very large. The unlucky young man thus seized by the hem of his garment, did not dare to fly in a state of shameful nudity. The young woman led him into the wood,—and then she took the garment off herself."

Lust of the Kanaka for the White Woman. The European woman, however modest may be her costume, and however moderate her degree of beauty seems a goddess descended from Olympus, compared to the horrible Popinée, the mere caricature of a woman. It may be imagined, *a priori*, that the Kanaka has few opportunities of gratifying his amorous taste, though he is very desirous to "break wood" with a White woman. In former days, he would have eaten her with great gusto, at a *pilou-pilou*, but now he is more modest, and would content himself with her favours. Unluckily for him, the wives and daughters of the colonists, who are generally of English birth, on the mother's side at least, their mothers having usually come from Australia, are of pure manners, and, with very rare exceptions, the Kanaka is considered by the White woman as a biped unworthy of her attention. However, I learned from an old colonist who had lived at la Poya for many years, and who escaped being murdered in the rebellion, that he had several times tried to bring up young Kanakas he had bought from the chief of the Farinos, but that these boys, as soon as they attained puberty, were a great bother, and were always hanging round the petticoats of the women

and girls.   On this account he was obliged to get rid
of them and take in their place men he had hired from
the New Hebrides, and this afterwards saved the lives
of himself and family.   He armed his New Hebrideans
with four or five old muskets he had on his farm, and
the Kanakas, seeing that he was prepared, did not
dare to attack him.

The Great Chief, Atai, and Madame F***   Commandant Rivière gives some curious details concerning
the passion of Atai, the principal leader of the revolt,
for Mme F*** the widow of an artillery captain, and
proprietress of a farm.

" Mme F*** was much admired by Atai, the chief
promoter of the rebellion.   He was a neighbour of hers,
and often came to see her.   He brought her fruit, and
she offered him coffee, bread, and wine.   He used to
smoke his pipe under the verandah, whilst she worked,
and talked to him.   On gala days, when he was full
dressed, he wore the tunic of an infantry officer, with
gold stripes, and a *képi*, like most of the other Chiefs,
but most usually he was naked.   But in a copper skin,
nudity does not seem to shock women, perhaps because
they are so used to seeing it.

" Atai was tall, of a remarkably strong build, and
very intelligent, but he was forty-five years old, which
is not young for a Kanaka, his head was large, the
top of his skull bald, and his ears hanging, and pierced
with large holes, according to the custom of the country.
He was much struck by Mme F***, and one day,
unexpectedly, but very quietly, asked her to marry
him.   She was greatly astonished, and refused.   Atai
renewed his proposal on several other occasions, but
always met with the same answer.   His vexation had,

perhaps, something to do with the insurrection ; there is generally a woman at the bottom of everything. I have many times told Mme F*** that she ought to have sacrificed herself, and she would have prevented the insurrection. She did not contradict me, but replied, that not even to save the colony from the greatest possible dangers, would she have contracted such a marriage."

CHAPTER IV.

Perversions of the sexual passions amongst the Kanakas.—The perversions of the Popinées.—Pederasty after the age of puberty.—A curious theory of sexual aberration.—The symptomatic characteristics of the pederasty of the Kanaka.—Cruelties and erotic mutilations committed by the Kanakas during the insurrection.—White women beheaded and violated.—Bechir, the Arab.—Louis, the Kanaka interpreter.—Acts of Sadism.—The mutilation and outraging of corpses.

The Perversions of the Popinées. The unhappy Popinée is not perverted, in the strict sense of the word; she permits the caresses of the man, but she knows nothing at all about the "spices of Venus." She is completely ignorant of the art of performing in a kneeling posture,—an art in which the Congai is so expert. Nor is she a sodomite. There are exceptions to every rule, it is true, but I found very few exceptions to this. I cannot say, whether the woman of New Caledonia has the same aversion for "the worship of Venus the wrong way," as the Negress of Senegal has, the number of Popinées I was able to question (and that with the greatest possible difficulty), being insufficient to enable me to deduce a general rule, from such observations as I was able to make.

Pederasty after the Age of Puberty. The Kanaka attains puberty at the age of thirteen or fourteen. He cannot become a warrior till he is of a certain age,—usually about the twentieth year,—and he must first

232

"prove himself to be a man," by undergoing certain trials. The Chief then gives him his share of a Popinée. Until that time, woman is forbidden fruit for him. The girls, as has been seen, belong to the Chief, and the vengeance of the Chief is a terrible thing to incur. However, now and then, a lad manages to find some young girl.

As to the woman who is the property of a squad of husbands, it is not advisable to have anything to do with her, for there is the danger of getting a crack on the head from a war club, and, moreover, a woman who is watched by such a lot of husbands is not easily got at. But the powers of generation have imperative rights at the age of from fifteen to twenty, and so the young Kanakas, who are brought up and taught together, follow the example of the Greeks of the sacred battalion of Thebes, and in default of women, "console" each other. Wherever human beings of one sex are collected together, the same result will follow, if moral sense is wanting, and the moral sense of the Kanaka is not that of the civilised man.

But, it must be confessed, to the disgrace of our civilisation, that in spite of the most attentive watchfulness, pederasty finds a secret asylum in our great educational establishments. If the past career of the poor wretches, whom pederasty has brought into the criminals' dock, were inquired into, it would probably be found that there was a vicious and depraved childhood. I know, for my own part, that several of my college friends were addicted to this vice. I have purposely abstained from speaking of one of them, an officer in the Navy, who left behind him in Cochin-China a deplorable reputation, on account of his hardly concealed weakness for boys. I should mention that he already had this vice when he was a pupil at the College of T***, and virility did but increase the sins of his youth.

Sexual Aberration in Antiquity. We make a pause here to quote the peculiar theory of Mantegazza and to show how wide-spread was this vice long before the modern European nations existed.

"Love between males is one of the most horrible facts of human psychology; in all ages and in every country it has been a far more common vice than is supposed. Let us first examine the facts, it will then be time to comment on them.

" Carthage was famous for its vices contrary to nature, and the Carthaginians gloried in them. Salvianus, a preacher of that period, said :

"'et illi se magis virilis fortitudinis esse crederent, qui maxime viros fœminei usus probrositate fregissent.'

(and they would think themselves to be of the greater manliness and vigour, in proportion as they had to the greatest extent broken men in with the abomination of using them as women).

" Mythological tradition traces pederasty back to Orpheus and the Thracians.

"'Ille etiam Thracum populis fuisse auctor amorem
In teneros transferre mares, citraque juventam,
Breve ver ætatis et primos carpere flores.' OVID.

(He too is related to have been the first who taught the peoples of Thrace to transfer their love to males of tender age, and before maturity to enjoy the brief spring-tide of their youth and pluck the blossoms of their early bloom).

" Aristotle says that this vice was authorised by law in the island of Crete in order to prevent an excessive increase of the population. Athenæus also speaks of the sodomy of the Cretans, but attributes it also to the Chalcidians of Eubœa. Licofronius accuses Achilles of having massacred on the altar of Apollo the youth Troilus, who had refused to submit himself to his shameful desires. Sodomy was certainly a Greek vice, for did they not introduce it even into Olympus in uniting Jupiter and Ganymede, Apollo and Hyacinthus, Hercules and Hylas. Sophocles and Æschylus dared to mention it in their tragedies, and Anacreon sang Bathyllus. The divine Socrates himself loved youths.

"Rome is not unworthy of her great mistress in this respect. Cæsar sells the first fruits of his youth to Nicomedes, King of Bithynia. Horace extols the charms of his male lovers, Ligurinus, Gyges, Lyciscus, etc. Virgil gives immortality, under the name of Alexis to his love for the youthful Alexander. The Roman people calls to mind Augustus when that famous verse is recited on the stage:

"'*Videtne ut Cinædus orbem digito temperet?*'

(See you how a Cinædus directs the world with his finger?)

"A Roman emperor has statues and temples raised in honour of his minion, and the immortal historian of Tiberius writes:

"'*Infantes, necdum tamen lacte depulsos, inguini ceu papillæ admovebat: pronior tunc ad id genus libidinis et natura et ætate.*'

(Young children, not yet weaned, he would put to his πριφατες as to their mother's teat,—being in fact better adapted to this form of indulgence both by constitution and age).

"And at another place:

"'*fertur etiam in sacrificando quondam captus facie ministri, nequisse abstinere quia pene vix dum re divina peracta, ibidem statim seductum constupraret, simulque fratrem ejus tibicinem, atque utique mox, quod mutuo flagitium exprobabant, crura fregisse.'*

(He is said, moreover, on one occasion when engaged in sacrifice, to have been captivated by the looks of a temple ministrant, and to have been unable to refrain from almost instantly, the service barely completed, taking him aside on the spot and polluting him, and along with him his brother, a flute-player; then presently because they were two living proofs of his infamy, to have had their legs broken)

" If now we turn from the Greco-Latin antiquity to the ancient Gauls, then to America or to contemporary savage tribes, we find sodomy not less prevalent.

" According to Diodorus of Sicily, the Gauls gave themselves up to orgies of debauchery and sodomy. In some parts of the North of Mexico, men dressed as women and who were forbidden to carry arms were espoused as wives. According to Gomara there were at Tamulipas houses of prostitution the inmates of which were men. [1] Diaz relates that, on the coasts of Mexico, pederasty was a common vice, although it was considered as a crime and severely punished. Duflot found these vices contrary to nature very common in California. Pederasty was general in Nicaragua. The first

---

[1] For further details on ancient pederasty and collateral vices the student is referred to *Geschichte der Lustseuche im Alterthume* by Dr. Julius Rosenbaum, an English translation of which, with literal rendering of the Latin and Greek passages, has been carefully done by Alfred R. Allinson, Esq. M.A. (Oxon) and will be published by the editor of the present work. The curious reader may also consult Dr. Virey, *De la Femme*, Paris, 1827, from which Mantegazza has borrowed the majority of his Latin references given in the text; and also Forberg's *Manual of Classical Erotology*, Paris, *Liseux*, 1882.

explorers found it implanted among the aborigines of Panama, although disapproved of by them. It was the same in ancient Peru, on the coast of Guayaquil.

"Many travellers have also met with it among the natives of North America. There men could be seen, dressed as women, and occupied in household work. From Alaoka to Darien are to be seen youths brought up and dressed like women, and who live in concubinage with the chiefs and great personages. The Aleoutians, the Codiaks and the inhabitants of Nutka had also this shameful custom. The ancient travellers often mention the existence of these horrible vices among the Caribs of the Continent; but at Cumanea, on the contrary, sodomy was execrated.

"It appears that at Madagascar vices contrary to nature are not wanting, as is proved by the existence of singers and dancers dressed as women.

"In the East, and unhappily in Europe also, neither children nor women are wanting for the satisfaction of this degrading pleasure, and in certain cities of Italy the sodomists have a language by signs to indicate that they can conjugate the verb in the active or in the passive tense (*cinedi* or *patici*)."

Prof. Mantegazza's Curious Theory. "This infamous vice is not confined to the lower classes of our society; it is to be found also among the richest and most intelligent. In the narrow circle of my acquaintance I have met with a French man of letters, a German poet, an Italian politician, and a Spanish lawyer, all of whom were addicted to it. Why is it that this disgusting form of licentiousness is so often to be met with? I think that I have found the solution of the problem.

" Anatomists are aware of the close connection that exists between the nerves that are distributed to the rectum and those which go to the genital organs. Perhaps by reason of some anomaly, in men given to this disgusting aberration the net-work of nerves which preside over the voluptuous sensations go to the rectum, and that it is their excitation which induces in the *patici* the venereal orgasm which, in ordinary cases, can be procured only by the sexual organ. What still further pleads in favour of this explanation, is that there are to be found female *patici*, women who, in the act of tribadism, like to have the rectum excited by the finger, men who can obtain erection only by foreign objects being introduced into the rectum. And I remember very well the case of a great writer who admitted to me that he had not yet been able to discern whether he experienced more voluptuous feeling during coition or during defecation.

" It is easier to explain the voluptuous sensation in the *cinedi* who experience a genuine orgasm on an ignoble track, preferred on account of its narrowness. That explains also why, in many countries, sodomy is practised on children only, whence the name pederasty, and why it is far more frequent in warm countries where the vagina becomes very large, and the continual aspect of naked bodies and the facility of obtaining women blunts the pleasure.

" However, it very often happens that sodomy is not of peripheric origin but resides in the nervous centres. I therefore admit *peripheric* or anatomical sodomy (by an abnormal distribution of the nerves), *lustful* sodomy (from desire of narrowness), and psychical sodomy. [1]

[1] Krafft-Ebing thinks that the above is " one of the strangest explanations of congenital contrary sexual feeling" that has been made. " How

"The author of the *Voyage d'Anacharsis* says that the laws of ancient Greece protected the prostitutes in order to combat pederasty.—Aspasia, the mistress of Pericles, of Socrates and of Alcibiades, encouraged the love between the two latter. Plato has preserved us a fragment of a dialogue between Socrates and Aspasia: 'Socrates, I have read in thy heart, it is burning for the son of Dynomaché and of Clinias. Listen, if thou would'st have the handsome Alcibiades respond to thy love; be docile to the counsels of my tenderness.—O, intoxicating words! exclaimed Socrates, O ecstasy! a cold sweat has gone through my body, my eyes have filled with tears.—Cease thy sighs, she interrupted, full of sacred enthusiasm, elevate thy mind to the divine intoxications of poetry; that enchanting art will open to thee the sanctuary of his soul. The sweets of poetry fascinate the intellect, the ear is the road to the heart which is the portal to all the rest.'— In the grand times of the Latin civilisation, pederasty was a tolerated form of prostitution and of slavery. Citizens were not to give way to the desires of a libertine, but slaves and emancipated slaves could and were indeed obliged to do so. In Rome masculine prostitution was more ardent and more general than the feminine, and the obscene traces of it are to be found in the verses of Catullus, of Martial and even

does this author," says he, "in other ways so acute, explain the great majority of cases, where pederasty is abhorred by those affected with contrary sexual feeling? Besides, Nature never makes such leaps. Mantegazza rests his hypothesis upon the statements of an acquaintance, a celebrated writer, who affirmed to him that he was not sure that he took a greater pleasure in coitus than in defecation! Allowing the correctness of this experience, still it would only prove that the man was sexually abnormal, and that his pleasure in coitus was reduced to a minimum." Krafft-Ebing, *opus cit.*, p. 227—8.

of Virgil. The ignoble Greek poet Sotades gave his name to some poems which were inspired him by the loves of three men.   In ancient Rome the barbers' shops were often houses of male prostitution:

" ' Quorum frequente opera non in tondenda barba, pilisque vellendis modo, sed vero et pygiacis sacris cinædice, ne nefarie dicam, de nocte administrandis utebantur.'

(Whose services were utilised frequently not only for shaving the beard and plucking out superfluous hairs, but also in serving by night à la cinædus, not to speak coarsely, the rites of *posterior* sacrifice).

(Commentaries of Douza on Petronius).

"Moses is perhaps the only legislator previous to Christ who has cast anathema upon pederasty—At Constantinople under Constantine there were even houses of prostitution where men sold themselves like women —In France, after the crusades, this vice became general and a poet of that period, Gauthier de Coincy, prior of the Abbey of Saint Medardus at Soissons, depicts the life in convents in far from edifying colours:

"'La grammaire *hic* à *hic* accouple
Mais Nature maldit le couple.
La mort perpetuel engenre
Cil qui aime masculin genre
Plus que le feminin ne face
Et Dieu de son livre l'efface.
Nature rit, si com moi semble
Quand *hic* et *hoc* joignent ensemble.
Mais *hic* et *hic*, chose est perdue,
Nature en est tost esperdue . . .'

"Philippe le Bel adopted energetic measures to prevent sodomy, and the celebrated trial of the Knights Templars revealed horrible things.   The following is the testimony of Jean de Saint-Just:

" ' *Deinde dixit ei quod poterat carnaliter commisceri cum fratribus ordinis et patι quod ipsi commiscerentur cum eo; hoc tamen non fecit nec fuit requisitus, nec scit, nec audivit quod fratres ordinis commiterent peccatum prædictum.*'

(Then he told him that he could have intercourse carnally with the brethren of the Order, and suffer them to have intercourse with him; this, however, he did not do nor was required to do, nor does he know nor has ever heard that the brethren of the Order committed the aforesaid sin).

" Still more explicit is the evidence given by Rodolphe de Taverne:

" ' *Deinde dixit ei quod, ex quo voverat castitatem, debebat abstinere a mulieribus, ne ordo infamaretur; verumtamen secundum dicta puncta, si haberet calorem naturalem, poterat refrigerare, et carnaliter commisceri cum fratribus ordinis, et ipsi commiscerentur cum eo; hoc tamen non fecit, nec credit quod in ordine fieret.*'

(Then he told him that from the time he had vowed chastity he was bound to abstain from women, that the Order should not be disgraced. Nevertheless, according to his words and ordinances, if he felt the natural heat of blood, he could have intercourse carnally with the brethren of the Order, and they have intercourse with him; however, he did not do this, and does not believe that it was done in the Order).

" Dufour attributes to the Italians who accompanied Marie de Medicis to France the spread of sodomy in that country. It is true that in Italy at that time the punishment of sodomy was a fine of only 36 livres tournois and 9 ducats, whereas in France the penalty of this crime was the stake (a punishment very seldom applied it is true).—It is curious to read the discussion of confessors on the various sins that can be committed in the way of sodomy by a man with a woman (see

Jean Benedicti, *Somme des péchés et remèdes d'iceux*, Lyons, 1534). Sanchez condemned sodomy between husband and wife as a mortal sin:

" ' *Duabus mulieribus apud synagogam conquestis se fuisse a viris suis sodomice cognitis, responsum est ab illis rabbinis: virum esse uxoris dominum, proinde posse uti ejus utcunque libuerit, non aliter quam is qui pisceno: ille enim tam anterioribus quam posterioribus partibus, ad arbitrium vesci potest.'* [1]

(Two women having made complaint before the synagogue that they had been known by their husbands *sodomically*, it was answered by those Rabbis: that the man was master of the woman, consequently that he could use her as he pleased, as does one who uses a vessel: for he can satisfy himself with the anterior or the posterior parts at his own will and pleasure).

" To return to psychical sodomy, several cases of which form I have had occasion to study. It more particularly attacks well educated, intelligent men who are often neuropathic subjects. A young man of high family and very chaste came to consult me because he perceived that he loved and desired persons of his own sex, whereas he remained insensible to the seductions of women. He was seized with violent erotic spasms whenever he kissed a child. In order to study himself, he went to a house of prostitution and remained insensible to all provocations. This unfortunate young man, who resisted with all his might, assured me that he would commit suicide if he could not come out victor from the strife. I do not know whether he succeeded for I have never seen him since.

[1] See the remarks of Havelock Ellis on the teachings, and the interest taken in sexual problems by the Catholic Church, Preface to *Sexual Inversion*, Lond. 1897.

"Psychical sodomy is not a vice, but a passion. A culpable, revolting and disgusting passion as much as you please, but a passion. These sodomists told me in their confession, which I read with tears, that they adored their lovers with real jealousy. They gave them tokens of love, wrote tender, chaste and poetical letters to them. In a certain Italian town, they walk out together in the evening in the darkest corners of the public gardens; they kiss each other and embrace with the most irresistible passion."

The Symptomatic Characteristics of the Pederasty of the Kanaka are guided by this rule: he uses a man when he cannot get a woman, and, when he *can* get a woman, no longer practises the vice. With him it is not a morbid passion, as it is in the old civilised countries of the Extreme East, where lust is satisfied indifferently on either men or women, and either the active or passive rôle assumed with the greatest facility. With the Kanaka, it is simply a mutual interchange of kindnesses which are quite simple and natural,—if that expression can be used in regard to acts which are unnatural. I may add that anal copulation is practised bestially, without any of the refinements of lust in which the Chinese, and more especially the Annamites, are so expert. But I will say no more on this filthy subject.

At what age do the young Kanakas commence to practise this vice? From the confessions made to me, I am able to state that matters are very much the same as they are in our large educational establishments. I say *our*, but should rather have said *the*, for sodomy is universal in Europe, and has taken root everywhere. Before puberty, the young Kanakas masturbate among themselves; after puberty, and the operation of demi-circumcision, and at an age when the yard is not yet fully developed, they take to anal coition. All the young sodomites I examined, bore the marks of being both active and passive agents.

Cruelties and Erotic Mutilations committed by the Kanakas during the Insurrection. I have explained at some length his innate ferocity. He never tortures his living enemies, but he abuses their dead carcases, and mutilates them erotically, after having glutted his brutal lusts on their still breathing bodies. I have also mentioned that the Kanaka lusts after the White woman. Not being able to possess her alive, in some cases, during the insurrection, he killed her, and made her dead body the instrument of his lust.

Many were the cases that came under my personal notice of rapes on White women, more often than not followed by mutilation and murder. And I could fill a fairly large size work with strange details of savage crimes. The question of the association of lust and cruelty will be examined a few pages further on. I shall not therefore stop to enquire into this matter here, but direct the student's attention to the close juridical analysis of this crime, which has been made by Krafft-Ebing:—By the term rape, the jurist understands coitus, outside of the marriage relation, with an adult, enforced by means of threats or violence; or with an adult in a condition of defencelessness or unconsciousness; or with a girl under the age of fourteen years. Immissio penis, or, at least, conjunctio membrorum (Schütze), is necessary to establish the fact. To-day, rape on children is remarkably frequent.

Hofmann ("Ger. Med." I, p. 155) and Tardieu ("Attentats") report horrible cases.

The crime of rape presumes a temporary, powerful excitation of sexual desire, induced by excess in alcohol, or by some other condition. It is highly improbable that a man morally intact would commit this most brutal crime. Lombroso (Goltdammer's *Arch.*) considers the majority of men who commit rape to be degenerate, particularly when the crime is done on children or old women. He asserts, that, in many such men, he has found actual signs of degeneracy.

It is a fact that rape is very often the act of degenerate male imbeciles, [1] where, under some circumstances, the bond of blood is not respected. Cases as a result of mania, satyriasis, and epilepsy, have occurred, and are to be kept in mind.

The crime of rape may follow the murder of the victim. [2] There may be unintentional murder, murder to destroy the only witness of the crime, or murder out of lust (*v. supra*). Only for cases of the latter kind should the term *lust-murder* [3] be used. The motives of lust-murder have been previously considered. The cases given in illustration are characteristic of the manner of the deed. The presumption of a murder out of lust is always given when injuries of the genitals are found, the character and extent of which are such as could not be explained by merely a brutal attempt at coitus; and still more, when the body has been opened, or parts (intestines, genitals) torn out, and are wanting. [4]

[1] Annal. médico-psychol., 1849, p. 515; 1863, p. 57; 1864, p. 215; 1866, p. 253.

[2] Comp. the cases of Tardieu, Attentats, p. 182—192.

[3] Comp. Haltzendorff, Psychologie des Mords.

[4] Tardieu, Attentats, Case 51, p. 188.

A Case of German "Lust-murder." However shocking the preceding case, and others I may later relate, may appear to the student, I hardly need to remind him of the fact that others, quite as bad, have been perpetrated in Europe by people, who were not held to be savages, at least not by race, and who had the advantage of being brought up "under the shadow of the Cross." Works on Medical Jurisprudence are filled with them. We will content ourselves with a case recited by Krafft-Ebing who points out that these "lust-murders are never committed with accomplices."

"On the evening of May 27, 1888, an eight-year-old boy, Blasius, was playing with other children in the neighbourhood of the village of S. An unknown man came along and enticed the boy into the woods. The next day the boy's body was found in a ravine, with the abdomen slit open, an incised wound in the cardiac region, and two stab-wounds in the neck.

"Since, on May 21st, a man, answering to the description given of the murderer by the children, had attempted to treat a six-year-old girl in a similar manner, and had only accidentally been detected, it was presumed to be a case of lust-murder. It was proved that the body was found in a heap, with only the shirt and jacket on; also, that there was a long incision in the scrotum.

"Suspicion fell upon a peasant, E.; but, on confrontation with the children, it was not possible to identify him with the stranger who had enticed the boy into the woods. Besides, with the help of his sister, he proved an alibi. The untiring efforts of the officers brought new evidence to light, and finally E. confessed. He had enticed the girl into the woods, thrown her down, exposed her genitals, and was about to abuse her; but, as she had an eruption on her head, and was crying loudly, his desire cooled, and he fled.

" After he enticed the boy into the woods, with the pretext of showing him a bird's nest, he was taken with a desire to abuse him. Since the boy refused to take off his trousers, he did it for him; and when the boy began to cry out, he stabbed him twice in the neck. Then he made an incision, just above the pubes, in imitation of female genitals, in order to use it to satisfy his lust. But, since the body grew cold immediately, he lost his desire, and, cleaning his knife and hands near the body, he fled. When he saw the boy dead, he was filled with fear, and his limbs became weak.

" During his examination E. looked apathetically at a garland. He had acted in a state of mental weakness. He could not understand how he came to do such a thing. He must have been beside himself; for he often became senseless, so that he would almost fall down. Previous employers report that he had periods when he was devoid of thought and confused, doing no work all day, and avoiding others. His father states that E. learned with difficulty, was unskilful at work, and often so obstinate that one did not think to punish him. At such times he would not eat, and occasionally ran away and remained all day. At such times he also seemed quite lost in thought, screwed his face up, and said senseless things. When quite a boy, he still sometimes wetted the bed, and often came home from school with wet or soiled clothing. He was very restless in sleep, so that no one could sleep beside him. He had never had playmates. He had never been cruel, bad, or immoral.

" His mother gave similar testimony; and further, that in his fifth year, E. first had convulsions, and once lost the power of speech for seven days. Some time about his seventh year he once had convulsions for forty days, and was also dropsical. Later, too, he was often seized in sleep, and he often then talked in his sleep; and mornings, after such nights, the bed was found wet.

" At times it was impossible to do anything with him. Since his mother did not know whether it was due to viciousness or disease, she did not venture to punish him.

" Since his convulsions, in his seventh year, he had failed so in mind that he could not learn even the common prayers, and he also became very irascible.

" Neighbours, persons prominent in the community, and teachers state that E. was peculiar, weak-minded, and irascible; that at times he was very strange, and apparently in an exceptional mental state.

" The examinations of the medical experts gave the following results:—E. is tall, slim, and poorly nourished. His head measures 53 centimeters in circumference. The cranium is rhombic, and in the occipital region flattened.

" His expression is devoid of intelligence; his glance is fixed, expressionless; his attitude is careless, and his body is bent forward. Movements are slow and heavy. Genitals normally developed. E.'s whole appearance points to torpidity and mental weakness.

" There are no signs of degenerative marks, no abnormity of the vegetative organs, and no disturbances of motility or sensibility. He comes of a perfectly healthy family. He knows nothing of convulsions or of wetting his bed at night, but he states that, of late years, he has had attacks of vertigo and loss of mind.

"At first, in circumlocution, he denies the murder. Later, in great contrition, before the examining judge, he confessed all, and gave a clear motive for his crime. He had never had such a thought before.

"He has been given to onanism for years; he even practised it twice daily. He states that, for want of courage, he had never ventured to ask coitus of a woman, though in dreams such scenes exclusively passed before him. Neither in dreams nor in the waking state had he ever had perverse instincts; particularly no sadistic or contrary sexual feelings. Also, the sight of the slaughter of animals had never interested him. When he enticed the girl into the woods, his desire was to satisfy his lust with her; but how it happened that he tried such a thing with a boy, he could not explain. He thought he must have been out of his mind at that time. The night after the murder he could not sleep on account of fear; he had twice confessed already, to ease his conscience. He was only afraid of being hung. This should not be done, as he had done the deed in a weak-minded condition.

"He could not tell why he had cut open the boy's abdomen. It had not occurred to him to handle the intestines, smell them, etc.

"He stated that, after the attempt on the girl in the day-time, and in the night, after the murder of the boy, he had convulsions. At the time of his crime he was indeed conscious, but he had not thought at all of what he did.

"He suffered much with headache; could not endure heat, thirst, or alcohol; there were times when he was perfectly confused. The test of his intelligence showed a high grade of weak-mindedness.

" The opinion (Dr. Kautzner, of Graz) showed the imbecility and neurosis of the accused, and made it probable that his crime, of which he had only a general recollection, had been committed in an exceptional (præ-epileptic) mental state, conditioned by the neurosis. Under all circumstances, E. was considered dangerous, and probably would require commitment to an asylum for life." [1]

It seems almost a relief after this, to get back to our Kanakas in the woods, for amongst them we are used to this sort of thing, and experience has taught us to wait for it, ever on the alert with horse and revolver to fight or to fly as circumstances may dictate. I would be the last to undertake the defence of the atrocious acts of the Kanaka, but *he* can at least plead his savage, " uncivilised" condition, and moreover, has centuries of inherited tendency behind him impelling him (" quien sabe?") irresistibly on towards the realisation of his necrophilic instincts.

White Women beheaded and violated. There is plenty of evidence that the unfortunate wives and daughters of the colonists, who were killed during the insurrection, were decapitated, and afterwards violated. Many were eaten;—the limbs and the breasts at least, if not the entire body. The bodies that were found, bore marks of erotic mutilations of a fantastic kind.

When war is declared, and hostilities commence, the warriors are ordered to avoid women. Copulation is forbidden to them, but to violate the headless trunks of White women is not considered an infringement of the rule. The reader may perhaps think I am exaggerating, so I will therefore ask permission to lay

[1] Krafft-Ebing, *Psychopathia Sexualis*, p. 397.

before him a couple of quotations, in support of my statements. The first is an account of the massacres of la Foa and la Fonwari, as related by Commandant Rivière.

"The Kanakas continue to murder, and to set fire to the houses. The waggons afford a proof of this. One is laden with wounded people, the other with sixteen dead bodies. Most of the wounded are insensible, some groan, and others are delirious. The wounds, which are nearly always on the skull, or back of the neck, are deep cuts, made with the axe, or the bird's beak club. All these persons have been struck from behind, at a moment when they did not expect it, by Kanakas whom they knew. The savages had amused themselves by practising on the dead bodies various refinements of cruelty or lust. Some of the limbs were wanting, and had been separated from the trunk by an axe. Others showed *ablations made with a knife, or even with the teeth*, or monstrous or derisive obstructions with wooden plugs."

In spite of the intentional reticence of the author, the reader will understand the nature of these ablations and obstructions. [1]

Bechir, the Arab. A short time after the insurrection had been put down, I became acquainted with one of the Arab convicts, who had acted as a scout against the Kanakas. This Arab, whose name was Bechir, had distinguished himself by his courage, and

[1] "Eunuchs and Eunuchism" (in course of preparation) will contain an account of a number of cases of similar mutilations which have been perpetrated *in Europe*. There does not exist, as far as we know, any work dealing specifically, and in a serious way, with this department of medical and juridical anthropology.

he was an eye-witness of the massacre of Bouloupari.
He had asked, as the sole reward for his services, to
be sent back to Algeria, and passed his time in writing
begging petitions, in which he naïvely recounted his
brave deeds. From one of these petitions, I extract
the following lines, which are also reproduced in the
Lettres d'un Marin.

" I arrived at Bouloupari, and first went towards
the Gendarmerie. There were four horses in the stables.
Near a hay-cart, two convicts lay, bathed in their
blood. I then went to the Kiosque, where the gendarmes usually took their meals. Ten yards from the
Kiosque, lay the body of the cook, face downwards.
He had been struck with an axe on the back of the
neck, and his hands were still holding in their death
grip a dish broken in two. Four gendarmes had met
their death as they were leaving the Kiosque,—no
doubt to fetch their arms. At the telegraph office, the
body of the clerk lay in the road, his face turned
towards the sky; his little black dog was watching
beside him. Behind the telegraph office was the house
of the Kleiches; the husband lay with his skull split;
his wife was naked, her body covered with wounds
and bruises, *and a broken bottle pushed into her belly.*

" Still keeping on my horse, for I was afraid of being
taken alive, I entered the convicts' camp. They lay
pell-mell, murdered during their siesta; two of them
were still in their dying agonies. At the overseers'
hut, the fire prevented me from counting the victims.
At Mostini's house, all were dead; Mme Mostini had
been violated, *and her abdomen torn open up to the
navel.* Her little sister had taken refuge under the
body. She had also been killed, and had suffered the
same mutilation as her sister."

Louis, the Kanaka Interpreter. Louis, a Kanaka, an interpreter on board a ship, and who spoke French very well, played an important part in the massacres of la Poya. He was employed by a European merchant. He fell in love with Mme V***, a superb blonde, the wife of an English colonist, and as she refused to favour his suit, he resolved to profit by the massacre of the Whites to satisfy his passion. Knowing that the husband was absent, he went to Mme V***'s house, with five other Kanakas. They began by murdering the children. Mme V*** seized a loaded double-barrelled shot gun, and killed two of the assassins. Then Louis, the interpreter, split her head open. At this moment M. V*** rode up on horseback, but seeing that the murderers were four to one, he had not the courage to attempt to avenge the murder of his wife and family, and rode off at full gallop. Louis satisfied his brutal passion upon the still palpitating body of the poor woman, then the Kanakas cut her in pieces, as they would a sheep, roasted her at a Kanaka stove, and Louis ate, for his share, the heart and one of the arms. These facts were notorious at Oubatche, where Louis was shot, and were related to me by a colonist, who was present at the execution of the interpreter. [1]

Acts of Sadism. The kind of crime last described falls into the category of what is known as "Sadism," by which term is meant the "association of lust and cruelty" as a means of satisfying the senses, the name of course being derived from that of the infamous Marquis de Sade. [2] It is possible that,

[1] Tardieu establishes the fact that, from 1851 to 1875 inclusive, 22,017 cases of rape came before the courts in France, and, of these, 17,657 were conmitted on **children!**

[2] Leo Taxil gives some interesting details of this sexual monster,

although violence would undoubtedly have been in
any case employed, murder would not have followed
the accomplishment of the sexual act had not this
courageous woman " shown fight ", and quietly submitted
to the monster's lustful attacks. Krafft-Ebing, the
great pathologist, than whom no other has made a
more profound study of these delicate matters, points
out that " the conquest of woman takes place to-day in
the social form of courting, in seduction and deception.
From the history of civilisation and anthropology we
know that there have been times, as there are savages
to-day that practice it, where brutal force, robbery, or
even blows that rendered a woman powerless, were
made use of to obtain love's desire. It is possible
that tendencies to such outbreaks of sadism are
atavistic." Under the section of " Paraesthesia of
Sexual Feeling"—" Perversion of the Sexual Instinct"
which must have been a case, Krafft-Ebing thinks, " of habitual satyriasis, accompanied by perverse sexual instinct." Sade was so cynical
that he deliberately sought to idealise his cruel lasciviousness, and took
glory in proclaiming himself, by all means available, the apostle of a
theory based upon it. Utterly corrupt both in mind and body, he lost
no opportunity of realising his lustful theories. Amongst other sensual
erraticisms, he threw an entire company of ladies and gentlemen into
an erotic paroxysm, who had responded to his invitation to dinner, by
causing them to be served with chocolate *bon-bons* which contained a strong
mixture of cantharides. His lewdness and perversity earned for him a
committal to the Insane Asylum at Charenton, from which he made
good his escape during the Revolution of 1790. He afterwards wrote
(the fruit of his meditations at the French " Colney Hatch " ?) obscene
novels filled with lust, cruelty and the most disgustingly obscene scenes
which the human imagination in the hour of its wildest nightmare has ever
bodied forth. He had the audacity to present Bonaparte with a mag-
nificently bound copy of these "precious" productions, on the latter's
attaining the Consulate. It is to the credit of Bonaparte that he had
these works destroyed, and the author again lodged at Charenton,
where he died, at the age of 64.

in that comprehensive work "Psychopathia Sexualis,"
the student will find quite sufficient fact and theory
to start him on the road of independent enquiry for
himself. The German doctor calls special attention to
the "Association of Active Cruelty and Violence with
Lust" to which phenomenon, he says, writers of all
kinds have invited notice. [1]

The Mutilation and Outraging of Corpses come
under the designation of sadistic acts, and are probably
amongst the most horrible of all sexual perversions.
The necrophiles form a group apart. They call for
the pitiful-loving study of the anthropologist and
alienist, for no other can relieve or understand their
awful state of mind.

"This horrible kind of sexual indulgence," says Krafft-
Ebing (p. 430), "is so monstrous that the presumption
of a psychopathic state is, under all circumstances,
justified; and Maschka's recommendation, that the
mental condition of the perpetrator should always be
investigated, is well founded. In any case, an abnormal
and decidedly perverse sensuality is required to overcome the natural repugnance which man has for a
corpse, and permit a feeling of pleasure to be experienced
in sexual congress with a cadaver.

"Unfortunately, in the majority of the cases reported
the mental condition was not examined; so that the
question whether necrophilia is compatible with mental
soundness must remain open. But anyone having
knowledge of the horrible aberrations of the sexual
instinct would not venture, without further consideration,
to answer the question in the negative."

[1] U. A. Novalis in his *Fragments;* Görres, *Christliche Mystik,*
vol. III, p. 460.

In these cases, just as with lustful murderers and analogous cases, an idea which in itself awakens a feeling of horror, and before which a healthy person would shudder, is accompanied by lustful feelings, and thus leads to the impulse to indulge in acts of necrophilia.

The cases of mutilation of bodies mentioned in literature seem to be pathological; but, with the exception of the celebrated one of Sergeant Bertrand, [1] they come far from being described and observed with exactness. In certain cases there may be nothing more than the possibility that unbridled desire sees in the idea of death no obstacle to its satisfaction. The seventh case mentioned by Moreau is perhaps such a one :—

A man, aged 23, attempted to rape a woman, aged 53. Struggling, he killed her and then violated her, threw her in the water, and fished her out again for renewed violation. The murderer was executed. The meninges of the anterior lobes were thickened and adherent to the cortex. French writers have recorded numerous examples of necrophilia. Two cases concerned monks, where they were performing the watch for the dead. In a third case the subject was an idiot, who also suffered from periodical mania, and after commission of rape was sent to an insane asylum, and there mutilated female bodies in the mortuary.

In other cases, however, there is undoubtedly direct preference of a corpse to the living woman. When no other act of cruelty—cutting into pieces, etc.—is practised on the cadaver, it is probable that the life-

---

[1] *Vide* Krafft-Ebing, *Psychopathia Sexualis*, Philadelphia, 1895, p. 69—70; Legrand, *La folie devant les Tribunaux*, p. 524; Tardieu, *Attentats aux Mœurs*, Paris, 1878, p. 114.

less condition itself forms the stimulus for the perverse individual. It is possible that the corpse—a human form absolutely without will—satisfies an abnormal desire, in that the object of desire is seen to be capable of absolute subjugation, without possibility of resistance. Brierre de Boismont ("Gazette médicale", July 21st, 1859) relates the history of a corpse-violator who, after bribing the watchman, had gained entrance to the corpse of a girl of sixteen, who belonged to a family of high social position. At night a noise was heard in the death-chamber, as if a piece of furniture had fallen over. The mother of the dead girl effected an entrance, and saw a man dressed in his night-shirt springing from the bed where the body lay. It was at first thought that the man was a thief, but the real explanation was soon discovered. It was afterward ascertained that the culprit, a man of good family, had often violated the bodies of young women. He was sentenced to imprisonment for life. The story of a prelate, reported by Taxil ("La prostitution contemporaine", p. 171), is of great interest as an example of necrophilia. From time to time he would visit houses of prostitution in Paris and order a prostitute, dressed in white like a corpse, to be laid out on a bed. At the appointed hour he would appear in the room, which, in the meantime, had been elaborately prepared as a room of mourning; then he would act as if reading a mass for the soul, and finally throw himself on the girl, who, during the whole time, was compelled to play the rôle of a corpse. [1] We have neither time nor space to go into Krafft-Ebing's ex-

---

[1] Simon (*Crimes et délits*, p. 209) mentions an experience of Lacassagne's, to whom a respectable man said that he was never intensely excited sexually except when a spectator at a funeral.

planation of the pathological conditions that give rise to these lustful obsessions; our aim will be sufficiently attained if we induce the student to go directly to the master's work.

Krafft-Ebing is careful to observe that "the not infrequent cases where individuals of very excitable sexual natures bite or scratch the companion in intercourse fall within physiological limits." In the course of my practice I have known numbers of both sexes resort to this where the harm done was very small and due to nothing else than intense passion for the beloved. I may be allowed to quote three lines from Alfred de Musset's ode to the Andalusian girl and am sure that the beauty of them will more than justify me in the reader's eyes for their introduction.

> " Qu'elle est superbe en son désordre—
>   Quand elle tombe les seins nus—
> Qu'on la voit béante, se tordre—
>   Dans un baiser de rage et mordre—
> En hurlant des mots inconnus ! "

CHAPTER V.

The convict in New Caledonia.—The motives for this chapter. — The Penitentiary of Nou Island.—The convict as a family servant.—The ticket-of-leave man.— The convent of Bourail.— Lesbians and "fellatrices".—Tribadism in Europe.— Tribads are not Sapphics.— The courtesans of Greece.—Lombroso on the causes of this vice.—Natural wantonness.—Environment as a Factor. —Secret clubs of vice.—Advanced age, another cause.—Disgust born of excess.—Congenital tendency.— The criminality of husbands.— The military post at Bourail.—The General's cap. —"Je m'emmerde, and I want a man".—Marriage of liberated convicts.—Sodomy and pederasty amongst the convicts.—Prisons as breeder of vice.— The universality of the vice.—Infamous passions.

The Motives for this Chapter. I will terminate the portion of the book relating to New Caledonia, by saying a few words about transportation, in order to complete the study of the subject I have already made concerning Guiana. I have said that as the worthy ex-convicts died like flies, in the unhealthy colony of Guiana, some philanthropic humanitarians had the ingenious idea of sending them to New Caledonia, one of the healthiest climates in the world, and one of the very few tropical climates in which a European can work without danger from the sun. I will not discuss here the future of this kind of colonisation, I will con-

tent myself with studying the special manners of these
not very interesting personages.

The Penitentiary of Nou Island. On Nou Island,
at the entrance to the harbour of Noumea, is the central Penitentiary, containing three to four thousand
convicts.   In the environs of Noumea, and in certain
other places in the Colony, are camps of convicts, employed in works outside the Penitentiary, which, however, contains all the central workshops.   The office
of the Penitentiary Administration is at Noumea, and
there application must be made to obtain convicts, who
are hired out for a certain sum.   All cannot obtain this
favour, but only those convicts whose conduct is "first-
class", who by their docility, and relative morality,
deserve the good opinion of the officers.

The Convict as a Family Domestic. From the
class last mentioned,—which, if not the most culpable
is, in my eyes at least, the most hypocritical—
are taken the *garçons de famille* who occupy, in
the households of civilians, and the functionaries of
the Penitentiary, the same position that the "orderly"
does in military households.   Commandant Rivière, in
his *Souvenirs de la Nouvelle Calédonie*, describes in
a sentimental and—in my opinion—much too flattering
manner, these *garçons de famille*. He makes them
out to be,—not men marked with the brand of infamy,
but valuable assistants, and companions, to whom you
easily get habituated.   With all due deference to him,
I think this glowing account must be considerably
toned down.   Those who employ the *garçons de famille*,
do so because their means do not allow them to take
other servants. A "hired man" from the New Hebrides

is much more trustworthy, and faithful, than a first-class convict. " The cask always smells of the herring," as the old proverb truly says. If the *garçon de famille* does not dare to steal, at least he will become, whenever you send him away, a valuable accomplice of his comrades who have escaped from Nou Island, and who at Noumea, rob almost with impunity. When this excellent servant learns where you keep your money, he will make it known to his friends and acquaintances, and some fine night, when you return home, you will find that your house has been cleaned out. Not. only money, but also clothes and arms, will become the spoil of the robber, who, thus rigged out, can hide himself in the suburbs of Noumea, and, if need be, defend himself against the Kanakas of the native police, who are always on the track of escaped convicts.

The Liberated Convict. When the transported convict, condemned to eight years or more of hard labour, has finished his time, he has to reside, for the same number of years, in some fixed residence. He then becomes *Monsieur le Libéré*, and the never failing manna of the favour of the prison authorities is rained upon him ever and always. For " Messieurs les Libérés " there has been created a real colony, in the valley of Bourail, the finest, largest, and most fertile valley in the island. Commandant Rivière has described this colony in his book, as he saw it through the enchanted prism of his imagination. To this work, from which I have already quoted, I refer the reader anxious to know his opinion. Mine is radically different, and the picture of the existence of the liberated convict, who has been granted an allotment, is, to my mind, quite

misleading.   He makes out these ex-convicts to be
repenting angels.   I venture to assert that they are
quite the reverse, and support my statement by the
general opinion of all the colonists of New Caledonia.
For, in the first place, it iş not in the power of any
regulations in the world, reformatory or not, to alter
human nature when it is vicious.   In the name of
common sense, what are we to expect from the union
of a thief, or an assassin, with a girl convicted of infanticide, or, at least, a thief, or a prostitute, or a jail bird
of some kind, from the central prison?

The Convent of Bourail.   Let us speak in the
first place of the celebrated convent of Bourail, the
inmates of which are sweet and docile lambs, according
to Commandant Rivière.   In this etablishment are penned
up (the word is not a whit too strong) a lot of women
sent from France, and who have been taken from the
central prisons to make future mothers of families.   On
their arrival at Noumea, on the steamers (generally
those of the Compagnie des Chargeurs Réunis of
Havre), they are sent direct to the convent at Bourail,
that they may recover from the fatigue of the journey,
and live in peace and piety, until the excellent Administration gives them husbands after their own heart.
The reader may easily guess, whether nymphs of this
sort are likely to spend their time in telling their beads,
knitting socks, or making baby linen.   The first thing
they demand with might and main, is a Government
grant, with a man attached to it.   Like the Greeks in
La Belle Hélène, they must have love if it was all
there was in the world.

Lesbians [1] **and Fellatrices.** [2] They continue in the
convent their habits as Lesbians and fellatrices which
they have learned in those convents of France, on the
doors of which are inscribed " No. 69", in large characters,
and from which many of them come. The others have
walked the streets of the large towns, and are not much
better, if they are not worse. The " *marmite* " of the
souteneur makes a worthy pair with the whore from
the brothel. It may easily be understood, that,—with
the best will in the world,— the sisters of Saint Joseph,
who have the charge of the souls of this flock of
scabby sheep, cannot be everywhere. Oh, those poor
sisters! To gain their place in Paradise, they must
suffer Hell upon earth. In spite of the means they
have for dissipating the *ennuis* of confinement, the
prisoners want the open air and liberty, and are inclined
to marry the first-comer who means business. No
matter what is the age, the appearance, or the skin,

[1] A verb exists, *lesbiare* (λεσβιάζειν), to depict this vice. Blondeau's
dict. defines it "*Aimer à la manière de Sappho; vouloir imiter les
hommes dans les caresses qu'on fait aux belles personnes de son
sexe; tribader; gamahucher.* Les Lesbiennes sont célèbres pour avoir
rendu la bouche le plus fréquent organe de là volupté. Elles employ-
aient la langue à se faire plaisir mutuellement, et elles affectaient la
blancheur aux lèvres. We have already spoken of the novels on the
vice; one of them, *Les deux Amies* of René Maizeroy was suppressed.

[2] Latin *fellator, fellatrix* from *fellare*, to suck; mettre dans la
bouche le membre en érection; also called *irrumare* which, as showing
the frightful distortion of words, meant (*vide* Forberg) "to give the
breast" It is strange that a disgusting habit of this kind should have
found an author. *Les Fellatores*, is a book that was suppressed, but
copies are still to be met with. See for fuller explanation of these
words, with illustrative passages from the ancient writers, Rambach's
Thesaurus Eroticus Linguae Latinae (Stuttgart, 1833); Forberg's
Manuel d'Erotologie Classique (Paris, 1882); and Blondeau's *Dictionnaire Erotique latin-français* (Paris, Liseux, 1885).

of Monsieur le Libéré who comes to ask their hand.
He brings liberty at the end of his Φαλλος, and that
is all they want.

We take this opportunity to go more fully into the
nature and causes of this frightful feminine perversion,
which, since I quitted the colonies, seems to have made
such terrible strides as a factor not to be counted with
lightly. Our observations to a large extent are based
upon the profound and extensive study of our master,
Lombroso, whom we have to thank for many a fertile
suggestion. His able work, *La Femme Criminelle et
la Prostituée* is a mine of information upon the vices
and waywardness of womankind.

Tribadism in Europe. The sole predominant anomaly which is really very prevalent among prostitutes,
is, says Lombroso, tribadism. Speaking of this vice,
Parent-Duchâtelet observes that all or nearly all prostitutes are given to it; others say, on the contrary,
that the number of them is very limited; according to
him this contradiction proceeds from their want of
frankness when confessing this vice; they reply warmly
and with impatience when the question is put to them:
" *I am a prostitute for men and not for women.*"
Others whom we have questioned, add: " *We do it,
but it is shameful.*" Some say: " *The male, that is
always lawful.*"

Moll, after what seems to have been a serious study,
concludes that in Berlin the number of tribads amounts
to 25 per cent of all the prostitutes.

Prostitutes in general maintain a certain reserve on that
subject; in their quarrels they insult each other in the
grossest language, but they never make any allusion to
this vice, even when they are certain that it is practised.

According to Parent-Duchâtelet, it is towards the age of from 25 to 30 that prostitutes give themselves up to this vice, after they have exercised their trade during eight or ten years, unless they have been in prison.

If there are any young ones and novices among them, it is that they are the victims of others who have seduced them.

Parent-Duchâtelet also very justly calls attention, as a remarkable phenomenon, to the remarkable disproportion of age and beauty between two women who unite in such manner; and what is still more surprising, is, that once the intimacy established, it is generally the younger and the handsomer of the two who feels towards the other the most passionate and tenacious love.

"I have been informed by many inspectors and by several overseers of prisons that pregnancy is more frequent among tribads than among the prostitutes. This is comprehensible and can be to a certain extent explained. The same observers have remarked that in such cases, the state of pregnancy becomes the subject of jokes and of quarrels in the prison, and there is not that pity, those attentions and care that female prisoners usually display towards their unfortunate companions who may be in that condition." (Parent-Duchâtelet).

The habits of these tribads differ, it appears, according to the country to which they belong.

Among the tribadic couples in Berlin, living in concubinage, says Moll, [1] there is always at least one who is a prostitute: the active and passive rôles are always distinct. The first, or the more active, belongs to that which they call the papa or the uncle, to whom,

[1] Moll, *Les inversions sexuelles*, Paris, 1893.

as in marriage, great freedom is permitted in her connection with men; these are mostly prostitutes.

The passive rôle is called mamma and woe betide her if she is unfaithful.

Some women become tribads all at once; but they admit, that from their infancy they were passionately fond of masculine games, liked to dress in manly attire, to dance with women, to smoke strong cigars, to get tipsy, to ride on horseback, to fight; others began to smoke at 5 years of age, were fond of male occupations and had a repugnance for needle-work; nevertheless they never assume a masculine air but when they know that they are not observed. They can recognise each other, it appears, by certain signs made with the eyes or the mouth; in general they sympathise only with one particular category, either for fair women or for dark, and they never change.

The Parisian tribads [1] often prefer to pawn their jewelry and their clothing rather than be unfaithful to each other: there is a distinctive sign which makes them recognisable: they usually wear exactly similar toilets; they have the same jewels, and call each other sisters. And in fact the expression *" petites sœurs "* (little sisters), in balls, cafés, on the Boulevards, and in the public gardens, has become synonymous of tribad.

Many of them remain faithful during many years; there were some who remained so for 17 years; but the majority of them change from month to month and even from one day to the other.

Tribads are not Sapphics. But it seems [2] that a distinction must be drawn here between the tribads

[1] Martineau, *Sur les déformations vulvaires*.
[2] Moraglia, *Archivio di Psichiatria et Anthrop. criminale*, vol. XVI, V.

properly so-called and the Sapphics or Lesbians (Cun-nilingues). The tribads have mostly a masculine gait, and aspect with virile passions, a taste for sport, for cigars and for manly attire. And, from their earliest age, they loved only for women: they did not fall into vice excited by others, but were born vicious as others are born-criminals; they have always a genuine repugnance for the male and all of them disdain marriage.

The Sapphists, on the contrary, are either led to Lesbian love, particularly by difficulties met with in love with men, or have been led astray by depraved companions. They have no virile character; they have no aversion to man, with whom they can repeat their Lesbian practice without repugnance.

The loves of Sapphists do not last nearly so long as those of tribads, except in colleges, and they provoke far fewer jealousies. Their epistolary correspondence is also very rare and never sentimental.

There is not here, as with tribads, one woman who imposes herself upon another, but two who agree together for some time, ready to separate without ill-feeling.

Among them, it is said, only one anomaly is observable: the gland of the prepuce in the form of a club and hypertrophy of the prepuce in the form of a hood: which is the effect of the exercise and of the abuse; they are therefore vicious by occasion.

The Courtesans of Greece. The same customs existed in ancient times. The *auletridæ* of the Greeks had also frequent and intimate intercourse among each other. In the *dicterions*, among the imprisoned hetæræ this paradoxal love reigned with great intensity.

A tribad courtesan was careful to hide this vice which met with more indulgence from her companions than from men.

The entire life of these tribads was an assiduous study of beauty; from the continuous contemplation of their own nakedness and the comparing of it with that of their companions, they created ardent pleasures to themselves without the aid of their lovers, who often left them cold and insensible (Lucian). The passions, which were thus inflamed between the *auletridæ*, were violent and implacable. In the dialogues of Lucian, we see the beautiful Charmidé complaining that her friend Philemation, old and painted, whom she has loved for seven years and has overwhelmed with presents, has abandoned her for a man. Charmidé, in order to forget this love which consumes her, tries to get another friend; she gives five drachmas to Triphena to share her bed, after a banquet at which she has not tasted a dish nor emptied a single cup; but hardly has Triphena laid herself down at her side than she thrusts her from her, seeming to avoid the contact of her friend.

Lucian, in his *Dialogues of Courtesars*, tells us that one woman could at one and the same time carry on two heterogeneous affections and be passionately in love with a man and with a woman.

Lombroso on the Causes of this Vice. Parent-Duchâtelet, who is not always so happy in his explications as he is precise and exact in the information he gives, explains tribadism by the forced privation of man and by promiscuous residence in prison or in brothels; but he has not thought of the invasion of this vice into the higher ranks of society, which have no connection with prisons or with the life in houses of prostitution; in order to prove this, as Sighele remarks, one has but to refer to the large number of novels in which allusion is made to it.

Amongst such works we may call to mind the following; some of them have been written by men of genius, and all by writers of great talent. This fact in itself is significant of the condition of "Society."

DIDEROT, *La Religieuse*, the romance of a devotee of Lesbian love; BALZAC, *La Fille aux yeux d'or*, Lesbian love; THÉOPHILE GAUTIER, *Mademoiselle de Maupin;* FEYDEAU, *La Comtesse de Chalis;* FLAUBERT, *Salammbô;* BELOT, *Mademoiselle Giraud ma femme.* In German literature KRAFFT-EBING cites the novels of WILBRAND: *Fridolin's heimliche Ehe;* of EMERICH COUNT STADION, *Brick und Brack, oder Licht in Schatten*, and of SACHER-MASOCH, *Venus im Pelz.* ZOLA also alludes to tribadism in *Nana* and in *La Curée*, and quite recently in Italy, BUTTI, in his novel *L'Automna.*

"There are in Paris," writes Leo Taxil, "in high society, genuine Lesbian assemblies, groups of women residing in fashionable quarters, who take the title of Lesbians, and rob and covet each the pathic victims that are supplied to them by special procuresses.[1]

"They also are Lesbian," adds Leo Taxil, "these *Kellnerinnen* who are to be seen together in the Paris beer-houses, wearing exactly similar clothing, whom the students call little sisters; these actresses who live together, these married women of 40 years of age, for whom a young and attentive friend quits everything and never leaves them for a moment. They are always accompanied by a little dog adorned with

[1] *Corruption fin-de-siècle.*

ribbons, etc.; they may also be recognised by their habit of protruding their tongue; I have distinguished some by a continual convulsive contraction of the hands, by the more masculine attitude and dress of one of the two."

The causes are here of various nature:—

Natural Wantonness. The first is the excessive lasciviousness of some of them, which the endeavour to satisfy by every means, even by the least natural. In this way we see one of them giving herself up to women after having used and made abuse of men; and who does not remember the words of Catherine II, who had also become a tribad: " Why has nature not given us a sixth sense? "

The same thing is noticed in men, and Caylus, the prototype of *Urnings*, admitted having made abuse of women until the age of 33 years; and as born-criminals are more lascivious, the observation of Parent-Duchâtelet becomes better comprehensible, that the most depraved tribads and the most inclined to deprave the others, had all of them remained during several years in prison.

Environment as a Factor. The second cause is the influence of the place of habitation ; some of us have verified, that in prison, some of these, unable to satisfy their desires with men, turned to women and became a centre of corruption, that spread even to the religious sisters on service. It is for this reason that although female prisoners are often criminaloids but little inclined to erotism, they often become tribads under the influence of the very lascivious born-criminals.

Parent-Duchâtelet observes that the prison is the

great school of tribadism, and that the most resisting
of prisoners finally gives way to the vice, if she has
to remain there from 18 to 20 months. Oldes remarks
that if several women are assembled together in a
prison, their erotic indecency, even when they are
closely watched, increases in cubic ratio; and when
they are locked up together, scenes take place which
far surpass the compass of any imagination (Liszt,
Archiv. 1891).

In this manner they come near to animals, which,
when they are unable to satisfy their sexual wants
on members of their species of the opposite sex, make
attempts upon those of their own.

The same fact has been observed in asylums, where
the entrance of one tribad is sufficient to contaminate
the entire establishment, where no tendency of the
kind had previously existed. (Lombroso, *Le Tribadisme
dans les Asiles*).

Secret Clubs of Vice. As a third cause we may
name the assembling together of a number of women,
particularly if among them there be prostitutes and
lascivious creatures. This assembling provokes, by a
sort of immoral ferment introduced into the community,
and by the multiplication of the vices of each of its
members, the formation of a more energetic collective
vice. Besides, the prostitutes are often naked or half
naked, living together in almost continual contact,
sleeping two and sometimes three in one bed. In the
higher classes the same thing is found in colleges, in
the orgies of the carnival and also in some convents.

Let us call to mind the scenes described by Juvenal:
" When, summoned to the dance by the sound of the
flute, excited by music and by libations, the priestesses

of Bacchus loosen their long tresses, exhaling passionate
sighs, then to what ardour are they not the prey,
impelling them to join one with the other! What
accents does not passion and the phrenzy of the dance
impress upon their voices! Nought any longer stops
the divine torrent which they let flow down their
thighs. Then Lasella provokes and defies them to
wrestle for the crown, the prize which she carries off
with more lascivious motions, from the most depraved
of prostitutes: and yet she cannot but admire Me-
dullina and her lascivious gests. Both of these great
dames have an equal glory. Nothing is simulated in
their play, so much so that, a son of Sparta, insensible
and frozen from his birth, and the venerable Nestor,
could not support the sight without being inflamed."

Similar collective orgies take place in certain houses
of prostitution in Paris, with participation of ladies of
fashion (Fiaux, *Les maisons de tolérance*, 1892); which
reminds us of the pederastic orgies of men assembled
together, which gave occasion to the prosecutions at
Padua, of Pavia, etc. The forbidden fruit seems only
to be enjoyable to the degenerate when accompanied
by the noisiest and most scandalous complicity.

Fiaux gives other reasons, hitherto ignored, for the
influence of the houses of prostitution on tribadism;
this is that the mistresses of these establishments favour
it in order to have greater tranquillity in the house,
to drive away from it fancy-men who are always
prejudicial to them, for, as they say: "When our women
have a lover, they go away on their out-days and spend
outside the money they have gained; whereas, on
the contrary, the tribads shut themselves up in their
room and treat each other to dainties and liqueurs
which are sold to them in the establishment."

Sometimes they visit the hospitals where they go to recruit and establish the preliminaries of these unions. Sometimes the mistresses of these houses are themselves sapphic; they dress and treat their pathics with much attention and care, or else suddenly act with such violence towards them as to oblige them to have recourse to the police.

More often again, they continue this infamous traffic for another sorry purpose: to make it the subject of *poses plastiques*, in which scenes of orgies there figured, to render the *tableaux* more exciting, the little dogs of these dames, sights which brought them in large profits. Lastly, as we have already said, it enabled them to supply a higher range of society with the pathics required by noble dames.

Carlier relates that there exist in Paris four or five houses of prostitution where women of the upper ten and of the *demi-monde* meet to abandon themselves to collective orgies and to sapphism. It may be here remarked that prostitutes, so inclined to reciprocal sapphism, are far less so towards outside lady visitors, unless they are obliged to do so by special agreement mentioned in their contracts and remunerated at stipulated price.

In the houses of prostitution the women also make bets, and have competitions and examens on their own secret beauties, which naturally excite to tribadism. It often happens that young girls, who are not born-sapphists, first of all resist and manifest a certain aversion to this vice; but the greater number succumb when tipsy and get gradually accustomed to it and become occasional sapphists.

There exists, according to Fiaux, a curious rite in connection with these strange nuptials. The woman

who seduces her companion, the *papa* we may say,
purchases a bottle of champagne and places it before her
sweetheart at their first dinner together.   All the others
then know of the new marriage and each one is bound
to respect it.   "In private life," says Martineau, "the
brasseries (beer-cafés) serve to bring about these unions;
and one can often see in these establishments two bar-
maids who live together.   They manage to suffice for
their household expenses with the gratuities they obtain
from their customers; they avoid as much as possible
all sexual contact with man, and when want of money
forces one of them to do so, it is always as much as
possible unbeknown to the other."

Advanced Age, another Cause. Maturity and
age, in changing the character of the female sex, also
favours sexual inversion in women.

Natural history also shows us that this tendency to
the sexual habits of the male may also be noticed in
the females of animals when they grow old.   As
Parent-Duchâtelet observes, almost all tribads are past
middle-age.   The princess R*** who wrote a letter to
a *chère amie* couched in terms of the most violent
Lesbian love, became a tribad at the age of sixty,
after having led an excessively gay life with men in
her youth; this is to some extent comprehensible, for
old age is in fact a sort of degeneracy.   It is true
that sapphism is also to be met with in quite young
girls, but only if they live in houses of prostitution
or in girls' colleges, where, according to Zola, they
are influenced and even compelled by their companions.

Disgust born of Excess may be regarded as a fifth
cause of this unnatural practice.   Among prostitutes

and also among some gay women, there is to be added the apathy and disgust caused by the too frequent use of the male; when the sexual passion is ardent, and fails to meet with satisfaction from the male, it takes another direction. It is known that fishermen object to eat fish. Martineau says: "Some of these tribads are driven to it by hatred of the bully who maltreats them; by disgust of the long file of males they have been obliged to satisfy, of whom they are satiated even to nausea." Illusions continually destroyed, even in the genuine love they may bear to their lovers, also contribute to it; impassioned and inconstant, they are continually subject to the ill-treatment of men, they then turn to women whom they trust will be more faithful and who to a certainty will be more gentle. Thus it was that Nana abandoned herself to women from disgust of men and of unclean amours, and after having been deserted by her fickle *amants de cœur*.

Fiaux relates that a poor girl, to explain the love she entertained for a bully, said, with wonderful truth: "*If I have nothing to love, I am nothing.*" It is this longing to love a stronger being, or merely for a love that is not mercenary, that is at the bottom of all these loves for bullies or fancy-men, even in those big brothels where their presence is unnecessary.

"One of the reasons of sapphism," writes Sighele (*Copia criminale*, p. 533), "is no doubt the sexual perversion of men. The sadists (and I gather under this name all the different sorts of voluptuousness against nature into which masculine love has been transformed) exact from prostitutes the most repugnant acts, and finally tire and disgust them. These women, who have almost abdicated their sex, can only feel disgust for such men, who are almost no longer males. Thence is born—as a logical and natural sequence—sapphism. To escape from one infamy, the prostitutes cast themselves into another."

But that is not limited to prostitutes.

Congenital Tendency. Krafft-Ebing informs us that a certain girl, aged 29 years, had an alcoholic father, who committed suicide; her brothers and sisters were also alcoholic or hysteric, and her maternal uncle was a madman. She was menstruated at 18 years; but already at the age of 14 she had chlorosis and later on serious hysteria; at the age of 18 she had sexual intercourse with a young man with whom she had fallen in love, and a little later on she masturbated herself in remembrance of him. In order to continue her romance with him, she dressed in male attire, became steward in a noble household, and on this occasion made her mistress fall in love with her; she afterwards became an employée in a shop, and must with her comrades have frequented houses of prostitution; she was then disgusted, and resumed female dress. She was sent to prison for theft, but being found to be hysterical she was sent to a hospital, where she fell violently in love with the female attendants. The medical officers pretended that this tendency was congenital, but she protested: "I feel as a woman; but the companionship of my male colleagues has disgusted me with men, and as I have an ardent nature, and feel the want of attaching myself to some one, little by little I felt myself impelled to bind myself to women and young girls with whom I can better agree."

It would seem that we have here a latent and feeble

congenital cause, upon which has been grafted an accidental cause precisely as is the case in the offences of criminaloids. (See Lombroso, *L' Homme criminel*, vol. II, 1895).

"Another cause of tribadism—which joins to, and becomes confounded with, the first—is," says Sighele, " the absence in rich houses of prostitution, of the bully or fancy-man. The prostitute longs for a more lasting, less ephemeral affection than what her trade procures her every day; unable to find it in men, she seeks for it in one of her companions. They live together, and the very intimacy of their obscenities, paves the slope down which they glide, without perceiving it, into Lesbian love.

" From the luxurious lupanars, sapphism has spread to other centres, if not less depraved, certainly less boldly vulgar.

" Sometimes a kept-woman of high degree, a courtesan of upper rank, has heard her friends speak of such turpitudes; after supper, she has had the curiosity to see it, and finally she has wanted to make the experiment.

" On the other hand, some young girl in rich houses of prostitution, who has managed easily to meet with an enthusiastic lover who takes her away to live with him, then communicates her infamous habits to other women whose acquaintance she makes. In this manner tribadism has become a very frequent exception even among married women. Leo Taxil says that 'the number of lady tribads in Paris is incalculable.'"

The Criminality of Husbands. There is another cause for tribadism for which man is wholly responsible.

Martineau knew married men, men living in con-

cubinage or having a passing *liaison* of only a few
hours, who, in order to excite genesic ardours that
have become more or less extinct, endeavour to awaken
in the woman powerfully voluptuous sensations. To
obtain this result, they do not hesitate to resort to
mercenaries. They may even be seen after a gay
supper, to take their female companion to some special
establishment, to be subjected to sapphism so as to
develop in her, who generally was ignorant of the act,
a genesic passion which she will be all the more
inclined to satisfy, that she has experienced more
voluptuous sensations. But from that moment the
woman will ardently seek for sapphism, accepts coition
but with repugnance and at once takes rank among
the professional or occasional tribads.

The Military Post at Bourail. The convent is
situated on the side of a little hill, some 170 feet high,
on the summit of which is a guard-house occupied by
a post of Marines. The palisades of the guard-house
overlook the walls of the convent, and are almost
within speaking distance. The women keep all the
soldiers in a quiver of excitement. In spite of the
sharpest look-out, and a punishment of thirty days in
prison from the officer commanding, entire squads of
the men sleep out every night, and scale the walls of
the convent. The women drop ropes down, if the
soldiers have no ladders. The janitress, who has the
key of the great door in her pocket, and the poor nuns
sleeping in their little cells, are far from suspecting
what scenes of lust go on in all corners of the convent.
But no notice was taken of this. The conduct of the
soldiers was so well known, that, whereas, in the other
posts in the Colony, the men are only relieved once

a year, the garrison of Bourail is relieved every three months. Generally, the soldiers, when they get back to Noumea, have to do a month's prison, for being absent at night without leave.

The General's Cap. One day, a General, who had been inspecting the troops, came down from the guard-house after the review. The damsels were all at the windows of the dormitory, to watch the proceedings. As the General passed under the walls of the convent, one of the inmates cried, " I say! You may have a fine gold cap, but you haven't got such a good head to put under it as my little trumpeter." The General had the good sense to laugh.

" Je m'emmerde, and I want a Man ". A Governor of the Colony, during one of his rounds, visited the convent at Bourail. After having " reviewed" all the inmates, who did their best to maintain a dignified and respectful attitude, he stopped in front of a pretty young blonde, who was standing in a corner of the room, her eyes modestly cast down, and with a sad and dreamy expression on her fair face. The Governor, who was anxious to pose as a paternal benefactor, said to the young girl, " Well, my child, are you glad to be so well cared for by these good Sisters? Is there anything you want?" The reply was forcible, and even more complete than that of Zola's La Satin in " Nana" : "I? Je m'emmerde, and I want a man!" The Governor turned on his heel, and walked away without saying another word.

The Marriage of the Liberated Convicts. When permission to marry is granted, the State, represented on this occasion by the Governor of the Reformatory, marries the well-assorted couple. The convicts, all numbered, pass in front of the immates of the convent, who are also ranged in order, and if the male prisoner, No. 3, takes a fancy to the female prisoner No. 5, for instance, they are granted an interview, which takes place through the bars of the grating, and under the sanctimonious eye of the good Sister.

The marriage occurs soon afterwards. The convict has granted to him a piece of land, with a small brick house built on it, some agricultural implements, seeds for sowing, kitchen utensils, the more indispensable articles of furniture, and for thirty months he receives his rations from Government,—bread, wine, meat, coffee and tafia. How many worthy peasants in France, who have never stolen a farthing, would be glad of such treatment! The marriage is celebrated at the Mairie, and the Church, and the neighbours are invited to the wedding feast, for there is always a wedding breakfast and attendant rejoicings. The State, however, does not carry its generosity so far as to pay the expenses. The modest bride procures the necessary money. She has sold, in advance, her wedding night to some admirer of patched-up virtue. The price varies, according to the quality of the chaste bride. It is usually fifty francs. At the end of the nuptial repast, it is the husband who himself conducts his better half to the house of the purchaser, and the next morning he comes to fetch her, and lead her, happy and smiling, to the legal domicile. I am inventing nothing; what I here state is known to everybody in New Caledonia, except the Government, which closes its eyes in order to see nothing. And, it is with people of this sort, that they seriously wish to colonise the island! The convict contents himself with hardly scratching the surface of the earth, and sowing some haricots, maize, pumpkins, and tobacco, which is very easy work. The conjugal field is the one he trusts in to bring in the money. The State furnishes the daily bread, and the woman procures the luxuries they require. What the domestic life of such a couple may be, can be guessed. Abuse and blows are showered upon the wife, if she is not a successful bread-winner, or if she has a fancy for putting any of her lovers on the free list. Sometimes, the husband uses the knife; and then the military tribunal interferes. In other cases, on the contrary, the wife poisons her husband, or employs one of her lovers to settle him. The children, when there are any—very fortunately, there are but few,—go to the devil their own way, as might be expected of the offspring of such cankered beings, the prime fruit of the hulks and the brothel!

Sodomy and Pederasty amongst the Convicts. We shall not be astonished to find amongst the convicts, both men and women, the vices of Sodom and Gomorrha flourishing vigorously. In the Reformatory, the convicts freely practise pederasty, and the liberated ones add thereto sodomy with their wives. A man is not usually condemned to hard labour for mere peccadillos, and the moral sense is almost extinct when they come to the Reformatory. Whether you call the condemned criminal a convict, or a transported prisoner; —whether he is dressed, as formerly in the hulks, in yellow trousers, a red coat and a green cap; or, as at present, in a very clean costume of white linen, with a neat straw hat, you do not change his nature. By the sole fact of living together, the bad become worse, and spoil those who are not yet completely corrupt. Put some damaged fruit into a basket with sound fruit, and it will make the good go bad; *a fortiori* when you put rotten fruit with fruit that is already damaged. The violent scoundrels, those of the redoubtable fifth category, use the knife, and end on the guillotine. The weak, and the cowards, are also hypocrites, that they may obtain the privileges reserved for the first-class, but, at bottom, they are not a bit better than the others. Crimes and assassinations are frequent amongst this evil crew. They have taught the Kanakas the use of certain poisonous solanaceæ, the effect of which is deadly, and which grow freely throughout all the Colony.

Prisons as Breeder of Vice. I see that my opinion as to the life spent by the convict in prison being a prolific breeder of unnatural vice is shared by Mr. Havelock Ellis, an English scientist who has had the courage to deal with this unpleasant subject. In his last work, *Sexual Inversion, Studies in the Psychology of Sex*, he quotes with approval the observations of my Italian *confrère*, Dr. Venturi. I reproduce the whole passage:—

"In a Spanish prison, not many years ago, when a new governor endeavoured to reform the homosexual manners of the women, the latter made his post so uncomfortable that he was compelled to resign. Sallilas, *Vida Penal en España*, asserts that all the evidence shows the extraordinary expansion of Lesbian love in prisons. The *mujeres hombrunas* receive masculine names—Pepe, Chulo, Bernardo, Valiente; new-comers are surrounded in the courtyard by a crowd of lascivious women, who overwhelm them with honeyed compliments and gallantries and promises of protection, the most robust virago having most successes; a single day and night complete the initiation. The frequency of sexual manifestations in insane women is well recognised. With reference to homosexual manifestations, I will merely quote the experience of Dr. Venturi in Italy: 'In the asylums which I have directed I have found inverted tendencies even more common than have other observers; and the vice is not peculiar to any disease or age, for nearly all insane women, except in acute forms of insanity, are subject to it. Tribadism must thus be regarded as without doubt a real equivalent and substitute for coitus, as these persons frankly regard it, in this unlike pederasty which does not satisfy in insane men the normal sexual desires.'" (Venturi, *Le Degenerazione psichosessuale*, 1892, p. 148.)

Mr. Ellis says (page 82) that " with girls, as with boys, it is in the school, at the evolution of puberty, that homosexuality *first* shows itself," and is later developed in the workshop, amongst servants at hotels or actresses in the theatre. " I quote," he says, " the following from a private letter written on the Continent: 'An English resident has told me that his wife has lately had to send away her parlourmaid (a pretty girl), because she was always taking in strange women to sleep with her. I asked if she had been taken from hotel service and found, as I expected, that she had. But neither my friend nor his wife suspected the real cause of these nocturnal visits.'

" At Wolverhampton, some years ago, the case was reported of a woman in a galvanising 'store', who after dinner indecently assaulted a girl who was a new hand. Two young women held the victim down and

this seems to show that homosexual vice was here common and recognised."

The Universality of the Vice. From very early times, and in lands widely removed from each other, this strange and unnatural practice has prevailed. Sir Rich. Burton has dwelt, in his final essay to the tenth vol. of the "Nights", on the ethnography of homosexuality; but few cases have been handed down with so much fidelity as to detail as the following. This is the case of Catherina Margaretha Lincken, who married another woman, somewhat after the manner of the Hungarian Countess V., in our own day, *i.e.*, with the aid of an artificial male organ. She was condemned to death for sodomy, and executed in 1721, at the age of 27 (F. C. Müller, "*Ein weiterer Fall von conträrer Sexualempfindung*," Friedrich's Blätter, Heft IV, 1891). This was in Germany, and it is somewhat remarkable that even at a much earlier period such an instrument appears to have been used by German women, for in the twelfth century Bishop Burchardt of Worms speaks of its use as a thing "which some women are accustomed to do." I have found a notice of a similar case in France, during the sixteenth century, in Montaigne's *Journal du Voyage en Italie en 1580* (written by his secretary); it took place near Vitry le Français. Seven or eight girls belonging to Chaumont, we are told, resolved to dress and to work as men; one of these came to Vitry to work as a weaver, and was looked upon as a well-conditioned young man, and liked by everyone. At Vitry she became betrothed to a woman, but, a quarrel arising, no marriage took place. Afterwards "she fell in love with a woman whom she married,

and with whom she lived for four or five months to
the wife's great contentment, it is said; but having
been recognised by some one from Chaumont, and
brought to justice, she was condemned to be hanged.
She said she would even prefer this to living again
as a girl, and was hanged for using illicit inventions
to supply the defects of her sex." (*Journal*, ed. by
D'Ancona, 1889, p. 11).

Infamous Passions. I have said that pederasty
existed amongst the convicts, a suitable ground in
which its pestilential growth could flourish freely. I
have said enough already on this loathsome subject,
apropos of the Annamite race, and do not wish to
tire the reader with repugnant details. There are
certain subjects with which I was obliged to deal in
the course of this work, but to which it is useless to
revert. I will simply state that,—in analogy to what
goes on amongst the Chinese of Saigon,—there are
to be found, amongst the transported convicts and
libérés, couples united by the bonds of an infamous
love. Of the two associates, the one plays the passive
part,—he is the wife; the other,—the husband—plays
the active part. *Rarely are the parts reversed*, and
in this circumstance we see that the pederasty of the
convicts differs greatly from that of the Annamites
and the Kanakas. Generally, in the couple, there is
one old, and one young, man, and, curious to say, it
is nearly always the old man who plays the woman's
part. The younger and more vigorous man is most
often the husband. The rule, however, has exceptions.

Coffignon, in his ably written book, " La Corruption
à Paris" (p. 327), divides active pederasts into " *amateurs*," " *entreteneurs*," and " *souteneurs*."

The " *amateurs* " ("*rivettes* ") are debauched persons, but also frequently congenitally perverse sexually, of position and fortune, who are forced to guard themselves against detection in the gratification of their homesexual desires. For this purpose they visit brothels, lodging-houses, or the private houses of female prostitutes, who are generally on good terms with male prostitutes. Thus they escape blackmail.

Some of these " *amateurs* " are cunning enough to indulge their vile desires in public places. They thus run the risk of arrest, but, in a large city, little risk of blackmail. Danger is said to add to their secret pleasure.

The " *entreteneurs* " are old sinners who, even with the danger of falling into the hands of blackmailers, cannot deny themselves the pleasure of keeping a (male) mistress.

The " *souteneurs* " are pederasts that have been, who keep their " *jesus*," whom they send out to entice customers ("*faire chanter les rivettes* "), and who then, at the right moment, if possible, appear for the purpose of plucking the victim.

Not unfrequently they live together in bands, the members, according to individual desire, living together as husbands and wives. In such bands there are formal marriages, betrothals, banquets and introductions of brides and bridegrooms into their apartments.

These " *souteneurs* " attach their " *jesus* " to themselves.

The passive pederasts are "*petits jesus*," "*jesus*," or " *aunts*."

The " *petits jesus* " are lost, depraved children, whom accident places in the hands of active pederasts, who seduce them, and reveal to them the horrible means of earning a livelihood, either as "*entretenus*" or as male street-walkers, with or without "*souteneurs.*"

The most suitable and promising "*petits jesus*" are given into the hands of persons who instruct these children in the art of female dress and manner. Gradually they then seek to emancipate themselves from their teachers and masters, in order to become "*femmes entretenues;*" and not unfrequently, by means of anonymous denunciation of their "*souteneurs*", are caught by the police.

It is the object of the "*souteneur*" and the "*petit jesus,*" to make the latter appear young as long as possible, by means of all the arts of the toilet.

The limit of age is about twenty-five years; then they all become "*jesus*" and "*femmes entretenues,*" and are then sustained by several "*souteneurs.*" The "*jesus*" fall into three categories: "*filles galantes,*" *i.e.*, those that have fallen again into the hands of a "*souteneur*"; "*pierreuses*" (ordinary street-walkers, like their female colleagues); and "*domestics.*"

The "*domestics*" hire out to active pederasts, either to gratify their desires, or to obtain "*petits jesus*" for them.

A sub-group of these "*domestics*" is formed by such of them as enter the service of "*petits jesus*" as "*femmes de chambre.*" The principal object of these "*domestics*" is to use their positions to obtain compromising knowledge, with which they later practise blackmail, and thus assure themselves ease in their old age.

The most horrible class of active pederasts is made up of the "*aunts*"—*i.e.*, the "*souteneurs*" of (male) prostitutes,—who, though normal sexually depraved, practise pederasty (passive) only for gain, or for blackmail.

The wealthy amateurs have their reunions and places of meeting, where the passive ones appear in female attire, and horrible orgies take place. The waiters, musicians, etc., at such gatherings are all pederasts. The "*filles galantes*" do not venture, except during the carnival, to show themselves on the street in female dress; but they know how to lend to their appearance something indicative of their calling, by means of style of dress, etc. They entice by means of gesture, peculiar movements of the hands, etc., and lead their victims to hotels, baths, or brothels.

What the author says of blackmail is generally known. There are cases where pederasts have allowed their entire fortune to be wrung from them.

Feminine jealousies and hates pale before the horrible passions excited in the hearts of these monstrous lovers. Revenge of unrequited love (it is sad to have to profane the word "love" by applying it such aberrations), often drives the neglected one to use the knife. If he has not the courage to do this, he seeks a new lover, who can avenge for him the disdain of the old one. Often are there related before the Council of War accounts of scenes too horrible to dwell upon, for these murders are often accompanied by atrocious aggravations, and erotic mutilations. The transported convict of the White race becomes as ferocious as the Kanaka, and has not, as he has, the excuse of being a savage. But here I will lay down my pen for the present, deeming it useless to tire the reader with an account of such disgusting turpitude. [1]

---

[1] A defence of uranism has been made by CARL ULRICHS writing under the name of "NUMA NUMANTIUS," and "all the latest literature," says Schrenck-Notzing, "shows traces of the influence of Ulrich's

theory." * Compare the following writings of the author mentioned:
" Forschungen über das Räthsel der mannmännlichen Liebe:

"VINDEX ": Social and legal studies of male love of males. Proof
that it deserves punishment as little as love of women, and that, according to the existing laws of Germany, it cannot be legally punished.
Leipzig, 1864.

"INCLUSA": Anthropological studies of male love of males. Proof
that in a certain class of individuals of masculine form sexual love of
males is congenital sexually. Leipzig, 1864.

" VINDICATE ": Struggle for freedom from persecution. Criminal
details and legislative proposals, looking to a revision of existing criminal
laws. Diary of an urning. Leipzig, 1865.

"FORMATRIX ": Anthropological studies of the love of urnings.
Description of the sexual nature of urnings in detail. Key to the
riddle of uranism and its varieties. Leipzig, 1865.

"ARA SPEI": Studies in moral and social philosophy in relation
to the love of urnings. Relation of the urning's love to morality,
Christianity, and the moral arrangement of the world. Moral justification of the urning's love. Love-bond of urnings. The conflict of urnings
and its solution. The exceptional place of love in the moral status of
the world. Hope. Leipzig, 1865.

"GLADIUS FURENS": The enigma of nature in the urning's
love, and error as a maker of laws. An arraignment of German laws.
Kassell, 1868.

" MEMNON ": The sexual nature of the male-loving urning. Psycho-
physical hermaphroditism. *Anima muliebris virili corpore inclusa.* A
study in natural science. Two parts. Schleiz, 1868.

"INCUBUS ": Urning's love and blood-thirstiness. A consideration
of abnormal states of mind and responsibility, occasioned by the case
of Zastrow, Berlin: with fifteen allied cases. Leipzig, 1869.

"ARGONAUTICUS ": Zastrow and the urnings belonging to the
camp of the pietists, ultramontanes, and free-thinkers, with considerations
concerning blood-thirstiness and responsibility, and brief reports from
the world of urnings and the criminal cases: Bishop Morell, of Edinburgh; Count Czarnechy, of Posen; Superintendent Forstner, of Vienna.
Leipzig, 1869.

* See *Theurapeutic Suggestion in Psychopathia Sexualis* by Dr. A.
von Schrenck-Notzing (Münich), trans. by Chas. G. Chaddock, M.D.
(Phil. and Lond., 1895).

CHAPTER VI.

A note by the Author.—Anthropological characteristics of the natives of the New Hebrides.—Their admixture with the Maori-Polynesian race.—Characteristics of the pure Melanesian race.—It is autochtnonous in Australia.—Anthropological importance of the genital organs in determining the origin of a race.—The genital organ of the African Negro, and of his various crossings with the White.—The genital organ of the Melanesian, compared to that of the African Negro.—The genital organ of the woman of the New Hebrides.

Note by the Author. I have not had the good luck to visit the New Hebrides, but I studied the race at Noumea, where many of the New Hebrideans were, in 188—, employed by the colonists. Besides this, I knew several " Copra-makers," who had resided in the islands for a time, and had returned to New Caledonia to recover their health, which had been weakened by marsh fever. Amongst these, I met one of my old college chums, formerly an officer in the Navy, who, after a series of adventures, had settled down in these islands, and who has since ended by leaving his bones there. I can confidently give the new and original information with which he supplied me. I have also gathered some useful knowledge from a book by M. Imhaus, formerly the manager of the French New Hebridean Company.

Anthropological Characteristics of the New Hebridean Race. The New Hebridean is a Melanesian

Black of almost pure race, in most of the islands.   In some of them he is crossed, like the Kanaka of New Caledonia, with the Maori-Polynesian race;—but these crossings form only a minority of the natives.   Usually, the New Hebridean is darker, less robust, and not so handsome as the New Caledonian.   I must remark, that the native of Loyalty Island is of Maori race, if not almost pure, at least not crossed to any great extent with the Melanesian race, and that he is in a much more advanced state of civilisation than the New Caledonian.   I may apply the same observation to the New Hebridean, who is lower in the scale than the New Caledonian.   In all these people the degree of civilisation may almost be ascertained by the lighter colour of the skin, which is the index of a greater or less infusion of Maori blood.

When speaking of Tahiti, I shall make a special study of the Maori race.   For the time being, I will content myself by saying that, in the New Hebrides, we are able to watch the effects of the crossing of the two races.

The Crossing of the Polynesian and Melanesian Races.   M. Imhaus gives a striking instance of this admixture.

" In the small island of Mélé, near the Sandwiches, the intrusion of the Maori only dates back about thirty years, which enables us to see clearly the progress made by the race.   The accident which caused this was the wreck of a vessel, which was taking some Kanaka Maoris back to Samoa.   The crew was murdered, and eaten, but the Maoris, braver and more vigorous than their companions, escaped from their enemies, and took refuge in a desert corner of the island.   There they organised their forces, and, thanks to the internal dissensions amongst the New Hebrideans, were able to hold their ground, and make themselves feared. They carried off wives for themselves, from the neighbouring tribes, and they formed, at last, a powerful tribe, which was upon the point of subduing the island, if it had not come across the White man in its progress."

Such an instance, of quite recent date; well explains why the mixed population of Cana and Aoba is now so different from that of the other islands, where the Melanesian race continues to be unmixed.

Characteristics of the Melanesian Race. Firstly, let it be said that the Melanesian Oceanean, who came from Australia, and who first peopled New Caledonia, the Loyalty Islands, and the New Hebrides, greatly resembles the African Negro. There is the same deep black coloration of the skin, the same woolly hair, on a high skull pressed down towards the front, the wide nose, thick lips, flat face, and low facial angle. But there the resemblance ceases. Primarily, I may remark that the African Negroes are stalwart, and physically handsome, whilst the Melanesian race is the most degraded of all, and undoubtedly occupies the lowest rank in the scale of humanity. The New Hebridean, who is a pure Melanesian, is still what he was in the time of Forster, one of the companions of Cook, in 1774, who closely studied the natives of Mallicolo.

"Being small and badly proportioned, with lanky limbs, a pot belly, a flat face, and thick, frizzy short hair, these savages are hideous; they remind one more of a monkey than a man." Those pseudo-scientific men, who have never taken their feet off their own footstools, have gravely discussed, at great length, the question whether the Australian Negro came from Africa, or, on the contrary, the African Negro came from Australia. They have never taken into consideration the distance which separates the nearest part of Australia from the coast of Mozambique,—a distance equal to 70º of longitude, or one fifth of the circumference of the equator, or something like five thousand miles, or rather more than 4500 nautical miles. And to accomplish this enormous distance the emigrants could only have at their disposal, a few clumsy canoes, with no water, no food, hardly any sails, and above all, no compass. The absurdity of such an hypothesis is palpable when we remember that Christopher Columbus, genius as he was, needed the compass, unlimited faith, three ponderous caravels, and the best and bravest sailors of Spain, to perform the voyage from Palos to San-Lucaye, which is less than that which divides Africa from Australia. No! the African Negro and the Australian Negro are two entirely distinct races.

The Melanesian Race of Australia is Autochthonous. Must we then agree with that theory of modern science, according to which Australia has its own peculiar race, and believe that the Melanesian race is autochthonous? That is Darwin's theory, who maintains that natural selection caused man to appear simultaneously or successively, in several parts of the earth. One point is now generally admitted by men of science, and that is that the Australian continent, the last discovered by European civilisation was, on the contrary, the first to appear above the waters, as we learn from geological data, and from the character of the fauna and flora. Was it the first to receive the human race, and does that explain the mental

inferiority of the natives, compared with other races?
I do not pretend to answer the question, but leave
the problem for others to solve.

But I am going to try to prove here, by means of
the difference existing between the anthropological
characteristics, that the Australian Black is not descended from the African Negro. He differs from him
less than do the other races, yellow, white, or red,
but that is all.

**Anthropological Importance of the Genital
Organ in Determining the Origin of Race.** I
revert to a question which I have already discussed.
Misplaced modesty has caused anthropologists generally to neglect to examine the male genital apparatus.
Apart from this, they give us minute details concerning
the facial angle, the prognathous jaw, etc. Like the
Norman peasant of Falaise, they have forgotten to
light the candle in their lantern. To me, it seems
evident that the genital organ gives us the key to
prove the descent of a race, for, in all the various
crossings the race may undergo, it is physically the
most powerful characteristic,—the one which lasts the
longest, and is the last to disappear. And this is but
logical. The genital organ ensures the continuity of
the race. It is the most important organ; it is the
last to appear, and the first to disappear. It lasts
hardly more than half the life of a man. For these
reasons it is the anthropological characteristic to which,
above all others, importance should be attached, and
I do not deem it more shameful and disgusting to
measure the length, the size, or the stiffness in
erection, of a Negro's penis, than it would be for a
surgeon to probe a urethra, or perform an operation

on a testicle. There is no false modesty in medical matters.

The Genital Organs of the Coloured Races.— Result of the Crossing of the Negro and the White.

Although this question has been thoroughly studied in the part of the book relating to Guiana, I refer to it again here to facilitate comparisons. The persistence of the characteristics of the genital organ of the Negro in all the crossings of the race first proved to me the importance of this sign. Thus the Zambo, who is one quarter White, is almost a Negro as regards his genital organ, and differs more from the White man than the Quadroon, who is one fourth Black, differs from the Negro. The Mulatto (half White and half Black) is genitally much nearer the Negro than the White. Taking the two extreme points of departure, the White and the Black, and comparing the two genital organs, I have shown the radical differences which separate them as to form, colour, and size, in the conditions of flaccidity and erection. The Zambo is, from this point of view, almost a Negro, the Mulatto much nearer a Negro than a White man, and we must come to the Quadroon before we find that the genital apparatus of the White man has regained its lost ground. But, I have been careful to state, that though the Quadroon, who has but one quarter of Black blood, may often have hair almost fair, and a skin lighter than that of a South European, a simple examination of the genital organs will reveal the "man of colour". The penis is always proportionally more developed than in the pure White, the difference between the flaccid condition and erection less considerable; and, finally, the mucous surface of the gland has never that red or pink colour which is peculiar to the European of the unmixed White race.

The influence of the genital organs of the Negro is still evident in the Octoroon (who, however, has but an eighth part of Black blood) and can be recognised by a gland of a rather dark brownish red colour, and a scrotum much darker than the skin of the body. I attribute this curious persistence to the fact that the crossing of the two races takes place in tropical countries, and in unhealthy climates, for which the Negro race was specially created. If a similar crossing took place in Siberia, between Russians and Negroes, perhaps the reverse would happen, and the White race would have the superiority over the Black.

Comparison of the Genital Organ of the Melanesian with that of the African Negro. By the aid of these facts, I am able to rebut the theory, that the two races of Negroes of Africa and Australia have the same ethnological origin. And here are my arguments. In the Melanesian Black, however dark the skin may be, and it is often as black as a pair of boots well polished with Day and Martin's blacking, you will never find the mucous surface of the gland *black*, as it is in the African Negro. The mucous surface, on the contrary, is of a fairly bright purplish red, such as may be obtained by a mixture of carmine, vermillion, and Vandyke brown, with neutral tint in the shadows.

This colour, being rather bright, contrasts forcibly with the dark ground of the skin of the penis and the scrotum. It resembles the penis of a Negro, the mucous surface of the gland of which has been flayed. As to the genital apparatus, it is less developed in the Melanesian than in the African Negro. The dimensions of the penis are very nearly those (as average and maximum) given for the New Caledonian; but the gland has a more obtuse shape, and there are cases of phimosis, when circumcision has not been performed. The testicles appeared to me to be a little less developed. The pubes is shaded with rather coarse, curly hair. In a flabby state, the penis is still fairly large, but the difference in the state of erection is very marked, which is not the case with the African Negro. These fundamental differences between the genital organs of the Australian and African Negroes are, to my mind, an unanswerable proof that the former are autochthonous in Australia, and that that country is the cradle of the race. From there it spread to New Caledonia, then to the New Hebrides, where later the Black race became mixed with the Maori-Polynesian.

The Genital Organ of the Woman of the New Hebrides is naturally in proportion to that of the male organ. It presents very little difference (except a darker colour of the skin and the mucous surfaces) from that of the New Caledonian woman. I therefore refer the reader to what I have already written concerning the latter.

CHAPTER VII.

A few words on the manners, customs, etc., of the New Hebri-
deans.—Costume.—The manou.—The woman's girdle.—Tattoo-
ing.—Habitations.—Food.—Arms and utensils.—The tam-tam;
the pilou-pilou.—The erotic dance.—The Kawa.

A Few Words on the Manners, Customs, etc.

Before studying the New Hebridean in contact with
the White man, it is as well to cast a rapid glance at
the manners and customs of the people. We will begin
by mentioning that the dialect varies in every island
throughout the group.

Costume.—The Manou of the New Hebridean.

Like that of the New Caledonian, the costume is of the
simplest possible kind, and, for the man, is confined to
the *manou*. But the *manou* is of a different shape.
The New Caledonian lets his hang between his legs
down to the knees. The New Hebridean, on the contrary, pulls his up, and passes the end under a girdle
of aloe fibre which he is never without.

At Santo and Aoba, instead of the *manou*, the men
wear a kind of short petticoat made of bark, and not
more than four or five inches in length (just sufficient
to hide the genital organs), which is fastened to a narrow
girdle. But, in the other islands, the upright *manou*
is used and it has the curious effect of letting the two
testicles stand out exposed to sight, owing to the lower
part of the scrotum being pulled up by the *manou*.

The Women's Girdle.   In all the islands the women are completely naked above the waist.   Those of Aoba wear a plaited petticoat; in the other islands, a few fibres of cocoa-nut are twisted into a wreath threaded on a cord, which passes round the hips and constitutes the whole costume.   This little petticoat only covers the abdomen and the buttocks.   At Tana the petticoat comes down to the ground, and resembles an old crinoline, rather flattened.

Tattooing   Tattooing is very little used, and is confined to a few blue rays on the face, and a scar or two on the body.   But the native smears himself all over, principally on the face, with red and white paint, which gives him a terrible appearance in war.

Habitations.—Food.   I will simply say that the hut much resembles that of the New Caledonian, and that, like the latter, the New Hebridean lives almost entirely upon vegetable food.   The introduction of poultry and pigs, by Cook, however, somewhat improved the diet.   On the coast, the tribes have a further resource, in the form of fish.   The New Hebrideans harpoon fish with their javelins.

Arms and Utensils.   The utensils are confined to some rude dishes of wood or bamboo, and the furniture to a few mats placed on the ground.   In the way of weapons, the New Hebridean possesses the war club with a rounded head and points projecting from it all round; javelins, ten feet long, armed at the tip with splinters of bone, and with a human shin bone fastened to the butt; and bows, throwing arrows furnished with human bones.   Arrows and darts are often poisoned, by means of a sticky extract made from the juice of certain plants. The Whites who trade (usually with the exchange of shots on both sides) with the natives, greatly fear the wounds of these poisoned weapons, and so they sold them a number of old muzzle loading muskets, shooting round bullets. They have also imprudently allowed them to possess some Snider rifles. This fault was due to the captains of some of the English vessels, but now the few Whites who inhabit the island, still manage to make themselves feared, by means of their American Winchester rifles, with sixteen shots in the magazine.

The Tam-tam; the Pilou-pilou. On the little open space in the middle of each village may be seen, fastened into the ground, enormous trunks of hollow trees, having the form of human heads and trunks, with an enormous phallus. This is the New Hebridean tam-tam, which gives, when it is struck with a thick stick, a dull sound, like that of a big drum. After the yam and banyan harvests, the natives assemble at the sound of this drum, and dance an interminable *pilou-pilou*, like that of the New Caledonian. During two or three days, they eat, drink, yell, beat the tam-tam, and play on bamboo pipes. These wild dances sometimes mimic war, and sometimes love.

"**The Erotic Dance.** "No art," observes Mr. T. M. Wheeler, [1] "dates back to a more hoary antiquity than that of dancing; nor is there any the history of which takes us over a wider survey of mankind. From prehistoric times only to be interpreted by such remains

[1] In *Footsteps of the Past, being Essays on Human Evolution,* Lond. *n. d.*

as gesture language, hieroglyphics, the customs of modern savages, and the games of children, down to our own ballets and ball-rooms; on every part of the globe, from China to Peru, alike among North American Indians and natives of Central Africa, dancing is found. It goes deeper than spoken language. Thoughts and feelings were expressed by actions long before they were communicated by words. Dancing is indeed, as Elie Reclus says, 'the supreme art and language of primitive men.' It even preceded humanity, an inheritance from ape-like ancestors." In case the latter remark may seem to go too far for a scientific work, we quote from Prof. Robert Hartmann's interesting account of a captive gorilla: [1]—

"He often expressed his feelings after quite a human fashion, by clapping his hands together, an action which no one had taught him; and he executed such wild dances, sometimes overbalancing himself, reeling to and fro, and whirling round, that we were often disposed to think that he must be drunk. Yet he was only drunk with pleasure, and this impelled him to display his strength in the wildest gambols."

The same writer adds that " among savage races the medicine-men, shamans, sorcerers, rain doctors, etc., often assume ape-like attitudes in the contortions, leaps, dances, and other gestures which are inseparable from their trade."

In unconscious excitement, action becomes automatic and atavistic. Savages dance off their emotions, whether of anger or entreaty, of passion for hunting, war, love, or religion.

Prof. Hartmann thinks that: " when we see a Zikr, an Islamite rite of worship, accompanied by obligatory howls and contortions of body, we are tempted to imagine ourselves in the midst of a troop of wild

[1] Anthropoid Apes, 263.

apes." The Zikr, be it said, is an ancient lunar dance, in honour of the moon as time-measurer.

A far greater authority even than the writer just quoted, Herbert Spencer, finds the origin of dance and song in the same instinctive motions. He says:

"Muscular movements in general are originated by feelings in genera. The violent muscular motions of the limbs which cause bounds and gesticulations, as well as those strong contractions of the pectoral and vocal muscles which produce shouting and laughter, become the natural language of great pleasure. Consequently, children shout and jump when they are pleased. So when primitive kings are honoured by their subjects, they are honoured by irregular jumping and gesticulation, with un-rhythmical shouts and cries, at first rising without concert, but which gradually by repetition become regularised into the measured movements we know as dances, and the organised utterances constituting songs."

It may be not uninteresting in this connection to recall a peculiar kind of chorographic display described by Colonel Dalton, [1] a gentleman I once had the honour to meet with abroad; I refer to the bear dancers of the Juangs, who with the exception of some leaves, are entirely nude. "The girls acting independently advance with bodies so much inclined, that their hands touch the ground; thus they move not unlike bears, and by a motion from the knees the bodies wriggle violently, and the broad tails of green leaves flap up and down in the most ludicrous manner. The pigeon dance followed: the action of a love-making pigeon when he struts, pouts, sticks out his breast, and scrapes the ground with his wings was well imitated, the hands of the girls doing duty as wings. Then came a pig and a tortoise dance, in which the motions of those animals were less felicitously rendered, and the quail dance in which they squatted and pecked at the ground

[1] Col. E. T. Dalton, *Descriptive Ethnology of India*, Calcutta, 1872.

after the fashion of those birds. They concluded with the vulture dance, a highly dramatic finale. One of the men was made to lie on the ground and represent a dead body. The girls in approaching it imitated the hopping, sidling advances of the bird of prey, and using their hands as beaks, snipped and pinched the pseudo-corpse in a manner that made him occasionally forget his character and yell with pain. This caused great amusement to his tormentors. I have heard," adds Col. Dalton, " of a ' ballet ', called ' the cocks and hens ', but this they could not be induced to exhibit. It was admitted that it was impossible to keep the leaves in proper position whilst they danced it. It was too much of a romp, especially for a day performance."

Kawa. To stimulate themselves, everybody drinks *Kawa*, a drink made from a root which is chewed by the woman, who spit juice and saliva into wooden basins, where it ferments. This beverage, which is not very enticing to a European, produces an intoxication quite as violent as that caused by alcohol.

CHAPTER VIII.

Forms and perversions of the sexual habit amongst the New Hebrideans.—Social condition of woman.—Marriage.—Sacrifice of widows in the islands of Tanna and Anatom.—Adultery and its punishment.

THE information on these heads I can only give subject to some reserve, for as regards most of these heads, I have had to content myself with information furnished by New Hebrideans, men and women, who had come to New Caledonia, to be hired as servants.

The Popinée of the New Hebrides. The social condition of the Popinée of the New Hebrides differs little from that of the woman of New Caledonia. As a girl, she is under the absolute control of her father; as a woman, she does but change her master. She is considered as much inferior to the man, and is not allowed to eat at the same time with him, but must wait till he has finished. Her husband has the right to beat her, or kill her, without anyone thinking of blaming him, or still less of punishing him. He takes no notice of her; never entrusts her with a secret; and is much offended if a White man offers the poor wretch a morsel of food or a cup of drink. She has, however, a great advantage over her neighbour of

New Caledonia, inasmuch as she is not obliged to give herself up to several men at the same time. Polyandry, which is caused by a disproportion in the number of women, is a rarity in the New Hebrides. No woman has more than one husband, and the chiefs of the tribes are even polygamists.

Marriage is performed with certain ceremonies which have no religious meaning, and are only intended to denote the husband's possession of the wife. It is at one of the *pilou-pilous* that the young man generally picks out his future bride. He does not worry himself at all about her heart, but makes a declaration of love to the girl's father. If he does not oppose the match, the future bridegroom has only to obtain the chief's permission to marry. When this permission is obtained, the girl has nothing to do but obey.

Wives are also obtained in another manner. When two neighbouring tribes are at peace, two young people of either tribe can exchange sisters,—of course with the father's consent. But then the chief of each tribe is entitled to a present from the young warrior of the other tribe. In this case, also, the girl's consent is not necessary. If a girl or woman has no male relatives, the chief of the tribe gives her away in marriage, or not unfrequently takes her himself.

If a woman is too much ill-treated by her husband, she may put herself under the protection of another man, and eventually become his wife. In this special case, which is very rare, the woman becomes the object of a deadly combat between the two men, who fight with war clubs like two knights of the Middle Ages at a tournament. If the woman's protector is vanquished, the husband generally clubs the two of them to death, and a grand *pilou-pilou* is danced round their bodies, as a sort of funeral ceremony.

When a chief dies, if he has several wives, the new chief picks out those which please him, and those he does not like are hanged or clubbed to death, at a grand *pilou-pilou* given in honour of the late chief.

Sacrifice of Widows in the Islands of Tanna and Anatom.

At Tanna the wife is frequently strangled after the death of her husband; this custom no longer exists amongst the tribes of the interior. It was imported, it would appear, from the island of Anatom, where it is still in force, for the women wear round their necks, from the time of their childhood, a cord, to incessantly remind them of the fate in store for them. The strangulation is performed in this manner. Two young men, whilst the woman is asleep, drive pegs into the ground on each side of her, and fasten the cord to them in such a manner that the neck remains compressed, until death ensues.

The husband-poisoner, who now and again crops up in England and France, would have little motive in these savage countries to play this unhappy rôle, it being to the obvious advantage of every married lady to keep her " lord" in the " land of the living " as long as possible. It is quite appalling to reflect upon the universality of widow-sacrificing. Westermarck says:—
Formerly among the Comanches, when a man died his favourite wife was killed at the same time. [1] In certain Californian tribes, widows were sacrificed on the pyre with their deceased husbands; [2] and

---

[1] Schoolcraft, " Historical and Statistical Information on the Indian Tribes of North America," vol. II, p. 133.

[2] *Ibid*, vol. IV, p. 226; vol. V, p. 217.

Mackenzie was told that this practice sometimes occurred among the Crees. [1] In Darien and Panama, on the death of a chief, all his concubines were interred with him. [2] When one of the Incas died, says Acosta, the woman who he had loved best, as well as his servants and officers, were put to death, "that they might serve him in the other life." [3] The same custom prevailed in the region of the Congo, as also in some other African countries. [4] "It is no longer possible to doubt," says Dr. Schrader, "that ancient Indo-Germanic custom ordained that the wife should die with her husband." [5] In India, as is well known, widows were sacrificed, until quite resently, on the funeral pile of their husbands; [6] whilst, among the Tartars, according to Navarette, on a man's death, one of his wives hanged herself "to bear him company in that journey. Among the Chinese, something of the same kind seems to have been done occasionally in olden times." [7] Writers of the stamp of Max Nordau are nevertheless enquiring vigorously whether in Europe the majority of widows are not also subjected to a species of "economic strangulation" when once the bread-winner has gone. But this question belongs rather to the domain of

[1] Mackenzie, "Voyages to the Frozen and Pacific Oceans," London, 1802, p. 98.

[2] Seeman, "Voyage of the Herald," Lond. 1853, vol. I, p. 316.

[3] Acosta, "Natural and Moral Hist. of the Indies," Lond. 1880.

[4] Reade (Winwood), "Savage Africa," Lond. 1863, p. 359. Waitz, "Anthropologie der Naturvölker," Leipzig, 1859—72, pp. 192, 193, 419.

[5] Schrader, "Prehistoric Antiquities of the Aryan Peoples," Lond. 1890, p. 391.

[6] Crawfurd, "Hist. of the Indian Archipelago" vol. II, p. 241. Zimmerman, "Die Inseln des Indischen Meeres," Berlin, 1863, vol. I, p. 19.

[7] Navarette, "An Account of the Empire of China," in Awnsham and Churchill's "Collection of Voyages and Travels", p. 77.

Social Economics than to a sober work on Anthropology and it must be strictly " tabooed " here.

Adultery. In certain islands, the outraged husband has the right of life or death on the wife and her lover. But the latter generally defends himself, and a combat takes place as related above. In other islands, on the contrary, the husband sells his adulterous wife, even if the lover is a White man. [1]

The Position in Coitu. Our friend, Dr. Ploss, thought it well to explain his standpoint in treating this question, and we can do no more than quote his words:—

" It may seem strange that we should give a particular attention to the situation and position of the actors in sexual connection.

" It is by no means our intention, in the manner of Pietro Aretino, to pass in review all the positions which

[1] Quite recently we English have somewhat restrained our inclination to pretend that morally we are better than any other nation. The records of the courts and the scandals of society prove that in sexual matters we are as culpable as any people on earth. And, owing to our Pecksniffian airs, care has been taken that the world shall be informed of this fact. Here, for instance, is " *Les Dessous de la Pudibonderie Anglaise*," a volume of **468 pages,** published in French, containing summaries of some of the most sensational divorce cases, beginning with that of Admiral Knowles in 1755. We are also treated to some choice passages from the English comedy writers, even in the present century. These are of a nature to make one wonder at the impudence of ignorant people in this country on the boldness of the foreign stage, which was never so coarse or so brutal as that of England. We have in this smartly edited and lively book a picture of British morals and manners sufficient to moderate our inordinate self-esteem and offensive hypocrisy. An effective chapter might have been added as to the terrible immorality prevailing at the present day among the clergy of the English Established Church.

may be invented by refined lechery and voluptuousness, but only to examine the positions adopted by certain peoples, and which are worthy of our attention because they differ from those usually known. It is therefore not from an erotic, but solely from the ethnographic and anthropological point of view that we feel called upon to study this question. For we must the more devote our attention to this subject, that the differencies noticed may raise the question, though perhaps not bringing an immediate answer, what are the causes and conditions which are here at work, if there is an instinctive imitation of the copulation of certain animals, or if we must see therein the result of certain anatomical modifications in the human races.

" It is quite natural to understand that man instinctively adopts, in all his physiological acts, the position which he finds the easiest and most convenient.

" It is therefore natural to suppose that this principle prevails in all countries and that there are certain modes and forms which exist and have become traditional among certain peoples, and this extends to the position occupied by man and woman *in coitu* and which we find to exist traditionally among different peoples.

" We find besides, in different countries, many differences of practice which are accepted by reason of their ancient customs and legendary habit."

Sodomy. We may remind the student that this offence is punishable under the **24 and 25 Vict.** C. **100, s. 61.** " Whosoever shall be convicted of the abominable crime of buggery, committed either with mankind or with any animal, shall be liable, at the discretion of the court, to be kept in penal servitude for life, or for any term not less than ten years."

" Sodomy is commonly understood," writes Taylor, " to signify unnatural intercourse between men and man, while bestiality implies unnatural intercourse with animals. Continental medical jurists have invented a new term *Pederastia* (Παιδὸς ἐραστής, pueri amator), comprising those cases, not unfrequent, in which boys at about the age of puberty are made the victims of the depraved passions of a certain class of men, but this term is not applicable to the crime committed by and between adults."

The New Hebridean Popinée has not the same horror of the vice of sodomy that the African Negress has. The girl mentioned in the foregoing story was not the only one of the hired women to whom I gave medical attendance, and it often happened that I found signs of inveterate sodomy.

We have little right to despise the savage for being addicted to this shocking habit if we take into consideration the frequency with which such cases come before European tribunals. Taylor states indeed that this crime is unhappily frequent in Lancashire, hardly an assize being held in Manchester or Liverpool where one or more of these cases are not tried. The crime is not unfrequent among seamen. In a case tried at Liverpool in 1884 it was proved that a sailor had induced a lad to go to sea in order that he might act as the prisoner's passive agent. The lad was unaware of this, and on the offence being committed denounced the prisoner to the rest of the crew, who complained to the captain, and the prisoner was given in charge to the authorities at the port in South America. The consular authorities inquired into the case, but sent the prisoner home for trial in England. The boy was examined by Lowndes, who found him suffering from pain in the anus and rectum, although this was some time after the committal of the offence. The prisoner was convicted, and sentenced to twenty years' penal servitude. In another case where Lowndes gave evidence the prisoner, a blind man, was charged with committing this offence upon his own son, a boy of twelve, who was himself the subject of partial paralysis. There were indications that the crime had been committed. The jury found the prisoner guilty of the attempt, and he was sentenced to ten years' penal servitude.

Unless an examination is made soon after the perpetration of the crime, the signs of it will disappear. In the case of one long habituated to these unnatural practices, certain changes have been pointed out as medical proofs, among them a funnel-shaped state of parts between the nates, with the appearance of dilatation, stretching, or even a patulous state of the anus, and a destruction of the folded or puckered state of the skin in this part. There may be also marks of laceration, cicatrices, etc., and sometimes the evidence derivable from the presence of syphilitic disease.

This condition of parts would represent the chronic state induced by these practices in the patient or succubus. In the recent or acute form, fissure and laceration of the sphincter ani, with bruising and effusion of blood, would be found. The appearances above described as belonging to the chronic stage were met with in the case of Eliza Edwards. Her history is curious. "An unclaimed body was sent to Guy's Hospital by the inspector of anatomy, as a female: on removing the dress, however, it was found to be that of a *male*. From some suspicion respecting the cause of death, and the habits of this person, a coroner's inquest was held. It turned out that the deceased, whose age was 24, had assumed the dress of a female at the age of 14, and had performed in many parts of England as an actress. The features had a somewhat feminine character; the hair was very long, and parted in the centre; the beard had been carefully plucked out, and the remains of this under the chin had been concealed by a peculiar style of dress. It was remarked during life that the voice was hoarse. The breasts were like those of a male, and the male sexual organs were perfectly developed. They had evidently been subjected to great stretching, and appeared to have been drawn forward and secured to the lower part of the abdomen. The state of the rectum left no doubt of the abominable practices to which this individual had been addicted. It was found that death had taken place from natural causes. The most remarkable circumstance in this case is, that the deceased had been attended in his last illness by an eminent physician for disease of the lungs; and so well was the imposition maintained, that this medical attendant did not entertain a suspicion of the real sex of his patient. [1]   This person was found after death to be a man, although he had passed himself off in dress and habits during life as a woman. On an examination of the body there was strong evidence that he had been for many years addicted to unnatural habits. It was noticed by all present that the aperture of the anus was much wider and larger than natural. There was a slight protrusion and thickening of the mucous membrane at the margin. The rugæ or folds of skin which give the puckered appearance to the anal aperture had quite disappeared, so that this part resembled the labia

[1] Med. and Phys. Journ., Feb. 1833, p. 168.

of the female organs. The lining membrane was thickened at the verge of the anus and was in an ulcerated condition. The male organs had been drawn up and secured by a bandage bound round the lower part of the abdomen. A short account of this remarkable case of concealed sex was published in the 'Lond. Med. and Physical Journ.', Feb. 1833, p. 168. Trials for this crime are not unfrequent, but the reports of evidence are not made public. There cannot be any doubt that false charges are as common as in cases of rape. They are made for the purpose of extortion, and as the publication of such a charge, even when unfounded, is really dreaded, and has actually led to suicide, it often proves a successful method of extortion. It is especially deserving of notice that such accusations are frequently made by soldiers and policemen."

Pederasty. The young New Hebrideans, who come to be hired, have a difficulty in finding at Noumea any opportunities of satisfying their amorous passions. The women of their own race prefer the White man, as being not only more pleasant, but more profitable. As for getting White women, they might as soon find a needle in a bottle of hay. The New Hebridean youth has not a farthing of money, and is not likely to be loved for his own sake, for he is an object of disgust even to the female freed prisoner, or the wife of the old convict, though they are not remarkable for delicate sentiments. As a matter of course, this state of things leads to pederasty amongst the hired men, as it does also with the New Caledonian. But it is not a morbid mental depravity, like that of the Annamite, who is ready to lend himself to any form of erotic turpitude. It seemed to me (though I cannot, however, affirm it with absolute certainty) that these unnatural acts were performed without any of the refinements of lust practised in the Far East. The New Hebridean acts according to the old French proverb, "If you can't get thrushes, you must eat blackbirds." And he eats his blackbird simply roasted, without any sauce, or even a bit of fat to grease the dish. He simply satisfies his amorous inclinations on the mutual aid system. He is very far from boasting about it, and it is only with great difficulty that he can be made to avow the truth. I was never able to obtain a confession without the bait of a bit of silver and the promise of absolute secrecy.

Bestiality with a She-goat. Taylor, the English writer on Medical Jurisprudence, [1] from whom we have already had occasion to quote, speaking of the unnatural intercourse of man with animals, points out that to this peculiar form of sexual aberration the Germans [2] apply the term "Sodomy," while specialists in England and France more commonly give to it the name of "Bestiality." Trials for this crime perpetrated with animals, such as the cow, the mare, and the she-ass, are not unfrequent at the assizes. They are not reported, and do not therefore attract any public notice. The criminals are commonly youths or men employed to look after the animals. In most of these cases the criminal has been caught *flagrante delicto*—or under such circumstances as to leave no doubt of the attempt, if not of the completion, of the act of unnatural intercourse.

[1] *The Principles and Practice of Medical Jurisprudence,* by the late Alfd. S. Taylor, 4th edit. by Thos. Stevenson, M.D., Lond., *Churchill,* 1894.

[2] Casper, *Gerichtl. Med.,* vol. 1, p. 180.

"Medical evidence is seldom required to sustain the prosecution.   There may be, however, circumstances which can only be properly interpreted by an expert. The hair of the animal may be found on the perpetrator, or marks of blood or feculent matter upon his dress, and in such cases analysis, or the microscope, may enable a witness to express an opinion in proof or disproof of the charge.   In one case tried at the assizes, where a man was charged with having had unnatural intercourse with a cow, the prosecution was able to show that some short coloured hairs found on the prisoner's person resembled those of the animal. In another case, [1] the editor found the peculiar coloured hairs of a mare upon the prisoner's clothes, and spermatozoa on his trouser-flap.

"The medical jurists of Germany have taken a great interest in cases of sodomy and bestiality; and in some of their reports they have contrived to throw an air of science over the details of this detestable crime. Kutter has published an elaborate report of a case of this kind, [2] in which a sub-officer was charged by his captain with unnatural intercourse with a mare, and in support of the charge Kutter was able to furnish good microscopical evidence.   The captain, on entering the stable suddenly, found the prisoner in the act of moving away from the stall of the animal.   Kutter was called to examine the mare, and found some small abrasions about the genitals of the animal, and a slight escape of bloody mucus from these parts.   The prisoner willingly submitted himself to examination.   Kutter found some stains of blood on his skirt; and on the penis between the prepuce and the glans, there were a num-

[1] REG. v. BRINKLEY, Lincoln Ass., Ap., 1887.
[2] "Fleischlicher Vermischung mit einem Thiere."

ber of short, dark, pointed hairs. The prisoner accounted
for them by saying that the night before he had had
connection with some woman. Kutter examined the
hairs carefully by the aid of a microscope, and found
them to be shorter, thicker, and more pointed than
those of a human being. They were also coarse, and
less transparent. Comparing them with hairs gently
rubbed off the back part of the mare, they exactly
corresponded in colour, form, and length, so as to leave
no doubt on his mind that there has been unnatural
intercourse. It was impossible to say with any certainty
that the blood-stains on the shirt were produced by the
blood of the animal. This, however, was not a necessary part of the evidence. [1] On these facts Kutter
gave an opinion that the prisoner had been guilty of
unnatural intercourse with the mare."

I will conclude by noting a case of bestiality
committed by a New Hebridean with a she-goat. At
the request of the master of this new sort of Corydon,
I examined both the animal and the culprit,—who
could not deny the charge, having been caught in the
act by his master. The goat showed a well-marked
anal infundibulum, very similar to that of professional
passive sodomites. The anus was much dilated, and
admitted two fingers, though, in its normal condition,
the anus of the goat is very constricted, the dung of
the animal being in small round balls. The genital
parts of the man presented all the marks of active
sodomy. The yard, which was normal as to length
(5¾ to 6 inches in erection) was very thick at the base,
where it was nearly two inches in diameter, but it
diminished gradually up to the gland, where the diameter,
at the crown, was hardly more than half that of the

[1] Horn's "Vierteljahrsschr.," 1865, 1, p. 160.

base, and the crown was further strangled by a rather well-pronounced phimosis. It terminated in a point, and the "ring" was but slightly marked. Altogether it was more like the penis of an animal than that of a man. The testicles were developed, and showed that the man often indulged in copulation. Having purposely asked if he had never tried to enter the natural way when the goat was "on heat", I received the following reply in the "Biche-la-Mer" language, which is the *patois* of Polynesia: "Me have no; belong me cue too large." This naïvely cynical response, devoid of all artifice, convinced me, in fact, that it was impossible for the human organ, on account of its great difference from the genital organ of the he-goat, to enter the long but narrow vulva of the she-goat. [1]

Artificial Hypospadias of the Natives of Santo.

I found a native of Santo with an artificial hypospadia, performed at the age of puberty by the Takata. With a well-sharpened piece of quartz, the urethra is slit from the gland to the root of the bag, the penis being first fastened to a piece of bark. The wound is covered with a bandage of fine bark, after being dressed with some herbs chewed by the Takata. This curious operation compels those who have been thus mutilated to stoop down to make water. In a state of erection, the member becomes large and flat, and when emitting, the sperm dribbles out over the bag. The native, who exhibited this curious mutilation, told me that he was not the only one, and that it was not unfrequently

---

[1] Compare also pages 159—160 of vol. I, *Gli Amori degli Uomini*, by Cav. Paolo Mantegazza, Milano, 1892, for two other curious cases of this strange lewdness. One can hardly dignify it with the name of passion.

performed by the Takata on persons specially named by the Chief. He could not explain to me the reason for this singular custom.

It is certain, however, that it comes from Australia (the original cradle of the New Hebridean race), where it is practised in the central and western parts of the country.

The natives of Santo are almost completely pure Melanesians.

CHAPTER IX.

Six weeks at Tahiti.—Panoramic view of Tahiti at sun-rise.—
Anthropological characteristics of the Tahitian Maori race.—
Beauty of the Maori race.—The portrait of Rarahu.

Six Weeks at Tahiti. On leaving New Caledonia
to return to France, I obtained, as an unexpected
favour, permission to make the journey at my own
expense *via* Tahiti and America, instead of returning
on the sailing transport vessel. The Government, however, paid me a sum equal to what my voyage on
the transport vessel would have cost. But I was
anxious not to lose such an opportunity of visiting the
famous New Cytherea, so much belauded by the old
navigators. Thanks to the kindness of the heads of
the Naval Department, I was also able to obtain a
furlough, and remain six weeks at Papeete, the capital
of Tahiti.

One of my colleagues, Doctor S***, who had been
three years in the colony, undertook to serve as my
guide, and owing to his kindness in putting his notes
at my disposal, and to the information of various kinds
which he procured for me, my voyage to Tahiti was
not devoid of profit.

Panoramic View of Tahiti at Sun-rise. The
three-masted sailing vessel, which carried me from
Noumea to Papeete, very luckily, arrived within sight
of land at evening and did not enter the harbour till

next morning. I was therefore able to enjoy the never to be forgotten spectacle of sun-rise when only a few miles from the coast of Tahiti.

At the moment when the shades of night gave place to the grey hues of dawn, the New Cytherea rose to view, and proudly raised its enormous pyramidal silhouette,—a gigantic mass of a uniform dark blue tint, crowned by Mount Orohena, about 7500 feet high. The great valleys of the island formed deep shadows on the sides of the mountains, the summits of which began to be gradually lighted up. The bright light of day spread rapidly, and the delighted eye watched undreamed of effects of colour, until the orb of day, rising like a golden disk behind the mountains, made their peaks glitter like diamond points.

The short duration of twilight, which, in the tropics, precedes the daylight by only a few minutes, made the spectacle seem like a panorama which was being slowly unrolled. Moorea, the sister island of Tahiti, with its mountain tops rising into the blue sky, formed a delightful background of a pinkish grey tint. The eye, used to the wild scenery of New Caledonia, with its arid mountains, rests with pleasure on the rich foliage of Tahiti. Beyond the girdle of reefs, on the edge of its pretty harbour, Papeete, the capital of the island, lies gracefully like a lizard in the sun. From a distance you can hardly see more than the church, and a few houses on the shore; all the rest is hidden under a luxuriant vegetation. I mentally compared this picturesque site with Saint Louis at Senegal; the one, a charming nest of verdure; the other, a dull glare of white walls.

A boat took me to land. Some narrow streets, planted with trees, forming a roof of foliage over the traveller's head, little, low houses, with red tiled roofs, and surrounded by gardens filled with flowers and foliage,—such is Papeete. In this delightful town I spent a few weeks, and the memory of it still makes my heart beat with pleasure. And yet Tahiti is no longer the New Cytherea of de Bougainville,—the paradise of love.

Anthropological Characteristics of the Tahitian Maori Race. The Tahitian Maori race is a product of the crossing of three races,—white, yellow, and black (the Melanesian),—the two former markedly dominating over the latter. The tint tends generally to a reddish white, and ranges from light brown chocolate (the darkest shade) to the warm, slightly olive tint of the Spaniards of Andalusia. In fact, reader, if you have never seen a Vahiné (a woman of Tahiti) nothing can give you a better idea of her than the Andalusian with the brown breasts, of Alfred de Musset. The almost white tint belongs exclusively to the families of the Chiefs, who have formed fewer *mésalliances* with the Black race, which came from Australia, evidently. In 1767 the navigator, Wallis, found at Maravai some Chiefs almost white, and with red hair. Generally, in the Maoris, the skull is enlarged at the level of the parietal bones, and its shape from front to rear, resembles that of the keel of a ship. The hair is black, fine, abundant, sometimes curly, but never woolly. It shades a projecting forehead, and eyes that are slightly oblique, and always very large, denoting, in the man, pride; and, in the woman, voluptuousness. Cheekbones slightly projecting, a nose sometimes flat, a large mouth with sensuous lips of a dark ruby red, magnificent teeth, a not very prominent chin, covered, in the case of the men, with a light black beard, a long neck, large shoulders and breast, a fine waist, a slim form, well-proportioned limbs, with fine and long extremities, complete, in the man, a most imposing ensemble.

Beauty of the Maori Race. Truly the *Tané* (Tahitian) of from twenty to twenty-five years of age, is a splendid fellow, and, in my opinion, one of the most perfect specimens of human beauty. If the Greek sculptors had but known him, what masterpieces of art they would have bequeathed us. A characteristic that is common enough amongst the young Tanés is a development, sometimes fairly considerable, of the buttocks, which are generally rounded, and of a slightly feminine shape, though the body, in its entirety, presents an appearance of strength combined with grace. The antique statue of the Indian Bacchus might serve as a type of many of the Tanés. We may remark that the flat nose is not a natural characteristic, and is due to the fact that the Tahitian nurses had formerly the habit of crushing the cartilage of the noses of the young children. The younger generation, on the contrary, have the nose aquiline, and of a very regular shape. In the Vahiné, the head is smaller than that of the man; the breasts have a splendid curve, slightly arched, of an average size, with small nipples standing out straight in front. The waist is slender, the belly, the haunches, and the buttocks, are rounded and beautifully proportioned, the thighs plump and well furnished, the calves and ankles splendid. The general appearance of some Vahinés of from eighteen to twenty years calls to mind the antique Venus of Arles.

To whom shall the prize of beauty be given? If

the Tané attracts our gaze by a beauty which is majestic, though still remaining graceful, and which makes him resemble the Indian Bacchus, the Vahiné fascinates the traveller by a languorous charm, and there shoots from her black, gazelle-like eyes, soft glances which are at once both sweet and impudent,— a seductive grace that promises every sort of voluptuous pleasure. A Vahiné of sixteen, leaving her bath, might serve as a model for Venus rising from the sea, her long hair spread over her shoulders like a royal mantle, and often falling below the bust. The pubes is well furnished with soft hair, in colour, black, dark chestnut, and sometimes red, for there are golden red blondes amongst the Vahinés.

The Portrait of Rarahu. I have tried my best to describe the nature of the beauties of the Tahitian race, but I feel how powerless my pen is to accomplish the task, and I have sought the help of that of Pierre Loti. The portrait of his mistress, little Rarahu, is a perfect jewel, and the reader will no doubt be pleased that I reproduce it here.

"Rarahu was a tiny creature unlike any other, though she was a perfect type of the Maori race which peoples the Polynesian archipelago, and which is deemed one of the most beautiful in the world; a distinct and mysterious race the origin of which is unknown. Rarahu had eyes of a russet black, full of exotic languor, and of a wheedling softness, like those of a kitten when you caress it; her eyelashes were so long, and so black, that you might have taken them for painted feathers. Her nose was short and small, like those of some of the Arab girls; her mouth, a little thicker and a little wider than the classic type, had deep corners

of a delightful contour. In laughing, she showed all
of a set of teeth which were a trifle large, and white
as white enamel,—teeth, which the years had not had
time to polish much, and which still retained the light
striæ of childhood. Her hair, which was perfumed
with sandal wood, was long, straight, and perhaps a
trifle coarse; it fell in heavy masses on her round,
naked shoulders. A uniformly tawny tint, tending
to redbrick, like that of the light terra-cottas of old
Etruria, spread over all her body, from the top of her
forehead to the tips of her toes.

"Rarahu was not tall, but admirably made, and
splendidly proportioned; her breast was pure and
polished, her arms perfect. Round each ankle was
a light blue tattoo mark, imitating a bracelet; on the
lower lip three little blue transversal rays, almost
imperceptible, like those of the women of the Marquesas
Islands; and upon her forehead a still paler tattoo
mark, in the form of a diadem. That which, above
all, characterised her race, was the excessive closeness
of her prominent eyes, as in all the Maoris; when she
was gay and laughing, this gave to her childish face
the cunning look of a young marmoset; but when
she was serious or sad, there was something about
her that you could not define better than by these
two words,—a Polynesian grace."

CHAPTER X.

Manners and customs of the Tahitians.— Social condition of the ancient Tahitians.— The Manahuné—Religion and the priests.— Origin of the Tahitian race.— The language.—The Tahitian Arii is an Aryan like the old Greek.—The priest's part in Tahitian civilisation.— The Maraé.— Human sacrifices.— The end of Tahitian civilisation.—Habitations.—Baths.—Food.—Amuraa.—Public festivals.— Costumes.

ALTHOUGH this chapter has only an indirect connection with sexual passions and habits, it seemed to me that it would not be altogether useless; however, I will be brief.

Social Condition of the Ancient Tahitians. The dynasty of Pomaré established by force its authority over Tahiti and the neighbouring isles. When Tahiti was discovered, only one Chief,—Oamma, the husband of Queen Oberea—possessed the " red maro", or insignia of royal power. The government was theocratic; the royal race descended from the God-King, Hiro. Under the sovereign, are the princes of the royal blood; under the princes, the lords, divided into two categories, and classed, according to their order of pre-eminence, into Arii (principal chiefs), and Raatira; the first have nearly all the power, and the second mere empty honours.

The Manahuné. Under these was the Manahuné (man of the people) who possessed nothing of his own.

His heritage was subject to certain feudal rights, but he could, nevertheless, transmit it intact to his children as a sort of permanent usufruct. He could enter into the sect of Arrioys, of which I shall speak more fully later on.

Religion and the Priests. Religion played an important part amongst the old Tahitians. Alongside of royalty and the nobility, was the sacred caste of the priests, possessing considerable privileges. Without entering on long dissertations, I will only say, that the old religion of the Tahitians resembled that of the Greeks, and showed the same characteristics. There was the same pantheism, the same anthropomorphism of the inferior gods, the same worship of the forces of Nature. The creator of the world was Taoroa, whose cosmic arrangements seem to have been distinguished by simplicity and energy. Man must die, but matter is eternal. The Divinities are of two orders; the Atorias, or great gods, who rule men's actions, but do not have to judge their morality. To enumerate all their names here, would take too long, but I find amongst the Tahitian gods, an Esculapius, a Hercules, a Mars, a Mercury, an Apollo, etc. Below these high gods, are inferior gods, who may be compared to the Naiads, Nymphs, Dryads, Fauns, etc., of the old Greek mythology. The gods could assume human form, when they wished to satisfy their passions; —exactly like the Greek Jupiter. Finally, in the lowest rank, we find the Oromatouas, domestic gods, or lares, absolutely identical with the lares and penates of the Romans. This resemblance of the Tahitian religion to that of the ancient Greeks would seem to indicate a common origin.

I have said above, that the Tahitians were the outcome of three races; the white, yellow, and black. The first is almost pure in the case of the kings, the princes, and the Arii. In the Raatira, the yellow race predominates. The Raatira were the first conquerors of the aborigines, and were subdued in their turn by the Arii, who left them barren honours and empty titles, but took away from them, in reality, all their power. The Manahuné has more black blood than the nobles, although this black blood has been greatly ameliorated by an admixture of yellow blood, and a little white blood.

Origin of the Tahitian Race. So much being understood, anthropology, the religion, and the language will enable us to discover the secret of the origin of the Maori race.

The Tahitian language is at once soft, sonorous, and harmonious, and by its grammar, its elegance, and its accentuation, reminds one of Greek, though of course much less perfect. To this opinion, Edward B. Tylor, the distinguished Oxford anthropologist, I consider gives his support by the following passage:—" Language, appearing as an art in full vigour among rude tribes, already displays the adaptation of child-like devices in self-expressive sound and pictorial metaphor, to utter thoughts as complex and abstruse as savage minds demand speech for. When it is considered how far the development of knowledge depends on full and exact means of expressing thought, is it not a pregnant consideration that the language of civilised men is but the language of savages, more or less improved in structure, a good deal extended in vocabulary, made more precise in the dictionary definition of words?

The development of language between its savage and cultured stages has been made in its details, scarcely in its principle. It is not too much to say that half the vast defect of language as a method of utterance, and half the vast defect of thought as determined by the influence of language, are due to the fact that speech is a scheme worked out by the rough and ready application of material metaphor and imperfect analogy, in ways fitting rather the barbaric education of those who formed it, than our own. Language is one of those intellectual departments in which we have gone too little beyond the savage stage, but are still as it were hacking with stone celts and twirling laborious friction-fire."[1] Besides the singular and plural numbers, the Maori possesses, like Greek, the dual, which is unknown to European tongues. The language of a people is the mark of its state of civilisation. We may then compare the Tahitian civilisation to that of the ancient Greeks, and by the connection existing between the languages and religions, assign to them both a common origin.

Consequently it is easy to trace the origin of the Tahitian race. The autochthone was the Melanesian Negro of Australia: he was conquered, at a very remote epoch, by men of a yellow race, evidently Malays. These latter partly allied themselves to the conquered people and formed the earliest race of nobles, those of the Raatira. Finally the White, the last conqueror, came, and founded,—like the Norman in England,—a superior hierarchy, a select caste (that of the Arii), which forced its religion and language on the conquered people. But the language has become corrupted by being mixed with that of the conquered

[1] *Primitive Culture*, third edit. London, *Murray*, 1891, vol. II, p. 445.

people, just as French is but a corruption of Latin; and English, a mixture of Saxon and old Norman French.

The close relationship between the Maori and the ancient Greek being thus established, it naturally follows that the two races must be derived from one common stock.

The Tahitian Arii is an Aryan, like the Old Greek. Greek civilisation is the daughter of Hindoo civilisation, and India is really the cradle of the civilised world. Philology and religion will prove this assertion. The names of the gods of the Greek mythology are, in fact, almost pure Sanscrit, and are nothing but translations of the titles given to the Hindoo gods. Hercules is in Sanscrit *Hora-Kala*, the hero of battles; Jupiter, in Sanscrit *Zu-pitri*, is the father of heaven, or *Zeus-pitri*, and became the Zeus of the Greeks, and the Jehovah of the Hebrews; Pallas is in Sanscrit *Pala-sa*, the goddess who protects; Minerva is in Sanscrit *Ma-nara-va*, she who supports the brave; Bellona is in Sanscrit *Bala-na*, warlike strength; Neptune is in Sanscrit *Na-patana*, he who masters the fury of the waves; Mars, the God of War, is in Sanscrit *Mri*, he who deals death; Pluto, the God of Hell, is in Sanscrit *Plushta*, he who strikes by fire; Orestes, celebrated for his madness, is in Sanscrit *O-rah-sata*, doomed to misfortune; Pylades, his friend, is in Sanscrit *Pa-la-da*, he who consoles by his friendship; Centaur is in Sanscrit *Ken-tura*, a man-horse. But here I will stop, though I could run through the entire mythology in the same way.

Let us take the names of the peoples of the Aryan race, whose migrations are shown by etymology.

The Hellenes, the ancient Greeks, are in Sanscrit *Hela-na*, warrior-worshippers of Hela, the Moon. In the Tahitian language, the moon is called *Hina !* The Italians, a name which comes from Italus, the son of the Trojan hero, are in Sanscrit *Itala*, men of low caste; the Celts, the first conquerors of almost the whole of Europe, are in Sanscrit *Kalla-ta*, the invading chiefs; the Gauls are in Sanscrit *Ga-la-ta*, the people who march conquering; the Belgians, in Sanscrit, *Ba-la-ja*, the children of the brave; the Scandinavians, in Sanscrit, *Skanda-nava*, worshippers of Skanda, the god of battles; the Alemanni (Germans), in Sanscrit, *Alamanu*, the free men; finally Ireland, which the poets call "Erin the green", is in Sanscrit *Erin*, rocks surrounded by salt water.

I am positive that there would be found in the Tahitian language many words derived from the Sanscrit, and that the White *Arii*, the invader of the island of Tahiti, who has conquered, and then peopled, the other large islands of Polynesia, New Zealand, the Hawaii Islands, etc., is an *Aryan* of pure extraction, the brother of the Aryan who conquered India and Europe.

The Priest's Place in Tahitian Civilisation. The caste of priests, like that of the Brahmins of India, and the bonzes of Cambodia, proudly maintained its privileges against the king and nobles. No people in the world, not even the Romans, allowed the ministers of their gods greater importance. In peace or war, no acts of political or civil life occurred without their interference. The person of the priest (Faaoura-Pouré) was sacred, and the sacerdotal authority hereditary, like that of the Brahmins of India ; their power extended even to life and death. They were the guardians of traditions, the historians of the nation. Below the priests, was a whole hierarchy, analogous to the deacons and sub-deacons of the Catholic Church; and also the Tiis, who were inspired by the inferior deities, and acted as exorcists and sorcerers.

I shall speak of the Arrioys, in the chapter on the perversions of sexual passion.

The Maraé, or sacred temple, offered some resemblance to the altars of the Gaulish druids, and it would even be possible to trace a curious resemblance between the analogous duties of the *Faaoura-Pouré* and the Druid, in their respective societies. It consisted of a parallelogram, terminated at one of its extremities by a pyramid of stone, surrounded by sacred trees. A kind of wooden platform, mounted on four legs, formed the *fata* or altar, and there the victim was offered, or the dead body of the chief deposited. In the maraé were to be seen,—cut by the inexperienced chisel of some Tahitian sculptor,—the *toos,* or images of the Atouas.

Human Sacrifices. To obtain the favour of the gods, recourse was had rather often to human sacrifices. Even in these horrible ceremonies, the mild nature of the Tahitian showed itself, and the unfortunate victims designated by the priests were killed unexpectedly. At the time when cannibalism prevailed, the victims were eaten, and the eye was the favourite morsel of the King, from whence came the name *Aimata* (eat eye), which was borne by many persons of the royal family. Captain Cook was present at a human sacrifice. But they ceased at the beginning of the present century, and since, in 1820, Pomaré II. abjured the religion of his fathers, the old Tahitian religion is quite dead, and the Maori race itself is dying out.

The End of Tahitian Civilisation. All this feudal organisation has disappeared under the influence of European civilisation, represented by the religious fanaticism of the English missionaries. The penal and religious code of Pomaré II. was drawn out by Englishmen, who endeavoured to bestow British manners and customs on a people whose civilisation was so different from that of prudish Albion. It was a repetition of the marriage of the cold Saxon carp with the lascivious Maori rabbit. The result obtained may be summed up in two words, hypocrisy and drunkenness. In the chapter relating to the sexual passions of the Tahitian race, I shall more fully discuss the question of the influence of the Anglican priest, importer of Bibles, but also trafficker in gin. Let us also add the small and great pox, with which the European has presented the Maoris.

At the time when I arrived at Tahiti, the old Queen Pomaré had died, leaving the throne to her second son, who took the title of Pomaré V. To spite his wife, an English half-breed, Pomaré V. ceded his royal rights to France, and Tahiti has now become a French colony. Loti is quite correct in saying that from the death of Queen Pomaré dates the end of Tahiti, as far as concerns customs, local colour, and the strange charms of an island that the French navigator, de Bougainville, had christened New Cytherea.

Habitations. The Maori does not live in a dirty hut, like the Kanaka of New Caledonia, or the New Hebrides. His house is a large rectangular building, a really airy cage, with bamboo walls hung with mats, and the roof covered with "tiles" made of the pandanus or the cocoa-palm leaf, and the roof ends in a verandah. The hut stands in the midst of a large enclosure, the property of the family, and under the shadow of cocoa-palms, bread-fruit trees, and mango trees. In the interior all is exquisitely clean.

Baths. The Maori race is exceedingly cleanly, and might give a lesson in this respect to many civilised Europeans. To bathe in cold spring water every day is a necessity to him, and in the shades of evening you may see in every pool of every brook,—which are numerous enough in the valleys,—couples of bathers playing joyously. I must have recourse to Loti again, to depict the grace and the charm of the Tahitian women bathing.

"Turning to the right through the underwood, we followed for half an hour the Apiré road, and then came to a large natural pool in the rock. Into this pool of Fataoua falls a cascade of delightfully cool running water. Here, all day long there is a numerous gathering; on the grass lie some of the fairest damsels of Papeete, who pass the hot tropical days in talking, singing, sleeping, or swimming and diving like gold fish. They go into the water dressed in their muslin tunic, which they still wear whilst they sleep after their bath, wet as it is,—like the Naiads of old. Sailors often come here to make the acquaintance of some of the girls."

Food. The food of the Tahitian is varied. Fish constitutes the main portion of the nourishment. It is often eaten raw with *taioro,* a sauce composed of grated

cocoa-nut, fermented with sea-water boiled to evaporation.   In this food there are two powerful aphrodisiacs,
phosphorus, and sea salt.   To this diet, the Maori adds
poultry, and on grand occasions, pork.   As vegetables
he has the yam, the taro, and the sweet batata.   He
has also bread-fruit, which grows everywhere, and the
fei, a kind of wild banana, can be found on the mountains.
As dessert, he possesses every variety of tropical fruit;—
oranges, bananas, mangoes, pine-apples, etc., which
grow wild.   All the blessings of heaven are showered
upon this island, and man has nothing to do but take
the trouble to live.   I would ask the reader to remark
how rich, abundant, and varied, this diet is.   As we
shall see a little later, it is not without its influence
on the amorous vigour of the Tahitian.

The Public Festivals of the Tahitians.   Every
Saturday, after gathering the *fei* in the mountains,
friends and neighbours assemble at a social gathering.
Besides these private gatherings, there are celebrated,
at certain periods of the year, in every district, grand
public banquets, called *amuraa*.   They are veritable
Gargantuan feasts, and will bear comparison with our
largest public banquets.   I do not know of any writer
who has ever dared to say that he saw a dinner of
five hundred covers, laid in a village.   Everybody sets
to work.   Yams, taros, *feis*, and *magori*, are heaped
up in profusion; whole herds of pigs, and hundreds of
fowls, are slaughtered, and roasted in the open air, in
front of enormous fires.

Costume.   The Tahitian Maori looks handsome in
his simple and artistic costume, which consists of a white
cotton shirt, or vest, falling loosely over a *pareo*,—a

large piece of cotton stuff of a large pattern and bright colours, which is draped round the hips, and hangs as low as the middle of the calf of the leg, and replaces the hideous trousers of civilisation, introduced by the English. Dressed in this costume, the young Tané carries his head high, and his chest stuck out, with an easy, manly, and proud bearing.

The Vahinés wear the "*gaule*",—a long robe without any waist, fastened under the breasts, like the dress of the time of the Directory. On the head is a light "straw" hat, made of the fine fibres of the bamboo; the hair falls loosely on the shoulders, or often hangs down to the thighs, or is twisted into two long plaits which hang down the back, à la Swiss peasant maiden.

Tané and Vahiné are alike ignorant of the use of the shoe, that instrument of torture of civilised man, and their feet consequently are well formed, and the insteps as arched as those of the Andalusians. The Vahinés wear this simple toilet with ease and grace, and charm the eye by their lissom bearing, and coquettish air. On fête days, and the evenings of the *upa-upa*, the hat is replaced by the *reva-reva*, bows of transparent ribbon of a yellow green tint, made from the pith of the cocoa-palm. The Vahiné fixes in her hair the *tiare miri*, a beautiful white flower, the scent of which is sweeter than the orange flower. Sometimes she perfumes her hair with powdered sandal wood, and crowns her head with a wreath of foliage interlaced with flowers. When she is thus attired, the dark daughter of Tahiti delights the eye, and captivates the senses. Unless a European is physically fitted to become the guardian of a seraglio. it would hardly be possible for him to resist the seductions of the Vahiné.

CHAPTER XI.

Moral characteristics of the Tahitians.—Marriages.—Woman's place amongst the Maoris.—Births.—The taboo.—Adopted children. —Songs.—The hymeneal chant.—The upa-upa, or lascivious dance of the Tahitian women.—A upa-upa in the interior of the island.—Diseases.—Rapid extinction of the pure Maori race.

Moral Characteristics of the Tahitians. I have spoken of the beauty of the Tahitians. I might also mention their physical strength, for the Tané is an athlete, as vigorous as he is handsome. Cook's sailors were easily overthrown at wrestling by the Tahitians, as Cook himself confessed, and yet it is well-known, that of all the European races, the Anglo-Saxon is that in which all species of physical exercise, especially wrestling and boxing, are most held in honour. Yet, with all his great physical strength, the Tahitian is mild, and good-natured. These qualities had led him to abolish cannibalism, before the island was discovered, and he spared the victims of the human sacrifices as much pain as possible, by killing them unexpectedly.

The old Tahitian was a bellicose warrior. European civilisation has made him peaceable, but nothing has altered his light, changeful character. The Tahitian is a real child, joyous and capricious; laughing one moment and weeping the next, without any reason. His head is full of folly, but his heart is sound. He has all the gay and careless nature of the Neapolitan lazzaroni, but he never uses the knife, as the Italian does. Sun and fine weather make him gay and joyful; bad weather makes him sad and dreamy. All the dreams and fancies of imagination appeal to his nature. The cold, formal Protestant religion has not been able to remove his belief in superstitions,—the last trace of the religion of his forefathers; he fears the solitude of the great woods, and the obscurity of night, for he is afraid of meeting the *Tupapan*, the shades or spirits of the dead. If his griefs are short but lively, his gaiety, on the other hand, is wild and contagious. Above all and before all, the Tahitian Maori loves pleasure.

Marriages. It is important to remark that the Tahitian priest, whose influence was formerly so considerable, never interfered in marriages, which at New Cytherea have always remained the manifestation of the formal wishes of the couple united, without any religious consecration. Cook describes, however, the Tahitian marriage ceremonies, as we shall see later on, when I come to speak of the ancient customs.

Woman's Place in the Maori Race. If the Tané does not purchase his wife, at least she was not his equal, amongst the old Tahitians. At table she did not eat along with her husband; she could not be a priestess; admission to the Maraé was forbidden to her. The daughters of the royal house could, however, inherit the throne. The Salic law has never been in force at Tahiti, but, on the contrary, descent is transmitted by the woman, the Tahitians considering, not without reason, that though a man was certain that he came out of his mother's womb, he was not sure who his male parent was, and the famous axiom of

Roman law, *Pater is est quem nuptiæ demonstrant*
(The father is he whom marriage demonstrates to
be so) has never been applied in Tahiti.

Births.—The Taboo. The mother of a newly-born
infant became *taboo*. She might not touch anything
with her hands during a period of two months, and
other women had to feed her. Under these circumstances, one consequence of the *taboo* was to prevent
the renewal of coition before the woman's organs of
generation had returned to their normal condition. I
have shown, in the case of the New Caledonian Kanaka,
what serious disorders might result from commencing
copulation too soon after parturition.

"An observer," says Frazer, 'Golden Bough' (vol.
I, page 168), "who knows the Maoris well, states
'Tapu [taboo] is an awful weapon. I have seen a
strong young man die the same day he was tapued;
the victims die under it as though their strength ran
out as water.' [1] A Maori chief's tinder-box was once
the means of killing several persons; for having been
lost by him, and found by some men who used it to
light their pipes, they died of fright on learning to
whom it had belonged. So, too, the garments of a
high New Zealand chief will kill anyone else who
wears them. A chief was observed by a missionary
to throw down a precipice a blanket which he found
too heavy to carry. Being asked by the missionary
why he did not leave it on a tree for the use of a
future traveller, the chief replied that 'it was the fear
of its being taken by another which caused him to

[1] E. Tregear, "The Maoris of New Zealand," in *Journ. Anthrop.
Inst.* XIX, 100.

throw it where he did, for if it were worn, his tapu'
(*i.e.* his spiritual power communicated by contact
to the blanket and through the blanket to the man)
'would kill the person.' [1]

" No wonder therefore that the savage should rank
these human divinities amongst what he regards as
the dangerous classes, and should impose exactly the
same restraints upon the one as upon the other. For
instance, those who have defiled themselves by touching
a dead body are regarded by the Maoris as in a very
dangerous state, and are sedulously shunned and
isolated. But the taboos observed by and towards
these defiled persons (*e.g.* they may not touch food
with their hands, and the vessels used by them may
not be used by other people) are identical with those
observed by and towards sacred chiefs. [2] And, in
general the prohibition to use the dress, vessels, etc.,
of certain persons and the effects supposed to follow
an infraction of the rule are exactly the same whether
the persons to whom the things belong are sacred or
what we might call unclean and polluted. As the
garments which have been touched by a sacred chief
kill those who handle them, so do the things which
have been touched by a menstruous woman. An
Australian blackfellow, who discovered that his wife
had lain on his blanket at her menstrual period, killed
her and died of terror himself within a fortnight. [3]
Hence Australian women at these times are forbidden
under pain of death to touch anything that men

[1] R. Taylor, Te Ika a Maui; or, New Zealand and its inhabitants,
p. 164.

[2] A. S. Thomson, The Story of New Zealand, I, 101 *sqq.; Old
New Zealand*, by a Pakecha Maori, pp. 94, 104 *sqq.*

[3] *Journ. Anthrop. Inst.* IX, 458.

use. They are also secluded at child-birth, and all vessels used by them during their seclusion are burned. [1] Amongst some of the Indians of North America also women at menstruation are forbidden to touch men's utensils, which would be so defiled by their touch that their subsequent use would be attended by certain mischief or misfortune. [2] Amongst the Eskimo of Alaska no one will willingly drink out of the same cup or eat out of the same dish that has been used by a woman at her confinement, until it has been purified by certain incantations. [3] Amongst some of the Tinneh Indians of North America the dish out of which girls eat during their seclusion at puberty 'are used by no other person, and wholly devoted to their own use.' [4] Again amongst some Indian tribes of North America men who have slain enemies are considered to be in a state of uncleanness, and will not eat or drink out of any dish or smoke out of any pipe but their own for a considerable time after the slaughter, and no one will willingly use their dishes or pipes. They live in a kind of seclusion during this time, at the end of which all the dishes and pipes used by them during their seclusion are burned. [5] Amongst the Kafirs, boys at circumcision live secluded in a special hut, and when they are healed all the vessels

[1] W. Ridley, "Report on Australian Languages and Traditions," in *Journ. Anthrop. Inst.* II, 268.

[2] Alexander Mackenzie, *Voyages from Montreal through the Continent of North America*, CXXIII.

[3] *Report of the International Polar Expedition to Point Barrow, Alaska* (Washington, 1885), p. 46.

[4] "Customs of the New Caledonian Women," in *Journ. Anthrop. Inst.* VII, 206.

[5] S. Hearne, *A Journey from Prince of Wales's Fort in Hudson's Bay to the Northern Ocean*, p. 204 *sq.*

which they had used during their seclusion and the boyish mantles which they had hitherto worn are burned together with the hut. [1] When a young Indian brave is out on the war-path for the first time the vessels he eats and drinks out of must be touched by no one else." [2]

Adopted Children. The Maori Polynesian is almost the only human race in which the child, in the old legislation, rarely belonged to its progenitors. The adoption of children was extremely common amongst the old Tahitians, and has not yet disappeared from amongst their customs. It is one of the most curious customs of the race. Between the *Metua* (the natural father) and the *Metua Faanu* (the adoptive father) there was an almost incessant exchange of infants at the breast, and this exchange created between the two families a sort of quasi tie of relationship.

Songs.—The Hymeneal Chant. I heard the hymeneal chant for the first time in the salons of the Government House at Papeete. The chant was sung in the garden. The chorus was composed of seventy to eighty persons. seated in the Turkish fashion, in several rows, the women in front. A woman commenced, on a very high chest note, a lively and curious air; the other women repeated it in a rather low key, and the men formed the bass, whilst some of these latter, swaying their bodies backwards and forwards, uttered real groans.

[1] L. Alberti, *De Kaffers* (Amsterdam, 1810), p. 76 *sq.;* H. Lichtenstein, *Reisen im südlichen Afrika,* I, 427.

[2] *Narrative of the Captivity and Adventures of John Tanner* (London, 1830), p. 122.

The ensemble was perfect, and the voices astonish-
ingly true. What a difference between this and the
cries and howls, as of wild beasts, at a New Caledonian
pilou-pilou. All the parts agreed in true harmony.
It was a strange kind of music, but it was music.
The Maoris sang as the Greeks doubtless did in
the plays of Sophocles and Euripides. To fully
understand the originality of the hymeneal chant,
you ought to hear it when a bright moon is shedding
its light on groups of women, excited by dancing
the *upa-upa.*

The Upa-upa. On the evening of a fête day, or
after the delights of a joyous feast, the *upa-upa* is
generally danced. This lascivious dance shows the
Tahitian in her true character. It is a national dance,
and there is nothing that resembles it in any part of
the world. It is performed at night, by the light of
the moon, or *Hina,* the ancient female divinity of
Tahitians, the silver rays of which light up the scene,
under a transparent sky, in which the stars of the
Southern Cross glitter like diamonds. There, under
the shadow of the trees, and on the green carpet of
a soft lawn, men and women dance wildly with infinite
pleasure. In vain has British prudery sought to repress
the license of the *upa-upa.* The young Queen Pomaré,
when she was but sixteen, and the English divines
sought to forbid her the *upa-upa,* replied by organising
an enormous *upa-upa* in the island of Moorea, and
before all her people, and simply clad in transparent
lace, which the missionaries had given her, and which
showed the shape of her royal form, performed this
most lascivious dance.

I must have recourse once more to the pen of Loti

to make the reader understand the nature of this dance.

"Every evening the wild scene was renewed. When night fell, the Tahitian girls decked their heads with the brightest flowers; the hurried strokes of the tam-tam called them to the *upa-upa*, and thither they ran, their locks dishevelled, their bodies hardly covered by their muslin tunics, and the maddening lascivious dance often lasted till the morning. The Tahitian women clapped their hands, and accompanied the tam-tam with a song, sung in chorus, to a fast and frenzied tune. Each of them in turn executed a figure. The steps and the music were slow at first, but grew faster till they attained a delirium, and when the girl dancing was worn out, and stopped suddenly at a loud bang on the drum, another darted into her place, and surpassed her in immodesty and frenzy The girls of Pomotou formed other, and wilder, groups, and rivalled those of Tahiti. Crowned with curious wreaths of the datura, wild as mad women, they danced to a more jerky and wilder rhythm, but in a manner so charming, that, between the two, one did not know which to prefer."

At present the *upa-upa*, as danced at Papeete, has lost a good deal of its original character, and has almost become an imitation of the *chahut* of Bullier. But in the interior it has still retained its original form, and has been thus described by the traveller, Desfontaines, who, more fortunate than I, was able to make the tour of the island.

"After lunch, a number of the young Tahitian girls, crowned with roses, and with their hair unloosed, came and formed a circle under the trees, squatting, in the Oriental fashion, on the grass. One of them possessed

an accordion; we were about to assist at a *upa-upa*,
a kind of lascivious dance, accompanied by songs.
Hardly had the accordion uttered the first notes, than
the singing began, to a lively and rapid air, and at
this moment the faces of the dancers seemed suddenly
to be lighted up; in their eyes, and in their smiles,
there appeared an indescribable expression, which
illuminated their faces with a look that seemed almost
divine; they appeared to no longer belong to the
earth. The head was inclined, and thrown slightly
backwards, the body swayed, the elbows struck the
sides in time with the air, with movements which
resembled tremblings, or the light beating of wings,
the lower limbs rose and fell according to the rhythm,
and thus they danced before us. And when they had
finished the verse, which ended with a long, high
note, they stopped in their dance, and the expression
suddenly died out of their faces; it was difficult to
believe that they were the same women. Then one of
them turned towards me in the most disdainful manner,
and said in a tone of command which admitted of no
reply, 'Frenchman, bring us some beer.' The woman
of this country is a wild animal of far too charming
a kind to be refused a request, so I hastened to offer
them some drink. Without loss of time, they passed
round the ring, glasses filled with beer or rum, and
which they emptied at a single draught. Then, transforming themselves anew into ethereal beings, they
began a second verse, which finished in the same
manner with a sudden stop, and another demand of,
'Frenchman, more beer.' Songs and dances thus
alternated with libations, without the least respite. The
excitement reached its height. Amidst these gardens
of cocoa-palms, these young and beauteous damsels,

in their light garments, with their beautiful black hair crowned with wreaths of roses, resembled Nymphs engaged in their voluptuous sports, and intoxicated with the exuberance of love. This was the time for us to slip away, for the dance would soon degenerate into orgies. We left the spot, being anxious to carry away, unchanged, the memory of this never to be forgotten vision."

Diseases.—Rapid Extinction of the Pure Maori Race. Before the discovery of the island, the principal diseases were rheumatic pains, generally caused by excessive bathing in cold water, and elephantiasis,—a disease derived from the Black race. On the other hand, since so-called modern civilisation has established a footing in the island, gin, the two poxes, and more especially phthisis, have caused enormous ravages. The royal family of Pomaré,—a race of giants, remarkable for their strength and beauty,—has almost entirely died out. In Cook's time, the island possessed a population of more than a hundred thousand inhabitants; at present, there are not ten thousand. If contact with the White race would quickly rid humanity of the cannibals of New Caledonia and the New Hebrides, that would be a benefit, but we must be allowed to deplore the extinction of the mild, good-tempered Maori race. It lived so happily in its terrestrial paradise before the arrival of the Europeans. There was hardly any work to be done, no moral troubles, free love, and every kind of pleasure. What have we given it in exchange? Alcohol, small-pox, and consumption, a terrible trinity alone,—to say nothing of drunkenness and hypocrisy. In a few years' time there will be (with some few exceptions) no Tahitians of pure breed left in New Cytherea,

What will the half-breed race, the cross between the European and the Vahiné, be like? Will it possess the moral qualities of the father, and the physical qualities of the Maori race? That is a question that the future alone can answer.

CHAPTER XII.

Importance of sexual intercourse to the Maoris.—Love the principal occupation of the race.—Manners of the former inhabitants of New Cytherea.—Public offerings to Venus.—Opinions of Cook and de Bougainville on the debauchery of the Tahitians.—Good Friday in Lancashire.—Timorodée, the lascivious dance.—Sacred orgies and erotic festivals.—Ancient rites.—The ancient Peruvians.—The sect of the Nicolites.—The aborigines of Australia. —The Hawaian Hula-Hula.—The West African Negroes.—The South American Puri.—Christian festivals.—New Britain Islands. —Esthonia.—Marriage amongst the Tahitians.—Circumcision and tattooing.—Tattooing on women.—The sect of the Arrioys, amongst whom woman is in common.—The happy life of the Tahitians.— The day's life of a Vahiné at Papeete.—Jealousy of the present race of Tahitians.—Tahitian hospitality.—The true character of the Vahiné.—Marriage after trial.—"If thee tak, I tak thee".—The "Come Nights".—The Philippine Islands.

Love is the Principal Occupation of the Race.

The *dolce farniente* in which men and women pass their day, the easiness of an existence which is almost devoid of material wants, the fact that family cares are almost unknown to this people, the last representatives of the age of gold of humanity, all combine to leave them the leisure necessary for consecrating all their nights to love.

Before studying the Tahitian as he now is, let us throw a backward glance at the manners of New Cytherea at the time of its discovery by the European navigators.

Manners of the Ancient Inhabitants of New Cytherea. In order to well understand the influence of "cant" and British mock-modesty on the present manners of the Tahitians, we must glance at the cynically frank and free manners of their ancestors at the time of the discovery of the island. What most especially struck the navigators of the eighteenth century, was the freedom with which the affairs of love were performed in open daylight, instead of in the obscurity and mystery of night. This led them to declare that the Tahitians were not jealous of their wives, because they offered them to strangers, and that the women had not preserved that natural instinct of modesty which is found almost everywhere. The Tahitians, after having listened to the Anglican divine service, showed Cook and his companions a ceremony of quite another kind, and which must have rather startled British cant.

Public Offerings to Venus. " A young man six feet in height, and a young girl of eleven or twelve years of age, sacrificed to Venus before several of our men, and a number of the natives, without attaching any idea of indecency to their action, but, on the contrary, seemed to imagine that they were merely conforming to one of the customs of the country. Amongst the spectators there were several women of high rank, and notably Oberea, the Queen of the island, who may be said to have presided over the ceremony, for she gave the young girl instructions how to play her part, but though the girl was very young she did not appear to need instructing."

Let us listen also to what de Bougainville, who has bestowed upon Tahiti the apt and pretty epithet of New Cytherea, has to say on the same subject.

"Every day our men walked about unarmed, either singly or in twos or threes: they were invited into the huts and provided with food. But the hospitality of the master of the house was seldom confined to the offer of a slight repast; they also offered young girls. [1] The hut was instantly filled by a crowd of men and women, curious to watch the proceedings, and who formed a ring round the altar on which the young victim to hospitable duty was to be sacrificed. The ground was covered with flowers and foliage, and the musicians sang to the strains of the flute a hymn of rejoicing. Venus is the goddess of their hospitality; her worship permits no mystery, and each act in her honour is a national feast; they were greatly surprised that we, on our side, showed any embarrassment."

We may note how differently the facts are related by the two celebrated navigators. Cook, the English-

---

[1] Compare Sir R. F. Burton on the Krumen:—"As regards morality, in its limited sense, the Krumen are not bright in the scale of creation. Adultery is punished, it is true, by a fine, and in the case of a wealthy or powerful man, there may be a 'great palaver.' The European stranger, however, travelling in their country is expected to patronise their wives and daughters, and these unconscious followers of Lycurgus and Cato feel hurt, as if dishonoured, by his refusing to gratify them. The custom is very prevalent along this coast. At Gaboon, perhaps, it reaches the acme; there a man will in one breath offer the choice between his wife, sister, and daughter. The women of course do as they are bidden by the men, and they consider all familiarity with a White man a high honour." Dr. Livingstone, chap. 25, asserts, "I have heard women speaking in admiration of a White man, because he was pure and never was guilty of any secret immorality." This is amongst the Makolokos: he would have heard them speak in anything but an admiring way about continence in these regions. "*Wanderings in West Africa from Liverpool to Fernando Po*," Lond. 1863, vol. II, p. 24.

man, mentions the offering to Venus, but says nothing
about his own men. De Bougainville, more frankly,
declares that the Frenchmen showed some embarrassment at being called upon to thus perform in public.
but he does not, from false modesty, deny that some
of the sailors (probably Provençals who are naturally
lewd and reckless) did commit such acts *coram populo*.

Let us, however, return to Cook's account. "It
cannot be supposed that these people can much esteem
chastity; men offer to strangers their sisters or their
daughters, out of civility, or as a return for some
service, and conjugal infidelity, even in the woman,
is only punished by a few hard words, or some light
blows. License and lust are carried to a degree that
no nation in the history of the world, from the creation
until now, has ever attained, and which it is impossible
to imagine."

Cook wrote the preceding lines after his first voyage;
on the second visit he was less severe in his opinion
of the lewdness of the Tahitians. "However," he
says, "those who have represented all the women of
Tahiti and the Society Islands as ready to grant the
greatest favours to all those who would pay them,
have been very unjust to them; it is a mistake. It
is as difficult in this country as it is in any other, to
have commerce with married women of a certain rank,
and even with those who are not, except the women
of the common people, and amongst these last there
are many who are chaste. Certainly there are prostitutes, as there are everywhere else, and the number
of them is perhaps greater than usual, and such were
the women who came on board our ships, or into the
camp which we had established on the coast. And
as these women mix freely with the chaste ones, and

with women of the highest rank, one is at first tempted to believe that they are all of the same sort, and that there is no difference between them except that of price. But, it must be confessed, that a prostitute does not seem to them to commit any fault which would cause her to lose the esteem or the companionship of her fellow countrywomen." [1]

Good Friday in Lancashire. [2] Some five-and-thirty years ago, on Good Friday, if the weather was at all favourable, a strange sight could be witnessed at any of the steam-ferry landing-stages along the quays of Liverpool. There were congregated motley crowds of men and women, mostly young, laughing, joking, and making fun in broad Lancashire dialect of the serious God-abiding folks passing by on their honest way to Church or Chapel, much to the latters' discomfiture and abomination.

But whence came these crowds and what was their destination?

They were Lancashire operatives with their wives, and they were waiting for steamboats to convey them to Eastham, some five or six miles higher up on the other side of the Mersey, where the river widens out into an estuary of considerable extent. The purpose of their trip was to have an "outing",—but a "Good Friday outing",—one of an altogether peculiar kind.

On arriving at Eastham, they formed into numerous groups and settled into comfortable nooks to enjoy the contents of their provision baskets, which they washed down with copious draughts of ale. Then there was

---

[1] For comparison with these customs, see the Excursus to present chapter, "Marriage after Trial."

[2] This account was sent to us by an old Lancashire resident.

dancing and games at hide and seek, and blind-man's buff, after which, well primed with fun and whiskey, they disappeared by couples into the neighbouring brush-wood; Eastham at that time was a wild region of little sand hills covered with sparse thickets, the only inhabitants being rabbits, to which the place was a perfect paradise.   To anyone wandering through the brushwood, a strange sight was now disclosed; nearly every bush sheltered some couple actively engaged in amorous conversation on the soft sand. Sometimes their legs only protruded from the protecting bush, sometimes, a little more of their persons, but their lively motions left no room for doubt as to the nature of their occupations.

These were all married couples, who believed that copulation in the open air on Good Friday would ensure them the birth of a boy during the year.

It is conjectured that this superstition dates back to the first invasion by the then heathen Anglo-Saxons and that it may be referred to the cult of the Scan-dinavian Venus, the goddess Freya, whose name appears in Friday.

The Lascivious Dance, Timorodée. " Amongst the amusements of these islanders, there is a dance called *Timorodée*, which is performed by young girls, whenever eight or ten of them meet together. This dance consists of postures and gestures which are extremely lascivious, but to which children are ac-customed from their earliest years; moreover, it is accompanied by words which plainly express lewdness. The Tahitians keep time as exactly as our best theatri-cal dancers in Europe. These amusements, which are permitted to the young girl, are forbidden to her as soon as she has become a woman; she can then practise for herself the lessons, and realise the symbols, of the dance."

Sacred Orgies and Erotic Festivals. My old friend, Dr. Ploss, has dwelt upon these with great wealth of detail:—Before terminating our observations concerning prostitution, we must once more refer to the delivery of women to this infamy as it was customary at certain festivals among various nations. It was often on the occasion of festivals of their divinities, which were connected with religious orgies, in other cases there were erotic feasts of profane nature, during which by special exemption the usually existing bounds of morals and honour were left aside, and the otherwise strictly forbidden extra-nuptial sexual intercourse was accepted and tolerated, and indeed sometimes ordered.

Ancient Rites. During the festivals of *Isis*, the *Pascht*, in ancient Egypt, the most fearful licentiousness reigned. It was the same in Byblos at the funeral rites of *Adonis;* and on these occasions the women who refused to abandon their bodies on that particular day in the temple of *Aphrodité,* were subjected to the punishment of having their hair cut off.

The festival of the *Bona Dea* in Rome was principally celebrated by the women. As Juvenal has recorded, it degenerated into the wildest orgies, in which ladies of the highest rank were not ashamed to have intercourse with the lowest people.

Similar things are reported from other centres of culture. Stoll [1] tells us for instance that in ancient

[1] Stoll (O.), Ethnog. v. Guatemala.

Guatemala on the days of the grand sacrifice there
were great rejoicings.

"The bounds of modesty ceased to exist, inebriated
individuals abandoned themselves without choice to
sexual depravity with their daughters, sisters, mothers
and concubines, and even little children of from six
to seven years old were not spared."

The Ancient Peruvians. Von Tschudi, [1] speaking
of the ancient Peruvians, says:

"In the month of December, that is at the approaching
moment of the ripening of the fruit *Pal'tay* or *Pal'ta*,
the participators in the festival prepare for it by a
five days' fast, that is to say, abstinence from salt,
utsu (chilies, *capsicum spec.*) and from female intercourse.   On the day fixed for the beginning of the
festival the men and women assemble at a certain
place among the gardens, all of them stark naked.
At a signal they all start off on a race to a distant
hillock.   Each man who overtakes a woman on the
road immediately takes advantage of the occasion then
and there to copulate with her.   This festival is continued
during six days and six nights."

This account was taken from an extremely rare do-
cument, a *Carta pastoral de exortacion é instruccion*,
fol. 47, from Don Pedro de Villagomez, archbishop of
Lima, who says that this festival is called *Akhataymita*.

The Sect of the Nicolites. Here we have to do
with heathen folks ; but similar things have been seen
in Christendom.   For instance, in the fourth century
the sect of the Nicolites, who thought it to be a reli-

[1] Tschudi, Beitr. über Peru. Denkschr. der K. Acad. der Wissensch.,
Wien, 1891, Vol. XXXIX, p. 214.

gious duty to put aside every feeling of modesty and to consider every form of sensual depravity right and holy (Lombroso). Similar opinions were defended by the disciples of Karpocrates and Epiphanius, as well as by the sects of the *Kanaits*, the *Adamites* and the *Picards*, and also, at the end of the 14th century, the *Turlupins*. For further details see Lombroso. [1]

But even up to the present moment such sexual depravations, pretended for the glory of God, have found enthusiastic disciples. This is to be seen in the description given by Dixon in his "Spiritual Brides" of certain bigotted religious sects; it is also to be seen in the religious service in Eva van Buttler and her similars, and is proved lastly by the judicial enquiries instituted in Russia concerning the members of the Skopzi seat.

The Aborigines of Australia. As it has been already mentioned, there are not only religious festivals to which are added such orgies, there have been and are still feasts celebrated of a profane character, in which the sexual connection between man and woman is either represented in pantomime or is really and naturally operated. For instance, Müller [2] relates the following concerning the Australian aborigines:

"It is remarkable and reminds one of the animal condition of the native Australian that marriage and copulation are generally accomplished during the warm season, when nature furnishes the necessary food in abundance and the body is therefore more disposed for sensual enjoyment. Among some tribes, the Watschandics for instance, marriage takes place in the

---

[1] Lombroso, *Anthropol. Studien*, Hamburg, 1894.
[2] Müller, *Allgem. Ethnogr.*, Wien, 1873, p. 293—300.

warm season and is the occcasion of a special festival,
called Kaaro.   This is celebrated at the first new moon
after the yams have become ripe, and is inaugurated
by the men with an eating and drinking bout.   For
this purpose the men smear themselves all over with
wallaby grease and ashes, and then execute an extremely obscene dance by moonlight roundabout a pit,
which is surrounded by bushes.   This pit and bushes
is supposed to represent the cunnus, of which they
present the shape, and the spears brandished by the men
represent the mentulæ.   The men jump in wild and
savage bounds expressive of their lust around the pit,
into which they finally cast their spears, singing at the
same time the following song in keeping with the obscene nature of the occasion:

> " Pulli nira, pulli nira,
> Pulli nira, Wataka "
> (*Non fossa, non fossa,*
> *Non fossa sed cunnus !*)

The Hawaian Hula-Hula.   In the island of Hawai
the natives have an extremely lascivious dance which
they call *Hula-Hula*.

" First of all the dancers of both sexes, as well as
the musicians, are seated in double rank on the ground
with their legs crossed, and they alternately rise and
sit down to the cadence of a chorus, whereby they
first of all slowly and then quicker and at last very
passionately agitate the upper part of their bodies,
waving their arms to and fro and shaking little calabashes in which are pebbles which rattle, so that
they make a most tremendous noise.   The melody is
far more complicated than in that of the Haka dance
of the Maoris of New Zealand or than the Meke-Meke

of the Viti Islands. The two female dancers wear a
peculiar ornament round their ankles, a sort of bodice
and raised frock; formerly the costume was limited to
a frock which could be easily lifted up. When the
dance has lasted a little time they spring about wildly
and with savage cries and exclamations make the most
indecent movements with their hind-quarters. The
native spectators participate most enthusiastically in
the amusement, laugh very heartily and imitate the
same obscene movements of the hind-quarters."

The West African Negroes. Staff-surgeon Wolff, [1]
speaking of the amusements of the Negroes in the
Congo territory (West Africa), says:

" The dance here consists mainly in thrusting the
hind-quarters backwards and forwards as quickly as
possible, they and the women posted opposite to each
other, advancing and retreating alternately, at last
taking hold of each other. In this position they
remain for a moment still, and then recommence
the previous backward and forward movements. In
many of the Mandinga villages during the embrace
they make the most unequivocal motions, after
which they hold each for some time still embraced, as
if exhausted."

The South American Puri. Spix and v. Martius [2]
had occasion to observe in the darkness of the evening
a dance of the Puri in South America, in the second
part of which the women began to give a rapid

[1] Wolff, *Verhandl. der Ges. f. Erdkunde* zu Berlin, Bd. 13, 1886,
p. 48, 49, 55, 56.
[2] Spix und v. Martius, *Reise nach Brasilien.*

rotary motion to their pelvis, thrusting it alternately
forward and backward. The men also thrust the
middle of their body forward, but forward only.

That such lust exciting dances, among people who
attach but slight value to maiden chastity, should
soon lead to acts, cannot be a source of astonishment,
and Kulischer [1] is of opinion that there is herein a
sort of elective choice. He cites a number of examples,
which tend to confirm his opinion. Among others the
following:

" The making of a choice by the women, and the
attention they pay to the exterior appearance of the
men, is clearly noticeable in one of the Kaffir dances.
In these, says de Albertis, any number of men,
usually naked, place themselves in close line together,
each with his right arm lifted, holding a war club, and
with the left arm holding his next man. Close behind
the men stand a line of women, but whose arms are
not entwined. They continue hopping in the air and
with both feet and without ever changing, while the
women are seen to make a sort of cramp-like movement of the entire body, consisting principally in a
backward and forward bending of the shoulders
combined with a movement of the head. From time
to time the latter go round about the men, following
one another at a very slow pace, and then re-occupy
their first position. During all this they are careful
to give themselves a most modest appearance particularly by lowering their eyes. But the real object
of this lowering of the eyes of the women, while
inspecting the men as they stand in rank, is easy
enough to divine. "

[1] Kulischer, *Zeitschr. f. Ethnol.*, Berlin, 1876.

Christian Festivals. [1] But in Christendom also there have been festivals, in which modesty was not one whit more respected than it is by these savages. It was particularly the Asses' and Fools'-feasts, and also the Church commemorations and Processions which led to the most shameless debauchery. There were certain dances that were not in best repute. As Prætorius [2] says, speaking of the Gallarda dance:

" Besides such a roundabout dance was accompanied by shameful obscene gestures and indecent motions." Kulischer [3] quotes a sermon by Spangenberg to the following effect:

" God preserve all pious souls from such maidens, who take delight in the dance at eventide and gladly allow themselves to be spun round and immodestly kissed and seized hold of. There can indeed be nothing good in them; they only excite each other to impudicity, and feather Satan's darts. At such dances many a woman has lost her honour and good fame. There many a maiden has learnt that it would have been better had she never known them. To sum up, there is naught honourable nor godly thereby."

As has been remarked the Fools'-feasts were the occasion of the grossest indecencies. The parody, of mass, used to be performed in the church, the actors being masked and in grotesque costumes, while gambling and dicing went on and ribald songs were sung. Dulaure [4] says: " After mass, there were renewed acts of extravagance and of impiety. The priests, mixed up with the population of both sexes, running about;

---

[1] *Vide* Lombroso, *loc. cit.*
[2] Prætorius, *Gestriegelte Rocken-Philosophia*, Chemnitz, 1707, cap. 36.
[3] Kulischer, M., *Zeitschr. f. Ethnol.* Berlin, 1876.
[4] Dulaure, J. A., *Culte du Phallus,* Paris, 1885, p. 96.

exciting each other to the most licentious acts that an unbridled imagination could suggest. No longer any shame or modesty; no barrier opposed this outbreak of folly and passion. In the midst of the tumult, of blasphemies and dissolute songs, some were seen to divest themselves entirely of their clothes, others abandoning themselves to the most shameful libertinism. Then the disorder was continued in the street. The most debauched among the seculars mingled with the clergy, and disguised as monks and nuns, performed lascive movements, taking all the postures of the most unbridled profligacy."

Quite similar monstrosities at the Asses' feasts. They throw a very curious light upon the moral conditions of mediæval Europe.

New Britain Islands. According to Weisser [1] the young maidens in the New Britain Islands are guarded with jealousy, and they are not allowed any communication whatever with the young men in the village; but on certain evenings a loud-sounding drum is heard in the bush, upon which they are allowed to go there to meet together with the youths.

According to other information concerning the same group of islands, Weisser seems to have made a mistake. This account says that in New Britain any woman without living relations may give herself to whomsoever she likes; but should she be killed, the tribe is not held bound to avenge her death. If a man marries her, she has the same rights as the other wives. If her father and mother are still living, their consent is necessary if she wishes to become a prostitute, which consent is often given. Otherwise the woman

[1] Weisser, *Zeitschr. f. Ethnol.*, 1885, XVII.

runs the risk of being killed by anyone of her relations, because she may have been destined to become the wife of an important man or have already been bought by a chief. On certain nights a drum is beaten, at sound of which all the prostitutes run into the forest and are there hunted by the young men. This is called "Lu-Lu", an expression which either relates to the women themselves or to something connected with this custom.

Esthonia. Kreutzwald says, concerning the inhabitants of Esthonia, that in the supplement to the Revel Esthonian Almanac for 1840, it is related that about 60 years ago thousands of people used to congregate on the eve of Saint John's festival (24th June) around the ruins of an ancient church where they lighted a votive fire into which they cast fire offerings. Women that were barren danced naked round the ruins, others gave themselves up to eating and drinking, while the youths and maidens amused themselves in the woods doing many naughty things. [1]

"Although we no longer meet with untrammelled intercourse between young people of both sexes, we may yet," thinks Dr. Ploss, "from an ethnographical point of view consider it as an echo of ancient days, when we find that in spite of all decency and modesty in words, on certain occasions youths and girls come together, and the most immodest and indecent things are allowed to be freely said and done to the great amusement of all parties.

"Even to-day these evil customs have not died out from amongst us, particularly in the country, and it is usually on a marriage evening that they take place,

[1] Kreutzwald, Fr. H., *Der Ehsten Gebräuche*, Petersburg, 1854.

whereas formerly in the Middle Ages, even in the best
society, when the young couple were taken home,
they were not spared the most abominably indecent
jokes and sallies. It may be added that in the
Spinnstuben (common spinning rooms in German villages) the conversation and songs are not always
strictly moral. Vambéry [1] relates something similar
of one of the Turkestan tribes, the Kumuken, in
Western Asia, as he says:

"Among the games of the Kumuken must be
counted the *Südjün-Tadjak*, that is to say Love-stick,
which is usually played by unmarried people on the
occasion of a marriage, and in which enamoured couples
strike each other with a stick on the shoulder, exchanging
at the same time a partly sarcastic and partly erotic
dialogue."

Marriage amongst the Tahitians. "It appears,"
says Cook, "that marriage at Tahiti is but an agreement between the man and the woman, in which the
priests do not interfere; the couple, however, does
observe certain ceremonies. The bridegroom sits by
the side of his wife, and takes her hand in his. He
is accompanied by ten or twelve persons, the greater
number of whom are women, who sing a monotonous
chant; the bride and bridegroom make some short
responses; then they have brought to them some food,
of which the husband offers part to his wife, and she,
in her turn, offers some to him. This action is accompanied by certain words, and then they both go to
bathe in the river. When a marriage is made, both
parties perform the conditions, but sometimes they
separate by common consent, and, in that case, the

[1] Vambéry, *Das Turkenvolk in Ethnogr. Beziehungen*, &c., Leipzig, 1885.

divorce is performed as easily as the marriage was made."

Circumcision and Tattooing. " The priests derive no income from their flock for the nuptial ceremony, but there are two other ceremonies by which they gain considerable sums. The one is circumcision, and the other, tattooing. These people have adopted circumcision from no other motive than that of cleanliness. The operation cannot be called circumcision, properly speaking, as they do not make a circular amputation of the foreskin; they only slit it across the upper part to provent it from covering the gland."

A learned friend of mine in the Berlin " Journal of Ethnography " has already dealt with this subject. I transcribe his remarks. [1] " Tattooing among the Pelau islanders is much less developed than in Japan, and nothing approaching to the majority of the men are now tattooed, though in former times the custom generally prevailed. The reason for this decrease in the practice was accounted for to me on the ground of the many serious maladies and even cases of death resulting from the operation of too extended tattooing. I have not heard the same complaint made either in Japan or in Samoa, where the natives are tattooed all over. Here, such things as serious illness or still less mortal effects subsequent to tattooing were said to be of very rare occurrence. But, as the natives of Pelau are great amateurs of tattoo ornamentation, and greatly admire a rich skin embellishment of the kind (such as may be seen in Japan, in Uleaï, and neighbouring islands), and as they are far from having weak constitutions compared with other Pacific islanders (the

[1] *Zeitschrift für Ethnologie*, Berlin, 1878, 80, p. 107.

Japanese for instance), there would evidently seem to
be here a sort of idiosyncracy."

Tattooing on Women.   " In Pelau the women are
more tattooed than the men.   On adult women it is
to be seen on the dorsal side of the hands, also up
to about the middle of the fore-arms, particularly on
the outside, the *mons veneris* is covered with ara-
besques, and with all sorts of almost continuous designs,
while the exterior sides of the legs, from the *trochanter
major* down to the exterior *malleolus*, is tattooed with
a series of crosses, stars, dots and simple zig-zag lines.
The tattooing of the *mons veneris* is not undertaken
until after the first menstruation.   The front part of
the exterior labia is also tattooed.—The tattooing on
this part is probably the reason for the practice of
depilating all the hairs from the pubes of women.   The
operation, in this case very painful, is, I was assured,
finished in an afternoon.—Wishing to see this tattooing,
I prevailed upon several young girls to strip off
together their 'Kariut', or garment made of pandanus
leaves, and was at once reminded of what Costanti
says of the tattooed bodies of the Suliotes: 'their
aspect does not in the least provoke a feeling of shame.'
At first view it seemed to me as if the girls wore a
triangular piece of stuff over their pubes." [1]

[1] The damsels in question, after assuring themselves that none of their
men could see us, made no difficulty whatever in complying with my
desire.—It would also seem that in Pelau there is no shame attached to
the exhibition of the naked body (except in certain positions). I have
constantly seen men stark naked working or walking about, without in
the least troubling themselves about passers-by. But among all of them
the long prepuce entirely covered the gland, and I was told that the
presenting to view of the *glans penis* was alone considered indecent,
that is to say " Mogull" or " Taboo " in Polynesian.

The Sect of the Arrioys (Woman in common).
" A considerable number of the Tahitians, of both sexes,
form singular societies, wherein all the women are
common to all the men. This arrangement affords
them a perpetual variety in their pleasures; which
variety it seems they so much need, that the same
man and woman rarely live together for more than
two or three days. These societies are known by the
name of *Arrioy;* those who belong to them hold
meetings at which the other islanders are not present.
The men amuse themselves with wrestling, and the
women dance the *Timorodée* in order to excite in
themselves desires, which, it is said, they satisfy upon
the spot. Nor is this all: if one of the women becomes
pregnant, which happens much more rarely than if
each woman lived with one man only, the infant is
strangled as soon as born, in order that it may not
embarrass the father, or interrupt the pleasures of the
abominable prostitution of the mother. Sometimes,
however, it happens that the mother experiences that
feeling which nature implants in the breasts of all
animals which bring forth young, and the maternal
instinct then overcomes the passions which had led
her into this society. But even in this case, she is
not allowed to preserve the child alive, unless she can
find one of the men who will declare that the child
is his, and adopt it. This will save the infant's life,
but the man and woman, being regarded as devoted
solely to each other, are driven out of the community,
and lose all rights to enjoy the privileges and pleasures
of the Arrioys.

" No people should be charged on imperfect evidence
with such horrible and strange practices, but I have
convincing proofs of the truth of the account I have

given. The Tahitians so far from regarding it as a disgrace to belong to this society, are quite proud of it, and deem it a great distinction. We were shown several persons who were members of an Arrioy, and we questioned them on the subject, and received direct from their mouths, the details that I have just given. Many of the natives confessed to us that they were affiliated to one of these abominable associations, and that many of their children had been put to death. "

As will be seen from the foregoing extract, the Tahitians long ago discovered the theory of free love, and free woman, which certain modern philosophers talk so much about. It may reasonably be supposed that this sect of Arrioys gave the Chevalier Andréa de Nerciat, an erotic writer of the 18th Century, the idea of his famous " Society of Aphrodité ", in which woman was common to all the men, though he placed the seat of the Society at Paris.

The sect of the Arrioys has long ceased to exist at Tahiti, the English missionaries having caused it to be suppressed by Pomaré II., when he was converted to Protestantism.

The Happy Life of the Tahitians. Modern civilisation has not been able to change the Tahitian race. If in the present day the Tahitian does not openly perform the acts of love, as his ancestors did, sexual lusts still form the sole object of his thoughts. He has simply become more of a hypocrite, but at bottom he is what he has been. The accounts of modern travellers leave no doubt on this point. The people of the Saxon and Semitic races say, " Business first and pleasure after, " but pleasure—sexual—is the sole occupation of the Tahitian.

Paul Branda, in his *Lettres d'un Marin*, thus depicts the life of the Tahitians.

" Nature seems to have created the Tahitian woman for nothing else but pleasure. She is not pretty, but her charm lies in her languid pose, and her graceful form; she breathes voluptuousness out of every pore. But,—as is but too clearly seen,—we were not put into the world for pleasure only, and he or she who seeks pleasure finds death. This graceful, artistic, idle race will soon disappear. There is no place for it in this world of business, science, and work. During the last five days I have travelled about a good deal. I will not say that the Tahitian women do nothing, but I will simply state that I have never seen them doing anything. In the town, they lounge through the streets, laughing and talking amongst themselves, or with the young men; in the country, they bathe and dive like Naiads, and then, with their long hair still dripping with water, they lie on the grass on the banks of the brooks, in lascivious attitudes, and gracefully smoke cigarettes, or they stroll about making wreaths of the yellow flowers of the *bouraos*, or cutting yellow stars from the golden fruit of the pandanus. "

Chartrier, the traveller, in his interesting work on Tahiti, also describes the present life of the Tahitians.

" The Tahitian, though richly endowed by nature with physical and muscular strength, shows a marked re-pugnance for all kinds of labour. Having few wants to satisfy, he does not feel the necessity of working; besides which the foreigner never refuses the Vahinés the little luxuries which they require.

" You can never get a Tahitian to undertake any cultivation of the ground, or perform any work that is ordered. As to his intelligence, his mental gifts are on a par with his bodily ones, but he never uses them except to gain the favours of the Vahinés, or to detect the business tricks of the Europeans. We remember an instance in which a midshipman had promised a native a gold ring in return for some services he had performed, but the ring he did give was copper-gilt. He had, however, not reckoned upon the exquisitely fine sense of smell of the Tahitian, who having put it to his nose, quickly detected the copper. As to the women they have preserved to the present day a sort of soft laziness, and Olympian carelessness. Dreaminess, a stroll, a siesta, a dance, a few songs, and a bath,—these form their principal occupations."

A Day of the Life of a Vahiné at Papeete. The Tahitian women pass their existence in playing and laughing, like the nymphs of Calypso's island; but unfortunately they add to these amusements, cards, tobacco, and beer, which European civilisation has brought them.

"In the morning, the Tahitian women who inhabit Papeete and the environs, after having made their purchases of fish and fruit, assemble at the market round the tables, were the Chinese sell them tea, coffee, butter, cakes, etc. Then they return home to take their principal meal, which they eat about eleven o'clock, and which is prepared by the men or the old women. As soon as it is finished, and the scraps given to the domestic animals, numbers of which wander round the house, the women attend to their toilet. The mats are then spread, and they take their siesta, the invariable custom throughout the tropics, and which lasts about two hours. Then, still reclining, but in a circle, they play cards,—an amusement of which Tahitian women are extremely fond; a cigarette rolled in a long leaf of the pandanus passes from mouth to mouth, and each Vahiné takes two or three whiffs, and leisurely breathes out the smoke through her nostrils. Those who do not care for écarté or poker, tittle-tattle about the incidents of last night's dance, or hum native songs to an accompaniment on the accordion or jew's harp. In the evening, if there is no *upa-upa*, or band, they meet in 'Little Poland Street', one of the principal streets of the capital, and the usual promenade. There they walk about in pairs, a sailor's hat, surrounded with wreaths of flowers and odorous plants, on their head, holding with one hand the little finger of their companion, and with the other gracefully raising the train of their long robe of white, pink, or blue muslin, and thus they stroll up and down, humming national airs. The youth of the Tahitian woman is passed in a continual fête. Alas! time has destroyed all their pleasures. Poor Vahiné! she must say farewell to the *upa-upa*, the hymeneal chant, and the long, idle reveries! "

Jealousy of the Tahitian in the Present Day. The inhabitants of New Cytherea no longer offer their wives to the European stranger. The Tahitian of the present day is as jealous of his wife as any other man can be. I am speaking of the native of the interior, and not of the native of Papeete, who has been corrupted by contact with the European.

The traveller, Desfontaines, from whom I have already quoted, gives some curious details, which I here reproduce, as to the present manners of the Tahitians: " Excessive hospitality prevails amongst the Tahitians, but they do not offer their wives, as certain travellers state. If by chance they do offer you a woman, it is one whom all the world can possess. On the contrary they are very jealous, as I found on more than one occasion, and this jealousy exists amongst the women as much as amongst the men. One night I was awakened by loud cries, and ran out of doors. A young Tahitian woman was being dragged along by the hair of her head. I questioned the people present and was told that the young man had been unfaithful to his wife, and that to punish him, the girl had left him and refused to return. Not being able to persuade her, he employed violence, and this, I was told, frequently occurred. Another time I heard that a woman had severely wounded her husband in the thigh, with the point of a pair of scissors, because he had gone astray with other women. I myself almost fell a victim to this blind and fierce jealousy. One day I asked for some information, from a pretty woman I met on the road. Suddenly, a man came out of the thicket, and seeing me talking to his better half, seized an enormous stake and rushed at me, foaming at the mouth with rage, and his eyes glaring. I thought my last hour had come, but conscious of my innocence, I stood firm, with my arms crossed. When within a yard of me, he stopped short, and lowered his weapon; then he poured forth a flood of words which I imagine could not have been compliments. I stood quite still and watched him, and when he had finished his harangue, I took him by the arm and tried to lead him to the *mutoi*, or rural policeman, of the district, but naturally, he refused to come.

" When you *do* interfere with his wife, the Tahitian threatens to harpoon you. I may add, too, that the native never misses his aim, and if he should throw his three-pronged harpoon at your back, you would die a most terribly painful death. Truth compels me to own, however, that such an occurrence is exceedingly rare. But though the Tahitian does not offer you his wife, he will offer you his best bed, or, if he has but one, he will not hesitate an instant to give you that, and will stretch himself on the mats."

Tahitian Hospitality. In the cordial hospitality he is always ready to give, the mild, good-natured character of the Maori shows itself in its true light. I again borrow from Desfontaines the following account. He had been invited to lunch with the chief of a district, to whom he had been recommended by a Frenchman of Papeete, a friend of the chief.

" In the afternoon I prepared to take leave of my hosts, and they watched me with surprise preparing my few articles of baggage. Then the daughter of the house, the lovely Tara, approached. 'Aita (no),' she said, 'you sleep here and stop with us.' The invitation was so prettily given, that it would have been bad grace on my part to refuse it. I was in no hurry, so I accepted the invitation. After a pleasant evening on the beach, spent in the company of some pretty girls, with whom I began to talk Tahitian with the help of my little dictionary, we returned to the hut. The drum began to beat to summon all the folks of the district to the hymeneal chant."

I will pass over the traveller's description of the hymeneal chant, and also of his dinner.

" My dinner being finished, I lay on my face on a mat, with my elbows resting on a cushion. The Kanaka cigarette passed from mouth to mouth round the circle of Tahitians of which I now formed part.

The beautiful Tara, who had disappeared for a minute, now returned with a magnificent wreath. As she advanced majestically, decked with flowers, and clad in a long loose robe which floated round her she looked like a queen. She came and sat by my side on the mat, and amidst these poetic surroundings, in which the exhalations of the flowers mingled with the scent of *monoi* (oil perfumed with sandal wood), in which my eyes rested on smiling faces, and my soul was captivated by the charms of this unexpected friendship, I found a happiness which I cannot describe. The little children themselves, pretty as Cupids, had lost their fear of me, and allowed me to caress them. I taught them how to blow kisses, and it was pretty to see them carry their little hands to their mouths, and quickly take them away again, or else waft kisses in the Australian way, that is to say, pretend to pick the kiss off the lips with the finger and thumb, then turn the palm of the hand towards me and prettily throw it.

" The hour of repose arrived, and I went to bed. In the morning the glare of a bright red band of light shining from under a dark cloud, awoke me. Nothing could be more beautiful than the landscape, as seen through the bars of this birdcage house. I rose with the sun, and prepared to leave; they still wished me to stay, but I was unwilling to abuse their kind hospitality, and excused myself on the ground that I was pressed for time. They compelled me, however, to stay to lunch. When I was finally about to take leave of my hosts, the charming Tara came to me with a bottle of *monoi*, some of which she emptied into the palm of her hand. She made me smell it, and asked if the perfume was agreeable to me. Upon

my replying in the affirmative, she anointed my hair
with this perfumed oil. Then everyone accompanied
me to the door-step, and shook hands with me cordially.
As I walked away, a last *ia-orana* (farewell) greeted
my ears: I turned and beheld the young and beauteous
Tara waving me a last farewell. I replied with a
kiss. The little girls insisted on conducting me, and
carried my baggage to the banks of the neighbouring
river. They absolutely refused to take the money I
offered them, when I took leave of them, and long after
I left them I could still see them blowing me kisses."

The True Character of the Vahiné. The Vahiné
is not only a beautiful creature of pleasure; under the
carnal covering that is swayed by her passionate
nature beats an ardent heart, that is susceptible of true
affection, and as capable of sincere love as that of any
European woman. This much can be learned from
the celebrated novel *Le Mariage de Loti,*—a book
which made the literary fortune of its author. The
romance is a strikingly lifelike picture. It would not
have been possible to invent such true sketches of the
manners and the character of the Tahitian as abound
in this book,—a remarkable work written by one who
is a psychologist as well as a lover. It will certainly
save from oblivion the Maori Vahiné, when the race
has finally disappeared, which, alas, will happen
ere long.

EXCURSUS TO CHAPTER XII.

Marriage after Trial. [1] We must now refer to a
particular form of marriage which may be denominated

[1] Translated from Dr. Ploss, "*Das Weib*" (Berlin, 1897).

"marriage after trial." This consists in the strange
custom, that an affianced couple live together in regular
sexual intercourse for a certain time, sometimes during
several years, and that marriage is only finally settled
when the future husband has succeeded in landing
his betrothed in the family way. If no pregnancy
intervenes it is taken for granted that these two people
are not suited for each other, and they therefore
separate. It is not seldom that the bride who has
been thus quitted very soon finds a new suitor ready
to take the place of his predecessor and to commence
another trial period with her. To abandon a girl who
has become pregnant under such circumstances, would
be considered a particular infamy and deserving of
general condemnation.

"If thee tak, I tak thee." G. v. Bunsen [1] relates
that in several parts of Yorkshire marriage after trial
still exists. The abandonment by the lover of the
bride after having made her pregnant is most severely
blamed by the neighbourhood. The solemn words of
the bridegroom when entering into such a trial contract
are: If thee tak, I tak thee (If thou conceivest I will
marry thee).

It is also reported that in 1864 marriage after trial
still existed in Masuren (East Prussia) where it was a
general custom among the peasants. Here also the
marriage was really contracted only after the girl had
become pregnant.

The "Come Nights." Fischer [2] reports a similar

[1] *Zeitschr. f. Ethnol.*, vol. XIX, p. 376, Berlin, 1887.
[2] Fischer (Frd.), Die Probenächte der deutschen Bauernmädchen, p.
101. Zurich. n. d.

custom in the Black Forest, where a distinction is made between the *Come Nights* and the *Trial Nights*. The first always precede the latter and the maidens begin with them as soon as they are grown up. "The country folk consider this custom so innocent, that it not unfrequently happens that when a village priest asks a peasant after the health of his daughter, the latter, to prove to him how well the child has grown up, quite openly and with fatherly satisfaction says that she has begun to hold her 'Come Nights.'"

The "Come Nights" are certainly of a rather innocent nature.

The young man is not permitted to enter the house through the door, he must go to the chamber of his sweetheart through the window, which may be sometimes a rather risky undertaking. In the chamber he finds the girl reclining on the bed, but completely dressed, and all his pains and efforts will at first procure him no other advantage than that of being able to pass an hour or two conversing with his darling. "As soon she falls asleep, he must leave on the instant, and it is only little by little that their interviews become more lively." The "Come Nights" now gradually change into the "Trial Nights". After a while the maid, with all sorts of teasings and country jokings, would let him get a stray glimpse of her hidden charms, receives him little by little in lighter vestment, and at last grants him all that a woman can. But in all this a certain gradation is always observed. Very often the girl refuses her lover the supreme favour until he uses violence to conquer. This is always when the coy maiden has some doubt as to the physical vigour of her lover.

It is not of unfrequent occurrence that after a few

" Trial Nights " the couple separate. But the maiden's
reputation does not thereby suffer in the least, and she
soon finds another lover ready to continue with her
the novel already commenced. Her reputation becomes
endangered when she is known to have gone through
several trial periods without any serious result. The
village gossips then think themselves authorised to
suspect in the girl some hidden infirmity.

It is highly probable that this custom of marriage
on trial also exists, if not so generally, in many other
parts of Germany among the peasants. The healthy
peasant girl who thus gets in child, now often seeks
for lucrative employment as wet-nurse in the nearest
large town, and as soon as her services are no longer
required, she returns to her native village and marries
her faithful swain. Fischer produces many examples,
from which it appears very probable, that this trial
before marriage was at one time very general among
both high and low. He further supports this opinion
by referring to the solemn public lying together of
bride and bridegroom before marriage, as it existed
of yore, and also the marriage by proxy of crowned
heads when the procurator of the prince put his leg
bared to the knee into the bed in which was the
princely bride, he standing at the side of the bed in
full armour, and this in presence of all the high
dignitaries of the State and of the Court assembled.
Pope Alexander III. ruled that of two affianced brides,
the one is to be proclaimed legitimate wife who has
already cohabited with her future husband; and the

¹ It exists in many parts of the Bavarian Alps, where the entry through
the window of the lover is called *fensterln* (windowing); only, these
lusty mountaineers brook no dallying *Come Nights*, but their courtship
is soon followed by marriage.

52nd law of the *Allemanen* (ancient Germans) notifies that whosoever has ruptured his connection with his betrothed, must swear " that it was neither from suspicion of any crime by her committed, nor that he had really discovered anything of the kind in her."

Ebers [1] also informs us that this trial before marriage is of very respectable antiquity, for, as he says, it already existed in long ages past among the ancient Egyptians.

The Philippine Islands. Hans Meyer [2] shows that some analogy with this custom is equally to be met with in uncivilised tribes. Speaking of the Igorrotes in the Philippine Islands, he says:

" When a loving couple have obtained the consent of their parents to their marriage, a feast is arranged, in which roast pork and boiled rice constitute the principal elements, and during the feast the married couple are shut up together in a hut, where provided with sufficient food, they remain together during four or five days, until the festival is over, either party is at liberty to relinquish the marriage. If it is the man who declines, he is obliged to give to the woman a robe, a spade, a cooking-pot, a bracelet and earrings and to pay the cost of the feast. But if the trial results in the woman becoming in child, the man is obliged to build her a hut and to give her a hog and a cock and hen."

[1] Ebers in Zeitschr. "Für Edle Frauen" von Heinrichsen, 1816.
[2] H. Meyer, "Eine Weltreise," Leipzig, 1890.

CHAPTER XIII.

Perversions of the sexual passion amongst the Tahitians.—The Tané.—Corruption of the Vahiné in contact with the European. —Sexual perversions of the Vahiné.—Masturbation and Sapphism. —The influence of race in genital perversions.

The Tané. This chapter will be brief so far as concerns the Maori Tané. From the age of puberty, he is a faithful worshipper of the natural Venus, and fervently adores her until old age. He commences the sports of love as soon as he finds a little Vahiné,— or perhaps even a nubile one,—who is obliging enough to give him his first lessons. Is he, when young, addicted to the vice of masturbation, peculiar to human kind, and its caricature, the simian race? I do not know; but from the moment that he has to do with his first mistress, the Tané cares only for women. That there may be amongst the race,—as amongst all others,—sodomites and pederasts, I admit; but they are very rare exceptions, and prove nothing against the relative morality of the Maori race. The cult of the Annamite " basket", and " boy ", has never existed at Tahiti, and from this particular point of view, the Tané is less depraved than certain European nations.

Corruption of the Vahiné in Contact with the European. European travellers, who now visit Tahiti, complain· bitterly of the want of morality, and the venality, of the Vahiné of Papeete. Desfontaines has faithfully re-echoed these statements, but he confesses that, if this picture of the immorality of the Tahitian women, "painted by the Frenchmen residing at Papeete, is a fair representation of the character of the natives of the capital, it is *absolutely false* as regards those of the interior." [1]

Of what then can the European complain? Is he not reaping the bitter fruit that he has sown? The accounts of Cook and de Bougainville have shown us the Tahitian race as attaining a very advanced degree of civilisation, worthy to be compared with that of the ancient Greeks. The Tahitian race was, at that moment, at the apogee of its physical and moral development. The Tahitians were good, docile, and hospitable, even to the point of offering their wives, not for money, but for "love"—in both senses of the phrase. In this fortunate island, the Vahiné bestowed her charms for the pleasure she derived, and not for filthy lucre. Is it not the European, with his pretended superior civilisation, who has destroyed these manners, —brutally frank, I admit, but simple and naïve? He has given the Tahitian artificial needs, by bringing him alcohol; he has morally poisoned him with his gold, and corrupted his blood by transmitting syphilis, which was absolutely unknown before the discovery of the island. It is the European who has made the

---

[1] Macdonald, cited by Westermarck, *Human Marriage*, p. 151, states that "in Efate, of the New Hebrides, sexual intercourse is regarded as something unclean" (See *Oceania: Linguistic and Anthropological*, Melbourne and London, 1889); and, according to the report of Cook, the Tahitians believed that, "if a man refrained from all connection with women some months before death, he passed immediately into his eternal mansion without any purification."

Vahiné drunken, selfish, and lustful after money. The Tané has become, by the force of circumstances, a *maquereau*, [1] and a pander. The Vahiné of Papeete is the worthy rival of the prostitute of Paris or London, and she has but too well profited by the lessons learned from the European.

All the worst faults of venal prostitution are now found at Papeete, as I can testify *de visu*. The grand-mothers of the present generation of Vahinés were "horizontals". Their grand-daughters have become "kneelers" (*i.e. agenouillée*, a fellatrice) in the Parisian fashion. How can she do otherwise than despise the European, who has taught her such disgusting practices? She reserves all her affection for her handsome Tané, the lover after her own heart, who, at least, does not beat her, as the *souteneur* [1] of la Villette thrashes his *marmite*, [1] when she does not bring in enough *galette*. [1] In his moral decay, although he has become a drunkard and a pander, the Maori still preserves an innate respect for woman. He is morally superior to the degraded beings, who grovel in the lowest depths of life in the great European capitals. He never uses the knife to kill a *pante*, [2] that he may rob him at his ease. Poor Maori, who is being quickly killed off by contact with the White, but who still retains his sweet disposition and good-nature!

There is, however, one thing to which the Vahiné resolutely objects, and to which she can be brought

---

[1] *Maquereau*, a prostitute's bully; *marmite*, a woman who keeps the same by her prostitution; *galette*, cake, but in slang, money; *souteneur*, a man who lives on the proceeds of a girl's whoring and maintains (*soutient*) her in her evil way; are all words used in Parisian fast, low life.

[2] Slang for customer.

only with the greatest difficulty. The practice of sodomy is almost unknown to her. We cannot say as much for the public "gay women" of old Europe; a perusal of the works of Tardieu and Martineau would set that point at rest. With many of them it is a mere question of price.

Besides, it must be confessed that Europe, the eldest daughter in civilisation of old Asia, cannot reproach her mother with immorality, for she is now as corrupt as ever her mother was,—but she conceals it better.

Sexual Perversions of the Vahiné. The contact of the corrupt White man with a woman of a nature so ardent, and so passionately fond of physical love, as the Vahiné, has had the natural result. He found in her suitable ground, and the seed of lust has sprung up: it is in the methods of copulation that it has first shown itself.

I do not know who introduced into Tahiti the "Manual of Classical Erotology" of Forberg, but all the different positions of copulation indicated by that experienced writer are known and practised by the "gay" Vahinés. It is the same with the thirty-six positions attributed to Pietro Aretino, on account of his indecent Sonnets, and under whose name it has circulated for the last three hundred years. I saw a copy of the French Aretin, which passed from hand to hand, and was used as a love breviary.

Among other Orientals also the artificial augmentation of the clitoris is far from rare and therein may be found the possible explanation of the fact that women, without having recourse to artificial means, are able to find a sensual satisfaction together.

Duhousset pretends that such Lesbian love once

long existed. It is supposed to have been imported thence to Greece, to Rome and to Egypt. This vice has also spread to the East and prevails particularly among the Arabs. And according to Parent-Duchâtelet [1] and other authors, it exists also among the nations of Western Europe, and is indeed more frequent than is supposed. Lucian has alluded to it in his dialogues of hetaerae.

An excessive development of the clitoris naturally facilitates active tribadism. In ancient Rome there were the so-called *Fricatrices* and *Subigatorices*, who particularly devoted themselves to this voluptuous work, and it is in the highest degree probable, that the efforts of many peoples to promote the greater development of the clitoris by repeated excitations, correspond to this vice. It is reported that the Bali women excell in this matter. Jacobs says: Almost in the same measure as pederasty, but more secretly, do the females practise among themselves the so-called Lesbian love (*metjengtjeng djocock*, literally: "rubbing the basins together without making any noise"). In Malay language: *bĕrtampoe laboe—tampoe*, the crown of a fruit, perhaps an allusion to the clitoris, with its digital and lingual variations. The considerable development of the clitoris among the Bali women would give some credence to this opinion.

Among other Orientals also the artificial augmentation of the clitoris is far from rare and therein may be found the possible explanation of the fact that women, without having recourse to artificial means, are able to find a sensual satisfaction together.

Duhousset [2] pretends that such Lesbian love once

[1] La Prostitution à Paris, Paris, 1857.
[2] Bull. de la Soc. d'Anthrop. d. Paris, 1878, vol. XII, p. 124.

resulted in pregnancy, but we must leave the proof of the fact to him. He relates that in Egypt two female friends, who practised this vice together, continued to do so even after one of them had been married; it then happened that the one who had remained single became pregnant, the explanation of this fact being that the married woman had retained in her vagina some of the semen given to her previously in cohabitation by her husband, and that she communicated the same to her friend while caressing her. This fact was communicated to the Anthropological Society of Paris in 1877.

Jan Mocquet [1] records a cruel punishment inflicted for tribadism. " A certain King of Siam having learned, that a great number of his wives and concubines, the most beautiful that could be found in the kingdom, sometimes amused themselves together, by imitating manly nature, to excite their lust, summoned them before him, and in condemnation of their unchastity, had each of them branded on the forehead and both cheeks with the image of a virile member, and then had them cast living into the flames."

That German women in the Middle Ages were also addicted to this vice appears from the ecclesiastical penalties edicted by Bishop Burchard of Worms, [2] which are quoted by Dulaure and are as follows:

" *Fecisti quod quædam mulieres facere solent, ut faceres quoddam molimen aut machinamentum in modum virilis membri, ad mensuram tuæ voluntatis, et illud loco verendorum tuorum, aut alterius, cum aliquibus ligaturis colligares, et fornicationem faceres cum aliis*

---

[1] *Itinerarium*, Lib. IV, p. 267, in M. Schurig, *Muliebra*, p. 107.

[2] Burchard, Bishop of Worms (12th century), De Poenitentia. Decretorum I, 19.

*mulierculis, vel aliæ eodem instrumento sive alio
tecum? Si fecisti, quinque annos per legitimas ferias
poeniteas. Fecisti quod quædam mulieres facere solent,
ut jam supradicto molimine, vel alio aliquo machina-
mento, tu ipsa in te solam faceres fornicationem? Si
fecisti unum annum per legitimas ferias poeniteas."* [1]

Communication contrary to nature between women
and beasts is not either an invention of modern times.
With regard to this Mantegazza says:

" Nor is woman either spared the shame of bestiality.
From the most ancient times, as Plutarch relates,
women gave themselves up to the unchaste vagaries
of the sacred goat in Mendes. Now, after a long
series of centuries, it is the dog that takes the place
of the goat. More than once do lovely women, in
the highest spheres of cultured Europe, adore their
lap-dogs, in a way they would not admit to a living
soul. Sometimes, but more seldom, it is not a lap-dog,
and then the aberration is still more base and despicable and instead of a bestial tribadism we have an
example of bestial coition, of an infamous and shameful
connection between the loveliest of creatures with the
ugliest and worst-smelling of domestic animals." [2]

In such disgusting matters the ape plays an important
part. In countries where the gorilla and Orang-Outang
live, numerous stories are related of girls carried off

[1] Dulaure, *Des divinités génératrices*, Paris, 1885, p. 96. A translation of this *bonne bouchée* of the good Bishop was made, but, on
reflection, it was decided not to give a translation of it in English. As
the Latin scholar will readily see, it is grossly improper, and we marvel.
at the state of morals that could allow German priests to put such
questions to female penitents, married and unmarried. No medical man
would *thus* question a woman to-day without risking his reputation.
See *infra* Havelock Ellis on the sexual teachings of the Catholic Church.

[2] Mantegazza, *Archiv. per Anthrop.*, IX, 1879.

by these big beasts, and their sexual connection with
their victims.   But in such cases the connection was
always a forced one.   But we have accounts of voluntary
intercourse between women and apes.   For instance,
the Indians on the banks of the Amazon river believe
that certain tailed men among the Uginas are the
result of such monstrous marriages between Indian
women and Coati apes. [1]   According to Francis de
Castelnau [2] such cohabitation with Coati apes still takes
place in those districts.   He relates as follows:—" As
I was going down the Amazon river, I one day saw
near to Fonteboa a black Coati of enormous size; it
belonged to an Indian woman, to whom I offered a
very considerable sum for this curious animal; but she
refused, at the same time bursting out laughing.   An
Indian who was in the hut said to me: your efforts
are useless, that ape is her husband."

Influence of Race on Genital Perversions.   I
deem it useless to extend my remarks, but I will say
a few words about the Sapphic couples at Tahiti,
formed of Vahinés having the same tastes.   This unnatural connection which tends to increase at the
antipodes, as, alas, it spreads and increases constantly
in old Europe, is it, as Moreau (of Tours) asserts, the
result of a mental aberration, a plainly defined psychical
malady?   Dr. Moreau extends his theory to all the
genital depravities exhibited by women or by men.
The subject is much too large to be treated here.
All that I simply wish to show is that the influence

[1] Bartels, *Die geschwänzten Menschen*, Archiv für Anthropologie,
Bd. XV, p. 52.   Braunschweig, 1883.
[2] *Expédition dans l'Amérique du Sud*, tome V, p. 104, 106.
Paris, 1857.

of race appears to me to be predominant. We have seen the Asiatic of the Far East, a sodomite and a pederast; the African Negro, simple in his tastes, a devotee of natural love; the Black, or rather the Melanesian half-breed of the New Hebrides, and his cousin with a skin a trifle lighter, a pederast when he cannot procure women; the Maori, a plain lover of the natural Venus, but his Vahiné practising, since she has come into contact with European civilisation, the vices of Lesbos. In fact, to sum up the whole, it is the European who fosters all kinds of genital depravity.

Fair-Play demanded for Present Work. There is, in this subject, ample matter for a work that I shall, perhaps, write, when I have collected evidence enough to be able to leave the beaten path, and arrive at some original conclusions. [1] I shall then discuss, proofs in hand, the opinions of modern psychologists, and seek to discover what is the real influence of atavism on genital depravities; which, until proof to the contrary is forthcoming, I shall, like Moreau (of Tours), regard as a special form of hereditary madness. I ask critics and students in the meanwhile for a fair hearing. Attack my facts, for it is on them that I rely, and not my crude manner of presenting them. I am no literary stylist of the De Goncourt school, and besides let it be borne in mind that in France greater liberty of pen is allowed on anthropological subjects than may perhaps be the case in England. My aim has been to write a work having

[1] See "Editor's note" at commencement of this volume concerning the new work promised by the Doctor, and which will practically amount to a HISTORY of the CRIMES and FOLLIES of the SEXUAL INSTINCT in the HUMAN RACE.

for object the good of humanity and the advancement
of science. Already several writers of great talent,
some of whom have been referred to in the foregoing
pages, have ably dealt with certain questions raised
by me. TARDIEU, in his "Etudes Médico-légales sur
les Attentats aux Mœurs"; my esteemed professor
MARTINEAU, in his "Lecons sur les Déformations vulvaires et anales produites par la Masturbation, le
Saphisme, la Défloration et la Sodomie"; my able
friend and *confrère*, CHEVALIER, in his remarkable
little "Manuel de l'Inversion sexuelle"; and finally the
REV. FATHER DEBREYNE, "prêtre de la Grande Trappe",
in his painstaking work entitled "La Théologie morale
et les Sciences médicales"; Dr. Rosenbaum, in the
"Geschichte der Lustseuche im Alterthume"; Dr. W.
Acton, "The Functions and Disorders of the Reproductive Organs" (published by Churchill, London); John
A. Symonds, in his suggestive little work, "A Problem
of Greek Ethics"; Moll, Laupts and Raffalovich, may
all be cited as workers in France, England, Russia and
Germany who have put forward the same ideas and
come to the examination, sometimes simultaneously, of
these painful problems, fearlessly unmasking the evil in
the hope of bringing relief. Neither they nor myself
believe for a moment in the possibility of destroying
unnatural practices, whether in the individual or in
entire tribes, by the process of violent uprooting. This
can never be done. Our only chance of success lies
in the frank envisagement of a given case. We hold
with the doctrine that John Morley puts into the mouth
of Chaumette [1] that to explain is to demolish, to clearly
diagnose is to destroy.

[1] In a magnificent passage in his Essay on "Robespierre"; See *Critical Miscellanies* by John Morley, Lond. *Macmillan*, 1888.

If sometimes my language seems crude and ill-chosen, I beg my readers to remember that the subject dealt with is ugly and ill-favoured, requiring a man of considerable mental courage to approach it who cares anything for his own reputation and that of his family. The world has learnt to judge harshly those who are not the favourites of the Gods. I am pleased to see that Englishmen and Americans of great talent and learning are taking a lively interest in questions relating to the sexual life. These are the proper men to handle such subjects. They possess discretion and courage, which, combined with their scientific attainments, sufficiently guarantee the honourableness of their aims and motives. One of these gentlemen, Havelock Ellis, a name we have more than once had the pleasure to quote in confirmation of our own views, defends his book on *Sexual Inversion* in a very eloquent passage which we beg to reproduce. We cite this with the more satisfaction because admirably expressing our own feeling:—"When the Catholic Church was at the summit of its power and influence, it fully realised the magnitude of sexual problems, and took an active and inquiring interest in all the details of normal and abnormal sexuality. Even to the present time there are certain phenomena of the sexual life which have scarcely been accurately described except in ancient theological treatises. As the type of such treatises I will mention the great tome of Sanchez, *De Matrimonio*. Here you will find the whole sexual life of men and women analysed in its relationships to sin. Everything is set forth, as clearly and as concisely as it can be— without morbid prudery on the one hand, or morbid sentimentality on the other—in the coldest scientific language; the right course of action is pointed out for

all the cases that may occur, and we are told what
is lawful, what a venial sin, what a mortal sin. Now
I do not consider that sexual matters concern the
theologian alone, and I deny altogether that he is
competent to deal with them. In his hands, also,
undoubtedly, they sometimes become prurient, as they
can scarcely fail to become on the non-natural and
unwholesome basis of asceticism, and as they with
difficulty become in the open-air light of science. But we
are bound to recognise the thoroughness with which the
Catholic theologians dealt with these matters, and, from
their own point of view, indeed, the entire reasonableness;
we are bound to recognise the admirable spirit in which,
successfully or not, they sought to approach them.
We need to-day the same spirit and temper applied from
a different standpoint. These things concern everyone;
the study of these things concerns the physiologist, the
psychologist, the moralist. We want to get into possession of the actual facts, and from the investigation
of the facts we want to ascertain what is normal and
what is abnormal, from the point of view of physiology
and of psychology. We want to know what is naturally lawful under the various sexual chances that may
befall man, not as the born child of sin, but as a
naturally social animal, what is a venial sin against
nature, what a mortal sin against nature. The answers
are less easy to reach than the theologian's answers
generally were, but we can at least put ourselves in
the right attitude; we may succeed in asking that
question which is sometimes even more than the half
of knowledge." [1] A last objection may be made against
the present work on account of the liberal way in

[1] Preface to "Sexual Inversion" (pages VIII and IX), by Havelock
Ellis, LONDON, 1897.

which reference has been made to other writers. I plead guilty to the charge. If I have quoted freely from other people it has been to show how closely the views of the eminent anthropologists and travellers of other nations coincide with my own independent studies and researches. In no case, however, have I made improper use of these authorities. Whenever a work has been cited, the fullest particulars in connection therewith have also been given, and no unfair use has been made of the labours of my predecessors. I ask only for a fair hearing. Where I am in the wrong, correct me by legitimate demonstration. I am ready to be taught. If additional knowledge may be imparted to strengthen the views enunciated, I shall be glad to receive information, regarding my work as I do, rather in the light of an *avant-coureur* to some more solid and possibly more scientific work, which may be put forth at a future date.

BIBLIOGRAPHY

TO THE TWO VOLUMES OF

UNTRODDEN FIELDS OF ANTHROPOLOGY

Sex contains all, bodies, souls,
Meanings, proofs, purities, delicacies, results, promulgations,
Songs, commands, health, pride, the maternal mystery, the seminal
[milk,
All hopes, benefactions, bestowals, all the passions, loves, beauties,
[delights of the earth,
All the governments, judges, gods, follow'd persons of the earth,
These are contain'd in sex as parts of itself and justifications of
[itself."

WALT. WHITMAN,
Leaves of Grass.

BIBLIOGRAPHY

LIST OF WORKS AND AUTHORS

CITED IN "UNTRODDEN FIELDS OF ANTHROPOLOGY."

A.

ACOSTA, *Natural and Moral Hist. of the Indies*, London, 1880.

ACTON, DR. W., *The Functions and Disorders of the Reproductive Organs*, Lond., *Churchill, n. d.*

ADAIR, JAMES, *History of the American Indians*, London, 1775.

ALBERTI, *De Kaffers aan de Zuidkust van Afrika*, Amsterdam, 1810.

ALBERTI, L., *De Kaffers*, Amsterdam, 1810.

AYMONIER, *Cochinchine, Excursions et reconnaissances* (Nº. 16: "Globus", 1885, vol. 48, Nº. 7).

————, *Notes sur les coutumes et croyances superstitieuses des Cambodgiens*, Saïgon, 1883.

B.

BALZAC, *Une dernière incarnation de Vautrin.*

BASTIAN, *Die deutsche Expedition an der Loango-Küste.*

BECKER, JÉRÔME, *La Vie en Afrique*, Paris et Bruxelles, 1887.

BEECHEY, *Hist. Univ. des Voyages*, London.

BELOT, A., *Mademoiselle Giraud, ma femme.*

BERTHERAND, DR., *Hygiène et médecine des Arabes*, 1885, Paris.

BEY, PRUNER, *Mém. sur les Nègres.* (*Mém. de la Soc. d'Anthropologie*, 1860—63).

BLEEK, *Brief Account of Busham Folk-lore.*

BLONDEAU, *Dictionnaire Érotique Latin-Français*, Paris, Liseux, 1885.

BOOTH, CHAS., *Work and the Poor in London.*

BOSE, *The Hindoos as they are.*

BOUGLÉ, DR., *Les Vices du Peuple*, Paris, 1888.

BOUCHARD, *Confessions de*, Paris, Liseux, 1881, in-8º.

394 BIBLIOGRAPHY.

BOWRING, SIR JOHN, *The Kingdom and People of Siam*, 2 vols., London, 1857.

BRAINE, CH., *Nouvelle Calédonie.*

BRANDA, PAUL, *Les lettres d'un Marin.*

BRANTÔME, *Vie des Dames Galantes*, Paris, 1857.

BROOKE, CHAS., *Ten Years in Sarawak*, 2 vols., Lond., 1866.

BRUNIUS, C. G., *Försök till Förklaringar öfver Hällristningar*, Lund, 1868.

BRUNY, L., *Zeitg. f. Literatur*, etc. (Hamburg. Correspondent, 1889, N°. 21).

BULLETIN DE LA *Société de Géographie de Marseille*, Avril-juin, 1883.

BURTON, LADY ISABEL, *Life of Sir Richard Francis Burton*, 2 vols., Lond., 1896.

BURTON, RICHD. F., *Pilgrimage to Al-Madinah, and Meccah*, Lond., 1873.

——————————, *Article in Memoirs of Anthropological Society of London*, Lond., 1863.

——————————, *Supplementary Nights*, 6 vols., Benares, 1886.

——————————, Translation of the "*Thousand Nights and a Night*", 10 vols., Benares, 1885—1886.

BUTTI, *L'Automna.*

C.

CABANÈS, DR., *The Secret Cabinet of History*, Paris, 1896.

——————————, *Curious Bypaths of History*, Paris, 1898.

CAMPBELL, *The Wild Tribes of Khondistan*, London, 1864.

CARLIER, *Les Deux Prostitutions*, 1864. (Ex-chef de la Sûreté).

CARLIER, F., *Rapport d'un officier de la Police Municipale de Paris.—Attribution des Mœurs*, 16 juillet, 1864.

CASPER, *Gerichtl. Med.*

CASTELNAU, FRANCIS DE, *Expédition dans l'Amérique du Sud*, Paris, 1857.

CHALMERS AND GILL, *Work and Adventure in New Guinea*, Lond., 1887.

CHARLEVOIX, *Histoire de la Nouvelle France.*

CHATEAUBRIAND, *Voyage en Amérique.*

CHEVALIER, DR. J., *L'Inversion Sexuelle*, une maladie de la personnalité, Paris et Lyon, 1893.

CHURCHILL, *Collection of Voyages and Travels*, London, 1704.

COLOMB, LIEUT.-COLONEL DE, *Notice sur les Oasis du Sahara et les grandes routes qui y conduisent.* ("Nouvelles Annales des Voyages", Juillet, 1860).

CORRE, DR., *Le Crime en Pays Créoles*, Paris, 1889.
CRAWFURD, *Hist. of the Indian Archipelago*, 3 vols., Edinburgh, 1820.

D.

DAILY TELEGRAPH of August 10th, 1897, *Piracy in the East Indies, Attack on a British Steamer.*
DALL, W., *Alaska and its Resources*, London, 1870.
DALTON, COL. E. T., *Descriptive Ethnology of India*, Calcutta, 1872.
DANKS, REV. B., *Marriage Customs of the New Britain Group*, in "Journ. Anthrop. Institute," London, 1889.
DAVENPORT, JOHN, *Aphrodisiacs and Anti-Aphrodisiacs*, London, 1869.
DEBREYNE (REV. FATHER), *La Théologie morale et les Sciences médicales.*
DEFOE, DANIEL, *Conjugal Lewdness, or Matrimonial Whoredom*, London, 1727.
DE GUBERNATIS, *Histoire des voyageurs italiens aux Indes Occidentales*, Livourne, 1875.
DELFOU, *Manuel des Maladies des voies urinaires.*
D'ENTRECASTEAUX, *Hist. Univ. des Voyages.*
DE ROCHAS, *Nouvelle Calédonie*
DESFONTAINES, JULES, *Dix-huit mille lieues à travers le Monde.*
DIDEROT, *La Religieuse*, Roman d'une dévote à l'amour lesbique.
DOSTOIEFFSKY, *Prison Life in Siberia.*
DU CHAILLU, *Journey in Equatorial Africa*, London, 1867.
DULAURE, J. A., *Culte du Phallus, ou Les Divinités Génératrices*, Paris, Liseux, 1885, orig. edit., 1802.
DUMAS, A., *La Princesse de Bagdad*, Paris.
DUNRAVEN, LORD, In "*The Times*" of May 15th and 18th, 1897.

E.

ELLIS, H., *Sexual Inversion*, London, 1897, in-8°. and a 2nd *castrated* edition 6 months later in same year.
EMIL UND LEONORE, *Sonnige Welten, Ostasiatische Reiseskizzen*, Wiesbaden, 1896.
EPP, *Schilderungen von Holländish-Indien*, Heidelberg, 1852.
ERAM, *De la Pratique des Accouchements en Orient*, Paris, 1860.

F.

FELDNER, *Voyage à travers le Brésil*, Leignitz, 1828.
FERRERO, GUILLAUME, *Le Crime d'Adultère, son Passé, son Avenir*, Paris, 1885.

FEYDAU, *La Comtesse de Chalis.*

FIAUX, *Les maisons de Tolérance,* 1892.

FINSCH, OTTO, *Neu Guinea und seine Bewohner,* Bremen, 1865.

FITZROY, *Voyage of Adventure, and Voyage of the "Beagle."*

FLAUBERT, GUSTAVE, *Salambo,* Paris.

FORBERG, *Manuel d'Erotologie classique,* 2 vols., Paris, 1882. The Latin text is given *en regard.*

FRAZER, J. G., *The Golden Bough,* London, 1890, 2 vols.

FRIEDLÄNDER, *Mœurs romaines.*

FRITSCH, *Die Eingeborene Süd-Afrikas,* Breslau, 1873.

FROLONG, MAJOR J. G. R., *Short Studies in the Science of Comp. Religions,* London, Quaditch, 1897.

G.

GABB, W. M., *Indian Tribes and Languages of Costa Rica,* 1875.

GALOPIN, DR. AUG., *Le Parfum de la Femme et le Sens Olfactif dans l'Amour.—Etude psycho-physiologique,* Paris, 1889.

GAUDEFRID IN DUCHESNE, *Recueil des Hist. de France.*

GAUTIER, THÉOPHILE, *Mademoiselle de Maupin.*

GAZETTE MÉDICALE DE PARIS, vol. 63.

GRAY, REV. ARCH-DEACON J. H., *China.—The Laws, Manners, and Customs of the People,* London, 1878.

GRÉGOIRE DE TOURS, *De Miracul. S. Martini.*

GRIMM, *Deutsche Mythologie.*

GUMILLA, *Histoire de l'Orénoque,* Avignon, 1758.

H.

HAMILTON, CHARLES, *Hedaya or Guide, a Commentary of Mussulman Law,* 4 vols., 4to., London, 1791. (Trans. from the Arabic).

HÄNTSCHE, *Physikalisch-Medicinische Skizze von Rescht in Persien;* in *Virchow's Archiv,* 1862.

HARTMANN, ROBT., *Anthropoid Apes,* p. 263.

HEARNE, S., *Journey to the Northern Ocean.*

HOCKER, DR. A., *De la Criminalité chez les Arabes au point de vue de la pratique médicale judiciaire en Algérie,* Paris, 1884.

HORN, *Vierteljahrsschr.,* 1865.

HUGHES, REV., *Dictionary of Islam,* London, 1887. (A most valuable book).

HUREAU DE VILLENEUVE, *De l'Accouchement dans la Race Jaune.*

HYADES ET DENIKER, *Mission scientifique du Cap Horn* (1882—83).

I.

ICARD, *La femme pendant la Période menstruelle*, Paris, 1883.

J.

JACOBS, *Reisebeschriving mit aanteekeningen betreffende Hygiene, Volkenkunde, etc.*, van de Eilanden Bali en Lombok, Batavia, 1883.
JEANNEL, DR., *De la Prostitution*, Paris, 1868. Contains much information on Ancient Brothels.
JOEST, *Allerlei Spielzeug* (*Intern. Arch. f. Ethnographie*).

K.

KAY, STEPHEN, *Travels and Researches in Caffraria*, Lond., 1883.
KRAFFT-EBING, DR. R. VON, *Psychopathia Sexualis*, London, 1895.
KREUTZWALD, FR. H., *Der Ehsten Gebräuche*, Petersburg, 1854.
KULISCHER, *Zeitschr. f. Ethnol.*, Berlin, 1876.

L.

LABAT, *Voyage du Chevalier des Marchais en Guinée, Iles voisines et à Cayenne*.
LAFITEAU, *Mœurs des Sauvages Américains*.
LA FONTAINE, *Tales and Novels* (English translation), London, 1896.
LAGARD, *Le Grand Voyage du Pays des Hurons*, Paris, 1865.
LAMAIRESSE, Traduction de: *Kama Sutra, Erotologie hindouic*, Paris, 1886.
LECAT, *Oeuvres de*, Paris, 1767.(In the "*Journal des Savants*," Paris, 1864).
LECKY, PROF., *History of European Morals*, 2 vols., Lond., *Longmans*, 1886.
LEGOUVÉ, *Hist. morale des femmes*.
LEGRAND, *La Folie devant les Tribunaux*.
LEMIUS, C., *De Lapponibus Finmarchiae eorumque lingua vita et religione pristina*, Copenhagen, 767.
LEOTY, ERNEST, *Le Corset à travers les Ages*, Paris, 1893.
LETOURNEAU, CH., *L'Evolution du Mariage et de la Famille*, Paris, 1888.
————, *La Sociologie d'après l'Ethnographie*, Paris, 1880.
LICHTENSTEIN, *Reisen im südlichen Afrika*.
LOMBROSO, PROF. C., *Anthrop. Studien*, Hamburg, 1894.
————, *La Femme Criminelle*, Paris, 1896.
LOSKIEL, G. H., *History of the Mission of the United Brethren among the Indians*.

LOTA, DR., *Deux ans entre le Sénégal et le Niger.*

LOTI, PIERRE, *Le Roman d'un Spahi*, Paris, 1896.

LUBBOCK, SIR JOHN, *Origin of Civilisation and Primitive Condition of Man*, London, 1882.

M.

MACDONALD, REV. JAMES, *Manners, Customs, Superstitions, and Religions of South African Tribes.* (In manuscript).

MACÉ (Ex-Chief-Detective), *Mémoires*, Paris.

MACKENZIE, *Voyages to the Frozen and Pacific Oceans*, London, 1802.

——————, *Voyages through the Continent of North America.*

MAIZEROY, *Deux Amies*, Paris. (Proscribed).

MANTEGAZZA, *Physiologie de l'amour*, Paris, 1895.

——————, *Gli Amori degli Uomini*, Milano, 1892.

MANUEL D'EROTOLOGIE CLASSIQUE, Paris, *Liseux*, 2 vols.

MARRIAGE-LOVE AND WOMAN *amongst the Arabs* (otherwise entitled in Arabic: *The Book of Exposition*, etc.), 350 pp., Paris, *Carrington*, 1896.

MARTINEAU, *Leçons sur les Déformations vulvaires et anales*, Paris, 1883.

MARTIUS, *Zur Ethnographie Amerika's.*

MAUREL, E., *Mémoire sur l'Anthropologie des divers peuples vivant actuellement au Cambodge* ("Mémoires de la Société d'Anthropologie de Paris"), 2e série, T. IV, Fascicule IV, Paris, 1893.

MENARD, *Morale avant les philosophes.*

MEYER, H., *Eine Weltreise*, Leipzig, 1880.

MOINAUX, *Les Tribunaux Comiques.—Règles pour former un avocat*, Paris, 1882.

MOLIERE, *Oeuvres de.*

MOLL, *Les inversions sexuelles*, Paris. 1893.

MONDIÈRE, *Monographie de la femme de Cochinchine* ("Mem. de la Soc. d'Anthropologie de Paris"), 1880.

MONRAD, H. C., *Gemälde der Küste von Guinea*, Weimar, 1824.

MORACHE, Art. "Chine", *Diction. Ency. des Sci. Méd.* ("Mem. Soc. d'Anthrop.", T. 1).

MORAGLIA, *Archivio di Psichiatria et Anthrop. criminale.*

MOREAU, DR. PAUL, *Aberrations du Sens Génésique*, Paris, 1880.

MOREL, *Traités des maladies mentales.*

MORLEY, JOHN, *Critical Miscellanies*, Lond., *Macmillan*, 1888.

MOURA, *Royaume du Cambodge.*

MÜLLER, *Allgem. Ethnogr.*, Wien, 1873.

N.

NAVARETTE, *An Account of the Empire of China*, London, 1704.
NEIS, PAUL, *Sur le Laos* ("Bulletin de la Société d'Anthropologie de Paris"), Paris, 1887.
NORDAU, MAX, *Conventional Lies of our Civilisation*, London, 1895.
NOTES SUR LA SODOMIE, *Lyon Médical*, 1880.
NOVALIS, U. A., *Fragments*.

O.

OGILVIE, *Imperial Dictionary*, London, 1897.
OLDFIELD, *Historical Memoirs on Australia*.
"OLD MAN YOUNG AGAIN," Paris, 1898.
O'NEILL, JOHN, *The Night of the Gods, an Enquiry into Cosmic and Cosmogonic Mythology and Symbolism*, London, 1897.

P.

PALLU DE LA BARRIÈRE, *Histoire de l'Expédition de Cochinchine*, Paris, 1888.
PARENT-DUCHATELET, A. J. B., *La Prostitution dans la Ville de Paris*, 3ème édit., Paris, 1857.
PARO, *Recherches philosophiques sur les Américains*.
PAUTHIER, *Chine Moderne*.
PAUW, *Recherches sur les Américains*.
PETRONIUS ARBITER, *Satyricon*, Amsterdam, 1669.
PLOSS, DR., *Das Weib in der Natur- und Völkerkunde*, Leipzig, 1895.
POLAK, *Persien, das Land und seine Bewohner*, 1, Leipzig, 1865.
POUILLET, DR., *De l'Onanisme chez la Femme*, Paris, 1894.
POWELL, W., *Wanderings in a Wild Country*.
POWERS, STEPHEN, *Tribes of California*.
PRÆTORIUS, *Gestriegelte Rocken-Philosophia*, Chemnitz, 1707.
PRITCHARD, W. J., *Polynesian Reminiscences*.

R.

RABUTEAU, *De la Prostitution en Europe depuis l'Antiquité jusqu'à la fin du XVI siècle*, Paris, 1851.
READE, WINWOOD, *Savage Africa*, London, 1863.
RELATIONS DES DÉCOUVERTES FAITES PAR COLOMB, etc., Bologna, 1875.
RELATIONS DES JÉSUITES, 1634.

RÉMUSAT, ABEL, *Mélanges asiatiques.*

RIEDEL, *De sluik- en kroesharige rassen tusschen Selebes en Papua.*

ROCHEBRUNE, A. FREMEAU DE, in the *"Revue d'Anthropologie,"* 1881, IV.

ROMILLY, *Proceed. Royal Geog. Soc.*

ROSE, *Four Years in Southern Africa.*

ROSENBAUM, *Geschichte der Lustseuche,* etc., Halle, 1889.

ROSS, ALEX., *Adventures of the First Settlers on the Oregon or Columbia River.*

S.

SALLILAS, *Vida Penal en Espana.*

SANCHEZ (LE PÈRE), *De Matrimonio.*

SCHEIDEN, *Das Salz.*

SCHLEGEL, DR. C. A., *La Prostitution en Chine,* Rouen, 1880.

SCHOMBURGK, *Reisen in British Guiana.*

SCHRADER, *Prehistoric Antiquities of the Aryan Peoples,* Lond., 1890.

SCHRENCK-NOTZING, DR. A. VON, *Theurapeutic in Psychopathia Sexualis* (Trans. by CHAS. G. CHADDOCK, M.D.), Phil. and London, 1895.

SCHWANER, *Borneo, Beschrijving van het stroomgebied van den Barito,* etc.

SEEMAN, *Voyage of the Herald,* Lond., 1853.

SIMON, *Crimes et délits.*

SPENCER, HERB., *Ancestor-Worship in general.—Principles of Sociology,* London, 1885.

SPENCER, HERB., *The Principles of Sociology,* Lond., 1885.

SPROAT, *Scenes and Studies of Savage Life.*

STEINE , KARL VON DEN, *Die Philosophie der Tracht, und Entstehung des Schamgefühls,* Ausland, 1891.

SYMONDS, J. A., *Problem in Modern Ethics,* London, 1896.

T.

TANNER, JOHN, *Narrative of the Captivity and Adventures of J. T.,* London, 1830.

TARDIEU, A., *Etude Médico-légale sur les Attentats aux Mœurs,* Paris, 1878.

TAYLOR, *Principles and Practice of Medical Jurisprudence,* Lond., 1894.

TAYLOR, R., *Te Ika a Maui; or, New Zealand and its inhabitants,* London, 1870.

THEVET, *Singularités de la France antarctique.*

TREGEAR, E., *The Maoris of New Zealand.* (In " Journ. Anthrop. Inst.",
XIX, 100).

TSCHUDI, *Beitr. über Peru, Denkschr. der K. Acad. der Wissensch.*,
Wien, 1891.

TYLOR, EDWARD B., Reader in Anthropology in the University of Oxford,
Primitive Culture, 2 vols., London, 1891.

V.

VERGA, PROF. ANDREA, *Si le Célibat prédispose à la Folie*, Milan, 1869.
——————————, *Si le Mariage contribue a la Folie*, Milan, 1871.

W.

WAITZ-GERLAND, *Anthropologie der Natur-Volker*, 1880.

WAKE, *The Evolution of Morality.*

WALLACE, A. R., *Narrative of Travels on the Amazon and Rio Negro.*

WAMBERY, *Das Türkenvolk in Ethnogr. Beziehungen*, etc., Leipzig, 1885.

WEBER, *Zwei Jahre in Africa.*

WESTERMARCK, *The History of Human Marriage*, London, *Macmillan*, 1894.

WHEELER, J. M., *Footsteps of the Past*, London, *R. Forder, n. d.*

WILBRAND, *Fridolin's heimliche Ehe.*

WILDER, DR. A., In : "*The Saturday Magazine*," February 8th, 1834.

WILKES, CH., *Narratives of the U.S. Exploring Expedition.*

WOLFF, *Verhandl. der Ges. f. Erdkunde* zu Berlin, 1886.

Z.

ZIMMERMAN, *Die Inseln des Indischen Meeres*, Berlin, 1863.

ZIPPE, *Wien. Med. Wochenschrift*, 1879, N°. 24.

ZOLA. EMILE. *La Curée. Nana.* Paris.

These things concern everyone; the study of these things concerns the Physiologist, the Psychologist, the Moralist. We want to get into possession of the actual facts, and from the investigation of the facts we want to ascertain what is normal and what is not normal, from the point of view of physiology and of psychology. We want to know what is naturally lawful under the various sexual chances that may befall man, not as the "born child of sin" but as a naturally social animal.

HAVELOCK ELLIS.

www.ingramcontent.com/pod-product-compliance
Lightning Source LLC
Chambersburg PA
CBHW070612270326
41926CB00011B/1672